Behavioral Police Management

Harry W. More
AUGUST VOLLMER UNIVERSITY
W. Fred Wegener
INDIANA UNIVERSITY OF PENNSYLVANIA

BEHAVIORAL POLICE MANAGEMENT

MACMILLAN PUBLISHING COMPANY
NEW YORK
MAXWELL MACMILLAN CANADA
TORONTO

Editor: Christine Cardone
Production Supervisor: Patricia F. French
Production Manager: Pam Kennedy-Oborski
Text and Cover Designer: Robert Freese
Cover illustration: Robert Freese
Photo Researchers: Diane Kraut and Sui Mon Wu
Illustrations: Precision Graphics

This book was set in Baskerville, Friz Quadrata, and Optima types by Publication Services, Inc., and was printed and bound by Hamilton Printing Company. The cover was printed by The Lehigh Press, Inc.

Macmillan Publishing Company
866 Third Avenue, New York, New York 10022

Macmillan Publishing Company is part of the Maxwell Communication Group of Companies.

Maxwell Macmillan Canada, Inc.
1200 Eglinton Avenue East
Suite 200
Don Mills, Ontario M3C 3N1

LIBRARY OF CONGRESS CATALOGING-IN-PUBLICATION DATA

More, Harry W.
Behavioral police management / Harry W. More, W. Fred Wegener.
p. cm.
Includes indexes.
ISBN 0-02-383350-5
1. Police administration. 2. Organizational behavior. 3. Police—Personnel management. 4. Police administration—United States. I. Wegener. W. Fred. II. Title.
HV7935.M62 1992
350.74'068'3—dc20 91-19955
CIP

Printing: 1 2 3 4 5 6 7 Year: 2 3 4 5 6 7 8

Dedication

This text is dedicated to one of the great pioneers of law enforcement education, the late V. A. Leonard. A native of Cleburne, Texas, Leonard died on October 28, 1984, in Denton, Texas, at the age of 86. His combined careers as a police administrator and academician spanned six decades. His expertise ranged from detection of deception to communications, records, and administration. Leonard started his career in law enforcement as a police officer in Berkeley, California, and then went on to become an administrator in Texas. Throughout his career he was active in professional organizations and was one of the founders of the Academy of Criminal Justice Sciences (initially known as the International Association of Police Professors).

He entered police education during its infancy as the chairman of the Police Science and Administration program at Washington State University during the early 1940s. He was awarded a Ph.D. from Ohio State University and was one of the first police educators to obtain this degree. Graduates in Dr. Leonard's master's program have entered the teaching field at two- and four-year institutions of higher education throughout the nation. V. A. Leonard left a legacy of criminal justice literature, including 32 books on a broad range of topics, from the administration of justice to records. One of his greatest contributions to the literature in the field was the classical work *Police Communications Systems*, published in 1938. Another significant contribution was *Police Organization and Management*, initially released in 1951.

A singular and highly significant contribution was the founding of the first chapter of Alpha Phi Sigma, the criminal justice honor society, at Washington State University. There are now more than 1,200 chapters of the honorary throughout the nation.

In his early writings, Dr. Leonard took the position that management was the act of working with and through individuals and groups to achieve organizational goals and objectives. V. A. inspired us to write this text, as he inspired many students who have contributed to the professionalization of law enforcement.

Preface

Management in contemporary police departments is constantly in flux. As we note in Chapter 1, police management has a rich history that, for the most part, is an integration of knowledge developed originally in the private sector. Most law enforcement agencies have evolved from a highly political style of policing to more of a professional model and are currently developing a style appropriately described as community policing.

Within this context, police managers have become increasingly aware of social and individual behavior in the organization. It is generally conceded that when the quality of working life within the organization is good, the organizational goals are more readily met and individual needs accommodated.

The creation of positive relationships between line officers, groups within the organization, and police managers at every level is critical to the success of any police department. Police managers must recognize the ecology of the organization, accepting it as a dynamic social system. We focus on organizational behavior as a means of understanding both the complexity of the criminal justice organization and the interaction between officers and managers as they work to resolve community problems.

Today's police managers have to develop behavioral and social skills to deal effectively with a rapidly changing community and the new breed of police officer. The modern police executive must integrate each member of the organization into the managerial process so the organization can improve both its internal and external adaptive capabilities.

Chapters 1 and 2 of *Behavioral Police Management* review the historical antecedents of management thought and consider the dimensions of management, including managerial functions and roles, and problem-solving.

Chapters 3 through 6 discuss how characteristics of the individual influence the organization and how, in turn, the organization affects the individual. Behavioral implications include a consideration of personality, attitudes, motivation, and organizational stress. An effort is made in these chapters to present information that provides a real understanding of behavior in the organization.

We are also concerned with social behavior and organizational processes. Groups and the group process are considered in detail, and extensive attention is given to key elements such as power, decision-making, communications, and leadership. Each of these are natural occurrences in the life of the organization, and they condition and recondition the organization.

Chapters 12 through 14 emphasize the interaction process in the organization. Special treatment is given to change, conflict, and developing the organization as a means of improving individual and organizational performance. The last chapter discusses several critical issues with which police managers must deal today, including minorities, women, unions, and the use of deadly force.

The text presents current behavioral theory and its application to the organization. The intent has been to help current and potential police managers understand the different beliefs and assumptions they hold about themselves, others, the organization, and the community. Our goal is to emphasize the importance of human behavior and its relationship to organizational processes.

The transition from theoretical to practical has been accomplished by providing numerous realistic examples throughout the text and by the inclusion of Focuses taken from journals, newspapers, and monographs. In addition, we offer real case studies in all chapters. Forty-five cases are provided. The instructor should use the issues raised in each case during classroom discussions.

Tables and figures amplify and reinforce important points discussed in each chapter. In addition to a summary, each chapter has sections entitled Learning Objectives, Key Concepts, Discussion Topics and Questions, and For Further Reading.

Each of these features makes the text user friendly and provides a range of activities to maximize instructor and student interaction. Lastly, the text has been written using an informal writing style. The experience of both authors is that students respond to it with a great deal of enthusiasm.

Behavioral Police Management is the product of many, including all the faculty members who were kind enough to share course outlines and review the text outline. Text reviewers were Paul Embert, Michigan State University; Richard N. Holden, Central Missouri State University; Max Futrell, California State University, Fresno; and James R. Farris, California State University, Fullerton. Police departments throughout the nation responded to inquiries and furnished information and data. In addition, special recognition and thanks must be extended to our wives, Ginger and Cheryl, for their assistance, patience, and support during the preparation of the manuscript.

Acknowledgments

Numerous individuals and organizations contributed to the completion of this textbook by either providing material or granting permission to reproduce material contained in other publications. We would like to thank the following people, who provided information utilized in preparation of *Behavioral Police Management*: J. Frank Acosta, Chief, Milpitas, CA; Joseph A. Bogan, Professor, Indiana University of Pennsylvania; Donald R. Burr, Councilman, Campbell, CA; William J. Winters, Chief, Chula Vista, CA; Victor Collins,

Assistant Chief, Salinas, CA; James D. Sewell, Chief, Gulfport, FL; Gary Leonard, Chief, Sandy City, UT; Joseph McNamara, Chief, San Jose, CA; O. Ray Shipley, Chief, Medford, OR; Robert R. Snow, Assistant Director, U.S. Secret Service; Louis A. Mayo, President, Murphy, Mayo and Associates; William Tafoya, Supervisory Agent, The FBI Academy; William Nay, U.S. Department of Energy; and Sam H. Killman, Chief, Charlotte, NC.

Additional thanks are extended to the following organizations and governmental units: Charles C Thomas, Publisher; Commission on Accreditation for Law Enforcement Agencies, Inc.; *Law Enforcement News*; Pennsylvania Commission on Crime and Delinquency; National Institute of Justice; The *San Jose Mercury News*; Alexander Hamilton Institute; Associated Press; Madison Police Department, Madison, WI; Los Angeles Police Department, Los Angeles, CA; *Success Magazine*; The *Pittsburgh Press*; The President's Commission on Physical Fitness and Sports; Police Foundation; U.S. Commission on Civil Rights; McGraw-Hill Publishing Co.; Scientific Methods, Inc.; Gulf Publishing Company; and the U.S. Equal Employment Opportunity Commission.

H. W. M.

W. F. W.

Brief Contents

Detailed Contents

CHAPTER 10
Managerial Communications: The Vital Process 329

CHAPTER 11
Leadership: The Integrative Variable 361

Behavioral Police Management

CHAPTER 1

Police Management: Evolving Strategies

LEARNING OBJECTIVES

1. Define the term *bureaucracy*.
2. Compare the findings of Leonhard Fuld and Elmer Graper.
3. List five characteristics of scientific management.
4. Identify the components of the acronym POSDCORB.
5. Describe why the Hawthorne effect is important.
6. Describe the impact of the human relations movement on the police field.
7. Differentiate between the following terms: input, throughout, output.
8. Compare an open to a closed management system.
9. List the key characteristics of the contingency approach to management.
10. Describe the organizational strategy of the political era.
11. Compare the organizational strategies of the reform and community policing eras.
12. List the methods used to organize a police department.
13. Describe a typical matrix organization.
14. Define the term *management*.
15. List the four management functions.

Focus 1.1 outlines a typical week for a typical police administrator. You can readily see that the job involves an extensive interaction with others. Management cannot be conducted in a vacuum—it involves many activities ranging from decision-making to problem-solving. But the primary concern is to utilize resources efficiently and effectively to achieve a goal—this is done *through* the efforts of others.

Resources are seldom adequate, so it is necessary for a police manager to choose carefully whether funds are to be used in acquiring personnel,

FOCUS 1.1

One Week in the Life of a Typical Chief Executive Officer

ACTIVITY/FREQUENCY	*PERCENTAGE OF TIME*
Desk/Mail (130 documents)	24.1
Telephone (33 calls)	6.6
Scheduled Meetings (14 meetings)	39.8
Unscheduled Meetings (37 meetings)	25.4
Tours (two tours of the department—usually when going from one meeting to another)	3.0
Miscellaneous/Personal (breaks, reading newspapers, etc.)	1.1
	100.00

SOURCE. Adapted from Louis A. Mayo, *Analysis of the Role of the Police Chief Executive* (Ann Arbor, MI: University Microfilms International, 1983).

purchasing materials or supplies, or developing an operational plan. The choices are seldom self-evident; hence, the manager will, in most instances, find it necessary to consult others before making a final decision. Once a decision is made, the management process is enhanced, and human, fiscal, and other resources are mobilized to accomplish objectives and goals.

The managerial process consists of the following general activities (Leonard and More, 1987):

1. Development of the departmental mission, organizational goals, and operational objectives.
2. Development of numerous plans including operational, procedural, tactical, fiscal, management, and program.
3. Structuring the organization to ensure goal attainment.
4. Directing activities with a leadership style that acknowledges the importance of human resources.
5. Controlling activities through adequate evaluation and taking corrective action when appropriate.

Police management is important in providing the necessary public safety services and in ensuring domestic tranquility in our democratic society. Specifically, it involves providing service to the total community by safeguarding lives and property, maintaining the quality of community life, and protecting the constitutional rights of everyone regardless of their political or social persuasion.

The importance of effective management cannot be underestimated. It is hard to imagine any department operating effectively when managerial activities are performed poorly. Management, as we know it today, has not just simply occurred. It is the result of an evolutionary process well over a century old. In order to put it into its proper perspective we must review the history of management thought: the ideal bureaucracy, scientific management, functional management (including POSDCORB), contributions of early researchers, human relations, systems management, and contingency theory. All of these concepts have impacted differently on police management.

Historical Antecedents

Through the years there have been different approaches to managing an organization. While the concern for managing organizations efficiently dates back to early times, what might be termed modern management thought can be traced to the launching of bureaucratic theory in the first part of the 20th century (McFarland, 1986). Keep in mind that many of the early management theorists relied heavily on military and religious models when developing their own theories. In addition, many police managerial theorists, as well as police managers, have repeatedly followed developments in business and industry. Creativity or originality in the police field has been negligible.

The Ideal Bureaucracy

Max Weber, a German sociologist (1864–1920), was the principal proponent of the systematic analysis of bureaucracy, or what has become known as "the *ideal bureaucracy*" (see Figure 1.1). This approach emphasizes administrative regulations, rational legal authority, and the principle of office hierarchy, and served as a model for police management for many years.

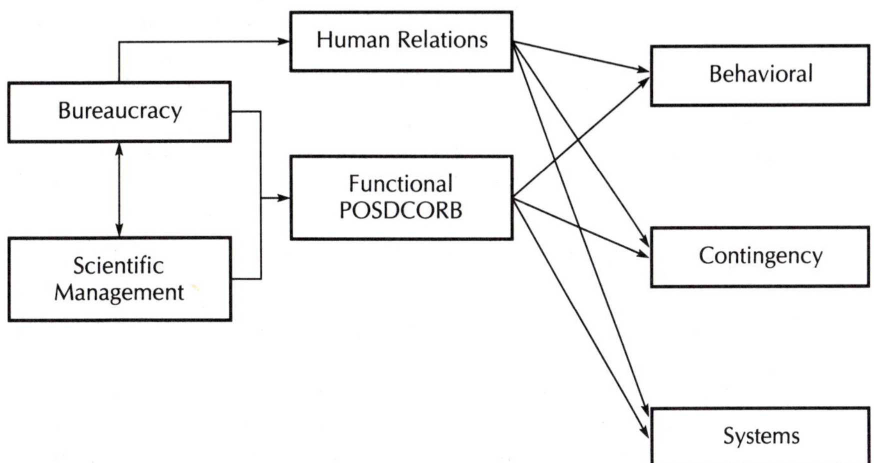

FIGURE 1.1 Theories of Management. Source Adapted from Robert J. Thierauf, Robert C. Klekamp, and Daniel W. Geeding, *Management Principles and Practices,* (New York: Wiley, 1977).

The following statements describe some of the characteristics of bureaucracy (Gerth and Mills, 1958):

1. Routine activities of the organization are distributed in a fixed way and are clearly identified as official duties. Authority is distributed to those who need it in order to accomplish assigned tasks.
2. Authority is vested in the position and not the individual, and the principle of office hierarchy provides for levels of authority.
3. Official records are maintained by the staff; management requires the preparation of numerous written documents.
4. Training is the best means of ensuring effective performance.
5. Management is a full-time job; every manager must respond accordingly.
6. It is essential to reduce management to a set of rules providing for stability within the organization.

While other organizational theories have lessened in importance, bureaucracy retains its place in competition with more recent theories. According to Weber, ideal bureaucracy is technically capable of attaining the highest level of efficiency. Bureaucracy has been viewed as the most rational means of controlling human behavior (Merton, 1952).

Max Weber, in describing the importance of the staff of an organization, pointed out their need to be rational and legal. The staff is viewed as functioning according to the following criteria:

1. Offices are organized hierarchically.
2. Every office is required to have a specific sphere of competence.
3. Open selection of staff is emphasized.
4. Selection is based on merit.
5. Salary is based on hierarchical rank.
6. The office is the primary occupation of the incumbent.

Many managers find the concept of the ideal bureaucracy to be viable because it is fundamentally logical, rational, and based on common sense (McFarland, 1986). Weber's views of bureaucracy dominate the managerial style of numerous police managers. Generally, police managers have risen from the ranks, so their organizational life is limited to serving in a bureaucratic organization. Even if a police manager has had the benefit of being introduced to more contemporary managerial theories, most police departments hold sacred the concepts of rational authority, hierarchy, specialization, and managerial authority (Leonard and More, 1987).

Detractors of bureaucracies point out the following drawbacks of organizations (Briscoe, 1980):

1. Too mechanistic to the extent that major facets of human nature are ignored.
2. Rigidly structured and nonresponsive to change.
3. Controlled by directives and procedures hindering real communications.
4. Inhibiters of innovation because of their hierarchical nature.
5. Designed to reward the job instead of the individual.
6. Control oriented and utilize coercion to gain compliance.
7. Encouraged to engage in make-work activities and job-defensive behavior.

Bureaucracies personify all that is perceived as being wrong with governmental agencies, expressed mainly in the term *red tape*. Red tape reflects the individual's frustration with highly specific rules and regulations and what seems to be the inability to get anything done. At the same time many employees of bureaucratic organizations feel they are reduced to being a cog in a big machine with limited opportunities to express themselves or to do anything but conform to organizational rules and regulations. It would seem the bureaucracy continues to dominate the police scene because it is a managerial theory ensuring stability and permanence rather than ambiguity and impreciseness. In addition, it provides for a means of responding to the demand for accountability. Managers can come and go, but the organization always remains intact.

Scientific Management

Frederick W. Taylor, an American efficiency engineer (1856–1915), is acknowledged as the founder of scientific management. He received his initial training as a machinist, becoming a foreman in a relatively short period of time. He found many workers did not work at top efficiency, a behavior he identified as "soldiering," where workers informally determined the work output. In attempting to resolve this problem, he realized that employees had little reason to work any harder because wage systems were based primarily on attendance.

It was Taylor's position that a piece-rate system would work if the employees knew it to be fairly structured. He believed it was essential to arrive at the rate by scientific and empirical procedures (George, 1968).

Taylor, in an effort to reduce soldiering by employees and to improve productivity, set out to find ways that work could be accomplished more effectively and with less effort. As the chief engineer of a steel company, he observed that some employees accomplished tasks with dispatch while others were producing less but, in some instances, expending more energy.

He carefully analyzed each job and broke each task down into the smallest possible denominator. He then rearranged the job into a sequence of steps and procedures in an effort to find the "one best way" of completing a task(s).

As a result of his analysis, Taylor found he could improve productivity dramatically and at the same time increase the wages of the workers. He also supported the concept of functional supervision, where an employee would be supervised by more than one foreman or expert (Taylor, 1947).

Scientific management can be accurately summarized as follows (Taylor, 1947):

1. Scientific designing of jobs rather than using the time-honored rule-of-thumb method.
2. Scientific selection of workers coupled with extensive training.
3. Replacement of individualism with cooperation.
4. Development of each employee to his or her greatest efficiency and prosperity.
5. Technique of fully explaining changes to employees as a means of reducing resistance to change.

Taylor's managerial philosophy was both idealistic and moralistic (McFarland, 1986). He felt the essence of scientific management involved a complete mental revolution by both management and workers. Employees had to change their attitudes toward work, fellow employees, and managers. At the same time, management had to change their views of workers, duties, and worker relationships (Taylor, 1947).

Government was highly skeptical of the scientific management movement, and unions also attacked the concept, vigorously describing it as mechanistic-oriented and totally ignoring the needs of employees.

Taylor, in testifying before a Special House Committee in 1912, stated management was unquestionably interested in the welfare of employees, pointing out (George, 1968),

> under scientific management the worker and the management are the best of friends, and in the second place, one of the greatest characteristics of scientific management is that all any employee working under scientific management has to do is to bring to the attention of the management that he thinks he is receiving an injustice, and an impartial and careful investigation will be made. And unless this condition of seeking to do absolute justice to the worker exists, scientific management does not exist. (p. 145)

Scientific management was never presented as a complete management theory, but it was the first scientific effort focusing on the individual task to be performed. It was embraced by some law enforcement agencies, but found greater acceptance by the industrial complex. It became a part of university curricula after the turn of the century (McFarland, 1986).

Functional Management

Henri Fayol, a French mining engineer, was the first to espouse a comprehensive statement on a theory of administration. He was very successful as a manager; consequently, many responded positively to his writings. He published a monograph in 1916, but the first English translation was not available until 1937. It was not until 1949 that it was widely distributed in the United States.

He identified the following elements of *functional management* (George, 1968):

1. Planning
2. Organizing
3. Commanding
4. Coordinating
5. Controlling

Based on his experience as a mining engineer and as the head of a coal mining and iron foundry company, Fayol developed 14 principles of management. A principle, as utilized by classical theorists, was defined as a general truth about the management of an organization. It was acknowledged such principles were not as infallible as principles in the hard sciences such as chemistry or mathematics, but it was believed the application of such principles would improve organizational performance. Fayol's principles included the following (Fayol, 1949):

1. Division of work allowing for specialization.
2. Authority (the right to give orders) coupled with employees' responsibility to do their best.
3. Discipline within the organization calling for obedience, application, energy, and respect.
4. Application of the concept of unity of command, pointing out subordinates should receive orders from only one superior.
5. Unity of direction, requiring that each objective have only one head and one plan.
6. Subordination of individual interest to the general interest.
7. Bonuses, profit-sharing, piece rates, and other methods should be used so as to ensure equitable payment to employees.
8. One central point in the organization should have control over all of the parts, but in a large organization some decisions may have to be made at lower levels.
9. There should be an unbroken chain of managers (scalar chain) from the bottom to the top of the organization. Authority and communications should follow this chain.
10. There should be a well-chosen place for everything, and everything in its place.
11. Equity should prevail, based on a combination of kindliness and justice.
12. Management should provide for the stability of tenure of personnel, and mediocre managers who stay are preferable to outstanding managers who come and go.
13. Plans should be well thought out before they are executed.
14. The group should work as a team, and every member should work to accomplish the organization goals (esprit de corps).

It must be emphasized that Fayol's contribution to management was highly unique and truly valuable. He outshone his contemporaries, and after the publication of his monograph, many others codified his principles. He was responsible for originating the organization chart, job specifications, and the idea of management training. Fayol's views on human relations clearly anticipated many of the findings of industrial psychology (Cuthbert, 1976).

In the application of his principles, Fayol advocated that different circumstances demanded flexibility in their application. Functional management as espoused by Fayol and others such as J.D. Mooney and Alan C. Riley had considerable impact on police departments during the first half of this century. Principles such as unity of command and esprit de corps dominated the police management scene (Leonard and More, 1987).

Early Researchers

As early as 1909 Leonhard F. Fuld published a very critical study of police organization in the United States. He concerned himself with the individual police officer as well as the police organization. He took the position that a police organization could only be effective when it was headed by a strong executive. He was especially critical of nonprofessional heads of police departments as well as police boards and commissions.

In his study he identified numerous problems confronting the police at that time, including the need for the following (Fuld, 1909):

1. The elimination of politics from police administration
2. Specialization of duties
3. Clearly defined duties
4. Constant supervision of duties
5. Strong executive leadership
6. Constant auditing by inspectors
7. Maintenance of discipline
8. Comprehensive training of patrolmen
9. Careful selection of personnel
10. Elimination of nonpolice duties

Fuld's overall approach placed a very serious emphasis on the management process of control (by exerting close supervision over subordinates) and the necessity of strong leadership to be provided by the chief. He also stressed the need for continually auditing the activities of all personnel.

The next study of the American police was released in 1915 when Raymond Fosdick completed his comprehensive study of 72 cities. He found the police departments were organizationally primitive, having developed without design or accurately determined purposes. He discovered that many cities had been saddled with organizations ill-fitted to local conditions, with ordinances spelling out the methods of operation which in turn were unadaptable to local needs. He also found police departments performing numerous extraneous and unrelated functions such as censorship and collecting taxes. Finally he observed departments were burdened with inept leadership (Fosdick, 1969).

Another major study was completed by Elmer D. Graper in 1921. In his handbook he supported the position that police departments should be administered by one individual and not a commission. Organizationally he supported the hierarchical arrangement of officers (military style), as a means of providing adequate supervision. He stated a department should be functionally organized, based on the activities undertaken by the police. He was also an advocate of a centralized police department and specialization (Graper, 1921).

POSDCORB

The managerial task was clearly set forth by Luther Gulick in 1937 in his paper that was part of the edited text he published in conjunction with L. Urwick under the title "Papers on the Science of Administration." Gulick was the originator of the acronym *POSDCORB* (Gulick, 1937):

P PLANNING concerns working out (in broad outline) what needs to be accomplished and then identifying appropriate methods to achieve departmental goals.

O ORGANIZING involves creating an authority structure in which work units are established and coordinated for the purpose of achieving organizational objectives.

S STAFFING refers to the personnel function of recruiting, selection, training, nurturing, and retaining competent human resources.

D DIRECTING is the process of making decisions, formulating policies, procedures, rules and regulations, and performing leadership tasks.

CO COORDINATING is the continuous process of developing harmonious interaction between organizational units.

R REPORTING requires keeping management and employees fully informed through inspection, records, and research.

B BUDGETING involves fiscal control by utilizing financial planning, resource allocation and accounting.

In the decades after Gulick's paper was released, POSDCORB was firmly embraced by the police, as evidenced by its appearance in police training programs. Writers in the field were also strongly influenced by the classical theories of management as indicated by the works of O.W. Wilson (police administration) and V.A. Leonard (police organization and management). Each of these authors were influenced by August Vollmer, the father of modern police administration, who served as the first marshal and then became the chief of police in Berkeley, California, from 1905 to 1932. In addition to his leadership position, Vollmer also served on the faculties at the University of Chicago and the University of California.

Vollmer fostered the concept of the police officer generalist and was a strong exponent of training and education. He led in the motorization of his force and the development of communications and records. He was an innovator and was instrumental in professionalizing the Berkeley Police Department (Leonard and More, 1987).

Up to this point, management theory addressed itself primarily to the organization itself. During the next phase, greater consideration was given to the needs of the individual as human relations management evolved (see Table 1.1).

TABLE 1.1 Historical Antecedents

The ideal bureaucracy
Scientific management
Functional management
Early police writers
POSDCORB
Human relations
Systems
Contingency theory

Human Relations

Human relations is simply relations among people. When two or more individuals work together, the potential exists for problems to arise. Every organization has human relations problems, and managers must deal not only with their own problems but with those of others (Laird, Laird, and Fruehling, 1983). Consequently the human relations school of management focuses on employee motivation and performance. It came into prominence in the 1920s, and two of the principal contributors were Elton Mayo, a psychologist, and Fritz Roethlisberger, a sociologist. These two (along with other researchers) were called on to analyze the puzzling results of the Hawthorne studies begun in 1924. The initial intent of the studies was to identify the relationship between productivity and physical working conditions. Initially the level of lighting was reduced, anticipating productivity would decrease; but, to the surprise of the researchers, productivity increased. Other factors were altered (such as rest periods, length of the workday, and wages), but production still increased.

These behavioral experts determined there were other factors affecting employees besides physical ones. Employees involved in the experiment were responding to human contact and the fact someone was paying attention to them. In other words, it was the psychological and social conditions of work that proved to be meaningful. This important variable became known as the *Hawthorne effect* (Tossi and Carroll, 1976).

Additional investigation was needed, so the two researchers studied six female employees who worked as a relay assembly group. The conditions of employment, such as work breaks, length of the workday, humidity, and the temperature were altered extensively. These changes occurred over a two-year period as the supervision emphasized humanitarian aspects and careful attention to employees. Numerous hypotheses were tested and then rejected. The only two that were retained were (1) wage incentives and (2) the method of supervision (Tossi and Carroll, 1976).

In the next phase of the study the effects of wage incentives on a group of relay assembly employees was studied. It was found production increased by 13 percent; but after a short period of time the study was abandoned because of the objections of other plant employees. The second variable, nature of supervision, was tested and found to be an unimportant variable.

In the last major area of study at the Hawthorne plant, an experiment was conducted involving 14 employees. The participants were assured that information obtained from the study would not jeopardize them. This group of men (including nine wiremen, three soldermen, and two inspectors) were responsible for connecting wires to banks of terminals that were parts of telephone switches.

Each participant was paid an hourly rate plus a bonus based on group production. Observers found behavior did not conform to the job descriptions. For example, workers assisted each other. When someone fell behind in his or her work, a faster worker would exchange jobs with the slower worker. Two cliques of friends were formed, each participating in their own social activities. The employees controlled the rate of production, as a group, and were well aware of what was an acceptable level of production (Tossi and Carroll, 1976).

It was found the workers had adopted a specific code of behavior including the following (Roethlisberger and Dickson, 1939):

1. The amount of work accomplished should be restricted. If you exceed what is expected of you then you are a "rate-buster."
2. You should not turn out too little work. If you do, then you are a "chisler."
3. You should never tell a supervisor anything that would harm a fellow employee. If you do, you are a "squealer."
4. You should never act officious even when functioning as a supervisor.

These studies demonstrated the importance of the individual within the organization and the need to consider something other than physical factors. The type of supervision was still viewed as important, but for the first time the significance of the impact of the group was brought out into the open. Near the middle of the century the human relations movement slowly came into disfavor as managers attempted to operate with a more simple interpretation of human relations (Scalan and Keys, 1979).

There has been considerable criticism of the Hawthorne studies, ranging from questioning the research methods utilized to challenging the conclusions reached by the researchers. The samples are considered by some to be too small, and the questions have been criticized for being too vague. One critic suggested the increased output of the employees was a result of the economic depression at the time (Rice, 1982). Others felt the researchers did not give enough consideration to the role of the unions and other factors influencing the attitudes of the workers. Some even felt Hawthorne was not a typical plant (Landsberger, 1958).

The human relations movement had a limited impact. As a general rule, the police field found bureaucratic management to be more acceptable.

In the first half of this century, police managers were strongly influenced by the reform movement that swept the United States. Corruption was rampant and the key words for resolving the problems were "efficiency" and "change." The goal of progressive chiefs was to gain control of their departments and to reduce political influence.

Bureaucracy and the functional approach to management dominated the police field inasmuch as they provided concrete recommendations to be followed. Human relations was viewed as being vague, and the military model with its rank and structure was looked on as almost an absolute panacea for resolving the problems of police managers.

Systems

Systems theory is a unique way of analyzing processes, and in recent years numerous administrative theorists have made a serious effort to apply the systems concept to management. It is a purely theoretical approach that was initially applied to the natural and physical sciences. The *systems* approach (physical, biological, or managerial) emphasizes the interdependence and interrelationship of each and every part to the whole. It contrasts sharply with the way many of the law enforcement agencies were organized during the first part of this century. It was and is common for the detective division to work in isolation from the remainder of the police department. In some instances the chief of detectives was appointed by the local governing body and did not report directly to the chief of police. In fact, this was true of a West Coast medium-sized police department having (until recently) three major units—patrol, records, and detective—each headed by a deputy chief with civil service status. Consequently the heads of these units could not be removed without cause or rotated to other administrative positions. Each unit functioned totally independent of the other. It was as if there were three entirely separate administrative units. Coordination and cooperation between the units was (and still is) often negligible.

Functionally, these three administrative units within one department can only be described as isolated subsystems with a limited interrelation. Generally the traditional organization with a strong bureaucratic orientation fosters (and in some instances actually supports) the isolation of one subsystem from another. The systems approach to management attempts to deal with this problem, and in the overall scheme of management thought, it can be looked on as taking up where the functional school of management left off in trying to unify management theory (Thierauf, Klekamp, and Geeding, 1977).

One expert has suggested that in order for someone to consider management as a system, it would be necessary to be totally aware of the following basic characteristics (Churchman, 1968):

1. An awareness of the objective of the total system and means of identifying and measuring performance.
2. The specific constraints that are fixed and impact the system's environment.
3. Identification of all the system's resources.
4. Identification of all the components of the system and the development of a clear understanding of their activities, goals, and how to measure their performance.
5. Consideration of the management of the system.

These considerations provide a means of analyzing one's reasoning and rechecking it continually. A systems-oriented manager must constantly review the total picture and evaluate each decision in terms of its impact on the mission, goals, and objectives of the organization. When a new policy or procedure is implemented, a police manager must be conscious of the effect change will have on each unit such as patrol, investigations, and special services. At the same time, consideration should be given to the potential impact on the police union, the community at large, the political environment, and other criminal justice agencies (see Figure 1.2).

Systems analysis is a specific technique that may be used to create a conceptual model. The following steps can be utilized (see Figure 1.3):

1. The desirable goals should be defined.
2. Alternative means of goal achievement should be developed.
3. Resource requirements should be developed for each of the newly created alternatives.
4. A model should be created for each alternative.

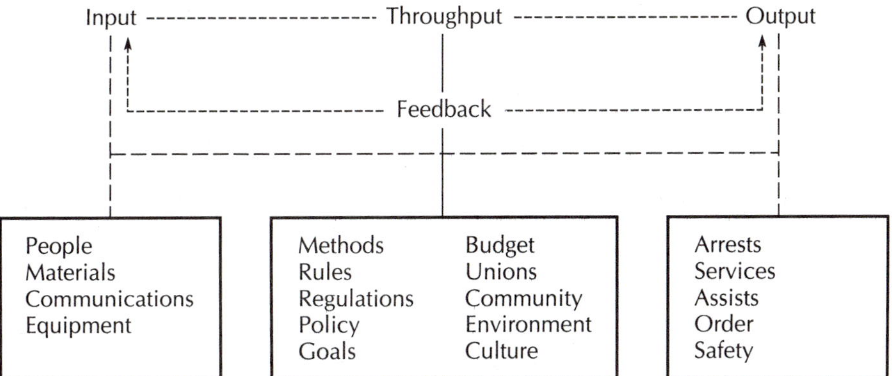

FIGURE 1.2 Simplified Police System. Source Adapted from Ernst K. Nillsson, "Systems Analysis Applied to Law Enforcement," *Allocations of Resources in the Chicago Police Department* (Washington, DC: Law Enforcement Assistance Administration, 1972).

5. Effectiveness measurements should be established in order to evaluate each alternative.

Upon completing these steps, management is provided with a comprehensive consideration of the police organization. It allows one to carefully consider each subsystem and the interrelationship between subsystems (Leonard and More, 1987). While theoretical, it holds promise as a tool to analyze an organization. Systems theory "provides a relief from the limitations of more mechanistic approaches and a rationale for rejecting 'principles' based on relatively 'closed-system' thinking" (Kast and Rosenzweig, 1972, p. 447).

All organizations are part of a larger system and have an interactive relationship with their environment. In other words, police departments do not function in isolation. Organizations must adapt to the larger environment or face extinction. Law enforcement, as we know it, has the potential for either becoming dysfunctional—or, in the extreme case—ceasing to exist. While it may be difficult to conceive of a situation where a law enforcement agency

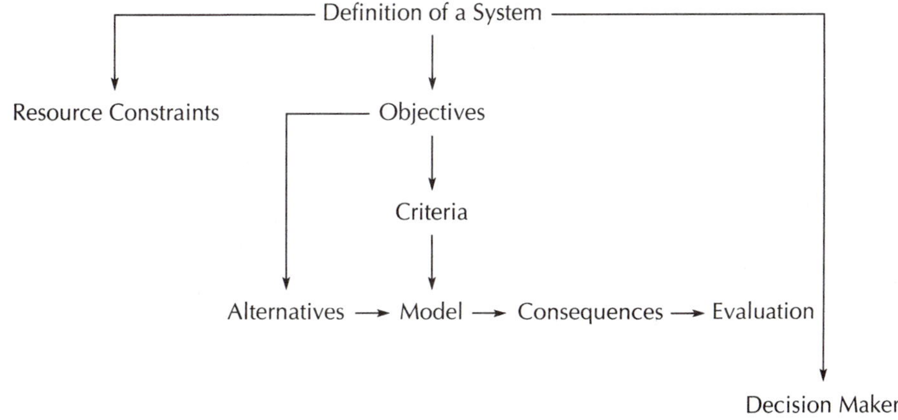

FIGURE 1.3 Systems Analysis.

could cease to exist, there is a slight trend to shift some police functions to private enterprise. Some wealthy Americans have turned to private security agencies to meet public safety needs. Part of this is due to the inability of some police departments to handle increasing workloads with limited personnel. For example, one major police department recently announced it will not investigate burglaries when the loss is under $1,000.

The changeover from a closed system to an open system is relatively new in law enforcement. For many years police executives chose to operate essentially as a closed system. The argument was that detachment from the community enhanced professionalism and allowed management to resist corruption. Needless to say, the police have not (as a general rule) been a totally closed system, but by limiting input from the environment and other elements of the criminal justice system, the police field has suffered from the lack of input that might allow them to do a better job.

The closed system is increasingly rejected because of its rigidity, impersonality, red tape, passivity of employees, and centralized control. It is also representative of organizations that reject creativity, limit communications, and can only be described as ignoring personal needs (Cordner, 1978; Woods, 1980).

It is best to view open and closed organizations as ideal types at the opposite end of a continuum. Keep in mind that the majority of police departments can be found to be somewhere between the extremes. Here are some of the characteristics of the open organizational model (Burns and Stalker, 1961):

1. Tasks are performed in a constantly changing environment.
2. The members of the organization have specialized knowledge.
3. Internal conflict is resolved within the organization.
4. Task accomplishment prevails.
5. Every member of the organization is expected to contribute to the organization.
6. Internal interaction stresses problem-solving.
7. Excellence of performance is emphasized.

Systems management presents itself as a challenge to police managers as they become more aware of the interdependence of all systems in our environment. The open model is not a panacea for the police administrator, but is a viable frame of reference, calling for more positive interaction between the organization and the rest of the community (Cordner, 1978).

Contingency Theory

Up to this point, we have seen that numerous attempts have been made to develop a specific approach to, and application of, a theory (scientific, functional, systems, or human relations) to the managerial process. In some instances the theories (in their application) have proven to be highly effective, whereas in other instances they were ineffective. Critiques of each theory abound. Some argue that "principles" are dogmatic and unrealistic. Others state that human relations ignores the actuality of the organization. Systems is viewed by some as being too esoteric and incomprehensible. There are, of course, truths as well as limitations in each of the theories.

What was needed was an integrated approach to management, which occurred in the late 1950s and the early 1960s when Burns and Stalker released a study of British industry and found that differences in the structure of the firms studied was the result of the type of market served and the nature of the technology. In some instances a loose organization proved to be effective; in other cases a traditional bureaucracy was found to be effective. The two researchers concluded that neither managerial systems could be considered to be superior in all situations, and there was no single management system that could be described as optimal (Burns and Stalker, 1961).

Joan Woodward (1965), in her studies of English companies, found organization structure and human relationships were in actuality a function of the existing technological situation. Her research marked the beginning of a situational approach to management and was supported by other efforts by F.E. Fiedler, Jay W. Lorsch, and Paul Lawrence, all of whom called for contingency management models (Thierauf, Klekamp, and Geeding, 1977).

Kast and Rosenzweig (1972) are two other theorists who have identified the *contingency approach* as a midrange level of analysis falling "somewhere between simplistic, specific principles, and complex vague notions" (p. 452). Their work was followed by that of Jay Lorsch and Paul Lawrence who summarized the contingency approach by pointing out that rather than searching for the one best way to do something, theorists have moved to examining a broad range of things such as organizational functions, the needs of employees, and the nature of external pressures (Lorsch and Lawrence, 1970).

In general, they concluded that in a stable environment, organizations are more effective if they have detailed procedures and centralized decision-making, while organizations in an unstable environment have decentralized organizations (allowing for participation) and place less emphasis on rules and regulations (Tossi and Carroll, 1976).

It is evident the contingency approach is (in actuality) a blend of different managerial approaches. It realizes that there is no *one* best way to do something when it comes to managing an organization, motivating people, or orchestrating change. It is obvious, then, a specific situation can trigger a variety of managerial responses before something can be accomplished.

In summary, a contingency management model consists of the following elements (Hellriegel and Slocum, 1976):

1. Environment
2. The individual
3. Organization
4. The group

A police manager must become adept at analyzing the relationships between the elements just listed when structuring an organization, developing a motivational program, or creating a task force. The major thrust of the contingency approach is to develop a managerial style that maximizes our knowledge of individual behavior, group dynamics, and their relationship to the organization and the environment.

Managerial principles are not forsaken, but are applied with intuition and practical judgment when the situation calls for it. At the same time, increasing emphasis is being placed on the human relations aspect of management. Today's police manager cannot ignore the fact that officers as well as nonsworn personnel have needs that evoke different perceptions, values, and emotional responses. Consequently increasing attention is being devoted to the human equation both within and outside the police organization. It must be understood that there are no simple conclusions for a police manager when organizational behavior is concerned. The contingency approach is widely accepted by behavioral scientists as a viable approach to assessing and dealing with the numerous interacting processes of the elements that make up the contingency model. The key is to give serious consideration to behavior in organizational settings (Baron, 1983).

Police Management in Transition

Two leading police experts, George L. Kelling and Mark H. Moore, have studied the development of police management by dividing the history of policing into three different eras: political, reform, and community policing. Each era has been dominated by a specific strategy. The *political era*, characterized by the close ties between the police and politics, came into existence in the 1840s and ended during the early part of this century. The reform era was a product of the desire to eliminate politics from policing. It lasted in varying degrees until the beginning of the 1980s, but now seems to be giving way to an era of community policing (Kelling and Moore, 1988).

The Political Era

During the first part of this century, police departments in the United States were at the focal point between numerous pressure groups working diligently to control the police. Departments derived their operational legitimacy and resources from local ward heelers and politicians. Two historians, K. E. Jordan and Robert M. Fogelson, have taken the view that the police were clear-cut extensions of the political process. Politicians recruited officers, and the police in turn supported political candidates to the extent of rigging elections when necessary.

During the political period, the police were not only active in traditional police functions such as crime control, prevention, and order maintenance, but they provided an extremely wide range of social services. Leonhard Fuld and Raymond Fosdick both called for the elimination of functions such as running soup kitchens, finding lodging, collecting taxes, and acting as a censor.

These early police departments, although they had all the trappings of the centralized, semimilitary organization with a definitive chain of command, actually functioned in a decentralized fashion. They were organized in such a way that each precinct was, in actuality, autonomous. A captain was in charge of each precinct, and it was quite routine for all personnel matters to be cleared with local politicians (Kelling and Moore, 1988). Principal tasks

TABLE 1.2 Organizational Strategy of the Political Era

1. Legitimacy and authority were primarily political.
2. Primary functions performed were the control of crime, order maintenance, and numerous social services.
3. Organizationally, police departments were decentralized.
4. Police were intimately connected to the political environment.
5. Demands for police services came either from citizens or politicians.
6. There was extensive use of foot patrol.

SOURCE: Adapted from George L. Kelling and Mark H. Moore, *The Evolving Strategy of Policing* (Washington, DC: National Institute of Justice, November 1988).

performed by the police during the political era included crime and riot control, maintenance of order, and providing a large number of social services (see Table 1.2).

Extensive decentralization and limited organizational control (coupled with the political appointment of officers) proved to be some of the reasons for the disenchantment with the police and the role they played in the community. As pointed out by Kelling and Moore (1988, p. 3), "the image of Keystone Cops—police as clumsy bunglers—was widespread and often descriptive of realities in American policing."

The Reform Era

During the latter part of the last century and the first part of this century, politicians and urban reformers were at loggerheads over who would control the police. Abuses of police power were quite common, and the close ties between the police and ward heelers led to a great deal of corruption (Walker, 1977). One expert pointed out that attempts at early reform usually failed, and it was not until this century that the combination of external and internal forces actually proved to be effective in altering the police forces of America in what is now called the *reform era* (Fogelson, 1977).

A leader in the reform movement was August Vollmer, the first police chief in Berkeley, California. He was followed by O. W. Wilson, who became the primary architect of the reform movement and espoused the belief that the purpose of leadership in the police field was to direct, control, and coordinate the members of the police force. He developed nine principles of organization a manager should practice when functioning as a police executive (Leonard and More, 1987):

1. Tasks similar in purpose, method, or clientele should be grouped together in one or more units under the control of a single person.
2. Duties should be defined precisely and made known to all members of the organization so that responsibility can be placed exactly.
3. Channels of communications should be established so that information can flow up and down the organization and authority can be delegated.
4. The principle of unity of command—one boss—must be applied.
5. The span of control should be limited.
6. Each task should be assigned to a member of the organization.
7. Line personnel must be supervised around the clock.

8. Each assignment of responsibility carries with it a commensurate authority.
9. Persons to whom authority is delegated are held accountable for its use.

As the reform movement came into its own, politics was rejected as the source of legitimacy and authorization. In some instances local control was usurped by state government. In a few cities the position of chief was placed under civil service. In other cities the chief executive officer was given lifetime tenure and could only be removed for cause. The purpose of all such changes was to isolate the police from political influence (Kelling and Moore, 1988).

As a result of such changes, law enforcement agencies became the most autonomous public departments in urban government (Goldstein, 1977). Policing became a legal matter under discretionary leadership. Political influence was perceived to be totally corrupting to the police field and was avoided no matter what the cost.

The police function changed considerably as crime control and suppression became the desirable goals of law enforcement agencies. In short order, anything that smacked of "social work" was rejected.

Police reformers adopted the *scientific,* or *classical,* theory of administration developed by Frederick W. Taylor. Management based on this theory implemented programs linked to economic rewards that, in turn, increased productivity. In addition, principles of division of labor and unity of command became the vogue, and specialization was supported along with hierarchical control. Police work was routinized and standardized, and a great deal of effort was expended to reduce officer discretion (Kelling and Moore, 1988).

The principal goal of law enforcement became the enforcement of the law. When special problems occurred, police management responded by creating separate and distinct units such as juvenile and traffic, which weakened the patrol function and centralized control. Bureaucratic control dominated and was expanded by close supervision and the creation of additional management layers. Meticulous record keeping was emphasized, and the chain of command became the desirable channel of communications.

The professional model of law enforcement became the goal of police reformers, and citizens were expected to be the relatively passive recipients of crime control services. Kelling and Moore placed this approach in perspective when they stated, "The metaphor that expressed this orientation to the community was that of the police as the *thin blue line*" (p. 4). Table 1.3 summarizes the organizational strategy of the reform movement.

TABLE 1.3 Organizational Strategy of the Reform Era

1. The authorization for the police was the law, and it was implemented by the professional model.
2. The primary function was crime control.
3. Organizationally the police were centralized and emphasis was placed on bureaucratic control.
4. The relationship to the community was characterized as professionally remote.
5. The demands for police service were channeled through central dispatching.

SOURCE: Adapted from George L. Kelling and Mark H. Moore, *The Evolving Strategy of Policing* (Washington, DC: National Institute of Justice, November 1988).

In retrospect, the reform movement swept the country. It made sense that the primary task of the police was to fight crime. In avoiding the pitfalls of the political era, professional law enforcement was looked on as a means of reducing discretion and providing police services in an impartial manner. While it seemed to be effective during the 1940s and 1950s it was found to be less than adequate during the subsequent decades.

During the 1960s and 1970s the United States underwent a series of social changes that altered the relationship of the entire system of government to the rest of the community. The civil rights movement, followed by antiwar movements, challenged the way the police handled riots, marches, and rallies. Television watchers saw minorities and demonstrators gassed, clubbed, and attacked by dogs, and police tactics were brought into disrepute.

Other changes were just as significant. Minorities moved into the cities, there were more youths, and the fear of crime rose substantially. During the 1980s researchers determined that the fear of crime was more closely correlated with disorder than with crime (Spelman and Brown, 1982). Unfortunately order maintenance was downplayed. In fact, few departments collected data on such offenses, and police management did not train officers in handling such activities. Nor did they reward officers for successfully performing order maintenance activities (Kelling and Moore, 1988).

The reform movement resulted in police managers becoming increasingly remote from line personnel. The problem was management style. While professionalism was the key word of the reform era, it did not extend to patrol. Management maintained the idea that the total organization was designed to support patrol, but such was not the case. The reality of the situation was that patrol officers were continually controlled. The police bureaucracy stifled initiative, and everything had to be done by the book—this policy even extended to personal conduct off duty. Specific rules and regulations were developed to ensure compliance with departmental policy. In many agencies any assignment except patrol was eagerly sought after, and over a period of time, patrol was performed by the youngest and most inexperienced officers. In fact, it became the dumping ground of many departments.

The Community Policing Era

During the latter part of the reform era, foot patrol was resurrected and in many cities, citizens, as well as politicians, not only demanded but funded additional foot patrols (see Table 1.4). The strategy proved to be successful because it helped to reduce fear, enhanced citizen satisfaction with the police, improved the attitudes of the police toward the public, and the police found that foot patrol was both personally and professionally rewarding (Trojanowicz, 1982).

Additional research in several communities revealed other police tactics that emphasized the quality and quantity of police-citizen interaction, resulting in the creation of new opportunities for the police to understand citizen concerns. The police discovered that citizens responded positively when asked about their priorities and concerns with crime and disorder. Citizens provided the police with valuable information, and in some instances, identified

TABLE 1.4 Traditional versus Community Policing: Questions and Answers

	Traditional	*Community Policing*
Question: Who are the police?	A government agency principally responsible for law enforcement.	Police are the public and the public are the police: The police officers are those who are paid to give full-time attention to the duties of every citizen.
Question: What is the relationship of the police force to other public service departments?	Priorities often conflict.	The police are one department among many responsible for improving the quality of life.
Question: What is the role of the police?	Focusing on solving crimes.	A broader problem-solving approach.
Question: How is police efficiency measured?	By detection and arrest rates.	By the absence of crime and disorder.
Question: What are the highest priorities?	Crimes that are high value (e.g., bank robberies) and those involving violence.	Whatever problems disturb the community most.
Question: What, specifically, do police deal with?	Incidents.	Citizens' problems and concerns.
Question: What determines the effectiveness of police?	Response times.	Public cooperation.
Question: What view do police take of service calls?	Deal with them only if there is no real police work to do.	Vital function and great opportunity.
Question: What is police professionalism?	Swift effective response to serious crime.	Keeping close to the community.
Question: What kind of intelligence is most important?	Crime intelligence (study of particular crimes or series of crimes).	Criminal intelligence (information about the activities of individuals or groups).
Question: What is the essential nature of police accountability?	Highly centralized; governed by rules, regulations, and policy directives; accountable to the law.	Emphasis on local accountability to community needs.
Question: What is the role of headquarters?	To provide the necessary rules and policy directives.	To preach organizational values.
Question: What is the role of the press liaison department?	To keep the "heat" off operational officers so they can get on with the job.	To coordinate an essential channel of communication with the community.
Question: How do the police regard prosecutions?	As an important goal.	As one tool among many.

SOURCE: Malcolm K. Sparrow, *Implementing Community Policing* (Washington, DC: National Institute of Justice, 1988).

problems that were unknown to the police. This led to the police seeking authorization from local citizens to intervene in disorderly situations (Pate et al., 1986).

At the same time, *community policing* was tested in a number of cities and proved to be successful. It is a process of rejecting the fragmented approach (where the police react to a single incident) and adopting a technique where the problem is viewed holistically. The police work with citizens and other agencies to solve problems (Goldstein, 1979).

This problem-confronting approach contradicts many of the key features of the professionalization occurring under the reform era. Foot patrol creates a closer relationship between officers and members of the community. Problem-solving was found to be totally foreign to previous efforts by police management to standardize the tasks performed by patrol officers. Lastly, relying on citizen endorsement of order maintenance activities (as a means of justifying police activities) acknowledges dependence on the political process and the broadening of the police function (Kelling and Moore, 1988).

Community Disenchantment A highly publicized 1991 incident thrust Los Angeles Police Chief Daryl F. Gates into a political and media spotlight when several members of the Los Angeles Police Department were videotaped beating a citizen. *(AP/Wide World Photos)*

TABLE 1.5 Organizational Strategy of the Community Policing Era

1. The authority for this strategy stems from community support, law, and professionalism.
2. Crime control and its prevention are considered to be the major functions of the police.
3. The organizational design emphasizes decentralization and the use of task forces.
4. This period is characterized by a consultive relationship with the community.
5. Community policing tactics include foot patrol, problem-solving, information gathering, counseling, and education.

SOURCE: Adapted from George L. Kelling and Mark H. Moore, *The Evolving Strategy of Policing* (Washington, DC: National Institute of Justice, November 1988).

Under the community approach, crime control remains one of the functions of law enforcement, but it also includes order maintenance, conflict resolution, problem-solving, and the provision of numerous services. Another difference is that the community approach treats each of the functions equally. In other words, as much attention is given to preventative activities as is given to crime control.

Organizational decentralization is emphasized under the community approach. Officers at the lowest level of the organization become involved in decision-making as community problems are identified, diagnosed, and responses implemented (see Table 1.5). Communications tend to flow up rather than down, and the organization is inclined to flatten as greater importance is given to maximizing dialogue between members of the community and the department. Typically, beat offices are established in community centers, schools, and churches; storefront stations serve as a vehicle for maintaining close contact with the community.

As decentralization occurs, problem-solving in the community enhances the power of lower-level management (especially the supervisor). At the same time, police executives become more involved in planning and implementation. Participative management prevails—this calls for involving operational personnel in an effort to solve community problems. Task forces are used extensively as a means of tapping internal talent and maximizing the skills of sergeants and patrol officers.

A realistic and positive community strategy requires the establishment of a continuing relationship between the police and the public. This is done by assigning officers to a specific beat for an extended period of time, conducting crime control meetings, solving problems, instituting educational programs, and any other activity that enhances a working relationship between the police and the public (Kelling and Moore, 1988).

Organization

Through the years the police have tested few alternatives to structuring the department other than establishing the formal bureaucratic organization. Typically it is a pyramid with the majority of the organization members finding themselves located at the bottom. Implicit in such a chart is the identification of those who have power and those who do not. Responsibility is clearly identified by boxes and lines—the higher the box location in the organization

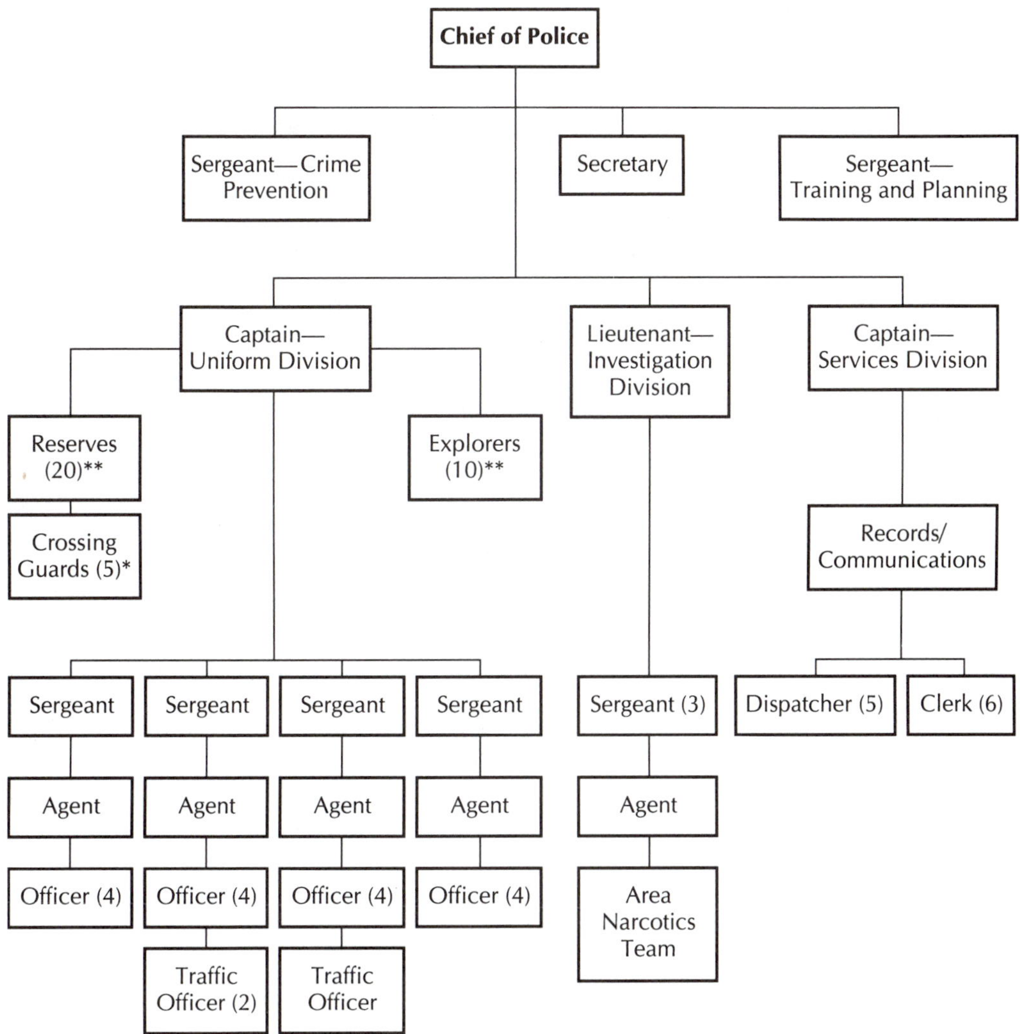

*Part Time
**Volunteers

FIGURE 1.4 Organizational Structure for a Small Police Department. Source Courtesy of Campbell Police Department, Donald R. Burr, Chief.

chart, the more knowledgeable and competent (presumably) the individual is. (Figures 1.4, 1.5, and 1.6 depict the traditional police organization.)

By virtue of such a formalized relationship, members of the organization are rewarded for appropriate behavior by promotions, fringe benefits, and other perks that go with the position. All these are done as a means of obtaining appropriate responses that ensure goal attainment. All the normal managerial functions such as planning, directing, and controlling are utilized in such a way that employee behavior is directed toward the efficient attainment of departmental objectives.

The desire of the police executive is to design an organization in such a way, through all the trappings of the bureaucracy, that the organization will make

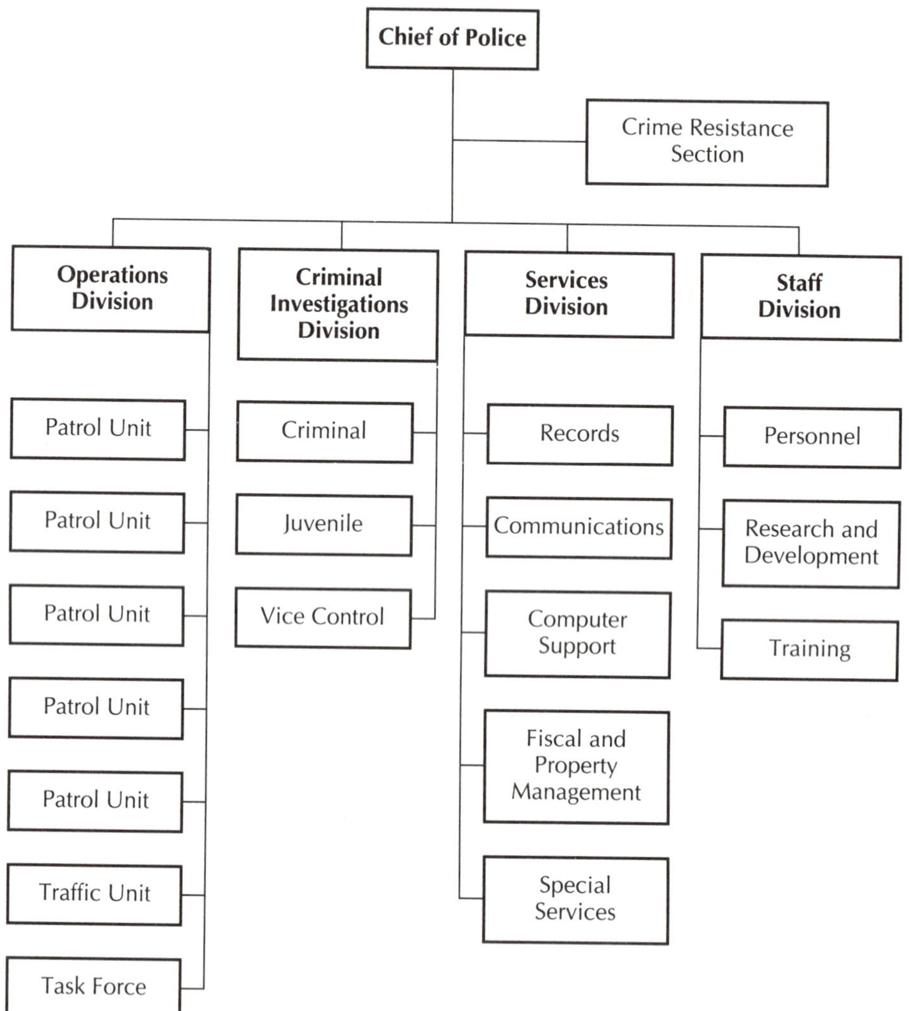

FIGURE 1.5 Organizational Structure for a Medium-Sized Police Department.

appropriate decisions and handle problems. Although this is a commendable goal, it is seldom attained because of numerous variables and events that cannot be controlled. People just cannot be fit into a box or treated as if they are a number instead of being human. Many police problems defy predictability. Expertise and knowledge vary considerably—in some instances, subordinates have the greater skills. In addition, the interaction between individuals, within an organization, seldom conforms to the rigidity depicted by boxes and lines of authority.

The human equation is forever present. While it might be desirable to always react intellectually, such is not the case. Emotions enter the picture, and such factors as personality, attitudes, perception, power, and group dynamics modify the relationship between managers and employees. All these factors

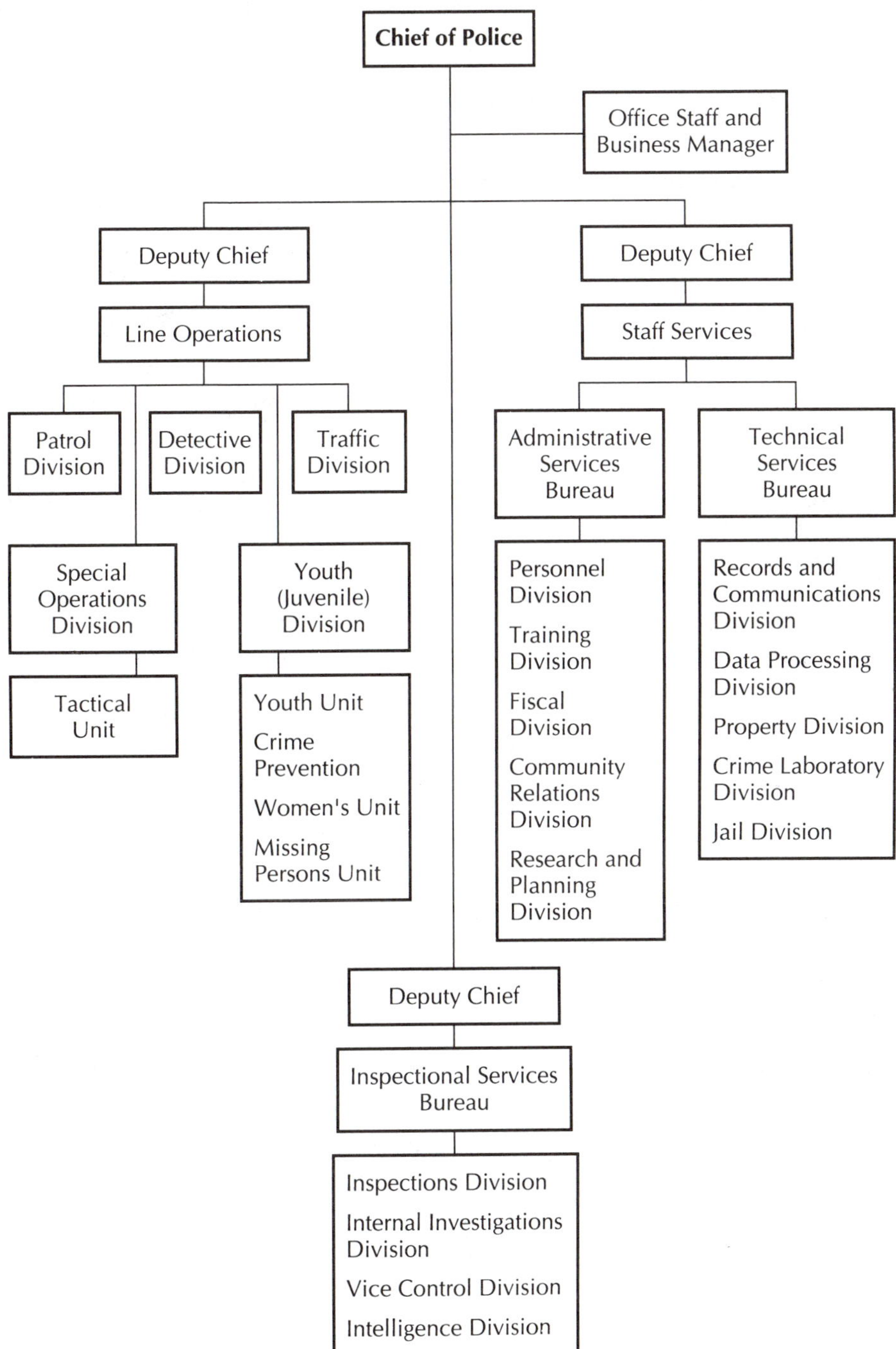

FIGURE 1.6 Organizational Structure for a Large Police Department.

influence the decision-making process and alter the organization's response to police problems (Cohen, Fink, Gadon, and Willits, 1980).

Types of Structuring

Traditionally, police executives have utilized a number of different approaches to structuring the organization. One approach has been to organize by *major purpose*. This allows for unified control over individuals who are performing similar tasks and has resulted in the creation of such units as patrol and traffic (see Table 1.6 for a list of approaches used when structuring an organization).

A second approach has been to organize by *major process*. An example is the crime laboratory organized to facilitate the examination of evidence. The same is true of the records division organized to receive, assemble, evaluate, and analyze data concerning police problems (Leonard and More, 1987). It should be pointed out that this functional specialization normally involves the combining of organization by purpose as well as by process.

Another way to organize is by responding to the *clientele* served. Typical of this is the juvenile unit organized to handle all juvenile offenders regardless of age or the crime committed. Foreign language speakers and racial clusters are other examples of creating special units to deal exclusively with groups from other countries.

The next way to organize is by *area,* or territory. The precinct station house has been a part of the structural organization for many years, especially in large cities. This type of organizing was prevalent during the political era, but during the reform era, efforts were made toward its elimination as an unnecessary burden on the taxpayer and because it diluted executive control.

The final way of organizing is by *time*. It provides police departments with the distribution of personnel over three shifts as a means of providing an around-the-clock operation. The amount, nature, and time of occurrence of offenses supply, in part, the information needed to allocate officers to one of the shifts.

The traditionalist used any one of these means or a combination of the methods in order to provide for the delivery of effective police service to the community. In more recent years, police managers in some agencies have turned to the matrix organization and the utilization of task forces as a means of adapting the structure to the human factor and providing a clearer representation of reality.

TABLE 1.6 Methods of Organizing a Police Department

Major purpose
Major process
Clientele
Area
Time

The Matrix Organization

The matrix structure is the antithesis of the traditional police organization. In fact, it violates the unity of command principle of functional management and in actuality replicates one of the concepts initially proposed by Frederick Taylor when he developed the scientific management theory. In the *matrix structure*, the individual or a group are supervised by two bosses, one commanding the special task being performed and the other heading one of the functional divisions. As illustrated in Figure 1.7, the sting operation is supervised by a sergeant (who is controlling the operation) and the head of the criminal investigations division. In the case of the problem-solving task force it is designed to solve household problems (drugs, burglaries, muggings) in a large municipal housing project. This unit is jointly supervised by the task force commander and the deputy chief of the operations division.

In both instances, members of the task force and the sting operation report to, receive direction from, and are evaluated by two managers. In other instances the matrix organization might find dual supervision at either a higher or lower level within the organization. Once personnel adjust to such a functional supervisory function, the reporting relationships are strengthened and formalized (Staft, 1980). The matrix organization provides for a balance between the functional need and the services provided by the department. For the traditionalist who is enamored with structural unity, the matrix organization can definitely be a source of serious irritation. It calls for managers and operational personnel who are interpersonally competent, are capable

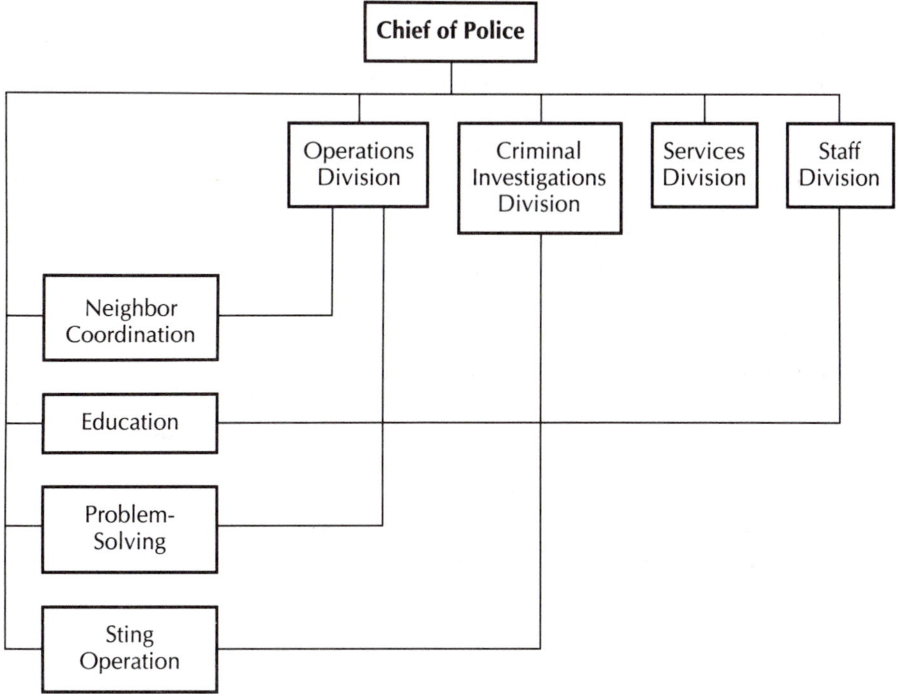

FIGURE 1.7 The Police Matrix Organization.

of accepting change, and can deal with the ambiguity of the two-boss system (Cohen, Fink, Gadon, and Willits, 1980).

Management Defined

There are probably as many definitions of management as there are individuals who have studied or written management texts. During the first part of this century Mary Parker Follett stated management was "the art of getting things done through people" (Steers, Ungson, and Mowday, 1985). Another definition widely accepted in management is the efficient utilization of resources (Rue and Byars, 1986).

In this text, *management is defined as a continuing process that includes all activities focusing on the identification, refinement, and attainment of objectives by the effective application of resources.*

This definition is dynamic and based on the fundamental concept that positive management of a police organization is the only way resources can be maximized in order to achieve departmental goals. It is a conceptual definition of managing in terms of what managers do.

Management Functions

Our definition of management is accepted and understood much more readily if the managers' functions are known. There are four primary functions that clearly represent the types of activities managers engage in. The time managers devote to each activity will vary, depending on their managerial level within the organization, but they must be performed to some degree and on a continuing basis if the department is to function effectively.

1. *Organizing.* The structuring of an organization is necessary in order to distribute the workload according to some type of logical plan. In law enforcement, the decision to group related activities usually takes into consideration such variables as the major purpose of the activity or function, the process or method to be utilized in order to achieve objectives, the nature of the clientele, the geographical distribution, and time. Most of these factors operate simultaneously.

2. *Planning.* A police department cannot function effectively if it strives to maintain the status quo in a changing community. A plan useful today can become obsolete tomorrow. There must be a continuing assessment and evaluation of police plans if departmental goals are to be attained. In law enforcement, the types of plans usually include operational, procedural, tactical, fiscal, management, and program (see Figure 1.8).

The purposes of planning varies from agency to agency, but generally includes the following (More and O'Neill, 1984):

1. Organizational flexibility is enhanced.
2. Goals are more easily attained.
3. Decision-making is improved.
4. Agency personnel become involved in the planning process.
5. Problems are identified more easily.

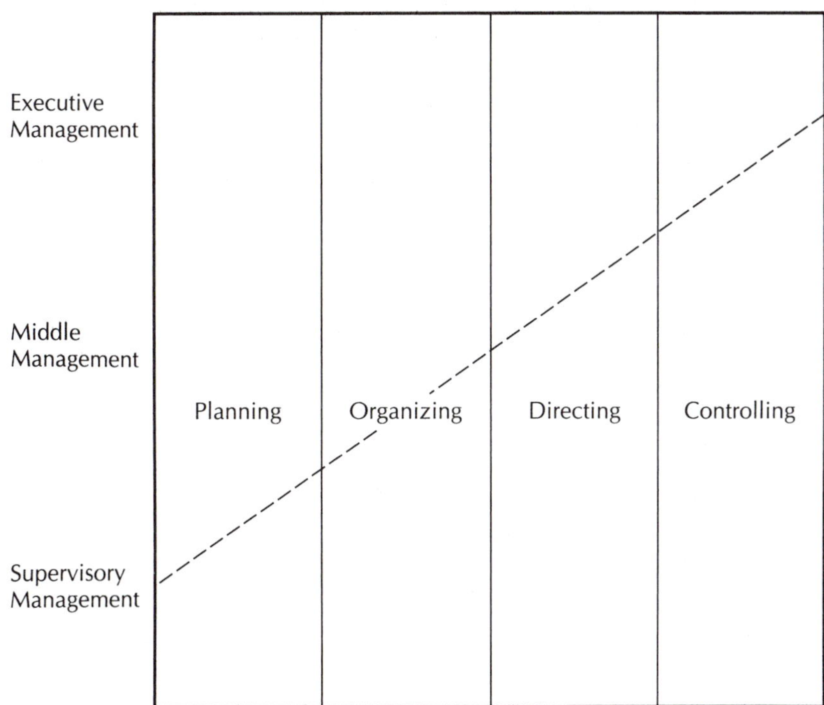

FIGURE 1.8 Relationship of Level of Management to Functions Performed.

6. Standards for measurement can be developed.
7. Needs can be identified.

Effective planning must be strongly supported by the police executive, to the extent there is no question that the police agency is committed to the planning process.

3. *Directing.* A police organization becomes a viable entity when fused with positive leadership. Direction is essential to the achievement of departmental goals, and it must be provided by the managers in the police agency. Inspired leadership is contagious, and officers will respond to positive direction allowing for the integration of personal and organizational needs.

The autocratic leadership style prevalent in law enforcement circles during the first half of this century is no longer generally acceptable or needed. Direction provided for an organization must be predicated on an awareness of motivational factors—not fear. Police managers must work with and through people. A serious and continuing effort must be made to create a results-oriented working environment. The complexity of relationships between managers and officers requires a unique insight into human behavior and a special awareness of individuals, groups, and the needs of the community.

4. *Controlling.* At some point, managers must become concerned with checking on progress in an effort to determine if previously agreed upon objectives have been attained. Effective managers obtain the data needed to review progress and share this data with superiors and subordinates. If corrective

TABLE 1.7 Management Functions

Organizing	Directing
Structuring	Leadership Skills
Grouping Related Activities	Coaching
Purpose	Style
Process	Results Orientation
Clientele	**Controlling**
Geographic	Standards
Time	Corrective Action
Planning	Development of
Types of Plans	Procedures
Operational	Policies
Procedural	Rules
Tactical	Regulations
Fiscal	Acquisition of Data
Management	
Program	
Setting of Objectives and Goals	
Development of Standards	

action is needed, it should only be taken after specific deviations are identified and measured against previously agreed upon standards (Lundy, 1986). Effective control activities, in which a manager engages, include the development of procedures and policies, rules and regulations, periodical reports, and budgets (see Table 1.7).

The four managerial functions just discussed are not mutually exclusive, but highly interrelated. They do not necessarily occur in the sequence we listed, but can happen at the same time. Keep in mind that managerial performance of these functions is continuously modified by any or all the following factors:

1. Managerial competence
2. Organizational level
3. Nature and type of activity
4. Competence of followers

Managerial Levels

As organizations become larger and more complex, the number of managerial levels increases. In a small police agency, a chief of police will be the only manager; in a very large agency, there can be 15 or more managers at the highest level in the organization. In general, there are three distinct levels of management in police organizations: executive, middle, and supervisory.

Executive managers in law enforcement have varying titles including commissioner, director, or chief. In addition, other top level managers may have titles such as assistant chief, deputy chief, assistant director, or in other situations they hold ranks similar to the military such as colonel or lieutenant colonel. At this level, these senior administrators are primarily responsible

Executive Managers
Middle Managers
Supervisory Managers

FIGURE 1.9 Managerial Levels.

for planning, creating organizational goals, developing organizational policies, and responding to political and community inquiries.

In one study of 96 law enforcement agencies, the percentage (median) of personnel in the chief's office was found to be 1.12 but the percentage of individuals serving in that capacity decreased slightly as the agency increased in size (Police Foundation, 1981). In one agency with approximately 1,110 sworn personnel, the chief's office had three secretaries, one administrative assistant, one sergeant (who was responsible for relationships with the media), and one captain.

Assistant chiefs normally function as the alter egos of the police chief executive and as key figures in the management team with in-line administrative responsibilities. Generally, deputy chiefs are responsible for supervising major functions such as line operations, staff services, or investigations (see Figure 1.9).

Middle managers in police departments supervise divisions or units carrying such titles as patrol, traffic, records, communications, personnel, or research and development. Managers at this level are responsible for interpreting policies and procedures and creating programs to meet departmental goals. In a survey of departments nationwide it was found that 18.99 percent (median) of police department employees functioned in various administrative capacities, and 5.46 percent (median) of the personnel held the ranks of lieutenant, captain, or major (Police Foundation, 1981).

Supervisory managers in police departments are more prevalent than at any other managerial level and constitute 61 percent of all administrative personnel who hold a managerial police rank (Police Foundation, 1981). Sergeant is the principal rank held, except for integrated police-fire organizations where the title is lieutenant. These first-line supervisors are generally held responsible for accomplishing short-term goals and carrying out day-to-day activities.

Line and Staff

Another way of viewing managers and the functions they perform is to distinguish between *line and staff,* similar to the distinction found in the military. As we indicated previously, American law enforcement has utilized the military model extensively.

The recognition of line and staff is the initial step to take in order to arrange related functions under unified supervision and command. Its value becomes readily apparent when functions are placed in their proper place, based on the distinction between the two principal functions—preparation for the delivery of police services and the actual delivery of those services.

The accepted classification of staff functions and line operations in police departments is clearly evident in the structure of a police agency as indicated in Figure 1.10 depicting a medium-sized agency. Staff functions deal

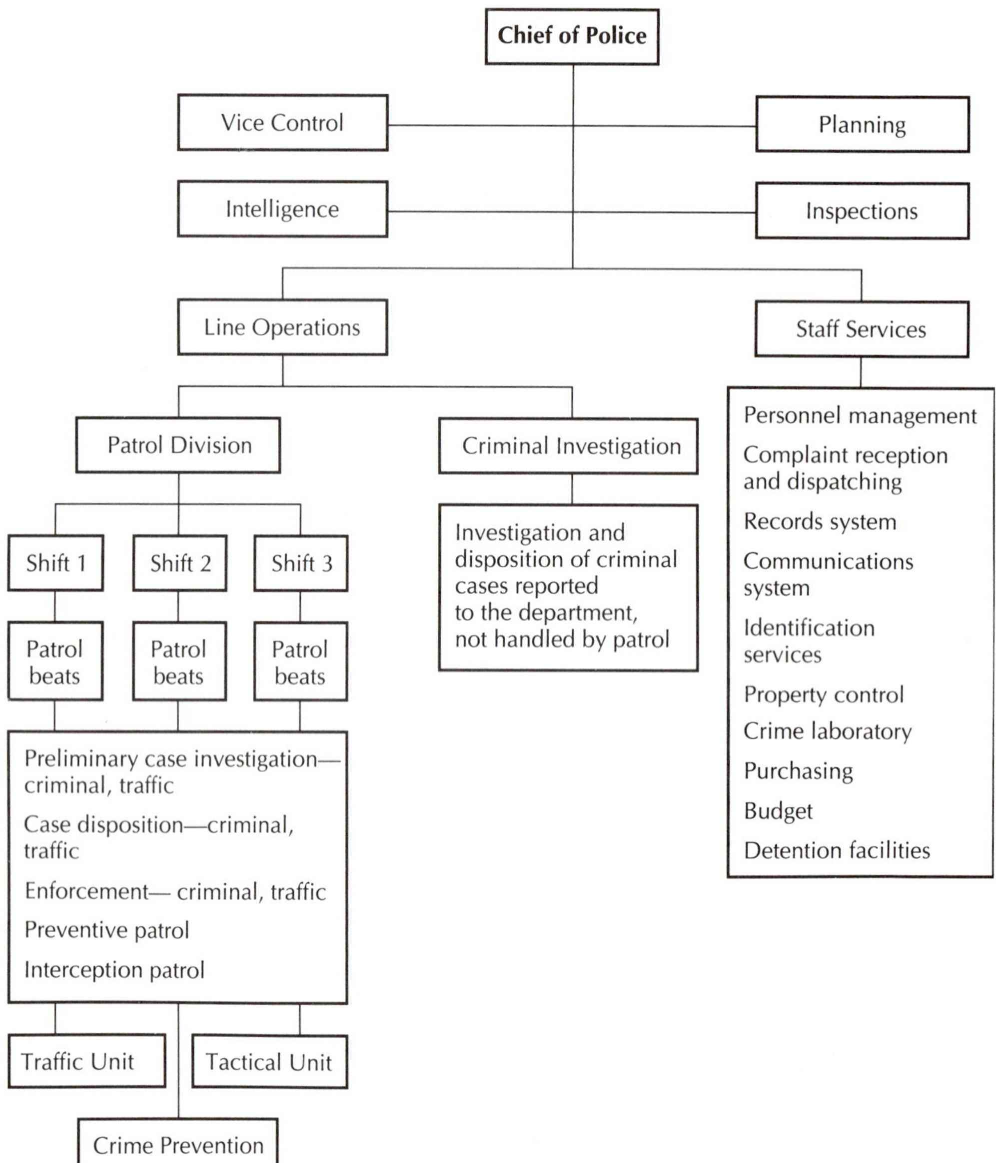

FIGURE 1.10 Organizational Structure of a Medium-Sized Police Department Distinguishing Line and Staff.

exclusively with supporting activities, and in some of the larger agencies, they have been broken down into administrative services and technical services. In any event, the key is that they function to support line operations and the attainment of organizational goals.

Operationally the line services translate policy into action. Ultimately the delivery of police services to the community is the responsibility of the line. On the other hand, staff services supply line services with personnel, records, and material, along with other services, so they can accomplish their job.

Within staff services the following trend is apparent as a number of agencies have subdivided support services into the following:

1. Administrative Services
    - Personnel
    - Training
    - Fiscal
    - Community Relations
    - Research and Planning
    - Crime Analysis
2. Technical Services
    - Records
    - Communications
    - Property
    - Crime Laboratory
    - Jail

This division of line services allows for the orderly arrangement of elements within the structure of the police organization. Such an arrangement provides for a clarification of lines of authority and the chain of command, and the distribution of power within the organization. A clear distinction between the two allows line services to devote total energies to the accomplishment of line objectives.

Summary

Management, as we know it today, is the result of an evolutionary process well over a century old. Many of the early management theorists relied on military and religious models. Other theories were developed in business and industry and later were adopted by the police field. These theories include ideal bureaucracy, scientific management, functional management (including POSDCORB), human relations, systems, and contingency management.

During the early part of this century, police departments in the United States were at the focal point between numerous pressure groups that worked diligently to control the police. During the political period, the police provided the traditional police services as well as a wide range of social services including collecting taxes, running soup kitchens, functioning as a censor, and finding lodging for the needy.

Disenchantment with the political control of the police and widespread corruption led to the reform era in which the goal was to isolate the police from political influence. Services that could be described as social work were eliminated, and the primary goal of the police became enforcement of the law. Professionalism became the dominant cry of the reformers, and every effort was made to reduce officer discretion and provide services in an impartial manner.

The reform movement dominated the police scene during the 1940s and 1950s, but during the following decades a series of social changes altered the relationship of the police with the public. The civil rights movement and the antiwar movements challenged the way the police handle marches, disorders, riots, and rallies. There was a cry for police review boards, television watchers saw minorities and demonstrators gassed, clubbed, and attacked by dogs, and police tactics were brought into disrepute. The reform movement resulted in the police becoming detached from the community served.

Today's approach is called the community policing era. It contradicts many of the key features of professionalism advocated during the reform era. Under the community approach, crime control remains as one of the functions of law enforcement, but equal consideration is also given to order maintenance, conflict resolution, problem-solving, and the provision of services. Officers at every level become involved in the decision-making process, and input from members of the community is actively sought. Under this concept, officers are assigned to a specific beat for an extended period of time to conduct crime control meetings, engage in problem-solving activities, and work diligently to improve the relationship between the police and the public.

Through the years the police have emphasized the need to organize bureaucratically by structuring the organization according to major purpose, major process, clientele, area, and time. As the police have moved into the community policing era, more and more agencies have responded by creating a matrix organization. In this type of structure the individual or the group is supervised by two bosses, one representing the special task being performed and the other the head of one of the functional units.

Currently police managers perform four primary functions: organizing, planning, directing, and controlling. The time a manager devotes to each activity varies, depending on their managerial level within the organization. In addition, the way the organization is divided into line and staff modifies the functions performed by each police manager at different levels within the organization.

Key Concepts

Ideal bureaucracy
Scientific management
Functional management
POSDCORB
Hawthorne effect
Systems approach
Contingency management model
Political era
Reform era
Community policing era
Organizing by clientele
Organizing by area
Organizing by time
Matrix structure
Line and staff

Discussion Topics and Questions

1. What are the characteristics of a bureaucracy?
2. What are the limitations of a bureaucracy?
3. Describe what employees do when they are "soldiering."
4. List Henri Fayol's elements of management.
5. Describe the series of Hawthorne studies.
6. What was the code of behavior adopted by workers in the Hawthorne plant?
7. How would you apply the open organizational model to a typical medium-sized police department?
8. What are the distinguishing features of a matrix organization?
9. What are the four major functions performed by police managers?
10. Why should there be a distinction between line and staff?

References

BARON, ROBERT A. 1983. *Behavior in Organizations*. Boston: Allyn & Bacon.

BRISCOE, DENNIS R. 1980. "Organizational Design: Dealing with the Human Constraint," *California Management Review,* Vol. XIII, No. 3.

BURNS, TOM, and G. M. STALKER. 1961. *Management of Innovation*. London: Tavistock.

CHURCHMAN, C. WEST. 1968. *The Systems Approach*. New York: Dell.

COHEN, ALLAN R., STEPHEN L. FINK, HERMAN GADON, and ROBIN D. WILLITS. 1980. *Effective Behavior in Organizations*. Homewood, IL: Richard D. Irwin.

CORDNER, GARY W. 1978. "Open and Closed Models of Police Organizations: Traditions, Dilemmas, and Practical Considerations," *Journal of Police Science and Administration,* Vol. 6, No. 1.

CUTHBERT, NORMAN H. 1976. "A Business Scientist." In Henry L. Tossi and Henry L. Carroll (Eds.), *Management: Contingencies, Structure, and Process*. Chicago: St. Clair Press.

FAYOL, HENRY. 1949. *General and Industrial Management*. London: Sir Isaac Pitman.

FOGELSON, ROBERT M. 1977. *Big-City Police*. Cambridge: Harvard University Press.

FOSDICK, RAYMOND B. 1969. *American Police Systems*. Montclair, NJ: Patterson Smith.

FULD, LEONHARD FELIX. 1909. *Police Administration*. New York: Putnam.

GEORGE, CLAUDE S., JR. 1968. *The History of Management Thought*. Englewood Cliffs, NJ: Prentice-Hall.

GERTH, H. H., and C. WRIGHT MILLS. 1958. *Max Weber: Essays in Sociology*. New York: Oxford University Press.

GOLDSTEIN, HERMAN. 1977. *Policing in a Free Society*. Cambridge: Ballinger.

GOLDSTEIN, HERMAN. 1979. "Improving Policing: A Problem-Oriented Approach," *Crime and Delinquency,* No. 2.

GRAPER, ELMER D. 1921. *American Police Administration*. New York: Macmillan.

GULICK, LUTHER. 1937 (reprinted in 1969). "Notes on the Theory of Organization." In Luther Gulick and L. Urwick (Eds.), *Papers on the Science of Administration*. New York: August M. Kelley.

HELLRIEGEL, DON, and JOHN W. SLOCUM. 1976. *Organizational Behavior.* St. Paul, MN: West.

KAST, FREMONT E., and JAMES E. ROSENZWEIG. 1972. "General Systems Theory: Application for Organization and Management," *Academy of Management Journal,* No. 4.

KELLING, GEORGE L., and MARK H. MOORE. 1988. *The Evolving Strategy of Police*. Washington, DC: National Institute of Justice.

LAIRD, DONALD A., ELEANOR C. LAIRD, and ROSEMARY T. FRUEHLING, 1983. *Psychology: Human Relations and Work Adjustment* (6th ed.). New York: McGraw-Hill.

LANDSBERGER, HENRY A. 1958. *Hawthorne Revisited.* Ithaca, NY: Cornell University Press.

LEONARD, V. A., and HARRY W. MORE. 1987. *Police Organization and Management* (7th ed.). Mineola, NY: Foundation Press.

LORSCH, JAY W., and PAUL R. LAWRENCE (Eds.). 1970. *Studies in Organizational Design.* Homewood, IL: Irwin and Dorsey Press.

LUNDY, JAMES. 1986. *Lead, Follow, or Get Out of the Way.* San Diego: Avant Books.

MCFARLAND, DALTON E. 1986. *Management Principles and Practices* (4th ed). New York: Macmillan.

MERTON, ROBERT K. 1952. *Reader in Bureaucracy.* Glencoe, IL: Free Press.

MORE, HARRY W., and MICHAEL O'NEIL. 1984. *Contemporary Criminal Justice Planning.* Springfield, IL: Charles C Thomas.

NILLSSON, ERNST K. 1972. "Systems Analysis Applied to Law Enforcement," *Allocation of Resources in the Chicago Police Department.* Washington, DC: Law Enforcement Assistance Administration.

PATE, TONY, et al. 1986. *Reducing Fear of Crime in Houston and Newark: A Summary Report.* Washington, DC: Police Foundation.

POLICE FOUNDATION. 1981. *Survey of Police Operational and Administrative Practices.* Washington, DC: Police Executive Research Forum.

RICE, BERKELEY. 1982. "The Hawthorne Effect: Persistence of a Flawed Theory," *Psychology Today,* February.

ROETHLISBERGER, F. J., and WILLIAM J. DICKSON. 1939. *Management and the Worker.* Cambridge: Harvard University Press.

RUE, LESLIE W., and LLOYD L. BYARS. 1986. *Management: Theory and Practice.* Homewood, IL: Richard D. Irwin.

SCALON, BURT K., and J. BERNARD KEYS. 1979. *Managing.* Garden City, NY: Doubleday.

SPARROW, MALCOM K. 1988. *Implementing Community Policing.* Washington, DC: National Institute of Justice.

SPELMAN, WILLIAM, and DALE K. BROWN. 1982. *Calling the Police.* Washington, DC: Police Executive Research Forum.

STAFT, JOSEPH. 1980. "Effects of Organizational Design on Communications Between Patrol and Investigative Function," *FBI Law Enforcement Bulletin,* June.

STEERS, RICHARD M., GERARDO R. UNGSON, and RICHARD T. MOWDAY. 1985. *Managing Effective Organizations.* Boston: Mass Kent.

TAYLOR, FREDRICK W. 1947. *Scientific Management.* New York: Harper and Row Brothers.

THIERAUF, ROBERT J., ROBERT C. KLEKAMP, and DANIEL W. GEEDING. 1977. *Management Principles and Practices.* New York: Wiley.

TOSSI, HENRY L., and STEPHEN J. CARROLL. 1976. *Management: Contingencies, Structure, and Process.* Chicago: St. Clair Press.

TROJANOWICZ, ROBERT. 1982. *An Evaluation of the Neighborhood Foot Patrol Program in Flint Michigan.* East Lansing, MI: Michigan State University.

WALKER, SAMUEL. 1977. *A Critical History of Police Reform: The Emergence of Professionalism.* Lexington, MA: Lexington Books.

WOODS, BRETT F. 1980. "Systems Management: An Overview," *Law and Order,* September.

WOODWARD, JOAN. 1965. *Industrial Organization.* London: Oxford University Press.

For Further Reading

ECK, JOHN, and WILLIAM SPELMAN. 1987. *Problem-Oriented Policing in Newport.* Washington, DC: Police Executive Research Forum.

This book describes the theory and practice of problem-solving policing. Building on over 20 years of research and innovative practice, problem-oriented policing seeks to focus police service on resolving problems that create crimes, calls for service, and the public's dissatisfaction.

HIGDON, RICHARD K., and PHILIP HUMER. 1986. *How to Fight Fear: The COPE Program Package*. Washington, DC: Police Executive Research Forum.

The authors offer a detailed prescription for law enforcement agencies and local government officials interested in understanding and implementing COPE's problem-oriented approach to reduce fear of crime. They describe the organization, management, training, and standard operating procedures of the COPE units, and present case studies of COPE officers in action.

KELLING, GEORGE L. 1988. *Police and Communities: The Quiet Revolution*. Washington, DC: National Institute of Justice.

Describes in brief how many departments are finding alternatives to responding rapidly to the majority of calls for service. Organizing citizens' groups has become a priority in many agencies. Discusses how, increasingly, police departments are looking for means to evaluate themselves on their contribution to the quality of neighborhood life, not just crime statistics.

TAFT, PHILIP B., JR. 1986. *Fighting Fear: The Baltimore County, COPE Program*. Washington, DC: Police Executive Research Forum.

Describes the genesis and operation of COPE units and how they fight fear by attacking the underlying problems which cause people to be fearful. Reviews how officers survey and work with neighborhoods and with all types of organizations on the community's own terms.

CHAPTER **2**

Dynamics of Management: Managers and the Community

LEARNING OBJECTIVES

1. Define organizational behavior.
2. Identify the four types of behavior with which a police manager should be concerned.
3. Compare individual and interpersonal behavior.
4. Write a short essay describing organizational history, emphasizing historical foundations.
5. List the three managerial levels.
6. Compare conceptual and technical skills.
7. Describe a typical police manager's work week.
8. List the three major police managerial roles.
9. Compare the managerial roles of figurehead and liaison.
10. Write a short essay describing a value statement for a police department.
11. Compare traditional and community policing.
12. List the components of the problem-solving process.
13. Identify the potential problems when implementing community policing.

The success of a police organization is generally dependent on the quality of working life within the agency. Managers can, in the short run, attain objectives by threatening employees (ordering them to do something or suffer the consequences), but experience has shown that in today's working environment, officers do not readily accept authoritarian management attempting to attain objectives by coercion or executive fiat.

The attainment of goals and objectives over an extended period of time can only be achieved by the efforts of individuals and groups of truly motivated employees. Realizing organizational objectives can be in jeopardy if a manager ignores the needs of employees. Most officers adjust well to their department, but for a variety of reasons there are always some who do not. There is no single solution to the conflict that may arise between officers and their department (Hellriegel, Slocum, and Woodman, 1983).

INTRODUCTORY CASE

Lieutenants Smits and Miles

In a large metropolitan police department two sergeants were promoted to lieutenant at the same time and both were assigned to field operations. Within six months Lt. Marge Smits proved to be a very competent and effective manager; Lt. Roger Miles was, unfortunately, less than successful. Upper management is becoming genuinely concerned about Lt. Miles's inability to function as a manager. Captain William Proctor is completing six-month reviews for each of the lieutenants and is truly perplexed about this situation. Both officers had performed outstandingly in their former positions but Smits has risen to the challenge while Miles demonstrates an inability to adjust to the new position.

Lt. Smits finds that the demands of her new position contrast sharply with what was expected of her when she was a sergeant. As a first-line supervisor she was expected to function as an operational expert with command or managerial decisions being left to upper management. Viewing her role as something entirely different from anything she has ever done, Smits relishes the interaction with the personnel she supervises and the challenge of accomplishing goals and objectives through others. On assuming her new job she immediately reviewed the personnel files for each of the officers in her unit and became familiar with their knowledge, skills, and abilities. Utilizing this information, she has little difficulty in attaining unit objectives, starting to identify individual weaknesses, and working with employees in order to improve their performance. When officers successfully accomplish assignments they are given immediate feedback as she works diligently to improve her coaching skills and provide positive leadership.

Roger Miles, who had an exceptional record in his previous position, is clearly lost as a lieutenant. His primary concern is to scrutinize every officer's performance to such an extent that he can always find an error or omission. In each instance the officer is made aware of inadequate performance, and Lt. Miles intensifies his supervision by paying careful attention to every incident and report. Nothing is too small to correct, and unit objectives fall by the wayside as intensive supervision dominates the relationship between Lt. Miles and the officers in the unit. Errors are not tolerated because Miles feels they are a reflection on his leadership skills. In fact, Lt. Miles personifies the "See me" syndrome where subordinates find their mailboxes filled with memos asking for further information or clarification. The officers have reached the point where it seems to be more important to respond to memos than to perform police work.

Lt. Smits is clearly functioning as a manager; Lt. Miles is performing as a technician. Obviously, Captain Proctor prefers the former. Management is a unique activity requiring the application of distinct skills. Lt. Miles feels comfortable performing tasks best performed by first-line supervisors. The situation in which Lt. Miles finds himself is not unusual but it is one that continually challenges managers such as Captain Proctor and is a dilemma demanding resolution.

Captain Proctor expects Lt. Miles to accomplish departmental goals through the officers he is supervising and to refrain from performing nonmanagerial tasks. What should Captain Proctor do to get Lt. Miles to perform as a manager? Some managers feel this is the $64,000 question—one that is easy to ask, but difficult to resolve. Our purpose here is to help you understand why such leadership problems occur, how they can be analyzed, and what techniques to use to resolve the problems.

Why an employee does not perform at the assignment level (or performs inadequately) will, in all probability, require a manager to not only view the employee as an individual but also to examine his or her relationship to the group and the organization.

In this instance, does Lt. Miles have the necessary skills to perform as a manager? Has he been trained? Does he need additional resources to accomplish his job? While these questions do not address every aspect of why Lt. Miles performs as he does, they illustrate the complexity of problems a manager encounters.

This case focuses on the reality of how and what occurs in an organization. Employees adapt to their position differently, and it is evident that a police manager must learn to deal with human behavior effectively.

The relationships between an individual officer, other officers, groups within the organization, and managers are critical to the success of any department. A police manager must recognize the ecology of the organization, accepting it as a dynamic social system. The most successful organizations make a serious effort to not only achieve organizational objectives but to help its members achieve their personal objectives as well (Higgins, 1982).

In our society, work is a fundamental and natural aspect of everyday life that plays an important role in the social, economic, and psychological aspects of our lives. Officers' identities are often obtained from their work—for example, most people describe themselves in terms of a work group or organization (Bureau of the Census, 1980). An adequately paying job not only provides the basic necessities of life, but also a sense of personal identity and accomplishment. The achievement of work-related goals is viewed by most officers as being just as important as material rewards.

The personal interaction in police departments provides a sense of belonging, which actually creates a social bond unique to the police culture. The sharing of duties and responsibilities circumscribed by the presence of danger generally results in officers becoming strongly committed to police work. Police work is more than just a job. The tasks to be performed become highly significant when properly accomplished and provide a feeling of well-being and fulfillment.

Police managers have great success when managing highly motivated employees. However, not all officers fit into this category. There is no simple answer as to why some employees are highly productive and others are not—it is a matter of human behavior. There is a plethora of misinformation about why employees do what they do and why they react differently to a situation. Some theorists argue that participation in the decision-making process is the answer to the problem of motivating, but some agencies have found that when this recommendation is implemented some highly motivated individuals prefer to follow instructions and not be involved. Other experts recommend continuous communication from top management. Some employees respond positively to this technique and want to know what is going on; others seem to care less and only want to hear from the top when it has to do with compensation or perks. One expert recommends close supervision and careful control of discretion. Experience has shown that although some employees respond positively to this technique, others object vigorously to close supervision. Human behavior is complex and panaceas have proven fruitless.

Police managers are increasingly aware of the need to understand human behavior in the workplace. They generally have a definite view (usually based on personal experience and observation) of how officers behave within the organization. In many instances managers' beliefs are based on myth or misinformation, so they deal with people in such a way that the results are either unproductive or inefficient (Higgins, 1982).

Through a study of organizational behavior, we can begin to understand not only the complexities of organizations, but something about managerial behavior and the interaction between officers, managers, and the organization (Hellriegel, Slocum, and Woodman, 1983).

If police managers are to deal effectively with all of the critical aspects of organizational behavior, it is essential that they develop and utilize motivational skills as well as enhance their conceptual skills. It is generally assumed that police executives have considerable technical skills and if they have any weakness it is in areas other than operational application.

In addition, if police managers are to be effective they must pay increasing attention to their managerial role with a special emphasis on its interpersonal aspects. This is especially true as more and more police agencies develop value statements and implement community policing.

Organizational Behavior

Organizational behavior, when defined in its broadest sense, is the systematic study of behavior and attitudes of individuals and groups in organizations (Johns, 1983). The behavioral sciences, such as sociology, psychology, and anthropology, provide a basis for understanding human behavior. Police managers utilize this information to manage individual and group behavior.

To really understand behavior in an organization is a difficult task because it involves not only understanding individual behavior, but the impact of the organization on the individual or groups. We must view the organization as a social system conditioned and reconditioned by the environment. Police organizations are not isolated entities but are part of a large social system. It is becoming increasingly apparent that law enforcement agencies cannot function in isolation.

Police managers are faced with many challenges, including understanding individual differences (skills, motivation, or learning abilities). When concerned with groups, factors like communications, decision-making, power, and leadership must be considered. Utilizing this knowledge as a basis, the manager can then focus on work itself and can consider such variables as attitudes toward work, conflict, stress, and work design.

When tasks, individuals, and groups are interrelated, a police manager coordinates and controls through organization design as a means of maximizing

TABLE 2.1 Types of Behavior in the Organization

Individual
Interpersonal
Group
Organizational

performance (Nadler, Hackman, and Lawler, 1979). The more successful a manager is in dealing with human behavior, the more successful the unit and the organization will be (Steers, 1984).

To understand organizational behavior, police managers should concern themselves with the following behaviors: individual, interpersonal, group, and organizational (see Table 2.1).

Individual

Behavior of the individual is highly significant when we consider the effectiveness of an organization. People are different and they both influence the behavior of others and exert influence on the organization. Individuals have different perceptions of organizational reality and consequently they react accordingly. Therefore it is important to understand how individuals develop their belief, attitudes, and values (see Chapter 4). It is also a continuing challenge for a manager to understand what motivates an individual (see Chapter 5). Another factor is that the values, attitudes, and perceptions officers bring to the job or those they acquire after employment become exceedingly significant when managers strive to achieve agency goals.

Another aspect of individual behavior is the personality of each officer. While there are many aspects of personality, our concern here is the influence of other individuals, groups, and the organization on the personality of the officer (see Chapter 3). A law enforcement agency exerts considerable influence on each individual, and this socialization process continues throughout the officer's career. Everyone makes assumptions about their peers, supervisors, and managers, and these assumptions influence our behavior toward others. It is essential that managers become truly aware of individual differences as they attempt to adjust individual needs with organizational needs. Finally, each individual can suffer from stress created by organizational life (see Chapter 6).

Interpersonal

When two people interact, the result is some type of interpersonal behavior that can be of considerable concern to managers. It can be the behavior between two officers, a superior and subordinate, or between two managers. In most instances it involves such factors as leadership style, power, influence, or communications (see Chapters 8 through 11).

Faulty communication can have a devastating effect on both behavior and performance in police organizations. Effective communication is essential and seldom just occurs—it must be cultivated. Poor communication can lead to poor decisions and in most instances is closely tied to such managerial variables as power, leadership, and influence. Power is a natural phenomenon in organizational life. When individuals compete for power, conflict can occur and it modifies interpersonal relationships within the organization. It is difficult to imagine an organization where power is not a key variable in the relationship between members of the organization. Power serves as a vehicle for achieving objectives and goals. In some police departments power serves as a positive feature that allows one to influence the actions of others in addition to serving as a vehicle that allows people to control their own destiny. Leadership proves to be the catalyst that makes an organization effective. The interpersonal skills that police managers possess impact directly on individuals, groups, as well as the total organization. Finally, managers are continually challenged by the need to reduce and manage interpersonal conflict in an effort to achieve departmental objectives and goals.

Group

Even though most police officers perform their duties singularly or in pairs, group behavior is becoming increasingly important to police managers. SWAT teams, task forces, and unions are all examples of formal groups exerting a great deal of influence on management. Chapter 7 discusses in detail the dynamics of the group and the group process. Groups, both formal and informal, are powerful forces working for the attainment of goals and assisting in the adaptation to change (see Chapter 12).

Groups exert influence over the attitudes and behavior of each officer. As a member of a group, officers often feel or act differently than they would alone. The group can foster teamwork that results in the attainment of objectives, or in other instances the group can sabotage innovative programs. A manager can be more effective when knowledgeable about the way groups are formed, the various types of groups, and the dynamics of groups. Groups have a strong influence on individual behavior. The manager who does not understand the role they play within the organization will prove to be less successful than the manager who directs group behavior in such a way that there is a positive contribution to the organization.

Organizational

The structure of the organization itself is significant because faulty organizational design can limit or inhibit coordination and cooperation between employees. Organizational design brings together like functions and provides for formal communications within the organization. In some instances police departments become fragmented and individual units within a department function with total disregard for other units. This was especially true in earlier days when detective units operated independently and in some instances the head of detective units were political appointments.

The work to be performed influences behavior—managers have to be especially concerned with how individuals and groups adjust to their assignments. A manager soon becomes aware of the need to deal with job stress, conflict, turnover, and absenteeism (Steers, 1984).

It is increasingly apparent that a law enforcement agency continually reacts to the external environment. The nature and type of ongoing interaction modifies the internal environment of the organization. It is the task of the police manager to enhance the working relationship between the external and internal environment and effectively manage resultant behavior. This is not an easy task, so managers must utilize every resource at their command in order to identify, understand, and solve organizational problems. The current trend toward community policing places an exceptional demand on all police personnel as the organizational structure becomes increasingly indistinct and the agency focuses on attaining the goals set forth in departmental value statements. This is especially true when temporary task forces come and go as community problems are resolved.

Historical Foundations of Organizational Behavior

Based on the foundations of the ideal bureaucracy, scientific management, and the human relations movement, we find the emergence of organizational behavior. Human problems became increasingly important—especially the employees' relationship with managerial style, the environment, and group dynamics.

With the growth of organizations and their increasing importance within society, greater attention is given to employees and their needs. Probably the most lasting of the early research are the motivational studies by Abraham H. Maslow. He studied the self-actualized individual, who he identified as a superior individual personifying a harmonious personality whose perceptions were less distorted by desires, anxieties, fears, hopes, false optimism, or pessimism (Maslow, 1962).

From his analysis of the self-actualized individual, Maslow created a theory of human behavior. Five levels of human needs were identified as hierarchical in nature. When basic needs were fulfilled (physiological and safety), the growth need came into play—belongingness, esteem, and self-actualization (see Chapter 5).

Another researcher, Douglas McGregor, believed that all management acts are based on specific assumptions, generalizations, and hypotheses about employee behavior. He suggested that if a manager holds workers in relatively low esteem then the majority of workers are viewed as being somewhat limited—whereas managers are part of an elite group.

Such a manager assumes most employees are inherently lazy, desire to have someone take care of them, and work best when subjected to firm control and positive direction (McGregor, 1960). This is known as Theory X. Conversely, a manager views employees from a Theory Y perspective when they are seen as not being lazy, stupid, irresponsible, or basically dishonest.

A manager functioning under a positive set of assumptions about worker behavior is concerned about relationships and the creation of an environment emphasizing the development of initiative and self-direction. Theory Y assumptions challenged the fundamental tenets postulated by the ideal bureaucracy and scientific management (see Chapter 5).

Frederick Herzberg postulated a two-factor theory of worker motivation. His research was concerned with job satisfaction or dissatisfaction. In other words, what is it employees want from their work? When subjects of his investigation reported feelings of unhappiness with their jobs he found they identified conditions external to task accomplishment (Herzberg, Mausner, and Snyderman, 1959). The factors that lead to workers being motivated include work itself, advancement, achievement, and recognition. This is in contrast to hygiene factors such as administration, supervision, salaries, and working conditions. Herzberg encouraged managers to create a working environment emphasizing satisfiers, rather than dissatisfiers (see Chapter 5).

Other researchers directed their attention to leadership. In what has become known as the Ohio State leadership studies, Rensis Likert identified management styles characterizing leadership in organizations arranged on a continuum from authoritarian to participative (Likert, 1961). According to Likert, it is necessary to consider human resources as a significant asset. Likert found, with few exceptions, the highest producing units within an organization were those in which the management style was participative (Likert, 1967).

During the same period of time, the 1950s, Robert Blake and Jane Mouton developed the highly popular managerial grid. The grid identified five different styles of leadership: impoverished, task, country-club, middle-of-the-road, and team. Each style was based on the relationship between a concern for production and a concern for employees. The most desirable style of management was found to be team management (Blake and Mouton, 1964) (see Chapter 11).

As behavioral researchers reviewed the numerous studies on leadership and motivation, they found them to be highly prescriptive and, in many instances, diametrically opposed. Efforts to identify universal principles, the best leadership style, or optimal motivational factors were rejected, and the contingency approach was born.

When discussing leadership, Fred Fiedler suggested a contingency approach where different situations and conditions require different management approaches (Fiedler, Chemers, and Mahar, 1976). Fiedler identified three dimensions determining the situational control of a job:

1. *Relationship between the leader and followers.* Do they get along together?
2. *Nature of the task structure.* Are the procedures, goals, and job evaluation techniques clearly defined?
3. *Amount of position power.* How much actual authority does the leader possess to hire, fire, and discipline?

Chris Argyris set forth (in a series of articles and texts) his theories concerning the difficulty of adjusting the individual to the organization. Argyris takes the position that conflict and frustration will tend to be high when the formal organization, the leadership style, and controlling techniques result in a "maturity-directed" individual functioning immaturely. On the other side of the coin, if the organization fosters immaturity, it will place an emphasis on task specialization, chain of command, unity of direction, and a limited span of control (Argyris, 1960).

Argyris viewed an effective organization as one requiring employees to be self-responsible, self-directed, and self-motivated. He argues that motivation can be maximized when each employee pursues goals and experiences psychological growth and independence (Argyris, 1957).

The contingency approach came into existence as a consequence of the frustration that behavioral scientists and consultants experienced in implementing ideas set forth by the traditional theories. Chapter 11 describes the contingency theory in detail. For the most part, the business world has been more receptive to evolving managerial theories whereas public administration (especially law enforcement) have trailed in their acceptance.

The implementation of organizational development programs in law enforcement agencies has received mixed responses. In some situations, organizational development, or OD, has proved to be highly successful, and in other situations it has been overwhelmingly rejected. Chapter 14 describes techniques for improving performance by utilizing OD.

It is almost like the search for the Holy Grail that, in ancient times, proved to be so difficult. Many of us are still looking for the one best way to do things, but those who accept the contingency approach realize that differing situations require different management approaches. Contingency supporters reject the concept of one best way to accomplish something and adopt the eclectic approach. For example, work simplification might prove to be highly successful in one situation, whereas in another, changing the relationships within a work group can be the best solution.

Our approach is to include the contributions from the major managerial theories with a primary focus on organizational behavior. When reviewing the management theories we can readily see that the early approach stressed that there was only one best way to manage people in organizations. Over the years the traditional approach received less and less support as researchers began to emphasize the necessity of understanding organizational behavior, and the foundation was laid for this new approach to management.

As previously indicated, law enforcement management, for the most part, still emphasizes traditional management approaches, but progressive police organizations are turning to more currently accepted managerial approaches.

Police managers should be fully aware of the advantages as well as the disadvantages of different managerial theories. Although the pragmatic police executive might feel somewhat uncomfortable with the ambiguity of diverse managerial theories, there is a definite need to become fully aware of new theories and ideas when implementing new programs. Change is always with us and rapid change demands an immediate response. What worked yesterday will, in all probability, not work today. The eclectic approach provides the law enforcement manager with tools benefiting not only the organization but also the employees and the public.

Managerial Skills

More than a decade ago Robert L. Katz identified three essential types of managerial skills: technical, human, and conceptual (see Figure 2.1). He defined a skill as the capacity to translate knowledge into action in such a way that a task is accomplished successfully (Katz, 1974). Each of these skills (when

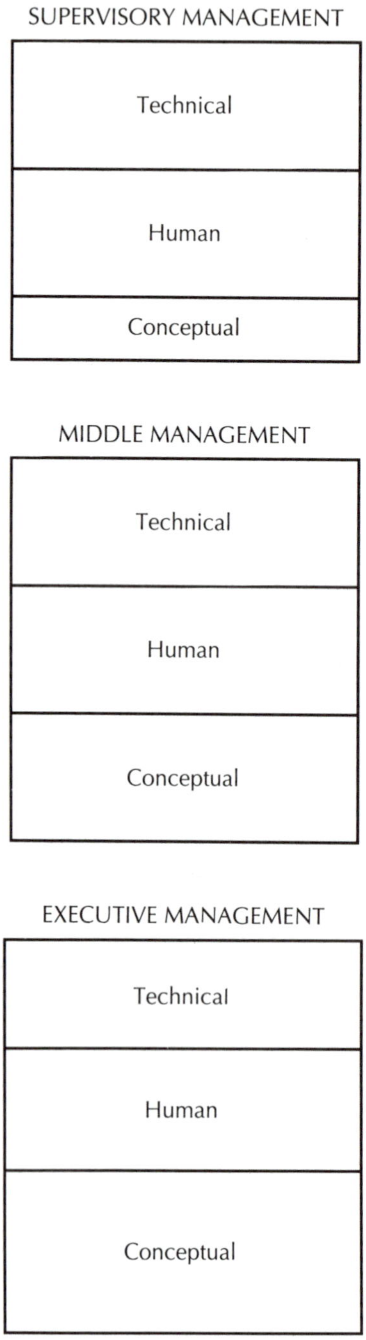

SUPERVISORY MANAGEMENT

Technical
Human
Conceptual

MIDDLE MANAGEMENT

Technical
Human
Conceptual

EXECUTIVE MANAGEMENT

Technical
Human
Conceptual

FIGURE 2.1 Managerial Skills Needed by Managers at Different Organizational Levels. Source Adapted from Robert L. Katz, "Skills of an Effective Administrator," *Harvard Business Review,* 52(5) (September–October, 1974, pp. 90–110).

FOCUS 2.1

Grand Jury Blasts Sheriff's Department

SAN BENITO PROBLEMS BLAMED ON INFIGHTING

The San Benito County grand jury has blasted the sheriff's department, castigating its leadership and rank and file members for letting infighting cripple service and jeopardize safety. The grand jury report, issued this week, includes recommendations ranging from a new jail to patching up personnel differences in order to solve a slew of problems.

The report says Sheriff Harvey Nyland is ultimately responsible for "failing service to the public and poor morale." But it also concludes most problems stem from budget constraints and conflicts with deputies who are out to sabotage the sheriff. Those deputies, unnamed in the document, were severely criticized for trying to get at the sheriff at the public's expense....

"Until the sheriff is able to communicate more effectively, take control of the department, and run it efficiently, he will have to assume the responsibility for the failing service to the public and poor morale within his department," jurors said.

SOURCE. Jack Foley, Mercury News Staff Writer, "Grand Jury Faults San Benito County Sheriff, Deputies," *San Jose Mercury News* (June 23, 1989, pp. 1B and 2B). Reprinted with the permission of the San Jose Mercury News.

performed effectively) results in the achievement of objectives and goals—that is what management is all about. In Focus 2.1 the skills of a sheriff are questioned.

Technical skills are those a police manager needs to ensure that specific tasks are performed correctly. They are based on proven knowledge, procedures, or techniques. An investigative supervisor, a patrol manager, or a records supervisor have all developed technical skills directly related to the work they perform. A manager of an investigative unit has to be knowledgeable in such areas as interviewing and interrogation techniques, proper utilization of informants, and surveillance techniques (Costley and Todd, 1978).

Human skills involve working with people including being thoroughly familiar with what motivates employees and how to utilize group processes. An awareness of human skills allows a police manager to provide the necessary leadership and direction, ensuring tasks are accomplished in a timely fashion and with the least expenditure of resources (Higgins, 1982).

Conceptual skills help managers be fully aware of the big picture so they reject a parochial view of the department's mission and goals. An effective manager utilizing conceptual skills not only understands the organization as a whole but is totally aware of the working relationship of its parts. When the interrelatedness of units and tasks are clearly understood, actions can be taken that are truly beneficial to the organization. Coordination is enhanced and effectiveness is the by-product.

As shown in Figure 2.1, all three of these skills are present in varying degrees for each of the managerial levels. As one moves up in the hier-

CASE STUDY

Chief Cindy Miller

Cindy Miller was appointed to the position of chief six months ago, after serving in a neighboring police department for 12 years. The last rank she held was lieutenant. The previous chief had served for many years. His managerial style may be described as "don't do anything that rocks the boat."

Soon after assuming the position, Chief Miller instituted a program of personally reviewing the daily reports of officers by randomly selecting them from different shifts. This new program went over like a lead balloon. Shock waves permeated the whole organization. The typical reaction was that the chief was treating everyone like children.

The chief's position is that it might be somewhat demeaning to make officers truly accountable for their activities, but in her judgment, daily reports should be a managerial tool, not a meaningless form.

The chief's review program created such dissent that several officers complained to members of the city council. The media soon picked up on the issue. The chief became very defensive and pointed out it was a departmental matter and officers had no business going outside.

In this instance, faulty communications may or may not have been at the center of the problem. What do you think? What might the chief have done to prevent this conflict from occurring? Is it a question of organizational behavior that is a function of interpersonal relations or of group dynamics? Did the officers have a right to challenge the chief? If you agree, explain why.

archy, conceptual skills become more important and technical skills less so. The common denominator for all levels of management is human skills. It is inconceivable that in today's working environment, human skills can be ignored. Their importance cannot be emphasized too strongly because it is readily evident managers are most effective when goals and objectives are attained through the efforts of others. In the majority of instances, managers must manage rather than perform technical tasks.

Actually, supervisory managers will find that human skills are exceedingly important and will, in all probability, dominate their working environment. Executive managers will find they utilize conceptual skills extensively as they expend a great deal of effort in planning and making decisions impacting on the future and the entire organization (Steers, Ungson, and Mowday, 1985).

Allocation of Managerial Time

If managers need the skills we just described to perform effectively, then it seems logical to look at how managers spend their time when actually working. One expert (Mintzberg, 1973) approached the problem of the allocation of managerial time by posing the question, "What do managers do?" He selected five managers for his study, including three from corporations, a hospital administrator, and a school superintendent. He observed and logged the activities of each executive for one week. Then he categorized the activities in terms of the purpose, individuals participating, and the duration of each activity.

Interestingly enough, Mintzberg found there were fundamental differences between the roles performed by public and private managers. In public agencies, the chief executive spent more time with outside groups and clients, and the specific roles of liaison, spokesperson, and negotiator were found to be highly significant (Mintzberg, 1973).

In the police field Louis A. Mayo refined the research format developed by Henry Mintzberg to study the activities performed by three managers. Each of these police executives had a reputation as a superior manager. The agencies they headed served countywide populations in high-income suburban areas (Mayo, 1983). For the consecutive five-day week in which the activities of each manager was logged, it was found the total hours worked ranged from 43.38 to 51.1; the average work week for the chief executives was 48.08. The study included evening meetings, but weekend engagements were not counted, in order to replicate the initial Mintzberg study.

Mail handling is required of public officials—police executives are no exception. Of the three managers studied, the actual documents handled during the work week studied ranged from 130 to 233, with 144 the average number. When this activity was compared to private enterprise executives, in every instance it was found the public official handled more documents. Many of the documents are of a routine type and in many instances are required by law. For example, a chief may have to sign a document requiring a separate signature for every member of the department certifying each member has completed a mandatory training program. The common belief that police bureaucracies are burdened with documents is certainly a proven fact. As noted in Table 2.2, the average time spent handling documents by police chief executives was slightly under 25 percent of the time (Mayo, 1983).

Each police executive also handled numerous telephone calls ranging from 33 to 46, with an average of 38 during a work week. The time devoted to this activity averaged 7.47 percent of the work week and illustrates the time a chief must devote to communicating with other officials or the public (Mayo, 1983) (see Table 2.2).

TABLE 2.2 Police Manager's Work Week

	Time in Percentage			*Average*
	Manager A	*Manager B*	*Manager C*	*Time*
Desk/Mail	24.1	20.6	29.0	24.57
Telephone	6.6	8.6	7.2	7.47
Scheduled Meetings	39.8	37.9	41.7	39.80
Unscheduled Meetings	25.4	27.7	16.1	23.07
Tours	3.0	2.2	2.5	2.57
Miscellaneous/Personal	1.1	3.0	3.5	2.52

SOURCE: Adapted from Louis A. Mayo, *Analysis of the Role of the Police Chief Executive,* (Ann Arbor, MI: University Microfilms International, 1983).

CRIMEBUSTERS ARRESTS YOUR PAPERWORK.

It's a crime how much paperwork your department has to battle, but now there's a powerful weapon to fight it. Crimebusters software from Modems Plus automates the incident-report process and lets you talk to major data sources such as NCIC and GCIC. It puts you in control over your paperwork.

Crimebusters is a menu-driven system that anyone can operate, so those tedious hours of writing are cut down to size. And your records inquiries are processed in half the time of old-fashioned systems. Plus, Crimebusters support people are on call 24 hours a day should you ever have any questions.

Hundreds of law enforcement organizations rely on Crimebusters, including the GBI and other state agencies. As one of America's oldest data communications companies, Modems Plus has installed law enforcement systems for over ten years.

Your department's job is to fight the Bad Guys, not paperwork, so write or call for more information today. Complete the coupon below and we'll send a free Crimebusters cap for every officer in your department.

YES, I want control over my paperwork. Send me more information and a FREE Crimebusters cap for every officer in my department.

Name ____________ Title ____________

Name of organization ____________ Population of city/county ____________

Address ____________ City ____________ State ____ Zip ____

Phone ____________ Number of law enforcement officers ____________

Who is the decision maker on a computer purchase? ____________

Do you have a computer-based law enforcement management system?

____ Yes ____ No If so, what kind? ____________

Do you have a computer-aided dispatch system?

____ Yes ____ No If so, what kind? ____________

How soon do you plan to buy a computer system? ____ 0-6 mo. ____ 6-12 mo. ____ 12-18 mo.

Technological Time-Savers Burdensome paperwork has long been an accepted aspect of police management, but, increasingly, computers are being used to ease the burden on managerial time. *(Courtesy of Modems Plus, Inc.)*

The most time-consuming of all activities for the three police managers Mayo studied was scheduled meetings. During the work week, the number of meetings ranged from 14 to 20; the average number was 17. In terms of the time devoted to scheduled meetings, it averaged 39.8 percent of the work week studied. It was generally assumed scheduled meetings involved issues of longer range importance; unscheduled meetings were more apt to involve current or crisis-oriented issues (Mayo, 1983).

Unscheduled meetings for the three police chief executives were found to be 37, 43, and 62, respectively, and the duration of these meetings ranged from 16.1 to 27.7 percent of the work week. Thus the chiefs used approximately 23 percent of their work week dealing with immediate issues. This clearly illustrates they had limited control over their time. The events of the day had a tendency to influence the type of activities requiring the chief executive's attention (Mayo, 1983).

Another area of activities in which police managers engaged, which was found not to be too time-consuming, was the time devoted to tours. Mayo found these to be most difficult to record because they were usually of an informal type, such as stopping somewhere while going from one meeting to the next. The number of tours taken by the chiefs ranged from 2.2 to 3.0; the average time devoted to this activity was 2.57 percent of the work week. This activity was born out of necessity, not out of desire, but the by-product could prove to be important to a chief because it calls for interaction with other members of the department.

The last category relating to the police manager's work week was identified as miscellaneous/personal, which involves activities that cannot be placed elsewhere and include going to the rest room or reading the newspaper. The time devoted to this category averaged 2.52 percent of the work week and is not enough time to impact negatively on the tasks that need to be performed. In fact, an argument can be made that a manager needs a few breaks each day from the tedious demands of the job (Mayo, 1983).

An important modifier of the time categories just described is the extent to which the police managers were responsible for initiating verbal activity when engaged in the following activities: scheduled meetings, unscheduled meetings, telephone calls, and tours. It is important because it is a definite indicator of the executives' managerial style. It is also a combination of a number of things including position power and the quasi-military style of police leadership.

The percentage range for the three police managers was from 46.5 to 55 for initiated verbal activity and averaged 50.17 (see Table 2.3). When com-

TABLE 2.3 Managerial-Initiated Verbal Activity

	Percentage of Time
Manager A	55
Manager B	49
Manager C	46.5

SOURCE: Adapted from Louis A. Mayo, *Analysis of the Role of the Police Chief Executive* (Ann Arbor, MI: University Microfilms International, 1983).

pared to business managers, it was found that the police officials studied were at the upper time range (Mayo, 1983). While it is difficult to pinpoint exactly when subordinates control a manager's time rather than the manager controlling the situation, it would seem reasonable to suggest that when manager-initiated activity falls below 50 percent, then self-analysis by the manager is essential. A manager's job is to manage—not to be managed.

Police managers devote a great deal of time to immediate issues that resemble fighting brush fires rather than dealing with fire-fighting policies. Unquestionably, the political environment in which a police executive operates calls for a more open management style, and politically sensitive issues demand an immediate response. But it is apparent that even a slight move toward greater concern for long-range issues would reduce the need to respond to the current issues that dominate the present police managerial style.

The nature of law enforcement management activities is such that a great deal of time is spent handling all types of correspondence. Some relief might be obtained from repetitive activities such as signing numerous documents. If laws or regulations were changed, this task could be delegated to other staff members. Another characteristic unique to their managerial activities is that police executive managers handle a large number of short telephone calls. Possibly this is a reflection of the public nature of the tasks they must perform. Many officials in other agencies and members of the community seem to believe the *chief* is the only one who can handle a problem.

Similar to tasks performed by managers throughout the business world, police executives spend an inordinate amount of time attending scheduled and unscheduled meetings that seem to be an inescapable requirement of the job. While these meetings are essential, there is a definite need to consider reducing their frequency and improving their quality. Within the context of *what a police executive does during an average work week* let us look at the roles a police executive performs when engaged in managerial activities.

Managerial Roles

Table 2.4 lists the ten managerial roles characteristic of the position of police executive officers. These roles can be concentrated under three major headings: interpersonal roles, informational roles, and decisional roles (Mayo, 1983; Mintzberg, 1973). A role is defined as an organized set of behaviors directly identifiable with a specific job (Sarlin and Allen, 1986). Formal authority gives a specific position status—and the two serve as a basis for the interpersonal roles of a manager. In turn, the interpersonal roles performed by a manager determine the specifics of informational roles. Lastly, both these major groups (interpersonal and informational) combine to place the manager in a position to perform specific decisional roles (Rue and Byars, 1986).

Managers at different levels in the organization perform each of the roles differently and to different degrees of intensity. Lower-level managers spend a great deal of time functioning as disturbance handlers or negotiators, whereas police chief executives are more apt to perform the roles of figurehead or liaison. In every instance, keep in mind that a manager's person-

TABLE 2.4 Managerial Roles

Figurehead
Liaison
Leader
Monitor
Disseminator
Spokesperson
Entrepreneur
Disturbance handler
Resource allocator
Negotiator

ality may affect how a role is performed, but not whether it is or should be performed (Steers, Ungson, and Mowday, 1985).

Interpersonal Roles

Interpersonal roles refer to the relationship between the manager and others—both within and outside the department. An effective manager soon develops the ability to enter into and maintain effective work relationships. In the study by Mayo (of three police chief executives) it was found this cluster of roles consumed the majority of the work week (Mayo, 1983) (see Table 2.5).

The first interpersonal role is *figurehead,* with the major activity being ceremonial. This type of activity accounted for 13.7 percent of an executive's time including activities varying from greeting visitors to such tasks as attending academy graduation ceremonies, funerals, or weddings (see Figure 2.2).

The *leadership* role took up 14 percent of managerial time and emphasizes such responsibilities as the coordination and motivation of employees. It

TABLE 2.5 Role of the Police Manager

	Percentage of Time			
Title	*Manager A*	*Manager B*	*Manager C*	*Average Time*
Interpersonal				
Figurehead	21.9	8.3	10.9	13.70
Leader	11.3	10.5	20.2	14.00
Liaison	26.3	19.8	26.0	24.03
Informational				
Monitor	10.8	14.5	4.7	10.00
Disseminator	2.6	1.6	2.2	2.13
Spokesperson	33.4	11.7	5.9	7.00
Decisional				
Entrepreneur	8.2	9.6	21.1	12.97
Disturbance handler	9.2	14.9	8.7	10.93
Resource allocator	3.4	7.0	.3	3.57
Negotiator	2.3	2.1	0.0	1.47

SOURCE: Adapted from Louis A. Mayo, *Analysis of the Role of the Police Chief Executive* (Ann Arbor, MI: University Microfilms International, 1983).

Interpersonal	Figurehead Liaison Leader
Informational	Monitor Disseminator Spokesman
Decisional	Entrepreneur Disturbance Handler Resource Allocator Negotiator

FIGURE 2.2 Groups of Managerial Roles. Source Adapted from Henry Mintzberg, *The Nature of Managerial Work* (New York: Harper & Row, 1973), and Louis A. Mayo, *Analysis of the Role of the Police Chief Executive* (Ann Arbor, MI: University Microfilms International, 1983).

also involves the integration of subordinate and organizational needs (Mayo, 1983).

Lastly, the *liaison* role is a component of the interpersonal cluster of roles and involves interaction with individuals outside the organization. This might include the managers' involvement with professional organizations or consulting with the prosecuting attorney or other agency heads. The average time spent was slightly over 24 percent and is the major time component of the interpersonal group of roles (Mayo, 1983).

Informational Roles

Managers at every level receive and exchange information. In one study it was found the average time spent by police managers on informational roles was 19.13 percent (Mayo, 1983). Managers at the executive level receive a great deal of information, therefore their initial role is identified as *monitor.* In this capacity, the executive can work at becoming the best informed individual in the organization. Information is primarily reviewed from the standpoint of approving items or ensuring the coordination of activities.

The second role in the informational cluster is termed *disseminator* and involves the least amount of time of the informational roles. The police manager transmits information to others in the organization. Usually it is timely information and involves current activities rather than information that might have long-range implications.

Lastly, the police manager performs the function of *spokesperson,* which involves the dissemination of information to individuals, agencies, and organizations external to the department. This is done formally and informally and can involve such activities as making presentations to the city council or holding a press conference (Mayo, 1983).

Decisional Roles

There are four areas of responsibility under the classification of decisional roles for a police manager. It was found they consumed 28.94 percent of the work week studied. The initial area is *entrepreneur,* which generally entails doing something to improve agency performance. Change is central to the activities performed in this area and includes either current or long-range issues. It can encompass such tasks as implementing a pilot project or evaluating a program (Mayo, 1983).

Managers also function as *disturbance handlers.* It was found this activity consumed almost 12 percent of their work week. Generally, it involves making a decision about unexpected situations needing corrective action.

Another decisional role is *resource allocator* and with the exception of budget preparation (which can be a time-consuming activity during certain periods of the year) generally relates to such responsibilities as the transfer of personnel, scheduling, or perhaps requesting additional funding to handle police emergencies.

The last area of activities involves functioning as a *negotiator.* Police managers spend less time doing this than any other role they perform (an average of 1.47 percent of time consumed during a work week). Generally, managers serve in this capacity because they have the authority and information negotiation requires (Stoner, 1982). In most instances, it involves settling internal conflicts or dealing with a union representative.

A careful analysis of the numerous roles a police manager performs clearly illustrates the complexity of managerial work. As one observer of the managerial process points out, managers are *doers* who perform in a dynamic environment (Mintzberg, 1973).

Value Statements

Community policing requires an entirely different approach in order to make the organization function effectively. All organizations have values. We can see these values expressed through the actions of the organization—what is taken seriously and what is rejected as irrelevant, inappropriate, or dangerous. Jokes, solemn understandings, and internal explanations for actions also express values. For example, in policing the strong belief among many police officers that they stand as the front line of defense against community lawlessness—reflecting what is often a narrow definition of order—conditions the organizational environment within which the police operate. These beliefs can easily become the prevalent values of the force.

Police departments are powerfully influenced by their values. The problem is that police departments, like many organizations, are guided by implicit values that are often at odds with explicit values. This breeds confusion, distrust, and cynicism rather than clarity, commitment, and high morale. Almost as bad, the explicit values articulated by some police organizations are unsuited to the challenges confronting today's police departments. Finally, there is a reluctance on the part of some police executives to rely on explicit statements of values as an important management tool for enhancing the

FOCUS 2.2

Traditional Policing Approach

At 1:32 A.M. a man we will call Fred Snyder dials 911 from a downtown corner phone booth. The dispatcher notes his location and calls the nearest patrol unit. Officer Knox arrives 4 minutes later. Snyder says he was beaten and robbed 20 minutes before but didn't see the robber. Under persistent questioning, Snyder admits he was with a prostitute he had picked up in a bar. Later, in a hotel room, he discovered the prostitute was actually a man, who then beat Snyder and took his wallet.

Snyder wants to let the whole matter drop. He refuses medical treatment for his injuries. Knox finishes his report and lets Snyder go home. Later that day Knox's report reaches Detective Alexander's desk. She knows from experience the case will go nowhere, but she calls Snyder at work.

Snyder confirms the report but refuses to cooperate further. Knox and Alexander go on to other cases. Months later, reviewing crime statistics, the city council deplores the difficulty of attracting businesses or people downtown.

SOURCE. Adapted from William Spelman and John E. Eck, *Problem-Oriented Policing* (Washington, DC: National Institute of Justice, January 1987).

performance of their organizations. Still, some police executives are working toward superior police performance by articulating a new set of values and by using these as a primary management tool.

The explicit statement and frequent pronouncement of organizational values becomes an important management tool in three circumstances: first, when management's explicit values are so well incorporated in the administrative systems and culture of the organization that they become workplace values; second, when management's values seem well suited to the challenges and tasks facing the organization; and third, when the organization's operations are such that management through values is superior to any other kind of management control. The executive of a law enforcement agency must work diligently to ensure that the values expressed by the organization are embraced and implemented by everyone in the organization. It requires defining a set of values reflecting internal and external consensus about what functions the police should perform and how the agency should operate (Wasserman and Moore, 1988).

An excellent example of a value statement has been articulated by Chief Lee P. Brown, formerly of the Houston Police Department (Wasserman and Moore, 1988):

1. The Houston Police Department will involve the community in all policing activities directly impacting the quality of community life.
2. The Department believes policing strategies must preserve and advance democratic values.
3. The Department believes it must structure service delivery in a way that will reinforce the strengths of the city's neighborhoods.

4. The Department believes the public should have input into the development of policies directly impacting the quality of neighborhood life.
5. The Department will seek the input of employees into matters which impact employee job satisfaction and effectiveness.

The articulation of values reflects a concern with the quality of police service delivery, the relationship between the police and the community, and the alliance within the police department between management and employees. The connection in the organization is of special concern to police managers who want to change an organization and accept problem-solving as the dominant technique to be utilized by the department.

Police managers must guide the change and development of the organization and help it adapt to the demands of community policing. It is not an easy task, but inside the department a manager can utilize organizational behavior in a systematic attempt to understand people in the organization in terms of the following behaviors: individual, interpersonal, group, and organizational.

Community Policing

Focus 2.2 relates the way the police have traditionally handled an incident reported by a victim. The response time was good, and the facts became apparent based on the investigation of the beat officer and the follow-up investigator. Needless to say, the results were typical of what has happened numerous times in many cities across the nation—forms are filed, statistics are generated, and the real problem is ignored.

Under incident-driven policing methods, many agencies act according to the following procedures:

1. Individual events reported by the public invoke a police response.
2. Information is gathered from victims, witnesses, offenders, and other sources.
3. When appropriate, the criminal justice process is invoked.
4. Crime statistics are utilized to evaluate police performance.

Table 2.6 compares traditional with community policing.

An alternative approach has been developed in recent years that is known as community problem-oriented policing. It is the outgrowth of research into police operations identifying three principal themes:

1. Effectiveness can be increased when the department deals with underlying problems that consume patrol and investigative time.
2. Solutions can be developed by utilizing the expertise and creativity of line officers.
3. Citizen needs should be identified by establishing a positive working relationship with citizen groups.

Rather than leaving the solution to planning and research units, the police officers, investigators, and supervisors become involved in the identification

TABLE 2.6 Traditional versus Community Policing: Questions and Answers

	Traditional	*Community Policing*
Question: Who are the police?	A government agency principally responsible for law enforcement.	Police are the public and the public are the police: The police officers are those who are paid to give full-time attention to the duties of every citizen.
Question: What is the relationship of the police force to other public service departments?	Priorities often conflict.	The police are one department among many responsible for improving the quality of life.
Question: What is the role of the police?	Focusing on solving crimes.	A broader problem-solving approach.
Question: How is police efficiency measured?	By detection and arrest rates.	By the absence of crime and disorder.
Question: What are the highest priorities?	Crimes that are high value (e.g., bank robberies) and those involving violence.	Whatever problems disturb the community most.
Question: What, specifically, do police deal with?	Incidents.	Citizens' problems and concerns.
Question: What determines the effectiveness of police?	Response times.	Public cooperation.
Question: What view do police take of service calls?	Deal with them only if there is no real police work to do.	Vital function and great opportunity.
Question: What is police professionalism?	Swift effective response to serious crime.	Keeping close to the community.
Question: What kind of intelligence is most important?	Crime intelligence (study of particular crimes or series of crimes).	Criminal intelligence (information about the activities of individuals or groups).
Question: What is the essential nature of police accountability?	Highly centralized; governed by rules, regulations, and policy directives; accountable to the law.	Emphasis on local accountability to community needs.
Question: What is the role of headquarters?	To provide the necessary rules and policy directives.	To preach organizational values.
Question: What is the role of the press liaison department?	To keep the "heat" off operational officers so they can get on with the job.	To coordinate an essential channel of communication with the community.
Question: How do the police regard prosecutions?	As an important goal.	As one tool among many.

SOURCE: Malcolm K. Sparrow, *Implementing Community Policing* (Washington, DC: National Institute of Justice, 1988).

and analysis of problems on a continuing basis. It is a comprehensive technique (see Figure 2.3) utilized to address the specific needs of members of the community. This strategy consists of four parts (Spelman and Eck, 1987):

1. *Scanning.* When appropriate, specific incidents such as armed robbery or burglary are related to broader community *problems.* For example, one or more criminal offenses might in actuality be related to a pattern of drug-related offenses committed in a specific part of town.
2. *Analysis.* Officers and supervisors define a *problem* and gather information from every known source of information (public and private). Once the underlying problem is identified, options for resolving the underlying cause(s) are proposed.
3. *Response.* Officers work with citizens, businesses, and public and private agencies to devise a program to deal with the identified problem.
4. *Assessment.* The program is evaluated in order to determine the degree of effectiveness.

This focus on underlying causes has been used in the police field for a number of years but never to the extent it is being used under the community policing approach. All officers become involved in problem-solving on a routine basis. In its implementation a *crime-analysis* model is used that, in part, is traditional, but is also nontraditional because it addresses a broader range of factors such as attitudes and lifestyles (see Table 2.7).

A principal feature of the community policing approach is how police managers treat and work with line officers. First, managers have found they are supervising many officers with college degrees who, for good reasons, view themselves as professional. Consequently they have and will continue to demand an involvement in the decision-making process (Spelman and Eck, 1987).

Today police officers in many departments have a need to be recognized and satisfied that performing in a professional capacity is acceptable to management. Job enrichment and job enlargement are viewed positively by officers. The rigidity of the quasi-military organization is increasingly being

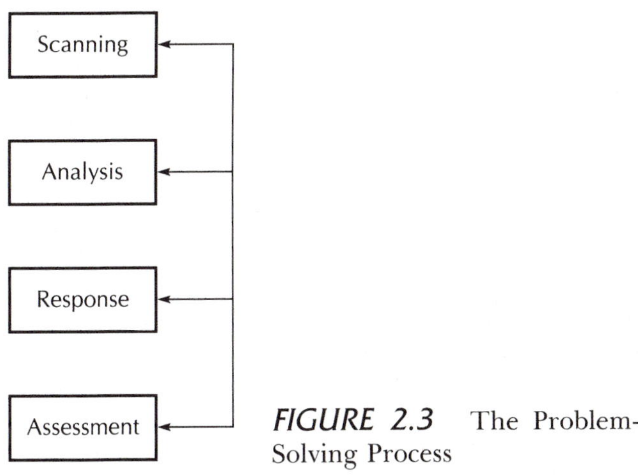

FIGURE 2.3 The Problem-Solving Process

TABLE 2.7 The Problem Analysis Model

Actors	*Incidents*	*Responses*
Victims	Sequence of events	Community
Lifestyle	Events preceding act	Neighborhood affected by problem
Security measures taken	Event itself	City as a whole
Victimization history	Events following criminal act	People outside the city
Offenders	Physical contact	Institutional
Identity and physical description	Time	Criminal justice agencies
Lifestyle, education, employment history	Location	Other public agencies
Criminal history	Access control and surveillance	Mass media
Third parties	Social context	Business sector
Personal data	Likelihood and probable actions of witnesses	
Connection to victimization	Apparent attitude of residents toward neighborhood	

rejected, and there is a desire to work in an environment more fluid and responsive to individual needs. Knowledge and skill are felt to be more important than rank or years of service, and coercive control is rejected as a means of gaining compliance. Above all, repressive rules and regulations are viewed as efforts to maintain the status quo and as a refusal by management to acknowledge the net worth of the *new breed* of officer. Lastly, today's professional wants to make a contribution to the organization and believes the goals of the organization are compatible with individual goals. This skilled person feels both can be attained in a modern police department that fosters and develops initiative and creativity.

The chief executive officer, when implementing community policing, can be confronted with a number of internal problems, but these can be overcome if the chief supports the concept without hesitation or reservation. The chief must be willing to challenge traditional assumptions about the goals of the department, its structure, and how it should meet its responsibility to the community. It is not an easy task. It takes courage and there will be many obstacles along the way—but once the organization accepts that community policing is what management really wants, things will start to fall into place. The key is personal commitment by the police executive.

The implementation of community policing is not easy. Organizational change is difficult to accomplish (see Chapters 12 and 13). The nature of the structure of the organization itself can be an obstacle when implementing a new value system. The larger the organization the greater the potential difficulty. Line operations are a long way from the chief's office and change demands effective communications (see Chapter 10).

The likelihood of effective change in policy and policing style also depends on the acceptance of the new focus by middle managers. In some cities team policing has been abandoned or proven to be ineffective because of the resistance of middle management. These managers have to be coached and reeducated as well as being allowed to participate in the change. Every effort must be made to obtain a personal commitment from those involved in the new community policing program.

FOCUS 2.3

The Community Policing Approach

Midnight-watch patrol officers are tired of taking calls like Snyder's. They and their sergeant, James Hogan, decide to reduce prostitution-related robberies, and Officer James Boswell volunteers to lead the effort. First Boswell interviews the 28 prostitutes who work the downtown area to learn how they solicit, what happens when they get caught, and why they are not deterred.

They work downtown bars, they tell him, because customers are easy to find and police patrols don't spot them soliciting. Arrests, the prostitutes tell Boswell, are just an inconvenience. Judges routinely sentence them to probation, and probation conditions are not enforced.

Based on what he has learned from the interviews and his previous experience, Boswell devises a response. He works with the Alcoholic Beverage Control Board and local bar owners to move the prostitutes into the street. At police request, the commonwealth's attorney agrees to ask the judges to put stiffer conditions on probation. Convicted prostitutes are given a map of the city and told to stay out of the downtown area or go to jail for three months.

Boswell then works with the vice unit to make sure downtown prostitutes are arrested and convicted and that patrol officers know which prostitutes are on probation. Probation violators are sent to jail, and within weeks, all but a few of the prostitutes have left downtown.

Then Boswell talks to the prostitutes' customers, most of whom don't know that almost half of the prostitutes working the street are actually men posing as women. He intervenes in street transactions, formally introducing the customers to their male dates. The navy arranges talks for him with incoming sailors to tell them about the male prostitutes and the associated safety and health risks.

In three months, the number of prostitutes working downtown drops from 28 to 6 and robbery rates are cut in half. After 18 months, neither robbery nor prostitution shows signs of returning to their earlier levels.

SOURCE. Adapted from William Spelman and John E. Eck, *Problem-Oriented Policing* (Washington, DC: National Institute of Justice, 1987).

Another potential difficulty of implementing community policing is that the process seems to be more applicable to white communities than minority communities. Community policing requires an empowered community that is able to deal with a sensitive and responsive police department. Unfortunately these conditions do not prevail in every minority community (Williams and Murphy, 1990).

Summary

Police managers are becoming increasingly aware of the need to understand human behavior in the workplace. Through a study of organizational behavior, we can begin to understand not only why organizations are such com-

CASE STUDY

Chief Max D. Kenney

Max D. Kenney had previously served as a chief in two other communities before being appointed chief of Websterville, a city of 110,000 population. The department has 120 sworn personnel and 21 civilians. Websterville can be described as a bedroom suburb in a large metropolitan area.

Chief Kenney when initially employed was known as a visionary, and the officials who hired him expected him to make the department the most professional in the area. Kenney has a master's degree in public administration, has been a police officer for 14 years, and is considered by most to be a comer.

As chief, Kenney spends the majority of his time performing the roles of figurehead, liaison, and spokesperson for the department. Operational activities are supervised by the assistant chief and Chief Kenney's internal supervision is limited to issues that might threaten the integrity or reputation of the department.

Chief Kenney holds numerous press conferences and does everything possible to maximize positive press relations. As a matter of policy, reporters are required to deal directly with the chief in any case of significance. The chief is also deeply involved in three major professional organizations and spends a great deal of his time attending meetings and serving on committees. In addition, he attends every city council meeting, neighborhood association meetings, and every cultural or social event his busy schedule allows.

From the preceding description it is apparent the chief believes the chief executive should spend most of his time engaging in activities external to the department. Do you think the chief is truly performing the roles required, or should he be more concerned with internal roles such as monitor and disturbance handler?

plex entities, but something about managerial behavior and the interaction between officers, managers, and the organization.

In order to really understand organizational behavior, it is essential to become aware of the following behaviors: individual, interpersonal, group, and organizational. Organizational behavior as a field of study did not just happen—it was a product of evolution and its historical antecedents included the ideal bureaucracy, scientific management, and the human relations movement.

In order to perform effectively, a manager must develop three areas of skills: technical, human, and conceptual. The common denominator for all levels of management is human skills—they are of the utmost importance. It is evident that managers are most effective when goals and objectives are attained through the efforts of others.

Police managers spend a great deal of time handling all types of correspondence, taking telephone calls, and attending both scheduled and unscheduled meetings. When performing these tasks, a good part of each day is spent handling issues of immediate importance rather than dealing with policy issues or activities related to long-range issues.

If a manager is to be successful it is necessary to perform in ten different roles that can be grouped under the headings of interpersonal roles, informational roles, and decisional roles. Slightly more than one-half of a manager's time is spent on interpersonal roles such as performing as the figurehead of the organization, engaging in leadership activities, and functioning in a liaison capacity. Just under 20 percent of a police manager's time is spent performing informational roles—in this capacity a manager functions as a spokesperson, a disseminator of information, and a monitor. Lastly, a police manager performs in four separate areas of responsibility when functioning as a decision maker. Altogether the numerous roles that a police manager assumes demonstrate the complexity and difficulty of successful management.

Management is a continuing process that focuses on the identification, refinement, and attainment of objectives by the effective application of resources. Operationally a police manager accomplishes this by articulating value statements that guide the department in its effort to attain defined goals.

In addition, it should be noted that community policing is the wave of the future and will soon become the primary style of policing.

Key Concepts

Individual behavior
Interpersonal behavior
Group behavior
Organizational behavior
Managerial skills
Self-actualized individual
Allocation of managerial time
Managerial roles
Police values
Incident-driven policing
Scanning
Assessment
Problem analysis model

Discussion Topics and Questions

1. Generally, what behaviors must be considered to fully understand the concept of organizational behavior?
2. Why is it important to understand the concept of organizational behavior?
3. Differentiate between the managerial skills needed by a manager at the supervisory level as compared to those performed by a middle manager.
4. Compare the interpersonal roles performed by an agency head in a large agency as compared to a small agency.
5. How can a police executive reduce the time spent attending unscheduled meetings?
6. Describe the figurehead role as it is performed by a typical police manager.
7. What does a manager do when functioning in the role of entrepreneur?
8. Why does a chief spend a great deal of time on the interpersonal role?
9. Discuss the importance of the chief's role as disturbance handler.

10. Discuss the problems that evolve when creating value statements.
11. What are the four components of the problem-solving process?
12. What distinguishes the problem analysis model from other research techniques?

References

ARGYRIS, CHRIS. 1957. *Personality and Organization.* New York: Harper & Row.

ARGYRIS, CHRIS. 1960. *Understanding Organizational Behavior.* Homewood, IL: Dorsey Press.

BLAKE, ROBERT R., and JANE S. MOUTON. 1964. *The Managerial Grid.* Houston: Gulf.

BUREAU OF THE CENSUS. 1980. *Social Indicators III,* Washington, DC: U.S. Government Printing Office.

COSTLEY, DAN L., and RALPH TODD. 1978. *Human Relations in Organizations.* St. Paul, MN: West.

FIEDLER, FRED E., and MARTIN M. CHEMERS with LINDA MAHAR. 1976. *Improving Leadership Effectiveness: The Leader Match Concept.* New York: Wiley.

HELLRIEGEL, DON, JOHN W. SLOCUM, JR., and RICHARD W. WOODMAN. 1983. *Organizational Behavior.* St. Paul, MN: West.

HERZBERG, FREDRICK, BERNARD MAUSNER, and BARBARA SNYDERMAN. 1959. *The Motivation to Work* (2nd ed.). New York: Wiley.

HIGGINS, JAMES, M. 1982. *Human Relations.* New York: Random House.

JOHNS, GARY. 1983. *Organizational Behavior.* Glenview, IL: Scott, Foresman.

KATZ, ROBERT L. 1974. "Skills of an Effective Administrator," *Harvard Business Review,* 52 (5).

LIKERT, RENSIS. 1961. *New Patterns in Management.* New York: McGraw-Hill.

LIKERT, RENSIS. 1967. *The Human Organization.* New York: McGraw-Hill.

MCGREGOR, DOUGLAS. 1960. *The Human Side of Enterprise.* New York: McGraw-Hill.

MASLOW, ABRAHAM H. 1962. *Toward a Psychology of Being.* New York: Van Nostrand.

MAYO, LOUIS A. 1983. *Analysis of the Role of the Police Chief Executive.* Ann Arbor, MI: University Microfilms International.

MINTZBERG, HENRY. 1973. *The Nature of Managerial Work.* New York: Harper & Row.

NADLER, D. A., J. HACKMAN, and E. F. LAWLER. 1979. *Managing Organizational Behavior.* New York: Little, Brown.

RUE, LESLIE W., and LLOYD L. BYARS. 1986. *Management: Theory and Practice.* Homewood, IL: Richard D. Irwin.

San Jose Mercury News. 1989. "Grand Jury Faults San Benito County Deputies," June 23, pp. 1B, 2B.

SARLIN, T. R., and V. A. ALLEN. 1986. "Role Theory." In G. Lindzey and E. Aronson (Eds.), *Handbook of Social Psychology* (Vol. 1). Reading, MA: Addison-Wesley.

SPELMAN, WILLIAM, and JOHN E. ECK. 1987. *Problem-Oriented Policing.* Washington, DC: National Institute of Justice.

STEERS, RICHARD M. 1984. *Introduction to Organizational Behavior* (2nd ed.). Glenview, IL: Scott, Foresman.

STEERS, RICHARD M., GERARDO R. UNGSON, and RICHARD T. MOWDAY. 1985. *Managing Effective Organizations.* Boston: Kent.

STONER, JAMES A. F. 1982. *Management* (2nd ed.). Englewood Cliffs, NJ: Prentice-Hall.

WASSERMAN, ROBERT, and MARK H. MOORE. 1988. *Values in Policing.* Washington, DC: National Institute of Justice.

WILLIAMS, HUBERT, and PATRICK V. MURPHY. 1990. *The Evolving Strategy of Police: A Minority View.* Washington, DC: National Institute of Justice.

For Further Reading

BLANCHARD, MARJORIE, and MARK J. TAGER. 1986. *Working Well.* London: Gower.

Presents an outstanding discussion of how managers can persuade employees to perform more effectively. Discusses such issues as participation, environment, recognition, and style.

LUNDY, JAMES L. 1986. *Lead, Follow or Get Out of the Way.* San Diego: Avant Books.

The author discusses the ten commandments for maintaining good personal relationships as part of a participative leadership style.

MAYO, LOUIS A. 1983. *Analysis of the Role of the Police Chief Executive.* Ann Arbor, MI: University Microfilms International.

A profile of time utilization is presented in this study of three police chief executives.

WITHAM, DONALD C. 1985. *The American Law Enforcement Chief Executive.* Washington, DC: Police Executive Research Forum.

This study focuses on four issues closely related to the performance of the law enforcement chief executive. Of special interest is the dual nature of their job—political and administrative.

CHAPTER 3

Personality: Understanding the Complexity of Human Behavior in the Organization

LEARNING OBJECTIVES

1. Define *personality*.
2. Identify personality determinants.
3. List the various personality theories.
4. Describe the concept locus of control.
5. Compare and contrast the defensive mechanisms of projection and avoidance.
6. Identify the personality traits of a Type A personality.
7. Describe the relationship of personality to work.
8. Identify the characteristics of a High Mach personality.
9. Describe an individual who has a strong bureaucratic orientation.

The behavior of an employee is often unpredictable because it usually involves an exceedingly complex interaction between an officer and a particular situation. Personality is an important element of behavior and cannot be discounted. At the same time, each person is influenced by others as well as the particular circumstances surrounding an event or occurrence. No two people are exactly alike, so each person brings unique characteristics to the work environment.

Personality alters the way people react to the same situation. Thus personality becomes an important concept with which a police manager must learn to deal. Personality is often described in terms of how we perceive someone. For instance, we describe some bosses as *hard nosed* and authoritarian, and others as really *nice guys*. Field officers describe their peers as "real street cops" or "wimps," depending on how they behave when confronted with a difficult situation. This process of employee personality labeling, if carried to

INTRODUCTORY CASE

Officer Jane Cooper

Jane Cooper is a member of the Sea View Police Department and is in her ninth year of service. She is married and has two children—three and six years old. She is a graduate of the local community college, with a degree in law enforcement. As a college student she interned in three different local law enforcement agencies. She was an explorer scout, and as a youth she spent weekends riding a dirt bike, which influenced her career goal—to become a motorcycle officer.

The Sea View Police Department has 642 sworn positions including 14 motorcycle officers who make up the traffic unit. Officer Cooper had been on a waiting list for six years before passing a series of rigid coordination and safety tests and receiving the appointment to the motorcycle unit.

As a patrol officer, she enforces the law aggressively and her orientation is almost totally *legalistic*. She considers the law to be "absolute" and a violation is a violation. There is no room for a consideration of the spirit of the law. She feels a transgressor of the law should always be arrested or cited; social consideration should be left up to social workers.

Officer Cooper really enjoys her work and finds days off to be boring unless she is riding her bike in the countryside. She had refused to take a promotional examination prior to her assignment to traffic, because it was more important to her to become a motor officer than to receive a promotion.

Within the department, the motor officers are looked upon as a different breed. They are viewed as overly aggressive and always in the thick of things, with a real love of facing danger. The unit members consider themselves to be the really elite unit in the department. All members have a great deal of pride not only in the work they perform, but in their uniform, which sets them apart from other members of the department.

Officer Cooper has been in three accidents since her appointment to the motorcycle unit. In every instance she was fortunate not to be seriously injured, but the motorcycles were totaled. Top management in the police department is becoming increasingly concerned about the aggressive behavior of the members of the motorcycle unit—not only in their contact with the public, but in the increasing number of accidents and injuries to officers. During the last calendar year, motorcycle officers have been involved in nine accidents. As a result of injuries, one officer has been retired on disability and three officers have been on sick leave for a total of 61 days. Unfortunately, during the same period of time, the number of citizen complaints against motor officers has doubled when compared to the previous five calendar years.

The officer in charge of the traffic unit, Captain Roger Miles, has been asked to devise a program for reducing motorcycle accidents and citizen complaints. The chief questions Miles's selection of Jane Cooper because of Cooper's aggressive nature, the number of recent accidents, and the fact that Cooper has received four citizen complaints during the last year. If you were Captain Miles how would you handle this problem? Do you think motor officers should be selected because they are aggressive? After reaching a conclusion, keep it in mind, and then after reading this chapter, review this case and see if your solution changes.

the extreme, can lead to misunderstanding and interpersonal conflict (Laird, Laird, and Fruehling, 1983).

Police managers must continually attempt to analyze human behavior. This is a difficult but necessary task, vital to their effective management of people with their various personality traits. Psychologists disagree as to how personality is acquired and what causes it to change. There is even disagreement about how to define personality (Griffin and Moorhead, 1986).

Notwithstanding, a manager must deal with the reality of each situation and employees' different personalities. A police department (in the final analysis) is a group of people joined together in order to achieve organizational goals and satisfy their personal needs. The method used to achieve these goals and whether or not the goals are in competition with each other depends in part on the personalities of managers and employees.

Definition

The term *personality* is usually used to characterize the unique nature of an individual. Many people use it in a very loose sense (to describe the primary behavior of an individual) by using such terms as "introvert" or "extrovert." When such labels are used, it tells something about the individual being described and leaves listeners with an impression concerning that individual (Schermerhorn, Hunt, and Osborn, 1988).

Although attempts to categorize personalities have pitfalls, the process can be useful to managers because there is evidence to show that personality can influence behavior. A realistic awareness of personality can be helpful to managers because it can allow them to predict the behavior of employees, peers, and superiors.

Here is one formal definition of personality (Maddi, 1980):

> Personality is a stable set of characteristics and tendencies that determine the commonalities and differences in the psychological behavior (thoughts, feelings, and actions) of people, having continuity in time, and that may not be easily understood as the sole result of the social and biological pressures of the moment. (p. 32)

This definition expresses a general theory of human behavior. It applies to everyone—not just to one individual or a class of individuals under a given circumstance. Personality is pervasive and descriptive of the total behavior under varying circumstances and at different times. Some feel personality is so important it describes the very essence of what it means to be a *Homo sapien*.

Another feature of this definition is it addresses both commonalities and differences. There are features of our personality we have in common with everyone else and then there are facets of personality exclusive and unique and not seen in others. Managers must look for what makes one person appear to be so different from other employees in some ways while identifying personality features similar to those possessed by other employees. This combination of similarities and differences is what makes humans so unique and what makes managing the human resources of an organization so demanding (Hellriegel, Slocum, and Woodman, 1983).

Admittedly, personality is relatively stable. Although it can change, it usually happens over a period of time. At the same time, situational factors can have a definite influence on personality. This is clearly apparent when we study individuals who have completed academy training, noting how much they are influenced by the socializing process of the organization once they spend some time working with other officers. Many officers have commented on the difference between what they were taught in the academy versus what was expected of them by officers with greater field experience. In this settling in phase, the new officer notes the emergence of the informal socialization process of peer values rather than the organizational values taught in the academy (Bahn, 1984).

Personality Determinants

How does one's personality develop? There are a number of theories describing the process, which involves the following assumptions about human behavior (Laird, Laird, and Fruehling, 1983):

1. Each and every individual has specific personality characteristics.
2. Life experiences, which are never the same for everyone, influence personality characteristics.
3. Each individual develops a distinct personality as a result of life experiences.

The concept of interactional psychology points out that human behavior is a function of both the individual and the situation which are continually interacting. Thus personality proves to be very important because it influences how an employee reacts to and evaluates work (Griffin and Moorhead, 1986). For example, an officer who is achievement oriented will, in all probability, evaluate each working situation in terms of its potential reflection on future promotions. Such an individual is more apt to volunteer for assignments, pursue special training or higher education, and develop an expertise needed by others—all with the intent of achieving the highest possible rank in the shortest time possible.

Heredity

Early research into personality stressed the importance of genetically determined characteristics. Heredity refers to those factors present at birth such as physical stature, gender, energy level, attractiveness, muscular composition, reflexes, and temperament. Heredity is then viewed as the final arbiter of how one acquires a personality. It is the result of the molecular structure of genes and chromosomes (Robbins, 1983). One of the earlier researchers, William Sheldon, went so far as to postulate that personality is directly correlated with body types. This theory has few supporters today, however.

More recent research suggests that while heredity is one of the major determinants of behavior it might not be as important as once thought. In fact, it is currently believed only a limited part of behavior can be definitely attributed to heredity. Current research in the field of genetic engineering may eventually answer many of our questions regarding the part heredity plays in determining personality—but as of today, those questions have not been answered.

The manager must remember that, based on our current knowledge, factors other than heredity probably exert more influence on personality development and the subsequent behavior of employees (Gray, 1984). If all personality characteristics were fixed at birth and solely the result of heredity, then one could not be influenced by experience, environment, or the situation. This is obviously a limited explanation of personality and cannot fully explain why individuals behave the way they do.

Culture

Another determinant of personality is culture, which has been clearly demonstrated by anthropologists who have studied cultures throughout the world. Culture exposes individuals to certain norms, attitudes, and values passed from parents to children. Over a period of time these elements condition and recondition each individual. In addition, friends, social groups, and work groups are other environmental factors influencing everyone.

In our culture such themes as competition, success, independence, and support for the Protestant work ethic are constantly reinforced by the educational system, family, friends, and fellow employees. Consequently, children raised in our culture tend to be more ambitious and aggressive than individuals raised in cultures that place greater emphasis on such things as cooperation and the importance of the job (Robbins, 1983).

With increasing frequency, members from different cultures are becoming police officers, placing a unique demand on police managers as these groups are assimilated into the working environment. The cultural variations become readily apparent as an increasing number of ethnic groups such as Chinese, Japanese, Mexicans, Cambodians, and Vietnamese enter the police field. Even though agencies are mandated by the courts to recruit minorities (so the composition of the police departments reflect that of the society), they are having a difficult time. One of the problems is that certain cultures foster a disdain for the police and in some instances have mistrusted the police for many years (see Chapter 15 for a discussion of minorities and law enforcement).

There are several factors that have a great deal of influence on organizational behavior. One is sociological constraints (that are culturally based and are important to a manager) including employee attitude toward authority and the perceived value of achievement. Another is educational constraints, reflected in literacy levels, attitudes toward education, and the amount of education an employee obtains. These cultural factors are important influences on managerial behavior and the attainment of organizational goals (Richman, 1965).

Concepts of actions that should or should not be exercised in a given situation are strongly influenced by the culture in which each person is reared. This determines to a great extent the values held by a group of people. Cultural influences are especially noticeable when determining employee motivation. For example, it may require managers to consider reassigning work because of the changing expectations of employees. This is especially true of many young men and women currently entering the police service who are less oriented to authority, who are not as competitive as their predecessors, and whose life can be complete without relying heavily on job satisfaction (Duncan, 1981).

Cultural diversity places unique demands on managers. While culture has a definite impact on the development of personality, it cannot be assumed every individual is influenced equally or that all cultures are homogeneous (Hellriegel, Slocum, and Woodman, 1983).

Situation

Different situations are another factor influencing personality. As we noted, personality is usually relatively stable, but a situation can occur altering that stability. Unfortunately our knowledge is somewhat limited in this area and there is not a system for categorizing specific situations and how they impact on personality (Robbins, 1983).

What we do know is that under certain circumstances individuals can react in a way seemingly almost foreign to their personality. Officers have, in numerous instances, performed heroically—placing their lives in jeopardy whereas if the event were reviewed logically and rationally, they may never have reacted as they did. Conversely, in other instances, officers who are fully aware of the potential outcome have been in a situation where they have acted unethically or engaged in illegal behavior for personal gain (Griffin and Moorhead, 1986).

Managers should be most careful when generalizing about the way employees behave unless they take into account the nature of each situation.

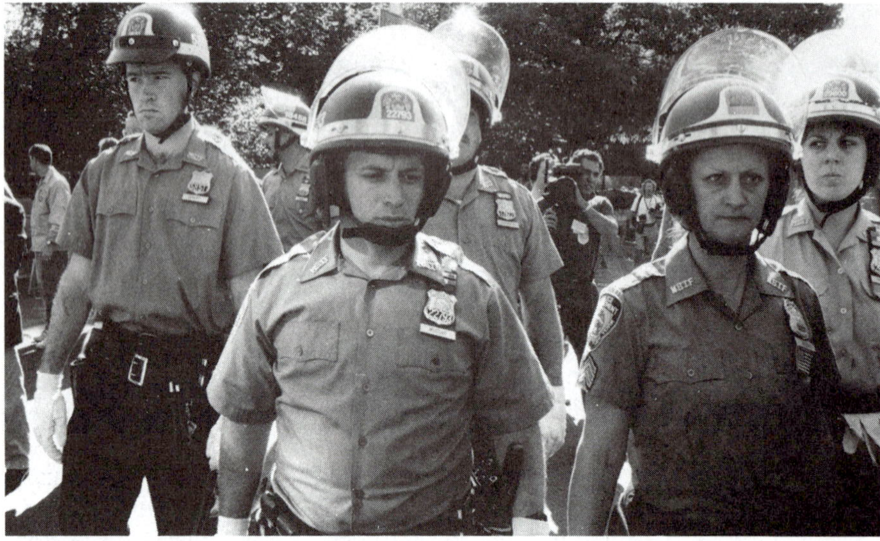

Diversity Although the public generally views the police force as a unit, it is important to note that a force is made up of individual personalities who are each affected by heredity, culture, and situation. *(©Robert Weinstein: Impact Visuals)*

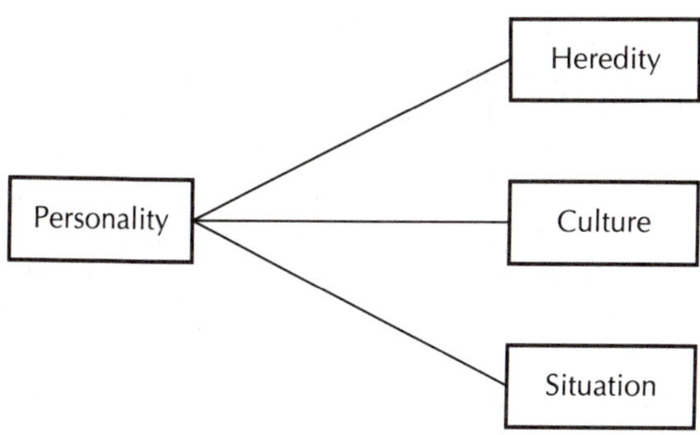

FIGURE 3.1 Personality Determinants

They must be knowledgeable about the strengths and weaknesses of each employee being supervised. When balancing this against a predictable situation, altering the situation rather than spending a great deal of time on human relations factors may be a reasonable alternative. For example, a first-line supervisor, when handling new employees, can limit the time they are not closely supervised to situations that will, in all probability, not lead to conflict.

The study of situational factors and their influence on personality is still subject to scrutiny. It is anticipated future studies might clarify the relationship between these determinants of personality and the extent to which they influence personality development (Pervin, 1985). The relationship between the three determinants and personality is illustrated in Figure 3.1.

Personality Theories

Organizational behavior stresses the importance of managers thoroughly understanding the various theories of personality in order to assess the behavior occurring in organizations. Numerous theories have been proposed during the last two centuries—the most prominent ones are the psychoanalytic, trait, and humanistic theories. Each of them presents a different view of personality.

There is no one theory of personality development that is totally right (Hellriegel, Slocum, and Woodman, 1983). Each has its supporters as well as its detractors. To date, no single theory of personality fully explains employee behavior or the reasons for their actions. But a manager who understands the theories of personality development has taken the first step in dealing with the complexity of human behavior whether it is individual, interpersonal, group, or organizational (Schermerhorn, Hunt, and Osborn, 1988).

Psychoanalytical Theory

Sigmund Freud developed the first comprehensive theory of personality. He believed the human mind is dominated by the unconscious; in other words, it is necessary to look inside the individual and analyze the unconscious motivations that underlie many of our thoughts, wishes, feelings, and memory (Myers, 1986). Personality is viewed as a dynamic process with a constant state of tension and conflict between the conscious and the unconscious.

Freud identified three different parts of personality—the *id,* the *ego,* and the *superego.* Each of these performs a different function and develops at a different time (Papalia and Olds, 1988). The three parts of personality were viewed by Freud as constructs, not physical entities, and were developed by observing and listening to his patients. The basic system of personality is the id, which is present at birth. The id strives to fulfill such basic needs as hunger, thirst, and sex. It operates on the pleasure principle and demands immediate and complete gratification. The individual is not aware of the id because it is not expressed consciously (Baron, 1983). The id is primitive, uninhibited, and not subject to rational control. At birth the id is the total personality of each person.

The second construct that develops is the *ego.* The ego begins to develop shortly after birth, when the child realizes everything wanted is not immediately available. The task of this construct is to mediate between the needs expressed by the id and the real world. It is the only part of Freud's theory of personality having access to and relating to the actual environment.

The ego distinguishes between what exists in the subjective mind as contrasted to reality. The ego may be described as the rational cognitive process that decides one's course of action (Wofford, 1982). The ego serves as the manager of one's personality structure and has the capacity of recognizing, evaluating, and testing reality. It reasons and learns from past experience and generally functions at the unconscious level. Freud was of the opinion that none of the three structures of personality operated solely at the level of consciousness (Baron, 1983).

The ego functions as the problem-solving element of personality as it deals with the real world and copes with life. This process becomes increasingly complex as the other element of personality, the *superego,* begins to develop (Ross, 1987).

Up to this point the ego need only check with reality to see whether the demands of the id can be met, but there is an added dimension once the superego is involved. This construct is shaped by society's concepts of what is right and wrong and what conduct is acceptable or noble. These ideals and values are acquired by everyone (by either having been taught or by learning from example) during childhood. Over the years, each person develops his or her own norms and standards of behavior, which are reflected in the superego (Ross, 1987).

Thus the superego is concerned with morality. It can tell what is right and what is wrong. It is formed early during childhood and relates to reality by going through the ego. The superego permits the fulfillment of id impulses only when they are found to be moral and not just when it is safe and reasonable as determined by the ego (Baron, 1983).

Generally speaking, when the id controls the actions, the individual tends to act in a selfish manner, is easily angered, and can be impulsive. If one's superego is overdeveloped, an individual will tend to feel guilty and unworthy. When the ego dominates an individual's personality, there is a more realistic behavior pattern, the person tends to react logically, and life is generally more satisfying (Laird, Laird, and Fruehling, 1983).

Freud's psychoanalytical explanation of personality is based on a conflict view, and involves the constant interplay between the id and the superego modified by the ego. Therefore the behavioral patterns of individuals are viewed as defensive mechanisms that respond to the anxiety created by the conflict.

Managers may encounter varying defensive mechanisms as they deal with employees and other managers. Each mechanism is designed to reduce an individual's anxiety resulting from the conflict between the three elements of personality structure (Bootzin, Bower, Zajonc, and Hall, 1986). One of the most common defensive mechanisms is projection. Individuals who are utilizing projection as a defensive mechanism have the tendency to see in others the traits or characteristics they have themselves. For example, an officer can project personal feelings, emotions, anxieties, and motives when judging other officers or supervisors. A supervisor who is highly judgmental and critical of everything done by subordinates will, in many cases, view the immediate manager as being too strict and demanding in never allowing freedom to perform assigned tasks (White and Bednar, 1986). Projection also occurs when managers assume all employees being supervised are like themselves—hardworking, industrious, goal oriented, and totally devoted to work. It can be a shock when a manager realizes that some employees have a greater orientation to their family or to personal activities than to work (White and Bednar, 1986).

Avoidance is another defensive technique. Officers who typically handle organizational conflict by withdrawing from adverse situations are utilizing this technique. It can be costly not only to the individual but to the organization (Baron, 1983). Officers have been known to respond too slowly to potential physical confrontations or they withdraw by sleeping on the job. It is also common to find an employee who will become a loner and withdraw from social interaction with other officers. Still others will use all their available sick leave (but not to the point of jeopardizing their job) as a means of avoiding organizational conflict and reducing anxiety (Duncan, 1981).

Each employee has been raised in a family with a culture circumscribing what is proper when exhibiting feelings such as anger, hostility, or aggression. Anger is a very powerful feeling and many officers have trouble dealing with it in their own personality as well as in situations where managers respond aggressively. It should be kept in mind that anger is (in and of itself) not good or bad, just like any other feeling, but most employees strive to repress or deny they are angry when dealing with others.

The fact is almost all people become angry from time to time and some act on this feeling by becoming aggressive. There is no one correct way to respond to anger. Within organizations there is a constant and continuing negotiation as to what is considered to be proper behavior (White and Bednar, 1986). Managers can respond to aggression in different ways—one, historically, has been to punish officers who express unacceptable aggression. Generally speaking, the concern is not with physical but verbal aggression.

One of the most promising ways of dealing with aggression is to respond with humor. This is because humor has been found to be incompatible with aggression—thus with its use the aggressive behavior is reduced. This approach to dealing with aggression is based on the premise that a human being is incapable of engaging in two totally incompatible activities at the same time. In other words, when an angry individual is exposed to humor, the angry behavior is subdued (Baron, 1983). Current research in this area holds considerable promise of providing managers with varying techniques for treating anger and aggression (Geen and Donnerstein, 1983).

Freud's psychoanalytical explanation of personality is not accepted by all behavioral scientists, but his early works have had a strong influence on others who have investigated the concept of personality. At the very least, the theory points out the complexity of human behavior and provides managers with an understanding of the interplay of subconscious conflicts and the resulting anxieties underlying human behavior (Wofford, 1982).

Trait Theory

Another way of identifying the key dimensions of human personality is by using trait theory. This approach to analyzing personality focuses on specific attributes peculiar to each individual. Personality is viewed as being consistent from situation to situation because of individual traits such as ambition, loyalty, and aggression.

Some of the trait approaches identify distinct categories and place individuals into the correct one. Other theories view behavior as resulting from a blend of different characteristics (Papalia and Olds, 1988). In contrast to Freud's emphasis on the unconscious, Gordon Allport believed the conscious determinants of behavior were what really counted (Hellriegel, Slocum, and Woodman, 1983). He theorized there were specific traits accounting for each person's unique behavior. Allport was concerned with the uniqueness of each individual's traits that were lasting, stable, and could be used to predict actual human behavior.

Allport identified three kinds of traits: cardinal, central, and secondary. He described a cardinal trait as a single trait dominating the behavior of an individual. He believed, however, that most individuals do not have a single trait controlling their behavior. A typical example of such a trait is shown when a police manager administers the agency in such a manipulative way that the performance can only be described as Machiavellian. This manager maneuvers individuals in order to obtain and hold power (Baron, 1983).

The second group of traits (identified as central) include such characteristics as being quick tempered, aggressive, or social. These traits are basic modes of adjustment as each individual interacts within both society and organizations. Allport felt that if an evaluator knows only five to ten of someone's traits, they are then in a position to know the individual's personality (Bootzin, Bower, Zajonc, and Hall, 1986).

The third group Allport identified were classified as secondary traits. These traits are sometimes displayed by individuals but they fluctuate and change from time to time. These surplus traits are not strong enough to influence individual behavior successfully. Allport's efforts were directed toward finding a way to identify personality rather than trying to explain it (Papalia and Olds, 1988).

Raymond Cattell, using a different identification system, distinguished between surface and source traits. The surface traits actually interact to produce source traits that account for the behavior of an individual. Surface

CASE STUDY

Oscar Williams

Oscar Williams has been a patrol officer for seven years in the Metropolitan Police Department. He is a graduate of the local university where he majored in political science. During his college years he was an outstanding football player and could favorably be described as a big man on campus. After graduation he served in the Marine Corps for two years and was discharged with the rank of first lieutenant.

In the police academy he was considered by his instructors to be the best cadet ever graduated from the program. Williams passed the probationary period with flying colors and each of his supervisors anticipated he would move rapidly through the ranks. After his second year in patrol, he served successfully as a member of the department's SWAT team and then with a special task force, monitoring the activities of paroled offenders with extensive criminal records.

Officer Williams has taken the sergeant's exam on two occasions, but in both instances he failed the written part of the examination. He responds by continually criticizing the promotional examination, pointing out that it is not actually a true measure of the skills an individual needs to be an effective supervisor. Over the last two years he has slowly but surely become disgruntled with the police department's management. He criticizes many of the department's policies and constantly questions the promotional process.

He has begun to function at a minimum level and only does what is necessary to keep out of trouble. He arrives late for roll call, but not late enough to be disciplined. He takes coffee and meal breaks exceeding the time set forth by departmental policy. His general negative attitude is rubbing off on younger officers and some of the older officers refuse to work with him.

During this same time he has become very active in the local police union and uses his membership as a platform for criticizing department management. He constantly finds fault with every immediate supervisor—pointing out they are exceedingly strict and refuse to give officers the freedom needed to perform effectively. Officer Williams is increasingly viewed as a thorn in management's side and a real problem employee.

His immediate supervisor has become increasingly strict in her supervision and is documenting the times he is late for roll call or takes too much time for meal and coffee breaks. Every arrest Officer Williams makes is reviewed with careful scrutiny and reports prepared by Williams are rejected with increasing frequency. Officer Williams filed a grievance against his immediate supervisor charging he has been singled out for punishment because he is active in the police union.

If you were Officer Williams's supervisor how would you deal with this distressful person? Is there something in Officer Williams's conduct that suggests he has a personality problem? If so, what is it? How should a manager work with an employee who is constantly negative? Can something be done to change the negative traits that Officer Williams exhibits?

TABLE 3.1 Personality Profiles

Reserved	Outgoing
Less intelligent	More intelligent
Affected by feelings	Emotionally stable
Submissive	Dominant
Serious	Happy-go-lucky
Expedient	Conscientious
Timid	Venturesome
Tough-minded	Sensitive
Trusting	Suspicious
Practical	Imaginative
Forthright	Shrewd
Self-assured	Apprehensive
Conservative	Experimenting
Group-dependent	Self-sufficient
Uncontrolled	Controlled
Relaxed	Tense

SOURCE: Stephen P. Robbins, *Organizational Behavior* (Englewood Cliffs, NJ: Prentice-Hall, 1983).

traits cluster together and are identified as those reflecting the behavior, easily observable, while source traits are somewhat difficult to identify because they are easily hidden (Griffin and Moorhead, 1986).

Using specialized statistical techniques, Cattell and his associates identified 16 distinct personality traits that form a unique pattern, termed a personality profile (Myers, 1986). Each of these traits are bipolar and have been found to be uniform sources of behavior allowing for identifying an individual's potential behavior when the observer carefully weighs each personality factor for situational relevance. Table 3.1 lists the 16 personality traits. Of these, Cattell felt the three most important traits for describing personality were how reserved or outgoing one is, how stable or emotional, and how intelligent (Papalia and Olds, 1988).

Humanistic Theory

Humanistic theory is a positive approach that views each individual as important in determining his or her own growth. It is represented by psychologist Carl Rogers who had a very optimistic view of human strength and who believed self-concept was the core of personality (Papalia and Olds, 1988). Self-concept includes the attitudes, values, thoughts, and beliefs that individuals have developed during a lifetime of experience. Rogers views the unconscious process as a positive motivator for individual behavior and points out that the concept of self evolves from one's early experience in dealing with the environment, the regard shown by others, and finally by reaching a point where the ideal self and the real self are congruent (Bootzin, Bower, Zajonc, and Hall, 1986).

The congruent individual functions at the very highest level. Such a person is open, does not react defensively, gets along well with others, and possesses high self-esteem. Rogers suggests this individual is seen as one whose fun-

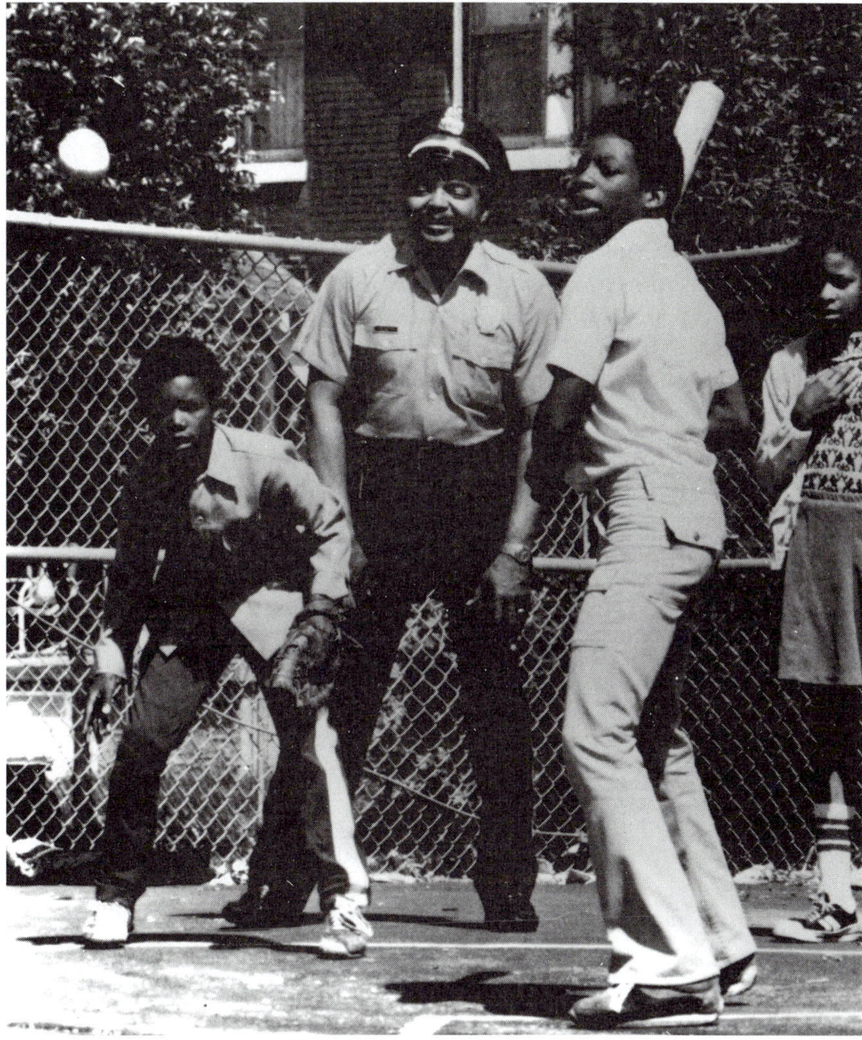

Adaptability Police personnel should be selected based on their ability to shift gears psychologically as they adapt to the demands of changing situations. *(©Tony O'Brien: Frost Publishing Group, Ltd.)*

damental desire is to become everything he or she is capable of being. This means that for each individual, self-actualization is something unique, specific, and totally individualized.

Other individuals may have an incongruent personal view, become tense or anxious, and react defensively as a means of protecting and preserving the view they have of themselves. From a managerial perspective it might be suggested that these types of employees must be treated positively, which can be done by respecting them as individuals. Employees must be viewed as such positive assets of the organization that when it is necessary to administer discipline, criticism must focus on the unacceptable or inadequate behavior and not on the individual. Under no circumstances should an employee be

TABLE 3.2 Personality Theories

	Motivation for Behavior	*Primary Interest*
Psychoanalytical	Unconscious	General behavior
Trait	Conscious	The individual
Humanistic	Conscious or unconscious	The individual

rejected as an individual. Feedback should emphasize tasks to be performed as a means of helping employees improve their job performance. The key is not to attack an employee's self-esteem because it will result in many undesirable effects (Baron, 1983).

Humanistic theory, like other personality theories, has its supporters as well as detractors, but its value is that it focuses on the positive aspects of human nature, acknowledging that the human organism seeks growth, self-actualization, and pleasant productive relationships with others (Bootzin, Bower, Zajonc, and Hall, 1986).

Personality is exceedingly complex, as is evident by the personality theories just discussed. Depending on education, preparation, training, and background, a manager may feel more comfortable with the explanation of one of the theories and find it meets specific needs. Each of the theories makes a significant contribution to the understanding of personality.

The essential ingredient is to utilize one or more of the theories as a means of gaining insight into organizational behavior. A manager might use the psychoanalytical approach by working to identify the nature and extent of conflict exhibited by employees and the defensive mechanisms they employ. Some managers might feel comfortable in evaluating personality by utilizing observable traits such as self-sufficiency, control, or conscientiousness. See Table 3.2 for an interpretation of personality theories. Another manager might find the most satisfactory approach is to assist employees in achieving goals and enhancing their self-esteem. Each of these approaches can be used to provide insight into an individual's total personality—including the actual character, behavior, and temperament of the employee (Duncan, 1981).

Dimensions of Personality

Researchers have identified a number of personality dimensions that have special relevance in the work environment. Their significance varies from organization to organization and situation to situation. Each of the dimensions are related to the total concept of personality rather than any specific personality theory. The dimensions we discuss here are locus of control, type A/type B behavior, Machiavellianism, and adapting to the bureaucracy.

Locus of Control

According to the concept of locus of control, people learn general expectancies about whether the source of control of what happens to them is outside them or inside them. Internals believe they control their own fate; externals believe luck and chance control their fate. Consider the following situation. Officer Cole has been studying for the promotional examination to be given next Wednesday. How should the test be approached? With the idea that passing or failing is primarily determined by how well officers are prepared for the test? Or would passing or failing be regarded as having very little to do with the amount of academic preparation but more with factors totally beyond personal control, such as the validity of the test? Or perhaps the test results are dependent on Cole's ability to obtain a copy of the examination.

If Cole believes individual performance on the test results from personal efforts, then locus of control is seen as favorably situated (Hampson, 1988). If Cole perceives passing or failing as beyond self-control, then locus of control is viewed as depending on fate, chance, or someone who exerts influence over the process. The first view illustrates a situation where an individual has *internal* locus of control, and the latter situation is one where the individual has an *external* locus of control (see Table 3.3).

Statements similar to the following are used in a test known as the I-E Scale to measure expectancies:

1. a. I am the master of my fate.
   b. A great deal of what happens to me is probably a matter of chance.
2. a. Getting along with people is a skill that must be practiced.
   b. It is almost impossible to figure out how to please some people.

If an individual taking the test selects items *a* in each of the questions, it indicates an internal orientation; items *b* show an external orientation (Baron, 1983). Locus of control is a continuous personality dimension, and employees actually are arranged somewhere on a continuum ranging from high external to high internal. There is some evidence that internals have greater control over how they behave in any given situation, are more social, and actively search out information needed to accomplish a task. Internals are more apt to be unsatisfied with the amount and type of information they have and generally will actively seek out new sources of information in order to achieve. Employees who have an internal focus are more apt to attempt to influence or persuade others and are less responsive to the persuasive power of others. They are definitely achievement oriented and respond readily to a type of supervision described as directive (Hellriegel, Slocum, and Woodman, 1983).

Locus of control that is internal in nature has additional implications for police managers. Internals are more likely to want some control over their jobs and will generally exhibit a strong desire to assume some responsibility

TABLE 3.3 Characteristics of Employees Who Have an Internal Locus of Control

Information seeking	Involvement in decision-making
Goal oriented	Self-control
Social	Limited risk taker
Extroverted	Achievement oriented
Responsive to motivation programs	Persuasive

FOCUS 3.1

Madison Police Department, Madison, Wisconsin

POLICE OFFICER POSITION

The Madison Police Department is nationally recognized for its innovation and leadership. The department is in the forefront of such concepts as employee involvement in decision-making, quality improvement, problem-solving, and community-oriented policing. We are an organization where individuals can and *do* make a difference.

The department wants to attract and retain men and women who reflect the diversity of our community. State law requires us to accept applications from those over 18 years of age. However, those who are successful in our hiring process usually have educational and/or life experience typically possessed by more mature individuals. New training classes commonly include a number of individuals who are changing careers. Previous experience may include work in teaching, social work, business, law enforcement, or a variety of other professions.

We want to recruit applicants who can communicate effectively both verbally and in writing. We need individuals who can enforce the law while protecting the constitutional rights of all and who want to work with citizens to improve the quality of life in Madison. We are looking for employees who are open-minded and sensitive to the needs of the community.

SOURCE. Hiring Information for Police Officer Position, Madison, Wisconsin (No date).

for decision-making. They want to be a part of the organization and control as much of the working environment as possible (Griffin and Moorhead, 1986).

Internals enjoy the work in which they have some control and usually gain satisfaction from work itself. They exhibit a great deal of self-control, conform to reasonable guidelines, and limit risk taking (Schermerhorn, Hunt, and Osborn, 1988).

Internals, as a group, are more extroverted in interpersonal relations and are more apt to relate to fellow employees as well as to the general public. They are responsive to motivation techniques and programs and advance at a more rapid pace than individuals who have an external orientation.

Locus of control has serious implications for police managers. Internals want to be involved, so each manager should strive to create their type of working environment. The working environment should foster individuality and reduce employee dependency. It should also be kept in mind that one's expectancies can be changed. They are not poured in concrete. Managers can make a difference—this is best done when the organization continually acknowledges and rewards outstanding performance. Focus 3.1 describes the type of candidate the department is recruiting.

An effective manager can change the expectancies of employees, thereby improving morale and impacting positively on employee performance. As employees become aware that hard work and the attainment of objectives are adequately rewarded, they are persuaded that what they do and how they do it can make a significant difference. The goal of the manager is to impact positively on performance by demonstrating that each individual has the potential to influence outcomes. Subordinates must be made to feel the things they do are significant (Baron, 1983).

Type A and Type B Behavior

Another personality dimension of interest to police managers is that of Type A and Type B behavior. Both of these types of behavior intrigue behavioral scientists because of their impact on the organization and its employees.

The Type A personality is characterized by a competitive striving for achievement, an exaggerated sense of time urgency, and a tendency toward aggressiveness and hostility (Franken, 1988) (see Table 3.4). The Type B personality can be described as easygoing and not especially competitive. Current evidence suggests approximately 40 percent of the general population is Type A and the remainder reflect Type B behavior (Baron, 1983). Obviously the two types impact a police organization differently.

Individuals who exhibit Type A traits are more than three times as likely to experience serious heart disease (Franken, 1988). Type A individuals tend to work rapidly on assigned tasks and their working relationships with others is often uncomfortable, impatient, irritating, and even aggressive (Schermerhorn, Hunt, and Osborn, 1988). Police managers who exhibit Type A behavior are usually hard driving, detail oriented, thrive on routine, and set high performance standards.

Type A individuals work fast even when there is no need to do so. When this tendency is carried to the extreme, the concern for details can become more important than the results they are trying to attain. In addition, Type A individuals dislike being interrupted and show outward signs of annoyance and impatience such as frowns and grimaces (Franken, 1988). When work becomes all important, this type of person will resist change, tightly control the activities of subordinates, and engage in activities having a negative impact on interpersonal relations (Schermerhorn, Hunt, and Osborn, 1988).

The impatient nature of Type A personalities causes them to perform poorly when the task requires a delayed response. Current research suggests Type *A*s perform better when they function under the pressure of a deadline, when they are required to respond to multiple demands, or when they are performing solitary work. On the other hand, they function below par when they have to perform tasks requiring complex judgment and when required to work as a member of a team (Baron, 1983).

TABLE 3.4 Type A Personality

Competitive	Hard driving
Achievement oriented	Impatient
Tendency toward aggressiveness	Easily irritated
Tendency toward hostility	Detail oriented

Type B personalities have to be handled differently than Type *A*s. They are easier-going, relaxed, deferent, and satisfied. In addition, they exhibit unhurried behavior. They are easier to manage because their behavior is predictable. Because they are non-competitive and prefer to work with others, they are good candidates for team assignments or working in two-officer patrol vehicles. When they assume supervisory and managerial positions, they prove to be people-oriented and interact well with peers and with those they supervise. Some Type B personalities have refused promotions because those in higher ranks function as administrators rather than as managers who must continually interact with subordinates. Type B managers are more apt to delegate authority, let employees work at their own pace, and provide detailed supervision. The ability to get along with others and the desire to work as a team are significant characteristics of Type B managers. On the other hand, the Type B personality needs closer supervision to ensure that deadlines are met and organizational objectives achieved.

Machiavellianism

Naturally, the personalities of police managers vary considerably. Occasionally a supervisor or manager exhibits the characteristics attributed to Niccolò Machiavelli who, more than four hundred years ago, wrote a book, entitled *The Prince,* that outlined a strategy for obtaining and keeping power (Baron, 1983).

Machiavellianism advocates manipulation as a way to attain goals. Some of the principles are "It is better to be feared then loved;" and "Humility not only is of no service, but is actually harmful" (Baron, 1983). Both of these suggest that the ends justify the means. A true Machiavellian is pragmatic, maintains emotional distance, and manipulates others for personal gain (Robbins, 1983). Making friends, being loyal, or expressing anything resembling ethics or morality are all viewed as inhibitors of true success.

Two psychologists, Richard Christie and Florence Geis, developed a short questionnaire termed the *Mach Scale.* Those who score high on the test are termed *High Machs* and behave in ways consistent with the principles espoused by Machiavelli (Schermerhorn, Hunt, and Osborn, 1988) (see Table 3.5). High Machs are not the least bit concerned about whether they lie or not, and will be as deceitful as necessary to achieve an objective. Morality can be ignored if necessary. In general, others are viewed as being gullible and not really aware of what is best for themselves. High Machs are usually convincing liars and are adept at identifying weaknesses in others (Johns, 1983).

TABLE 3.5 High Mach Personality

Power hungry	Deceitful
Manipulative	Logical
Pragmatic	Adept at identifying weaknesses in others
Emotionally distant	Influential
Not concerned with morality	Detached

Individuals with a High Mach personality orientation approach tasks logically and thoughtfully, do not respond to persuasion, and have little regard for the opinions of others. They consider their problems with a cool detachment and never allow emotions to enter into the equation. High Machs function best when they control the situation and operate in a nonstructured position (Schermerhorn, Hunt, and Osborn, 1988).

Interestingly enough, High Machs feel no guilt as they manipulate others for personal gain. It is a game, and the winner takes all. They perform at their zenith when dealing with others face to face, when emotions cloud the judgment of others, and when the situation is loosely structured (Robbins, 1983).

Bureaucratic Orientation

Police departments, for the most part, are bureaucratic organizations. Many agencies hold sacred the concepts of rationality, hierarchy, specialization, and positional authority (Leonard and More, 1987). Rules and regulations dominate daily operations. It is the view of many that a bureaucracy thwarts communications and stifles innovation and creativity. It is also felt that such an organization demands conformity and group-thinking but limits personal growth.

The question then becomes, Is there such a thing as a bureaucratic personality? In other words, are there certain personality dimensions that best describe those who achieve rank in bureaucratic organizations? Bureaucracies are very demanding in their own special way, and it appears individuals who exhibit the following attitudes and behaviors seem to be the best adjusted individuals within the organization (Baron, 1983; Johns, 1983):

1. Absolute conformity and adherence to rules and regulations. Individualization is minimal; abstract rules dominate operations.
2. Social interaction is impersonal and not allowed to interfere with decision-making and other organizational processes.
3. Acceptance of higher authority: The chain of command dominates, so acquiescence to authority is essential.
4. Traditionalism: Organizational members are expected to identify with the department and accept the traditions developed over the years.
5. Merit: Only the best qualified individuals are hired and promotion is based on performance. Consequently only the best attain higher rank.

Those who are out of step with the demands of a bureaucratic organization are more apt to seek employment elsewhere. It is also quite apparent some personalities have no difficulty in accepting bureaucratic standards and adjusting well to an organization. Many individuals find bureaucracies meet their personal needs because rules dominate, positional authority is viewed as important, and the organization is looked on as more important than the individual (Johns, 1983).

CASE STUDY

Lieutenant Robert F. Taylor

Robert F. Taylor has been a member of the Continental Police Department for eight years. He is currently assigned to the chief's office and is responsible for supervising the investigation of complaints against sworn personnel. He has been a lieutenant for two years, having assumed his current position after serving as a watch commander in the patrol division. Lt. Taylor graduated from the local university where he majored in public administration. Within the department there are a number of officers and supervisors who feel Taylor achieved his current rank because of his skill at manipulating people and his total disregard for the feelings of others.

Lt. Taylor is viewed as someone who clawed his way to the top in a relatively short period of time, and the general consensus is that he is power hungry, using deceit without any thought of the moral consequences. He is very pragmatic in his approach to decision-making and has demonstrated the special capacity to influence the brass in the organization. Many feel he is being groomed for an early promotion to captain.

Taylor goes by the book and is a stickler for the application of each and every rule or regulation. He may be described as a real traditionalist and is totally devoted to the job. Whatever comes down from the top is viewed as gospel and is never questioned. There is considerable anxiety about whether Taylor will use his new position in such a way as to ensure his next promotion.

Taylor is aware of how he is viewed by some of the members of the department and states he believes some of it is sour grapes, but he is still concerned about the potential negative influence on his career.

How would you describe Lt. Taylor's personality? Does he have a strong bureaucratic orientation? Would you describe him as a Type A or as possessing a High Mach personality? If you were Taylor how would you deal with those who object to the way he operates? Would it be detrimental to try to change in the new position? If you were Taylor's immediate supervisor how would you relate to him?

Summary

Police managers must continually deal with analyzing personality as it impacts on human behavior.

There are a number of theories describing how personality develops. Each of these makes the following assumptions about human behavior: (1) Every individual possesses specific personality characteristics; (2) Life experiences influence personality characteristics; and (3) Each individual develops a distinct personality as a result of life experiences.

Early research into personality postulated heredity as the final arbiter of how one acquires personality, but it is currently believed heredity plays a limited part in determining behavior. Culture is another factor influencing personality development. Culture exposes everyone to certain norms, attitudes, and values that are passed from parents to children. Culturally based factors exert a great deal of influence on organizational behavior, and police managers must respond not only to cultural variance, but to the different ways it influences each person.

Another factor influencing personality is situational in nature. A situation may alter the behavior of an individual, causing a manager a great deal of difficulty when trying to supervise an employee. Unfortunately situational factors and their influence on personality are still subject to scrutiny and their actual relationship is unknown.

There are numerous theories of personality development. The most prominent are psychoanalytical, trait, and humanistic. Each theory can provide a manager with insights regarding the complexity of human behavior, whether it is individual, interpersonal, group, or organizational.

Researchers have uncovered a number of personality dimensions having a special relevance in the work environment. These dimensions include locus of control, Type A/Type B behavior, Machiavellianism, and bureaucratic orientation.

Key Concepts

Personality
Personality determinants
Heredity
Culture
Situational
Psychoanalytical
Ego
Superego
Id
Traits
Humanistic
Locus of Control
Type A behavior
Type B behavior
Machiavellianism
Bureaucratic orientation
High Machs

Discussion Topics and Questions

1. How does personality develop?
2. How important is culture in the development of the individual?
3. Why do individuals who have a bureaucratic orientation seem to perform effectively in police organizations?
4. Differentiate between individuals who have external and internal locus of control.
5. How would you deal with a manager who uses avoidance as a defensive technique?
6. In what ways do situational factors determine personality?
7. Differentiate between psychoanalytical and trait theories.
8. Describe three kinds of traits.
9. What are the characteristics of employees who have an internal locus of control?
10. Describe the personality orientation of a High Mach employee.

References

BAHN, CHARLES. 1984. "Police Socialization in the Eighties: Strains in the Forging of an Occupational Identity," *Journal of Police Science and Administration,* 12 (4).

BARON, ROBERT A. 1983. *Behavior in Organization: Understanding and Managing the Human Side of Work.* Boston: Allyn & Bacon.

BOOTZIN, RICHARD R., GORDON H. BOWER, ROBERT B. ZAJONC, and ELIZABETH HALL. 1986. *Psychology Today* (6th ed.). New York: Random House.

DUNCAN, W. JACK. 1981. *Organizational Behavior* (2nd ed.). Boston: Houghton Mifflin.

FRANKEN, ROBERT E. 1988. *Human Motivation* (2nd ed.). Pacific Grove, CA: Brooks/ Cole.

GEEN, R. G., and E. DONNERSTEIN (Eds.). 1983. *Aggression: Theoretical and Empirical Reviews.* New York: Academic Press.

GRAY, JERRY L. 1984. *Supervision: An Applied Behavioral Science Approach to Managing People.* Belmont, CA: Wadsworth.

GRIFFIN, RICKY W., and GREGORY MOORHEAD. 1986. *Organizational Behavior.* Boston: Houghton Mifflin.

HAMPSON, SARAH E. 1988. *The Construction of Personality* (2nd ed.). London: Routledge.

HELLRIEGEL, DON, JOHN W. SLOCUM, and RICHARD W. WOODMAN. 1983. *Organizational Behavior* (3rd ed.). St. Paul, MN: West.

JOHNS, GARY. 1983. *Organizational Behavior—Understanding Life at Work.* Glenview, IL: Scott, Foresman.

LAIRD, DONALD A., ELEANOR C. LAIRD, and ROSEMARY T. FRUEHLING. 1983. *Psychology: Human Relations and Work Adjustment* (6th ed.). New York: McGraw-Hill.

LEONARD, V. A., and HARRY W. MORE. 1987. *Police Organization and Management* (7th ed.). Mineola, NY: Foundation Press.

MADDI, S. R. 1980. *Personality Theories: A Comparative Analysis* (4th ed.). Homewood, IL: Dorsey.

MYERS, DAVID G. 1986. *Psychology.* New York: Worth.

PAPALIA, DIANE E., and SALLY W. OLDS. 1988. *Psychology* (2nd ed.). New York: McGraw-Hill.

PERVIN, LAWRENCE. 1985. "Personality." In Mark Rosenzweig and Lyman Porter (Eds.), *Annual Review of Psychology,* Vol. 36.

RICHMAN, BARRY M. 1965. "Significance of Cultural Variables," *Academy of Management Journal,* 8 (2).

ROBBINS, STEPHEN P. 1983. *Organizational Behavior.* Englewood Cliffs, NJ: Prentice-Hall.

ROSS, ALAN O. 1987. *Personality: The Scientific Study of Complex Human Behavior.* New York: Holt.

SCHERMERHORN, JOHN R., JAMES G. HUNT, and RICHARD N. OSBORN. 1988. *Managing Organizational Behavior* (3rd ed.). New York: Wiley.

WHITE, DONALD D., and DAVID A. BEDNAR. 1986. *Organizational Behavior: Understanding and Managing People at Work.* Boston: Allyn & Bacon.

WOFFORD, JERRY C. 1982. *Organizational Behavior: Foundations for Organizational Effectiveness.* Boston: Kent.

For Further Reading

HAMPSON, SARAH E. 1988. *The Construction of Personality* (2nd ed.). London: Routledge.

This book is organized around three different perspectives on personality. It includes explicit theories of personality from the personality psychologists' perspective, implicit theories of personality from the layperson's perspective, and the perspective that people have about their own personality.

LAIRD, DONALD A., ELEANOR C. LAIRD, and ROSEMARY T. FRUEHLING. 1983. *Psychology: Human Relations and Work Adjustment* (6th ed.). New York: McGraw-Hill.

Presents four major objectives for individual adjustment to the work environment: learning to cope with and handle stress; learning the job and producing results; developing healthy interpersonal relationships; and learning to communicate effectively. Consideration is also given to the stages of personality development and to a discussion of why people act the way they do.

ORGAN, DENNIS W., and W. CLAY HAMMER. 1982. *Organizational Behavior: An Applied Psychological Approach* (Rev. ed.). Plano, TX: Business Publication.

Includes a very good discussion of the uniqueness of every person and the development of personality. Consideration is also given to locus of control, neuroticism, and extroversion as dimensions of personality.

ROSS, ALAN O. 1987. *Personality: The Scientific Study of Complex Human Behavior.* New York: Holt.

Surveys the principal measures used in assessing individual differences. It also reviews motivation and emotion, ending with the topic of self-concept. Includes an excellent review of personality in a historical context.

CHAPTER 4

Beliefs, Values, and Attitudes: Determinants of Human Behavior

LEARNING OBJECTIVES

1. Define *operant behavior.*
2. Define *culture* and identify the steps involved in the socialization process.
3. Discuss the nature of and need for introspection.
4. Compare and contrast ideas, beliefs, values, attitudes, opinions, and motives.
5. Identify various *levels of existence* and discuss them in terms of value conflict.
6. Demonstrate the relationship between attitudes and job satisfaction in complex organizations.
7. Define *perception.*
8. Identify the principal components in the perception formation process.
9. List and describe the steps involved in perception formation.
10. Describe the sources of perceptual distortion.
11. Define motivation and show how it is affected by prior experience, beliefs, values, attitudes, opinions, and expectations.
12. Show how behavior is a function of the interaction between people and their environment.
13. Describe the manager's role in changing improper attitudes and behaviors that are exhibited by the employees.
14. Identify the steps involved in a planned intervention designed to produce a change in employee attitudes and behaviors.
15. Illustrate the complex relationship between environmental stimuli and goal-directed behavior.

Police departments are organic social systems created by and composed of human beings. They are microcosms of the society at large and provide a sociocultural milieu in which people interact with, react to, and influence one another as they pursue common goals and objectives. The individual

INTRODUCTORY CASE

Captain Harvey Adams

Harvey Adams is a captain in charge of the midnight patrol shift in a large urban police department located in the Midwest. The captain is 57 years old and has been a police officer for nearly 30 years. Once considered a progressive Young Turk (radical), he has been having great difficulty dealing with many of the social changes taking place in society. Adams is, in fact, being investigated by the State Human Relations Commission. He has been charged with sexual discrimination against a female police officer.

Officer Jo Andleman, 26 years old, has been with the department for two years. She is the only female officer. Andleman has been working the midnight shift for about eight months. An avowed feminist, she "marches to her own drummer." She is outspoken in her support of equal rights, comparable worth, and affirmative action. Officer Andleman is also a pro-choice activist.

When Capt. Adams heard rumors that Andleman was living with a male police officer assigned to the same shift, he called her into his office and ordered her to sever the "immoral" relationship immediately. Even though she had a "clean slate," he gave her a written reprimand for "conduct unbecoming an officer." When she objected, he criticized her for "living in sin" and subjecting the police department to ridicule. Adams told Andleman that if she had to "shack up" with a policeman that she should "make it legal" and become his "little mama." Adams told her that he would do all he could to get her fired if she failed to heed his "advice."

Because the department's rules regarding conduct do not prohibit fraternization between or cohabitation with other police personnel, Officer Andleman filed a grievance to have the written reprimand removed from her folder. She also filed a sexual discrimination charge with the Human Relations Commission. Capt. Adams is upset by the incident and has put in for retirement. He told the chief he could no longer stand to work in the same department with "morally bankrupt people."

The Human Relations Commission investigation revealed that Harvey Adams was raised in a traditional and very religious family. As a fundamentalist, he interprets the Bible in literal terms. Adams was taught that women are subservient to men and should function as homemakers. He feels that women have no place in a "man's job" like police work. Thus Capt. Adams has a very negative attitude toward female police officers. He belittles them and expresses his opinions in overtly sexist terms.

Is Capt. Adams a dinosaur and out of step with society? Or is he representative of the male chauvinists who were attracted to police work in the past? Prepare a memo for the mayor explaining—based on the information contained in this chapter—what you think happened in this situation. Indicate whether or not you feel that the captain's resignation was in the best interest of the police department.

is the fundamental subsystem upon which organizations are built. Individuals consist of interdependent physiological and psychosocial systems that work in concert with environmental factors to produce distinctive behavior. The dynamic interdependence between human (internal) and environmental (external) factors helps to account for the complexity of human behavior (Sheehan and Cordner, 1979).

Human Behavior

Human beings are social animals who exhibit recurrent, regular, and recognizable patterns of behavior. In a general sense, *behavior* can be defined as anything an organism does that involves self-initiated action and/or reaction to a given stimulus. From an organizational point of view, behavior is comprised of adaptive adjustments people make as they cope with one another, with problems, with opportunities, and with synergistic aspects of specific situations (Bittel, 1980). All human behavior involves the conscious or subconscious selection of particular actions from among those that are possible and over which a person exercises some influence, control, or authority. At times the selection or choice of alternatives is almost automatic and done without very much thought. In other cases, it is the product of a complex chain of behaviors called planning and design activities (Simon, 1976). Learning to be a good shot with a 9mm pistol, for example, requires a series of behavioral adaptations keyed to internal as well as external factors.

According to H. Joseph Reitz (1981), there are two basic types of behavior: (1) inherited behavior and (2) learned behavior. Normal human beings exhibit both types of behavior simultaneously and are able to integrate them into a fairly stable persona.

1. *Inherited behavior.* Inherited, or innate, behavior refers to any behavioral response or reflex exhibited by people due to their genetic endowment or the process of natural selection. The survival of the species is contingent on behaviors like breathing, ingesting food, voiding wastes, mating, and defending oneself. These behaviors are modified through adaptation as the environment acts on the individual.

2. *Learned behavior.* Learned, or operant, behavior involves cognitive adaptations that enhance a human being's ability to cope with changes in the environment and to manipulate the environment in ways which improve the chances for survival. Learned behaviors (such as verbal communication, logical problem-solving techniques, job skills, etc.) give people more control over their lives. The key to this behavior lies in its consequences for the person and for the environment.

It is learned (self-initiated and goal-oriented) social behavior that sets human beings apart from other animals. Abstract thinking leads to vicarious learning and activates the adaptive process.

Social Relationships

Human beings—as social animals—live and work in groups. A *group* is ordinarily defined as a collection of individuals who derive satisfaction from interacting with each other in some consistent and coordinated way as they strive to achieve a common goal or objective. Groups are held together by multiform social relationships. A social relationship exists when people possess reciprocal expectations about one another so that they act in relatively patterned ways. This concept is based on the fact that almost all human behavior is oriented toward others. Not only do people live and work together, they share common beliefs, values, attitudes, and normative understandings. They continuously interact with and respond to significant others. People shape their (conscious and unconscious) behavior in relation to the behavioral expectations of significant others within groups (Chinoy and Hewitt, 1975). Figure 4.1 depicts the dynamic aspects of social interaction.

Groups, like the society at large, develop a distinctive way of life, or culture, that defines appropriate ways of feeling, acting, and thinking. Culture reflects the shared language, events, symbols, rituals, and values indigenous to a particular group. While culture is derived from past behavior, it is

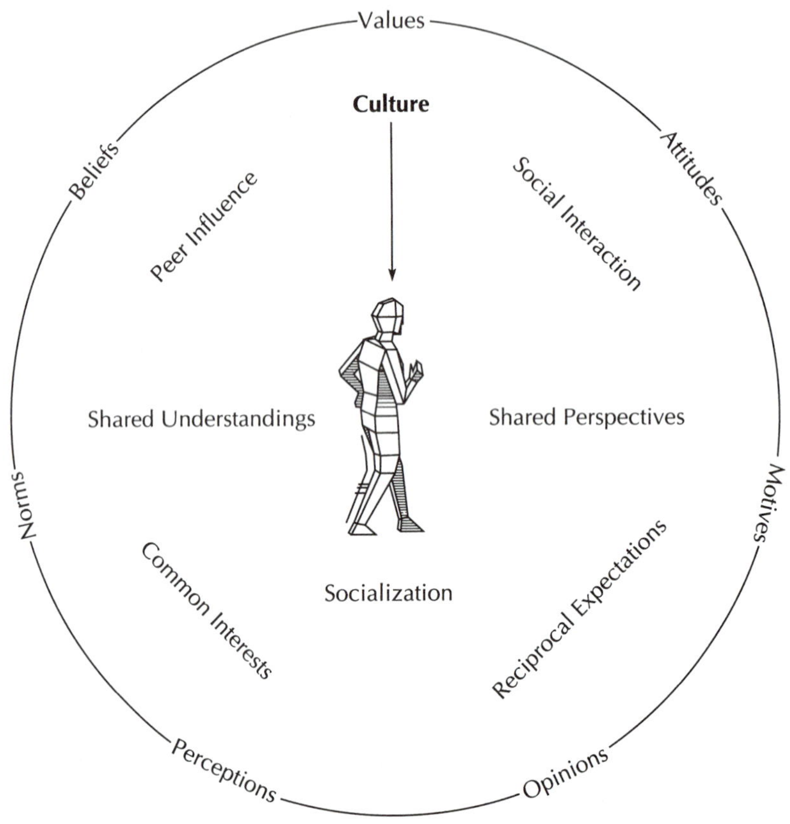

FIGURE 4.1 Group Dynamics, Social Relationships, and Learned Behavior.

perpetually reconstituted in current members via the socialization process. From a pragmatic point of view (Uttal, 1983), culture embodies shared beliefs (how things work) and values (what is important) that are internalized by members of a group to produce behavioral norms (the way things "ought to be done"). The culture must be learned before it can be internalized. In this context, learning is defined as a dynamic process which manifests itself in changed behavior that is based on prior experience. People possess few—if any—instinctive skills and no instinctive knowledge which will enable them to survive. They only survive by virtue of what they have learned. The central idea is that culture is learned from, shared with, and modified through interaction with other human beings in group settings (see Figure 4.2).

As groups mature they begin to develop their own unique personalities. In other words, each group evolves into an impersonal form that cannot be identified solely with the biography of one specific person. In fact, individual characteristics are almost always overshadowed by those of the group itself. A police work group, for example, will usually exhibit characteristics apart from and beyond the mere sum of those who make up the group. To a large

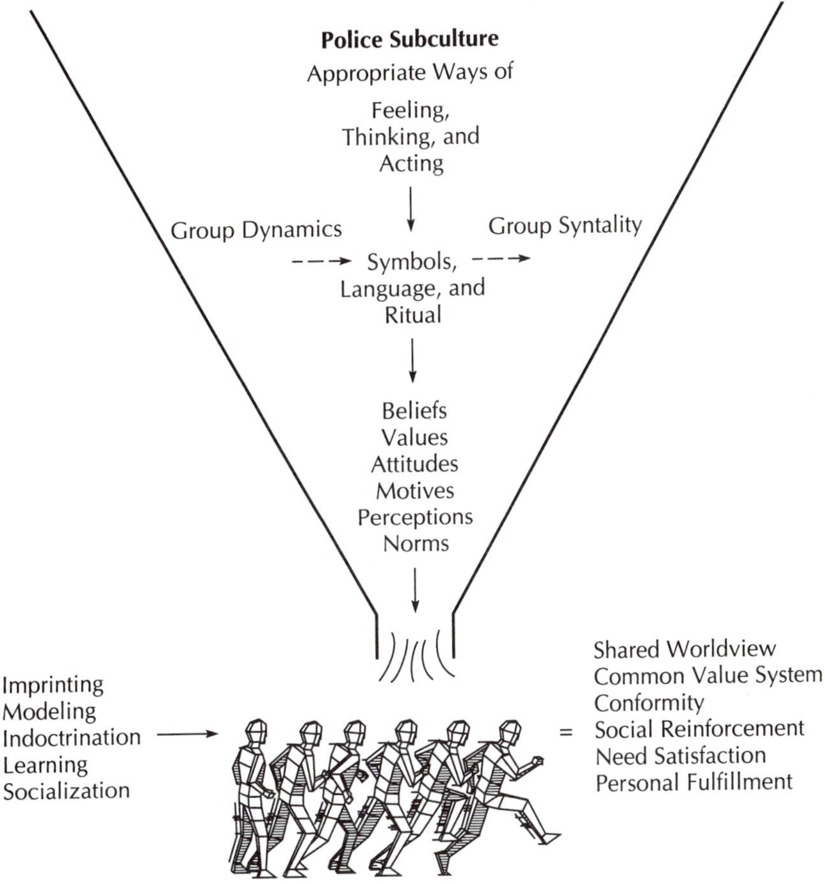

FIGURE 4.2 Learning, Internalizing, and Exhibiting Culture.

degree, a formal group (like the Chicago Police Department) becomes an independent entity. It "thinks!" It "acts!" It is in this sense that specialized groups are regarded as functional units with a distinctive personality. This counterpart to the human personality has sometimes been referred to as *syntality* (Champion, 1975). New police officers are socialized to feel, think, and act not as autonomous individuals but as constituent members of a goal-oriented group.

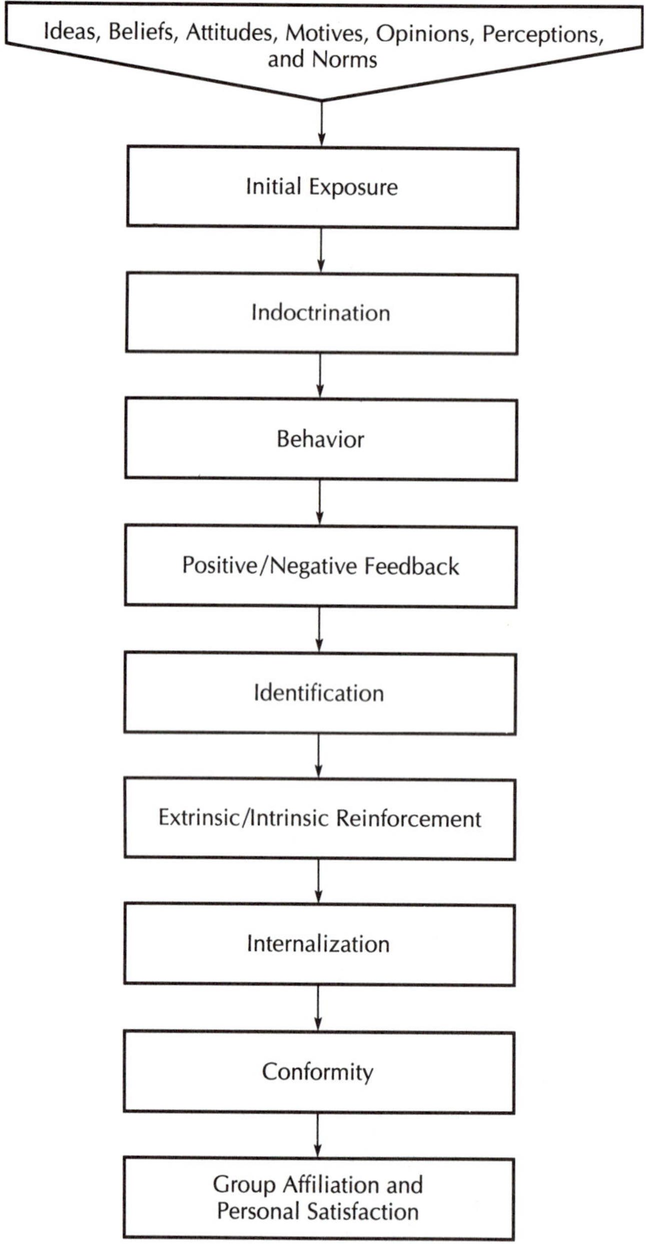

FIGURE 4.3 The Human Socialization Process.

TABLE 4.1 Glossary

Ideas	Abstract mental images of something imagined, seen, or known.
Beliefs	Ideas accepted as true and acted on as an article of faith.
Values	Strong and enduring beliefs about appropriate conduct and/or end states of existence (i.e., goals) which are preferable to opposite or inverse conduct or end states of existence.
Value System	Enduring values arranged hierarchically in terms of relative importance to a particular individual.
Attitudes	Predispositions, based on one's beliefs and values, to react either positively or negatively to various ideas, persons, events, or things.
Motives	Cognitive variables that activate, direct, sustain, or inhibit a person's goal-oriented behavior.
Opinions	Judgments about ideas, persons, events, and things translated into words that reflect one's ideas, beliefs, values, attitudes, and motives.
Perception	Filtering process through which individuals transform, attach meaning to, and structure information coming from their experience or memory.
Norms	Shared beliefs, values, attitudes, expectations, and rules—spoken or understood—that guide human behavior in specific situations.

Every social group attempts to socialize its members as they move through the cycle from initiation to full participation. *Socialization* is the process by which group-shared beliefs, values, attitudes, and norms are inculcated into each member's psyche (see Figure 4.3). Once these beliefs, values, attitudes, and norms have been internalized, they serve as prescriptive guides to appropriate behavior. See Table 4.1 for a definition of these terms. Consistent beliefs, values, attitudes, and norms produce conformity with group-shared expectations. Inconsistency creates ambivalence and conflict. The resulting anomie, or sense of normlessness, frequently leads to deviant behavior (Smith and Preston, 1982).

By the time young men and women become police officers, most of them have developed a fairly stable worldview and fixed personality structure. They have a repertoire of beliefs, values, attitudes, and norms that they bring with them into the workplace. These neophytes incorporate newly acquired ideas, beliefs, values, attitudes, motives, and norms into their preexisting frame of reference. Consequently, a police officer is a dynamic composite of past experience as modified by current events.

People-Oriented Management

It is clear that the beliefs, values, and attitudes of individual police administrators help to determine their capacity to work effectively with subordinates. The philosophical base of modern management lies in the following beliefs:

1. Human beings are social animals who engage in purposeful goal-oriented behavior.
2. People "exist" in terms of their interrelationships with other human beings and life-forms.
3. The welfare of individual workers and the work group cannot be separated from one another.

4. Every employee—as a human being—possesses intrinsic worth.
5. All human beings have the need to grow and develop toward the realization of their own unique potential.
6. Workers and work groups have an inherent propensity for change.
7. People are not by their nature passive and/or resistant to organizational needs.
8. The individual and the sociocultural environment can be understood through use of the scientific method.
9. The essential task of management is to arrange organizational conditions and methods of operation in such a way that individual workers can achieve their own goals best by directing personal efforts toward the accomplishment of organizational goals and objectives (McGregor, 1960).

Managers who subscribe to this philosophy are known as "organizational humanists." They believe in achieving productivity through people and seek to instill in all employees an awareness that their best efforts are essential for the success of the enterprise.

Thomas J. Peters and Robert H. Waterman, Jr., are the leading proponents of organizational humanism in America today. Their book, *In Search of Excellence* (1982), is still a nationwide bestseller. Based on their research, Peters and Waterman conclude that there is hardly a more pervasive theme in excellent organizations than respect for the individual. They found an abundance of structural devices, systems, styles, and values interacting to reinforce one another so that these organizations are able to "achieve extraordinary results through ordinary people." Workers are permitted to exert control over their own destinies. Peters and Waterman do not advocate mollycoddling people. They are talking about tough-minded respect for individual workers and a willingness to train them, to set clear and reasonable expectations for them, and to grant them the genuine autonomy to step out and make a meaningful contribution to the organization. Peters and Waterman contend that managers in excellent organizations are quite different from their counterparts in less healthy organizations. They are more open and trusting. They treat people as adults and as partners in the collective enterprise. They respect their subordinates and see them as the wellspring of productivity. They make people feel like winners and celebrate winning ways with a variety of nonmonetary, psychosocial rewards.

In a sense, all intentional behavior is the product of intrinsic motivation. People, based on psychosocial needs and/or environmental stimuli, set their own goals and expend the amount of effort necessary to demonstrate to themselves that they can, or almost can, reach these goals. There is an implicit question of values in all goal setting. Setting personal goals and activating goal-oriented behavior is inextricably linked to one's judgment of good and evil, right and wrong, and desirable and undesirable. These judgments are rooted in each person's cultural heritage, ethical perspective, and normative orientation. The heterogeneous nature of modern American society promotes ethical relativity and anomie. For all practical purposes, monolithic value systems like the Protestant ethic are now obsolete. Since police administrators perceive reality in terms of their own values, attitudes, and expectations, they must learn a great deal more about themselves in order to minimize distortion and prevent interpersonal conflict.

In order to become truly effective managers who have the ability to get things done through others, police administrators must learn to understand themselves as well as their subordinates. Introspection is a key to good management. Effective managers are not only empathetic but have some idea of their own values, attitudes, and motives. Good managers understand that who they are (in terms of background, experience, beliefs, values) almost always determines what they do with the organization's human resources. This self-awareness allows them, when necessary, to reevaluate their style and to adjust their behavior accordingly. Being comfortable with their role as an administrator in a complex criminal justice organization is much easier when police managers can do the following:

1. Be aware of and have the ability to accept themselves as fallible human beings with strengths and weaknesses.
2. Develop realistic expectations so as not to demand perfection from themselves and/or subordinate personnel.
3. Have the capacity to recognize and deal effectively with the negative attitudes and less than acceptable behaviors exhibited by some others within the organization.
4. Come to realize that self-esteem is dynamic and subject to change.

Successful police administrators know that their own personal beliefs, values, attitudes, and expectations have a substantive influence on perceptions, interpersonal relations, and work-group dynamics. Thus good managers

1. Understand that they are a "walking system" of conscious and unconscious values which is so much a part of their personality they are scarcely aware of its existence or influence.
2. Use all means at their disposal to identify personal predilections or biases that reduce objectivity in assessing the on-the-job behavior of others.
3. Strive to evaluate themselves and their personal values in a rational and objective manner.
4. Endeavor to change those values (and concomitant behaviors) that, based on serious self-evaluation, need to be changed.

If police administrators are secure within themselves, have adequate coping mechanisms, and understand their own feelings, beliefs, values, attitudes, and motives, they ordinarily will not find it difficult to identify with and respect healthy differences in other people (Brill, 1978).

Ideas, Beliefs, and Values

Human beings are intelligent social animals with the mental capacity to comprehend, infer, and think in rational ways. People convert raw physical and social data into psychological imagery. They use the power of reason to draw conclusions, make judgments, and guide their goal-oriented behavior. A healthy mind produces a continuous stream of ideas. Ideas are generated during the thought process and can be described as relatively abstract mental

Negative Reflection The actions of several Los Angeles Police Department officers during the 1991 beating of an African-American motorist were widely believed to be a reflection of management's values and attitudes. *(AP/Wide World Photos)*

images of something imagined, seen, or known. They are cognitive representations of what is or what could be. Ideas are untested concepts which may or may not reflect reality. Creative people have the ability to translate good ideas into positive action.

Ideas, once formed, are cycled through the mind for (conscious or subconscious) evaluation. Some seem implausible and are discarded outright. The rest are arranged along a continuum of support ranging from *some* to *complete*. Beliefs are ideas accepted as good or true (whether they are or not) and acted on as an article of faith. Since the person involved makes an emotional commitment, beliefs take on an existence of their own. Selective perception is used to confirm and reinforce them. Consequently, they can withstand virtually any challenge. Facts become irrelevant! Logic becomes irrelevant! A Theory X police administrator who believes that people lack ambition, dislike responsibility, and prefer to be led will, for example, reject Peters and Waterman's assertion that giving employees respect and autonomy will help police departments achieve extraordinary results through ordinary people. Theory X administrators find it very difficult if not impossible to share power with rather than exercise power over their subordinates. (See Chapter 5 for a discussion of Theory X management style.)

As human beings, we learn and share the values by which we live. Values represent the ideas and beliefs through which we define our personal goals, choose particular courses of action, and judge our own behavior in relation to that of others. Focus 4.1 illustrates that many of our values are acquired

FOCUS 4.1

And we wonder why kids have no values...

as the result of vicarious learning. According to Ely Chinoy and John Hewitt (1975), values are not specifically defined rules for action but general precepts to which people are expected to give their allegiance and about which they are likely to have strong sentiments. Values are very important in that they have a direct influence on our perceptions, preferences, aspirations, and choices. In addition, personal fulfillment depends—in large measure—on how well our values find expression in our daily life (Yukl, 1981).

Paul M. Whisenand (Whisenand, 1981; Whisenand and Ferguson, 1978; Whisenand and Rush, 1988), one of the best-known police management theorists in America, contends that "we are what we value." He argues that police administrators need to know and understand their own values because values are the linchpin in the foundation of one's character, personality, management style, and on-the-job behavior. Past values help determine who we are and what we want out of life. Current values give substance to our personal and professional being. Future values will influence our behavior at some point down the road. In a generic sense, values are mental constructs representing behaviors and end states of existence (goals) that are considered important to us as individuals (Gordon, 1975).

From a practical point of view, a value is a strong and persistent belief that certain behaviors and/or end states of existence are preferable to an opposite or inverse action or end state of existence. A *value system* is an enduring set of beliefs about preferred conduct (instrumental values) and end states of existence (terminal values) in a hierarchical ranking of relative importance (Rokeach, 1973). Because all people possess more than one value, managers need to adopt a broader perspective and think in terms of value systems. Those managers who value honesty and openness in human relationships will do everything in their power not to manipulate or appear to be manipulating their subordinates.

Values are enduring yet changeable beliefs about appropriate ends (goals) and acceptable goal-oriented behaviors (means). Basic values are acquired through imprinting, modeling, and socialization in a group setting (see Chapter 7). These values influence virtually every aspect of life. According to Paul Whisenand (1981), there is enough evidence to support the following general propositions concerning human values:

1. The actual number of values that people possess is relatively small when compared to their interests, attitudes, and motives.
2. All human beings tend to have the same values to one degree or another.
3. Values are organized into hierarchical value systems.
4. The origin of human values can be traced back to one's formative years, culture, institutions, and society.
5. The influence of values is manifest in everything a person feels, thinks, and does.
6. A police administrator's effectiveness or lack of effectiveness ultimately depends on that person's value system.
7. Improved or continued effectiveness is directly related to a police manager's awareness of personal values and the values of co-workers.

Individual values and value systems are critically important variables in that they automatically filter the way people, as human beings, perceive the world around them. They serve as ethical as well as moral standards. Values and value systems help resolve internal conflicts and facilitate the decision-making process. They encourage analytical thinking about legitimate goals and the socially acceptable means for achieving those goals. Values and value systems also motivate people to get off of dead center and move toward the accomplishment of important organizational goals and objectives.

Evolving Value Systems

Clare Graves (1970) has theorized that normal people, regardless of their intelligence, evolve through various levels of existence. As they develop psychosocially, they move away from a very limited set of values to a more expansive system of values that gives much more meaning to their life. Old values give way to and are replaced by new values that are more appropriate to the elevated level of existence. Individual values and value systems are manifested in the behavior of police officers at work. The seven levels of psychosocial existence identified by Graves are as follows:

1. *Reactive.* This is the basic level of existence in the evolutionary chain. Reactive people are childlike. They exist in the here and now and have no conception of cause or effect. They are not aware of themselves or others as individuals. Their only real interest is in the physiological aspects of work (pay, benefits, safety, working conditions, etc.). Relatively few people become fixated at this stage of development.

2. *Tribalistic.* This is the first established "way of life." Employees at the tribal level are mainly concerned with their own safety and the principal value is tradition. People at this particular level have a strong need for direction from the boss. They are impressed by the use of power and authority in the workplace. Group values are considered to be binding. Violation of group-shared expectations elicits strong negative sanctions.

3. *Egocentric.* Rugged self-assertive individualism is prevalent at this level. Egocentric people are inclined to be suspicious and disruptive at work. They are often selfish, thoughtless, unscrupulous, and dishonest in dealing with others because they have not learned to live within the constraints imposed by the group. Rights become absolute and are perceived as the prerogatives of management. Power is viewed as the inalienable right of those who have claimed it. Egocentric employees respond well only to managers who are strong and willing to exert control.

4. *Conformist.* Conformists accept their position in life and inequity as a fact of life. They subscribe to the work ethic and believe in self-sacrifice, duty, loyalty, and achieving perfection in one's assigned role. Conformists accept department policy, procedures, rules, and regulations. They go by the book. They have very low tolerance for ambiguity, resist innovation, and seek to perpetuate the status quo. Conformists tend to judge themselves and others in terms of absolute moral law.

5. *Manipulative.* Manipulators are wheeler-dealers who constantly strive to get ahead. They are ambitious, pragmatic, and utilitarian in their efforts to achieve recognition, status, and material rewards. Manipulators see everything as a game. They are on the lookout for the surest and best way to beat the system. They excel in unsettled situations in which they can use ingenuity to achieve, advance, and garner psychological as well as economic rewards.

Manipulators are goal-oriented moral entrepreneurs with a desire to meet their own needs regardless of the cost to others within the organization.

6. *Sociocentric.* In a sociocentric state of being, people feel that getting along with others is more important than getting ahead of them. Their value system centers around interpersonal relationships, positive human relations, empathetic supervision, and goal-oriented collaboration within the work group. Emphasis is placed on sensitivity and collegiality rather than utilitarian exploitation. Sociocentric police administrators share power with instead of exercising power over their subordinates. Conflicting values often lead to conflict between managers and others within the organization.

7. *Existential.* At the existential level, people focus their attention on themselves as autonomous individuals. They believe in meaningful work through job enrichment. They value spontaneity over conventionality. Continuing growth and development is very important to them. Existentialists have a need to set their own performance standards, seek opportunities to solve problems, participate in the decision-making process, and perform work that is imaginative as well as challenging. They are at the self-actualization stage of development and have a distinctively different value system than those at the other six levels. They are intolerant of closed systems, overly restrictive policy, and the arbitrary use of authority. People who are existential are quite often viewed as troublemakers and may be forced out of the work group because they do not or will not conform to culturally mandated expectations. Existentialists have difficulty dealing with rigid structure, formal roles, rules, and regulations (Steinmetz and Todd, 1986).

Some people, for a variety of reasons, do not move up the evolutionary ladder from one level of existence to the next (see Figure 4.4). They become

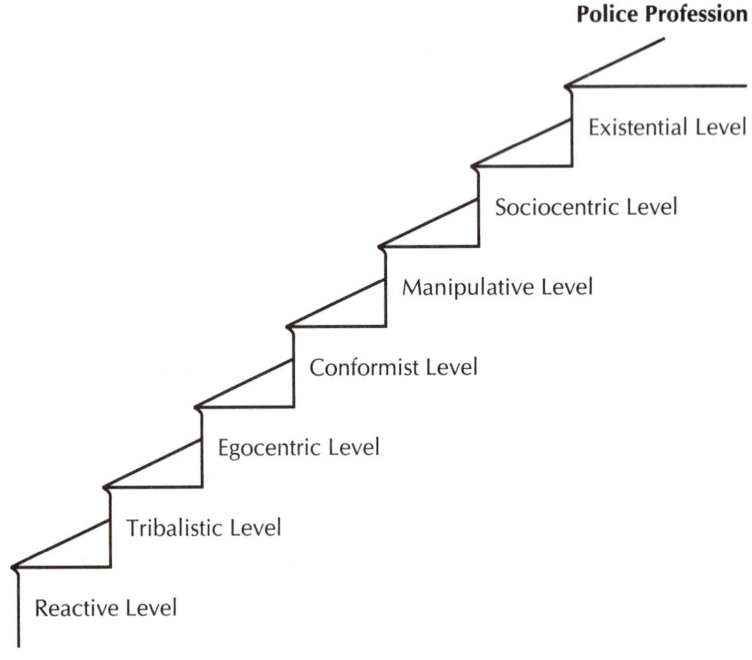

FIGURE 4.4 Seven Levels of Existence.

fixated at a particular level or, for any number of reasons, actually regress from one level to another. This process is fluid. Research by Scott and Susan Myers suggests that more and more managers are finding themselves out of sync with their subordinates in terms of basic values. This problem is frequently caused and exacerbated by the fact that these managers are on a different level of existence than other employees (Leonard and More, 1987).

Bureaucratic values define the public interest, shape organizational goals, and set performance standards. Utilitarian values like efficiency, effectiveness, productivity, and accountability stress the rational aspects of work and virtually ignore what Douglas M. McGregor called "the human side of enterprise." According to Warren Bennis (1966), police administrators who are preoccupied with materialistic values are badly cast to play the exceedingly complex managerial roles now assigned to them. He feels their ineptitude in dealing with human resources leads to internal strife and a demonstrable reduction in the problem-solving capacity of complex organizations. Like other organizational humanists, Bennis places a great deal of emphasis on goal-oriented communication, interaction, and collaboration. Good managers are viewed as pragmatists who understand they must temper bureaucratic values with genuine empathy (for employees and clients) if they are to accomplish the mission, goals, and objectives of the police department.

Humanistic Values

While mechanistic values like efficiency, effectiveness, productivity, and accountability are still very important, much more emphasis is now being placed on the quality of work life (Certo, 1986). This shift in values is based on profound dissatisfaction with traditional bureaucracy. It is also related to the rising influence of humanism in contemporary American society. Humanism has been nurtured by the following trends:

1. Generally higher levels of education in the work force.
2. New technology that frees most people from routine physical labor, yet makes them much more dependent on goal-oriented social interaction.
3. Sociocultural change that is more challenging than threatening.
4. Affluence that opens up opportunities for experiences never before so readily available to the population as a whole.
5. Escalation in the revolution of rising expectations.

As police managers have eased themselves into an existential/humanist philosophy of work, more and more of them are questioning and moving away from traditional bureaucratic values. They are constructing new multidimensional value systems that stress efficiency, effectiveness, productivity, and accountability while addressing employee needs for personal growth, self-esteem, competence, and autonomy (Tannenbaum and Davis, 1969).

Since management is often defined as "the art of getting things done with and through the efforts of others," all credible management theories have a humanistic component. They are based—to one degree or another—on the value-laden assumption that organizations should be designed to meet the legitimate needs of people (including employees) as they seek to accomplish their mission, goals, and objectives. Even the infamous "paramilitary mentality" of seasoned police administrators is not impervious to humanistic values. Most mainstream police managers know that organizational productivity in a labor-intensive enterprise is contingent on appreciation for and effective use of human resources. They understand the importance of job enlargement, job enrichment, shared decision making, and team management. Little by little their values are shifting away from the following:

1. Viewing people as essentially bad toward viewing them as basically good.
2. Evaluating individuality negatively toward confirming unique individuals as human beings.
3. Perceiving people as fixed or unchanging toward seeing them in process.
4. Fearing and/or resisting individual differences toward accepting and utilizing them to strengthen the organization.
5. Viewing employees solely in terms of their job description toward visualizing the individual as a whole person.
6. Walling off the expression of feelings toward encouraging appropriate expression and use of feelings in order to improve interpersonal communication.
7. Relying on marksmanship and game playing toward emphasizing more authentic human behavior.
8. Using status for maintaining power or personal prestige toward utilizing status only for organizationally relevant purposes.
9. Distrusting people toward trusting and having confidence in them.
10. Avoiding confrontation with others based on the use of relevant (cultural, social, and organizational) data toward using controlled conflict as an organization development technique.
11. Avoiding risk taking toward showing a willingness to assume reasonable risks.
12. Viewing group process work (involving guided group interaction) as unproductive effort toward seeing it as an essential management function in all complex criminal justice organizations.
13. Emphasizing competition toward depending on collaboration among all of those who toil in the workplace (Tannenbaum and Davis, 1969).

Based on this shift in basic values, police work is moving toward its own unique brand of industrial democracy. These new values have provided an impetus for unionization and are almost always incorporated into collective bargaining agreements. Some of them have been factored into community-based policing strategies and collegial organization models like the one depicted in Figure 4.5.

It is clear that modern police administrators have been compelled to abandon the overly simplistic push-button view of man embodied in bureaucratic theory. They have replaced it with a new concept of human resources which takes into account the complex and shifting needs of subordinates. Since their values have changed, they also view power in a much different way than their predecessors. The new concept of power is based on competence, collaboration, and reason rather than assigned status (rank) and coercion (formal authority). There is no doubt that humanistic-democratic values have slowly been replacing the impersonal, mechanistic, and authoritarian value system

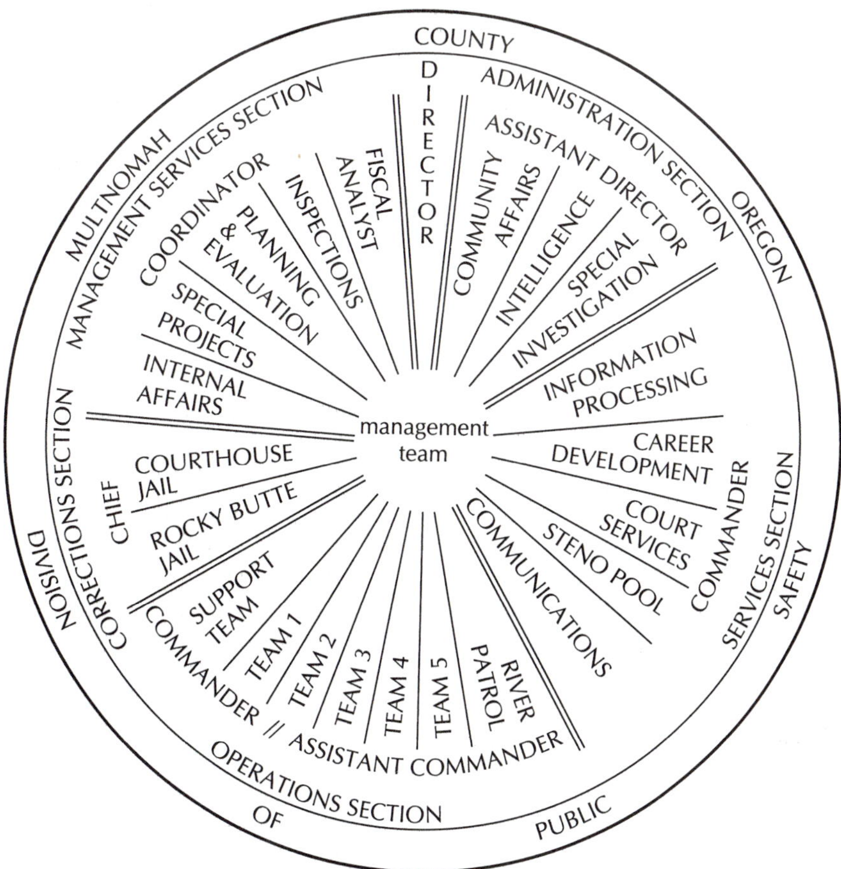

FIGURE 4.5 Colleague Organizational Structure.

glorified by Max Weber and his colleagues (Bennis, 1969). According to Stanley Vanagunas and James Elliott (1980), humanistic police managers believe that most police officers want to be good at their job and have a need to exercise self-direction and self-control. Under the right set of circumstances, they seek out and accept responsibility. They have the knowledge, imagination, creativity, ingenuity, and practical skills necessary to help the police department accomplish its mission, goals, and objectives. A police administrator's primary job is to get things done through others. In order to do it, they are expected to marshal resources, motivate personnel, supervise employees, set the moral tone, and perform all of the other specialized work required to keep the organization in operation (Barnard, 1976).

Attitudes and Opinions

As noted earlier, the term *culture* refers to the way of life of a particular group. Police officers are members of a unique occupational group and share a distinctive cultural orientation. Beliefs are major components of that culture. *Beliefs* are ideas that people in a group share about themselves and the physical, biological, and social world in which they live. Beliefs, regardless of their accuracy or merit, influence perception and regulate our relations with other human beings, society, and nature itself. *Values* are very strong beliefs about what is good and/or what is bad. A *personal value system* is a relatively permanent perceptual framework that influences and shapes our attitudes, opinions, motives, and behavior (England, 1975).

Values and attitudes are similar in that they are beliefs about appropriate ways of feeling, thinking, and behaving. Values are much broader, however, and cut across specific situations to which personal attitudes are tied (Schermerhorn, Hunt, and Osborn, 1982). Values are also more enduring than attitudes. They transcend attitudes and serve as a guide to our attitudes, judgments, choices, and behavior. An attitude is a composite of our beliefs concerning a particular person, object, event, or situation.

An attitude is a general point of view. It represents a way of looking at someone or something and is coupled with a predisposition to react to a specific stimulus in a predetermined manner. An attitude can also be described as a state of mind in which one's likes and dislikes are translated into an opinion concerning the intrinsic worth of a certain person, event, or thing. An opinion is the verbal expression of this judgment and a reflection of each evaluator's personal beliefs, values, and attitudes. Police administrators can learn a great deal about the beliefs, values, and attitudes of other people if

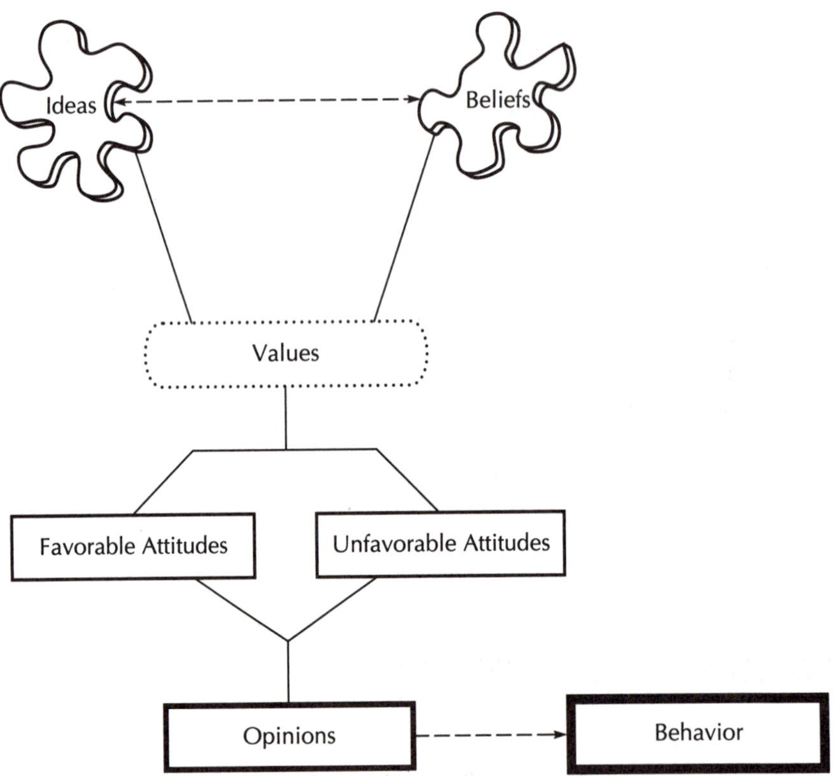

FIGURE 4.6 Values in Action.

TABLE 4.2 Behavior Formation

	Example 1	*Example 2*	*Example 3*
Value	Belief in the ethical use of police power to protect and serve the community.	Belief in and respect for people regardless of their station in life.	Belief in the legitimate use of authority to accomplish management goals and objectives.
Attitude	Feeling criminal activity by police officers violates the Law Enforcement Code of Ethics (see Focus 4.2) and should not be tolerated.	Feeling empathetic understanding and support will help others to achieve their full potential.	Feeling police officers are to carry out all legitimate orders given to them by their superiors.
Opinion	"Blue-coat crime" should be rooted out and police officers who violate the crimes code ought to be prosecuted to the full extent of the law.	Police officers should have an opportunity to be involved in making those decisions that directly affect them.	Insubordination should not be tolerated and must be dealt with in a forthright manner.
Behavior	A police officer reports his partner for stealing jewelry from the body of an accident victim.	The police chief forms a task force to recommend ways to improve the overall quality of work life in the police department.	An acting lieutenant suspends a senior patrol officer for failure to follow a direct order.

they take the time to analyze their opinions (Plunkett, 1983). This is true because *values* (general principles) generate *attitudes* (favorable or unfavorable feelings) which are translated into our *opinions* (personal judgments) and lead to specific *behavior* (cognitive response to stimuli). This process is illustrated in Figure 4.6. Table 4.2 gives examples and demonstrates the dynamic interaction between these variables. Focus 4.2 contains the official code of ethics for law enforcement officials.

Paul Whisenand and George Rush (1988) have analyzed the relationship between values and attitudes. They point out the following characteristics of values:

1. A value is a single belief; an attitude refers to several related beliefs concerning a single object or situation.
2. A value transcends particular objects and situations; an attitude focuses on a specific object or situation.
3. A value is a standard; an attitude may or may not function as a standard.
4. Values are few in number; the number of object-specific or situation-specific attitudes is incalculable.
5. Values are more central to the personality and the cognitive process than attitudes.
6. Values are global and more dynamic; attitudes are normally linked to particular objects or situations.
7. Values explicitly reflect adaptive, ego-defensive, and knowledge functions; attitudes do so only through inference.

Attitudes are identifiable predispositions to react in a favorable or unfavorable way to a particular person, event, or object in the environment.

FOCUS 4.2

Law Enforcement Code of Ethics

As a Law Enforcement Officer, *my fundamental duty is to serve mankind; to safeguard lives and property; to protect the innocent against deception, the weak against oppression or intimidation, and the peaceful against violence or disorder; and to respect the Constitutional rights of all men to liberty, equality and justice.*

I will *keep my private life unsullied as an example to all; maintain courageous calm in the face of danger, scorn, or ridicule; develop self-restraint; and be constantly mindful of the welfare of others. Honest in thought and deed in both my personal and official life, I will be exemplary in obeying the laws of the land and the regulations of my department. Whatever I see or hear of a confidential nature or that is confided to me in my official capacity will be kept ever secret unless revelation is necessary in the performance of my duty.*

I will *never act officiously or permit personal feelings, prejudices, animosities or friendships to influence my decisions. With no compromise for crime and with relentless prosecution of criminals, I will enforce the law courteously and appropriately without fear or favor, malice or ill will, never employing unnecessary force or violence and never accepting gratuities.*

I recognize *the badge of my office as a symbol of public faith, and I accept it as a public trust to be held so long as I am true to the ethics of the police service. I will constantly strive to achieve these objectives and ideals, dedicating myself before God to my chosen profession . . . law enforcement.*

Acquiring Attitudes

Attitudes are learned. They are not inherited. People acquire positive as well as negative attitudes as the result of their personal experiences and maintain them if there is sufficient reinforcement to justify their retention. Police officers, like all other human beings, acquire their attitudes in three distinct ways: (1) direct experience, (2) association, and (3) the vicarious learning process.

1. *Direct experience.* Attitudes can develop from a personally rewarding or painful experience with a person, event, or object. A rookie police officer who loses an important criminal case because of the exclusionary rule may—whether he or she was at fault or not—develop a very cynical attitude toward procedural due process and argue that public safety is in jeopardy because the courts are "handcuffing the police."

2. *Association.* Attitudes toward a person, event, or object may develop from associating them with others about which attitudes have already been formed. A police captain may be predisposed to give all college graduates preferential treatment based on the spectacular accomplishments of one or two college-educated police officers.

3. *Vicarious learning.* Attitudes may also develop based on what someone is told about some person, event, or object by another person. A squad leader exercises very close supervision over women police officers because his peers have convinced him that "women are members of the weaker sex" and cannot perform the physical aspects of police work as well as their male counterparts.

Attitudes which are value specific and have been acquired through personal experience are almost always more resistant to change than those learned through association or from other people. According to H. Joseph Reitz (1981), if attitudes formed as the result of association and/or the vicarious learning process are integrated into a mutually reinforcing cluster of values and attitudes, they became much more stable and resistant to change.

Characteristics and Functions

While specific attitudes are idiosyncratic, all attitudes exhibit three common characteristics. They are *cognitive* (reflect beliefs), *affective* (express feelings), and *conative* (indicative of a predisposition to act). Attitudes also serve four very distinct functions for the individual:

1. *Knowledge function.* An attitude can help people organize and make some sense out of their knowledge, experiences, and beliefs. As such, an attitude serves as a standard or frame of reference. A stereotype, for example, is an attitude that ascribes certain traits or characteristics to all members of a particular group regardless of their individual differences. Accuracy is irrelevant.

2. *Instrumental function.* An attitude may develop because it (the attitude) or its object (person, event, or thing) is instrumental in obtaining rewards or avoiding punishments. Attitudes serve as a means to an end. A lieutenant's positive attitude toward police work and co-workers could be instrumental in achieving a promotion (reward) or in helping to avoid rejection by other command personnel (punishment). In other cases, the object itself becomes a means to an end, and attitudes develop from associating the object with

its outcome. For example, a sergeant may develop a very favorable attitude toward police personnel who are easily controlled and a negative attitude toward subordinates who question the need for so much control. The sergeant clearly associates "success" with the ability to exert control and "failure" with the lack of control.

3. *Value-expressive function.* Attitudes may serve as a concrete expression of one's basic values and/or self-image. A police officer who places great value on social order, for example, is certain to have a negative attitude toward ambiguity, individuality, and the so-called excesses caused by too much freedom. A white captain, on the other hand, who views himself as a firm, fair, and unbiased manager may exhibit a very positive attitude in relation to EEO (Equal Employment Opportunity), AA (Affirmative Action), and PER (Proportional Ethnic Representation). A person's real values can be inferred through the analysis of personal attitudes only if the attitudes displayed are, in fact, genuine. Any type of game playing is detrimental in that it distorts the process and reduces the accuracy of the analysis.

4. *Ego-defensive function.* According to H. Joseph Reitz (1981), attitudes also serve to protect people's egos from unpleasant or threatening knowledge about themselves and their psychosocial environment. Accepting this kind of negative data induces stress and causes anxiety. Consequently, we develop and deploy defense mechanisms. Rationalizations are used to (1) block or (2) alter this negative data in an effort to control physical stress and emotional anxiety. Under these circumstances, rationalizations function as a homeostatic device designed to control cognitive dissonance (i.e., tension that occurs whenever a person holds conflicting cognitions—ideas, beliefs, values, attitudes, motives—which are psychologically inconsistent) and create a dynamic equilibrium between different, yet interrelated elements of the thought process. To hold opposing attitudes is to flirt with the absurd (Aronson, 1976). A police chief who views himself as a natural leader yet treats lower level uniformed police personnel as chattel—without regard to their personal feelings or professional competence—may adopt an ego-defensive attitude that they lack interest and are ill-equipped to do their job in an efficient, effective, and productive manner. This particular rationalization makes it unnecessary for the chief to come to grips with the fact that as an autocratic person there is a compulsive need to control subordinates. It tends to justify the chief's innate, albeit psychologically well-camouflaged, need for superiority based on differential psychosocial status. Police officers who develop ritualistic attitudes about their work may be trying to protect themselves against deep-seated feelings of inadequacy, insecurity, inequity, and so on.

An attitude is a psychological mind set that influences our opinions, perception, and behavior. Attitudes are the positive and negative predispositions that people interject into virtually everything they do.

Our attitudes have a number of identifiable characteristics. They are ordinarily discussed in terms of their valence, multiplicity, relation to need, centrality, and determinance.

1. *Valence.* The valence, or magnitude of a particular attitude is indicative of the degree to which it is positive or negative toward a particular attitude object. For the purpose of this discussion, an attitude object is an idea, person, place, or thing. Most attitude research involves the empirical measurement

of valence. We want to know the intensity of feeling. Valence is fairly easy to quantify.

2. *Multiplicity*. Multiplicity refers to the total number of factors incorporated into one's attitude. Police officers might have a very positive attitude toward the department (because it takes care of its own) yet feel free to criticize it when their sense of fair play is violated by the arbitrary actions of some administrators. Other officers in the department may feel loyal, respectful, and totally dependent. Criticizing the department would be equivalent to a mortal sin. Due to the dynamics involved in formulating and maintaining attitudes, it is nearly impossible to find a one-dimensional attitude. The more factors that we incorporate into and use to support a particular attitude, the less susceptible it will be to substantive change.

3. *Relation to Need*. Attitudes differ widely in terms of their relation to individual needs. As we indicated, attitudes are keyed to and reflect our level of existence. A humanist police administrator's attitude about sharing power with instead of exercising power over subordinates is the manifestation of personal needs for social interaction, collaboration, achievement, and self-actualization. Other attitudes are more peripheral in nature. They cluster around aesthetic, intellectual, occupational, and recreational interests.

4. *Centrality*. Some attitudes are—for various reasons—more central or salient than others. They cluster around high-priority values. They are fully integrated into our personality. Central attitudes become motives or cognitive variables which activate, direct, sustain, or stop goal-oriented behavior. They are easily reinforced and almost always resistant to change. Racial prejudice is an attitude built on our predisposition to react very negatively toward other human beings due to their race or ethnicity. Discrimination, on the other hand, involves prejudicial action or treatment. While a particular attitude may change, our central attitudes are almost never changed through the use of reason alone.

5. *Determinance*. Determinance measures the degree to which our attitudes directly influence our personal behavior. A police officer's negative attitude toward restrictive Supreme Court decisions could lead to apathy, mechanistic performance, and absenteeism. Countervailing factors may be more influential, however (Albanese, 1981). The fear of being fired may act as a constraint. Under these circumstances, fear keeps the negative attitude in check. Male police administrators with a negative attitude about women may bend over backward not to discriminate against female police officers because they have developed strong feelings about equity, equal employment opportunity, and affirmative action. The stronger the attitude, the more likely it is to evolve into a motive for goal-oriented behavior.

Attitudes are important variables in the psychosocial landscape of collective behavior. They influence perception and serve as guides for human conduct. Police administrators must learn how to identify and analyze their own attitudes vis-à-vis those of superiors, subordinates, and society at large. This knowledge will help individual managers to understand themselves and should provide them with a vehicle to identify their own values, understand their own motives, explain the behavior of others, develop healthy (empathetic) relationships, and avoid interpersonal conflicts caused by the misinterpretation of someone else's motives (see Table 4.3).

TABLE 4.3 The Benefits of Attitude Analysis

Introspection and attitude analysis helps police administrators to
1. Identify their basic beliefs.
2. Clarify their personal values.
3. Explore their own attitudes.
4. Understand their own motives.
5. Accept individual differences.
6. Understand behavior of others.
7. Develop healthy relationships.
8. Avoid interpersonal conflict.
9. Manage personnel effectively.

Attitudes and Work

Work plays a dominant role in our life. According to Robert Baron (1983), work occupies most of our time and consumes more energy than any other single activity. Work is a critical factor in development of the self-concept. Most people learn to define themselves, in part, by their occupation, profession, or career. Job performance is influenced by factors such as our (1) level of aspiration, (2) pride in the work group, and (3) interest in the job itself (Whisenand and Ferguson, 1978). While there is no clear-cut scientific evidence to show that job satisfaction and job performance are directly related, there is no doubt a police officer's attitude toward work can have a positive or a negative effect on how well the job gets done.

In simple terms, job satisfaction is an attitude. It is a reflection of our general attitude (composed of beliefs, feelings, and a predisposition to act) toward work and a set of relatively specific attitudes concerning certain aspects of a particular job. From a conceptual point of view, job satisfaction and dissatisfaction are a function of the perceived relationship between what employees expect from their job and what they actually get (Locke, 1969). Morale (job satisfaction) is the degree to which the needs of individuals are satisfied and the extent to which they perceive that satisfaction as coming from the total job situation (Fulmer, 1983). The main components of job satisfaction are as follows:

1. Relevant and meaningful work
2. Acceptable working conditions
3. Positive work-group dynamics
4. Satisfaction with the agency
5. Adequate general supervision
6. Accessible and fair rewards
7. Intrinsic satisfactions

While these components may not be applicable to all work environments, they are viewed as significant variables in most employment situations involving complex criminal justice organizations.

Poor morale (job dissatisfaction), like any other bad attitude, is contagious. It can spread throughout a police department just like a virus. Poor morale tends to lower the efficiency, effectiveness, and productivity of human resources. It often manifests itself in the form of (1) apathy, (2) disruptive behavior, (3) interpersonal conflict, (4) absenteeism, and (5) employee turnover. It is the police administrator's job to counteract the job dissatisfaction that leads to these behaviors. In order to carry out this responsibility, administrators use a variety of techniques:

1. Participation
2. Job analysis
3. Job redesign
4. Job enlargement
5. Job enrichment
6. Job rotation
7. Organization development

These techniques are normally incorporated into a motivation strategy. (For a full discussion of motivation, see Chapter 5.)

Perception, Motives, and Human Behavior

Human beings are rational animals who have the ability to convert raw data into conceptual representations of reality. Beliefs, values, attitudes, and opinions help to shape a person's understanding of the physical, social, and psychological world. People do not react to each event in their life as something unique. They construct a perceptual frame of reference that establishes a sense of order and gives meaning to their experiences (Dunham and Alpert, 1989).

People assume that they possess a fairly clear and relatively undistorted view of reality. They believe ideas, people, places, and things are pretty much as they perceive them to be. This belief is so strong that it is given little or no thought. The problem is that our perceptions are not always accurate. As human beings, we do not experience the world around us in simple and direct terms. Our cognitive picture of it is synthesized and constructed out of information derived from the five senses. The process by which people organize and interpret sensory input is known as perception (Baron, 1983). Due to the subjective nature of this process, reality exists only in the eye of the beholder. Truth becomes relative and is merely a reflection of an individual's point of view (Holden, 1986).

Perception is a mental screen or filter through which information must pass before it can be integrated into human thought processes and behaviors (Schermerhorn, Hunt, and Osborn, 1982). People use this perceptual apparatus to help them do the following:

1. Relate their past experiences to current situations.
2. Choose the various stimuli to which they will react.
3. Group stimuli into a manageable number of categories.
4. Fill in missing data about persons, places, or things.
5. Defend themselves against serious threats to the ego.

It is through the manipulation of perception that we create and maintain a sense of consistency and order in a complex world where rapid change is the rule rather than the exception (Bobbitt, Breinholt, Doktor, and McNaul, 1978). Perception is used to process environmental stimuli. It converts the stimuli into useful information and then links that information to an appropriate behavioral response. In this context, perception helps to protect the human mind from systemic overload.

Perceptions

Every perceptual event has three components. Perceptions are formed based on interaction between (1) the perceiver, (2) the target, and (3) the situational context in which the perception takes place. These factors influence the perceiver's interpretation of all sensory data related to an idea, event, person, place, or thing.

1. *Perceiver.* While there is some disagreement, most social scientists contend that there is really no such thing as objective reality. They operate on the assumption that perception depends, to a large extent, on the personal characteristics and background of the perceiver. Research in organizational behavior (OB) indicates that emotions, beliefs, values, attitudes, motives, interests, experiences, and expectations skew perception (Robbins, 1989). They also help to determine the actual behavioral response in any given situation.

2. *Target.* In addition to the factors just noted, perception is affected by the characteristics of the target itself. Two of the most important characteristics are the degree of ambiguity of the target and the target's social status (Johns, 1988). Since perception involves the attribution of meaning as well as interpretation, ambiguous targets that are not well defined are particularly susceptible to perceptual distortion. Research clearly indicates that in the case of person perception, the social status of the target influences the perceiver's perception of the person as well as what that individual says and does. Status and perceptual distortion go hand in hand. Because targets are not looked at in isolation, the relationship of a target to its background (or perceptual field) also influences perception (Robbins, 1989). People have a natural inclination to group close things and similar things together. Proximity is frequently translated into cause and effect. Stereotypical thinking may be the rule rather than the exception.

3. *Situation.* There are a number of situational variables with the potential to influence an individual's perception of people, places, and things. The physical surroundings, social setting, emotional atmosphere, and time frame are important factors in perception formation (Schermerhorn, Hunt, and Osborn, 1982). While the perceiver and the target might remain the same, our perception of the target is anchored to and changes with the situation. Perception is an inherently complex psychosocial process by which human beings attach meaning to those things they experience through the senses. There are forces in each of us (perceiver), in the stimuli (target), and in the environment (situation) that cause perceptions to differ. Focus 4.3 illustrates this phenomenon. It is no wonder that sincere people adopt opposing points of view and exhibit radically different behaviors (Albanese, 1981).

FOCUS 4.3

A Matter of Perception

PORTRAIT OF A . . .

Is it a portrait of a young woman or an old lady?
(Source: Unknown.)

THE STRAIGHT LINE

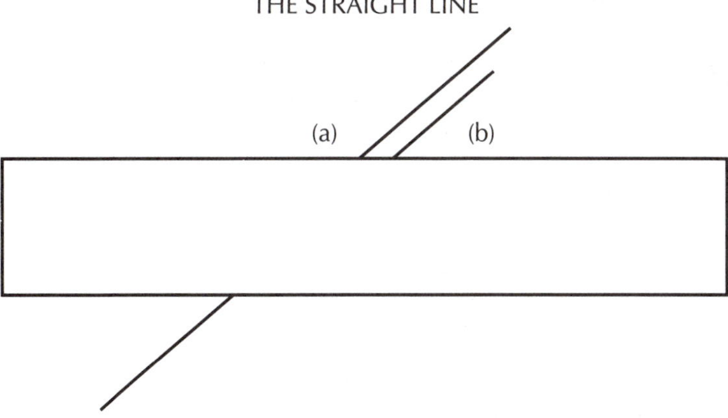

Using just your eyes, which line (a) or (b) goes through the box?
(Source: Unknown.)

The Perception Process

Behavior, in its simplest form, can be viewed as an individual's response to a stimulus in a given situation. This is known as the stimulus-response (S-R) model and is often used to explain reflex actions. In more complicated behaviors, however, there is a discrete chain of events between the stimulus and the operant (or intentional) response. There are three intervening subprocesses—*reception, organization,* and *interpretation*—that work to convert information input into decisions or behavioral outputs (Bobbitt et al., 1978). The perception process is illustrated in Figure 4.7.

Sensing is the first step in the perception formation process. In other words, a stimulus is encountered by one of the five senses: touching, tasting, seeing, hearing, or smelling. Since people simply cannot deal with all of the stimuli in the physical, social, and psychological environment, they become selective in picking out those stimuli they feel are important and tuning out the others. This is known as selective perception.

Selective perception is the psychological predisposition to see and evaluate raw data (about people, places, and things) in light of our own ideas, beliefs, values, attitudes, opinions, motives, and past experiences. People sort through the data related to sensory stimuli and select information that is supportive and satisfying (Leavitt, 1978). They tend to ignore negative information that is painful and/or disturbing. Whether a particular stimulus captures our attention and elicits a behavioral response will depend on

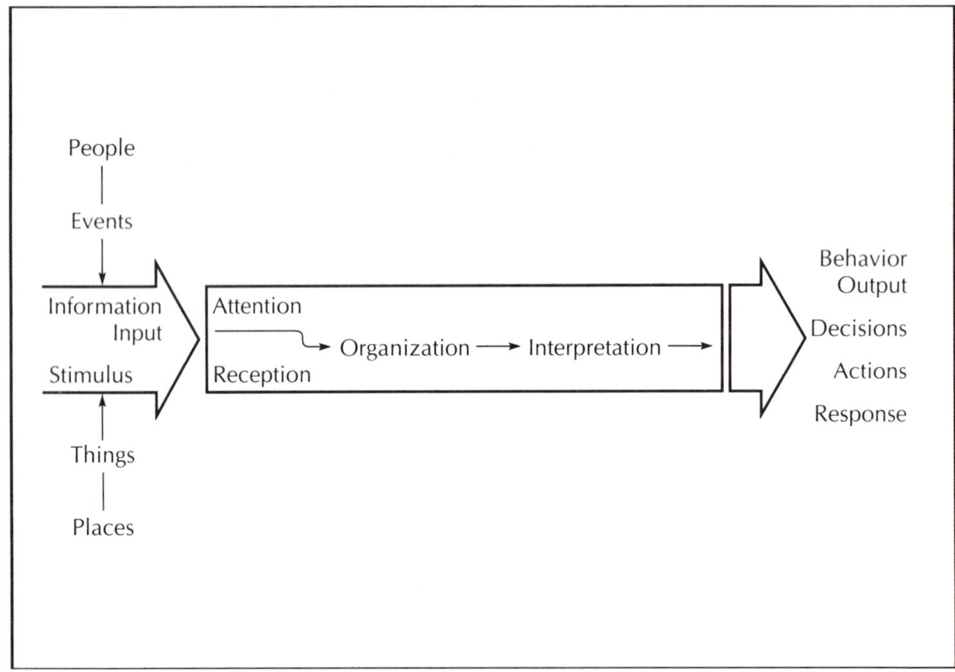

FIGURE 4.7 The Perception Process.

1. The properties of the stimulus itself (in terms of its size, intensity, contrast, repetition, motion, etc.).
2. Past experience in relation to it and other stimuli within the environment.
3. The preparatory set (based on our personality, values, motives, and past learning) to see certain things and not others, regardless of the properties of the target itself.

Selective attention leads to selective perception and serves as the springboard for all purposeful human behavior.

Once attention has been focused, the bits and pieces of information derived from a target as well as the situation must be organized in such a way that it can be incorporated into one of the perceiver's cognitive systems. A cognitive system is a set of interrelated perceptions and cognitions about people, places, and things. Our perceptual mechanisms operate to organize this information into patterns and categories that make some sense. This is known as perceptual organization.

Perceptual organization is the psychological predisposition to avoid the discomfort normally associated with unorganized information by reconfiguring and attributing meaning to it based on each person's beliefs, values, attitudes, interests, motives, experiences, and expectations. Our mind automatically sorts all sensory information into patterns or categories in an effort to avoid systemic overload. Consequently, there is a natural tendency to do the following:

1. Distinguish a central object (person, event, place, or thing) from its surroundings. Leaders tend to stand out more than support players do in crisis situations.
2. Respond to people, things, and situations based on anticipated rather than actual information input. A mind set is a compulsive proclivity to think and act without rational analysis.
3. Combine bits and pieces of information into wholes by creating groupings based on proximity, similarity, closure, and continuity. (See Figure 4.8 for additional information.)
4. Perceive the characteristics of a target (a person, place, or thing) as remaining relatively constant despite variations in the stimuli that produced the original information. This helps people deal with the instability caused by change (Toffler, 1972).
5. Predict behavior and ascribe meaning to the motives of others. Attribution is designed to make the behavior of others more understandable.

These perceptual organizers are beneficial most of the time. There is a downside, however. They add to and distort reality. When it comes to person perception, there are several other perceptual tendencies that influence how people organize their perceptions and convert them into cognitive systems. Following is a discussion of these perception organizers.

1. *Frame of reference.* A frame of reference is a perspective, or vantage point from which people view people, events, and things. Perception is dependent on the context in which it occurs and on the frame of reference used by the

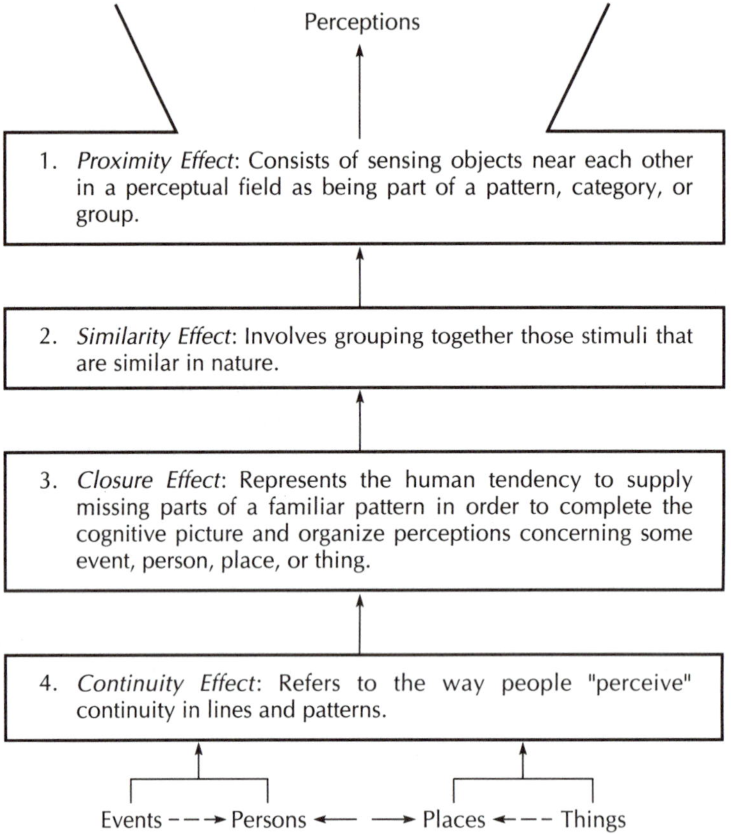

Perceptions
1. Proximity Effect: Consists of sensing objects near each other in a perceptual field as being part of a pattern, category, or group.
2. Similarity Effect: Involves grouping together those stimuli that are similar in nature.
3. Closure Effect: Represents the human tendency to supply missing parts of a familiar pattern in order to complete the cognitive picture and organize perceptions concerning some event, person, place, or thing.
4. Continuity Effect: Refers to the way people "perceive" continuity in lines and patterns.
Events
Persons
Places
Things

FIGURE 4.8 Perceptual Organization Through Grouping.

perceiver. A person who feels secure and is in a festive mood may not pick up on sensory cues that would ordinarily alert him or her to impending danger.

2. *Stereotyping.* Since it is impossible for one person to know everyone else in terms of their distinctive traits, people develop and use stereotypes. One way to organize sensory data about other people is to simply assume they all have the same characteristics because of some category (or group) they fall into. Putting police officers into pigeonholes, or categories and responding to them based on their ethnicity might conserve cognitive energy but usually results in the loss of information and spread of misinformation. Stereotypes based on race, gender, and age skew perception if they predispose the perceiver to ignore information concerning the individual and rely on preexisting stereotypical images.

3. *Halo effect.* The halo effect occurs when one personal trait or attribute is used to develop an overall impression of another person. It involves generalizing from one characteristic to the total person. The halo effect tends to obscure individual differences. People are perceived as being either good or bad. Once they have been assigned to a particular category, we tend to ascribe only good qualities to those labeled as being good and all bad qualities to those labeled as bad. Selective perception is used to confirm our expectations.

CASE STUDY

Officer Michael Byrne

Mike Byrne was, at age 29, the youngest detective sergeant in the history of the Milesburg Police Department. Byrne's meteoric rise in the police hierarchy began three years ago. As we might say, "it was in the cards." Byrne was a relatively undistinguished patrol officer in this industrial city of 38,000. After five years on the street as a patrolman, he was temporarily assigned to the five-member detective bureau. Byrne was filling in for another officer who was on sick leave. As duty officer on the midnight shift, he was dispatched to investigate the abduction of a three-year-old boy who had been taken from the home of his mother's boyfriend. The child's body was found a week later. It had been dismembered and discarded in a landfill in another county. After an extensive investigation, the police came up with the name of a prime suspect and put out a bulletin on local radio stations. A confidential informant contacted Officer Byrne and told him where the suspect could be found. Byrne and his partner, Leonard Smitts, went to the suspect's hideout. After several gunshots were exchanged, the suspect surrendered. Because he captured the suspect, Byrne became the darling of the media.

The trial itself became a media spectacular. Officer Byrne seized the opportunity and used the media to his advantage. He made the local news almost every night for two weeks. The suspect was convicted, and after an emotional episode in which he admitted he had killed the boy, he was sentenced to death by electrocution.

The trial took place in an election year. The leading candidate for mayor liked Byrne and, sensing his popularity, announced publicly that he would—if elected—promote Byrne to the rank of detective sergeant. The candidate won the election. The incumbent detective sergeant was transferred to a new assignment, and since all command officers are appointed by and serve at the pleasure of the mayor, Mike Byrne was promoted to the exempt rank of detective sergeant. The other detectives resented the fact that the mayor was politicizing the bureau. They saw Byrne as an opportunistic political hack. There was an informal work slowdown, an escalation in the level of interpersonal conflict, and productivity declined drastically. Byrne was like a fish out of water. He was not a leader and had no real experience as a supervisor. Things became intolerable. After ten months of continuous rancor, Mike Byrne was reduced in rank and quietly reassigned to the patrol division. He resigned from the department after three years. He now owns a private security company.

What happened here? Was a perceptual distortion involved in this case? What is the lesson to be learned? How would you as the police chief executive deal with the mayor in this type of situation?

4. *Projection.* Projection refers to the fact that perceivers tend to ascribe their own characteristics to other people and use themselves as the norm for judging others. It is much easier to comprehend the behavior of others if we assume that they are similar to us. Consequently, our own characteristics influence what we are likely to see in others. A classic projection error is for managers to assume they and their subordinates have the same unmet needs or motives.

5. *Expectancy.* Expectancy is the tendency for people to find or create in another person what they expected in the first place. This is also known as the *pygmalion effect* and is similar to selective perception in some respects. People often see what they want to see in order to validate their original expectations.

Once sensory stimuli garner attention and are organized in a way to facilitate their integration into the thought process, normal people use the power of reason to interpret that data, generate useful information, and select an appropriate operant response. Perceptions are interpretations of sensory data (Sheehan and Cordner, 1979).

Interpretation is the psychological process by which people evaluate information input concerning a particular stimulus and choose an operant behavioral response. The cognitive context for interpretation is in the mind and consists of the concepts, theories, and cause-effect models we use to construct our own version of reality. How police officers interpret sensory stimuli will depend, in large measure, on their past experience, their value system, and their attitudinal propensity to think or act in certain ways. This helps to explain why different people see different things even when they are looking at the same person, event, or thing. In a sense and as we noted before, there is no such thing as objective reality. Sensory inputs are transformed through perception into interpretive or "normative" reality (Hodgetts, 1979).

Interpretation is the final step in and completes the perception formation process. It attaches meaning to our experiences in relation to other people, events, and things. Figure 4.9 illustrates the dynamics involved in perception formation.

In order to survive and thrive in a complex sociocultural milieu, we must be prepared to receive, organize, interpret, and react to all kinds of environmental stimuli. The accuracy of our perception is a critically important factor in the struggle for physical as well as psychosocial survival. The inability to perceive the cues and cope with dangerous situations can lead to tragedy in police work. Pierce Brooks (1975) has noted that most of the police officers killed by criminals in this country made fatal mistakes. They committed one of "ten deadly errors" by missing or misinterpreting the "danger signs." Faulty perception is a fatal flaw in a manager as well. It all but dooms that person to failure.

Successful police administrators understand the psychosocial dynamics involved in perception formation and are aware of the inherent potential for perceptual distortion. They have learned that personal beliefs, values, motives, experiences, and expectations put subjective constraints on their perception. Truly perceptive managers

1. Have a relatively high level of self-awareness and know how to avoid most of the perceptual pitfalls that we discussed earlier in this chapter.

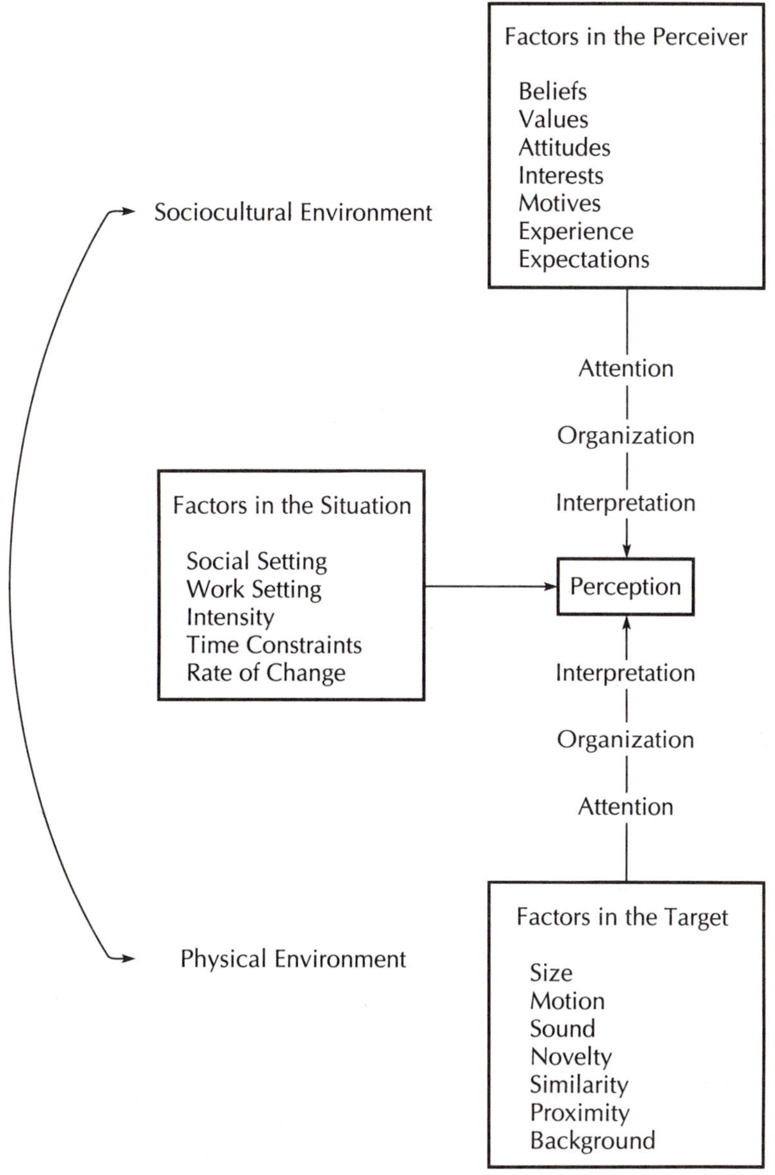

FIGURE 4.9 Dynamics of Perception Formation.

2. Seek information from a variety of sources to confirm or disconfirm their personal impressions of a given person, event, or thing.
3. Tend to form empathetic relationships and are often able to see situations as they are perceived by others.
4. Know when to intervene and how to influence the perceptions of significant others who are drawing incorrect impressions about people, events, or things in the work setting.
5. Appreciate individual differences and seek to avoid those perceptual distortions that bias performance evaluations (Schermerhorn, Hunt, and Osborn, 1982).

There is no doubt that perception has an effect on managerial decision-making, and these decisions affect work unit efforts to accomplish the police department's mission, goals, and objectives. It is also clear that values and value-based perceptions are motivators. They trigger and shape operant behavior.

Motivation

Motivation is the inner state that causes a person to behave in a way designed to satisfy a need. In other words, motivation explains why we—as human beings—act the way we do (Certo, 1986). The motivation process begins with physical and psychosocial needs (or deficiencies) which lead to the accomplishment of certain goals. A *motive* is a stimulus which produces an action that satisfies a need (Rue and Byars, 1980). The intense need to satisfy an unmet need is known as a *drive*. Perceived needs which are linked to basic values become potent motives and are always accompanied by powerful drives. Perception is the psychodynamic variable that activates goal-oriented behavior. (See Chapter 5 for a more detailed discussion of human motivation.)

Stephen Robbins (1989) argues that unsatisfied needs stimulate people and almost always exert a strong influence on their perceptions concerning sensory stimuli. Intense primary (instinctive) and secondary (learned) needs command attention. They are the focal point of our interests and a catalyst for action. A truly hungry person may, depending on the degree of hunger, perceive unrelated sensory data in terms of food. Some psychological studies have shown that the extent of hunger influences a subject's interpretation of blurred pictures. Those who had not eaten for 16 hours perceived the blurred images as depicting food far more frequently than did the subjects who had eaten only a short time earlier. In an organizational context, police administrators who are insecure often perceive a subordinate's efforts to do an outstanding job as a threat to their own position. In other words, personal insecurity can be incorporated into a perception that other people are out to get your job irrespective of their real intent. In a Machiavellian sense, those people who are devious and/or manipulative are prone to see the same traits in others. This is known as selective attribution and attaches meaning to sensory stimuli. It is not surprising that traffic officers are more likely to notice and react to moving violations than are absentminded professors. A sergeant who has just been written up by the lieutenant for the sloppy way subordinates handled an arson investigation will, in all probability, seek to identify the cause of the problem and try to be more on top of things than was the case before this incident occurred.

Good managers understand the psychodynamics involved in motivating their subordinates. They know that their own motives, tucked away in the subconscious mind and difficult, if not impossible, to define, turn them on, influence their perceptions, and serve as springboards to purposeful behavior. This self-awareness, based on introspection, is a key ingredient in effective management. Good managers also make it their business to anticipate how significant others will behave in given situations. In order to do this, they learn to understand other people in terms of their unique

1. Wants
2. Needs
3. Beliefs
4. Values
5. Attitudes
6. Motives
7. Experiences
8. Expectations
9. Perceptions
10. Perspectives
11. Situations

This anticipation helps mangers understand why the behavioral response to a given stimuli differs from person to person and for the same person at a different time or under a different set of circumstances.

On-the-Job Behavior

Behavior refers to the conduct of human beings as they react to environmental stimuli. According to Lester Bittel (1980), behavior refers to the actions people take or things they say with regard to

1. Objects
2. Events
3. People
4. Problems
5. Opportunities
6. Situations

Based on knowledge derived from the behavioral sciences, there is every reason to believe that behavior is (1) caused, (2) motivated, and (3) goal oriented. In other words, most human behavior is purposeful (Roberg and Kuykendall, 1990). Operant behavior is intentional behavior involving some choice among alternative responses. In very simple terms, behavior is a function of the interaction between people and their environment. The basic equation is as follows:

$$B = F(P \times E)$$

This means that factors within the individual and the environment determine behavior both directly and indirectly due to their effect on each other (Reitz, 1981). Purposeful human behavior is produced by a sequential process utilizing a feedback loop. The essential steps in the behavior formation process are outlined as follows:

1. There is an implicit or explicit goal to be achieved.
2. The behavior related to goal accomplishment is caused by reaction to an environmental stimulus of some kind.

3. The stimulus is generated by needs (or wants) which—if not satisfied—cause tension and discomfort.
4. The reduction of tension and discomfort becomes a hedonistic imperative, or goal (Leavitt, 1978).

The steps in the behavior formation process are illustrated in Figure 4.10.

While the behavior formation process is exactly the same for all human beings, actual behaviors vary substantially. Because people are unique (with different backgrounds, value systems, perceptions, and motives), they react idiosyncratically to environmental stimuli. This is compounded by the fact that an individual's needs, wants, and expectations are subject to change. Consequently, a person's response to the same stimuli will ordinarily deviate from time to time. A patrol captain, for example, may give a subordinate a verbal warning for a minor infraction one day (depending on the captain's

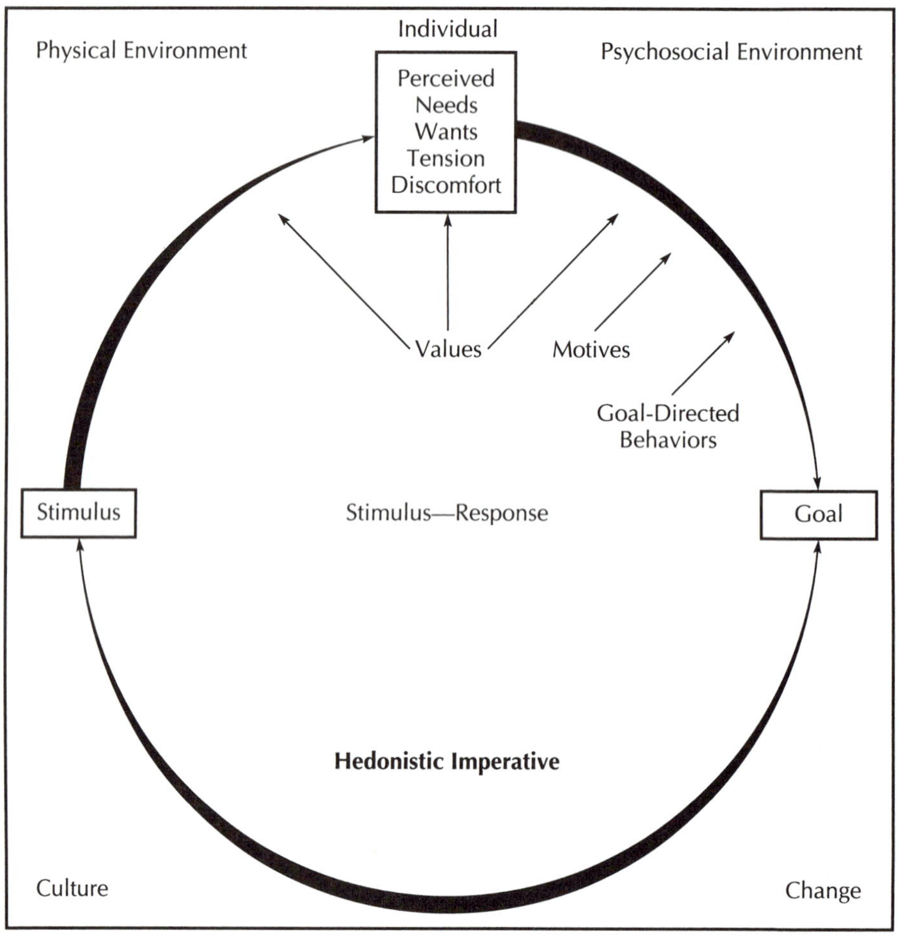

FIGURE 4.10 Steps in the Behavior Formation Process. Source Adapted from H. J. Leavitt, *Managerial Psychology* (4th ed.) (Chicago: University of Chicago Press, 1978).

needs, wants, and expectations), whereas he or she might write up the subordinate for the same behavior in a different situation or at a different time. Good managers know that because of individual and situational differences with respect to needs, wants, tension, and discomfort, human behavior—even under similar circumstances—is difficult to predict (Roberg and Kuykendall, 1990).

Management's Role in Changing Attitudes and Behavior

As noted earlier, attitudes are the product of related beliefs and values. They are incorporated into our motives, opinions, and behaviors. Positive attitudes toward work in general, our job, and the organization (as a whole) are indicative of high morale. High morale produces an esprit de corps which is conducive to cooperation and collaboration. Negative attitudes, on the other hand, often lead to interpersonal conflict and have been linked, at least indirectly, to poor on-the-job performance. It is the police administrator's job to accentuate the positive and minimize the influence of negative attitudes.

Police administrators have three basic options when it comes to dealing with employees who exhibit negative attitudes:

1. *Do nothing.* They attempt to contain negative attitudes through benign neglect. This "let the sleeping dog lie" strategy seldom works and almost always makes the situation worse.

2. *Intervene.* They seek to transform negative attitudes into neutral or positive attitudes. The success of any attempted intervention will depend on the strength of the negative attitude and the skill of the change agent.

3. *Terminate.* They try to fire the employee. In a unionized and litigious environment, discharging someone for having a bad attitude is a very difficult task. Managers are required to make a good faith effort to change the person's unacceptable behavior before they are permitted to hand out a pink slip.

In order to do their job properly, police administrators must learn to be effective change agents. This is not an easy task. Since attitudes are anchored to beliefs and values, they are always resistant to change. There are two principal barriers that tend to limit the extent to which employees are likely to change their attitudes. These are (1) insufficient justification and (2) previous commitments. In the absence of a compelling need to change, people prefer to maintain the status quo. This inertia is very difficult to overcome. The second barrier encompasses past promises and gut-level values. A person's link to the past may be powerful enough to block a change in attitude and accompanying behavior. People are prone to take a position and defend it. They invest their ego, reputation, resources, and so on (Whisenand and Rush, 1988).

Change Agents

Change agents know that personal dissatisfaction and significant emotional events can modify attitudes. According to Paul Whisenand and George Rush

(1988), there are six other modifiers. They act independently or in concert with each other to change attitudes and behavior. They stem from our values and relate to our needs:

1. *Leadership by example.* The police chief executive and other members of the management team are in an excellent position to change attitudes by setting an example for their employees.

2. *New information.* When employees receive new information they accept as truthful and significant, they are apt to change their attitudes about ideas, events, people, places, and things.

3. *Intimidation.* While it might be temporary, fear and the use of threats can bring about a change in attitudes.

4. *Individual discrepancy.* When attitudes and behavior do not mesh, people experience cognitive dissonance and have a need to change one or both of them to make them congruent.

5. *Organizational discrepancy.* When employee attitudes are at odds with those which are part of the organizational culture, they experience the need to alter their own attitudes, the cultural attitudes, or to remove the discrepancy by leaving the department.

6. *Participation.* When employees are allowed to participate in events and decisions that affect them, their attitudes are exposed to either confirmation or challenge.

Whether or not police administrators succeed in changing the attitudes (and behavior) of employees will depend, to a large extent, on their credibility and believability as *communicators.* We see others as credible and believable when they are perceived as expert, unbiased, and likable. Success will also depend on the *intervention techniques* used to effect attitudinal change. (See Table 4.4 for a list of intervention techniques.) The *audience* is the third variable. Some groups are—based on their history and cohesiveness—much more resistant to change than others (Johns, 1988).

Initiating Change

Managers can usually bring about a change in their subordinates' attitudes (and accompanying behavior) if they use the following five-step process. Once managers observe improper behavior or hear improper attitudes expressed, they should (1) identify the improper attitude, (2) determine root causes, (3) weaken the root causes, (4) offer a practical substitute, and (5) reward all of those employees who exhibit the new attitude or behavior.

1. *Identifying the improper attitude.* Once managers determine that a subordinate's behavior is improper, they must look for the attitude behind it. The attitude should be defined in specific terms. By investigating an improper attitude, showing genuine concern, and making constructive comments, managers are frequently able to resolve the problem without further intervention. Employees may come to the realization that their behavior is unacceptable and change it to conform with the general expectations of the manager.

2. *Determining the root causes.* The manager should collect and analyze all relevant information in an effort to determine the roots (or primary causes) which support and feed the attitude in the employee's mind. The best way

TABLE 4.4 Intervention Techniques

1. *Force field analysis*: Study of the dynamic relationship between the "driving forces" that promote change and the "restraining forces" which inhibit change.
2. *Effective communications*: Opening up channels of communications for employees, peers, and outside specialists in an effort to deal with fears, negative attitudes, and the lack of motivation.
3. *Persuasion techniques*: Methods designed to convince employees to change attitudes and/or behavior. Here are some examples of effective change agents:
   - Explain why change is necessary.
   - Explain how it will affect them.
   - Be honest and tell them the truth.
   - Try to reach a realistic compromise.
   - Give them examples of past success.
   - Plant seeds and let them germinate.
   - Seek information by asking questions.
   - Offer them a choice of alternatives.
   - Present change as a challenge.
   - Promise to evaluate them regularly.
   - Request cooperation and avoid orders.
   - Give them a demonstration.
   - Involve them in the decision.
4. *Participation techniques*: Methods designed to keep subordinates informed about departmental activities and let them participate in making those decisions which affect them.
5. *Training programs*: Formal methods for teaching personnel the skills, knowledge, attitudes, and behaviors needed to do their job efficiently, effectively, and productively.
6. *Organization development*: OD is an educational strategy intended to change the beliefs, values, and attitudes of people and organizations as they seek to improve their ability to achieve common goals and objectives.

SOURCE: W. Richard Plunkett, *Supervision: The Direction of People at Work* (3rd ed.) (Dubuque, IA: Wm. C. Brown, 1983).

to accomplish this objective is to get employees talking about their beliefs, feelings, attitudes, motives, and expectations. Some of the root causes that nurture and support improper attitudes are listed here:

- Group pressures
- Faulty logic
- Ambiguous standards
- Prior experiences
- Selective perception

3. *Weakening the root causes.* Once the root causes have been identified, they can be analyzed in terms of strength and vulnerability. A program of action should be developed to attack these causes systematically through the use of reason. One way to attack an improper attitude (and the accompanying behavior) is to point out flaws in the employee's assumptions or draw attention to the changes that have taken place to weaken those assumptions since they were originally formed.

4. *Offering a substitute.* While managers may be able to change an employee's attitude by constant harping and the use of criticism, this approach takes too long and leaves some noticeable scars. As a rule, people will change only

CASE STUDY

Chief M. Lawrence Glick

Corona is a small, yet relatively prosperous city located in the corridor between New York City and Washington, D.C. The police department has an authorized strength of 113. Virtually all of the officers on the police force have taken college courses and a large percentage of the younger officers hold AA degrees. Some of them are working toward a BS in criminal justice. Sworn police personnel are covered by civil service. All members of the department—except the chief and commanders in exempt positions (with the rank of captain or above)—are represented by the same labor union. Commanders have formed a team to serve as their bargaining agent.

The former chief of police was a politically astute autocrat who maintained power through tight administrative control and manipulation of the reward system. He was, in terms of his values system, anything but an organizational humanist. He found it impossible, regardless of the composition of the work force, to share power with rather than to exercise power over others. The chief used selective perception to protect his ego and vilify those with the audacity to question his authority and/or style of management. Everything "hit the fan" when a study conducted by the State Department of Community Affairs concluded that the police department was "plagued by labor/management conflict, bad attitudes, low morale, and disruptive infighting." As a result, the city manager asked for and received the chief's resignation.

Larry Glick, an administrative lieutenant with 22 years of experience, was promoted to chief. He was given a mandate from the mayor to "clean up the mess at police headquarters." Chief Glick is a pragmatist. He is convinced that the only way to increase the efficiency, effectiveness, and productivity of the police department is to improve officer attitudes and morale. The chief knows that he does not have the expertise to accomplish these objectives by himself. He has been authorized to hire a consultant/change agent. The person he has chosen is an organization development (OD) specialist with experience in law enforcement. Dr. Karl Helms is set to begin the project later in the month.

Did Chief Glick make the right decision? If you were Dr. Helms, how would you approach this project? What type of intervention seems most appropriate? Prepare a memo for the chief in which you explain, compare, and contrast the traditional approach and the behavior modification approach discussed at the end of the chapter. Outline some of the change strategies that can be used to achieve the goals of the project.

when they determine the attitudes they hold are no longer worth keeping. Orders and threats tend to suppress natural and observable behavior and drive it underground. Employees become sneaky and do what managers want only when management personnel are present. When managers are absent, old attitudes and behaviors resurface. Permanent change comes about when employees begin to question their own beliefs, values, attitudes, and motives (Plunkett, 1983).

5. *Rewarding proper attitudes.* Change is normally reinforced by positive social sanctions. In order to make any attitudinal change permanent, managers should practice what Michael LeBoeuf (1985) has called the greatest management principle in the world: *"Things that get rewarded get done."*

While these five steps sound simple enough, good managers know it takes a great deal of time, energy, skill, and expertise to bring about substantive attitudinal change on the part of personnel in any complex criminal justice organization.

The traditional view held by most police management theorists is that changed beliefs and/or values produce new attitudes that lead to changes in on-the-job behavior. Some management theorists contend it is more sensible to change a person's behavior first. This is based on research indicating that people realign their attitudes in support of their behavior. This effect has been observed in experiments where subjects were required to role-play behaviors that were inconsistent with their attitudes (Johns, 1988). A few management theorists argue that people should be taught specific behaviors they can apply on the job and which correspond to the desired attitude change. When the trainees learn that they will be rewarded for their behavior, their attitudes will change to agree with the newly learned behaviors. In order to teach these appropriate behaviors, trainers use modeling techniques, role playing, and social reinforcement (Goldstein and Sorcher, 1974). While this approach is still experimental, it is reasonable and offers opportunities for further exploration.

Summary

Human behavior involves the conscious or subconscious selection of actions over which the person exercises some degree of influence, control, or authority. People differ from other animals in the sense that they are social animals who live in groups and engage in purposeful (self-initiated and goal-oriented) behavior. Groups develop a unique way of life, or culture. Culture is the cement that holds a group together and defines appropriate ways of feeling, thinking, and acting. Beliefs, values, attitudes, motives, and expectations are passed from one generation to the next through the socialization process. Values are the linchpin in one's personality, character, management style, and goal-directed behavior.

Police administrators at the existential (or humanistic) level of existence find themselves questioning and moving away from traditional bureaucratic values. They adopt multidimensional value systems that stress efficiency, effectiveness, and productivity while responding to each employee's need for personal growth, self-esteem, competence, and autonomy. Good managers try to cultivate positive attitudes in their subordinates because employee attitudes are critical variables in the success or failure of any goal-oriented enterprise. Attitudes reflect values, express feelings, and indicate a predisposition to act in a certain way with regard to a given stimulus.

Human beings are rational animals with the unique ability to convert sensory data into cognitive representations of reality. Attitudes (which are based on values and past experiences) influence perceptions and are factored into the motives that produce operant behavior. Motivation is the inner state which causes a person to behave in ways designed to satisfy a need. Perceived needs that are linked to basic values become potent motives and are always accompanied by powerful drives. Good managers understand the link between values, attitudes, perception, and motivation.

Positive attitudes toward work, the job, and the organization are indicative of good morale and may lead to increased productivity. Negative attitudes, on the other hand, can lead to interpersonal conflict and have been linked, indirectly, to poor on-the-job performance. Good mangers work to transform negative attitudes into positive attitudes. Some use the traditional five-step process in which they identify improper attitudes, determine root causes, weaken the root causes, offer substitutes, and reward those who exhibit appropriate new attitudes and concomitant behaviors. Other managers reverse the process. They seek to change behavior first on the assumption that people will realign their ideas, beliefs, values, attitudes, motives, opinions, and expectations to support the new behavior. They emphasize the importance of modeling, role playing, and social reinforcement.

Key Concepts

Behavior
Operant behavior
$B = F (P \times E)$
Group dynamics
Culture
Socialization
Ideas
Beliefs
Values
Value system
Value conflict
Attitudes
Opinion
Motives
Motivation
Job satisfaction
Morale
Perception
Perceptual distortion
Cognitive dissonance
Change agents
Introspection
Behavior modification

Discussion Topics and Questions

1. How do organization/management theorists define behavior and differentiate between inherited and operant behaviors?
2. Where do our beliefs, values, attitudes, and motives come from, and how are they transmitted from one generation to the next?
3. What is introspection? Explain why it is necessary in order to become a truly effective police administrator.
4. Define ideas, beliefs, values, value systems, attitudes, motives, and opinions. How are these psychosocial concepts related to one another?

5. Based on an analysis of your own behavior, what is your "level of existence?" What is the next step that you can expect to attain if there is a normal progression? Where does organizational humanism fit in?
6. What does it mean to say that attitudes are cognitive, affective, and conative?
7. What is an attitude? Explain its functions. Does the positive attitude associated with job satisfaction always produce better on-the-job performance?
8. Define perception. What three components interact to produce our perceptions? What psychosocial processes are involved in perception formation? Discuss perceptual organization, interpretation, and distortion.
9. What are motives? How are they formed? How do they influence our expectations, perceptions, and behavior?
10. Discuss the six strategies police administrators use to modify the attitudes of their subordinates. What three variables help determine the success or failure of a planned intervention?
11. How does the behavior modification/attitude change approach differ from the traditional five-step attitude/behavior change process?

References

ALBANESE, ROBERT. 1981. *Managing: Toward Accountability for Performance.* Homewood, IL: Richard D. Irwin.

ARONSON, ELLIOT. 1976. *The Social Animal.* San Francisco: Freeman.

BARNARD, CHESTER I. 1976. *The Functions of the Executive.* Cambridge: Harvard University Press.

BARON, ROBERT A. 1983. *Behavior in Organizations: Understanding and Managing the Human Side of Work.* Boston: Allyn & Bacon.

BENNIS, WARREN G. 1966. *Changing Organizations.* New York: McGraw-Hill.

BENNIS, WARREN G. 1969. *Organization Development: Its Nature, Origins, and Prospects.* Reading, MA: Addison-Wesley.

BITTEL, LESTER R. 1980. *What Every Supervisor Should Know: The Basics of Supervisory Management.* New York: McGraw-Hill.

BOBBITT, H. RANDOLPH, ROBERT H. BREINHOLT, ROBERT H. DOKTOR, and JAMES P. MCNAUL. 1978. *Organizational Behavior* (2nd ed.). Englewood Cliffs, NJ: Prentice-Hall.

BRILL, NAOMI I. 1978. *Working with People.* New York: Lippincott.

BROOKS, PIERCE R. 1975. *Officer Down, Code Three.* Schiller Park, IL: Motorola Teleprograms.

CERTO, SAMUEL C. 1986. *Principles of Modern Management: Functions and Systems.* Boston: Allyn & Bacon.

CHAMPION, DEAN J. 1975. *The Sociology of Organizations.* New York: McGraw-Hill.

CHINOY, ELY, and JOHN P. HEWITT. 1975. *Sociological Perspective.* New York: Random House.

DUNHAM, ROGER G., and GEOFFREY P. ALPERT. 1989. *Critical Issues in Policing.* Prospect Heights, IL: Waveland Press.

ENGLAND, G. W. 1975. *The Manager and His Values: An International Perspective.* Cambridge: Ballinger.

FULMER, ROBERT M. 1983. *The New Management* (3rd ed.). New York: Macmillan.

GOLDSTEIN, A. P., and M. SORCHER. 1974. *Changing Supervisor Behavior.* New York: Pergamon.

GORDON, LEE V. 1975. *The Measurement of Interpersonal Values.* Chicago: Science Research Associates.

GRAVES, CLARE W. 1970. "Levels of Existence: An Open System Theory of Values," *Journal of Humanistic Psychology*, Vol. 10, No. 2.

HODGETTS, RICHARD M. 1979. *Management: Theory, Process and Practice*. Philadelphia: Saunders.

HOLDEN, RICHARD N. 1986. *Modern Police Management*. Englewood Cliffs, NJ: Prentice-Hall.

JOHNS, GARY. 1988. *Organizational Behavior: Understanding Life at Work* (2nd ed.). Boston: Scott, Foresman.

LEAVITT, HAROLD J. 1978. *Managerial Psychology* (4th ed.). Chicago: University of Chicago Press.

LEBOEUF, MICHAEL. 1985. *GMP: The Greatest Management Principle in the World*. New York: Barkley Books.

LEONARD, V. A., and HARRY W. MORE. 1987. *Police Organization and Management*. Mineola, NY: Foundation Press.

LOCKE, EDWARD A. 1969. "What Is Job Satisfaction?" *Organization Behavior and Human Performance*, Vol. 4.

MCGREGOR, DOUGLAS M. 1960. *The Human Side of Enterprise*. New York: McGraw-Hill.

PETERS, THOMAS J., and ROBERT H. WATERMAN, JR. 1982. *In Search of Excellence: Lessons from America's Best-Run Companies*. New York: Warner.

PLUNKETT, W. RICHARD. 1983. *Supervision: The Direction of People at Work*. Dubuque, IA: Wm. C. Brown.

REITZ, H. JOSEPH. 1981. *Behavior in Organizations*. Homewood, IL: Richard D. Irwin.

ROBBINS, STEPHEN P. 1989. *Organizational Behavior: Concepts, Controversies, and Applications* (4th ed.). Englewood Cliffs, NJ: Prentice-Hall.

ROBERG, ROY, and JACK KUYKENDALL. 1990. *Police Organization and Management: Behavior, Theory and Processes*. Pacific Grove, CA: Brooks/Cole.

ROKEACH, MILTON. 1973. *The Nature of Human Values*. New York: Macmillan.

RUE, LESLIE W., and LLOYD L. BYARS. 1980. *Management: Theory and Application*. Homewood, IL: Richard D. Irwin.

SCHERMERHORN, JOHN R., JAMES G. HUNT, and RICHARD N. OSBORN. 1982. *Managing Organizational Behavior*. New York: Wiley.

SHEEHAN, ROBERT, and GARY W. CORDNER. 1979. *Introduction to Police Administration*. Reading, MA: Addison-Wesley.

SIMON, HERBERT A. 1976. *Administrative Behavior*. New York: Free Press.

SMITH, RONALD W., and FREDERICK W. PRESTON. 1982. *Sociology: An Introduction*. New York: St. Martin's Press.

STEINMETZ, LAWRENCE L., and H. RALPH TODD. 1986. *First-Line Management: Approaching Supervision Effectively*. Plano TX: Business Publications.

TANNENBAUM, ROBERT, and SHELDON A. DAVIS. 1969. "Values, Man, and Organizations." In Wm. B. Eddy et al. (Eds.), *Behavioral Science and the Manager's Role*. La Jolla, CA: University Associates.

TOFFLER, ALVIN. 1972. *Future Shock*. New York: Bantam Books.

UNIFORM CRIME REPORTS. 1988. *Crime in the United States—1987*. Washington, DC: Federal Bureau of Investigation.

UTTAL, BRO. 1983. "The Corporate Culture Vultures." *Fortune*, Oct. 17.

VANAGUNAS, STANLEY, and JAMES F. ELLIOTT. 1980. *Administration of Police Organizations*. Boston: Allyn & Bacon.

WHISENAND, PAUL M. 1981. *The Effective Police Manager*. Englewood Cliffs, NJ: Prentice-Hall.

WHISENAND, PAUL M., and R. FRED FERGUSON. 1978. *The Managing of Police Organizations*. Englewood Cliffs, NJ: Prentice-Hall.

WHISENAND, PAUL M., and GEORGE E. RUSH. 1988. *Supervising Police Personnel: Back to Basics*. Englewood Cliffs, NJ: Prentice-Hall.

YUKL, GARY A. 1981. *Leadership in Organizations*. Englewood Cliffs, NJ: Prentice-Hall.

For Further Reading

FULMER, ROBERT M. 1983. *The New Management* (3rd ed.). New York: Macmillan.

Management text containing an excellent chapter on the need for and types of managerial introspection. The content is based on the assumption that managers must know themselves (in terms of their own beliefs, values, attitudes, motives, and expectations) before they can get things done through others in an efficient, effective, and productive manner.

MONDY, R. WAYNE, ET AL 1986. *Management: Concepts and Practices* (3rd ed.). Boston: Allyn and Bacon.

A comprehensive management text. It explores the dynamics involved in a planned intervention designed to change the attitudes of employees in complex organizations. Emphasis is placed on environmental factors and the change sequence leading to alteration of the status quo.

SISK, HENRY L., and CLIFTON WILLIAMS. 1981. *Management and Organization* (4th ed.). Cincinnati: South-Western.

Organization and management text with a good discussion of ethics and social responsibilities. The authors propose a profile approach using (1) operative values, (2) adopted values, (3) intended values, and (4) values with low behavioral relevance. The personal, organizational, and environmental determinants of ethical behavior are also discussed.

SWANSON, CHARLES R., LEONARD TERRITO, and ROBERT W. TAYLOR. 1988. *Police Administration* (2nd ed). New York: Macmillan.

Police management text. Concluding chapter deals with the various types of planned interventions: (1) People Change Technology (PCT), (2) Analysis from the Top, and (3) Organization Development. PCT is explored as a remedy for negative attitudes, low morale, and poor performance.

ZIMBARDO, PHILLIP, and EBBE B. EBBENSEN. 1969. *Influencing Attitudes and Changing Behavior.* Menlo Park, CA: Addison-Wesley.

A practical how-to book designed to help managers understand how to change attitudes and operant behavior. There is a discussion of behavior/attitude change as well as attitude/behavior change.

CHAPTER 5

Motivation: The Force Behind Behavior

LEARNING OBJECTIVES

1. Discuss the etiology of goal-oriented human behavior in the workplace.
2. Define motivation and those terms associated with the motivation process.
3. Describe the interplay between individual, social, and situational factors related to human motivation.
4. Explain needs and the adaptive behavior they elicit in the motivation process.
5. Differentiate between content theory and process theory as they relate to the human motivation to work.
6. Compare and contrast major content and process theories.
7. Identify various motivation strategies that can be used to motivate police officers to improve individual performance and increase personal productivity.

In a generic sense, modern-day management can be defined as the proactive process of getting things done with and through other people by guiding their individual efforts toward the accomplishment of common goals and objectives. While police administrators are expected to allocate and manage time, equipment, material, and money, the most significant aspect of their particular job is the management of people. Human beings represent a far different type of resource than any other resource they are asked to deal with. This is complicated by the fact that people are truly unique and bring various attitudes, values, sentiments, motives, behaviors, and skills with them into the workplace. According to Theo Haimann and Raymond Hilgert (1972), the challenge to manage people efficiently and effectively is undoubtedly the greatest challenge confronting police administrators today.

INTRODUCTORY CASE

Chief David Gunther

David Gunther is the new chief of police in a small rural community in upstate New York. The department has an authorized strength of six full-time and four part-time police officers. Chief Gunther is anxious to fill the vacant sergeant's position created when he was promoted to chief three months earlier. The sergeant is second in command. Since the department is not covered by civil service, the chief has the authority to promote whoever he chooses, subject only to the advice and consent of the mayor.

After a very careful review of the situation, Chief Gunther has concluded that Charles Zanich, a five-year veteran, is the best person for the job. Officer Zanich is a personable, energetic, and talented man who possesses excellent analytical skills. He is a natural leader with a commitment to public service. Officer Zanich is and always has been a high achiever. He was the (1) Top candidate on the eligibility list the year that he was hired; (2) Outstanding trainee at the academy based on academic achievement, marksmanship, self-defense, and professionalism; (3) Officer of the Year for a heroic rescue of three drowning children; (4) Recipient of four commendations for exemplary police work; and (5) Coordinator of the police department's in-service training program. As far as the chief is concerned, he really has no alternative but to offer the position to Charles Zanich. He feels they are simpatico and would complement one another.

After securing the mayor's authorization to fill the vacant position, Chief Gunther asked Officer Zanich to stop by his office. They exchanged pleasantries and then the chief advised Officer Zanich he would be promoted to the rank of sergeant (at a higher pay grade) effective the first of the month. Much to the chief's surprise, Zanich declined the promotion. The chief did everything he could to get Officer Zanich to change his mind, but the officer maintained he was simply not interested in taking on the responsibility of a first-line supervisor. He said pay was not the issue. He thanked the chief, left the office, and returned to work.

Chief Gunther's surprise turned into anger. He felt Officer Zanich was being selfish. He considered him an ingrate with no sense of loyalty to the department. He swore he would never do anything for Officer Zanich and Zanich would, in fact, rue the day he had refused "to stand up and be counted." Although he was unhappy with the situation, Chief Gunther promoted James Wooten.

The chief's hostility toward Officer Zanich festered to the point where it turned into open conflict. He watched Officer Zanich closely and frequently criticized him behind his back. Over a period of time, Officer Zanich became increasingly dissatisfied with his job. He became a chronic complainer. Poor morale reduced his performance and led to increased absenteeism. Charles Zanich found himself in a box. He got so frustrated that he resigned from the police department and left police work altogether.

What happened in this particular situation? What assumptions did Chief Gunther make, and why did he become so angry with Officer Zanich? If you were the chief of police, how would you deal with an officer who does not see promotion per se as the preferred path to job satisfaction and/or career advancement?

Pursuing Excellence

Leading others as they pursue an organization's mission, goals, and objectives is the essence of police management. Leadership does not exist in a vacuum, however. There is a symbiotic relationship between leadership, motivation, and performance in complex goal-oriented police departments. Most management theorists believe that highly motivated individuals working smarter are more productive and produce a better quality product or service than their less motivated co-workers (Holt, 1987). Many of them subscribe to the axiom that overall, "Productivity is achieved through excellence, and excellence is achieved by having an organization of highly motivated individuals."

Human motivation is a fascinating topic. Motivating people to work has become one of the most pervasive concerns in contemporary management theory. Motivation is a buzzword in industry, an "in" term in the lexicon of police management, and the goal of staff development. There is probably no other topic in which police administrators express more interest. The motivation of police personnel is viewed as an antidote for poor performance, a magic key to productivity, and the answer to all sorts of organizational problems (Albanese, 1981). The application of simplistic solutions to very complex social problems rivals baseball as America's favorite pastime, however.

The motivation perspective just discussed is not the panacea it was made out to be by the theorists and practitioners who argued that it had ushered in a new era of enlightened human resources management. After nearly a half century of rigorous scientific inquiry, we still do not know what motivates a human being to act in a certain way. It is very difficult to tell why some police officers are self-starters and seem to be high achievers in almost everything they do, whereas other police officers need prodding and external incentives to do anything productive. It is hard to explain why activities that generate enthusiasm and energy in one person might well trigger boredom and apathy in someone else (Steinmetz and Todd, 1986). After years of research, motivation still remains one of the most misunderstood psychosocial phenomena. David Holt (1987) contends there is relatively little definitive information about human motivation and that when recent research data is analyzed, it is unable to answer succinctly the question of how to motivate people systematically to accomplish more or how to achieve excellence.

Assumptions of Contemporary Theory

While there is no universally accepted theory of motivation, most contemporary theories are based on the following set of assumptions: (1) all behavior is caused, (2) human beings are alike in a great many ways, and (3) motivation per se is only one of the variables that influence a person's on-the-job performance.

1. Social scientists generally accept the proposition that behavior does not occur spontaneously or as a matter of chance. They believe all behavior is caused by human needs, some kind of external stimuli, or by dynamic interaction between the two. Under these circumstances, motivation is viewed

as the key ingredient in purposeful behavior (Fulmer, 1983). Motives are very influential psychological abstractions that are simply not subject to verification through direct observation. Even though it is difficult to tell what motivates human beings to act as they do in given situations, a person's motives can be inferred from their behavior.

2. While every person is a unique physical, psychological, and social being, all people—as social animals—are alike in many ways. They think in abstract terms, use rational problem-solving techniques, and communicate with one another. Behavioral scientists place an emphasis on the recurrent aspects of social interaction and regularities in individual behavior. Motivation and management theorists now emphasize how people are alike rather than how they are different. They believe the real key to human motivation lies in capitalizing on similarities rather than exploiting differences (Chinoy and Hewitt, 1975).

3. Job performance is produced by a tripartite motivational system composed of the individual, the work situation, and the particular job that is to be done (Longenecker, 1977). Put in more succinct terms, job performance (P) is a function (f) of the interaction between the individual (I) and the work situation (S); P = f(I,S). Based on this formula, a person's overall job performance is dependent on the interplay between individual and situational variables. Motivation (see Figure 5.1) is just one of the individual variables that determine what workers will do as opposed to what they can do or are

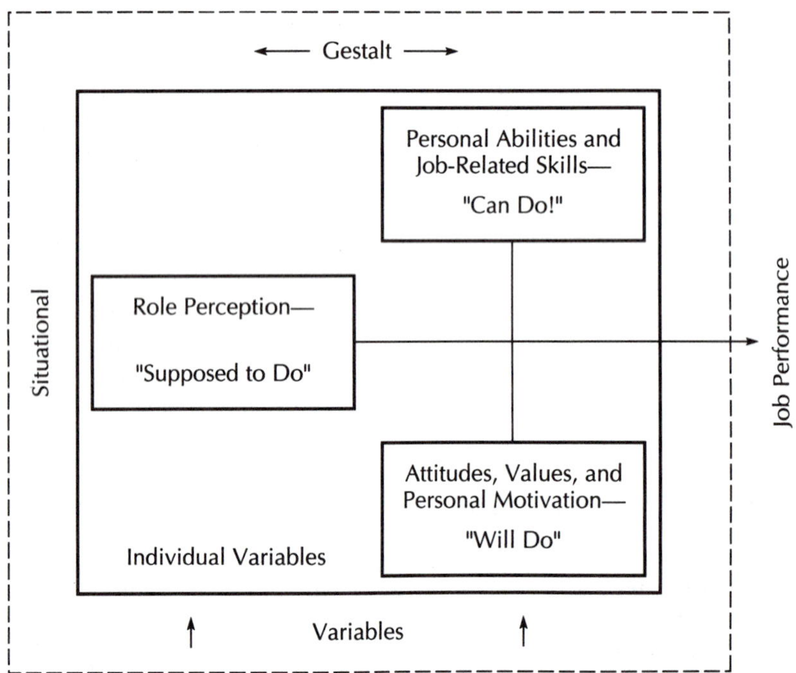

FIGURE 5.1 Interplay Between Individual and Situational Variables in Human Motivation. Source Adapted from Robert Albanese, *Managing: Toward Accountability and Performance* (Homewood, IL: Richard D. Irwin, 1981).

supposed to do. Behavioral scientists contend that a single goal may explain a variety of motives and a single motive can often help to explain various goals (Albanese, 1981).

This particular set of assumptions, while not all inclusive, provides police administrators with a conceptual frame of reference concerning the complexity of the motivation process.

Motivation to Work

Motivating human beings to work, to produce more, and to seek excellence is one of the simplest yet most complex tasks in management. It is simple in the sense that people are hedonistic. They have been programmed socially as well as genetically to minimize pain and to maximize pleasure. Consequently, motivating them should be fairly easy. It is up to management to determine what a person wants and to use it as a reward or incentive. According to Michael LeBoeuf (1985), this is, in fact, "the greatest management principle in the world." Establishing a functional link between appropriate behavior and meaningful rewards is the key to improving organizations and achieving results. Whenever people act in any way, good or bad, it is because they have been motivated to act (Colling, 1982). Reward people for proper behavior, and you usually get the right results. Fail to reward the right kind of behavior, and you will most likely get the wrong results.

Awaiting Motivation Equipped with the necessary skills, knowledge, and uniform, these recent police academy graduates will look to management for motivation. (*UPI/Bettman*)

Things are not as simple as they may appear at first glance, however. Different people have different desires and needs they want to satisfy through their work. In some cases, the needs of employees are not the same as those of the organization. Irreconcilable differences can lead to dysfunctional conflict, disorganization, and deterioration in performance. Rewards one police officer considers to be important may be viewed as undesirable or merely superfluous by others. Even an enticing reward is not a surefire motivator. Rewards, in themselves, do not ordinarily motivate people unless there is a belief that an effort on their part will lead to a payoff. Police personnel, like all other human beings, differ from one another in how they size up their chances of earning meaningful rewards or achieving their own personal goals (Dessler, 1979).

Police administrators have a managerial responsibility to recruit, screen, select, and develop human resources with the potential to be efficient, effective, and productive employees. Unless these individuals are motivated to draw on this potential, they are not likely to achieve the level of performance that is desired from them. Managers at all levels are faced with the problem of motivating subordinates to unleash their own potential so that the mission, goals, and objectives of the organization can be accomplished. One way to deal with the so-called motivation problem is to create conditions in which people acting to satisfy personal needs and to achieve their own goals act in such a way that the work desired by the organization gets done as well (Tansik, Chase, and Aquilano, 1980). Police managers must learn to recognize symptoms and to design jobs and reward systems to alleviate the problem. Failure to act will only compound the motivation problem and could eventually destroy the organization.

Organizations as Social Entities

Organizations are unique social entities that are created by human beings in order to accomplish certain goals that require cooperative effort. A formal organization is a social unit that has been designed to achieve a common objective or set of objectives. As instruments created for a specific purpose, all formal organizations have similar structural characteristics; they have (1) a fairly distinct division of labor, (2) built-in mechanisms to regulate, coordinate, and control the activities of members, and (3) the capacity to replenish depleted human resources. Healthy organizations have the ability to adapt to changes in the environment, alter internal processes, reconfigure job assignments, and withstand the influx of replacement personnel. Consequently, formal organizations usually acquire an identity independent of their members. Organizations develop their own distinctive persona that—while it may change based on situational factors—tends to perpetuate itself from one generation to the next (Reitz, 1981). An unhealthy organization, like its counterpart in the animal kingdom, is very likely to wither away and risks extinction.

In order for a police department to survive and thrive, management personnel must learn to deal effectively with the behavioral requirements of the individuals who work for them. According to Paul Whisenand and George Rush (1988),

1. Competent human beings must be attracted to join and be encouraged to remain with the police department.
2. Police officers must perform the tasks they were hired to perform consistently.
3. Police officers must go beyond routine tasks by becoming more involved in spontaneous, creative, and innovative behavior at work.

These behavioral requirements deal directly with the issue of motivation. In order to become effective managers, police administrators must learn to understand and appreciate the importance of their role in the motivation process. They must also develop a repertoire of motivational techniques that will not only encourage qualified people to join and remain in the police department but also to perform their duties in an enthusiastic, competent, consistent, and professional manner. Motivation is the linking pin between employee needs and job performance within organizations. It is the key to a productive and satisfying life. On the other hand, highly motivated, productive, and satisfied employees are the mainstay of quality police service.

Organizations should be viewed as living organisms rather than inanimate things. Police departments, for example, are deliberately constructed social systems (with a structure and process) designed to coordinate the activities of workers as they seek to accomplish group-shared goals and objectives. An organization is a coalition of many participants with diverse needs, values, attitudes, and behaviors (Pfeffer, 1978). Organizations are social entities in which members take part and to which they react (Porter, Lawler, and Hackman, 1975). The essence of an organization, according to Robert Albanese (1981), is in the pattern of human relationships that exists in order to achieve goals. For the purpose of our discussion, motivation is the energizing force that brings people together and serves as the springboard to individual effort as well as goal-oriented group interaction.

Motivation and the Motivation Process

The study of motivation and the motivation process can be traced back to antiquity. There have always been attempts to describe, explain, and predict goal-oriented human behavior. The ongoing interest in motivation is based on the assumption that those in authority need to know what turns people on or off about their work. Until quite recently, the emphasis was on the use of coercive power to increase individual productivity and/or organization output. Things began to change around the turn of this century, however. Most police administrators now subscribe to the old adage, "You can lead horses to water, but you can't make them drink."

Defining Motivation

Motivation is not a particularly easy term to define. While just about everyone agrees that it has something to do with human behavior, no one has been able to formulate a single definition that is acceptable to all of the behavioral scientists and management personnel with an interest in this topic. Some writers avoid definitions altogether. They are content to focus their attention on the consequences of human behavior. Others, in the classical tradition of Frederick W. Taylor, explain motivation in terms of economic rationality. As dyed-in-the-wool hedonists, they see human beings as goal-oriented individuals who have been programmed to avoid pain (punishment) and to seek pleasure (rewards). Many organization/management theorists reject utilitarian views and contend that motivation is a subconscious psychological process that evolves in people as the result of personality, background, environment, and cultural factors. Still others are convinced that motivation is a conscious and continuous process in which individuals make choices about what they will or will not do in given situations (Levine, 1975).

There are conflicting definitions of motivation based on etiological considerations. In much simpler times, motivation was thought of as the means, methods, and techniques used by management to stimulate workers to engage in activities designed to achieve the organization's mission, goals, and objectives. Leaders, managers, and other authority figures were expected to use extrinsic motivators like pay, promotion, fringe benefits, and camaraderie as carrots to induce employees to increase their output and to upgrade the overall quality of their product or service. Extrinsic motivators are external to the person. They are regulated, dispensed, and controlled by significant others in the organization. On the other side of the coin, the famous Hawthorne experiments conducted during the mid-1920s clearly demonstrated that intrinsic factors also motivated people to behave in certain ways. Intrinsic motivators like instinct, drives, desires, values, feelings, and needs are internal to the individual and, as such, are largely unaffected by environmental stimuli. People strive to achieve, to be competent, to make a contribution, and to derive real satisfaction from work. The theorists, researchers, and practitioners who subscribe to this human relations school of thought place most of their emphasis on internal as opposed to external variables. The primary function of management is to create a situation in which worker needs and organization needs are not only congruent but mutually reinforcing (Whisenand, 1981).

Police officers, in reality and like all other human beings, are motivated by a combination of intrinsic and extrinsic factors. Both are necessary. According to Craig Pinder (1984), the motivation to work is caused by a set of energetic forces originating within and beyond the individual which initiates work-related behavior and determines its form, direction, intensity, and duration.

Motivation has been defined as the state or condition of being induced to do something (Chruden and Sherman, 1976). The term itself comes from the Latin word meaning "to move" and implies that something is causing someone to move toward the accomplishment of a goal (Fulmer and Franklin, 1982). Motivation to work can be described as dynamic forces within an individual which account for the intensity, direction, and relative persistence of the effort expended at work. Researchers have found a direct link between motivation and effort. In fact, motivation is a predictor of overall effort. In the long run, it is effort, individual ability, and organizational support that determines the level of our on-the-job performance.

Many contemporary writers believe internal tensions are the root cause of all motivation. They argue that motivated behavior is aimed at reducing these tensions (Dessler, 1979). According to Richard Plunkett (1983), motivation is the drive within people to alleviate the discomfort caused by internal tensions. A drive is an energetic force fueled by human needs. These needs become motives for action. Mental and physical actions are the conscious and unconscious efforts to achieve goals. Goals are desired outcomes an individual feels will lead to a reduction in internal tension. Once their needs, desires, and wants are fulfilled, people experience a measure of personal satisfaction.

Related Terminology

Before proceeding with a discussion of the motivation process itself, let us review some basic terminology one more time. A precise vocabulary is very important because ambiguity leads to confusion and helps perpetuate misunderstanding.

1. *Needs.* Something that exists within people that moves them to engage in work-related behavior in an effort to accomplish personal goals.
2. *Drives.* Dynamic inner forces created and energized by human needs.
3. *Tension.* The frustration or discomfort caused by unfulfilled human needs.
4. *Motives.* Inner impulses, drives, needs, and abstract values that energize, activate, move, and direct behavior that is designed to achieve specific goals.
5. *Goals.* Objects, conditions, or activities toward which a particular motive is directed.
6. *Incentives.* Internal and external incentives, such as anticipated satisfaction (positive as well as negative), social reinforcement, and financial rewards provide the impetus for goal-oriented behavior designed to reduce the tension caused by unfulfilled human needs.
7. *Performance.* The purposeful activity that results from an individual's goal-oriented behavior and normally evaluated in terms of specific outcomes.
8. *Motivation.* Psychosocial process which produces an attitude that results in an action leading to a particular result.
9. *Internal motivation.* Comes from within the person (based on needs, drives, feelings, desires, and values) and activates certain conscious and unconscious behaviors designed to produce satisfaction.
10. *External motivation.* Involves the application of incentives to encourage patterns of behavior that will contribute to accomplishment of an organization's mission, goals, and objectives.

While there is no simple answer to the question of what turns on, or motivates, human beings to act as they do in a given situation, police administrators will be ahead of the game if they learn to view motivation as a dynamic, interactive process as opposed to a collage of marginally related managerial tasks. It is through knowledge and the skillful use of motivation that modern managers attempt to mold their people into productive units capable of achieving a new and much higher level of performance (Lynch, 1986).

Motivation Cycle

According to Calvin Swank and James Cosner (1983), the motivation cycle or process consists of needs setting up drives to accomplish goals. They argue that the intensity of the drive toward a goal is always proportional to the severity of the need. A police officer's absolute need for peer acceptance, for example, could supersede his or her desire to be considered a professional. Driven by the need for acceptance, the officer may elect to conform to the code of silence rather than testify against a fellow officer involved in a brutality case.

Herbert Chruden and Arthur Sherman (1976) also describe the motivation process in dynamic terms. They see needs as something in people that prompts them to engage in work-related behaviors that are directed toward the attainment of goals they feel are capable of satisfying their needs. Chruden and Sherman contend that the motivation process consists of four sequential steps: (1) need, (2) goal-directed behavior, (3) goal achievement, and (4) tension reduction.

Need (tension)	→	Goal-directed behavior	→	Personal goal achievement	→	Tension reduction

The simplicity of the diagram is somewhat deceptive, however. Behavioral scientists and experienced police administrators know that human behavior is multimotivated, in that any number of conscious, subconscious, and (at times) conflicting needs demand satisfaction all at the same time. It is the intensity of a need or the relative mix of needs that determines behavior in a given set of circumstances. We will never know, for example, exactly what motivates an otherwise passive police officer to become a supercharged hero in a dangerous or life-threatening situation involving very young children. It is always difficult to isolate a single causal factor in relation to job-related behavior in complex criminal justice organizations.

While many police administrators still believe that motivation is something they do to their subordinates, they are wrong. Motivation is an internal (dynamic and goal-oriented) process. It is—in essence—what individual police officers feel and do in relation to their own particular needs. From this standpoint, the only true form of motivation is self-motivation (Haimann and Hilgert, 1972). Almost all successful police managers have the unique ability to elicit from and reinforce self-motivation on the part of their employees by creating environments in which police personnel are able to satisfy inner needs through affiliation, competence, recognition, and productive police work itself (Iannone, 1987).

W. Richard Plunkett (1983) has done a good job of synthesizing the prevailing ideas concerning motivation and the motivation process. He describes motivation as a process in which one's personal needs act as motives for behavior. Plunkett contends motivated people find themselves in a state of discomfort because they feel or perceive that they lack something or some state of being that seems to be desirable or necessary. Motivated people continuously set new goals because their needs, desires, and wants are nearly insatiable. It is

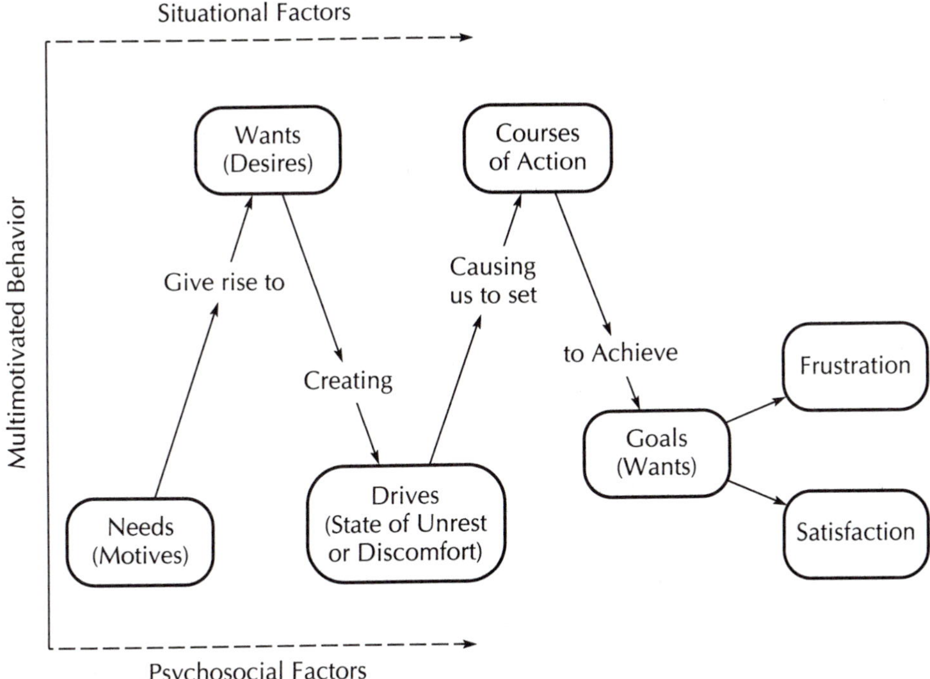

FIGURE 5.2 The Motivation Process. Source Adapted from W. Richard Plunkett, *Supervision: The Direction of People at Work* (Dubuque, IA: William C Brown, 1983).

only human nature to want more, to strive to progress, to improve ourselves and our condition, to acquire new things, and to improve our position vis-à-vis others within the organization. Figure 5.2 illustrates Plunkett's concept of the motivation process.

For our purpose, motivation is a continuous internal process composed of three very distinct steps: (1) need, (2) goal-directed human behavior, and (3) goal attainment.

1. *Personal need.* An individual experiences a need caused by internal or external forces which mobilizes the energy to act.
2. *Direct action.* A need is responded to in terms of instrumental behavior that is designed to accomplish a specified goal.
3. *Goal attainment.* Achievement of appropriate goals results in the satisfaction of specific personal needs (Associates, 1976).

An individual's motivation to act in a given situation depends on two salient factors:

1. The relevance and relative strength of a particular need.
2. The probability that action will lead to satisfaction of a given need.

The completion of one motivation cycle is not the end of the process, however. Other needs arise. They trigger a new cycle and perpetuate the motivation process.

Even though motivation is something inside of each person, police administrators activate and guide the motivation process as they seek to improve the performance of a department's human resources. Performance is the bottom line in management. According to H. Joseph Reitz (1981), performance (P) is a function (f) of ability (A) interacting with motivation (M): $P = f(A \times M)$. Based on this formula, the manager's job is to select competent personnel and motivate each of them to achieve group-shared goals and objectives as they strive to satisfy their own personal needs.

Based on the preceding discussion, it is evident there is no simple answer to the question, "What motivates people to act as they do in a given set of circumstances?" Behavioral scientists have, in fact, developed an array of different theories to explain the dynamics involved in human motivation. Fortunately, most of these theories tend to reinforce each other to one degree or another (Steinmetz and Todd, 1986). We devote the remainder of this chapter to categorizing and describing some of the major theories. Our purpose is to provide information and not to say a particular theory is right or wrong. It is—in the final analysis—up to each police administrator to abstract, synthesize, and reconfigure this information in such a manner that it will work in a given environment with a specific clientele. Broad generalizations usually lack substance and are of little or no real value in motivating personnel to work in complex criminal justice organizations.

Approaches to Motivation Theory

As noted earlier, the motivation to work has been the subject of serious scientific inquiry for more than a half century. Behavioral scientists normally approach the study of human motivation from two general perspectives: (1) content theory and (2) process theory.

1. *Content theories.* Content theories attempt to explain what motives (needs, desires, and wants) are and how they influence human behavior. They focus on internalized human needs that serve as an impetus for our goal-oriented behavior. These theories are built around the assumption that people have psychosocial and physiological needs that elicit some type of instrumental behavior designed to meet those needs. Content theories provide various ways to profile and analyze people in order to identify their motives. They have little or nothing to say about the process by which needs are aroused and manifested in actual behavior. Understanding motivation is primarily a matter of recognizing basic needs and the process by which they are satisfied.

The centerpiece of content theory is that unmet needs motivate people to act. They seek to reduce inner tension by fulfilling these needs. Satisfied needs are not considered to be motivators. While content theory does not explain how people are motivated to do something, it does provide some insight into individual needs and may help police administrators understand what their subordinates will or will not value as work incentives. Content theories have been criticized as being static and overly descriptive (Schermerhorn, Hunt, and Osborn, 1982).

2. *Process theories.* Process theories explain how people are motivated. These theories examine performance based on the degree of satisfaction associated with rewards used to initiate goal-oriented behavior. Process theory focuses on the motivation process rather than on motives per se. Process theories strive to shed light on the cognitive (or mental) processes by which human beings choose to engage in certain behaviors designed to satisfy their own needs. While content theories emphasize needs themselves, process theories zero in on decision-making as it relates to job performance. Process theories are built on the assumption that people make conscious and subconscious evaluations of contemplated behavior and assess the consequences of their actions. These personal expectations are critical in determining how a person is motivated to perform in any given situation (Holt, 1987).

These theoretical approaches are not mutually exclusive. In fact, most content and process theories reinforce one another and provide police administrators with an information base which can be transformed into action designed to help subordinates become more efficient, effective, and productive workers. The theories provide clues about people, explain why people (do or do not) work, and examine how the psychosocial environment influences job performance. Job performance is the bottom line in management and is the key factor in determining the long-term health of any complex criminal justice organization.

Content and process theories represent a radical departure from the classical concept of motivation advocated by Frederick W. Taylor in the early 1900s, as discussed in Chapter 1. Taylor was a utilitarian looking for practical ways to increase the productivity of available human resources. He believed maximum organizational efficiency could be achieved by identifying the one best way to do a particular job and segmenting the task into a series of simple operations or steps. Each worker would be trained to perform a few task-related operations. The combined efforts of all workers would then maximize efficiency and productivity. Taylor also believed that workers were not capable of self-motivation. They had to be motivated by external forces (managers) in order to overcome their natural inclination for "soldiering." Increased productivity would be achieved by creating incentives (in the form of financial rewards) to work harder during a specific period of time. Taylor devised a bonus system to reward and reinforce the behavior of those who exceeded the minimum expectations set for them. In a Pavlovian sense, improved performance and increased productivity reflect a conditioned response activated by external reward systems (Champion, 1975).

Content Theories

Interest in content theory can be traced back to the Hawthorne studies conducted in Chicago during the mid-1920s. The researchers wanted to know how productivity is affected by negative environmental factors. (See Chapter 1 for more information on the Hawthorne studies.) The researchers concluded that unanticipated "psychological factors" had somehow influenced the productivity of the experimental group. While they were unable to find a direct relationship between physical working conditions and worker outputs, it became clear that organizations do not exist for production alone. They are organic social settings in which people seek to satisfy their own intrinsic psychological and social needs. The experiment itself became a motivator. The assembly workers felt they were being treated as people rather than machines. Management's interest in their situation made them feel special. It was a recognition of their worth as human beings. The researchers came to the conclusion that when human needs are met, workers develop a very positive attitude toward work, management, and their organization. This often leads to greater job satisfaction, improved performance, increased productivity, and a commitment to the goals and objectives of the organization (Steinmetz and Todd, 1986).

Content theory attempts to explain what motivates people to behave as they do in relation to their work. While most of the theories are consistent with one another, there are some important differences. The theories presented here are representative of this genre.

Hierarchy of Needs

Abraham Maslow's progression theory of employee needs is one of the best known content theories. As a positive humanistic theory of motivation, it stresses the importance of both biological drives and psychosocial needs. According to Maslow (1970), five basic human needs activate, fuel, and shape the internal drive to overcome inertia affiliated with the status quo. He classified them as physiological (survival) needs, safety (security) needs, belongingness (social) needs, self-esteem (ego) needs, and self-actualization (fulfillment) needs. These terms are ordinarily defined as follows:

1. *Survival needs.* The most basic of all human needs is to sustain life. Biological maintenance requires food, water, air, shelter, sex, and so on. Due to the nature of the life cycle, the satisfaction of physiological needs is of limited duration. As soon as one need is satisfied, it is replaced by another. When police managers concentrate on meeting survival needs to motivate personnel they are operating on the assumption that most people work based on economic incentives. Emphasis is placed on pay increases, improved working conditions, and better fringe benefits as the best way to motivate their personnel (Hellriegel, Slocum, and Woodman, 1983).

2. *Security needs.* Security needs emerge once basic survival needs have been met. People have an intrinsic need to be relatively free from fear, to feel safe, and to have some stability in both the physical and interpersonal events involved in day-to-day living. According to Frank Goble (1970), dominant security needs can be grouped into two categories: (1) the need for order and stability and (2) the need for freedom from anxiety and insecurity related to personal safety, job security, financial survival, and the capricious actions of others. Police administrators who place primary emphasis on meeting the security needs of their personnel rely on policies, procedures, rules, and regulations to produce order, promote safety, improve performance, and increase productivity.

3. *Social needs.* Once physiological and security needs have been satisfied, social needs emerge as a very important source of motivation. Human beings have an inherent need to interact with significant others. People derive personal satisfaction from group membership. Groups fulfill their need for human companionship, love, affection, and a sense of belonging. Police administrators who understand and appreciate the importance of the social needs of subordinates know that employees have a strong tendency to identify with and internalize the norms and values of the work group. Effective managers facilitate communication, promote purposeful interaction, and encourage meaningful participation in order to improve on-the-job performance and the individual productivity of their human resources (Whisenand and Ferguson, 1978).

4. *Ego needs.* The ego-esteem need has two dimensions. First, people have a need to be respected by significant others for who they are and what they can contribute to the work group. They have a desire to be competent and look to the work group as a source of recognition, acceptance, prestige, and status. Second, people have an absolute need for self-esteem. In other words, they need to feel they are worth something to themselves as well as to others. Self-esteem is manifested in feelings of adequacy, worthiness, fulfillment, and self-confidence. Managers who understand the importance of ego-esteem needs do everything they possibly can to ensure that their employees become competent and exhibit self-confidence, harbor few self-doubts, and have a good self-image. Effective police administrators help their subordinates to realize that they, as public employees, are "important people, doing important work, in an important place" (Feldman and Wright, 1982).

5. *Self-actualization needs.* The need for self-actualization is triggered when people achieve a measure of satisfaction for their physiological, security, social, and ego needs. Self-actualization is the need to grow, to be creative, and to fulfill one's potential. While self-actualization varies from one person to another, it causes people to pursue interests and knowledge for their own sake and for the joy of the pursuit (Plunkett, 1983). Self-actualized people have a need to become increasingly competent and to gain mastery over their own life. All of their talents and potential are put to use. At this stage, motivation is an internal process. External stimulation is unnecessary. Management's job is to provide resources and to create an environment in which self-actualized people are given the freedom to make truly significant contributions to the organization. To paraphrase the U.S. army's advertising slogan, self-actualized people have become all they are capable of becoming.

Maslow divided these human needs into two distinct categories: (1) lower order (survival, security and social) needs and (2) higher order (ego and self-actualization) needs. He also depicted them in a hierarchy ranging from the most basic instinctive drives to the most abstract psychosocial motives (see Figure 5.3).

Maslow's hierarchy of needs theory assumes that human needs affect on-the-job performance in accordance with three basic principles: (1) countervailing needs, (2) satisfaction deficit, and (3) progressive fulfillment:

1. *Countervailing needs.* Human beings are viewed as multidimensional social animals who sort through, prioritize, and strive to satisfy a variety of competing (lower and higher level) needs on a simultaneous basis.

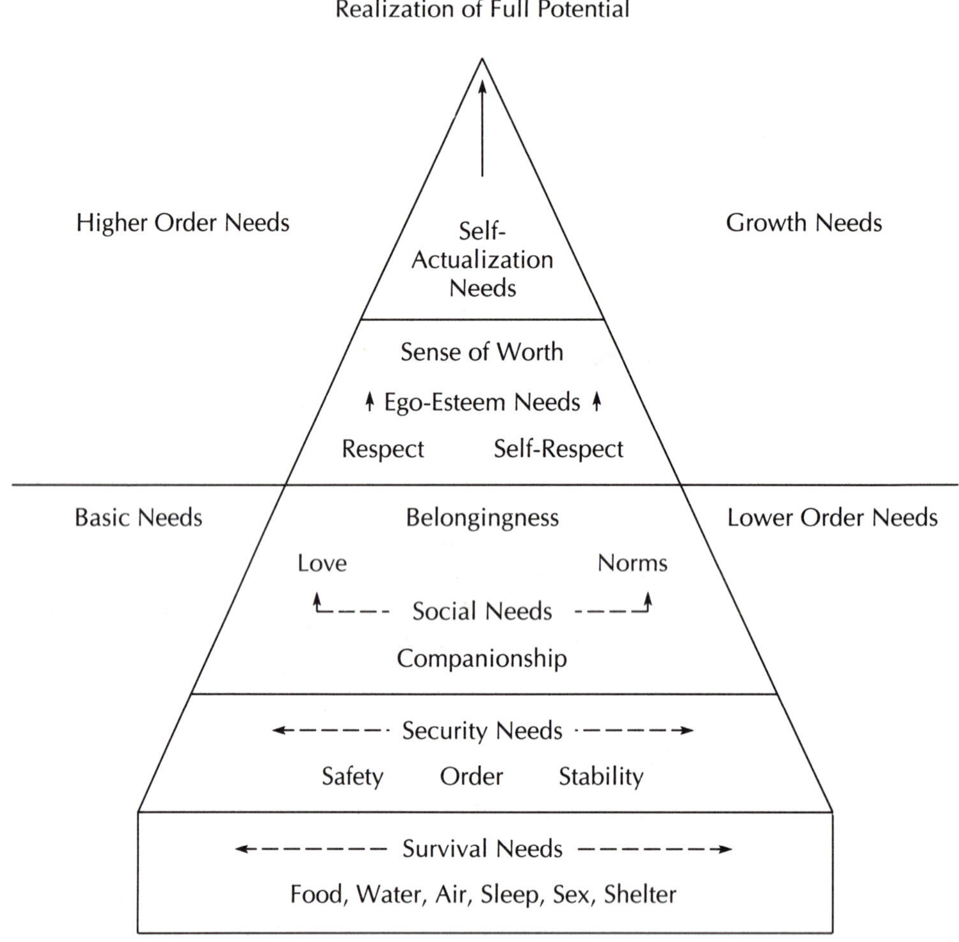

FIGURE 5.3 Maslow's Hierarchy of Needs.

2. *Satisfaction deficit.* Unsatisfied human needs create a state of tension, a perception of deprivation, and the impetus to act in a way to satisfy those needs.
3. *Progression principle.* The five need categories form a hierarchy of needs based on their relative prepotency and are activated only when the next lower level of need has been satisfied.

A deprived need creates a satisfaction deficit that commands individual attention and determines goal-oriented behavior. When deficits are reasonably well satisfied, they cease to act as motivators. This allows people to focus more attention on higher order needs. Progression up the hierarchy takes place, and the next higher level of human need is activated (Schermerhorn, Hunt, and Osborn, 1982). The key to understanding the dynamics of this process lies in accepting the idea that people are motivated by the lowest level of their unsatisfied needs. If all four lower levels are reasonably well satisfied (as determined by one's expectations, personality, and past experience), a person will seek self-actualization. It should also be noted that once a lower level need is satisfied, there is a natural tendency to reevaluate the definition of what is reasonable and to upgrade expectations. Consequently, people cycle back to lower level needs when the reasonable level of satisfaction is defined upward or when satisfaction of a need is jeopardized (Tansik, Chase, and Aquilano, 1980). A police officer who accepted a low starting salary to launch a career, for example, will redefine what is reasonable pay as the officer becomes more competent and moves up the career ladder. A new definition of what is reasonable may create a satisfaction deficit and motivate one to seek a promotion or look for another, higher paying, position.

According to Maslow's hierarchy of needs, police administrators should identify the unfulfilled needs of their subordinates. This will give them a better understanding of why police officers may or may not perform as expected. Management must find incentives which will stimulate and reinforce desired work-related behavior. In practical terms, police departments should provide employees with sufficient financial compensation to meet their basic needs, a reasonably safe environment in which to work, and a nonmonetary reward system that reinforces individual esteem. Enlightened police administrators recognize the need for and support the personal growth of their subordinates by providing opportunities for career advancement, encouraging self-development, and creating environments in which police officers are allowed to explore their own talents and dreams (Holt, 1987).

While very few people (probably less than 10 percent of the general population) achieve self-actualization, most professional police officers are acutely aware of their higher order needs. As they have moved in the direction of self-actualization, their need structure has changed. Growth needs (for competence, fulfillment, and autonomy) have displaced survival needs as primary motivators. Consequently, modern police administrators must be willing to deemphasize their short-term goals and pay more attention to developing human resources. Failure to meet the growth needs of professional employees is certain to have a negative effect on the efficiency, effectiveness, and productivity of the police department. As Tom Peters and Robert Waterman (1982) pointed out in their book, *In Search of Excellence*, outstanding companies go to great lengths to meet the higher order human needs of professional employees. This type of proactive management strategy is designed to counteract the dysfunctional influence of stress, absenteeism, shoddy workmanship, interpersonal conflict, and poor morale.

While there is little or no scientific proof to validate Maslow's theory, it is still accepted as an article of faith by organizational humanists and theoreticians who currently subscribe to the human relations school of management. Maslow's concepts have been repackaged in many ways and serve as a foundation for most content theories.

E.R.G. Theory

As we noted earlier, behavioral scientists have been unable to validate Abraham Maslow's theory. While it has a great deal of humanistic appeal, there is simply no consistent evidence to prove the contention that the satisfaction of a human need at one level actually decreases its importance vis-à-vis an appreciable increase in the importance of the next higher need (Lawler and Suttle, 1973). Consequently, some motivation theorists have attempted to modify the hierarchy of needs concept to make it more realistic in terms of its application to goal-oriented behavior. Clayton Alderfer's E.R.G. theory has become one of the better known content theories.

Alderfer's E.R.G. (existence/ relatedness/ growth) theory was developed in an effort to simplify Maslow's hierarchical model. The theory collapses the original five human need categories into just three and contends they are active in all human beings:

1. *Existence needs.* These needs include all of the drives, desires, and wants related to a person's physiological and material well-being. Survival and security needs are combined in a single category focusing on the need for food, water, shelter, safety, pay, fringe benefits, working conditions, and so on.
2. *Relatedness needs.* These needs involve the innate sociability of human animals as they search for meaningful and mutually satisfying relationships with significant others individually or in groups. The satisfaction of social (interaction) and ego (esteem) needs is keyed to the process of sharing.
3. *Growth needs.* These particular needs are directly related to the psychosocial processes that produce a sense of self-esteem (personal worth) and/or self-actualization (personal fulfillment). When growth needs are reasonably well satisfied, people exhibit confidence in themselves and engage in tasks that not only require the full use of their capabilities but may also require the development of new skills.

People, as very complex social animals, exhibit a myriad of behaviors as they consciously or subconsciously strive to satisfy a variety of competing and, at times, conflicting human needs (Baron, 1983). Figure 5.4 compares Alderfer with Maslow in terms of their need categories.

E.R.G. theory does not contain a hierarchical progression component. There is absolutely no assumption that lower level human needs must be satisfied before higher level needs can be activated. In fact, any need may be activated regardless of whether or not any other needs are satisfied (Alderfer, 1972). Since E.R.G. theory does not require lower level needs to be satisfied before higher level needs can be activated, people may be multiple motivated at any given time. As a result, it is very difficult to tell exactly what motivates people to behave as they do in a particular situation.

Alderfer's E.R.G. theory is straightforward and fairly simple to understand. It is built on a set of three basic principles: (1) the need-escalation principle, (2) the satisfaction-progression principle, and (3) the frustration-regression principle:

1. *Need-escalation principle.* The less each level of human need has been satisfied, the more it will be desired by the individual.
2. *Satisfaction-progression principle.* The more that lower level needs have been satisfied, the stronger the desire for higher level needs.

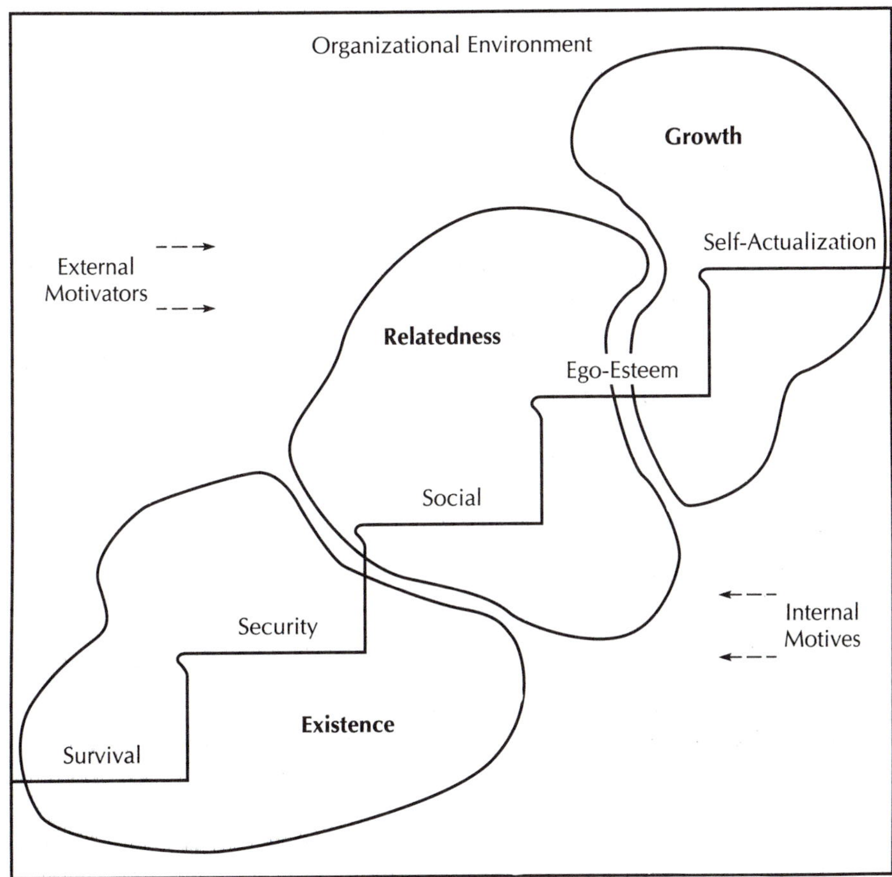

FIGURE 5.4 E.R.G. Modification of Maslow's Hierarchy. Source Adapted from David A. Tansik, Richard B. Chase, and Nicholas J. Aquilano, *Management: A Life Cycle Approach* (Homewood, IL: Richard D. Irwin, 1980).

3. *Frustration-regression principle.* The less that higher level needs have been satisfied, the more likely a renewed emphasis will be placed on previously satisfied lower level needs.

E.R.G. theory is based on dynamic interaction between perceived needs. Robert Albanese has described the E.R.G. motivation process in succinct terms. According to Albanese (1981), there is a definite E.R.G. motivation cycle:

1. The less existence needs are satisfied, the more they will be desired;
2. The more existence needs are satisfied, the more relatedness needs are likely to be desired;
3. The less relatedness needs are satisfied, the more both existence and relatedness needs are desired;
4. The more relatedness needs are satisfied, the more growth needs will be desired;

5. The more growth needs are satisfied, the more growth needs will be desired; and
6. The less growth needs are satisfied, the more relatedness needs will be desired.

E.R.G. theory provides police administrators with a workable approach to motivation in complex criminal justice organizations. Alderfer has simplified Maslow's model by reducing the number of need categories and eliminating emphasis on the specific order in which particular human needs are activated. The frustration-regression aspect of E.R.G. theory gives managers the opportunity to direct employee behavior in a constructive manner even though higher level needs may be temporarily frustrated (Whisenand, 1981).

While there has not been much applied research on E.R.G. theory, some behavioral scientists believe that it is the most current, valid, and researchable theory of human motivation based on the need concept (Ivancevich, Szilagyi, and Wallace, 1977).

Acquired Needs Theory

David McClelland, a psychologist, used the Thematic Appreciation Test (TAT) to identify and measure basic human needs. The TAT asks people to look at pictures and write about what they see. Based on extensive data, McClelland and his colleagues identified three basic human drives: (1) need for achievement, (2) need for affiliation, and (3) need for power. He defined these needs in the following way:

1. *Need for achievement.* Human beings have a basic need for achievement (nAch). It relates to each person's desire to be competent, to solve problems, to accomplish complex tasks, and to make a meaningful contribution to the organization.
2. *Need for affiliation.* The human need for interpersonal contact and group affiliation (nAff) is insatiable. It is reflected in a person's desire to establish and maintain meaningful social relationships with significant others.
3. *Need for power.* People strive to acquire power (nPower) in order to influence or control the behavior of others. "Positive power" combines the desire to influence others with a genuine concern for the organization's goals and objectives.

These three needs (nAch, nAff, and nPower) exist in all people all of the time. One need is predominant, however. It motivates people to act and shapes their on-the-job behavior (Holt, 1987).

McClelland's theory is based on the fundamental assumption that the needs for achievement, affiliation, and power are acquired over time and as a result of various life experiences. They are learned motives that are given substance by an individual's personality, background, and values. People are normally motivated by their dominant need. This dominant need is almost always translated into a person's work preferences. People with a high nPower usually become much better managers than the high achievers. They have a sincere desire to influence others in an effort to accomplish the organization's mis-

CASE STUDY

Chief L. J. Clayborn

L. J. Clayborn is the chief of police in a wealthy suburban community of 21,000 located just outside of a large midwestern industrial city. He was appointed chief 31 years ago when the municipal government was first incorporated. The chief is a very powerful man with an institutionalized political base. His word is law and has never been challenged.

Chief Clayborn is autocratic (in that he distrusts the judgment of his subordinates and makes virtually every decision that affects the police department) but paternalistic in the sense that he takes care of those officers who are loyal as well as obedient. The department has the highest pay scale and the best equipment in the metropolitan area. On the surface, it is a model police agency.

The older officers (who refer to themselves as "donkeys") are content to let the "old man" run the show. Most of them have retired intellectually and want to avoid responsibility like the plague. They have absolutely no desire to jeopardize their lucrative pensions by making "decisions." Most of them are ritualistically counting the days until they can "hang 'em up."

Younger officers—who are ordinarily better educated, more participative, and often risk oriented—have been challenging the status quo. They want more input into the decision-making process. Several of the renegades have formed an association and are calling for an election to identify an exclusive bargaining agent. Chief Clayborn, in a knee-jerk antiunion move, fired the president of the police officers' association. This action only fueled the fire of discontent. Members of the police officers' association have voted no confidence in the chief and asked for his resignation.

The chief is being pressured by the news media to resolve the police department's internal problems. He believes that his job may be in jeopardy. Consequently, he has approached the city council and the mayor with a final proposal designed to reduce the tension. His plan calls for the "prompt resolution of all grievances by the chief of police," "a substantial increase in pay and fringe benefits," and more "job security." The police association's board of directors has labeled the chief's plan as a sham designed to perpetuate the status quo and to "camouflage the real issue."

What is the real issue? How would Abraham Maslow and Douglas McGregor describe the dynamics of this situation? If you were the chief of police, what would you do to defuse this problem? Is it time for the chief to go? Why or why not?

sion, goals, and objectives. They thrive on ambiguity, seek responsibility, and feel comfortable being involved in the executive decision-making process. McClelland's theory encourages managers to learn how to recognize dominant needs in themselves and others and to create work environments that are responsive to the personal need profile of each employee (Schermerhorn, Hunt, and Osborn, 1982).

TABLE 5.1 Work Preferences Based on a High Need for Achievement, Affiliation and Power

Individual Need	*Work Preferences*	*Exemplar*
High need for achievement	Skill Competence Responsibility Autonomy Challenging goals Feedback Competitiveness	A rookie police officer with a dominant need to master his craft and be a true professional
High need for affiliation	Interaction Relationships Communication Participation Camaraderie Sharing Group-orientation	A community relations specialist assigned to help ease the conflict between the police and the black community
High need for power	Manage Influence Control Direct Decide Instruct Motivate	A newly promoted major with the will to manage human resources in order to achieve a police department's goals and objectives

The nAch, nAff, and nPower are very similar to those identified by Maslow and Alderfer. They help police administrators understand why people act the way they do and what determines their work preferences (see Table 5.1). The identification of the employee's dominant need gives managers a unique opportunity to match the right person with the right job in the right set of circumstances. This takes much of the guesswork out of the motivation process and increases the likelihood that management will achieve a harmonic mean between the psychosocial needs of the individual and the needs of the organization (Souryal, 1977). Finding the right mix is a critical variable in determining the productivity of a complex criminal justice organization.

Theory X and Theory Y

Taking his cue from Maslow and other content theorists, Douglas C. McGregor developed a humanistic theory of management. It is based on two distinct sets of assumptions about people. He called them Theory X and Theory Y and argued that the assumptions managers make about employees influence their management style. Theory X (the traditional approach to direction, control, and management) is based on a fairly negative view of people. Theory Y (a humanistic view of the innately motivated person) is much more upbeat. According to McGregor (1960), managers organize, control, and attempt to motivate employees based on their assumptions about human nature. McGregor constructed his now famous Theory X–Theory Y continuum in order to illustrate this very important concept.

Theory X, the traditional framework for much of management's thinking, is, as we noted earlier, based on negative assumptions about human nature and human behavior:

1. The average human being has a natural dislike for work and will avoid it whenever possible.
2. Because they really dislike work, most people must be coerced, directed, controlled, and threatened with punishment in order to get them to work toward the achievement of organizational goals and objectives.
3. Most humans lack ambition, avoid responsibility, and need constant direction.

Their chief concerns are survival and job security. Consequently, employees are viewed as expendable resources with little or no value in and of themselves (Sennewald, 1985). They simply become a means to an end.

The tragedy of Theory X, according to W. Richard Plunkett (1983), is that it is a self-fulfilling prophecy. Police administrators who subscribe to Theory X assumptions treat their subordinates in a suspicious and authoritarian manner. They threaten them, exploit them, and look down on them. New employees soon learn that their drive, ideas, initiative, and commitment are neither respected or rewarded. They learn to behave the way they are expected to behave. Police officers who find themselves in Theory X environments adapt quickly. They adopt a nonproductive, what's the use attitude. As poor morale robs an organization of vitality, the organization becomes progressively more dysfunctional.

Theory Y represents the other end of the continuum and is based, in large measure, on Maslow's hierarchy of needs. Theory Y assumes that once people's lower level needs (for survival, security, and belongingness) have been reasonably well satisfied, they are motivated by higher order needs for self-esteem and self-actualization. If they are deprived of the opportunity to satisfy these higher level needs at work, they become frustrated. They often react to this frustration by becoming indolent, passive, resistant to change, nonproductive, and unhappy. Poor morale creates a dilemma for proactive managers, and its resolution calls for a totally different set of assumptions about what motivates people to work (Wren, 1987).

Douglas McGregor offered Theory Y as a "modest beginning for a new theory" with respect to the day-to-day management of human resources. Theory Y is built on the following set of assumptions:

1. The average human being does not inherently dislike work. In fact, the expenditure of physical and mental effort is as natural as play and rest.
2. External control and the threat of punishment are not the only means by which to elicit individual effort. Employees exercise self-direction and self-control in order to achieve goals to which they are committed.
3. Motivation, the potential for development, the capacity to assume responsibility, and the readiness to direct one's behavior toward organizational goals are present in every person. Management does not put them there.
4. Commitment to goals is a function of the rewards that are associated with their achievement. The most important rewards are to be found in the ego satisfaction and the self-fulfillment aspects of commitment.

5. The most important function of management is to create an organizational environment and arrange internal processes so people can achieve their own goals best by directing their own efforts toward organizational objectives. The manager's job is to create opportunities, release potential, encourage growth, and provide guidance.
6. The capacity to exercise a relatively high degree of imagination, ingenuity, and creativity in seeking solutions to organizational problems is widely spread throughout the population (McGregor, 1960).

Intrinsic motivation is viewed as the key to improved performance and increased productivity. Theory Y, in sharp contrast to Theory X, emphasizes managerial leadership through motivation by objectives and by permitting subordinate personnel to experience need satisfaction as they contribute to the achievement of the organization's mission, goals, and objectives (Chruden and Sherman, 1976).

Theory Y managers respect their personnel and, as indicated in Focus 5.1, use rewards to enhance performance. They also seek to motivate their people through meaningful participation in the organization's decision-making process. Police officers who feel like they are part of the team and receive psychosocial satisfaction from their job are much more likely to invest time, talent, energy, and expertise in the organization.

As with Theory X, Theory Y may have a Pygmalion effect. Assuming the best about people often results in their giving their best. All other things being equal, people learn to give what they are expected to give. According to J. Sterling Livingston and his colleagues (1979),

1. What managers expect of employees and the way they treat them will help determine their performance and career progress.
2. Superior managers have the unique ability to create high performance expectations their subordinates strive to fulfill.
3. Less effective managers usually fail to develop the same level of expectation and, as a result, the overall productivity of their subordinates tends to suffer.
4. Employees, more often than not, seem to do what they are expected to do by those with whom they identify.

By treating subordinates as mature, fully functional human beings who are capable of making a significant contribution to the police department, Theory Y administrators frequently motivate police personnel to achieve extraordinarily high levels of performance.

Theory X and Theory Y are not mutually exclusive managerial strategies; they represent the assumptions on which managerial strategies are built. While McGregor did not argue that either Theory X or Y is always correct, he did suggest that managers tend to adopt Theory X assumptions more often than can be justified by the characteristics of their employees. He argued that, where and whenever appropriate, management practices that are consistent with Theory Y would produce much greater personal and organizational benefits (Albanese, 1981). His message seems to be that police administrators should tailor their managerial approach to meet the profile (X or Y) ex-

FOCUS 5.1

Motivating Police Personnel

Good police administrators know instinctively that those things that get rewarded get done. They are also aware that people work harder and smarter when there is something in it for them.

Effective managers use incentives like money, recognition, time off, a piece of the action, work assignments, advancement, freedom, and personal growth in an effort to motivate their subordinates. They attempt to

Reward:	Rather than:
1. Solid solutions	1. Quick fixes
2. Risk taking	2. Risk avoidance
3. Applied creativity	3. Mindless conformity
4. Decisiveness	4. Paralysis by analysis
5. Smart work	5. Busy work
6. Simplification	6. Needless complexity
7. Quietly effective behavior	7. Squeaky wheels
8. Quality work	8. Fast work
9. Commitment	9. Absenteeism/turnover
10. Collaboration	10. Debilitating conflict

SOURCE. Michael LeBoeuf, *GMP: The Greatest Management Principle in the World* (New York: Berkley Books, 1985).

hibited by police personnel (Tansik, Chase, and Aquilano, 1980). Perhaps the optimal theory should take into account the police administrator's need to employ both approaches at one time or another depending on the orientation of his personnel and the demands of the situation (Fulmer, 1983). Figure 5.5 explores the relationship between McGregor's concepts and other content theories.

Motivation-Hygiene Theory

Another view of human needs has been developed by Frederick Herzberg and his associates. His motivation-hygiene, or two-factor theory was originally derived from an analysis of critical incidents reported by 200 engineers and accountants. They were asked to describe the times when they felt exceptionally good and exceptionally bad about their jobs. The respondents identified different things as sources of satisfaction and dissatisfaction in their work. Based on the data he gathered, Herzberg isolated two vital factors found in all jobs: (1) maintenance or hygiene factors and (2) motivational factors. He described these terms as follows:

1. *Maintenance factors.* Maintenance or hygiene factors are those things in the work environment that meet an employee's hedonistic need to avoid pain.

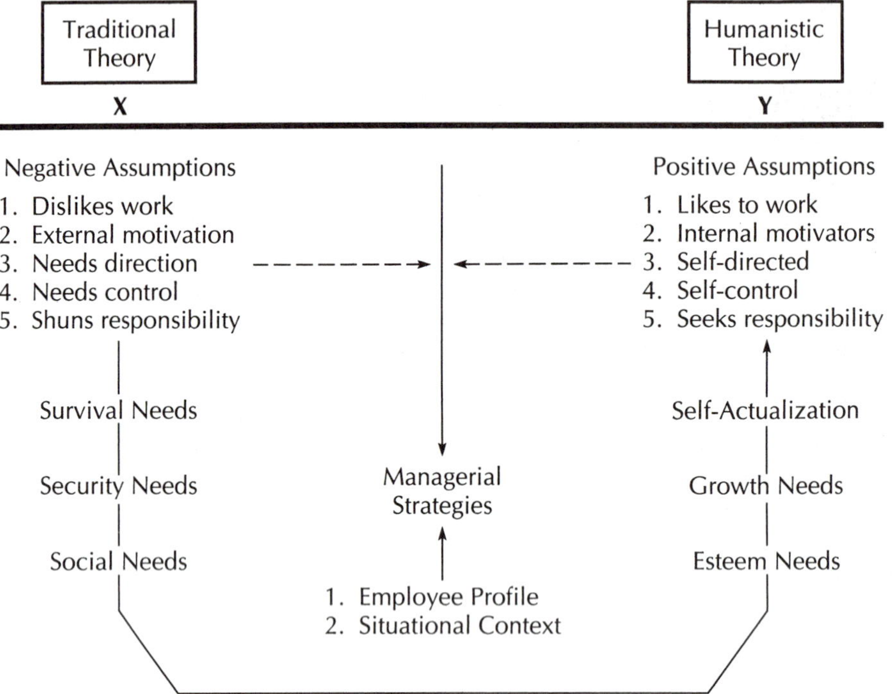

FIGURE 5.5 McGregor's Theory X and Theory Y.

Hygiene factors include the necessities of any job (i.e., adequate pay, fringe benefits, job security, decent working conditions, supervision, interpersonal relations, managerial practices and realistic policies, procedures, rules, and regulations). Hygiene factors do not satisfy (or motivate); they set the stage for motivation. They are, however, the major source of job dissatisfaction when they are perceived to be inadequate.

2. *Motivational factors.* Motivators are those psychosocial factors in work that provide intrinsic satisfaction and serve as an incentive for people to invest more of their time, talent, energy, and expertise in productive goal-oriented behavior. The primary human motivators are (1) achievement, (2) recognition, (3) advancement, (4) the work itself, (5) the potential for growth, and (6) responsibility. The absence of motivators does not necessarily produce job dissatisfaction (Herzberg, 1978).

While these concepts are obviously related, they represent completely different dimensions of satisfaction.

In terms of motivation, hygiene factors provide the milieu within which motivators (or satisfiers) function. They create a neutral state by meeting lower level human needs and preventing negative or dysfunctional behavior. Actions designed to improve hygiene factors can prevent or help to eliminate job dissatisfaction but cannot increase job satisfaction per se. While motivators can lead to more job satisfaction, they cannot prevent job dissatisfaction. In other words, people can—and almost always do—experience job satisfaction and dissatisfaction simultaneously (Whisenand and Rush, 1988).

John Schermerhorn and his colleagues (1982) contend that people at work normally fall into one of the four basic categories listed below:

JOB DISSATISFACTION (HYGIENE)		*JOB SATISFACTION (SATISFIERS)*
High	⟷	High
Low	⟷	High
High	⟷	Low
Low	⟷	Low

The least desirable situation from a management point of view is to have police officers experiencing *low satisfaction* (of higher level human needs) and *high dissatisfaction* with the organization's efforts to meet lower level survival, security, and social needs. The best mix involves *high satisfaction* and *low dissatisfaction* (see Figure 5.6). The police administrator's goal under the two-factor theory is to minimize job dissatisfaction and to maximize job satisfaction. Once improved hygiene factors reduce job dissatisfaction, managers must be prepared to shift their attention to motivational factors if they are to create more job satisfaction.

The best way to motivate workers (to be more efficient, effective, and productive) is to give them a bigger stake in the job itself. In fact, upgrading the

Job Satisfaction (Satisfiers)		Job Dissatisfaction (Hygiene)	Adaptive Behavior
High	←――――――――→	High	Competition Conflict Normlessness Wheel spinning Individualism
High	←――――――――→	Low	Cooperation Self-direction Self-control Responsibility Productivity
Low	←――――――――→	High	Stress Low morale Poor workmanship Absenteeism Turnover
Low	←――――――――→	Low	Ritualism Apathy Status quo Soldiering Resists change

* Motivational factors interact with hygiene factors to produce adaptive behavior.

FIGURE 5.6 Satisfaction/Dissatisfaction* and Adaptive Behavior.

job itself is the core component of Herzberg's theory. According to Herzberg, managers motivate their subordinates by eliciting their input, encouraging participation, involving people in the decision-making process, and enlarging or enriching the job (Herzberg, 1978).

Frederick Herzberg's motivation-hygiene theory draws heavily on Maslow, Alderfer, and McGregor. It emphasizes the importance of dynamic interaction between maintenance needs (hygiene) and motivation needs (satisfiers). Like all other content theories, it has been criticized for its methodological imprecision. A major debate concerns Herzberg's contention that hygiene factors function only as dissatisfiers, not as satisfiers. Researchers have found little or no support for this position. Nevertheless, there does seem to be some substance to the rest of Herzberg's theory. According to Lyman Porter and Raymond E. Miles (1974), much of the evidence supports the conclusion that job content factors are considered to be critically important to those workers who are asked to report their most highly satisfying experiences.

Content Theory Revisited

While it is virtually impossible to tell exactly what motivates people to act as they do in a given situation, theorists like Maslow, Alderfer, McGregor, and Herzberg have made important contributions to our knowledge of the psychosocial processes that produce goal-oriented human behavior. They have provided us with food for thought and a springboard to further inquiry. Many motivation theorists have shifted their attention to process theories dealing with how employees are motivated to work toward organizational goals and objectives.

Process Theories

Many behavioral scientists have been frustrated by subjective, introspective content theories. They are much more interested in how people are motivated to engage in goal-oriented behavior. Some of them subscribe to the behavior modification approach based on classic reinforcement theory. With Pavlovian zeal and Skinnerian logic, they believe workers can be trained to be more efficient, effective, and productive through the use of stimulus/response techniques with money as the primary reward. Some behaviorists recommend the use of operant conditioning to make people operate in a certain way to receive a certain reward. They contend people are what they are and do what they do based on environmental factors, not because of internal drives, needs, or abstract intellectual calculations. Operant conditioning theory is based on the assumption that when an operant response (the desired behavior) is followed by a pleasant incident (a reward), it causes people to associate that pleasant behavior with the desired response. Since human beings are hedonistic animals who prefer pleasure to pain, people almost always repeat the behavior that brings them pleasure. In order to use operant conditioning effectively, managers are encouraged to avoid the use of punishment as their primary means of motivation and to take the following actions:

1. Specify the desired behavior in clear operational terms.
2. Use positive reinforcements (rewards) whenever possible.
3. Minimize the time lag between desired behavior and reinforcement.
4. Use a variable-ratio schedule as opposed to continuous reinforcement.
5. Determine the response level and use shaping techniques to obtain appropriate behavior.
6. Manipulate environmental factors so that they will all reinforce the desired behavior.
7. Keep the positive reinforcement at the lowest level needed to maintain performance (Fulmer, 1983).

The operant conditioning process became the centerpiece of Frederick W. Taylor's scientific management and is still popular in some management circles. Most newer process theories stress the decision-making dimension of work performance.

Newer process theories represent a dynamic alternative to the more descriptive content theories discussed in the last section. They have been designed to help police administrators understand the cognitive (thought) processes by which individual workers choose to engage in specific behaviors in order to satisfy their personal needs. Two of the most popular process theories are expectancy theory and equity theory. They are both based on the assumption that people make conscious and subconscious assessments of contemplated actions and the consequences of those actions. Personal expectations of the outcomes associated with goal-oriented behavior are critical variables in determining how people are motivated to perform at work. Let us take a closer look at expectancy theory and equity theory.

Expectancy Theory

Expectancy theory assumes that people are not only driven by intrinsic needs but that they also make substantive decisions about what they will or will not do based on what they think will result from their effort. The motivation to work is determined, in large measure, by the individual's belief concerning effort-performance relationships and the desirability of the work outcomes (rewards) that are associated with different levels of performance. In other words, police officers will evaluate behavioral alternatives and choose the one they believe will lead to a valued work-related reward. All other things being equal, they will perform as expected if the following are true:

1. The task appears, based on their level of competence, to be possible.
2. The intrinsic or extrinsic rewards (outcomes) are seen as desirable.
3. They believe that performance of the behavior or task will bring the desired outcome.
4. There is a reasonably good chance that better performance will lead to greater rewards (Schuler, 1981).

The higher the expectation that a given behavior will pay off (in terms of an anticipated reward), the more likely people are to invest their time, talent, and expertise in order to do it well. Victor Vroom's expectancy theory is designed to explain the dynamics involved in this type of choice behavior.

Victor Vroom, a well-known management consultant, introduced his expectancy theory in the early 1960s. He identified five critically important variables: (1) expectancies, (2) valences, (3) outcomes, (4) instrumentalities, and (5) choices. Vroom described these variables in the following manner:

1. *Expectancy.* Expectancy is a probability estimate made by a person concerning the likelihood that a particular behavior will be followed by a particular outcome. The degree of expectancy ranges from zero (none) to one (absolute certainty). There are two levels of expectancy: Expectancy 1 (E → P) is a person's perception of the chances that a certain level of effort will lead to first-level outcomes that result in adequate job performance. Expectancy 2 (E → O) is a person's perception of the chances that performance will lead to desired second-level outcomes.

2. *Valences.* A valence is the strength of one's preference for a particular outcome. Unlike expectancies, valences can be positive or negative and are measured on a scale from −1 (very undesirable) to +1 (very desirable). The level of motivation will depend on how much someone wants the ends (goals) of work effort as well as the means (or tools) needed to achieve these ends.

3. *Outcomes.* An outcome or reward is any need-related consequence of behavior. First-level outcomes are the outcomes of work effort that result in job performance (a sense of accomplishment, feelings of competence, goal achievement, etc.). Second-level outcomes are the consequences to which first-level outcomes are expected to lead (a pay increase, promotion, professional status, etc.). Some outcomes are intrinsic to the person; others are extrinsic.

4. *Instrumentality.* An instrumentality is the belief that if the necessary level of performance is achieved, the anticipated outcome (reward) will be forthcoming. The overall strength of an instrumentality ranges from zero (none) to one (certainty).

5. *Choice.* A choice concerns the selection of a particular pattern of behavior. People weigh the potential value and consequence of each action they contemplate in order to estimate the probability that certain outcomes can be attained by choosing a particular behavior.

These components interact with each other and affect the motivation to work. Three of the variables, expectancy (E), instrumentalities (I), and valences (V), interact multiplicatively to determine the extent of the motivation to perform. All of them must have high positive values to produce goal-oriented choices. If the value of any one of these three variables approaches zero, the probability that a person will be motivated to perform well also approaches zero. Vroom (1964) contends these factors are interrelated as manifested in the equation $M = E \times I \times V$.

When people believe they have the ability to accomplish a certain task or perform at a particular level, their self-confidence may produce a *high* level of expectation (expectancy). This belief will not, in and of itself, motivate goal-oriented behavior, however. They must also feel that if they put forth the necessary effort and perform at a *high* level, anticipated rewards can be achieved (instrumentality). These factors do not produce motivated goal-oriented behavior by themselves. People must place *high* value on the reward or other anticipated outcomes (valence). A patrol officer, for example, may have the skill, steady performance, and the intradepartment support for appointment to the SWAT team but may turn the opportunity down because this special assignment is far less important to him than maximizing the amount of time he can spend with his terminally ill wife.

Managers play a key role in operationalizing expectancy theory in the workplace. The multiplier effect (just discussed) requires police administrators to attempt to maximize expectancy, instrumentality, and valence when they seek to create high levels of work motivation among their subordinates through the allocation of certain work-based rewards (Schermerhorn, Hunt, and Osborn, 1982). In order to motivate personnel based on expectancy theory effectively, police administrators should do the following:

1. Establish reasonably high expectations and a climate of police professionalism.
2. Recruit, screen, select, and retain well-qualified human resources.
3. Create an incentive system based on equal access to meaningful rewards.
4. Supervise subordinates in such a way that they are always learning, growing, and expanding their horizons.
5. Implement an effective in-service training program keyed to the concept of staff development.
6. Forge a direct link between on-the-job performance and positive reinforcement.
7. Analyze the total situation for conflicting expectancies and take appropriate action to minimize conflict.
8. Check to make sure there is an equitable distribution of rewards based on actual performance levels.
9. Perform the executive function of keeping the motivation system in a state of dynamic equilibrium.

From an expectancy perspective, the greatest management principle in the word is, *The things that get rewarded get done!* Establishing the proper link between job performance and meaningful rewards is the single most effective way to improve organizational efficiency, effectiveness, and productivity (LeBoeuf, 1985).

Expectancy theory has evolved into a very complex explanation of motivation built around the assumption that human beings are rational animals who voluntarily choose to engage in those behaviors that their expectancy calculation tells them will consistently produce anticipated rewards (see Figure 5.7). The complexity of the expectancy model has made it very difficult to validate through applied research. The lack of supportive data does not invalidate the concept, however. Common sense tells us that motivation depends on the dynamic interaction between our expectations, opportunity, desired outcomes, and the intensity of the desire for particular rewards. While they may not be able to explain it in technical terms, most effective police administrators have incorporated expectancy theory into their overall philosophy of management.

Equity Theory

One of the most sensitive issues confronting modern management is achieving equity in rewarding individual workers for their job performance. Equity

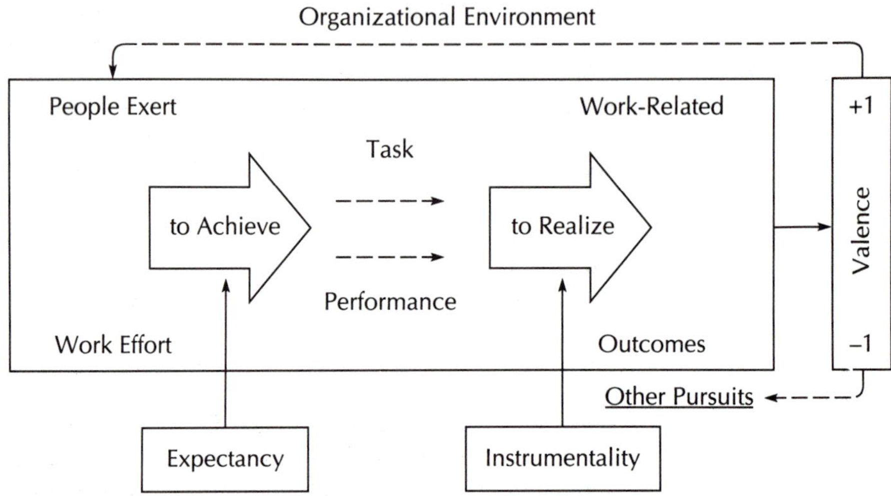

Human beings are rational animals who voluntarily choose those behaviors their expectancy calculation tells them will consistently produce anticipated rewards.

FIGURE 5.7 Simplified Version of Expectancy Theory.

means fairness. From a motivation standpoint, equity refers to the perceived fairness of rewards and of the reward system itself. J. Stacy Adams (1965) formulated one of the best known equity theories. He contends that a feeling of inequity is a motivating state of mind. In other words, when people feel there is an inequity in the way they are being treated, they will be moved psychologically to eliminate the discomfort and to restore a sense of equity to the situation. Inequities exist because people believe the rewards or incentives they receive for their work output are unequal to the rewards other workers appear to be getting in proportion to their input. This violates the widely accepted norm that people should be treated equitably (not equally). Workers expect meaningful rewards that are commensurate with their on-the-job performance. They are motivated to maintain fair relationships with other people and attempt to rectify unfair relationships by making them fair (Baron, 1983).

According to Adams's equity theory, a key element in determining the fairness of a particular relationship lies in some type of social comparison. A perceived inequity involves the comparison of an existing state or condition with a given standard. Employees instinctively compare themselves and their particular situation with others in the workplace. It is common for police officers to compare what they do (in terms of their specific job) with better paid sergeants assigned to what are often perceived as "rubber gun squad" details requiring little or no real police work. Comparisons of this type tend to lower morale. It is often impossible for management to justify the status quo. It does not matter what managers believe is fair and equitable because fair play and equity are in the minds of those affected. Even if police officers and sergeants are rewarded in exactly the same way, inequities would still exist.

According to David Holt (1987), injustice exists when unequals are treated as equals as well as when equals are treated as unequals. The bottom line is that perceived inequities are inevitable whenever large numbers of people interact with one another in complex criminal justice organizations. They are caused by factors such as

1. Pay differentials and discretionary monetary incentives.
2. Racial, religious, sexual, and social discrimination.
3. Variable access to organizational resources.
4. Political as opposed to merit-based promotion.
5. Favoritism and selective communication.
6. Preferential assignment based on length of service.
7. Differential status and the distribution of perquisites.

Equity theory is based on the assumption that all workers have been socially programmed to make a comparison between themselves and other employees with respect to what they get out of their job (outcomes) and what they invest in their job (inputs). *Outcomes* include pay, fringe benefits, prestige, a feeling of achievement, a sense of personal satisfaction, and so on. *Inputs* are factors such as special skills, training, ingenuity, perseverance, and hard work. These comparisons are then translated into ratios that reflect their inputs and outcomes vis-à-vis those of others within the work force. A negative inequity exists when a police officer feels he is receiving relatively less of a valued outcome than other officers in proportion to work inputs. A positive inequity, on the other hand, exists when an investigator feels she is receiving relatively more of a valued outcome than other detectives doing the same type of work. If an individual's input/outcome ratio is equal to that of the others, the person will experience a sense of equity. Both negative and positive inequity are motivators (Schermerhorn, Hunt, and Osborn, 1982).

According to Robert Fulmer (1983), when the reward for performance equals or exceeds what is considered to be fair, the satisfaction will produce repeat behavior. If a reward falls short of perceived equity, dissatisfaction will reduce the motivation to continue the effort. Adams noted that when either positive (overpayment) or negative (underpayment) inequity exists, those experiencing psychosocial discomfort will consciously or subconsciously engage in one or more of the following behaviors in order to reduce cognitive dissonance, disequilibrium, and the perception of inequity:

1. Increase performance, work load, and other kinds of inputs to justify higher rewards when there is a perceived positive inequity.
2. Decrease performance, work load, and other kinds of inputs when there is a perceived negative inequity.
3. Change outcomes (or rewards) through personal persuasion, collective bargaining, legal action, or dysfunctional behavior like misappropriation, employee theft, and outright corruption.
4. Change comparisons by persuading low performers with equal pay to increase their efforts and by discouraging high performers from being rate busters.

5. Distort the comparison psychologically by rationalizing that the perceived inequities are justified in light of the situation.
6. Avoid dealing with perceived inequity through absenteeism, malingering, the misuse of sick leave, and fraudulent disability claims.
7. Leave an inequitable situation via reassignment, promotion, or career change when perceived inequities cannot be resolved.

While equity is not a motivator per se, the maintenance of comparative equity is the goal of all ethical management systems. If there is a sincere attempt to determine the worth of every job and each person's performance, police officers will be much less inclined to perceive themselves as victims of inequity (Chruden and Sherman, 1976).

Figure 5.8 outlines equity theory and shows that the equity comparison takes place after the allocation of rewards yet before the onset of goal-oriented behavior. Rewards accompanied by feelings of equity can lead to job satisfaction, improved on-the-job performance, and increased productivity. Rewards depreciated by negative inequity, on the other hand, ordinarily fuel conflict, lower employee morale, and lead to a diminution in the quality of products and services produced by a particular organization.

It is the police administrator's job to take control of the situation and to minimize, or eliminate, the dysfunctional aspects of the equity comparison.

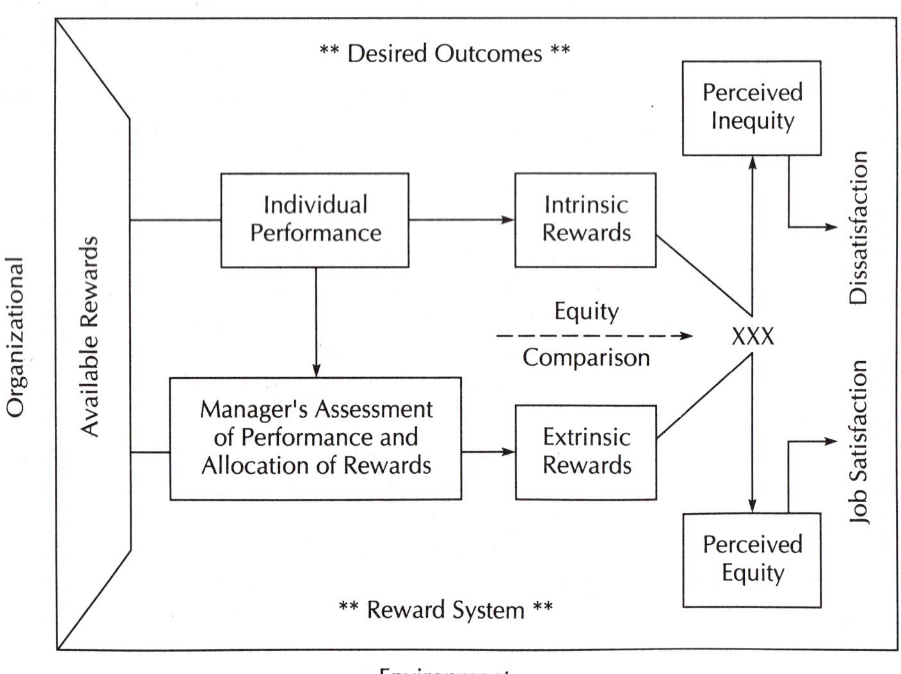

FIGURE 5.8 Equity Theory and Job Satisfaction.

Schermerhorn and his colleagues (1982) contend managers can maintain control of the equity dynamic in their work unit if they follow three basic rules:

1. Be equitable in allocating extrinsic rewards. Treat all subordinates fairly. Establish a direct link between meaningful outcomes and on-the-job performance.
2. Recognize that psychosocial equity comparisons will almost always be made by each subordinate whenever highly visible rewards (e.g., pay, promotions, special assignments, perquisites, etc.) are being distributed. Equity comparisons are natural and normal. Cognitive dissonance takes place when outcomes do not conform to expectations.
3. Anticipate felt inequities. Superior managers convey their assessment of the reward, the performance on which it was based, and the evaluative factors used to make the final selection. Openness is critical because sunshine tends to reduce suspicion and helps defuse the perception of inequity.

While these relatively simple rules will not cure all of the very complex problems associated with psychosocial equity comparisons, they should help to make the process more objective. Since most Americans equate objectivity with fairness, there could be a genuine reduction in labor-management conflict.

Even though recent research has consistently demonstrated that the perception of inequity leads to reduced input, more absenteeism, and higher employee turnover (Dittrich and Carrell, 1979), some motivation theorists feel it is of limited value because it is a special purpose theory rather than a general theory of motivation. They argue that the equity theory does not explain how people select a person to compare themselves with or how they arrive at the value placed on inputs and outcomes. Nevertheless, equity theory provides police administrators with an intellectual framework for thinking about issues like equity, fairness, and justice in the allocation of rewards (Albanese, 1981). In fact, feelings of inequity and injustice have served to motivate human beings throughout all of recorded history.

Implications for Police Management

Police administrators must come to grips with one simple fact of life. They are dealing with a new breed of employee. Modern police personnel are more sophisticated than their predecessors. They are better educated, more participative, and much less resistant to change. They demand respect and expect to be treated as professionals. While money is still a magical word in the police subculture, it has a much different meaning than it did a generation ago. Salaries and fringe benefits have been improved to the point where more money, in and of itself, no longer serves as the primary motivator. Police officers demand more. Most of them want to do meaningful work that meets their conscious and subconscious higher order needs for growth, self-esteem, and a sense of fulfillment (Souryal, 1977).

Police managers, who are expected to get things done through others, are in a position to help satisfy the higher order needs of their subordinates. Their job is to translate individual effort into collaborative action. Effective managers tend to be proactive people developers (LeBoeuf, 1985) who subscribe to the Theory Y assumptions of Douglas McGregor. They emphasize the importance of (1) participation, (2) job design, (3) job enlargement, (4) job enrichment, and (5) job rotation:

1. *Participation.* As police officers move up the professional ladder, they have an increased need to become involved in charting the course of an enterprise. They experience a strong desire to help shape its mission, set its goals, and determine its objectives. Meaningful participation in the organization's decision-making process creates a sense of ownership in and a strong commitment to those decisions produced by the process. Since collective decisions are often superior to those made by a single individual, managers should solicit input from their personnel and employ strategies designed to facilitate full participation. A police department will be much stronger when management is comfortable sharing power with rather than exercising power over its professional employees (Follett, 1973).

2. *Job design.* A job is comprised of a task or series of tasks a person performs in support of the organization's mission (purpose). Job design involves deliberate and purposeful planning in order to bring both the structural and psychosocial aspects of the activity together in one basic process. It is the police administrator's responsibility to design the task and the work setting so employees will have intrinsic motivation to perform and will derive satisfaction from a job well done. Properly designed jobs are interesting, challenging, achievable, and rewarding. Managers usually prepare job descriptions that spell out the duties, processes, authority, responsibility, and accountability inherent in a given job (Tansik and Elliott, 1981).

3. *Job enlargement.* One of the first modern methods of motivating employees through job redesign was job enlargement (Baron, 1983). Job enlargement refers to taking a fairly repetitive, boring job and injecting some variety by introducing different, yet similar, kinds of tasks. Instead of doing just one repetitive task for eight hours, police patrol personnel might do three or four different, but related, tasks requiring the same level of skill. The use of job enlargement has regained some of its popularity. The team approach to motor vehicle assembly is a very good example of job enlargement. The police agent concept in law enforcement represents a practical application of this idea. Police agents are patrol personnel who have responsibility for performing many of the routine duties usually assigned to detectives. They are often allowed to conduct preliminary investigations in misdemeanor and lower level felony cases. These job enlargement strategies are built on the assumption that variety is the spice of life. Job enlargement motivates employees to improve on-the-job performance and increase their productivity.

4. *Job enrichment.* Job enrichment is a job redesign strategy implemented to counteract the negative aspects of specialization by building motivating factors into job content. Frederick Herzberg referred to this as vertical loading, calculated to meet higher order human needs for autonomy, growth, and

self-actualization. Job enrichment is similar to enlargement, except where enlargement introduces task variety at the same horizontal skill or decision-making level, job enrichment provides for task variety on the same level while adding new tasks demanding higher levels of skill and/or decision-making ability (Tansik, Chase, and Aquilano, 1980). According to Herzberg (1978), the purpose of job enrichment is to motivate people by

1. Removing some controls while maintaining overall accountability.
2. Increasing the accountability of each person for their own work.
3. Giving employees responsibility for performing a natural and complete unit of work.
4. Granting additional authority to people in their area of responsibility.
5. Encouraging autonomy in decision-making as it relates to the task being performed.
6. Introducing new and more difficult tasks not previously handled by employees at a particular level.
7. Assigning individual police officers to enhanced or highly specialized tasks to help them become experts.

Because of the rigid bureaucratic structure of most American police departments, job enrichment programs have not been widespread. Where job enrichment programs have been implemented, they have produced encouraging results. They motivate police personnel by targeting their higher order needs for achievement, responsibility, recognition, advancement, and personal growth. As a police department's human resources become more and more sophisticated, it will take innovative strategies like job enrichment to motivate them to become team players whose personal goals coincide with those of the organization.

5. *Job rotation.* Job rotation is a motivation strategy in which people are moved into different jobs, usually on a temporary basis, in order to give them additional experiences, understandings, and challenges. It is most often used to cross-train employees so they gain a better appreciation for the importance of different jobs and the relationship between jobs in an organization. Employees who become involved in job rotation programs are usually more valuable to themselves and their employers because they develop the ability to perform more than one fairly limited function (Plunkett, 1983). Job rotation tends to give employees more self-confidence. It helps prepare them for promotions and transfers. While many police departments have experimented with job rotation programs, they have not been as effective as originally envisioned. The enemy is bureaucracy and the lack of good management. Bureaucracy prevents police administrators from becoming leaders by turning them into paper shufflers rather than people developers (LeBoeuf, 1985).

Almost all of the available evidence suggests that these motivation strategies work if managers are careful about when, how, and with whom they are used. Their success in improving efficiency, effectiveness, productivity, and morale will depend on the composition of the work force, the managerial skill of the police administrator, and the dynamics of the situation. These motivational strategies will probably have more influence on quality than quantity (Dessler, 1979).

CASE STUDY

Captain Marsha Darley

Captain Darley is the commander of a patrol division in one precinct of a very large city. Based on tradition and operational policy, the department has a rigid bureaucratic structure keyed to job specialization. Patrol officers answer calls, do preliminary investigations (when minor crimes are involved), and engage in preventive patrol when time allows. All other investigations are conducted by the Bureau of Criminal Investigations. Job descriptions are specific and binding. Deviation from a job description results in immediate disciplinary action. The work load is used to justify this particular division of labor.

The dehumanizing aspect of bureaucratic specialization has taken its toll on the personnel assigned to the patrol division. Statistics indicate the extent of the problem (vis-à-vis the specialized work units within the police department):

1. The job is viewed as dissatisfying.
2. Morale is low.
3. The crime rate is up.
4. Response time is high.
5. The clearance by arrest rate is down.
6. Use of force is at a record high.
7. The number of citizen-initiated complaints is up.
8. More officers are filing disability claims.
9. Absenteeism is rampant.
10. Abuse of sick leave is epidemic.
11. Employee turnover is exceeding projections.

The situation has become critical and imperils the division's ability to function efficiently, effectively, and productively.

Capt. Darley has just returned from a four-week course on the quality of work life at the FBI Academy. She has been asked to devise a plan (and motivation strategies) to counteract the overspecialization in her unit. If this pilot program is successful, it will be implemented in other parts of the city.

Capt. Darley is being given financial as well as moral support to carry out this project. Management has finally come to the conclusion that increased productivity must be keyed to improved performance by line personnel. Police work is a labor-intensive enterprise. Most of the budget (between 75 and 85 percent) is spent on human resources. Dissatisfied employees are a liability. The solution is to design a motivation program that meets the needs of employees.

What philosophical approach do you believe Capt. Darley should take in carrying out this project? What specific motivational strategies would you recommend that she consider? Give several concrete examples.

Summary

Management can be defined as getting things done with and through the efforts of others. Thus it is the police administrator's job to create an environment within which professional employees motivate themselves. This is done by establishing a concrete link between appropriate on-the-job behavior and meaningful rewards. Motivation is a psychosocial process. It produces an attitude that results in actions which lead to anticipated results. All other things being equal, well-motivated police officers are more efficient, effective, productive, and satisfied than their unmotivated counterparts.

Most motivation theories are based on the assumption that psychosocial tensions caused by intrinsic and/or extrinsic factors are translated into human needs. Needs elicit instrumental behaviors that are designed to reduce the tension. Needless to say, different needs generate different and unique adaptive responses. The intensity of a felt need (or needs) activates and energizes people as they interact with one another in the workplace.

The motivation theories discussed in this chapter fall into two very distinct categories: (1) content theory and (2) process theory. Content theory attempts to explain exactly *what* motivates people to act as they do in a given set of circumstances. Process theory, on the other hand, deals with *how* people are motivated. While none of these theories provides a complete explanation of motivation or the motivation process, they tend to supplement one another and provide the police administrator with a fairly comprehensive perspective on this very complex psychosocial phenomenon.

Key Concepts

Caused behavior
Organizations as social entities
Psychosocial adaptation to tension
Organizational humanism
Motivation
Motivation process
Needs
Drives
Incentives/Rewards
Performance
Content theory
Process theory
Hierarchy of needs
E.R.G. theory
Acquired needs theory
Theory X and Theory Y
Motivation-Hygiene theory
Expectancy theory
Equity theory
Participative management
Job design
Job enlargement
Job enrichment
Job rotation

Discussion Topics and Questions

1. What do social scientists mean when they say that all human behavior is caused? Why is this concept so important to the study of motivation?
2. What is the basic function of any organization? List and discuss the behavioral requirements that allow complex criminal justice organizations to survive and thrive.
3. Define the term *motive*. What are the basic steps in the motivation process? What role do motives play in this process?
4. Explain the difference between content theory and process theory. Why is this distinction important? Are these theories mutually exclusive?
5. Explain Maslow's hierarchy of needs and show how his theory has been factored into other major content theories. What contribution did the Hawthorne experiments make to Maslow's thinking?
6. Why do motivation theories ordinarily not view a satisfied need as a motivator?

7. What, from Herzberg's perspective, is the difference between a hygiene factor and a motivator? Give an example and explain why poor hygiene leads to dissatisfaction but good hygiene does not serve as a motivator.
8. Discuss the basic assumptions on which the Theory X and Theory Y continuum is built. How does the theory's self-fulfilling prophecy influence job performance? Is Theory Y always superior to Theory X? Explain your answer.
9. What are the five elements in expectancy theory? What does it mean when expectancy theorists say that the three key elements interact multiplicatively to determine the intensity of motivation? Give an example.
10. How do people ordinarily adapt their on-the-job behavior to compensate for a perceived inequity in the way they are being treated vis-à-vis others in the work force? What can police administrators do to control the equity dynamic in their work unit?
11. Identify the major strategies used to motivate police officers who have developed beyond the need for more money. What is the difference between job enlargement and job enrichment? Which one do you feel would be the best for motivating police personnel? Why?

References

ADAMS, J. STACY. 1965. "Inequity in Social Exchange." In L. Berkowitz (Ed.), *Advances in Experimental Social Psychology*, Vol. 2. New York: Academic Press.

ALBANESE, ROBERT. 1981. *Managing: Toward Accountability for Performance*. Homewood, IL: Richard D. Irwin.

ALDERFER, CLAYTON P. 1972. *Existence, Relatedness, and Growth: Human Needs in Organizational Setting*. New York: Free Press.

ASSOCIATES. 1976. *A Study of Organizational Leadership*. Harrisburg, PA: Stack Pole Books.

BARON, ROBERT A. 1983. *Behavior in Organizations: Understanding and Managing the Human Side of Work*. Boston: Allyn & Bacon.

CHAMPION, DEAN J. 1975. *The Sociology of Organizations*. New York: McGraw-Hill.

CHINOY, FLY, and JOHN P. HEWITT. 1975. *Sociological Perspective*. New York: Random House.

CHRUDEN, HERBERT J., and ARTHUR W. SHERMAN, JR. 1976. *Personnel Management*. Cincinnati: South-Western.

COLLING, RUSSELL L. 1982. *Hospital Security*. Boston: Butterworth.

DESSLER, GARY. 1979. *Management Fundamentals: A Framework*. Reston, VA: Reston.

DITTRICH, J. E., and M. R. CARRELL. 1979. "Organizational Equity Perceptions, Employee Job Satisfaction, and Departmental Absences and Turnover Rates," *Organizational Behavior and Human Performance*, No. 24.

FELDMAN, P. E., and GEORGE B. WRIGHT. 1982. *The Supervisor's Handbook*. New York: Frederick Fell.

FOLLETT, MARY PARKER. 1973. "Power." In Elliot M. Fox and L. Urwick (Eds.), *Dynamic Administration*. New York: Hippocrene Books.

FULMER, ROBERT M. 1983. *The New Management*. New York: Macmillan.

FULMER, ROBERT M., and STEPHEN G. FRANKLIN. 1982. *Supervision: Principles of Professional Management*. New York: Macmillan.

GOBLE, FRANK G. 1970. *The Third Force*. New York: Pocket Books.

HAIMANN, THEO, and RAYMOND L. HILGERT. 1972. *Supervision: Concepts and Practices of Management*. Cincinnati: South-Western.

HELLRIEGEL, DON, JOHN W. SLOCUM, JR., and RICHARD W. WOODMAN. 1983. *Organizational Behavior* (3rd ed.). St. Paul, MN: West.

HERZBERG, FREDERICK. 1978. "One More Time: How Do You Motivate Employees." In Walter E. Natemeyer (Ed.), *Classics of Organizational Behavior.* Oak Park, IL: Moore.
HOLT, DAVID H. 1987. *Management: Principles and Practices.* Englewood Cliffs, NJ: Prentice Hall.
IANNONE, NATHAN F. 1987. *Supervision of Police Personnel.* Englewood Cliffs, NJ: Prentice Hall.
IVANCEVICH, J. M., A. D. SZILAGYI, and M. J. WALLACE, JR. 1977. *Organizational Behavior and Performance.* Santa Monica, CA: Goodyear.
LAWLER, EDWARD E., III, and J. LLOYD SUTTLE. 1973. "A Casual Correlation Test of the Need Hierarchy Concept," *Organizational Behavior and Human Performance,* Vol. 7.
LEBEOUF, MICHAEL. 1985. *GMP: The Greatest Management Principle in the World.* New York: Berkley Books.
LEVINE, F. M. (Ed.). 1975. *Theoretical Readings in Motivation.* Chicago: Rand McNally.
LIVINGSTON, J. STERLING. 1979. "Pygmalion in Management." In *Harvard Business Review on Human Relations.* New York: Harper & Row.
LONGENECKER, JUSTIN G. 1977. *Principles of Management and Organizational Behavior.* Columbus, OH: Charles E. Merrill.
LYNCH, RONALD G. 1986. *The Police Manager: Professional Leadership Skills.* New York: Random House.
MASLOW, ABRAHAM H. 1970. *Motivation and Personality.* New York: Harper & Row.
MCGREGOR, DOUGLAS M. 1960. *The Human Side of Enterprise.* New York: McGraw-Hill.
PETERS, THOMAS J., and ROBERT H. WATERMAN, JR. 1982. *In Search of Excellence.* New York: Warner.
PFEFFER, J. 1978. *Organizational Design.* Arlington Heights, IL: AHM.
PINDER, CRAIG C. 1984. *Work Motivation.* Glenview, IL: Scott, Foresman.
PLUNKETT, W. RICHARD. 1983. *Supervision: The Direction of People at Work.* Dubuque, IA: William C. Brown.
PORTER, LYMAN W., EDWARD E. LAWLER, and J. RICHARD HACKMAN. 1975. *Behavior in Organizations.* New York: McGraw-Hill.
PORTER, LYMAN W. and RAYMOND E. MILES. 1974. "Motivation and Management." In Joseph W. McGuire (Ed.), *Contemporary Management: Issues and Viewpoints.* Englewood Cliffs, NJ: Prentice-Hall.
REITZ, H. JOSEPH. 1981. *Behavior in Organizations.* Homewood, IL: Richard D. Irwin.
SCHERMERHORN, JOHN R., JAMES G. HUNT, and RICHARD N. OSBORN. 1982. *Managing Organizational Behavior.* New York: Wiley.
SCHULER, RANDALL S. 1981. *Personnel and Human Resource Management.* New York: West.
SENNEWALD, CHARLES A. 1985. *Effective Security Management.* Boston: Butterworth.
SOURYAL, SAM S. 1977. *Police Administration and Management.* St. Paul, MN: West.
STEINMETZ, LAWRENCE L., and H. RALPH TODD, JR. 1986. *First-Line Management: Approaching Supervision Effectively.* Plano, TX: Business Publications.
SWANK, CALVIN J., and JAMES A. CONSER. 1983. *The Police Personnel System.* New York: Wiley.
TANSIK, DAVID A., RICHARD B. CHASE, and NICHOLAS J. AQUILANO. 1980. *Management: A Life Cycle Approach.* Homewood, IL: Richard D. Irwin.
TANSIK, DAVID A., and JAMES F. ELLIOTT. 1981. *Managing Police Organizations.* Monterey, CA: Duxbury Press.
VROOM, VICTOR H. 1964. *Work and Motivation.* New York: Wiley.
WHISENAND, PAUL M. 1981. *The Effective Police Manager.* Englewood Cliffs, NJ: Prentice-Hall.
WHISENAND, PAUL M., and R. FRED FERGUSON. 1978. *The Managing of Police Organizations.* Englewood Cliffs, NJ: Prentice-Hall.
WHISENAND, PAUL M., and GEORGE E. RUSH. 1988. *Supervising Police Personnel: Back to the Basics.* Englewood Cliffs, NJ: Prentice-Hall.
WREN, DANIEL. 1987. *The Evolution of Management Thought.* New York: Wiley.

For Further Reading

FORD, ROBERT N. 1979. *Why Jobs Die and What to Do About It.* New York: AMACOM.

Discusses the causes of job stagnation and what can be done about them. The author explores the relationship between job redesign, personal satisfaction, and individual productivity. He presents 22 practical suggestions and strategies for their implementation.

MELTZER, H., and WALTER R. NORD (Eds.). 1981. *Making Organizations Humane and Productive: A Handbook for Practitioners.* New York: Wiley.

Various authors explore motivation from an organizational humanist perspective. Work redesign theories are reviewed in terms of their anticipated outcomes. Emphasis is placed on interpersonal dynamics in an organizational setting.

RICE, CRAIG S. 1982. *Your Team of Tigers.* New York: AMACOM.

This text has two excellent chapters dealing with human motivation. One concerns motivating average to below-average employees. The other discusses how to motivate high achievers. Realism and practical utility make this volume very good reading.

SUOJANEN, WAINO W., et al. (Eds.). 1975. *Perspectives on Job Enrichment and Productivity.* Atlanta: Georgia State University School of Business Administration.

Contains a variety of articles emphasizing orthodox as well as experimental approaches to human motivation through job enrichment. The editors focus attention on sociotechnical systems, participative management, job satisfaction, and industrial democracy.

CHAPTER 6

Stress in Organizational Life: Its Nature, Causes, and Control

LEARNING OBJECTIVES

1. Define *stress*.
2. Compare and contrast the two basic forms of stress: frustration and conflict.
3. Identify the types of stress unique to law enforcement.
4. List the operational items that can be identified as stressors.
5. Describe the positive aspect of stress.
6. List the types of psychological reactions possibly caused by stress.
7. Explain the relationship between stress and job performance.
8. Describe three elements of a stress reduction program.

Stress is an integral part of life and can have both positive and harmful effects. It is difficult to imagine a society without stress. In fact, normal stress is always present. Individuals who are well adjusted seem to have no difficulty in handling everyday stresses of life. It is only in recent years that stress has become a concern to those who study organizational behavior (Albrecht, 1979).

Stress is looked on as a part of organizational life and an inevitable consequence of the relationships occurring between the individual, groups, and the department. Stress is a part not only of work but of life itself. It can contribute to the personal growth and development of each officer, as well as to his or her good mental health (Rue and Byars, 1986). An officer who works at peak efficiency because of stress will be satisfied, have a feeling of well-being, and accept success as part of the working environment. On the other hand, excessive and prolonged stress in the same situation can cause an officer to perform inadequately because of its negative impact on the body (Hellriegel, Slocum, and Woodman, 1983).

INTRODUCTORY CASE

Lieutenant Stanley Clark

Lt. Stanley Clark supervises 12 investigators in the robbery unit of a fairly large police department. He is 51 and has spent the majority of his career in the investigations unit of the department. Until recently he has thoroughly enjoyed his work, as reflected in his semiannual performance evaluations, which have always been excellent.

Two years ago he failed the captain's test for the third time. In each instance he was unable to complete the oral section of the Assessment Center successfully. No matter how much he studied prior to each examination the results were negative.

Police work is his life, and promotion means everything to him. His failure places him in an unfavorable light and hurts him a great deal. Several officers who used to work for him have been promoted to captain, thus leading to even greater frustration.

Lt. Clark had always been a moderate drinker but since failing the last examination he has begun to drink heavily and his work performance is becoming increasingly poor. He has been late to work numerous times. During a one-month period he took 12 days of sick leave. Following the last sick leave, he was asked to bring a doctor's report when returning to work, which he failed to do. In his last performance evaluation he was rated below average and given a list of five ways in which to improve his job performance, but he has not complied with any of the recommendations.

Lt. Clark is scheduled to have a special performance evaluation at the end of the month. Knowing the probable outcome, he has decided to apply for a disability retirement. This type of retirement would allow him to retire four years earlier than planned at a higher pension rate. Clark has obtained reports from three doctors who are ready to testify that Clark's drinking problem is related to on-the-job stress.

What responsibility does the police department have for reducing on-the-job stress? If you were the chief would you make an effort to salvage Lt. Clark? Why? What should the department do when a police officer becomes an alcoholic? Is police work so unique that on-the-job stress is inevitable?

It is clear, then, that certain stresses are normal in life. What we have to do is learn how to live with stress. A leading expert suggests three realistic antidotes to the stress problem (Selye, 1974):

1. Determine your personal stress levels.
2. Determine your life goals.
3. Learn how to be needed by others.

This chapter explores some of the ways managers can deal with stress by identifying it, determining its causes, and finding ways to relieve it in the working environment. First we define stress, both as a general term and as it applies to the organization.

Definitions of Stress

Stress creates different problems for each and every manager. Some handle stress very well; others have a great deal of difficulty coping with its effects. If a manager understands stress, then it is more probable it can be handled with dispatch and effectiveness.

Stress is defined as *the resulting physical and psychological condition that occurs when one attempts to adapt to one's environment* (Higgins, 1982). From this definition, you can readily see that stress is (in part) a function of personality and at the same time partly a function of environmental *stressors*.

Before any stressor becomes important to us, it must cause a feeling of uncertainty concerning its potential negative impact. If the stressor inhibits our ability to do something, stress will be rather high, since we have no idea whether we are going to win or lose. If the constraint is of no consequence and winning is a certainty, then we will view stress as inconsequential. Another factor to consider is the degree of importance. If the situation created by the stressor is not important then there is no stress. In the case of Lt. Clark (discussed in the introductory case) it was highly important to him to get promoted to captain, but his continual failure to do so resulted in his becoming an alcoholic. He was unable to cope with the constraints preventing him from achieving his goal (Robbins, 1986).

There is a way to view stress from a totally positive viewpoint called *eustress,* which means *good stress* (Cherry, 1978). It does not matter whether the stressor is good or bad—only how the individual responds to the constraints and whether the stressor is important or not. Our response to stress may depend on a positive view of various life events.

Our attitude is what determines whether a specific stressor, such as poorly defined departmental policies, is perceived as pleasant or unpleasant. Poor policy can be viewed as a challenge not a detriment. Thus a positive view of a stressor converts negative stress into eustress (Leonard and More, 1987).

Positive stress, fostered and developed by management, can serve to integrate officers into the department. A certain degree of stress, resulting from the differing value system of individuals and the organization, can in most instances serve as the basis for creating a goal-oriented organizational culture. Managers must accept the fact that different individuals respond to stress differently, so it is important to foster eustress and strive to eliminate aspects of the work environment creating negative stress.

Organizational stress is defined as *the general, unconscious, patterned mobilization of an individual's energy when confronted with any organizational or work demand* (Quick and Quick, 1984). When an officer is disciplined for violating a regulation (e.g., firing a weapon at a moving vehicle) and is suspended for five days without pay, the officer will react to this stressor either positively or negatively, depending partly on departmental opinion. In some police organizations the suspension could be viewed as a badge of honor for enforcing the law while in other agencies it could be viewed as the action of a potential troublemaker.

Conversely there is evidence showing that when an officer is promoted, stress is experienced even though it is a positive event (Griffin and Moorhead, 1986).

When *organizational stress* occurs, it can have an effect on individuals as well as the organization itself. For the individual, stress can result in problems such as alcohol or drug abuse, psychosomatic disorders, or rigidity of behavior. A person under constant and continual stress may exhibit any of the following behaviors: anger, thoughtlessness, defensiveness, and irritability (Higgins, 1982). Organizationally the manager can see productivity drop, morale decline, tasks not accomplished on time, an increase in sick leave, or other signs of employee rebellion.

Stress Unique to Police Work

Behavioral scientists in recent years have expressed a special concern about the amount and types of stressors unique to law enforcement. Emotionally unbalanced people must be dealt with, street people must be confronted on a daily basis, alcoholics must be handled again and again, domestic disputes must be settled, and child abusers arrested. On the other hand, there are positive aspects of the job (such as giving first aid, finding a lost child, and arresting a bad actor), but unfortunately they do not occur as often as the negative encounters.

Other stressors include boredom, danger, shift work, lack of public support, unfavorable court decisions, unfair administrative policies, and poor supervision. The police task is circumscribed by negative stressors that present a very strong challenge to police managers.

Altogether the research to date supports the following conclusions. First, stress can be extremely costly to a police department. In many states, a police officer's heart attack will result in early disability retirement. For example, courts in the state of California have continually ruled coronary heart disease as being occupationally related.

Second, experts support the position that stress is additive (Robbins, 1986). A single stressor may or may not have any consequence, but if added to other negative stressors they become cumulative. An assessment tool used for a number of years is the Holmes-Rahe life-stress inventory. The scale devised by the two experts was based on the examination of a large number of medical case histories in which specific life experiences were correlated with adjustments required (Leonard and More, 1987).

The table provides a rough measure of the degree of adjustment required of a person over a specified period of time and points are associated with each life event (Organ and Hamner, 1982). It is postulated that if an individual earns 200 or more points during a single year, there is a 50-50 chance a serious breakdown in health will occur within two years. The risk increases dramatically when the points exceed 300 and the potential for illness moves up to 75 to 80 percent. Some of the events measured were positive while others were negative, such as death of a spouse, 100 points and marriage, 50 points.

Of the 43 life events identified in the scale, 6 were job-related incidents (Ruch and Holmes, 1971):

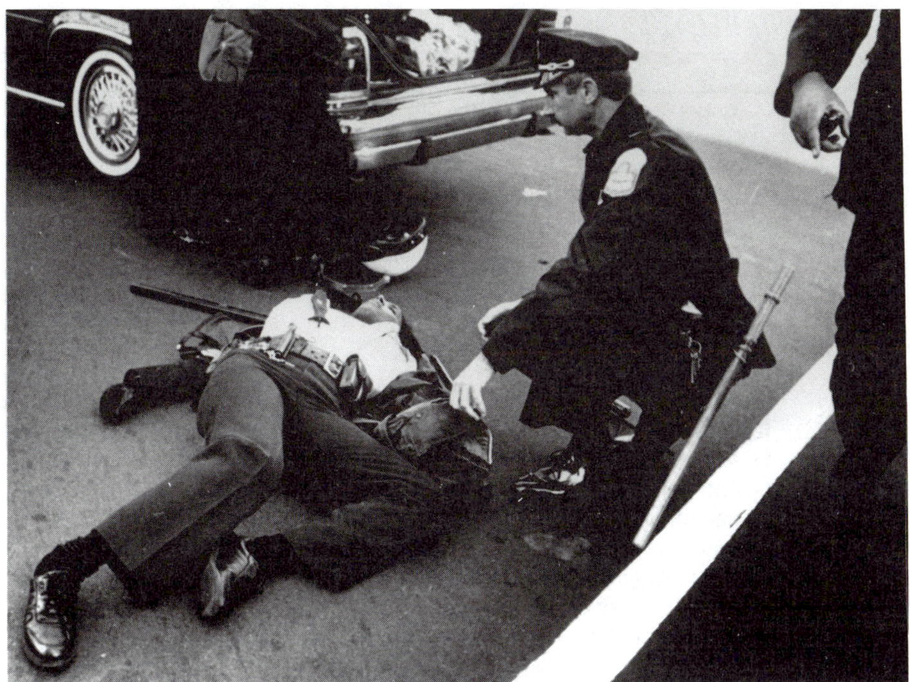

Officer Down, Code 3 Stress is endemic to police work and is often triggered by situations involving significant others. *(©Carol Guzy: The Washington Post)*

ITEM	*POINTS*
Being fired	47
Retirement	45
Major readjustments such as merger or reorganization	39
Major changes in responsibility such as promotions, demotions, or lateral transfer	36
Trouble with the boss	29
Major changes in working hours or conditions	20

Not everyone has supported the use of the standardized weights used in the Holmes and Rahe scale. One expert has suggested that life events should be classified as being good or bad, rated as to the effect (none to great), and whether the individual filling out the instrument had any control over the event (none to complete). Sarason also added some life events to the instrument, but this study has not received the attention given to the Holmes and Rahe scale (Sarason, 1982).

James D. Sewell constructed a questionnaire of 144 events experienced by police officers, then had them rate each event on a scale of 1 to 100. The highest rating (88) was given for the most stressful situation, violent death of

TABLE 6.1 Law Enforcement Critical Life Events Scale

Life Event	Value
1. Violent death of a partner in the line of duty	88
2. Dismissal	85
3. Taking a life in the line of duty	84
4. Shooting someone in the line of duty	81
5. Suicide of an officer who is a close friend	80
6. Violent death of another officer in the line of duty	79
7. Murder committed by a police officer	78
8. Duty-related violent injury (shooting)	76
9. Violent job-related injury of another officer	75
10. Suspension	72
11. Passed over for promotion	71
12. Pursuit of an armed suspect	71
13. Answering a call to a scene involving violent nonaccidental death of a child	70
14. Assignment away from home for a long period of time	70
15. Personal involvement in a shooting situation	70
16. Reduction in pay	70
17. Observing an act of police corruption	69
18. Accepting a bribe	69
19. Participating in an act of police corruption	68
20. Hostage situation resulting from aborted criminal activity	68
21. Response to a scene involving the accidental death of a child	68
22. Promotion of inexperienced/incompetent officer over you	68
23. Internal affairs investigation against self	66
24. Barricaded suspect	66
25. Hostage situation resulting from a domestic disturbance	65
26. Response to "officer needs assistance" call	65
27. Duty under a poor supervisor	64
28. Duty-related violent injury (nonshooting)	63
29. Observing an act of police brutality	62
30. Response to "person with a gun" call	62
31. Unsatisfactory personnel evaluation	62
32. Police-related civil suit	61
33. Riot/crowd control situation	61
34. Failure on a promotional examination	60
35. Suicide of an officer	60
36. Criminal indictment of a fellow officer	60
37. Improperly conducted corruption investigation of another officer	60
38. Shooting incident involving another officer	59
39. Failing grade in police training program	59
40. Response to a "felony in progress" call	58
41. Answering a call to a sexual battery/abuse scene involving a child victim	58
42. Oral promotion review	57
43. Conflict with a supervisor	57
44. Change in departments	56
45. Personal criticism by the press	56
46. Investigation of a political/highly publicized case	56
47. Taking severe disciplinary action against another officer	56
48. Assignment to conduct an internal investigation on another officer	56
49. Interference by political officials in a case	55

(cont'd)

TABLE 6.1 (*continued*)

Life Event	*Value*
50. Written promotional examination	55
51. Departmental misconduct hearing	55
52. Wrecking a departmental vehicle	55
53. Personal use of illicit drugs	54
54. Use of drugs by another officer	54
55. Participating in a police strike	53
56. Undercover assignment	53
57. Physical assault on an officer	52
58. Disciplinary action against partner	52
59. Death notification	51
60. Press criticism of an officer's action	51
61. Polygraph examination	51
62. Sexual advancement toward you by another officer	51
63. Duty-related accidental injury	50
64. Changing work shift	50

SOURCE: This table lists the top 64 critical life events out of the 144 developed by James D. Sewell. A copy of the instrument was obtained from the author. For a detailed explanation of the scale see James D. Sewell, "The Development of a Critical Life Event Scale for Law Enforcement," *Journal of Police Science and Administration,* Volume 11, No. 1, March 1983, or James D. Sewell, "Police Stress," *FBI Law Enforcement Bulletin,* April 1981.

a partner in the line of duty, to a low point value of 13 for the least stressful, completion of a routine report.

Of the officers who participated in the development of the law enforcement critical life events scale, slightly over half (52.1 percent) indicated they had experienced at least one of eight stress-related illnesses. The ailment most frequently cited was digestive disturbances (25.4 percent), and the second most frequent was an increased use of alcohol (19.9 percent).

While the Sewell instrument (see Table 6.1) has not been tested extensively, it can still be used by paying special attention to critical life events when they occur. When this is coupled with events listed in the Holmes and Rahe scale such as the death of a spouse, divorce, or marital separation, a police manager should react by personally providing appropriate support or by seeing that support is offered by a professional counselor. Table 6.2 combines a number

TABLE 6.2 Combined Stressful Life Events Occurring in One Year That Require a Managerial Response

Event	*Value of Life Change Units*
Divorce	73
Oral promotion review	57
Written promotional review	55
Changing work shifts	50
Reassignment/transfer	46
Unfair administrative policy	46
	327

TABLE 6.3 Law Enforcement Officers Killed and Assaulted

Year	*Assaulted*	*Killed*
1986	64,259	131
1985	61,724	148
1984	60,153	147
1983	62,324	152

SOURCE: Bureau of the Census, *Statistical Abstracts of the United States, 1988* (108th Ed.) (Washington DC: U.S. Government Printing Office, 1987).

of critical life events, the combined values of which exceeds 300. If these events happened during one year they could possibly lead to an increased risk of psychological or physiological symptoms arising within two years (Sewell, 1981, 1983).

Other studies have compared male and female officers (in a relatively large law enforcement agency) on ratings of stressful events. The most significant stressors were found to be those emphasizing the importance of human resources, equipment, and supervision. Interestingly enough the male officers expressed a greater concern about career issues; female officers had their greatest concern with personal safety issues (Pendergrass and Ostrove, 1984).

In another study of officers in two states, the researcher found female officers did not generally experience any more work-related stress than white male officers in the same departments. At the same time, the study showed women police officers felt danger was viewed as an important stressor in contrast to male officers who gave it a low rating (Davis, 1979).

Danger in police work is *real*—annually, a considerable number of law enforcement officers are the victims of felonious assault or murder. Table 6.3 shows the number of officers assaulted and killed over a four-year period from 1983 through 1986. During this period, the number of incidents have shown a slight decrease, but the statistics are higher than a decade ago.

Francis A. Graf presented some interesting observations in his study of a Canadian police department. He found two-thirds of the police officers felt they never or almost never successfully handled problems created by work, change was not conducted effectively, and they had little confidence in their ability to deal with work hassles (Graf, 1986).

Transitory Stages of Life

Perceived stress is viewed somewhat differently by Violanti and Marshall who found transitory stages during a police officer's career affecting stress perception (Violanti and Marshall, 1983):

1. *Alarm stage* (0 to 5 years). The early period of an officer's career involves adjusting to the reality of the street. Life is usually entirely different from circumstances the officer experienced while attending the police academy. Actual police work also happens to be entirely different from what is depicted by police shows on television. Faced with the demands of the job, the new

TABLE 6.4 Transitory Stages of a Police Career

Alarm	(0–5 years)
Disenchantment	(6–13 years)
Personalization	(14–19 years)
Introspection	(20 years and over)

officer has the tendency to question personal ability to handle police work. Stress increases during the first five years of police service.

2. *Disenchantment stage* (6 to 13 years). Stress increases during this stage and is a period in which an officer finds all crimes cannot be solved—there is a limit to what can be done. Officers continue to question their ability to do good police work and control their personal destinies (see Table 6.4).

3. *Personalization stage* (14 to 19 years). In this stage there is a dramatic decrease in stress. An officer who has been working long enough does not find the demands of police work so great. There is also a lessening of concern because the fear of failure loses its importance. This is a period when an officer becomes more concerned with personal goals.

4. *Introspection stage* (20 years and over). With the exception of concern for retirement, stress continues to decrease during this stage. An officer is usually more secure in the job by this time, and it might even be described as a coasting period. Failure is of limited concern.

If this longitudinal model just described remains constant under additional scrutiny and replication in other departments (besides the 21 police organizations studied in western New York state) then it will prove that police managers should initiate stress reduction programs during the early stages of an officer's career. If a department has a field training officer (FTO) program, it is an excellent place to educate new officers about the nature and type of stress occurring during a career.

Stressors at Work

It is very important for police managers to recognize the varying sources of stress because an officer's on-the-job behavior can be influenced by work-factor stress (Schermerhorn, Hunt, and Osborn, 1988). Increasingly, managers are becoming interested in stress and its potential impact on job behavior. But keep in mind the impossibility, based on our present level of knowledge, of developing a comprehensive list of stressors and their possible consequences.

It is also essential to remember there is both malstress (bad or negative stress) as well as eustress (good or positive stress). One officer can view a specific stressor as being inimical while another finds it rewarding and enjoyable. In law enforcement, there are easily identified stressors and then there are those subtle ones, emerging only after careful consideration. The first thing to do is to identify specific stressors peculiar to a specific task or assignment

TABLE 6.5 Stressors Related to Work

Job Characteristics	Personal Variables
Role ambiguity	Personality
Role conflict	Age
Nature of work	Family
Amount of work	Sex
Physical factors	Ethnicity
Use of force	Group Characteristics
Organizational Characteristics	Norms
Leadership style	Support
Rules and regulations	Cohesiveness
Policies	Role conflict
Authority	Informal leaders
External Factors	Resource Management
Community	Promotion
Individuals	Training
Victims	
Criminal justice system	

SOURCE: Michael T. Matteson and John M. Ivancevich, *Controlling Work Stress* (San Francisco: Jossey-Bass, 1987), and Stephen P. Robbins, *Organizational Behavior* (Englewood Cliffs, NJ: Prentice-Hall, 1986).

and then work out a way of modifying the stressful working environment (Pelletier, 1984).

When one of the stressors identified in Table 6.5 is found to be of concern to managerial and operational personnel, it should be carefully analyzed to see if it is actually causing stress in the organization.

We discuss many of the work-related stressors peculiar to law enforcement in the following sections. There is no attempt here to discuss all stressors, but only those important to police managers.

Job Characteristics

Role conflict and ambiguity represent quite significant sources of stress for law enforcement personnel and problems for their agencies. Role conflict is defined as *the simultaneous occurrence of two (or more) sets of pressures such that compliance with one would make more difficult or impossible, compliance with the other* (Organ and Hamner, 1982). The role to be performed by a contemporary police department is certainly not cut and dry. There is much a police officer does other than enforcing laws.

If we suggest that the primary function of law enforcement in a democracy is the prevention of crime, then it immediately requires us to carefully define what we mean. Is prevention of crime something unique and distinct or does it merely mean the *control of crime?* The conflict becomes immediately apparent when the police try to balance the competing roles of maintaining the peace as a means of providing for domestic tranquility while at the same time providing needed police services (More, 1985). What is an officer to do when told by the first-line supervisor to spend more time handling inebriated individuals on the beat but is also being pushed for comprehensive report writing (a time-consuming process), and there is not enough time to do both?

Role Conflict and Ambiguity

How the officer reacts to the competing expectations results in what is known as *role pressures*. Hence role conflict occurs. It is generally accepted that conflict is a stressor (Matteson and Ivancevich, 1987). The greater the amount of conflict generated by inconsistent demands, the greater the potential for the stressors to impact negatively on the individual.

Another type of role conflict occurs when a supervisor communicates incompatible or conflicting expectations. For example, a lieutenant in charge of a burglary unit expected an improvement in the conviction rate, but found it difficult to accept investigators' needs to spend a great deal of time developing informants. Needless to say the investigators viewed these two demands as diametrically opposed (Quick and Quick, 1984).

Personal role conflict occurs when there is a perceived incompatibility between an individual's values and the expectations of others in the organization. This is especially apparent in police work when an officer is pressured by other officers to conform to informal production standards. In other words, don't disturb the status quo by writing more tickets than other officers or conducting more field interrogations during a shift.

All these forms of role conflict contribute to increased stress levels, greater levels of interpersonal tension, a lowering of job satisfaction, and a decreased confidence in the organization. Interestingly enough, research has found the more authority possessed by the individual sending the conflicting message the greater the job dissatisfaction (Fraser, 1983).

Role ambiguity is the uncertainty resulting from a lack of clarity about tasks and the way they have to be performed by an individual.

Such a situation can be stressful for an officer, especially if a structured environment has a great deal of meaning for that individual. On the other hand, there are officers who readily accept and actually thrive on ambiguity (Organ and Hamner, 1982).

Managerial jobs in law enforcement are prone to ambiguity by virtue of the way law enforcement is organized. Information needed for decision-making is controlled by line officers, but police managers also need such information to perform their job. In an effort to control the discretion of officers, police organizations constantly generate rules and regulations, making outcomes predictable and reducing ambiguity in the working relationship between managers and officers (Johns, 1983).

At the operational level, this effort to reduce role ambiguity is especially apparent in the situation whereby police administrators have eliminated the choke hold as a means of restraining someone, but have never been provided with an alternate means of restraint. In the new policy, they have left it up to line personnel to interpret what is meant by the dictum, use restraint appropriate for the situation. This is a policy the officers view as inadequate and open to conflicting interpretations.

Role ambiguity has been found to decrease general life satisfaction as well as to create job dissatisfaction. It also lowers individual self-esteem, and can lead to anxiety and feelings of resentment (Caplan and Jones, 1975; Margolis, Kroes, and Quinn, 1974).

Work Overload and Underload

From time to time almost everyone has experienced *work overload*, but it is of special concern when it becomes chronic. It can cause an employee to feel absolutely helpless. Time constraints or deadlines can become such a burden to managers that the job seems to be out of control. Almost everyone has felt the stress caused by having too much to do whether their job is dispatcher, sworn officer, clerk, or manager (Pelletier, 1984).

Work overload is a stressor normally occurring as quantitative or qualitative. The most obvious is quantitative. There is just too much to do. It is difficult for a criminal investigator to handle a caseload of 123 residential burglaries (Matteson and Ivancevich, 1987). Even when cases are prioritized in terms of solvability there is only so much time which can be devoted to investigating each case.

Qualitative overload is best described as a situation in which employees feel they are not competent enough to perform certain tasks or that performance standards are unrealistic and too high (Matteson and Ivancevich, 1987). For example, this type of overload is evident when a highly qualified line officer is promoted to a supervisory management position and (even though operationally competent) does not have the capacity to shift gears and accomplish tasks through the efforts of others (Quick and Quick, 1984).

Finally, work overload can be a stressor when a manager has too many separate types of tasks to perform. If one must constantly shift from one type of task to the next, the adjustment to the new situation can be frustrating and at some point becomes a stressor. This occurs quite often at the middle management level when the incumbent of a position has no sense of the real responsibilities of the job or there is a failure to delegate tasks to subordinates (Organ and Hamner, 1982).

The other side of the coin occurs when there is too little work to do and boredom sets in, especially when the work underload occurs over an extended period of time (Ellison and Genz, 1983). In many police departments, officers working the midnight shift find the limited number of calls for service can make the hours drag on endlessly.

Whether the job to be performed involves work overload or underload, the employee can respond by feeling frustrated and anxious about the working environment. Work can become a burden rather than a rewarding experience. As pointed out by one expert, the majority of workers prefer to be busy performing rewarding tasks rather than loafing or being idle (Albrecht, 1979).

Use of Force

In an earlier part of this chapter, danger as a component of police work was discussed. We now consider the *use of force*. One study showed police officers have killed an average of one person per day since 1970, and the ratio of police killed to police killings has, over the years, remained at 1 to 5 (National Institute of Law Enforcement and Criminal Justice, 1979).

In the United States there are approximately 1,700 police departments with nearly half a million sworn police personnel who are confronted with an untold number of violent situations every day. When these statistics are compared to the estimates of killings by police officers, only 1 officer in 60 has killed someone during the last 15 years. The evidence also suggests the majority of police shootings occur in large cities, hence the vast majority of officers are never involved in a police shooting (Fyfe, 1981).

While police shootings do not occur often, when they do, there are severe legal, physical, and emotional implications. The officer can suffer from psychological trauma, be sanctioned by the department, and/or be sued and have to spend an inordinate amount of time in court defending the action (Matula, 1982).

Police managers should be fully aware of the need to give officers who have been involved in a shooting the opportunity to deal with the emotional consequences of their actions. It is in the best interests of the department, the community, and the officer to have a psychological debriefing process allowing an officer to express feelings about the incident. It has been found to be a successful means of reducing malstress (Carson, 1987).

Poor *physical* settings can cause police officers to suffer from stress when their working environment extends beyond a reasonable comfort zone. Factors include temperature, humidity, sunlight exposure, weather, noise, air pollution, or chemicals. For example, a reasonable temperature comfort zone ranges from 65° to 80° F. In one police department located in a valley, the police cars were not air conditioned, even though the summer temperatures often exceeded 100° F.

The chief of police in this valley town had a vehicular temperature study conducted. On an average summer day, in a vehicle without air conditioning, the temperature was recorded at 135° F. The city manager refused to purchase air-conditioned vehicles until it was pointed out that the increased cost of air-conditioning vehicles was negligible when compared with the car's resale price (with air conditioning) which exceeded the actual air-conditioning cost by 50 percent (Albrecht, 1979).

Organizational Characteristics

Police managers at every level may create situations leading to stress for themselves as well as for their employees. A leader in an organization is in a position to exert a tremendous amount of influence on how tasks are accomplished and the methods used to attain goals.

Dealing with an authorization leadership style is difficult for many individuals. It generally causes tensions and pressures beyond the control of the individual. One way for the subordinate to respond is to accept this type of supervision and suppress the resulting stress and hostility. Another style of response is to object to such arbitrary leadership behavior by becoming hostile. The former response, over a period of time, will (in all probability) result in undesirable physiological changes; the latter response will serve to release

CASE STUDY

Lieutenant Tom Phelps

Lt. Tom Phelps has been a member of the Sycamore Police Department for nine years and has held his present position for two years. He has recently been transferred to field operations and placed in charge of the SWAT unit with a team of nine officers. During a typical month, the unit responds to three calls. When not engaged in such operations, the unit works from 7 P.M. to 3 A.M. and may be deployed anywhere within the city limits.

Generally, when the unit is not training, emphasis is placed on identifying career criminals by placing suspects under surveillance, following them, and attempting to apprehend them when committing a crime. The unit has been highly successful in this endeavor and has arrested numerous suspects in the act of committing felonies.

When operating as a SWAT unit involving barricaded subjects, Lt. Phelps found it necessary to have marksmen shoot the last two suspects. In each instance, the subjects were armed and were threatening hostages. Each of the officers who shot a suspect underwent extensive psychological debriefing and the departmental psychologist worked with their families in order to reduce their mental strain.

Unfortunately the press and several pressure groups object to the actions of the team, taking the position, that neither life should have been taken. This is part of the public's overall position concerning this aspect of police work—the police should severely curtail the use of deadly force.

Departmental policy holds that an *officer may use deadly force to defend others against deadly force,* so it is clear that Lt. Phelps, in both instances, acted within the parameters of departmental policy. The opponents of police use of deadly force are demanding a complete revision of departmental policy and calling for the creation of a civilian review board.

At this same time, the city manager is calling for a 10 percent cut in the police department's budget with one specific recommendation—the elimination of the department's psychological support unit.

The city council responded to public clamor and established a special commission to review departmental policy when using deadly force. Lt. Phelps has been selected by the chief to prepare a position paper setting forth a rationale for the department's use of a psychologist.

If you were Lt. Phelps how would you deal with this issue? In other words, is there a real justification for employing a psychologist to provide counseling services or should officers be expected to handle their own personal problems?

some tension, but at the same time create a stressful environment (Quick and Quick, 1984).

Certainly some employees function effectively under an authoritarian leadership style, but most officers in today's departments respond more readily to expert and referent power than to legitimate and positional power (see Chapter 8 for an extended discussion of power).

Leadership studies to date have not supported any one style as being best in terms of creating the least amount of stress. So at our present level of knowledge, we must assume that a style of leadership which might be stressful for one officer might not be stressful for another (Matteson and Ivancevich, 1987).

There is some indication that present-day police managers are not effective at providing performance feedback. Unfortunately a great deal of feedback is viewed negatively by the employee because it is presented in a highly authoritarian manner. For the most part, this type of feedback emphasizes one-way communications and is stress inducing. The manager must, then, create an atmosphere fostering two-way communications which (when properly handled) can prove to be stress reducing.

If there is anything characteristic of American law enforcement, it is its bureaucratic nature and its excessive reliance on rules and regulations. Carefully delineated policies are a standard feature of police departments. Rules and regulations outline the authority, responsibility, and duties of every individual in a department. In many instances it seems there is a policy on everything. One police department has six manuals covering everything from how to operate a radio to how to give an informant a control number (Leonard and More, 1987).

Some policies are just a restatement of state law, others are precise and technical, while still others prove to be moral statements. Some policies are only a few sentences long; others ramble on for pages. Of the many police departments in the United States, one can find agencies with carefully delineated policies and other departments where it is almost impossible to find written policies (More, 1985).

If an agency has a *policy,* it should be written so it becomes a firm commitment between the agency and its personnel. If correctly written, it promotes uniformity and continuity. A good policy is one that includes enough detail to ensure the desired results are attained, but at the same time does not unnecessarily restrict the exercise of discretion.

Rules, regulations, and policy should be developed jointly between management and agency personnel through formal and informal meetings. In this manner, all those responsible for working within policy guidelines are more apt to work for its successful implementation. Jointly developed policy can serve as a stress reducer. It also fosters creative decision-making because it acknowledges the need for discretion.

When rules and regulations are exceedingly detailed and circumscribe discretion to the extent that agency personnel feel stifled and suppressed, then the rule or regulation can become a stressor. A manager should constantly monitor supervised employees in order to identify potential sources of stressors and then work to minimize them in the organization (More and Shipley, 1987).

External Factors

In recent years, increasing attention has been given to the relationship of law enforcement to the community. The police managers of tomorrow will have to meet the challenges of unprecedented societal transformations. Numerous communities are changing rapidly because of urbanization, technological advancement, population explosion, a changing morality, and a transient lifestyle (Wilson, 1981).

By the end of this century, approximately 56 percent of the population will be under 25 and the vast majority of people will be living in metropolitan areas. During the same period of time, in a phenomenon called the *graying of America,* those over 65 will increase by 21 percent (More, 1985). All these factors will place an increasing demand on the police, so their role will have to be highly flexible. Laws will have to be enforced in such a way to ensure that a reasonable balance is maintained between collective needs and individual rights.

Community relations has been a constant problem in many police departments. For example, in one large agency study, community relations was ranked fourth as an external stress inducer. Slightly more than one-third of the officers studied cited community conflict as contributing to stress (Kroes, Hurrell, and Margolis, 1974). In a more recent study of women police officers, a negative public attitude was cited as a source of stress (Wexler and Logan, 1983). As the police are called on to perform different and more numerous tasks and the public increases its scrutiny of police activities, we can speculate that a negative community attitude will continue to prevail in many towns and cities. It is anticipated that police departments adopting a community problem-solving orientation will find negative relations with citizens reduced considerably.

The *criminal justice system* (especially the courts), is a significant stressor for police officers. Many officers feel that courts are too lenient and that judges show a greater consideration toward the defendant than the community. Another problem is the courts demonstrating a lack of regard and interest when court appearances are scheduled. The police express a similar concern for defense attorneys, public defenders, and the tactics used in court.

These concerns are well demonstrated when a defense attorney diligently shops around in order to find a "lenient" judge or the postponement game is played to the hilt in an effort to delay the trial as much as possible. Another tactic of many public defenders is to attempt to discredit officers' testimony and actually do everything possible to put the officer on trial rather than the defendant (Ellison and Genz, 1983; More, 1985; Wexler and Logan, 1983).

Recent research supports the proposition that the impact of stress on an employee's behavior is definitely altered by that person's personality. This includes such personality traits as tolerance for ambiguity, extrovertedness, dogmatic personality, and the extent of personal rigidity (Brief, Schuler, and Van Sell, 1981).

Every person has distinct personality and behavioral traits which are in turn modified and influenced by such variables as gender, age, ethnic origin, and family. The overall life expectancy for women is almost eight years longer than men (Bureau of the Census, 1987). The difference might be explained genetically, but it is believed much is attributable to men smoking more, consuming more alcohol, and being more apt to exhibit the Type A behavior pattern (Quick and Quick, 1984).

As more women enter law enforcement it is anticipated they will assume a higher rate of risk factors and react to stress just like their male counterparts. In one study it was found the levels of work anxiety were the same for both sexes. However, as we mentioned, women found danger to be a more important stressor than did male police officers. Female officers were found to intervene more often when infractions occur, possibly because they were found to be more cynical about human behavior. Such intervention (in spite of the concern for danger and a lesser degree of self-confidence) suggests policewomen try harder (Davis, 1979).

In another study, women present a different perspective. Out of 19 different stressors, the most common one centered around their being women. Even after women were in the department for six years, male officers did not fully accept them. The actions of the male officers definitely increased the stress level of the female officers as they were *ignored, harassed, watched, gossiped about, and viewed as sexual objects* (Wexler and Logan, 1983).

Women are starting to assume managerial positions in law enforcement agencies and it is anticipated that their reactions will parallel women managers in business. That is, they will smoke more and increase their use of alcohol, tranquilizers, antidepressants, and sleeping pills. All these reactions are in response to the stressors women face working in law enforcement (Quick and Quick, 1984).

With affirmative action programs and a broadening recruitment base in many law enforcement agencies, members of *minority groups* are entering the managerial ranks and subsequently are affected by occupational stress. In some instances it is the result of racial prejudice. Carried to its extreme, a minority manager can begin to feel inadequate, develop a sense of inferiority, or experience a loss of self-esteem (Kirkpatrick, 1987).

When minority managers are few in number, it becomes difficult for them to have access to the informal organization, thus denying their ability to obtain information and contacts they may need in order to do their job effectively. In some agencies even the formal organization does not provide them the support needed for success. This is currently occurring in one large department, under court order to promote a certain percentage of minority officers to managerial positions. These managers are isolated from the formal organization and denied access to the informal organization. In some instances their exclusion impairs their ability to perform at an acceptable level. Special training and support is needed if all new managers are to succeed. This is especially pertinent when the new manager is a member of a minority group (Matteson and Ivancevich, 1987; Quick and Quick, 1984).

Many *groups* in an organization place pressures on their members so it becomes a source of stress and tension (for a detailed discussion of groups and their characteristics see Chapter 7). Members of a team or working together on a shift exert pressure on each other in order to get members to behave in a certain way (Matteson and Ivancevich, 1982). Informal groups can resist the attainment of departmental objectives, reduce individual freedom, and force members to conform to production standards. Managers who are knowledgeable enough to understand thoroughly how a group behaves can use the group to build individual members' self-confidence, assist in providing a means of self-expression, and reduce tension within the organization (Kirkpatrick, 1987; Terry, 1983).

Career development opportunity stressors occur frequently in law enforcement agencies. In one nationwide survey it was found only 18.99 percent (median) of the personnel held administrative positions ranging from supervisory management positions up to the chief executive officer. What it actually means is most police officers will be very fortunate to attain the rank of corporal or sergeant and have only a limited chance of achieving a rank beyond the supervisory management level (Police Foundation, 1981).

Career variables become organizational stressors to an individual when they cause frustration or anxiety. Just the process of pursuing a promotion can prove to be stressful. One has to compete for promotion by taking a test(s), either written or oral, and in some instances a candidate either fails or is ranked so low as not to be promoted. As an officer becomes older and promotions fail to occur, dissatisfaction with the job increases (Matteson and Ivancevich, 1987).

Management training is a necessary function of human resource management—when this is lacking, it can contribute to stress felt by managers. When one assumes a managerial position, the organization has an obligation to provide training, the skills and knowledge necessary to allow the individual to work toward the attainment of organizational goals. Managers need to be given the opportunity to grow, develop, and contribute (Quick and Quick, 1984).

Occupational stressors occur in the majority of occupations—law enforcement is no exception. It is not actually a question of trying to classify police work as being highly stressful as compared to other occupational groups, but of dealing directly with the occupational stress employees report. Figure 6.1 depicts the potential impact of low employee participation in the decision-making process. It can be seen that all these items can limit the effectiveness of the organization. Community policing, emphasizing problem-solving, is a style of management actively soliciting officer participation.

A decentralization of tactical decision-making down to the beat level does not imply abdication of executive obligations and functions. It means first-line supervisors assume greater managerial responsibilities and every effort is made to tap the wisdom and experience of line officers. It also means the chief executive must become personally involved in the participative management process from its inception to the point of active involvement when implementation and subsequent assessment occurs (Kelling and Moore, 1988).

Symptoms of Stress

Organizational stress can be tremendously important to both the individual and the organization. These reactions to stress can be divided into three categories: behavioral, psychological, and physiological. Stress and response to it varies from individual to individual so it is best to look at organizationally induced malstress (bad stress) in terms of three groups of employees who are part of the average police department. Our perception of work is important and while perceptions can change, evidence seems to support the position that we will remain in our group rather than move from one group to another.

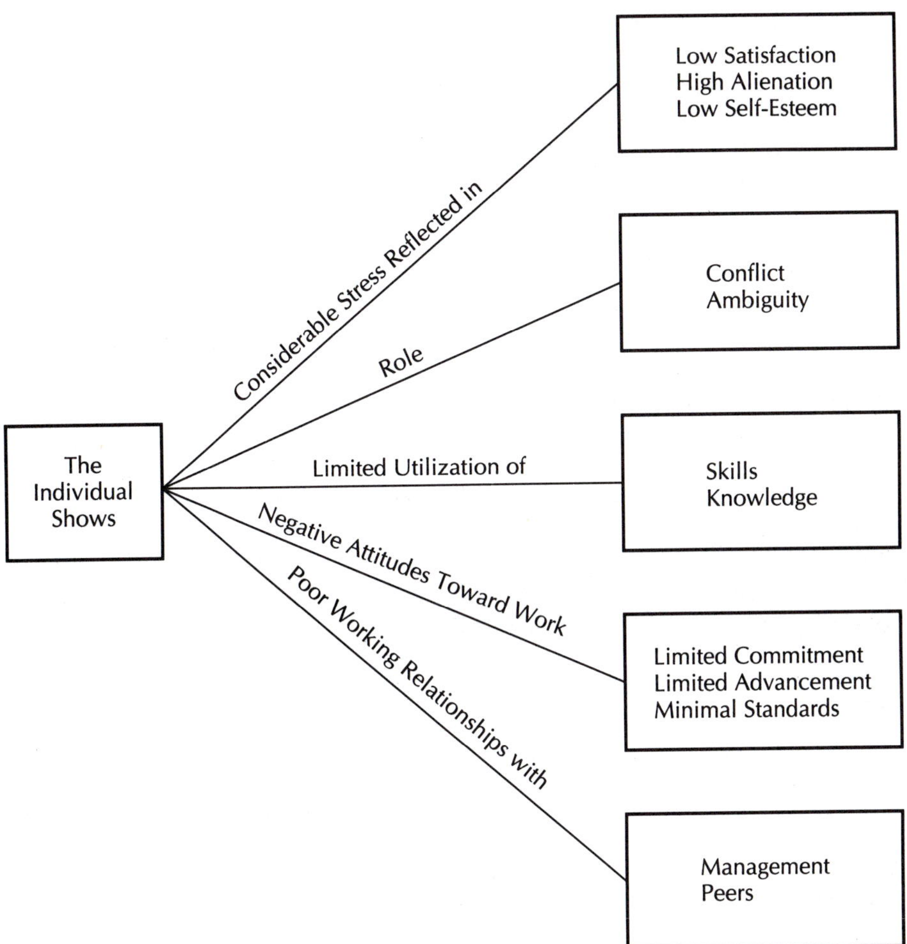

FIGURE 6.1 The Impact of Low Participation. Source Adapted from Jerrod S. Greenberg, *Comprehensive Stress Management* (Dubuque, IA: Wm C Brown, 1983).

Ascendant

One group, called *ascendant,* describes employees who are on the fast track for the sole purpose of moving through the ranks as fast as possible. Even if it takes playing musical chairs to accomplish it, the ascendant individual will strive to attain as much rank as soon as possible and then apply for every vacancy occurring in other agencies, with the goal of attaining the rank of chief (generally in a small department), then moving up to a larger agency.

The ascendant manager relates positively to the job and department, reacts favorably to feedback from superiors, and above all, is goal oriented. Such an individual generally is known as a Type A person. Work is more important than anything else, and social as well as family matters generally take second or third place. Advanced academic degrees are pursued vigorously. In order to become as eligible as possible for promotion to the top, the goal of attending the FBI's National Academy is sought.

Stress is of little consequence to the ascendant individual. In fact, stress is accepted as an important part of a managerial position—something to thrive on (Davis, 1979). However, not everyone can make it to the top—those who fall by the wayside suffer extensively from job stressors (Steinmetz and Greenridge, 1976).

Indifferent

The *indifferent* individual typifies most of the rank and file of a police organization. The attainment of rank in the organization is not something actively sought and power is viewed as an interest of others. Change proves to be threatening and the real goal is to maintain the status quo. In some instances, the indifferent officer reacts to malstress by leaving the organization either actually or symbolically. Mentally they escape by daydreaming or just putting in their time (see Table 6.6).

The indifferent officer is apt to seek protection from management decision by joining and becoming active in a police association or union. The indifferent officer also views peers as a primary support group and the department's informal organization is strengthened by their participation. Both these groups help the officer deal with organizational stressors (Davis, 1979).

Ambivalent

The last group of officers is appropriately described as ambivalent. These individuals accept the alarm stage (0 to 5 years) of police service in stride, but when the disenchantment stage (6 to 13 years) starts, they become very

TABLE 6.6 Attitudes Toward Work

Ascendant
Strong task orientation
Identifies with the department
Work is primary
Thrives on stress
Readily accepts feedback from superiors
Problems can be solved by working harder
Indifferent
Power is never sought
Identifies with the informal organization
Obtains support from work groups
Active in police unions
Accepts change with reluctance
Gravitates toward off-the-job satisfaction
Feels an inability to control own destiny
Ambivalent
Resists new rules and regulations
Avoids commitment to the department
Does not like to make decisions
Frustrated by the inability to do the job well
Eventual commitment to the department is lessened

frustrated with the job. As they begin to feel they cannot control their destiny, they become anxious about work. Things are not as clear-cut as they once were—the shadow of doubt enters the picture. Over a period of time this type of individual becomes out of step with the organization, and if they attain the level of first-line supervisor, it is usually their highest rank. This individual finds it increasingly difficult to make anything other than a routine decision, and eventually becomes less committed to the department. Anxiety about the job can create stress resulting in one or more behavioral changes.

Physiological Symptoms

A great deal of the early research on stress concentrated on physiological symptoms. One of the early researchers, Hans Selye, set forth a three-stage process of stress damage called the *general adaptation syndrome* (GAS) (Albrecht, 1979):

1. Alarm reaction
2. Resistance
3. Exhaustion

The initial stage is one of mobilization, as the body responds to a stress-inducing situation. This is followed by the resistance stage which usually begins as the first stage subsides and the body increases its reaction to the threat. The battle for survival begins. When resistance becomes ineffective, the final stage, exhaustion, takes over as adaptive energy lessens and lessens. Eventually the individual dies.

Studies of physiological reactions to stress have centered on the cardiovascular system with a special emphasis on heart attacks. This is especially applicable in law enforcement as many cardiovascular irregularities have been determined by several different state court systems to be job related and a reason for retiring on disability.

In some police departments, retirement on disability (with various medical reasons) appears to be quite easy to acquire; in others it is very difficult to obtain. In one department with more than 1,000 employees, 91 percent of the officers have received a disability retirement. This seems to make a mockery of the intent and purpose of the disability retirement system. In fact, one police executive was given a disability retirement because of a bad back, but he is an avid hunter and has no difficulty carrying deer carcasses great distances or performing house remodeling activities requiring him to lift very heavy objects.

On the other hand, another police chief was in his attic moving some items when he thought his wife had turned the lights off by accident. He soon discovered, however, that he was blind from a stroke. Even though he subsequently recovered part of his eyesight, he was unable to continue work. The city vigorously fought his efforts to receive disability retirement. Eventually the court ruled in his favor.

Stress-induced physiological symptoms vary considerably and include the items listed in Table 6.7. Note it includes such maladies as headaches, ulcers, backaches, and changes in metabolism (Quick and Quick, 1984). The link

TABLE 6.7 Specific Physiological Symptoms of Stress

Headaches	Backaches
Stroke	High blood pressure
Changes in metabolism	Cancer
Lung disease	Liver cirrhosis
Skin disease	Chest pains
Heart disease	Chronic fatigue
Diabetes	Chronic pain
Insomnia	Constipation
Trembling	Nausea
Stomach pain	Diarrhea
Irregular menstrual periods	Difficulty breathing

SOURCE: Barry L. Reece and Rhonda Brandt, *Effective Human Relations in Organizations* (3rd ed.) (Boston: Houghton Mifflin, 1987), and James C. Quick and Jonathan D. Quick, *Organizational Stress and Preventive Management* (New York: McGraw-Hill, 1984).

between any specific stressor and a particular physiological symptom is not clear, as most studies have compared the incidence of certain risk factors to specific occupations. Unfortunately, correlation does not imply causation, but in time, researchers anticipate they will be able to measure the relationship objectively (Johns, 1983; Robbins, 1986). The important aspect to the police manager is the behavioral and psychological consequences of the stressors, which we discuss next.

Behavioral Symptoms

An individual who is experiencing a high level of stress (too intense and too frequent) and is unable to find a suitable outlet may respond by exhibiting behavioral symptoms that can affect performance on the job (Quick and Quick, 1984). Research still needs to be accomplished in this area, but it seems reasonable to assume that stress, and its impact on performance, is the result of the interaction between individual factors, the task being performed, and the working environment (Matteson and Ivancevich, 1987).

The relationship between stress and performance is depicted in Figure 6.2. In this inverted-U relationship it can readily be seen that as we move from a low to a moderate level of stress, productivity increases. At the very low level of stress, employees may not be challenged to perform effectively. As stress increases, most employees are stimulated to perform better and more rapidly. An optimal level of stress exists for each situation and for each individual. Poor performance occurs when either excessive stress causes individuals to be constrained to the extent of agitation or when demands are unrealistic (Hellriegel, Slocum, and Woodman, 1983).

Moderate levels of stress can have a negative influence on employee performance if the continuing and constant presence of stress reduces the ability to deal with it constructively. This is especially true of officers assigned to vice or narcotics, so police administrators have learned to rotate personnel assigned to such units after two or three years.

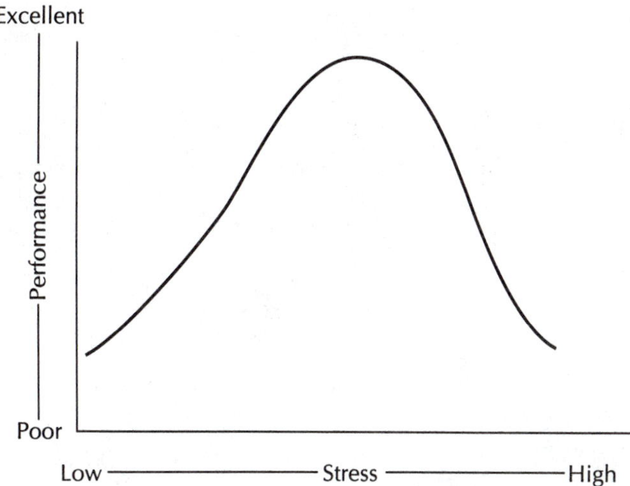

FIGURE 6.2 The Relationship Between Stress and Performance. Source Adapted from Stephen P. Robbins, *Organizational Behavior* (3rd ed.) (Englewood Cliffs, NJ: Prentice-Hall, 1986), and Donald Hellriegel, John W. Slocum, and Richard W. Woodman, *Organizational Behavior* (St. Paul, MN: West, 1983).

Behavioral symptoms related to rising levels of stress include an increased use of tobacco products, alcohol abuse, drug abuse, appetite disorders, and (possibly) involvement in accidents.

The excessive consumption of alcohol or the use of other drugs can have severe consequences for both the individual and the organization. Alcohol abuse has always been recognized as a problem. One expert estimated that 25 percent of police officers were dependent on alcohol (Kroes, 1976). Another study of the problem found that 67 percent of the officers admitted to drinking on the job (Van Raalte, 1979). In a study of 500 officers in 21 police departments, researchers concluded that police officers used alcohol as a socially acceptable coping technique in an effort to deal with stress (Violanti, Marshall, and Howe, 1985).

Managers can look for the early signs of poor work performance by monitoring the following employee behaviors (More and Unsinger, 1987):

1. Excessive absenteeism
2. Unreported absences
3. Arriving late and leaving early
4. Poor quality of work
5. Erratic work performance
6. Failure to meet work standards
7. Friction with co-workers
8. Increased accident rates

Not all these behaviors mean an officer is under malstress, but they are indications that stress should be considered (Davis, 1979). On the positive side,

Family Stress It is management's responsibility to recognize that the stress of police work is not unique to the officer but extends to the entire family. *(©Robert L. Snow)*

a manager should monitor employee performance in an effort to identify behavioral indicators shown to be related to excellent performance.

These indicators include work habits reflecting a high energy level, alertness, strong motivation, calmness under pressure, thorough problem analysis, sound decision-making, and a positive attitude toward work (Matteson and Ivancevich, 1987).

Psychological Symptoms

Dissatisfaction with one's job is the most obvious psychological manifestation of malstress (bad stress). Psychological reactions to stress generally are emotion-laden and involve thought processes rather than some overt behavior (Johns, 1983). Psychologically based stress is usually characterized by increased tension, irritability, anxiety, procrastinating, or becoming bored with the job (Robbins, 1986).

Psychologically, an officer usually reacts to stress by turning to defense mechanisms in an attempt to reduce the anxiety associated with malstress. The officer or manager never deals directly with the malstress involved, and in some instances might not even be aware of the actual process.

Psychologically based malstress can result in numerous problems including marital discord and family conflict, sleep disturbances, sexual dysfunction, depression, and job burnout (Quick and Quick, 1984).

A good marriage can serve to sustain a police officer when dealing with job-related stress and can contribute to a successful police career. In this respect, spouses of law enforcement officers are no different than those of individuals in other occupational areas. Some relationships end in divorce, but evidence shows that police divorce rates are lower than originally believed (Terry, 1983).

When departmental policy encourages sound family relationships, extra support can be provided by training programs for spouses. In such training, an emphasis is placed on teaching coping techniques, improving communications, and working out problems (More and Unsinger, 1987).

Organizational stress can, in some instances, lead to *sleep disturbances*. Many officers suffer from insomnia caused by a very common stressor—shift work. Furthermore, worries about being promoted, conflict with a fellow employee, or testifying in court are all typical work-related problems in law enforcement that can, in some instances, lead to debilitating sleep disturbances. Excessive use of caffeine and/or alcohol can disrupt sleep patterns. When sleep deprivation becomes chronic, it can have a negative impact on an individual's mood, which in turn can affect job performance (Quick and Quick, 1984).

Stress Reduction

Employees and managers of police organizations are not only the most important components of the agencies, but consume the largest portion of an agency's budget. Their physical and mental well-being contribute directly to the effectiveness of the organization. With the awareness of eustress and malstress and their potential impact on the individual as well as the organization, increased consideration is being given to developing programs fostering greater production with less stress and more enthusiasm for work (Albrecht, 1979).

Individual Response to Stress

Techniques have been developed to allow an individual to cope with stress effectively. The methods include exercise, planning ahead, proper nutrition, and mental relaxation. In many instances, stress begins to be meaningful to individuals only when things seem to be out of control. Many of us work from day to day and give little consideration to planning ahead. Part of this is the failure not only to consider our life goals realistically, but also to contemplate how to deal with job demands, a changing society, and all the other pressures we feel when encountering issues and preventing a crisis situation (Reece and Brandt, 1987).

TAKE CHARGE OF YOUR LIFE One measure to take in solving the malstress problem is to review job expectations realistically, comparing them to what is currently happening in the organization. It is entirely possible some behavior can be identified and changed. In other instances, it might become necessary to accept the reality of the working environment and quit fighting the organization.

The thing to do is to take charge of your own life—do not wait for the organization to solve problems you can solve yourself. As a manager, perhaps exposure to a stressor can be reduced by delegating part of the work load to qualified subordinates. Or possibly a better time-management plan can be devised. For example, at the beginning of the day, a manager can prepare a schedule and follow it as closely as possible (Johns, 1983). If we really take control of our own lives, work can become enjoyable and rewarding. It is important not to rely on additive sustenances as a behavioral response to malstress (Reece and Brandt, 1987).

RELAXATION Job-related stressors are inevitable. Deadlines occur, people do not get along, someone will have to be disciplined—there are any number of stressful events. Relaxation techniques provide a means for reducing or preventing stress buildup. When we begin to feel tense or anxious, it should be a signal to employ some type of stress reliever as soon as the opportunity becomes available.

Most experts agree that relaxation techniques can play a key role in the control and reduction of stress (Matteson and Ivancevich, 1982). In the early 1970s Herbert Benson and his colleagues developed the relaxation response. Utilization of one of the numerous relaxation techniques will generally decrease the heart rate, the metabolic rate, and the respiratory rate. Although blood pressure may remain the same initially, over a period of time it will be lowered (Quick and Quick, 1984).

After studying the various techniques eliciting the relaxation response, four common elements were found (Benson, 1975):

1. It is necessary to select a place free of distraction, noise, and interruptions, all of which can inhibit placing the relaxation response into operation.
2. Select a mental device that helps focus thoughts and prevents the mind from wandering. The mental device can be as simple as using the number *one* (monosyllabic and emotion free). Or it can be the use of another word or phrase. Some people fix their gaze on an object or concentrate on the rhythm of breathing (Quick and Quick, 1984).
3. Retain a passive attitude. If something distracts you, it is essential to refocus on the mental device being used.
4. While some find it helpful to assume the classical lotus position, it is not an essential part of the process. To be comfortable and relaxed the sitting position is adequate. Lying down is not recommended because you could easily fall asleep.

In addition to these four elements, if the relaxation response is to work, it is essential to heed the following guidelines (Benson, 1975):

1. Remain in a comfortable position. Sit quietly and refrain from moving or fidgeting.
2. Prevent visual distractions by closing eyes.
3. Relax all muscles by starting at the feet and working upward. With practice, total relaxation can be accomplished in one minute or less.
4. Breathe through your nose and concentrate on the breathing activity. When exhaling, repeat the mental device we discussed.

5. Engage in this activity for 10 to 20 minutes once or twice a day. Upon completion, sit quietly for a few minutes before opening your eyes; stay in the same position with eyes open for a few minutes.
6. Do not be anxious about achieving a deep relaxation. Permit relaxation to occur at its own pace.

A real advantage of the Benson relaxation response is that it does not require any formal training. The evidence clearly supports the innumerable benefits from its utilization which have a practical and realistic application to the workplace (Quick and Quick, 1984).

A number of relaxation techniques are listed in Table 6.8 ranging from muscular relaxation to biofeedback. All these techniques may be used by police managers in dealing with their own stress or as part of an organizational effort to reduce and control malstress (Matteson and Ivancevich, 1982).

EXERCISE If you are committed to reducing stress in your life, consider participating in an exercise program. It is not only good for physical well-being but for peace of mind as well. It is increasingly common for law enforcement agencies to support physical conditioning programs including such activities as 10 km runs, the police olympics, and the "Pig Bowl" (football).

In addition, numerous agencies have opened weight rooms and provide officers with exercise equipment including bicycles and tread machines. All this has been in response to an increasing awareness of the value of vigorous exercise, which (Dintiman and Greenberg, 1980)

1. Improves the performance of the lungs and the circulatory system
2. Delays degeneration of the body
3. Reduces the pulse rate
4. Tones muscles
5. Improves posture
6. Increases endurance
7. Burns calories
8. Strengthens the heart muscles
9. Decreases low density lipoproteins (harmful cholesterol)

Aerobic exercises performed on a regular basis (four or more times per week) and for a reasonable period of time (30 minutes to an hour) will prove

TABLE 6.8 Mental Relaxation

Relaxation response
Meditation
Breathing
Muscular relaxation
Progressive muscle relaxation
Imagery
Hypnosis
Centering
Prayer
Biofeedback

TABLE 6.9 Energy Expenditure In Various Activities (150-Pound Person)

Activity	Gross Energy Cost—Calories per Hour
A. Rest and Light Activity	50–200
Lying down or sleeping	80
Sitting	100
Driving an automobile	120
Standing	140
Domestic work	180
B. Moderate Activity	200–350
Bicycling (5½ mph)	210
Walking(2½ mph)	210
Gardening	220
Canoeing (2½ mph)	230
Golf	250
Lawn mowing (power mower)	250
Bowling	270
Lawn mowing (hand mower)	270
Fencing	300
Rowboating (2½ mph)	300
Swimming (¼ mph)	300
Walking (3¾ mph)	300
Badminton	350
Horseback riding (trotting)	350
Square dancing	350
Volleyball	350
Roller skating	350
C. Vigorous Activity	over 350
Table tennis	360
Ditch digging (hand shovel)	400
Ice skating (10 mph)	400
Wood chopping or sawing	400
Tennis	420
Water skiing	480
Hill climbing (100 ft. per hr.)	490
Skiing (10 mph)	600
Squash and handball	600
Cycling (13 mph)	660
Scull rowing (race)	840
Running (10 mph)	900

SOURCE: President's Council on Physical Fitness and Sports, *Exercise and Weight Control* (Washington, DC: President's Council on Physical Fitness and Sports, 1976).

to be personally beneficial. Table 6.9 lists the calories expended per hour for various activities from sleeping to running. It can readily be seen that vigorous activities provide the greatest benefit. For example, "If you need to lose weight, you'd be advised to jog; but if flexibility is your concern you'd be better off doing calisthenics, playing handball or squash" (Greenberg, 1983).

Numerous professional organizations have cautioned that before starting an exercise program a medical evaluation is in order. In police departments requiring an annual physical examination, the physician should screen each officer before allowing him or her to engage in vigorous exercising.

Aerobics, in the view of some, is almost synonymous with jogging, but experts encourage individuals to select an exercise they enjoy. In fact an exercise classified as moderate will suffice if it is done over a reasonable period of time. Other aerobic exercises include pedaling a stationary bike, jumping rope, running in place, swimming, or playing organized sports such as basketball, water polo, tennis, or racquetball (Bullard, 1980).

The goal of aerobics is to replace oxygen during exercising. Lifting weights, for example, is an excellent way to build up skeletal muscles, but it has limited effect on improving endurance or cardiovascular conditioning (Bullard, 1980). Aerobics is an integral and essential part of a stress reduction program. Whatever exercise is selected, it must be vigorous enough to raise the heart rate to approximately 80 percent of what has been established as the maximum heart rate. This is easily calculated by subtracting your age from 220 and multiplying that number by 0.8. For example, the target heart rate for someone 25 years of age would be 156 (80 percent of the maximum 195). During workouts, the heartbeat should be within 10 beats of that number (Bullard, 1980).

An exercise program should be designed to ensure what is described as *functional fitness.* It consists of the following: cardiorespiratory endurance, muscular strength, body composition, and muscular flexibility. Focus 6.1 explains the concept of functional fitness in detail.

Employee Assistance Programs

The *employee assistance program* (EAP) is new to law enforcement, but it has been a part of many businesses for more than 40 years. Initially these programs concentrated on alcoholism, but in the 1970s consideration widened to emotional and stress-related problems. Today some EAPs offer a broad range of services to help employees deal with anxiety, depression, death in the family, and more recently, retirement (Matteson and Ivancevich, 1987).

An increasing number of psychological services have been offered through the auspices of EAPs. A comprehensive program can address many problems (see Table 6.10).

When planning for the implementation of an EAP in a law enforcement agency, a manager should first determine the current conditions in the department. Such a survey should include an analysis of the organization, a detailed study of the need for such a program, and a survey of community resources (Matteson and Ivancevich, 1987).

An effective EAP can be of benefit not only to the organization but also to the individual. As organizations become increasingly concerned about the quality of working life it is anticipated that EAPs will play a very important part in reducing organizational stress and helping officers deal with malstress. Today there is a critical need for law enforcement agencies to provide counseling, rehabilitative, and health promotion services for all personnel (Smithers, 1988).

PEER COUNSELING Peer counseling is relatively new to law enforcement; the first such program was offered by the Boston Police Department and directed

TABLE 6.10 Problems That Can Be Addressed by an Employee Assistance Program

Alcoholism	Grief
Substance abuse	Smoking
Job stress	Nutrition
Job burnout	Exercise
Anxiety	Weight control
Depression	Divorce
Parent-child conflict	Separation
Single parenting	Police shootings

SOURCE: John G. Stratton, "Employee Assistance Programs: A Profitable Approach for Employees and Organizations," in Harry W. More and Peter C. Unsinger (Eds.), *Police Managerial Use of Psychology and Psychologists* (Springfield, IL: Charles C Thomas, 1987).

by two recovering alcoholics (Donovan, 1985). The concept was picked up by other departments and has been successful because of the general hesitancy of police officers to seek professional assistance. A fellow officer is cut from the same cloth and because he or she shares common experiences and special training can be highly successful when counseling others (Graf, 1986).

A police psychologist (in those departments where one is available) can train peer counselors and serve as a consultant and referral source (Stratton, 1987). Peer-counseling groups in law enforcement have been successful in dealing with alcoholism, widows of slain officers, police shootings, retirement issues, death in the family, terminal illness, and officers injured on duty. (Graf, 1986; Stratton, 1987).

Summary

Stress is unique not only to the situation, but to the individual. Some handle stress very well; others have a great deal of difficulty coping with its effects. Outlook on life is important. A specific stressor, such as a poorly defined policy, can either be viewed as greatly significant or of little importance. If viewed positively, a negative stressor can be converted into eustress (positive stress).

Stress is not unique to law enforcement, but there are certain stressful events and situations peculiar to police agencies—danger, boredom, lack of public support, unfavorable court decisions, and unfair administrative policies.

An assessment tool used for a number of years is the Holmes-Rahe life-stress inventory. It provides a rough measure of the degree of adjustment required of an individual over a specified period of time and points are associated with each life event (e.g., death of a spouse, 100 points). There is also a law enforcement critical life events scale consisting of 144 events

FOCUS 6.1

Functional Fitness

Physical fitness has been defined in numerous ways over the years. In some cases, the concept was restricted to athletic ability, speed, or coordination. In other cases, physical fitness was embodied in a heavily muscled individual or a fast runner. None of these definitions are an accurate explanation of fitness.

Physical fitness is the functional fitness or the ability of the body to function efficiently. Functional fitness consists of four major areas, equally balanced in an individual's personal fitness program. These four areas relate directly to health and well-being, and not to athletics or skill. Functional fitness consists of the following:

1. *Cardiorespiratory Endurance.* This relates directly to the efficiency of the heart-lung system and its ability to deliver oxygen to the muscles when performing work.

Attaining a reasonable level of cardiorespiratory endurance has been proven to enhance the efficiency of the total individual. Increased respiratory endurance allows an individual to sustain work for a longer period of time. In law enforcement, such work can entail chasing or wrestling felons, working long and varied hours, and a myriad of other functions requiring physical exertion.

Medical research also shows that an efficient cardiorespiratory system prevents certain degenerative diseases (e.g., stroke and heart disease). Regular aerobic exercise like swimming, cycling, jumping rope, jogging, and circuit weight training can reduce body fat, make positive changes in blood lipid levels (i.e., cholesterol and triglycerides), and can reduce the degenerative effects of stress.

2. *Muscular strength.* Functional muscular strength relates to the ability of the muscles to contract efficiently. There are two types of muscular strength: dynamic strength and absolute strength. Dynamic strength is muscular endurance—the ability to perform repetitive muscle contractions without undue fatigue as in push-ups, sit-ups, or any activity necessitating the dynamic use of one's muscles for an extended period of time (30 seconds or 3 minutes).

Absolute strength is the force an individual can generate with one single contraction of a muscle like that required to bench press 300 pounds, one time.

Dynamic strength most closely represents functional fitness because most physical activities require an individual to contract muscles more than once to perform a task.

Muscular strength is also related to health and disability prevention. Since the abdominal muscles support the torso, an individual with weak abdominal muscles is more susceptible to lower back injury. Supporting the spine with good abdominal muscle tone is, therefore, very important to prevent injury to the lower back.

3. *Body composition.* The human body consists of two types of mass: lean body mass and fat. Lean body mass consists of muscle, bone, organ, and fluids, such as blood. The remainder of the body is composed of fat. To be functionally fit and healthy, it is imperative the percentage of fat in the body be kept to a minimum. Males should keep their percentage body fat between 3 percent and 19 percent, and females between 13 percent and 22 percent.

Statistically, an individual increases the risk of heart disease and stroke if the percentage of body fat is above this range. If an individual is below the low percentage rate, he or she is on the brink of starvation and is metabolizing muscle mass to stay alive.

Body weight in relation to height, a standard improperly used for years, bears no importance when referring to functional fitness. For example, an individual weighing 250 pounds can be as fit as an individual weighing 150 pounds. If both are 90 percent lean body mass and 10 percent fat, the 250-pound person has the same level of efficiency as the lighter individual.

4. *Muscular flexibility.* A functionally fit individual must also have good muscular flexibility and range of movement. A shortened range of movement will interfere with daily tasks and cut an individual's efficiency in performing many of life's functions.

Medical research has also indicated a shortened range of motion in the lower back directly related to lower back pain and the susceptibility of serious lower back injury. The lack of flexibility in the lower back compounds the postural deviations caused by lack of abdominal strength and results in a high risk of structural damage to that area. Since flexibility exercises do not cause visible changes in the body, like running or weight lifting do, it is quite often deleted from an individual's personal fitness program, but its importance should not be overlooked.

To be healthy and efficient, an individual must engage in a fitness program. This program should be enjoyable and suitable to the needs of that person. When engaging in a fitness program, a person should find something recreational and vigorous.

The well-rounded fitness program includes following the proper dietary guidelines and addressing all four components of functional fitness. This balance will provide for increased health and the ability to perform daily tasks more efficiently.

SOURCE. Office of Training, U.S. Secret Service, "Functional Fitness," *Service Star,* 1983, Vol. 4, p. 11. Adapted with permission.

---

experienced by police officers. It has not been extensively tested, but can be used by a police manager to deal with stressful events.

One expert has found there are several transitory stages affecting stress perception: alarm, disenchantment, personalization, and introspection. These stages can be used as bench marks for the initiation of stress reduction programs.

Stressors in law enforcement vary, but generally can be categorized as follows: job characteristics, organizational characteristics, external factors, personal variables, group characteristics, and resource management.

Organizational stress and the response to it will vary from individual to individual, but is usually described as being behavioral, psychological, or physiological. Studies of physiological symptoms have centered on the cardiovascular system, but stress-induced symptoms such as headaches, chronic fatigue, stomach pain, backaches, and chest pains are extensive.

Police managers usually witness behavioral symptoms because of their impact on job performance. Symptoms related to rising levels of stress include an increased use of tobacco products, alcohol abuse, drug abuse, appetite disorders, and accidents. Managers looking for the early signs of poor work

CASE STUDY

Captain James Stevens

Capt. James Stevens supervises the 12th station house in a large metropolitan police department. There are 221 sworn officers assigned to the station, who are divided into three shifts, with the largest number assigned to the swing shift. Detectives are centralized and work out of headquarters—consequently Captain Stevens's primary concern is administering the station house in such a way that called-for services are answered rapidly. The area patrolled is primarily commercial with some residential sections. The crime rate is very high (when compared to similar sized cities), an average of 85 felonies to be investigated annually per officer. Besides this crime, there are a large number of misdemeanors.

Even with computerized printouts, a state-of-the-art dispatching system, and a large number of civilian support personnel, the overall workload is excessive. Priority calls become backed up, and the paperwork is overwhelming, to where it seems everyone is drowning in reams of paper circumscribed by red tape.

Capt. Stevens has been requesting additional personnel for the last five years. Even though the requests have been thoroughly justified, additional officers have never been assigned. The city just does not have the resources to support the police department. The city manager has made the decision to treat all departments in the city alike, even though the police department demonstrates a greater need than any other city department. There are no new funds and the foreseeable future is quite bleak economically. Status quo seems to be the byword of the day.

During the last 18 months, morale has dipped considerably. Many of the officers have always complained, but now it seems to be pervasive. Seldom does one hear truly positive statements. In the past, the locker room was a place for jokes and free interchange between officers, but for the most part it is now quiet and subdued. The primary focus of discussion usually revolves around the inability to keep up with the demands of the job.

The captain has noticed a number of officers are late in attending role call, sick leave is being used more frequently, and there is a tremendous increase in what can only be termed sloppy police work. First-line supervisors and watch commanders are spending a great deal of time dealing with the line officers' increasingly poor performance. All these problems seem to be mushrooming.

After consulting with all the managers under his command and with other key officers including staff personnel in headquarters, Capt. Stevens finds his observations unanimous and knows something has to be done to improve working conditions and reduce the stress created by the job.

The desirable action plan is to conduct a comprehensive survey in order to determine the current conditions in the department and the community resources. Capt. Stevens has been advised it will take 18 months to complete the survey. With this in mind, the captain decided to appear at each roll call to discuss the problem. If you were Capt. Stevens what would you do next? If malstress is the real problem, what should be done while the survey is being conducted?

performance should monitor the following employee behaviors: excessive absenteeism, poor quality of work, erratic work performance, failure to meet work standards, friction with co-workers, and any other type of behavior that seems unusual.

Psychologically an officer usually reacts to malstress (bad or negative stress) by turning to defense mechanisms in an effort to reduce the anxiety associated with the offending stress. This usually means an officer will react psychologically by becoming tense, irritated, anxious, and even bored with the job. In turn when such behavior continues over an extended period of time it results in marital discord, family conflict, sleep disturbances, sexual dysfunction, depression, and job burnout.

With the awareness of eustress and malstress and their potential impact on the individual and the organization, increasing consideration is being given to developing programs fostering greater production with less stress and more enthusiasm for work.

Key Concepts

Stressors
Eustress
Organizational stress
Life-stress inventory
Critical life events scale
Alarm stage
Disenchantment stage
Personalization stage
Introspection stage
Malstress
Role conflict
Role ambiguity
Role pressures
Ascendant
Indifferent
Ambivalent
General adaptation syndrome
Behavioral symptoms
Psychological symptoms
Physiological symptoms
Stress reduction
Employee assistance programs (EAPs)

Discussion Topics and Questions

1. Compare and contrast eustress and malstress.
2. What are some of the consequences of organizational stress?
3. What can a manager do to reduce the organizational stress felt by women police officers?
4. As a supervisory manager, what types of stress might occur when managing officers who have been on the force for 6 to 13 years?
5. What are some of the behavioral symptoms a manager should look for that might indicate the presence of malstress?
6. What are some of the things a police manager can do to reduce personal stress?
7. How does role conflict and ambiguity create stress?
8. Describe the characteristics of an ambivalent officer.
9. Describe stress-induced physiological symptoms.
10. What problems should an employee assistance program address?

References

Albrecht, Karl. 1979. *Stress and the Manager.* Englewood Cliffs, NJ: Prentice-Hall.

Benson, H. 1975. *The Relaxation Response.* New York: Avon Books.

Brief, A. P., R. S. Schuler, and M. Van Sell. 1981. *Managing Job Stress.* Boston: Little, Brown.

Bullard, Peter D. 1980. *Coping with Stress: A Psychological Survival Manual.* Portland, OR: ProSeminar Press.

Bureau of the Census. 1987. *Statistical Abstracts of the United States, 1988* (108th ed.). Washington, DC: U.S. Government Printing Office.

Caplan, R. D., and K. W. Jones. 1975. "Effects of Work Load, Role Ambiguity, and Type A Personality on Anxiety, Depression, and Heart Rate," *Journal of Applied Psychology,* 60.

Carson, Stephen L. 1987. "Post Shooting Stress Reaction," *The Police Chief,* 49 (10).

Cherry, L. 1978. "On the Real Benefits of Eustress," *Psychology Today,* March.

Davis, Richard H. (Ed.). 1979. *Stress and the Organization.* Los Angeles: University of Southern California Press.

Dintiman, George B., and Jerrold S. Greenberg. 1980. *Health through Discovery.* Reading, MA: Addison.

Donovan, Edward. 1985. "The Boston Police Stress Program," *The Police Chief,* February.

Ellison, Katherine, and John L. Genz. 1983. *Stress and the Police Officer.* Springfield, IL: Charles C Thomas.

Fraser, T. M. 1983. *Human Stress, Work, and Job Satisfaction.* Geneva, Switzerland: International Labour Organization.

Fyfe, James J. 1981. *Readings on Police Use of Deadly Force.* Washington, DC: Police Foundation Press.

Graf, Francis A. 1986. "Police Stress and Social Support," *Journal of Police Science and Administration,* 14 (3).

Greenberg, Jerrold S. 1983. *Comprehensive Stress Management.* Dubuque, IA: Wm. C. Brown.

Griffin, Ricky W., and Gregory Moorhead. 1986. *Organizational Behavior.* Boston: Houghton Mifflin.

Hellriegel, Don, John W. Slocum, Jr., and Richard W. Woodman. 1983. *Organizational Behavior* (3rd ed.). St. Paul, MN: West.

Higgins, James D. 1982. *Human Relations.* New York: Random House.

Johns, Gary. 1983. *Organizational Behavior—Understanding Life at Work.* Glenview, IL: Scott, Foresman.

Kelling, George L. and Mark H. Moore. 1988. *The Evolving Strategy of Policing.* Washington, DC: National Institute of Justice.

Kirkpatrick, Thomas, D. 1987. *Supervision.* Boston: Kent.

Kroes, W. 1976. *Society's Victim: The Police Man; An Analysis of Job Stress in Policing.* Springfield, IL: Charles C Thomas.

Kroes, W. H., Joseph Hurrell, and Bruce Margolis. 1974. "Job Stress in Police Administrators," *Journal of Police Science and Administration,* 11 (1).

Kroes, W. H., Joseph Hurrell, and Bruce Margolis. 1974. "Job Stress in Policemen," *Journal of Police Science and Administration,* 11 (4).

Leonard, V. A., and Harry W. More. 1987. *Police Organization and Management* (7th ed.). Mineola, NY: Foundation Press.

Margolis, B. L., W. H. Kroes, and R. P. Quinn. 1974. "Job Stress: An Unlisted Occupational Hazard," *Journal of Occupational Medicine,* 16.

Matteson, Michael, and John M. Ivancevich. 1987. *Controlling Work Stress.* San Francisco: Jossey-Bass.

Matteson, Michael T., and John M. Ivancevich. 1982. *Managing Job Stress and Health.* New York: Free Press.

Matula, Kenneth J. 1982. *A Balance of Force.* Gaithersburg, MD: International Association of Chiefs of Police.

More, Harry W. 1985. *Critical Issues in Law Enforcement* (4th ed.). Cincinnati: Anderson.

More, Harry W., and O. R. Shipley. 1987. *Police Policy Manual—Personnel.* Springfield, IL: Charles C Thomas.

More, Harry W., and Peter C. Unsinger. 1987. *Police Managerial Use of Psychology and Psychologists.* Springfield, IL: Charles C Thomas.

National Institute of Law Enforcement and Criminal Justice. 1979. *Use of Deadly Force by Police Officers.* Washington, DC: U.S. Government Printing Office.

Organ, Dennis W., andW. Clay Hamner. 1982. *Organizational Behavior: An Applied Psychological Approach.* Plano, TX: Business Publications.

President's Council on Physical Fitness and Sports. 1976. *Exercise and Weight Control.* Washington, DC: President's Council on Physical Fitness and Sports.

Pelletier, Kenneth R. 1984. *Healthy People in Unhealthy Places.* New York: Delacorte Press.

Pendergrass, Virginia E., and Nancy M. Ostrove. 1984. *Survey of Stress in Women in Policing.* Unpublished paper presented at the American Psychological Association.

Police Foundation. 1981. *Survey of Police Operational and Administrative Practices—1981.* Washington, DC: Police Executive Research Forum.

Quick, James C., and Jonathan D. Quick. 1984. *Organizational Stress and Preventive Management.* New York: McGraw-Hill.

Quick, Thomas L. 1980. *Understanding People at Work.* New York: Executive Enterprises.

Reece, Barry L., and Rhonda Brandt. 1987. *Effective Human Relations in Organizations* (3rd ed.). Boston: Houghton Mifflin.

Robbins, Stephen P. 1986. *Organizational Behavior—Concepts, Controversies, and Application.* Englewood Cliffs, NJ: Prentice-Hall.

Ruch, L. O., and T. H. Holmes. 1971. "Scaling of Life Change: Comparison of Direct and Indirect Methods," *Journal of Psychosomatic Research,* 15.

Rue, Leslie, and Lloyd L. Byars. 1986. *Management Theory and Practice* (4th ed.). Homewood, IL: Richard D. Irwin.

Sarason, I. G. 1982. *The Revised Life Experience Survey.* Unpublished paper.

Schermerhorn, John R., James G. Hunt, and Richard N. Osborn. 1988. *Managing Organizational Behavior* (3rd ed.). New York: Wiley.

Selye, Hans. 1974. *Stress Without Distress.* New York: New American Library.

Sewell, James D. 1981. "Police Stress," *FBI Law Enforcement Bulletin,* 50 (7).

Sewell, James D. 1983. "The Development of a Critical Life Events Scale for Law Enforcement," *Journal of Police Science and Administration,* 11 (1).

Smithers, Robert D. 1988. *The Psychology of Work and Human Performance.* New York: Harper & Row.

Steinmetz, Lawrence, and Charles D. Greenridge. 1976. "Realities That Shape Managerial Style: Participative Philosophy Won't Always Work." In Lawrence Steinmetz and Charles D. Greenridge, (Eds.), *Participative Management: Concepts, Theory and Implementation,* Atlanta: Georgia State University.

Stratton, John G. 1987. "Employee Assistance Programs: A Profitable Approach for Employees and Organizations." In Harry W. More and Peter C. Unsinger (Eds.), *Police Managerial Use of Psychology and Psychologists.* Springfield, IL: Charles C Thomas.

Terry, W. C. 1983. "Police Stress: The Empirical Evidence," *Journal of Police Science and Administration,* 9 (1).

U.S. Secret Service, Office of Training. 1983. "Functional Fitness," *Service Star,* 4 (11).

Van Raalte, R. C. 1979. "Alcohol as a Problem Among Officers," *The Police Chief,* 44.

VIOLANTI, JOHN M., and JAMES R. MARSHALL. 1983. "The Police Stress Process," *Journal of Police Science and Administration,* 11 (4).

VIOLANTI, JOHN M., JAMES R. MARSHALL, and BARBARA HOWE. 1985. "Stress, Coping, and Alcohol Use: The Police Connection," *Journal of Police Science and Administration,* 13 (2).

WEXLER, JUDIE W., and DEANA D. LOGAN. 1983. "Sources of Stress Among Women Police Officers," *Journal of Police Science and Administration,* 11 (1).

WILSON, MARLENE. 1981. *Survival Skills for Managers.* Boulder, CO: Johnson.

For Further Reading

ELLISON, KATHERINE W., and JOHN L. GENZ. 1983. *Stress and the Police Officer.* Springfield, IL: Charles C Thomas.

A definitive work that covers a wide range of topics from the nature of stress to techniques for individual stress management. Of special interest is the chapter on stress in policing that reviews the research conducted on police stress.

MATTESON, MICHAEL T., and JOHN M. IVANCEVICH. 1987. *Controlling Work Stress—Effective Human Resource and Management Strategies.* San Francisco: Jossey-Bass.

Of special interest to police managers is the part of the book discussing guidelines for assessing the extent to which stress is a problem in an organization. Suggests ways of improving relationships between the individual and the organization and offers techniques for dealing with dysfunctional stress.

QUICK, JAMES C. and JONATHAN D. QUICK. 1984. *Organizational Stress and Preventive Management.* New York: McGraw-Hill.

Emphasizes the diagnosis of stress and the philosophy and practice of preventive management. It is a blend of organizational, medical, and psychological views of stress. Police managers will find the chapter on individual methods for managing work and personal demands of special interest.

SMITHERS, ROBERT D. 1988. *The Psychology of Work and Human Performance.* New York: Harper & Row.

Presents an excellent discussion of addictive behavior in the workplace with a special emphasis on alcoholism, drug abuse, and gambling. There is also a section on how to evaluate employee assistance programs (EAPs).

CHAPTER 7

Groups and the Group Process: Human Dynamics at Work

LEARNING OBJECTIVES

1. Analyze the behavior of human beings as social animals.
2. Discuss groups and group dynamics.
3. Differentiate between formal groups and informal groups.
4. Identify reasons why people become members of informal as well as formal groups.
5. Compare and contrast leadership in formal and informal work groups.
6. Define *culture* as it applies to groups, subgroups, and cliques in complex criminal justice organizations.
7. Describe the concept of group culture and the mechanisms used to instill self-control.
8. Identify the elements of the interactionist perspective.
9. Define *socialization* and trace the steps in the socialization process.
10. Compare and contrast the categories currently used to classify groups.
11. List and explain the structural components that make a social group a distinct entity.
12. Explain the influence of structural variables on individual and/or group performance.
13. Assess the role of the police administrator in managing group dynamics.
14. Discuss managerial strategies designed to minimize group conflict and maximize individual or group performance.
15. Evaluate the impact of group dynamics on organizational productivity.

Many police administrators have been reluctant to accept the group-dynamics approach to management and have gone to great lengths to maintain the illusion that an organization is little more than an aggregate of individuals performing a common function. There are several reasons why they prefer to deal with their subordinates in these individualistic terms:

INTRODUCTORY CASE

Chief Maynard K. Bear

Maynard Bear is the chief of police in a large southern city. He was just appointed to the position by the mayor. The chief, a college-educated pragmatist who worked his way up through the ranks, has been ordered by the mayor to streamline the bulky, top-heavy bureaucracy in an effort to make the police department more efficient, effective, and productive. While the new chief has good intentions, he is having a difficult time overcoming institutional inertia.

After a very careful analysis of the situation, the chief has concluded that his managerial options are limited by legal, organizational, and cultural constraints beyond his immediate control. In a memorandum to the mayor, Chief Bear cites the following limitations:

1. Autonomous civil service commission charged with recruiting, screening, ranking and de facto appointment (based on a rank order) of all entry-level police personnel.
2. Civil service commission control of promotions via compilation of an eligibility list and a contractual requirement for selection based on rank order.
3. Civil service status for all classified positions (including detective) up to the rank of division chief.
4. Permanent duty assignment based on seniority and by bid.
5. Rigid chain of command with an emphasis on control through executive decision-making.
6. Traditional limitations on the delegation of authority.
7. Union opposition to major changes in police operations.
8. Little or no support for reform from members of the city council.
9. Anticipated budget shortfall for the next several years.

The chief points out that he has some flexibility in allocating financial resources and the temporary reassignment of police personnel.

While the mayor is sympathetic, he still wants the department to become more efficient, effective, and responsive to the community.

This conflict is being brought to a head by a series of obviously related and particularly grotesque homicides that are causing panic in the city. After the traditional methods and procedures failed to produce results, the city's leading newspaper decried what it called "bureaucratic bungling" and demanded immediate "action" by the police department. The chief is convinced that inappropriate personnel assignments, organizational rigidity, bureaucratic infighting, and a battle over turf are hindering the investigation. He feels his job is on the line.

Although the constraints he identified are real, Chief Bear does have options. What are they? What would someone with a knowledge of groups and group dynamics do in this particular situation?

1. They become accustomed by training and through experience to handle problems on a one-to-one basis. As a result, they are simply not conditioned to look for systemic variables or interaction patterns that might have contributed to a problem.
2. The individualistic approach to resolving personnel problems is quicker and easier than identifying and analyzing systemic and/or group factors. Learning to understand and deal with groups often requires more time, energy, effort, and expertise than a manager is willing to give.
3. Maintaining an individualistic perspective helps managers retain control over all legitimate authority within the organization. This existing mythology justifies department rules, managerial prerogatives, and limitations on interaction with employees.

According to some police management theorists (Munro, 1977), it is far less threatening for a manager to condemn individual police officers as lazy, inept, or corrupt than it is to raise substantive questions about the department's structure, operating procedures, and goals. Many police administrators do not have the knowledge, technical expertise, conceptual ability, or human skills needed to understand and deal effectively with group dynamics in the workplace.

Competent police managers have a knack for resolving problems and handling personnel. They have learned to appreciate the importance of groups and the group process. They know that people and groups are the human resources upon which all social organization is built (Schermerhorn, Hunt, and Osborn, 1982).

The Group Phenomenon

Effective police managers never forget that human beings are social animals (Aronson, 1976). They know all of us need to have interpersonal relationships with other people. Meaningful social interaction is absolutely essential for human development and is a very important source of personal fulfillment. Virtually everything we do is done in conjunction with or through others. Our unique personality (attitudes, values, and behaviors) evolved in response to the interaction we had with other people in a variety of very different situations (Chruden and Sherman, 1976). In more succinct terms, people do not exist apart from social groups. All people are born into them, transformed through them, and eventually buried by them.

Based on the idea that each person exists and develops a sense of self largely in response to meaningful interaction with significant others, many social scientists believe groups are the basic unit of social organization and that they perform a wide variety of very distinct functions. Groups provide their members with companionship, a frame of reference for collective behavior, a normative perspective, and emotional support. People behave based on how they perceive themselves and how they feel they are perceived by significant others within the group (Holden, 1986). The group-based interpersonal relationships that police administrators are most concerned with are those which occur in the work environment. These interpersonal transactions are normally initiated and maintained to facilitate the accomplishment of work. From this perspective, good interpersonal relationships are those which are productive in terms of task achievement and satisfying in terms of meeting the work-related needs of those people within the group (Albanese, 1981).

Collective Behavior

A group is more than a mere collection of individual human beings who happen to be in physical proximity to one another or who share a common interest or characteristic. According to Ronald Smith and Fred Preston (1982), a group consists of a number of persons who interact with each other in an organized way. They share common traits, views, values, circumstances, and a sense of togetherness. More specifically, a group is composed of (1) two or more people, (2) who are consciously aware of one another, (3) who consider themselves to be a functional unit, and (4) who share in the quest to achieve one or more goals or other common benefit (Plunkett, 1983). Two basic requirements must be met before an *aggregate* (a number of persons who happen to be clustered in one place) qualifies as a group. First, the individuals must interact with each other in some organized manner. Members share norms, role expectations, and social status. Second, there must be a consciousness of kind. In other words, they feel bound together by common traits, perspectives, and circumstances. When fused together, these two elements create a single, dynamic, and goal-oriented social entity.

Groups differ tremendously with respect to their size, function, structure, and sophistication. Some groups are one dimensional, in that they exist for a single purpose. Others have one dominant purpose and various ancillary functions. Some very complex groups juggle a number of coordinated purposes simultaneously. Groups exhibit their own unique personality. They can carry on their activities with great vigor and enthusiasm, or they may be laid back and even lackadaisical. Groups can be composed of just two people, or they may be as large as the New York Police Department, the federal government, or the entire United States. The purpose, size, and composition of a particular group helps determine the nature of the interpersonal transactions between members:

1. *Primary groups.* Primary groups are those in which members develop close, personal, intimate, and enduring relationships based on frequent and meaningful interaction.
2. *Secondary groups.* Secondary groups are less intense and more segmented than primary groups because the occasional interaction between members is superficial, impersonal, and utilitarian in nature.

People are born into certain social groups like the family, the nation, and the church. Membership in other groups (school, military service, or a jury) may be imposed on some individuals. In other situations, membership is more or less voluntary. The groups that people join voluntarily may be (1) open to everyone, (2) limited to certain categories of people in the population, or (3) open only to those who are willing to go through some type of screening and/or initiation. Groups can be deliberately organized or may evolve slowly through the process of natural selection without conscious intent. Social scientists often describe groups vis-à-vis a continuum. They note that groups can be formal or informal, functional or dysfunctional, highly structured or relatively unstructured, related to other groups or unattached, unified or segmented by subgroups, directive (autocratic) or participative (democratic), proactive or reactive, receptive to change or resistant to change, task-oriented or human relations-oriented. Regardless of their characteristics, it is clear that groups provide the context within which almost all human behavior occurs (Rose, 1977).

It is the police administrator's job to maximize employee productivity within the context of the work group. For our purpose, a *work group* is best defined as a task-oriented group that has been created by formal authority of an organization to transform *resource inputs* (like money, material, equipment, ideas, and personnel) into *product outputs* (reports, decisions, services, and law enforcement activities). A police department, like all other very complex and task-oriented organizations, is composed of an interlocking network of work groups. Police administrators and first-line supervisors perform what Rensis Likert (1961) described as the linking-pin function in the network. It is through the activities of these managers and supervisors, acting as superiors in one groups and subordinates in another, that work groups are interconnected in such a way as to create a sense of totality for the organization as a whole (Schermerhorn, Hunt, and Osborn, 1982). Figure 7.1 illustrates the linking-pin principle in supportive relationships.

Work Groups

A work group, as we use the term, is a formal task group consisting of two or more people who come together as the result of a managerial decision to achieve some aspect of the department's mission, goals, and objectives. All formal work groups are created as the result of the organizing function inherent in management and through which police officers are assigned to different tasks and task groups by some higher authority (chief executive officer) or the head of a particular subgroup (unit commander). The productivity of any work group depends on how managers handle the division of labor and delegation of authority within the group.

Formal work groups are normally classified as temporary or permanent. Both are created by management to contribute to the organization's productive purpose as articulated in its mission, goals, and objectives. Permanent work groups are relatively stable and usually appear on organizational charts as (1) departments, (2) divisions, (3) bureaus, and (4) units. See the generic organization chart presented in Figure 7.2. It represents an inverted hierarchy of function based on work-group membership, component interaction, and formal structure. Temporary work groups, on the other hand, are normally created by managers and assigned to special tasks that permanent groups are, for whatever reason, not equipped to deal with efficiently or effectively. Ad

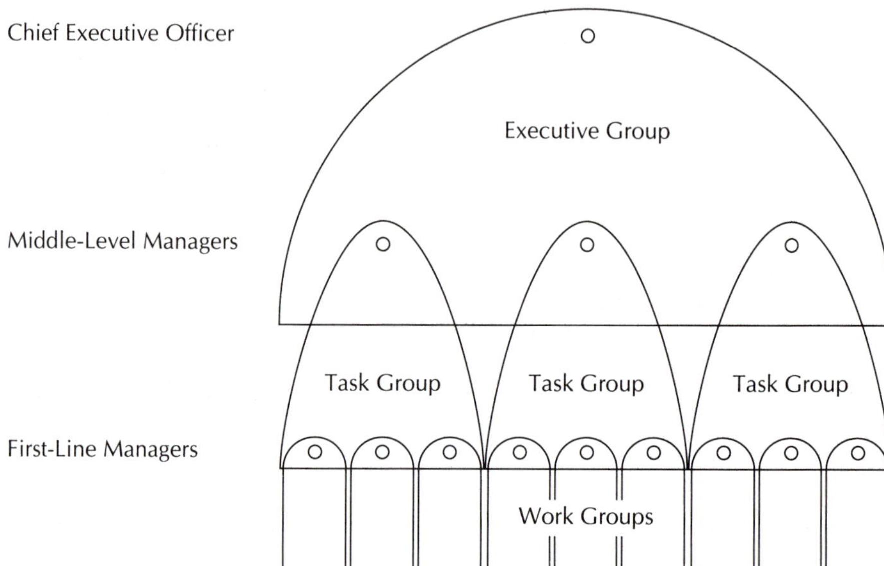

o indicates managerial leaders at various hierarchical levels in the organization. Expectations, instructions, and orders flow down the "chain of command" to first-line managers who supervise work groups. Administrators below the executive level have overlapping memberships. They are members of superordinate as well as subordinate work groups. As a "linking-pin," they serve to integrate and coordinate various groups as they seek to achieve the mission, goals, and objectives of the organization.

FIGURE 7.1 Interlocking and Supportive Relationships in Complex Police Organizations. Source Adapted from Rensis Likert, *New Patterns of Management* (New York: McGraw-Hill, 1961).

hoc committees, project teams, and task forces are temporary work groups designed to accomplish a specific objective. Once the temporary work group achieves its objective, it is dissolved and all personnel are returned to their permanent duty assignment (Holt, 1987).

Every formal group has a designated leader. The leaders who head up work groups in police departments are usually managers who have been selected for that specific purpose. Under normal circumstances they have the rank, power, and legitimate authority needed to coordinate the on-the-job behavior of subordinates (Plunkett, 1983). Whether police administrators succeed or not depends in large measure on their knowledge, expertise, and leadership skills.

Although work groups always have one or more leaders, the officially designated manager may not exert the most influence over the job-related behavior of fellow employees. Formal leaders are usually task oriented. They are eager to get the job done in the quickest and most effective manner even if they are required to use their official position, power, and authority in a

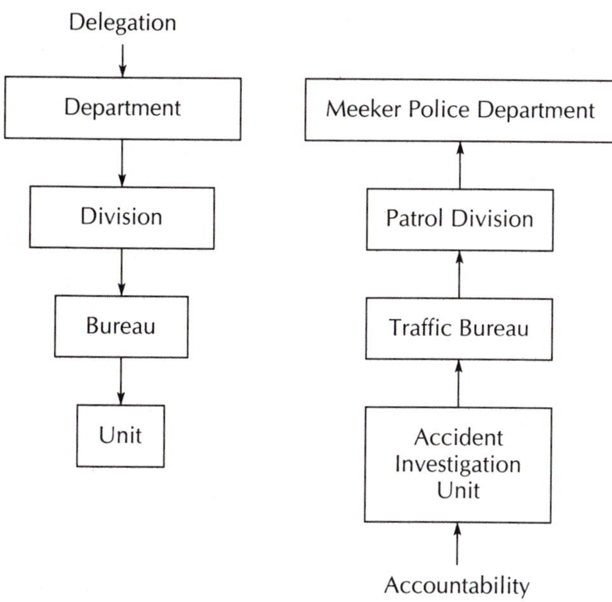

FIGURE 7.2 Formal Work Groups.

negative way. According to Robert Fulmer (1982), formal leaders almost always have the institutionalized power and authority to direct, discipline, or fire members of their own particular work group. He also notes that these authority figures use negative motivation. They rely on the use of differential status, discipline, and punishment to accomplish their objectives.

Cliques

Natural subgroups, or cliques, can be found in nearly all formally designated work groups. When two or more employees come together in an effort to satisfy mutual needs or share common interests, they form an *informal group*. These informal groups evolve from spontaneous interactions among compatible individuals who are looking for validation as human beings and social reinforcement for appropriate behavior. Informal groups help satisfy member needs for companionship, security, belonging, and self-esteem. Although they are not created by those in authority, seldom have defined goals, and are almost always transitory, informal groups are influential in complex organizations. They provide their members with social acceptance, friendship, and an opportunity to develop meaningful interpersonal relationships (Holt, 1987). They also provide satisfactions that are often denied or thwarted by formal group affiliations (Schermerhorn, Hunt, and Osborn, 1982). These groups are formed to fulfill very important psychosocial needs for security and camaraderie among members. A formal group can also function as an informal group if members freely choose to associate with each other on and off the job (Plunkett, 1983).

Informal groups or cliques are shadow organizations because they do not exist officially. They arise out of the interactions, attractions, and needs of individuals. Members are not assigned to these groups. Membership is voluntary and dependent on the mutual attraction the individual and the group have for each other. Informal groups create intricate patterns of influence that extend far beyond the mechanical representations drawn on an organization chart. Members identify with one another, share common perspectives, and feel a sense of solidarity. They often manipulate the work environment in an effort to meet group needs. As a result, the flow of legitimate authority may be altered and/or circumvented altogether (Reitz, 1981). Effective police administrators know how to recognize and deal with informal groups.

According to contemporary management theory, three basic types of informal groups tend to develop within the social environments created by complex organizations. Dalton Melville (1959), in his classic study of industrial organizations, identified these naturally occurring groups as (1) horizontal, (2) vertical, and (3) random or mixed, depending on the predominant interaction pattern. These informal groups are often referred to as cliques and, for our purposes, are best described in the following manner:

1. *Horizontal cliques.* Horizontal cliques are composed of two or more people from the same functional area who are at the same level (or rank) in the hierarchy. A patrolman may find himself in a small informal group within the SWAT (Special Weapons and Tactics) team because he and a few of his colleagues share a common concern about the group's safety based on the commander's lack of field experience or his inability to incorporate their ideas into the decision-making process. Due to the nature and complexity of police work, almost all police officers belong to horizontal cliques.

2. *Vertical cliques.* Vertical cliques consist of two or more people from the same functional area (or department) who are at different levels in the hierarchy. Police officers at various ranks often socialize with each other. These informal groups are formed and maintained based on a consciousness of kind, similar interests, and common needs for acceptance, security, self-esteem, and a genuine sense of accomplishment. Many police officers are members of vertical subgroups within their department.

3. *Random cliques.* Random or mixed cliques involve two or more people who come from various departments, ranks, and locations. This type of informal network is often made up of individuals who get things done and share a common desire to avoid the red tape normally associated with bureaucracy. Active participation in a random clique is often facilitated by a common membership in other organizations like the Masons, the Knights of Columbus, or the FBI National Academy Alumni Association. Many police officers become involved in random or mixed cliques in an effort to maximize their overall influence as law enforcers.

Because of the nature of their work, police managers should expect to interact with virtually every type of informal group just described. They must learn to identify informal leaders and help them (and their group) achieve personal goals and objectives that are consistent with those of the organization as a whole.

Every informal group has at least one leader. While they have no formal authority or tenure, these informal leaders have the ability to influence group members so they respond favorably to suggestions, instructions, and direct orders. Informal leaders, in contrast to formal authority figures, derive power from their followers. Group members voluntarily subject themselves to the will of the informal leader because of that particular individual's personality, knowledge, abilities, and skills. No formal action is needed to create leadership. In its most natural form, it is predicated on voluntary submission and willing compliance. Since informal leadership is both dynamic and situational, it can almost never be delegated. Formally appointed leaders seldom, if ever, continue to function as informal leaders of cliques within the work force (Plunkett, 1983). These two roles are almost always mutually exclusive.

Membership

Groups, whether they are formal (created by authority) or informal (spontaneous goal-oriented), can also be categorized in terms of their criteria for membership. There are two basic classifications: (1) open groups and (2) closed groups. They are often described in the following terms:

1. *Open groups.* An open group is one that has relatively few restrictions on who is allowed to join. There are few specific requirements. Open groups are constantly adding and losing members. New members bring enthusiasm, creativity, and an insatiable appetite for change. As a result, group leaders spend a great deal of time and effort socializing new members. They strive to create an equilibrium between continuous change and the need for stability. Open groups are future-oriented, energetic, unpredictable, and usually hard to manage.

2. *Closed groups.* A closed group restricts its membership to a select few through the imposition of stringent requirements. Membership is relatively stable. Power and status relationships are well established and fixed. Groupthink is a common characteristic of closed and highly cohesive groups. They tend to lose their flexibility and adopt one perspective. Elitism is often used to mask the absence of critical thinking. Tightly closed groups quickly become "self-perpetuating" cliques (Reitz, 1981).

"Open" and "closed" are maximum terms and represent opposite ends of the continuum. Most groups fall somewhere in between the two extremes. All police organizations are composed of relatively open and closed groups. Once again, it is the manager's job to coordinate the activities of these groups in such a way that they all make a positive contribution to the organization as a whole.

Groups as Functional Units

The key to understanding the group phenomenon is to think about it in terms of action as well as structure. From this perspective, a group consists of people acting together as a functional unit. In other words, a group is a collection of people who are capable of consistent, coordinated action that is consciously or unconsciously directed toward some common objective in anticipation that they will receive some type of gratification (Shibutani, 1961).

Social interactionists place emphasis on participation in collective activity, not on group membership per se. They are not concerned with individuals as total organisms, but with those aspects of their behavior that contribute to the collective enterprise. Group action is regarded as something that is constructed out of the diverse efforts of independently motivated human beings moving together toward some shared goal or objective. According to Robert Albanese (1981), this particular concept of group implies some degree of interdependence, mutual influence, and interaction among those people seeking to accomplish a common purpose.

Social interactionists explore group-based human behavior from the interaction/influence perspective we discuss in Chapter 11. They contend that a group does not really exist until its members are involved in something together. They define a group as two or more persons who (1) interact with some or all members on an individual or network basis; (2) share one or more goals; (3) allow themselves to be governed by a normative system of attitudes, values, and behavior; (4) maintain stable relationships; and (5) form subgroups based on interpersonal attraction or rejection. Interactionists view groups as synergistic in the sense that they are much more than a composite of the personalities of their members. In this particular context, *synergism* means that the simultaneous action of various people working together within the group is likely to produce a greater total effect than individuals who work independently. In other words, the whole is usually greater than the sum of its parts (Fulmer, 1983).

People join and continue their membership in formal as well as informal groups for a variety of different reasons. As noted earlier, human beings are social animals with an innate need to interact with others. In addition, most people—as a condition of employment—are assigned to work with other people in groups. From a utilitarian point of view, people join groups and remain active in them because they have expectations that membership will benefit them in some way. They associate groups with positive outcomes or have formed positive attitudes about group participation. Social scientists argue that most people continue to join and remain in groups because they receive positive reinforcement from group behavior.

Police officers join formal and informal groups within the organization for exactly the same reasons other people join them. They are looking for ways to fulfill their occupational role while trying to meet personal needs. These personal needs fall into two fairly broad categories: (1) psychosocial needs and (2) economic needs. While both of these needs promote purposeful interaction among employees, psychosocial factors are the most influential.

1. *Affiliation*. One reason why police officers join (formal and informal) subgroups is that they have a need to interact with other people and enjoy the companionship of those with whom they have something in common. These subgroups provide structured environments in which police personnel pursue their collective interests and establish lasting friendships. Due to the clannish nature of police work and the 24-hour-a-day rotational scheduling usually associated with the delivery of police services, the requirement for affiliation is often met on the job or not at all.

2. *Security*. All human beings have a basic need for safety and security. People want protection from real as well as imagined external threats. Many

police officers experience feelings of insecurity that can only be alleviated through interaction with supportive group members. Probationary police officers sense that there is safety in numbers. By joining a group whose members have already experienced and survived the probationary period, they are able to reduce their anxiety. Rookie police officers can learn the ropes faster and become part of the grapevine information network much more quickly by joining a group than by going it alone. The capacity for informal groups to indoctrinate and socialize new members into the organizational routine gives these groups a great deal of power.

3. *Self-esteem.* Membership in groups can assist police officers in developing a sense of worth and self-esteem. Police officers acquire self-esteem by becoming members of high-status groups. Being a member of the in group is both intrinsically and extrinsically rewarding. In addition, the close interpersonal relationships that police officers develop as members of subgroups provide them with great opportunities for recognition and praise usually unavailable to those outside of the group. Groups provide acceptance, perspective, support, and a milieu in which members feel safe and secure. Self-esteem is a natural by-product of subgroup affiliation.

4. *Power.* Group membership can serve as a source of power in two totally different ways. First of all, subgroup solidarity contributes to an employee's sense of safety and security. Police officers believe in the old adage, "United we stand, divided we fall." There is little or no doubt that workers organized into cohesive groups enjoy far greater power than they do as individuals. This is the principle upon which the labor union movement was built. Secondly, subgroup membership gives members the opportunity to become leaders. As leaders they are permitted to exercise power over others in the group. They can exert influence even though they do not occupy a formal position of authority within the police department. Informal group leaders normally avoid all of the responsibilities that go along with positions of formal authority.

5. *Self-concept.* Subgroup membership helps individual police officers deal with the introspective question, "Who am I?" People have a need to establish an identity and locate themselves as objects in their symbolic environment. According to Charles H. Cooley's concept of the "looking-glass self," people do not see themselves directly, but only as reflected in the behavior of others toward them (Smith and Preston, 1982). In other words, our conception of self is essentially a reflection of our attitudes as they are mirrored in the groups to which we belong. Self-conceptions develop through social interaction in groups. Groups are a very good source of evaluative feedback. Each person's experience with other members lends to the credibility of the assessment. Continuous interaction gives subgroups a good basis for a collective evaluation of the officer's personality and behavior. Significant others are more willing to provide colleagues with the positive as well as the negative feedback police managers often try to avoid.

6. *Accomplishment.* Some groups form simply because it takes more than one person to complete a task or because the task is made easier through cooperative effort. In other situations, the etiology of group formation is much more sophisticated. Human beings are social animals who have an innate need to collaborate with one another in order to achieve their individual and collective goals. Police officers join in groups to pursue mutual interests.

Group Dynamics A SWAT team's success or failure in achieving goals and objectives depends heavily on the interaction pattern of the work group. *(©Bill Green: The Frederick News-Post, Frederick, MD 1990)*

They pool their knowledge, energy, expertise, talent, and tools to accomplish certain tasks. They derive natural satisfaction from achievement and a sense of fulfillment from voluntary interaction with their peers.

7. *Economics.* Police officers may join groups to pursue their own economic self-interests. They often become members of (promotional examination) study groups, fraternal organizations, labor unions, and professional associations with a utilitarian expectation that they will benefit financially from membership in these groups. While economic security is subsumed as part of a police officer's basic need for safety and security, it also represents a pathway to self-actualization. Fanned by years of financial deprivation, the quest for economic security has become one of the most inflammatory issues in American law enforcement. Police officers are now one of the most heavily unionized groups of public employees in the country (Reitz, 1981).

One of the most important factors leading to interpersonal attraction and group formation in complex criminal justice organizations is the opportunity to interact. Paul Whisenand and George Rush (1988) contend that proximity is a critical variable. Many subgroups form simply because police officers are assigned near one another. All other things being equal, those police officers who live near each other or who work closely together have far greater opportunities for interaction than those officers who are physically separated.

Group Survival

Whether or not a particular formal or informal subgroup survives and makes a substantive contribution to the organization depends on its success in (1) achieving goals and objectives, (2) meeting the psychosocial and economic needs of group members, and (3) facilitating smooth, meaningful interaction between those members who were involved in goal-oriented transactions. The long-term survival of a group is almost always contingent on bringing these three factors into a state of dynamic equilibrium.

Groups overlap one another in all complex police departments. As a result, it is not unusual for a police officer to be an active participant in several informal as well as formal subgroups simultaneously. A police captain, for example, could conceivably belong to the chief's staff, the Command Officers' Association (union), the department's Precision Shooting Team, the Black Caucus, the Police Athletic League, and the Blue Knights' Motorcycle Club all at the same time. Under normal circumstances, the captain will play a variety of different roles (leader, follower, technician, facilitator, counselor, teacher, etc.) in these groups. Versatility is a key ingredient in successful role playing.

Types of Groups

One way to classify groups is to construct intellectual models, or ideal types that can be used in conjunction with a continuum to describe relative differences in group behavior. As noted earlier, groups can be classified in a number of different ways.

1. Primary—Secondary
2. Formal—Informal
3. Voluntary—Involuntary
4. Horizontal—Vertical
5. Open—Closed
6. Esoteric—Utilitarian
7. Ingroup—Outgroup

Groups can also be categorized in terms of their principal function. According to Leonard Sayles (1957), there are four basic categories that may be used for categorizing groups based on functional type: (1) command groups, (2) task groups, (3) interest groups, and (4) friendship groups. He described these categories as follows:

1. *Command groups*. Command groups are vertical groups in complex organizations in which orders are given. The group's structure is determined by a formal organization chart and chain of command. It is composed of all subordinates who report to one particular police manager. A captain, lieutenant,

sergeant, and the sergeant's immediate subordinates form a command group. Activities normally take place on orders from a superior. While these orders may be phrased as requests, the command group remains intact because the rank relationship between group members still exists.

2. *Task groups.* Task groups are created by formal authority. They are usually temporary in nature and are created to deal with a specific project or task. Police administrators are finding that smaller, less formal task forces move faster and are more productive than most traditional command groups. Task boundaries are not limited to those in the immediate chain of command. In fact, they often cross command relationships. The activities of task groups and project staffs create situations in which members are able to communicate and coordinate with each other to determine the best way to achieve the goal. If a police officer is suspected of being an alcoholic, for example, communication and coordination between the sergeant, the shift commander, the employee assistance program manager, the personnel director, and the chief may be necessary to resolve the problem. In a command group, the emphasis is on following directions. In a task group, on the other hand, emphasis is placed on the task and its accomplishment.

3. *Interest groups.* Interest groups emphasize the group itself. While they may have a chain of command and assigned tasks, they exist because of the mutual interests of all their members. Police personnel who band together to have their work schedule changed, to support a colleague who has been disciplined, to protest the establishment of a civilian review board, or to seek improvements in wages, hours, and working conditions choose to engage in collective action in order to advance their common interests. Interest groups usually exist for a shorter period of time than other groups because the objectives that bring them together are likely to be achieved or abandoned.

4. *Friendship groups.* Friendship groups exist primarily because members like being together. Members normally have one or more characteristics in common. Their interaction, which frequently goes beyond the workplace, may be based on sports, hobbies, religious affiliations, interest group activities, professional memberships, or fraternal associations. While members of these groups may have met at work or through other groups, it is real friendship that sustains their interpersonal relationships (Whisenand and Rush, 1988).

These categories are not mutually exclusive. While they often overlap and intertwine, they still provide police administrators with a frame of reference for understanding the structure and function of groups (Fulmer, 1983). Every organization has its own constellation of informal as well as formal groups that create a unique personality or climate that differentiates it from all other organizations.

Anatomy of a Group

No two groups are ever the same and individual groups are never the same over time. They are distinct and evolving entities within an environmental setting. While each group develops a unique personality, all groups have certain structural components that differentiate them from aggregates. Researchers have identified five primary structural components that are common in formal as well as informal groups: (1) role, (2) norms, (3) values, (4) status, and (5) culture. Every police administrator needs to understand these basic sociological concepts because they are often used to analyze behavior in and by certain groups.

One way to analyze groups is to look at the various roles played by group members. A *role* is a set of expectations and behaviors that is associated with a given position in a social unit (i.e., group, organization, or institution). The sociological use of this term is similar to the theatrical definition for role. For every function that is performed in the group there is a role. Most groups, for example, have roles labeled leader and follower. The group also has expectations about how these roles should be performed. As in a drama, a role makes sense only if there is a supporting cast interaction based on a pattern of reciprocal claims and obligations. A *claim* consists of those things we expect others to do by virtue of their role. An *obligation,* on the other hand, is what we feel bound to do because of the part being played. What constitutes a claim by one party to the transaction is an obligation for the other (Shibutani, 1961). Without socially defined roles and the regularized behavior these roles produce, collaborative goal-oriented human behavior would be absolutely impossible.

Police personnel play multiple roles within police departments and adjust their role to the expectations of the group they are part of at a given time. Role playing involves living up to the obligations of the role that has been assumed and insisting the other players perform their own appropriate role-related duties. Role behavior can be classified into three categories: (1) task-related, (2) maintenance-related, and (3) individual-related. While these categories were developed more than 40 years ago (Benne and Sheats, 1948), they are still relevant today. Task-related roles require behavior directly related to establishing and achieving the mission, goals, and objectives of the group. "Maintenance-related" roles call for those behaviors that are directly related to the well-being, continuity, and development of a particular group. "Individual-related" roles—the "joker," "chronic complainer," "hedonist," "opponent," "troublemaker," for example—are scripted to meet the needs of individual members rather than those of the group. Even though these individualistic roles can, under certain circumstances, be functional, they are usually dysfunctional and have a negative effect on the group as a whole.

Roles within Groups

Researchers have identified an almost endless array of different roles that can be found in complex organizations. Whether or not one of these roles emerge will depend on the nature of the group, its task, and the situation involved. Here are some of the most common social roles:

1. The *leader* influences, motivates, and coordinates the goal-oriented activities of other group members.
2. The *follower* does willingly those things the leader asks in order to accomplish the organization's goals and objectives.

3. The *expert* provides technical information and practitioner skills relevant to achievement of the group's task.
4. The *enforcer* sees to it that group norms and values are understood, adhered to, and that violations result in the appropriate application of negative sanctions.
5. The *facilitator* works to avoid destructive intragroup conflict through consensus building and compromise.
6. The *devil's advocate* questions virtually every suggestion or managerial decision affecting the group.
7. The *scapegoat,* for a variety of social and psychological reasons, gets the blame for group failures.

As noted earlier, most people occupy several roles simultaneously. For each of these roles there is a role set. The role set of a patrol officer is depicted in Figure 7.3. A *role set* consists of those (in other roles) who interact with them in some way and have legitimate expectations concerning their behavior. Role sets are important because they pressure individuals to conform to their role-related expectations (Reitz, 1981).

Role conflict, like that discussed in Focus 7.1, is produced when a person tries to perform two roles that impose contradictory or incompatible demands on the actor (Smith and Preston, 1982). Due to the fact that most people play a variety of very different roles, there is bound to be role conflict. This conflict results from varying expectations concerning how the person should behave in a given set of circumstances. According to Dean Champion (1975), there are several kinds of role conflicts that managers must learn to deal with; there are conflicts based on (1) the disparate demands of two different roles, (2) too many roles being played at once, (3) internal stressors like the lack of time or expertise, and (4) different expectations about how a particular role should be carried out. Role conflict is inherent in group dynamics.

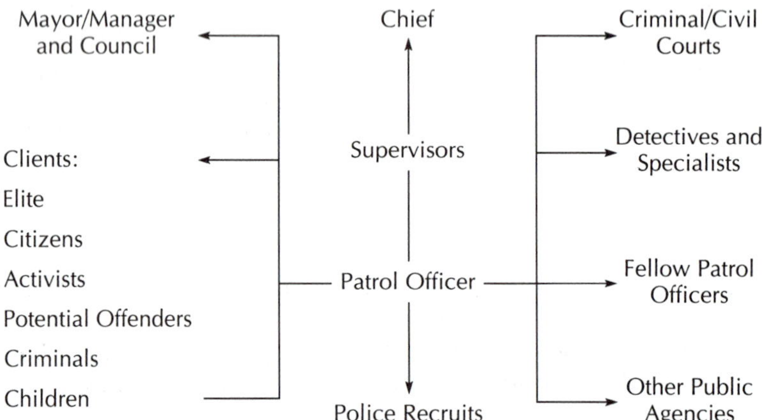

FIGURE 7.3 The Role Set of the Patrol Officer. Source Adapted from John J. Broderick, *Police in a Time of Change* (Prospect Heights, IL: Waveland Press, 1987).

CASE STUDY

Captain Oliver Dixon

The city of Rinert is located in the northeastern United States. The city was founded in 1764 and the police department can trace its history back to the early 1800s. The department is proud that it has employed individuals from the same family lines from one generation to the next. As a relatively homogeneous group, members of the work force share similar values, attitudes, norms, and social perspectives. Consensus has become the rule rather than the exception.

Most of Rinert's police officers were trained to use separation and mediation as a tool in domestic violence cases. They viewed domestic conflict as a civil matter. Arrests were infrequent and almost always precipitated by truly outrageous behavior or other kinds of aggravating circumstances.

A new law was enacted by the state legislature requiring arrest in any domestic dispute involving physical injury or imminent threat of such injury. Capt. Dixon, the department's training officer, immediately distributed a copy of the new law to all police personnel. He also incorporated the information into the basic training curriculum at the police academy. The captain and his staff continually emphasized the importance of the new law and the rationale for arrest in domestic violence cases. A counselor from the local domestic violence shelter made an audiovisual presentation and gave an impassioned plea for full enforcement of the new law. An assistant district attorney was brought in to discuss civil liability in these cases. Once rookies graduated from the academy and assumed their duties, a senior police officer, selected at random, was assigned to serve as a field training officer (FTO) and mentor for each rookie.

The department's planning and research unit did a follow-up study to determine the effect of the new law on arrest rates. The data was obtained at six-month intervals (beginning six months after the law took effect). The phase 1 data revealed there had been a moderate increase in the number of arrests made by veteran officers. Rookies, on the other hand, had a very high ratio of arrests in relation to the number of domestic dispute calls they answered. In phase 2, the number of arrests made by both groups declined. Phase 3 data indicated that arrest rates for veteran officers and rookies had converged and stabilized at a point slightly higher than the departmental average before the new law was passed.

Capt. Dixon has been asked to explain why the number of arrests has leveled off and what can be done to increase the effectiveness of the department's training program.

Based on the concept of group and group dynamics, how would the captain explain this situation? What could and should be done to make sure this type of cosmetic change does not take place in the future?

FOCUS 7.1

Minority Perspective of Lena Williams

Not everyone is considered to be a "brother in blue." According to Lena Williams, the police establishment has not matured to a point where it fully embraces blacks or women. This is true, at least in part, because many black officers have isolated themselves from whites in order to be a force for their own people. Black cops are members of a distinct racial minority within an equally distinctive minority group.

SOURCE. Lena Williams, "Police Officers Tell of Strains of Living as a 'Black in Blue,' " *The New York Times*, Feb. 14, 1988, p. 1.

Group-Shared Norms and Values

Groups, based on meaningful interaction among members, formulate definitions of appropriate and inappropriate behavior. These definitions become normative standards by which all members of the group are judged. Social norms are group-generated, accepted, reinforced, and internalized expectations that are translated into informal as well as formal rules of conduct that guide human behavior in a given situation. Norms require (prescribe) or prohibit (proscribe) certain types of conduct depending on the circumstances. Members of the group are rewarded (with positive sanctions) if they conform to group-shared expectations. They are punished (through negative sanctions) if they deviate from the group's norms. Virtually all of our actions are influenced by the norms of one group or another. Most of these norms have been internalized to the extent that well-conditioned people conform to them without being aware cognitively that they are conforming. Norms are internalized in the subconscious and become part of our very existence (Chinoy and Hewitt, 1975).

Norms can ordinarily be categorized in terms of the intensity of the feeling, the extent of the social reaction, and the consequences (in terms of negative sanctions) generated when a group-shared expectation is violated. There are four basic types of social norms: (1) folkways, (2) mores, (3) taboos, and (4) laws.

1. *Folkways.* Folkways are customs, conventions, or traditions of formal or informal groups that members tend to follow almost automatically. Police officers, for example, learn to use a unique job-related vocabulary. They are also expected to remain calm and collected even in stressful situations. Violation of a folkway normally elicits a relatively mild negative reaction from other members of the group.

2. *Mores.* Mores are the morally binding customs of a group. They are among the strongest norms and compromise the basic ethical/moral/

behavioral judgments of a particular group. Mores represent those standards of behavior the violation of which elicits intense feelings and very serious consequences. Some mores are considered to be more important than others and are condemned much more strongly. While "blue coat" crime violates the mores of the average police officer, turning in the officer may be even more repugnant to a loyal group member who has been socialized to believe that maintaining "the code of silence" and supporting "the officers in blue" are more important than eliminating crime and/or corruption within the police department.

3. *Taboos.* Taboos represent an absolute prohibition against behavior that is considered so despicable that it is almost unthinkable. Taboos are the strongest norms, and they elicit maximum consequences. Police work has its taboos, for example, lack of courage or failure to back up an officer who is in danger and needs assistance. Those who break taboos may face criminal sanctions as well as complete ostracism by the group and, in some cases, by the society at large.

4. *Laws.* Laws have been defined as customs in decay. They represent group-shared expectations that have, for whatever reason, been translated into statute. The severity of group reaction is measured in terms of the behavior's classification as a summary offense, misdemeanor, felony, or capital crime. From an organizational perspective, policies, procedures, rules, and regulations are laws. The failure to abide by departmental policies, procedures, rules, and regulations elicits the imposition of negative sanctions ranging from a verbal reprimand to termination for cause. The articulation of legitimate norms can also be found in civil service legislation, police department accreditation standards, and the Law Enforcement Code of Ethics.

Although we have distinguished between folkways, mores, taboos, and laws, it is important to note that determining exactly what type of behavior goes in which category is somewhat arbitrary. It is often based on selective perception. In reality, norms fall on a continuum in terms of importance and social significance. They do not apply equally to every individual and/or group. In addition, the boundaries between norm categories often overlap. Norms are produced through a dynamic interactive process and continue to change over time. They are best viewed as fluid, shifting guidelines for thinking and behavior (Smith and Preston, 1982).

Group-generated and shared values play a crucial role in the personal and professional lives of police personnel. Values are abstract and general beliefs about what is right, good, and desirable (Zastrow and Bowker, 1984). Values are the heart and soul of a group. They also provide the philosophical glue that holds the group together. Values are not specific rules for action but general precepts to which people give allegiance and about which they have strong feelings. Values constitute a general guidance system for thinking and behaving. Interests, attitudes, norms, and behaviors originate in and are reflected by some value or set of values.

The word *value* has a variety of different meanings. In the most general sense, values are global beliefs concerning what is good (freedom, justice, the American way) and what is bad (war, poverty, dishonesty). These values provide a cultural base for determining the appropriateness of our behavior.

From a managerial point of view, a value is an enduring belief that a specific mode of conduct or goal is preferable to others in a given set of circumstances. Paul Whisenand and George Rush (1988) define a value as a fairly stable yet changeable belief that a particular means to a particular end is preferred over the alternatives. Since police officers have more than one value, police managers must learn to think and to judge on-the-job behavior in terms of a value system. A *value system* is a set of beliefs concerning preferred modes of conduct and goals in a hierarchical ranking of relative importance. A personal value system is a relatively permanent perceptual framework that influences and shapes the general character of each individual's behavior.

People are what they value. They discipline themselves and interact with significant others according to their personal value system. Values produce attitudes that generate and shape all purposeful human behavior. An attitude represents a state of mind that is focused on an object, event, or person existing in that individual's psychological world. Attitudes are a concrete manifestation of a police officer's basic values (Albanese, 1981). Fair treatment of a very unpopular black subordinate is indicative of a commitment to administrative due process and fundamental fairness in the workplace. Values cut across specific situations to which attitudes are tied.

The Learning Process

While genetics shape broad patterns of human behavior, most value-specific behavior is learned from birth on. People are exposed to and internalize values throughout life. The most intense learning takes place during the first 20 years and normally consists of three very distinct phases: (1) imprinting, (2) modeling, and (3) socialization.

1. *Imprinting*. From a sociological point of view, babies are born tabula rasa, or as absorbent blank slates. They learn by osmosis to react, think, and cope with the exigencies of life through interaction with significant others during the first six or seven years of life. Their personality (consisting of the id, ego, and superego, or social conscience) is formed and sets the stage for virtually all their future mental, emotional, and social development. The principal actors in the imprinting process are parents and other members of the primary group who have a responsibility to nurture children so they can survive, thrive, and move toward far greater autonomy. The infrastructure of a person is the child as formed during these very critical early years.

2. *Modeling*. During the modeling phase (from about age 7 to 14), children begin to identify with and pattern their behavior after an expanding number of family members, peers, and heroes in the outside world. Group membership also begins to play a much more prominent role in their life. They identify with the group per se and with significant others within the group. As a result, new values and patterns of behavior are integrated with those learned as the result of earlier imprinting. Children construct ego models (based on information from a variety of sources) and try to measure up to the ideal. A child's value system is a composite produced by imprinting and modeling.

3. *Socialization.* From age 14 to 20, social life is organized primarily in terms of friends. Peer influence reaches its zenith and meaningful interpersonal relationships center around common interests or activities. These young men and women spend a great deal of time defining and integrating the beliefs, standards, and values of peers into their own unique personality. It is during this particular phase of the developmental process that young people achieve physical maturity and adopt a dominant value system. This value system is a guide for internal self-control and molds the individual's personality. Adolescence almost always involves experimentation, verification, clarification, and validation of group-shared values (Massey, 1979). Once a value system is in place, it serves as an internalized set of standards designed to guide human behavior in ambiguous situations.

From about age 20 on, the value system that was developed during childhood and adolescence locks in and becomes the standard by which to determine what is good and what is bad in a given set of circumstances. While much of the socialization we experience occurs during childhood and adolescence, the inculcation of norms, values, and ethics continues throughout life. New police recruits are taught the values of police service and are expected to perform their duties in certain ways. Police officers are rewarded when they conform to group-shared expectations and/or exhibit appropriate values. They are punished when they fail to do so. Values activate, sustain, and legitimize human conduct.

Status in Groups

Social status is a very important concept in the study of group dynamics. Behavioral scientists point out that each and every person is involved in a complex web of social relationships. We all interact with other human beings in a variety of group settings. Social groups consist of a number of people whose relationships are based on a set of interrelated roles and statuses. They interact with each other in a more or less standardized way based on the norms and values they accept. They are united by a consciousness of kind and similarity of interests that enables them to differentiate members from various nonmembers.

In a very general sense, status refers to any position that is held within a group. It also refers to a person's position or rank in relation to other members of the work group. Status is a measure of worth (in terms of prestige or esteem) conferred on a person or on a position by a social group. Persons or positions with high status in a group are considered more valuable in certain respects than most of those to whom they are compared. Many have legitimate authority and real power in the organization. They also have corresponding duties and responsibilities. This ranking is important because it contributes to the ordering of social interaction and structuring of social relationships. The complex array of roles and statuses that defines the behavior of individuals and specifies their relations with one another constitutes what social scientists call social organization and/or social structure (Chinoy and Hewitt, 1975). A police department is a formal organization built on patterned regularity in behavior and interaction.

Few people or positions have universally high status in all situations. In fact, a high-status person or position in one group may have no status at all in another group setting. It is complicated because human beings belong to many groups and occupy different statuses simultaneously. According to behavioral scientists, much of our group-oriented behavior consists of acquiring, enhancing, and preserving social status (Shibutani, 1961).

Statuses are designations assigned to individuals and/or positions by the group. They emerge from the process of collective living and are normally broken down into two basic categories: (1) ascribed status and (2) achieved status. An *ascribed status* is derived from attributes over which individuals have no control (age, gender, race) or from membership in groups to which they are assigned by others (family, religion, nationality). Based on this ascribed status, the person is expected to acquire and perform certain socially defined roles. *Achieved status,* on the other hand, is acquired as the result of some direct or positive action. Achieved status is earned status. Potential occupants compete for status and are required to demonstrate that they have the ability to fulfill a particular role. Officially designated leaders, for example, are usually given the respect and esteem due a superior based on the authority inherent in their formal position within the organization. Natural (often informal) leaders, regardless of their rank, earn the respect and esteem of their colleagues. They exercise power with as well as power over followers. Followers do willingly what is asked of them by their leaders. Under ideal circumstances, formal authority and real leadership come together in the police department's official chain of command. Behavioral scientists refer to this state of affairs as *status congruence* (Schermerhorn, Hunt, and Osborn, 1982).

Group Culture

Social groups—including work groups—are produced by and reflect certain aspects of the culture in which they exist. Groups also create subcultural milieus of their own. Culture consists of all the knowledge, values, attitudes, norms, behavioral patterns, language, and artifacts that are passed from one generation to the next and form a way of life for those within the group. In the most general sense, culture is a way of life that defines appropriate modes of thinking, acting, and feeling. It exists because human beings are able to share their creations and pass knowledge on to subsequent generations (Smith and Preston, 1982). A common culture is the glue that holds any group together.

Culture is often referred to as the collective personality of the group. Some work groups—like the police—develop a distinctive, at times unique, social orientation. In fact, the police are frequently described as a culture within a culture (Skolnick and Gray, 1975). The police subculture is a vocational group that is somewhat isolated from the rest of American culture. Police officers share common knowledge, values, attitudes, norms, and behavioral patterns.

They share a common language or argot. There are strong bonds of loyalty and secrecy and a feeling of "we against them" among police personnel (Thibault, Lynch, and McBride, 1985). Police officers see themselves as "the thin blue line" and/or the "blue minority." The police academy is the first formal step in the socialization process and is designed to influence the police recruit's values, attitudes, and behaviors. Socialization is the process through which individuals learn proper ways of thinking, acting, and feeling in a particular culture. Academy training serves to separate trainees even further from the society at large. In addition, various on-the-job experiences provide for continued socialization that draws police officers more deeply into the existing police subculture (Alpert and Dunham, 1988). While they do not seem to produce either job satisfaction or equitable law enforcement, loyalty, solidarity, esprit de corps, and secrecy are the pillars on which the police subculture is built. They become an integral part of each police officer's "working personality" (Broderick, 1987). See Chapter 4 for more on socialization.

Most police administrators have been promoted through the ranks. Their friends, colleagues, and on-the-job experiences have shaped their management style and their approach to discipline, training, and supervision. A knowledge of informal groups and subcultural values, norms, and group dynamics will help ensure the success of contemporary police management. According to Edward Thibault and his colleagues (1985), understanding the subcultural context within which police work takes place may be more important than all other knowledge and administrative skills combined.

Group Dynamics

According to Muzafer and Carolyn Sherif (1956), a *group* can best be defined as a social unit which consists of a number of individuals who stand in (more or less) definite status and role relationships with one another and possesses a set of values, norms, and ethical orientations that regulate the behavior of members in matters of consequence to the group as a whole. It is the group process that transforms resource inputs into group outputs. Group dynamics are those forces within the group which affect task performance and member satisfaction. Effective police managers learn to harness and deploy the energy created as the result of positive group interaction.

Work groups grow and mature just like individuals do. As groups begin to mature, members learn to understand and trust each other. They are better able to work together in decision-making and problem-solving situations. There are four recognizable stages in the group development process: (1) formation, (2) differentiation, (3) integration, and (4) maturity.

1. *Formation.* The formation stage of group development begins with a consciousness of kind and/or a recognition of common interests. Prospective members tentatively identify with a group and cautiously enter into a give-and-take relationship with other members. They seek mutual acceptance and focus their attention on the task to be performed, the ways that the group can satisfy their psychosocial needs, the ground rules for behavior, and the status

a particular group or task has within the organization of which it is a part. Much of the person's knowledge about a particular group is derived from a subjective evaluation of the characteristics and behaviors of other group members.

2. *Differentiation.* The differentiation stage in group development involves the process of getting a better feel for the composition of the group and for its assigned task. New members learn how to do the job and what to expect in terms of need satisfaction. It is not uncommon for competition and conflict to emerge. Coalitions are often formed to work out strategies for making the job easier or to enhance the chances for need satisfaction. As members work together, they learn each other's strengths and weaknesses. Joint problem-solving and group decision-making reinforces the team concept. In most cases, meaningful participation cements relationships and promotes efficiency, effectiveness, and productivity. As a result, individual members are much more likely to invest their time, energy, effort, and expertise in psychologically satisfying and socially rewarding group-oriented activities.

3. *Integration.* The integration stage of group development is the point at which everything comes together. Member motivation changes from being strictly hedonistic to being much more altruistic in nature. There is a realization that the group—as a unit—can accomplish more than individuals acting on their own. Consequently, there is an incentive for members to channel their individual efforts into group solidarity and teamwork. Members receive a psychological as well as a social payoff when they cooperate with each other, encourage others within the group to achieve their full potential, and create an environment in which goal achievement becomes a form of need satisfaction. Under these conditions, the group becomes a goal-oriented and cohesive social entity in which common values, norms, and ethical orientations regulate individual as well as collective behavior. At this stage, the individual members and the group find themselves in a state of dynamic equilibrium.

4. *Maturity.* The maturity stage of group development reflects group needs for both stability and flexibility. In a mature group, the group itself assumes the control function and sets standards for regulating member behavior. Members seek to avoid anomie (a sense of normlessness) and willingly submit to the will of the group as embodied in its values, norms, ethical standards, and other mechanisms designed to guide behavior or ensure conformity. They tacitly agree to abide by informal rules and regulations that are designed to keep them performing successfully without surrendering their individual autonomy. The group controls itself and individual members control themselves in an effort to benefit the rest of the group. According to Robert Fulmer (1982), mature work groups tend to be self-regulating, self-motivating, and self-directing. They take care of their own needs and have the ability to solve problems arising within the group. At the same time, mature groups seek to avoid groupthink and try to remain flexible enough to adapt to changing tasks and environmental factors (Heinen and Jacobson, 1976).

Work groups go through life cycles just like all other living organisms. New groups are being formed all of the time. Others are in the process of coming together as distinct and identifiable entities. Some become fully integrated and reach the stage of dynamic equilibrium. While some groups achieve a degree of stability and permanence based on their maturity, others lose their capacity to change and they move toward extinction. Police administrators need to understand the life cycle of groups so they can harness a group's energy and make the adjustments necessary to increase its efficiency, effectiveness, and productivity.

Work groups are mechanisms through which goal-oriented human beings learn relevant knowledge, job skills, and appropriate behaviors. Members interact with one another and communicate their mutual expectations concerning exactly how work is to be performed. Membership in the work group gives participants the opportunity to model correct behaviors, provide instruction or technical assistance to neophytes, and exchange evaluative feedback about on-the-job performance. Group members are in a position to exert a direct influence on each other's beliefs and/or predispositions concerning work and how it is to be done. They are in a unique position to encourage or discourage high levels of individual effort (DuBrin, 1985). Functional work groups also provide members with security, emotional support, and an in-group perspective. They give members a sense of identity (vis-à-vis their work) and the opportunity for ego involvement in mutually satisfying activities. An effective work group is multidimensional in that it achieves high levels of task performance and human resource maintenance over a protracted period of time (Sutermeister, 1976).

Human Relations and Management

The human relations school of management and the organizational humanists (discussed in Chapter 11) emphasize the importance of group dynamics in task performance and human resource maintenance. The human relations movement can be traced back to two pioneering studies that were conducted during the mid-1920s at the Hawthorne Works of the Western Electric Company. The famous Relay Room Experiments and the Bank Wiring Room Study produced concrete evidence that work groups and work-group participation have a direct influence on individual productivity. Elton Mayo and his colleagues discovered that social variables—like interaction patterns, supervisory styles, and group pressure to raise or lower production—played a key role in determining the level of effort expended by those employees within a particular work group. In one case, these factors operated to increase overall productivity; in the other, it acted to restrain it. In both instances, however, the research team concluded that insight into on-the-job performance could be obtained by paying attention to important aspects of human behavior (Baron, 1983).

Some theorists have a totally negative view when it comes to the human relations approach to management. Their opposition is ordinarily based on two basic assumptions: (1) social groups, per se, do not exist or (2) groups are bad. Other theorists have a completely positive attitude toward the group process. Organizational humanists and group dynamists argue that social groups exist in all complex goal-oriented organizations. The reality of groups is demonstrated by the difference it makes to individuals whether they are accepted or rejected by social groups and whether they are part of a healthy or unhealthy work group. Secondly, groups are considered to be good. Groups satisfy the deep-seated needs of employees for affiliation, affection, recognition, and self-esteem. Group membership promotes altruism, loyalty, and a sense of belonging. Group membership provides a means through cooperative interaction by which human beings can achieve objectives they could not accomplish by themselves. Some extremists believe that everything should be done by and in groups. They contend that individual responsibility, person-to-person supervision, and even individual problem-solving are bad.

Dorwin Cartwright and Ronald Lippit (1976) reject the assumption that individual and group interests are incompatible. They have formulated five assertions about individuals, groups, and group dynamics to challenge the belief that individuals and groups must necessarily have incompatible or even compatible interests:

1. Groups do exist. They are a natural part of the social landscape. There is dramatic evidence—from a wide variety of different sources—to show that group decisions often produce changes in human behavior which are much more substantive and durable than those normally associated with attempts to modify the behavior of people as isolated individuals.

2. Groups are both inevitable and ubiquitous. Human beings are social animals with an instinctive need to interact with one another in a group-generated milieu built around communications and supportive interpersonal relationships. There is absolutely no way to conceive of people living in geographical proximity without forming groups and/or rewarding participative group membership in one way or another.

3. Groups mobilize powerful synergistic forces that produce effects of utmost importance to people. The members' position (based on role and status) in a group will affect the way others behave toward them as well as how they feel about themselves. Group membership itself could be a prized possession or an oppressive burden. Tragedies have resulted from the exclusion of individuals from groups. Equally profound consequences have stemmed from enforced membership. It is also clear that events occurring within a group can have repercussions on others—members and nonmembers—who are not directly involved in these events.

4. Groups may produce both good and bad consequences. The assumption that groups are completely good or bad is likely to lead to selective perception and tunnel vision. Under these circumstances, research tends to be ideological rather than scientific. Groups are multidimensional, and their value almost always depends on the situation.

5. Group dynamics theory is based on the assumption that the desirable consequences resulting from group interaction can be deliberately enhanced. Through knowledge of the group process, police administrators can help make work groups more efficient, effective, and productive. It is the recognition of this fact that produces ethical concerns on the part of behavioral scientists. It raises the problem of social manipulation explored by George Orwell in his chilling book, *1984*.

Based on the preceding discussion, it is clear that many police administrators need to rethink their position concerning groups in the workplace. There is no doubt that groups exist; they are inevitable as well as ubiquitous; they mobilize powerful forces having profound effects on people; these effects may be good or bad; and through an understanding of group dynamics, it is possible to maximize work group efficiency, effectiveness, and productivity.

Work groups play a critically important role in attitude formation and provide members with the repertoire of appropriate skills to do the job. Group standards (based on shared values) become the gauge by which to measure individual performance. While group standards may be articulated by management, they are normally internalized by employees via the socialization process. Socialization is designed to promote overall uniformity in thought and action based on the group's values, norms, and ethical orientation. This emphasis on the group—as opposed to the individual—leads to a tendency on the part of work-group members to change their opinions to conform with significant others in the group, to change the opinions of others, and to redefine the boundaries of the group to exclude those individuals holding deviant points of view. The success of any work group, as a group, will have a direct impact on the job performance of individual members.

Collaboration

There is ample evidence to demonstrate that when individuals work cooperatively with rather than competitively against one another in the workplace, the work group's cohesiveness increases and the work itself becomes more satisfying in terms of meeting employee needs (Fox and Urwick, 1973). Research data suggests that both cooperation and group cohesion have a positive influence on an individual's productivity. D. W. Johnson and his colleagues (1981) examined the findings of 120 studies designed to evaluate individual productivity in terms of three prevailing reward structures:

1. *Cooperative reward structure.* Cooperation involves conditions in which goal attainment by each member facilitates goal attainment by others within the work group.
2. *Competitive reward structure.* Competition creates a reward structure in which goal attainment by one member blocks the attainment of goals by other group members.
3. *Individual reward structure.* Individual rewards involve conditions in which goal attainment by one member is unrelated to the activities of other members.

In most cases, cooperation yielded higher levels of group productivity than competition and/or an individual effort. This is a much more important factor in small groups than in large groups and in groups where members work interdependently rather than independently. Other researchers have noted that the addition of even a small element of competition into a cooperative situation can sharply lower overall productivity (Rosenbaum et al., 1980).

Influences on Behavior

It is clear, based on the material just presented, that there are a number of factors which exert an influence on the way people perform in group settings. The task, work environment, maturity level, ambient stimuli (related to group membership), and discretionary stimuli (like social acceptance, rejection, communication, etc.) transmitted from one group member to another on a selective basis have an indirect influence on performance. There are seven other variables that have a much more direct impact on performance: (1) complexity, (2) need orientation, (3) size, (4) composition, (5) norms, (6) cohesiveness, and (7) groupthink.

1. *Complexity*. Simple tasks ordinarily place fewer demands on the group process than tasks that require greater knowledge, technical know-how, or social skills. As the overall complexity increases, it usually becomes more difficult for members of a work group to achieve a productive balance between quantity and quality. Members must distribute their efforts more broadly on increasingly complex tasks that require greater interdependence, cooperation, and coordination. If the group process does not adjust to these new demands, individual performance begins to suffer and there will be a concomitant reduction in job satisfaction.

Job satisfaction and performance tend to increase as the complexity of the task increases if group members are competent, have needs that are in sync with those of organization, and can work collaboratively with other members of the group to achieve mutual goals and objectives. Whether complexity has a negative or a positive effect on job performance of individual police officers will depend on the situation as well as the collective attributes of those involved.

2. *Need orientation*. Group members with conflicting needs march to different drummers. The willingness of one individual to exert an effort voluntarily on behalf of the group is always contingent on a variety of factors. A key element in the functioning of a work group is the degree to which there is some interpersonal compatibility—based on needs—among its members.

William C. Schutz (1958) developed his fundamental interpersonal orientation theory of behavior (FIRO-B) more than 30 years ago. It is designed to help explain how people orient themselves to each other based on the assessment of how strongly they need to express and receive feelings of inclusion, affection, and control. Those with a need for inclusion strive for prominence, recognition, and prestige. People with a need for affection manifest it in the desire to be friendly and to seek emotional bonding with others in the work group. Members with a need to control have a tendency to rebel against those with authority; they resist being controlled by others and refuse to be compliant or submissive.

Work groups in which members have reciprocal and compatible needs are almost always more efficient, effective, and productive than those groups that are plagued by incompatibilities. Group members who are motivated by very different and/or conflicting needs are much less likely to work well together. Antagonistic needs, drives, aspirations, and goals hinder collaboration and have a negative influence on the performance of individuals within the group as well as that of the group itself. Symptoms of these debilitating incompatibilities include widespread apathy, open hostility, struggles for control, poor job performance, lowered productivity, and domination of the group by an oligarchy composed of a few powerful and politically adroit members who operate on the principle of divide and conquer.

3. *Size.* Based on the definition of a group that we developed earlier, it is clear that formal and informal groups vary greatly in terms of their size. Most of the groups with which we interact are relatively small, however. They have fewer than ten members. One approach to the analysis and understanding of behavior in work groups focuses on activities, interactions, and sentiments. It is through the study of activities that we can tell exactly what a person does in a productive enterprise. Interaction occurs when individuals within the group respond to each other (or to the group as a collective entity) and normally involves some type of interpersonal communication. Sentiments refer to personal and/or group shared and reinforced values, attitudes, beliefs, and feelings (Dessler, 1979).

As the size of a particular work group increases, competing forces are unleashed and the number of potential relationships is increased in a geometric progression. Some of these changes foster better individual performance while others hinder it. On the positive side, an increase in group size tends to increase the human resources available to the group. It also brings in the additional skills needed to accomplish the assigned task more efficiently and effectively. Expanding the group may make it more representative of the population at large and, as such, could offer greater opportunities for affiliation and meaningful participation. On the downside, any real growth in size increases the potential for problems in communication, coordination, and quality control. Individual members may become more inhibited and less productive with the imposition of a more formal group structure composed of well-defined tasks, roles, and statuses. As the work group moves away from primary face-to-face interaction, more of its (human and financial) resources will be invested in the group maintenance function as opposed to task achievement.

The complexity of the coordination problems that must be resolved before a work group can achieve its full potential tends to increase faster than group size. It is very difficult to attain and maintain optimum motivation, morale, performance, and productivity as more and more people join the work group. According to John Schermerhorn and his colleagues (1982), larger groups suffer some real disadvantages in terms of individual performance and group effectiveness. Many of these problems can be overcome in law enforcement through proactive management of the group process.

4. *Composition.* On-the-job performance, group effectiveness, and group dynamics are all influenced to one degree or another by the demographic, competency, and psychosocial characteristics of individual group members. In order to fulfill their role and take advantage of their competencies (intelligence, maturity, motivation, personality, technical skill, physical ability, etc.), individuals must be capable of functioning in a group setting. This is extremely important because the performance of an individual member can be greatly enhanced or restricted—deliberately or unintentionally—by other members of the work group.

Homogeneous work groups are composed of members who have similar backgrounds, interests, values, attitudes, and other traits. Heterogeneous groups, on the other hand, tend to accept and thrive on diversity. Open groups are heterogeneous in nature. They bring a fairly wide variety of skills and perspectives to bear on problems. This diversity can, at times, lead to competition, conflict, and a lack of direction. Closed groups are much more homogeneous. Homogeneity produces common goals and increases the likelihood that there will be relatively harmonious working relationships among group members. Due to their innate similarities, it is fairly easy for individual members to buy into the group's culture. Conformity to group-shared values, norms, and ethical orientations becomes the rule rather than the exception.

Equal Employment Opportunity and Affirmative Action notwithstanding, the police profession still belongs near the closed group end of the continuum. The selection process is designed to identify men and women who possess an affinity for membership in the informal culture as well as the formal organization. According to Thomas Gray (Skolnick and Gray, 1975), affinity represents a predisposition to adhere to a distinctive set of sentiments that can be expanded and reinforced through training and socialization. Affinity is the operative concept used to separate those who are technically qualified to become police officers from those who will probably be able to absorb the requirements of the legal system, the formal police organization, and the police subculture.

Managers must exercise judgment in selecting human resources in order to create a healthy balance between homogeneity and heterogeneity. Individual performance and group productivity are directly related to the degree of fit experienced by those involved in a collective enterprise. Police work is undergoing a fundamental transition. It is in the process of moving away from resisting and fearing individual differences and moving toward accepting and utilizing them. The more diverse the membership, the more skilled an administrator must be in reconciling individual differences and managing group dynamics.

5. *Norms.* As defined earlier, norms are guidelines for accepted and expected social behavior that are inculcated in an individual's subconscious mind through the socialization process. They reflect group-shared ideas about how individual members are supposed to behave inside and outside of the group. Group norms not only regulate formal and informal relationships between members of the work force but control the overall quantity and quality of the work itself. Socialization is a dynamic process whereby the culture of the work group is transmitted from one generation of workers to another. It is through the socialization process that new members learn to identify with, model, internalize, and derive intrinsic social satisfaction from conformity with the values, norms, and ethical standards of the group.

As the result of socialization, the police officer develops a distinct consciousness of kind, a self-concept, and a reaffirmation of personal worth expressed in terms of approval and support (Souryal, 1977). Work groups exert a strong influence on the behavior of their members by providing them with security, support, encouragement, and positive reinforcement for appropriate behavior. Work groups also punish those members who deviate from their group-shared expectations. They use ridicule, shame, and the threat of expulsion to elicit conformity (Munro, 1977).

Virtually every aspect of a police officer's behavior is regulated by norms. As a result, the norms of the work group determine what is to be done, how it is to be accomplished, who is to do it, and and how much value it has to the group as a whole. The work group sets the standard for productivity and quality against which an individual's on-the-job performance is judged.

6. *Cohesiveness.* Some work groups are much more cohesive than others. Used in this context, cohesiveness is regarded as a characteristic of a group in which all of the forces acting on members to remain in the group are greater than those forces acting on them to leave it. According to Robert Albanese (1981), cohesive forces—those holding a work group together and strengthening interpersonal relationships among members—can be grouped into two very basic categories: (1) those that positively influence the achievement of the personal goals of group members and (2) those that satisfy group members' needs for meaningful and supportive interaction with significant others in the group. In a best case scenario, there will be congruence between organizational needs (for efficiency, effectiveness, and productivity) and members' needs (for belongingness, achievement, meaningful participation, and recognition) within a dynamic, synergistic, and hospitable social milieu.

Police officers find themselves in closed and relatively cohesive work groups. They work under hazardous and stressful conditions that draw them into a kind of brotherhood (Baker, 1985). Confronted with the demands of the public, expectations of administrators and pressures from their peers, police officers find themselves caught up in a web of insecurity, confusion, and frustration. Since it is almost impossible to resolve these personal dilemmas on their own, they identify with the group and cultivate its support by strengthening interpersonal relationships with each other. As the police have become more occupationally cohesive, their bonds with the public have grown weaker. These two groups have become polarized and treat each other as adversaries (More, 1985).

Most police officers have now adopted the attitude that no one can understand them but another cop. Recruits are screened and selected based on how well they will fit the police mold. They are then very carefully socialized to internalize the values, norms, and ethical orientations of the work group. At this point, they become full-fledged members of the police subculture. They think and behave and operate by the same rationale as their colleagues.

Cohesiveness and performance are directly related in several ways: (1) the successful performance of group tasks can increase cohesiveness, (2) even failure can lead to cohesiveness in a threatening or win-lose situation, and (3) cohesiveness can produce an increase in individual and/or group performance. The highest levels of performance are normally found in highly cohesive groups that value productivity and have established uniformly high performance norms (Ivancevich, Szilagyi, and Wallace, 1977). On the other side of the coin, cohesiveness can have a negative effect on performance if there is a conflict between organizational objectives and group members' needs. A high level of cohesiveness coupled with low performance goals promotes low performance. Under these circumstances, both individuality and innovation are discouraged (Whisenand and Rush, 1988).

7. *Groupthink.* As just described, group cohesiveness is the degree to which individuals are attracted and motivated to maintain their affiliation with a group. Cohesiveness can be a double-edged sword. Although it can have a very positive effect on performance, too much cohesiveness can become pathological. It discourages individuality, critical thinking, and innovation. Groupthink is a common characteristic of excessively cohesive groups. Loyalty to the group (in terms of its values, norms, and subcultural perspectives) becomes the most powerful group-shared expectation. Any behavior—from the inside or the outside—that harms the group or diminishes its solidarity is viewed as divisive, illegitimate, and totally unacceptable. Conformity and consensus replace analysis. It becomes "us" versus "them." "Them" refers to anyone outside of the group even if that person has legitimate authority and administrative responsibility related to the group's function.

Groupthink is a real hazard in police work. It is nourished by an obsession with loyalty, solidarity, esprit de corps, dependability, and secrecy. Many police officers are willing to tolerate incompetence, corruption, brutality, and "blue coat" crime rather than to "blow the whistle" or "hang dirty linen in public." They openly resist civilian control and have deep-seated antipathy for whistle blowers, internal affairs personnel, civilian review boards, and officers induced to break "the code." Police managers must be alert to the following symptoms of groupthink:

1. A shared illusion of invulnerability.
2. Application of pressure on those who deviate from the majority viewpoint.
3. Fear of the consequences of deviating from the majority viewpoint.
4. A shared illusion of unanimity and consensus in the group.
5. A perception of outsiders as evil, stupid, or weak.
6. An unquestioned belief in the morality of the in group.
7. The presence of self-appointed mind guards who shield the leader and other group members from information contrary to the party line.
8. An attempt to channel out negative feedback to the group (Albanese, 1981; Janis, 1976).

Conformity is a natural and normal aspect of group dynamics. Conformity becomes pathological when it manifests itself in groupthink and has a negative effect on individual performance as well as work group productivity.

Accepting and Managing Work Groups

The traditional Theory X (autocratic) approach to management is slowly but surely giving way to the kind of participative self-management that Douglas McGregor called Theory Y (Leonard and More, 1987). Experienced police administrators understand that groups and the group process are a permanent part of the landscape in police work. They know that without the work group's energy, effort, expertise, and support the chances of achieving the organization's mission, goals, and objectives are slim. The division of labor and task specialization associated with work in complex criminal justice organizations places a premium on cooperation, collaboration, and coordination in the workplace. Purposeful interaction and synergy provide an impetus for productivity. A lack of healthy group involvement and support is a kiss of death in those situations requiring collective behavior. Successful administrators see the management of group dynamics as a critical variable in effective task accomplishment. Consequently, they spend a great deal of their time in group development and maintenance. They seek to identify and resolve those problems that make the work group dysfunctional. It is their job to dismantle the barriers that obstruct intergroup as well as intragroup communication, neutralize destructive conflict, and encourage all members to become active participants in the group process.

Participatory management evolved from the concept of organizational humanism espoused by some members of the human relations school of management. It consists of a proactive and integrated strategy designed to increase organizational productivity as well as individual satisfaction by giving members of the work force a substantive role in the decision-making process. Members of the work group are permitted (within the parameters established by management) to establish their own goals and to achieve these goals through a collaborative effort. Once this participatory group process is set in motion, administrators can garner much needed support by allowing work groups to function with minimum intervention. Under these circumstances, managers assume a different role. They do less directing and more coordinating. They help guide and give substance to the group process by serving as resource persons, role models, teachers, and coaches. Modern police administrators are expected to convert the work group's synergistic effort into productive outputs (Holt, 1987).

Skillful police administrators utilize their knowledge of group and group dynamics to meet human needs as well as to motivate their immediate subordinates. They know that membership in a goal-oriented group tends to enhance the satisfaction, performance, and productivity of its members in relatively ambiguous and unstructured situations where they exercise a great deal of discretion. Ethical managers avoid using the group process to manipulate police personnel. They view employees as basically good and are committed to confirming them as whole persons. Ethical police administrators oppose game playing and cultivate genuine collaboration. They build supportive relationships with individuals and groups based on mutual respect and trust. Mutual respect and trust are part of the glue that holds any productive enterprise together.

Managerial Strategies

W. Richard Plunkett (1983) has identified seven basic principles he believes managers should follow in order to minimize a work group's tensions and conflicts and to maximize its performance, cooperation, collaboration, coordination, and contribution to the organization:

1. Accept groups, subgroups, and cliques as a fact of organizational life. Consider these informal groups as allies and additional forces to be won over and brought to bear on mutual problems. The trick is to learn to work with these groups, not to fight them or try to destroy them.
2. Identify and seek cooperation from informal leaders. They are a force to be reckoned with and might become future managers. Their informal power can be of great value in resolving organizational problems. It may be appropriate to share formal authority (through delegation) with them in certain situations. Informal leaders often recognize the advantage of cooperation and try to avoid conflict. Informal leaders are influential with their followers and other informal leaders. They know the opinions and attitudes of their group and serve as its spokesperson when communicating with management.
3. Prevent intergroup competition and the development of win-lose situations. Conflict debilitates the individual and reduces overall productivity. Hold out standards to be achieved and surpassed. Emphasize—through word and in deed—the importance of cooperation and collaboration. Treat all subordinates fairly, regardless of their group, subgroup, or clique affiliation. Solicit input from all groups and, when appropriate, incorporate it into the decision-making process.
4. Do not force people to choose between you and their group. If a manager backs them into a corner, based on an "either or" basis, they will usually pick the group. Loyalty to and membership in a subgroup or clique is not necessarily a negative. Members can serve the organization and the group if their goals are congruent and coincide with one another. They can be loyal and unopposed to a manager as long as that manager is fair, predictable, and loyal to them in return.
5. Adopt a coach's attitude toward all groups, subgroups, and cliques within the organization. Foster a team spirit and nurture the type of camaraderie that these informal groups promote. Be firm, play fair, and demand that subordinates behave in the same way. Team players know the value of rules and fair play. Enlist their meaningful participation as a group and give them a chance to enhance their self-esteem.
6. Appeal to individual group members and to each group's sense of competence. All members of the organization have a need to be good at what they do and to know what others think of them. Give people a series of challenges that, when met, will instill a sense of accomplishment, confidence, and pride. By setting organizational objectives and helping subordinates set their own goals, administrators motivate employees to excel and find ways in which to build confidence and self-respect. Point out how poor performance hurts others and makes everyone's job much more difficult.
7. Use the traditional and not-so-traditional levers to encourage cooperation. Levers are tools used to influence people in specific situations. None can be used in every situation. Levers like job assignments, overtime, disciplinary action, merit pay, and sincere praise may be effective. Most of them are effective if they are used by a manager who has the trust and respect of subordinates. Trust and respect comes as the result of the manager's knowledge, ability, (technical, interpersonal, and group) skills, and demonstrated concern for the group and its members.

CASE STUDY

Officer Bob Franklin

Officer Bob Franklin joined his hometown police department 14 years ago. He was a high school graduate who came from a working class family. His fellow officers came from similar backgrounds, and most of them had lived in town all of their lives. They shared many values, attitudes, perspectives, and dreams. The officers felt they belonged and were comfortable interacting with one another. They were a source of mutual support in times of stress.

Bob Franklin, like most of his peers, started out as an idealist. He wanted to be a supercop. His goal was to preserve the peace, protect people from criminals, and save society. Bob Franklin placed a relatively high value on individual rights and due process of law. He really wanted to protect and serve.

After three years in the patrol division, Officer Franklin was reassigned. He was placed in an undercover drug enforcement unit known as NARCON, which consisted of six investigators and one supervisor who formed a tightly knit work group. They had been together for nearly five years. Bob Franklin's goal—based on his need to belong—was to become a full-fledged member of the group.

NARCON could be described as a subculture within the police department. It consisted of a homogeneous and cohesive group of people who identified with each other and shared a unique set of values, attitudes, and beliefs related to their job. Based on continual face-to-face interaction among themselves and with criminals, they had become cynical reactionaries. They rewarded loyalty, secrecy, and conformity to group-shared expectations. The highest priority was to get addicts and dealers off the street regardless of the cost. Members of NARCON were more than willing to lie, deny due process, and violate constitutional rights to accomplish their objectives. The end justified the means as far as the members of NARCON were concerned.

Although Bob Franklin tried to remain neutral and adhere to his set of values, he needed recognition, support, and approval from the group. Subconsciously, he wanted to be considered "a stand-up guy" and was willing to sacrifice his ethical standards to achieve acceptance by and status in the work group. Membership in the group became an end in and of itself. He learned that abstract notions of right and wrong were irrelevant. Virtue consisted of loyalty to and protection of the group.

As Bob Franklin's partner was making a bust for possession with the intent to deliver, he accidentally shot and killed an unarmed suspect. After declaring that the dealer deserved to die, the officer placed a throw-down gun in the dead man's hand and told Franklin to call the NARCON supervisor. After the three police officers discussed the situation and agreed on a story, the supervisor summoned the department's shooting team.

Officer Franklin and his partner were interviewed by members of the shooting team. Bob Franklin was asked to describe what had happened. After a moment's hesitation (during which he thought about his duty to protect and serve and his loyalty to the group), he lied. Even though he knew it was wrong and that he could be fired or prosecuted for providing false information,

Bob Franklin told the shooting team member the story that had been concocted to cover his partner. Because the dead man was considered "a low life," no further action was taken. Bob Franklin had successfully negotiated a rite of passage. He could now claim to be a full-fledged member of NARCON.

Using concepts related to groups and group dynamics, explain what happened in this situation. When does group cohesiveness cease to be positive and become pathological? What steps might you take, as a police administrator, to prevent this from occurring?

This is a tall order to fill. While it is very difficult to deal effectively with groups, subgroups, and cliques in the workplace, managing groups and the group process now consumes a lion's share of the police administrator's time.

Summary

Human beings are social animals who live, work, and find varying degrees of psychosocial validation in groups. Groups, as the basic unit of social organization, provide people with a cultural milieu in which to satisfy their personal needs as well as their social need for interaction with significant others. Each person develops a social identity, a unique sense of self, and an internalized set of normative controls through meaningful interaction with other people during the socialization process.

Most people belong to and participate in a wide variety of formal organizations and informal cliques. Some groups are task-oriented and highly structured. Other groups are much more casual and coalesce around some vague—loosely defined—common interest. These groups tend to emphasize the importance of meaningful interpersonal relationships as opposed to the task itself.

Groups develop a distinctive social orientation, or collective personality. New members are socialized to behave in certain ways. They are expected to learn and internalize appropriate roles, norms, values, and cultural perspectives. All members are rewarded for conformity to group-shared expectations and punished if they deviate from them. Consciousness of kind and internalized self-control reduce conflict and promote collaboration.

Work groups are mechanisms through which goal-oriented human beings learn relevant knowledge, technical skills, and job-related behaviors. Groups have life cycles just like all other living organisms. Group dynamics have an effect on individual performance. Group dynamics also exert an influence on the efficiency, effectiveness, and productivity of the organization. Whether these effects are good or bad will depend on member needs, the complexity of the task, the size, composition, norms, and cohesiveness of the group, the prevailing reward structure, and so on.

Experienced police administrators accept that groups, subgroups, and cliques exist within the police department. They understand that groups are inevitable and ubiquitous. They also know groups unleash powerful synergistic forces that can have either good or bad consequences depending on the situation. The police administrator's principal job is to manage the department's human resources in such a way as to increase its overall efficiency, effectiveness, and productivity. In order to accomplish this objective, they must do the following: (1) accept the group phenomenon as a fact of organizational life, (2) identify and seek cooperation from informal group leaders, (3) prevent dysfunctional competition and the development of win-lose situations, (4) avoid forcing members to choose between allegiance to management or their group, (5) adopt a coach's attitude toward groups, subgroups, and cliques within the organization, (6) motivate work groups by appealing to their sense of competence, and (7) utilize traditional and nontraditional methods to encourage individual as well as group collaboration.

In order to be successful in working with groups, police administrators must have knowledge, good interpersonal skills, and a positive attitude concerning subgroup participation in the organization's decision-making process. This will enable them to channel the energy, effort, and expertise of group members in such a way as to achieve the mission, goals, and objectives of the police department. In a very real sense, knowledge is power and skill is the ability to translate knowledge into action.

Key Concepts

The social animal
Social interaction
Collective behavior
Formal groups
Informal groups
Need orientation
Group structure
Role
Role set
Norms
Values
Sanctions
Culture
Socialization process
Initiation
Conformity
Reinforcement
Self-control
Group dynamics
Group growth cycle
Structure and performance
Cohesiveness
Groupthink
Groups and productivity
Managing group dynamics

Discussion Topics and Questions

1. List and discuss the distinct social functions that groups perform for their members.
2. What is a group? What are the characteristics of formal work groups and how do they differ from informal groups within complex criminal justice organizations?
3. How do social interactionists define a group, and why do they place such a great emphasis on action?
4. What are the principal psychosocial needs that motivate human beings to join and remain active in informal as well as formal groups?

5. Name and discuss four categories commonly used to classify groups in terms of their function. Which are most often associated with the division of labor in bureaucratic organizations?
6. Identify and describe the primary structural components that are common to both formal and informal groups.
7. The police are referred to as a subculture. What is a subculture? What are values and norms, and how are they passed on to new members?
8. How does the prevailing reward structure influence individual performance and work-group productivity?
9. Identify, list, and discuss the characteristics of work groups that have a direct effect on individual performance and organizational productivity.
10. If police administrators accept the assumptions on which organizational humanism and social interactionism are founded, how do you expect them to approach their job as managers in a complex criminal justice organization?

References

ALBANESE, ROBERT. 1981. *Managing: Toward Accountability for Performance.* Homewood, IL: Richard D. Irwin.

ALPERT, GEOFFREY P., and ROGER G. DUNHAM. 1988. *Policing Urban America.* Prospect Heights, IL: Waveland Press.

ARONSON, ELLIOT. 1976. *The Social Animal.* San Francisco: Freeman.

BAKER, MARK. 1985. *Cops.* New York: Pocket Books.

BARON, ROBERT A. 1983. *Behavior in Organizations: Understanding and Managing the Human Side of Work.* Boston: Allyn & Bacon.

BENNE, K. J., and P. SHEATS. 1948. "Functional Roles of Group Members," *Journal of Social Issues,* 4, Spring.

BRODERICK, JOHN J. 1987. *Police in a Time of Change.* Prospect Heights, IL: Waveland Press.

CARTWRIGHT, DORWIN, and RONALD LIPPIT. 1976. "Group Dynamics and the Individual." In Robert A. Sutermeister (Ed.), *People and Productivity.* New York: McGraw-Hill.

CHAMPION, DEAN J. 1975. *The Sociology of Organizations.* New York: McGraw-Hill.

CHINOY, ELY, and JOHN P. HEWITT. 1975. *Sociological Perspective.* New York: Random House.

CHRUDEN, HERBERT J., and ARTHUR W. SHERMAN, JR. 1976. *Personnel Management.* Chicago: South-Western.

DESSLER, GARY. 1979. *Management Fundamentals: A Framework.* Reston, VA: Reston.

DUBRIN, ANDREW J. 1985. *Contemporary Applied Management.* Plano, TX: Business Publications.

FOX, ELLIOT M., and L. URWICK. 1973. *Dynamic Administration: The Collected Papers of Mary Parker Follet.* New York: Hippocrene Books.

FULMER, ROBERT M. 1982. *Supervision: Principles of Professional Management.* New York: Macmillan.

FULMER, ROBERT M. 1983. *The New Management.* New York: Macmillan.

HEINEN, J. S., and E. JACOBSON. 1976. "A Model of Task Group Development in Complex Organizations and a Strategy for Implementation," *Academy of Management Review,* 1.

HOLDEN, RICHARD N. 1986. *Modern Police Management.* Englewood Cliffs, NJ: Prentice-Hall.

HOLT, DAVID H. 1987. *Management: Principles and Practices.* Englewood Cliffs, NJ: Prentice-Hall.

IVANCEVICH, J. M., A. D. SZILAGYI, and M. J. WALLACE. 1977. *Organizational Behavior and Performance.* Santa Monica, CA: Goodyear.

JANIS, I. L. 1976. "Groupthink Among Policy Makers." In G. M. Kren and L. H. Rappoport (Eds.), *Varieties of Psycho-history*. New York: Springer.

JOHNSON, D. W., et. al. 1981. "Effects of Co-operative, Competitive and Individualistic Goal Structures on Achievement," *Psychological Bulletin,* Vol. 89.

LEONARD, V. A., and HARRY W. MORE. 1987. *Police Organization and Management*. Mineola, NY: Foundation Press.

LIKERT, RENSIS. 1961. *Organization Theory*. New York: McGraw-Hill.

MASSEY, MORRIS. 1979. *The People Puzzle: Understanding Yourself and Others*. Reston, VA: Reston.

MELVILLE, DALTON. 1959. *Men Who Manage: Fusions of Feeling and Theory in Administration*. New York: Wiley.

MORE, HARRY W. 1985. *Critical Issues in Law Enforcement*. Cincinnati: Anderson.

MUNRO, JIM L. 1977. *Administrative Behavior and Police Organization*. Cincinnati: Anderson.

PLUNKETT, W. RICHARD. 1983. *Supervision: The Direction of People at Work*. Dubuque, IA: William C. Brown.

REITZ, H. JOSEPH. 1981. *Behavior in Organizations*. Homewood, IL: Richard D. Irwin.

ROSE, PETER I. 1977. *The Study of Society: An Integrated Anthology*. New York: Random House.

ROSENBAUM, M. E., et. al. 1980. "Group Productivity and Process," *Journal of Personality and Social Psychology*, Vol. 39.

SAYLES, LEONARD R. 1957. *Research in Industrial Human Relations*. New York: Harper & Row.

SCHERMERHORN, JOHN R., JAMES G. HUNT, and RICHARD N. OSBORN. 1982. *Managing Organizational Behavior.* New York: Wiley.

SCHUTZ, WILLIAM C. 1958. *FIRO: A Three-Dimensional Theory of Interpersonal Behavior.* New York: Rinehart.

SHERIF, MUZAFER, and CAROLYN W. SHERIF. 1956. *An Outline of Social Psychology*. New York: Harper & Row.

SHIBUTANI, TAMOTSU. 1961. *Society and Personality: An Interactionist Approach to Social Psychology*. Englewood Cliffs, NJ: Prentice-Hall.

SKOLNICK, JEROME H., and THOMAS C. GRAY. 1975. *Police in America*. Boston: Little, Brown.

SMITH, RONALD W. and FREDERICK W. PRESTON. 1982. *Sociology: An Introduction*. New York: St. Martin's Press.

SOURYAL, SAM S. 1977. *Police Administration and Management*. St. Paul, MN: West.

SUTERMEISTER, ROBERT A. 1976. *People and Productivity*. New York: McGraw-Hill.

THIBAULT, EDWARD A., LAWRENCE M. LYNCH, and R. BRUCE MCBRIDE. 1985. *Proactive Police Management*. Englewood Cliffs, NJ: Prentice-Hall.

WHISENAND, PAUL M., and GEORGE R. RUSH. 1988. *Supervising Police Personnel: Back to Basics*. Englewood Cliffs, NJ: Prentice-Hall.

WILLIAMS, LENA. 1988. "Police Officers Tell of Strains of Living as a 'Black in Blue,' " *The New York Times,* Feb. 14, p. 1.

ZASTROW, CHARLES, and LEE BOWKER. 1984. *Social Problems: Issues and Solutions*. Chicago: Nelson-Hall.

For Further Reading

JOHNSON, THOMAS A., GORDON E. MISNER, and LEE P. BROWN. 1981. *The Police and Society: An Environment for Collaboration and Confrontation*. Englewood Cliffs, NJ: Prentice-Hall.

Contains a well-written section dealing with role theory and the police organization. The authors explore the recruitment, selection, and socialization of police personnel. They also discuss the subculturalization and microsocialization of patrol officers within the police subculture itself.

NATEMEYER, WALTER E. (Ed.). 1978. *Classics of Organizational Behavior.* Oak Park, IL: Moore.

Reprints many of the classics dealing with interpersonal and group behavior. Selections range from Maslow to Schein.

O'NEILL, MICHAEL E., and KAI R. MARTENSEN. 1975. *Criminal Justice Group Training: A Facilitator's Handbook.* La Jolla, CA: University Associates.

Deals with the use of group dynamics in the organization development (OD) process. Emphasis is placed on team building to resolve organizational problems in American law enforcement.

SHAFRITZ, JAY M., and PHILLIP H. WHITBECK. 1978. *Classics of Organization Theory*. Oak Park, IL: Moore.

Reprints many of the classics dealing with organization theory. Selections range from Mary Parker Follett to Rensis Likert.

CHAPTER 8

Power: Its Nature and Use

LEARNING OBJECTIVES

1. Define *power*.
2. Distinguish between power and influence.
3. Identify the types of power.
4. Describe how power is acquired.
5. Distinguish between referent and expert power.
6. Identify the sources of power in terms of their applications and effects.
7. Compare and contrast coercive and legitimate power.
8. Describe the positive aspects of power.
9. Explain the relationship between power and responsibility.
10. Contrast leadership and power.

A phrase used extensively in newspapers, magazines, journals, and in the lexicon of police training programs is, *Power corrupts, and absolute power corrupts absolutely*. The implication is that when one has an excess of power, it will be used unwisely (Kotter, 1985). The concern that managers have too much power is definitely invalid. Indeed, the real problem is that managers in today's organizations in many instances do not have the power they need in order to function effectively.

The reality is, managers' power is becoming increasingly circumscribed by legal and social constraints. Laws and regulations such as the Civil Rights Act, the Age Discrimination in Employment Act, the Equal Employment Opportunity Act, and rulings by federal courts have resulted in restrictions and limited the power base of police managers (Reece and Brandt, 1987; Dressler, 1983).

Managerial power is further reduced by the pressure exerted by interest groups, citizens, the city manager or mayor, the city council or board of supervisors, the state legislature, civic groups, and unions (Lee, 1980). All these combine at different times to limit or restrict the power exercised by managers. An illustration of this is officer membership in unions or associations, coupled with legislation mandating memorandums of agree-

INTRODUCTORY CASE

Lieutenant Fred Weaver

Lt. Fred Weaver currently commands the Youth Services Bureau in a medium-sized police department in a city that is primarily a bedroom community with a large commercial section and no industry. There are a large number of young citizens in the community, thus making it especially important for the police department to emphasize the prevention of crime. This is done through a Police Athletic League that sponsors various sports activities throughout the year.

Lt. Weaver attended the local university, earning a degree in psychology. He was very active in campus activities and earned a letter in both baseball and track. As a high school student, he joined a police-sponsored Explorer Scout unit and played baseball in the Police Athletic League. He continued these activities as a college student. He joined the police department after graduation.

He then attended the regional police academy and graduated first in his class. Weaver's first assignment was to patrol, where he served for three years with distinction. In his fourth year of service he was promoted to sergeant and assigned to the Youth Services Bureau where he both supervised the Explorer Scout unit and coached the baseball team.

In his seventh year of service he was promoted to lieutenant and became the commander of the Youth Services Bureau. During the three years assigned to the bureau he has become indispensable as a fund-raiser. He is an excellent speaker and appears before community groups frequently. Under his leadership, the bureau's influence has extended greatly, and many public officials as well as important citizens in the community view Lt. Weaver as the real spokesperson of the department.

During the last three years, Lt. Weaver has quadrupled the unit's income from outside sources and has introduced an annual circus and a Youth Olympics program. Both these programs were instant successes and clearly enhance the reputation of the bureau.

The chief of police is beginning to sense that he has lost control of the bureau and that it is almost becoming an independent police unit. It is a tenuous situation. The chief feels Lt. Weaver is becoming a threat to his position and is attempting to gain all the power he can.

Lt. Weaver's point of view is that he is only trying to do his job, he is not searching for power, and he simply makes decisions to ensure that the bureau stays the primary crime prevention unit in the community.

If you were the chief how would you deal with the potential problem? Could Lt. Weaver have done things differently to avoid being perceived as a power threat? What types of power do both leaders have?

ment/understanding between police departments and unions (Unsinger and More, 1989).

In addition, the personality of the manager and the organization itself serve as modifiers of power. Some police managers are viewed as *power hungry*; others' behavior suggests they do not like to exercise power. This dichotomy is especially apparent when it involves discipline. Some managers will go out of their way to avoid confronting deviant organizational behavior while others relish the prospects of conflict.

Structurally the bureaucratic nature of a police organization is such that power (of the type causing things to happen) is distributed from top to bottom. The higher the rank the greater the amount of power.

Definitions of Power

Power is a concept with negative connotations. Managers who have power deny it. Power seekers do everything possible to make it look otherwise. Lastly, those who are adept at securing power are reluctant to discuss how they acquired it (Kanter, 1979).

Taken most negatively, power implies a master/slave relationship or at the very least, a superior/subordinate relationship. When power is criticized, it is generally for one of two reasons (Cohen, 1980):

1. It is being used to manipulate, coerce, or force someone to do something. In this instance it is an abuse of power.
2. The goal to be achieved is totally undesirable, possibly even illegal, morally wrong, or corrupting.

Power has been defined differently by researchers who have analyzed the concept. The following definitions demonstrate the variability:

1. The ability to command or apply force, not necessarily accompanied by authority (Rue and Byars, 1986).
2. The ability to influence others through some personal or situational characteristic (Duncan, 1981).
3. Simply the ability to get things done the way one wants them to be done (Salancik and Pfeffer, 1983).
4. The capacity to exert influence (Cohen, Fink, Gadon, and Willits, 1980).
5. The capacity or ability to get things done . . . to exercise control over people, events, situations, and oneself (Cohen, 1980).

Each of these definitions describe either the ability or the capacity to control the behavior of an individual or a group in order to attain some goal. The negative connotations of power can be dealt with best by defining it as *the ability, the vigor, and the strength to influence others and to control one's own destiny* (Waitley and Witt, 1985).

This definition accepts the premise that everyone in an organization possesses some power giving them the capacity to choose between alternatives. In this context, power is viewed as the ability to adapt to a situation, negotiate alternatives, plan for event(s), or assume responsibility (Waitley and Witt, 1985). Needless to say, not everyone in an organization has equal power or even the power needed to completely control their future. Implicit in the definition is a degree of dependency between members of an organization, and at the same time some discretion for the individual when responding to efforts designed to influence behavior.

Power is, in reality, a paradox. It can be used to achieve organizational goals, group objectives, and individual goals or it can be used to thwart goal attainment. In recent years a number of pertinent books from pop psychology have received a great deal of attention: *The Power Broker* (Korda, 1977); *Power: How to Get It and How to Use It* (Ringer, 1974); *Looking Out for Number One* (Ringer, 1983); *No More Mr. Nice Guy* (Epstein, 1979); and *Scrambling* (Chapman, 1981). All these place a great deal of emphasis on the acquisition of power and in some instances, its use for personal gain.

It is clear that managerial power, when used correctly, generally involves bringing together resources to accomplish something. Effective managers understand the uses, limitations, sources, and characteristics of power. If power is used to make employees totally dependent, then it is being used ineffectively. If it is used sparingly or in a helping mode, it is more apt to be effective.

Managers use different techniques to make employees dependent (Grothe and Wylie, 1987) (see Table 8.1).

1. *The Bureaucrat.* This type of police manager worships the manual. There is a place for everything and everything must be in its place. Exceptions, if ever, are few and far between. An officer must go by the book. To deviate is to court disaster. Officers being supervised are made dependent and are required to conform to every rule and regulation. This type of boss can cite departmental policies in their entirety.

2. *The Controller.* This type of police manager is most likely to have had military experience; the tough drill-sergeant approach to management typifies the working relationship between the manager and subordinates. Subordinates are never allowed to question the authority of such a manager and dependency must be absolute. The managerial style is autocratic, authoritarian, and in some instances, tyrannical.

3. *The Competitor.* This kind of boss is selective when developing dependency relationships. The bottom line is to rise to the top as fast as possible and dependency is used as a tool to achieve promotion and positions of influence. Competitors are the movers and shakers in the organization and while they have the capacity to be inspirational leaders, they only show that side if it is to their advantage. They are competitive and tend to be risk takers, but when threatened, they can become pushy and overwhelming.

4. *The Incompetent.* Incompetents are always looking for someone who can help them solve a problem, and they become very adept at blaming others

TABLE 8.1 Managerial Style and Dependency

1. The Bureaucrat
2. The Controller
3. The Competitor
4. The Incompetent
5. The Realist

SOURCE: Mardy Grothe and Peter Wylie, *Problem Bosses: Who They Are and How to Deal with Them* (New York: Warner-Tamerlane, 1987).

for their inadequacies. They clearly are functioning at a level beyond their capabilities. This category also includes managers who have become stymied and will never move beyond their present position. They know they are not going anywhere and everyone in the organization knows it too. They become negative and preoccupied with how they have been treated unfairly. In terms of dependency they are neutral.

5. *The Realist.* Managers in this category limit employee dependency to situations where someone has to be trained in order to achieve an organizational goal, when confronted with an unusual occurrence, or during an emergency. When the realist delegates work it includes the authority needed to accomplish the task. This leader makes every effort to give each employee a degree of control over his or her own destiny. Realists are risk takers and understand that errors and mistakes are inevitable if employees are allowed to grow and become competent.

Different types of managers, then, use power for different reasons, but to some degree managers are continually using power as a means of influencing others. Influence apparently is the behavioral response to the application of power (Schermerhorn, Hunt, and Osborn, 1988). When people are convinced to change their behavior, to change their opinion, to complete a certain act or activity, or to support a different position, then a manager can be said to have exerted influence over a follower, a peer, or a superior.

The Power Base

Power has meaning not only to the individual but to groups and organizations. Everyone has heard, at some time or another, an individual referred to as powerful, and it is always someone who can influence behavior. Decisions are made, goals attained, or changes instituted. Power involves the interaction between two individuals. This personal interaction is described as consisting of five types of power: reward, coercive, legitimate, referent, and expert (French and Raven, 1959) (see Figure 8.1).

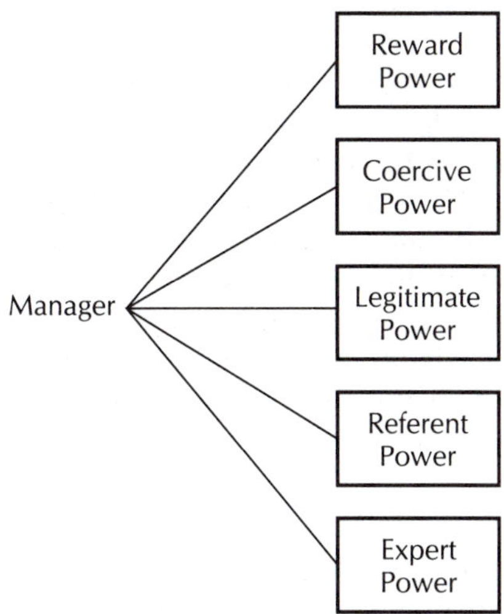

FIGURE 8.1 The Power Base of the Manager.

Reward Power

Rewarding an employee for performance is one of the best ways a manager can influence behavior. For example, a manager can use pay and promotions to encourage acceptable behavior. In the few police departments having a merit program, officers can be rewarded monetarily for engaging in acceptable behavior. This has proven to be an excellent tool for motivating employees when they have strived for the recognition accompanying a merit increase. In other departments the creation of levels for police officers such as Officer I, Officer II, and Officer III (some departments have a Senior Patrol Officer position) has provided police managers at every level with another tool useful in the rewards process. Hopefully this system will be adopted by other police departments because law enforcement has been constrained for years by the lock-step promotion system wherein an officer (after receiving four salary increments), remains at the same pay level (other than cost of living raises) until promoted.

Most police officers pursue promotions actively and find it to be one of the best ways to obtain status and receive recognition both in the organization and within the community. In a law enforcement agency a manager gains increasing control over the rewards system as additional rank is attained. Normally a sergeant can recommend someone for promotion, but the final action is taken by the chief.

In recent years the reward power of the police chief executive officer has been extended as the typical promotion list has expanded and the chief has been given greater latitude in the selection process. For many years a chief was required to select from the top three candidates, but in recent years this has been increased in many agencies to the top eight candidates.

As police departments have grown in size, the reward power (in the hands of the chief executive officer) has, however, been diluted as it has become increasingly necessary for the chief to rely on recommendations of other managers. This is in sharp contrast to the situation in smaller police departments where the chief is personally acquainted with every officer being considered for promotion—except for instances where lateral transfers from other police organizations are also being considered.

In law enforcement, intrinsic rewards have a great deal of importance, for example, special assignments, praise, and awards. Many officers can be motivated because of their desire to be recognized and accepted as a productive member of the organization. Managers at various levels within the organization can satisfy these needs by assigning an officer to special units such as K-9 or SWAT. In most instances officers find assignment to these units highly desirable. In some departments the same holds true for assignment to crime prevention, traffic (motorcycle), and investigations.

Police managers have a special obligation to acknowledge exemplary police action, which can range from apprehending an offender to solving a complex crime or providing assistance to someone in need. Most agencies have a written policy specifying how police managers will take official notice when an officer deserves commendation. Commendations can be classified as follows (More and Shipley, 1987):

1. Class A: Outstanding, exceptional work beyond the call of duty.
2. Class B: Meritorious police work, but not outstanding.

TABLE 8.2 The Manager's Reward Powers

Promotion
Increases in pay
Special assignments
Additional responsibility
Praise
Commendations
Establishing a trusting relationship
Participation
Two-way communications

SOURCE: James M. Jenks and John M. Kelly, *Don't Do. Delegate!* (New York: Ballantine, 1985).

3. Class C: Above average police work of a routine nature.
4. Class D: Ordinary police work of a routine nature, but deserving official notice.
5. Class E: Not requiring official notice.

There are a number of other intrinsic rewards of importance to officers including a wide range of managerial actions (see Table 8.2). Managers should strive to encourage participation whenever possible.

Thus power has to be shared—this is done by delegating authority commensurate with responsibility. There is considerable evidence showing most people gain satisfaction from exercising power (Swingle, 1976). It is important to remember some officers are not ready to exercise additional organizational power because they cannot accept the responsibility. Managers are advised to limit delegations to those who potentially can benefit, then monitor it, and when necessary, teach the employee how to exercise the newly acquired power to support departmental goals.

Whenever possible a manager should strive for consensus during the decision-making process as a means of increasing mutual trust. The goal is to create an atmosphere whereby subordinates respond to this type of reward by becoming more creative, demonstrating a higher degree of initiative, and exhibiting a greater dedication to the department which in turn makes for a better operating department. This does not mean a police manager abandons a leadership position, but the leadership style is facilitative, not repressive. When the situation demands, a police manager must still respond to the situation (especially during emergencies) and orders must be issued and followed without any thought of participation or achieving consensus.

Coercive Power

Coercive power is at the other end of the continuum from reward power. It is based on fear of punishment and the sanctions police managers can utilize to control the behavior of subordinates. Punishment can take many forms including suspension, demotion, official reprimand, or more subtle sanctions such as giving an officer an undesirable assignment.

The extreme sanction is termination. Even if it is a first offense, many departments will dismiss an officer for the following:

1. Soliciting, accepting, or offering a bribe.
2. Theft of cash or city property.
3. Falsifying city records.
4. Destroying city records.
5. Falsifying time reports, mileage reports, or expense accounts.
6. Deliberately withholding information (relating to work) from supervisors.

In many police departments (because of the 24-hour orientation) the midnight shift is imposed on officers to punish them or to put them where they are out of sight and mind. The same strategy transfers employees to undesirable locations. For example, officers can be disciplined by being assigned to a station many miles from home thus requiring a long commute.

Not every assignment in law enforcement is sought after. Some officers like to work traffic and others do not. Others enjoy the action of working a high crime beat while still others would rather do anything but this task. In most instances a police manager, especially the supervisory manager, will know what an officer likes and dislikes and can use this knowledge for purposes of punishment.

Overly strict supervision is another way to administer punishment. An officer who is perceived as recalcitrant can have incident reports returned repeatedly for rewriting. Rules and regulations can be enforced down to the last crossed t or dotted i. Every deviation is written up and documented. Another punishment technique utilized by first-line supervisors is excessive monitoring of the procedures and techniques utilized when stopping someone for a traffic violation. In most instances the supervisor can find reasons to write a negative report, for example, the police vehicle was parked incorrectly, the officer's approach to the car was wrong, the radio was not used properly, or the officer detained the offender too long (see Table 8.3).

All this harassment can result in a punishing working environment. The repeated application of negative sanctions can result (at its extreme) in a decision by an officer to quit—or in some instances, file a grievance against the supervisor. In other cases an officer can respond to the sanctions by treading water, that is, doing just enough to get by, or ignoring field conditions leading to a possible reprimand such as a questionable car stop or field interrogation.

Table 8.4 lists what is considered to be improper behavior in relations with supervisors, fellow employees, and the public. Potential corrective action is also given.

In recent years the coercive power of police managers has been reduced because of the influence of police unions and associations.

TABLE 8.3 The Manager's Coercive Powers

Termination	Transfer
Suspension	Relocation
Official reprimand	Strict supervision
Undesirable job assignment	Enforcement of rules and regulations

TABLE 8.4 Standard of Employee Conduct: Employees must cooperate and work well with other employees and the public.

Improper Behavior in Relations with Supervisors, Fellow Employees, or the Public	*Potential Corrective Actions*		
Offense	*First Offense*	*Second Offense*	*Third Offense*
a. Flagrant refusal to perform reasonable work assignments or to cooperate with supervisors or management in the performance of duties (insubordination).	1 to 6 days suspension	Dismissal	
b. Failure to cooperate with or using abusive language toward other employees or the public.	Oral warning or written notice	Written notice to 5 days suspension	6 days suspension to dismissal
c. Unnecessarily disrupting the work of other employees.	Oral warning or written notice	Written notice to 5 days suspension	6 days suspension to dismissal
d. Using threats or attempting to harm another employee or the public.	6 days suspension to dismissal	Dismissal	
e. Making false, vicious, or malicious statements about any employee, or City government or Department management.	Oral warning to 30 days suspension	6 days suspension to dismissal	Dismissal
f. Unauthorized possession of dangerous weapons, such as firearms or knives, on City or Department property.	Oral warning to 30 days suspension	6 days suspension to dismissal	Dismissal
g. Unauthorized use of dangerous weapons, such as firearms, knives, or tools which could result or results in harm to another employee or the public.	30 days suspension to dismissal	Dismissal	
h. Actions on the job intended to destroy property or to inflict bodily injury (whether or not the destruction or injury actually occurs).	Written notice to dismissal	10 days suspension to dismissal	Dismissal
i. Creating unsanitary conditions.	Oral warning to 5 days suspension	6–10 days suspension to dismissal	Dismissal

SOURCE: Harry W. More and O. R. Shipley, *Police Policy Manual—Personnel* (Springfield, IL: Charles C Thomas, 1987). Reprinted with permission.

Legitimate Power

Legitimate power is associated with one's position, role, and status in the organization. The incumbent possesses legitimate power as long as assigned to the office or position, and that power is transferred when another individual assumes the position. In law enforcement, rank is closely associated with legitimate power. Power generally increases with each higher rank. For example, a chief executive officer's position will usually be described as follows: "The Chief of Police is the chief executive officer of the department and the final departmental authority on all matters of policy, operations, and discipline. The chief exercises all lawful powers of the office and issues such lawful orders as are necessary to assure the effective performance of the department" (More and Shipley, 1987).

In law enforcement the boss has the right to command. The authority identifying that right is usually quite specific, as the following police directive shows (More and Shipley, 1987):

> *Compliance with Lawful Orders.* The department is an organization with a clearly defined hierarchy of authority. This is necessary because unquestioned obedience of a superior's lawful command is essential for the safe and prompt performance of law enforcement operations. The most desirable means of obtaining compliance are recognition and reward of proper performance, and the positive encouragement of a willingness to serve. However, negative discipline may be necessary where there is a willful disregard of lawful orders, commands, or directives. (p. 98)

This directive clearly illustrates that a superior has accompanying reward and coercive powers. Unity of command is also stressed and there is a definite chain of command. Everyone is aware of their relative position in the organization, whom they are immediately responsible for, and to whom they are accountable.

In law enforcement, departmental directives will also spell out command responsibilities at unusual occurrences. A field commander or the assigned senior officer will have the authority to direct the operation and is held responsible. A senior commanding officer may make suggestions, but actual supervision is left up to the field commander unless properly relieved. Most senior command officers will assume command of an unusual occurrence because it is normal for a police department to have a policy specifying this officer will be held accountable for unfavorable developments even if he or she has chosen not to take command (More and Shipley, 1987). For example, at a bombing scene departmental policy will specifically state the responsibilities of the first officer at the scene, and what is required of the responding field commander. Procedures for collecting evidence will be specified, and experts identified who can assist in the search of the crime scene.

Referent Power

Referent power is difficult to define because it is intangible. It is related to the ability of a manager to influence subordinate behavior because the employees identify with the manager. It can be the result of the manager's intelligence or some aspect of their personality that subordinates like or admire. When a leader's personal characteristics are seen as exceptional in the eyes of followers, the leader is usually described as charismatic.

Charisma is defined as a personal magic of leadership arousing special popular loyalty or enthusiasm for a public figure. It is usually used to describe a political leader or a military commander such as John Kennedy or George Patton. In law enforcement, J. Edgar Hoover at the federal level and O. W.

Wilson, Bill Parker, and August Vollmer at the local level are examples of charismatic leaders who had a large number of supporters.

If a manager is perceived as charismatic it seems everything falls nicely into place. Values and attitudes become positive and tasks are accomplished with ease. Such a leader is found to be unusually persuasive and followers respond because they want to—not because they have to (Wofford, 1982).

When a manager is someone with whom employees identify easily, that person has referent power. A key element of this type of power is trust. When an officer trusts a police manager it enhances the working relationship. Trust is something given by an employee—not something that demands or manipulates (Hawkins, 1981). Trust is a positive variable engendering acceptance and a real desire to follow. When trust is present, the manager is in a position to influence outcomes. Current research suggests referent power is still a somewhat unknown quality and not completely understood.

Expert Power

When managers are able to control the behavior of others because of their knowledge, experience, or judgment they are said to have expert power. This special information might have been acquired over an extended period of time or as a consequence of special training, but in every instance such expertise provides a base for obtaining subordinate compliance.

When managers have relevant, useful, and important information, they are in a position to exert influence extending beyond their other powers. In recent years, law enforcement agencies have increasingly relied on the expertise of professionals, especially in the areas of law and psychology. It is quite common to find police departments employing police legal advisers and police psychologists.

In addition, as police departments have grown in size, supervisors have developed an expertise in numerous areas including the investigation of auto theft, bunco, forgery, sex, and computer crimes. In other instances managers have been placed in staff positions where they have developed unique skills in planning, budgeting, or other administrative tasks giving them additional power.

Expert power (if it is to be of benefit to a department) should not be autocratic, but a process of balancing technical competence and allowing subordinates, superiors, and peers to achieve goals and objectives. We anticipate that technical knowledge will become increasingly important. Experts will have to learn how to manage the complexities of interdependent relationships they encounter if the organization is to be responsive and adapt to changing conditions (Kotter, 1985).

Power Sources

An effective manager influences the behavior of others in the work environment. The power used is derived from two sources: personal and positional (Schermerhorn, Hunt, and Osborn, 1988). The five bases of power are distributed differently between the two sources. The extent to which a manager

CASE STUDY

Lieutenant Luis Gonzales

Lt. Luis Gonzales has been a member of the Crater Police Department for 11 years and been a lieutenant for 2 years. Crater has a population of 83,000 and is part of a metropolitan area in the northwestern United States. When still a sergeant, Gonzales was assigned to the Support Services Bureau and became involved in the electronic automation of the department.

Lt. Gonzales attended City University where he majored in business administration and minored in computer sciences. This academic preparation, coupled with his intense interest in computers, served as a base of knowledge when the department decided to automate its communications and records center.

Gonzales first surveyed other police departments to determine what computer-aided dispatching systems they used. In addition, he visited state and federal agencies to obtain the latest information on computer applications to law enforcement. Then he wrote a prospectus, obtained its internal approval, and submitted the proposal to various computer vendors.

Once the city selected a vendor, Lt. Gonzales was assigned to work full time monitoring the installation of the computer-aided dispatch system. This process took nine months, and after the system was put on line, it proved to be most effective. Problems were solved with dispatch. The chief of police then assigned Lt. Gonzales to head a team to computerize the records system.

With this new assignment, Lt. Gonzales became a real expert in the application of computers to law enforcement. His advice is sought by other departments as he has proven to be very skillful. He runs hands-on training programs for the department, receiving enthusiastic acclaim from all the attendees.

The investigative unit now is capable of accessing computerized criminal records, case files, and field interrogation reports. Patrol units find their response time for service calls has been reduced drastically, and the immediate access to departmental records enhances their ability to have the information they need.

Lt. Gonzales is the leading departmental expert on computers. Other managers in the department have limited computer experience so they have had to turn to Lt. Gonzales for help. As other departments call on him, his reputation is enhanced and he spends more time away from the department. In every instance the other departments reimburse the city for Lt. Gonzales's expenses.

During the last two years, Lt. Gonzales became a real power within the department. It seems everyone relies on him. Since Lt. Gonzales has a unique expertise, there is a great deal of resentment. Part of it can be attributed to a forthcoming promotional examination for captain at the end of the year. Four other eligible lieutenants feel Lt. Gonzales has the inside track because of his expert power.

The conflict is apparent and known to everyone in the department. Lt. Gonzales is at a loss about what to do. He is perplexed by the whole problem and is considering discussing it with the chief. If you were Lt. Gonzales how would you deal with this problem? What would you tell the chief? Would you ask to be assigned to another position?

uses one power base can definitely modify power from another base. Unquestionably, when a manger is adept at rewarding, employees respond to a greater extent and prove to be more supportive. On the other hand, when a manager uses coercive power as a consistent managerial style it can reduce referent power (Hellriegel, Slocum, and Woodman, 1983).

The interaction between power sources varies considerably and is modified by how subordinates perceive a manager, whether or not the unit is important to the organization, and whether subordinates are dependent. Legitimate power provides a manager with a supporting base for the utilization of reward or coercive power. This can be altered, as was done recently, for example, in a large police department when the chief of police transferred a deputy chief from a position as head of investigations to an administrative position. This was really a disciplinary transfer and by changing the location where the deputy chief functioned, there was a reduction in legitimate power, reward power, and coercive power.

Position Power

The formal position a police manager holds in an organization provides the manager with positional power. In police organizations, it is a matter of the hierarchical relationships identified by the organizational chart. There is a definite division of labor identifying lines of control (More and Shipley, 1987).

The departmental manual specifically identifies the duties of members of the organization and spells out the legal basis by citing statutes and ordinances. Police departments are especially concerned with command responsibility and specify that police managers be responsible and accountable for each aspect of their command. A commanding officer is required to work within policy guidelines and legal constraints when coordinating and directing subordinates. The following Focus illustrates the power of one chief of police.

Position power is further reinforced by policy requiring police managers to enforce departmental rules and regulations and ensure compliance with department policies and procedures. Because of the potential negative impact of certain situations or unusual occurrences, most police departments have a policy carefully spelling out when the watch commander will notify the chief of police. Table 8.5 lists a wide range of occurrences requiring such notification. This notification allows the chief executive officer to either be present or at least be knowledgeable when something unusual occurs.

Knowledge is power. The higher the position in the department the greater the amount of information one can process. When we are in the know, we are more apt to be involved in the decision-making process, and when we have the capacity to make or have input prior to a decision, there is an acquisition of power (Hellriegel, Slocum, and Woodman, 1983).

Another symbol of power is the ability to obtain resources whether they are personnel, equipment, or supplies. Resources are important to success and a manager who obtains the resources needed to accomplish tasks and achieve departmental goals adds to positional power.

FOCUS 8.1

Outspoken, Provocative Police Chief Will Be Missed

Even Joseph McNamara's admirers say his complexity has both helped and hindered the department at times. A charismatic police chief, he commands respect from people throughout the ranks. At the same time, he serves as a lightning rod for their criticism.

In many ways, McNamara was the right man at the right time for San Jose. When he arrived, the department was in chaos. Leaders of the city's minority groups were at war with their police force. Outraged residents were demanding the police establish a citizens' review board. Through a deft marriage of style and substance, McNamara managed to join his strengths with those of the troubled department.... What he did was put San Jose on the map nationally.

At the same time, McNamara took a series of controversial steps. He instituted a deadly force policy forbidding officers from shooting except in life-threatening situations, he strengthened the internal affairs division, and he forced a number of people into retirement—and took heat for all these from within the ranks. He survived a no-confidence vote by the Police Officers Association and slowly earned respect for his political skills within the department and at City Hall. Relations between the department and the community improved steadily....

SOURCE. Betty Barnacle, Maline Hazel, Brad Kava, Bill Romano, and David Schrieberg, "Outspoken, Provocative Police Chief Will Be Missed," *San Jose Mercury News*, Sunday, August 14, 1988, pp. 1A and 19A. Reprinted by permission of the San Jose Mercury.

(Note: The chief took a leave for medical reasons and has since returned to the department.)

TABLE 8.5 Notification of Chief of Police

It is the policy of the police department that the chief of police be notified (by the watch commander, as soon as is practical) concerning any of the following incidents or situations:

1. Any incident where a police officer is injured to the extent it is necessary to consult a physician or medical facility.
2. Any incident where firearms have been used, or where it is reasonable to believe such firearms will be used.
3. Any incident where this department requests assistance (from an outside agency) of an unusual or emergency nature.
4. Any incident where an outside agency requests assistance of an emergency nature.
5. In the event of a major disturbance, or reports are received indicating there may be a major disturbance.
6. Any general alerts issued over regular communications circuits requesting the assistance of this department.
7. Any case where a dangerous person is at large in the city or adjacent thereto, particularly by virtue of escape or evasion during pursuit.
8. Any major signal or power failure, either wire, radio, or the transmission line affecting (or potentially affecting) the operations of the department.
9. Any matter of an unusual or uncommon nature likely to attract wide public or media interest.

SOURCE: Harry W. More and O. R. Shipley, *Police Policy Manual—Personnel*, (Springfield, IL: Charles C Thomas, 1987). Reprinted with permission.

Personal Power

Personal characteristics and traits are also a source of power. It is a power an individual develops and is not related to the formal position he or she occupies within the organization. Referent and expert powers provide the base for personal power and supporting powers can be reward, coercive, and legitimate.

Managers can reinforce personal power by expanding their expert power as much as possible. They should take advantage of every opportunity to attend special training programs. As police departments become more sophisticated, the police manager who has computer and information management expertise will prove to be influential (Robbins, 1986). Specialization reinforces personal power as one becomes an expert, for example, computer specialist, labor negotiator, or polygraph examiner.

A police manager can enhance and reinforce personal power by becoming an astute observer and participant in the decision-making process whenever possible. If asked for information, it provides an opportunity for face-to-face interaction and the potential to influence the ultimate decision (Wilson, 1981).

Perceived Power The classic example of personal and position power is J. Edgar Hoover, the first director of the Federal Bureau of Investigation, who served from 1924 until 1972. *(Culver Pictures)*

Follower loyalty and responsiveness allow a manager to get things accomplished easily. It can be just a request—the response to which is usually positive. The key is, the followers respond because they want to, not because it is required. When the boss is liked, things just seem to get done—this serves to reinforce a manager-subordinate relationship (Schermerhorn, Hunt, and Osborn, 1988).

It is difficult to imagine any manager (other than the most charismatic) being able to rely solely on personal power without the support of other power bases. In terms of command responsibility, a police manager is obligated to the full range of administrative functions, relying on personal initiative in order to ensure the highest level of performance possible (More and Shipley, 1987).

One can have both positional and personal power. When they are combined, a police manager will have the highest possible level of influence over subordinates, superiors, and peers (Griffin and Moorhead, 1986).

Utilizing Power

The manner in which a police manager utilizes power sources and bases is important if he or she is to be truly effective. There are times when one technique can be used effectively to influence subordinates or peer behavior and other times that call for the choice of a different tactic (Robbins, 1986). There are seven different techniques managers use to influence others (Kipnis, Schmidt, Swaffin-Smith, and Wilkinson, 1984):

1. *Reason.* Persuading or influencing others by the process of reason.
2. *Friendliness.* Showing kindly interest and goodwill as a prelude to a request.
3. *Coalition.* Creating a temporary alliance of distinct parties or persons for joint action.
4. *Bargaining.* Coming to an agreement as to what each gives and receives.
5. *Assertiveness.* Stating a position positively and with force when needed.
6. *Higher authority.* Obtaining the support of departmental superiors.
7. *Sanctions.* Utilizing rewards and punishment that are organizationally derived.

The power tactic used most often when dealing with either superiors or subordinates is reason. Circumscribed by the need to comply and exist in a legal environment, law enforcement officers are prone to go by the book and utilize rules, regulations, and policies when reasoning with other members of the organization. When managers have an abundance of power they are more apt to use a variety of power techniques as compared to managers who have a limited amount of power (Kipnis, Schmidt, Swaffin-Smith, and Wilkinson, 1984).

Assertiveness is a backup strategy that powerful managers use when the situation dictates or when other techniques have proven to be ineffective. It can start with a simple request or an effort to reason with someone and then shift to a more forceful approach in an effort to obtain compliance. If a manager encounters resistance by a subordinate, the technique utilized can reach the point where sanctions come into play.

When managers attempt to influence subordinates, as a means of obtaining compliance and ensuring the attainment of goals, the techniques most frequently used are reason, assertiveness, and friendliness (Schermerhorn, Hunt, and Osborn, 1988). The normal sequence of occurrences is this—as managers exert both positional and personal power when attempting to influence officers being supervised, there is a greater reliance on personal power.

When managers have had a favorable experience utilizing a power strategy (such as reason), they are more apt to rely on that method in the future. If reason proves to be ineffective, a manager will then try to obtain compliance by using other techniques such as assertiveness or friendliness.

Effective managers are those who utilize power with restraint tailored to the specific situation. They are fully aware of both the positive and negative consequences of power. They apply power with care and concern for personnel as well as for the organization (Hellriegel, Slocum, and Woodman, 1983).

An interesting approach to power is to turn it into influence by specifically utilizing power bases. However it is done, it is an effort to obtain true commitment, not just mere compliance. A manager wants employees to work diligently at a task until it is accomplished. It is not a question of just doing one's job, but doing it with dispatch and effectiveness. Workers who just plod along and control the amount of work to a level just barely acceptable are responding to power with compliance, not commitment. When power is used effectively it results in commitment (Griffin and Moorhead, 1986) (see Table 8.6).

TABLE 8.6 Guidelines for Utilizing Power

Power Base	*Guidelines*
Reward	Subordinate needs to be recognized. Recognition must be given publicly. Acknowledgment should be specifically related to work performed.
Coercive	Subordinates must be informed of all rules and regulations. Punishment has to be reasonable. Communicate. Document reprimands. Punishment has to be uniform. Warnings and discipline must occur privately.
Legitimate	Utilize chain of command. Present a rationale when requesting something. Follow up to ensure the request is understood. Ensure a request is accomplished. Present request in such a way it will be readily accepted.
Referent	Subordinates must be treated fairly. Select competent subordinates. Provide support when needed.
Expert	Keep up to date. Readily admit a lack of knowledge. Conduct yourself decisively. Be believable.

SOURCE: Gary L. Yukl, *Leadership in Organizations* (Englewood Cliffs, NJ: Prentice-Hall, 1981).

Exercising Reward Power

Most employees respond positively to reward power, and the same holds true for managers. If subordinates have a need for rewards from the organization, it will result in commitment to the department. If organizational rewards are perceived as being used to exploit employees or if rewards are given to employees who do not deserve them, then the reward power has less meaning. When promotions are made, they should be based on measurable performance criteria not subjective evaluations, and the specific reason(s) for the promotion should be made known to everyone (Yukl, 1981).

If the rewards are being given a desirable assignment or being assigned to a critical investigative team, for example, the same principle holds; tell people why the assignment is being made and do it publicly at roll call, in a departmental bulletin, or by special memorandum.

Other rewards a manager can give range from acknowledgment of a task well done to officially commending an officer. Public recognition should be used whenever the situation allows. The problem is, it takes time. But a manager must make the effort if the officers in the organization feel such publicity is important.

The giving of rewards is a pleasurable experience for both the recipient and the manager. One useful technique is to acknowledge police officers' special accomplishments publicly every spring during a "Police Week" ceremony.

Exercising Coercive Power

The best exercise of coercive power is to never exercise it at all. Unfortunately situations do occur when it becomes necessary for a police manager to discipline an officer. There are few managers who enjoy exercising coercive power. It is usually a time-consuming process and can be emotionally exhausting. Disciplined officers can become resentful, minimal performers, and if carried to an extreme, become so negative they are just not pleasant to be around.

Managers are striving to get officers to comply with official procedures or rules and regulations. While commitment is a desirable product of any power source, it seldom happens when coercive power is used. Instead, the best result may be mere compliance, and it is very possible to encounter resentment or even obstructionism (Griffin and Moorhead, 1986).

Most police departments have numerous rules and regulations carefully spelling out how tasks should be performed and what can and cannot be done. Infractions are specifically identified as is the punishment, for example, for disclosing confidential information, the first offense can result in anything from a one-day suspension to dismissal. For a second offense an employee can be given anything from a ten-day suspension to dismissal; for a third offense the punishment is dismissal (More and Shipley, 1987).

It is imperative for the manager to make sure all employees are fully aware of policies, procedures, and regulations, especially when procedures are changed or modified (Yukl, 1981). As the old saying goes, ignorance is no excuse nor is the failure to advise. The key is to communicate—often and effectively.

There is clear-cut logic requiring a manager to not only inform those being supervised of the punishment but (when a violation occurs) warn them of the action to be taken against them. This action should be documented. A paper trail must be left whenever an employee is warned of possible punishment, so it can serve as a basis for later disciplinary action if needed. It is much more effective to tell an officer "You were warned of the failure to comply with departmental procedure on July 1, August 5, and August 15," than it is to say, "Well, I warned you."

The same idea applies to performance reviews. The process should be a real dialogue between the employee and the manager, in other words, two-way communication. At the time of a performance evaluation, employees should never be informed by the boss for the first time of their inability to perform their job properly (Gordon, 1985).

If coercive power is to be used effectively it should only be administered after a careful investigation to ensure an actual infraction or violation has occurred. In addition, if there is latitude as to the exact nature or type of punishment to be administered, every effort should be made to ensure it is appropriate to the situation and commensurate with the seriousness of the infraction or offense (Yukl, 1981).

Lastly, every employee has the right to be warned or reprimanded privately. The manager has this obligation. Punishing in public has the potential of permanently straining a manager's relationship with employees. Punishment is a no-win situation for everyone involved (Griffin and Moorhead, 1986).

Utilizing Legitimate Power

Legitimate power represents a type of power a police manager possesses because subordinates believe that he or she has the right to command (Schermerhorn, Hunt, and Osborn, 1988). It is the same as formal authority and in law enforcement it is legitimized because managerial duties are usually set forth in legal documents.

Most officers readily accept legitimate power. It is a natural phenomenon to follow the dictates of someone of higher rank when the request is reasonable and clearly authorized by policy or rules and regulations. Legitimate power can be used forcefully, but there is little reason to do so. Forcefulness should be limited to those situations in which it is obvious that it is the only way to obtain compliance.

When a formal request is sent to subordinates, it should be done in a solicitous manner with a concern for those who must respond or react to it. It should be sent through the chain of command, which serves to reinforce its legitimacy. Whenever possible, a formal request should include a reason(s) for its transmittal in order to set a positive frame of reference for the request.

In every instance, a request should be followed up as a means of ensuring that the recipient understands the request and the request is not only legitimate but necessary (Yukl, 1981).

Utilizing Referent Power

The key element of the effective utilization of referent power is subordinate compliance because the subordinate does not want to disturb the working relationship. Requests are complied with because subordinates like their manager and they identify with his or her personal traits.

A manager wanting to enhance referent power should do everything possible to create a working relationship based on mutual respect. Fairness and equity are essential when dealing with subordinates. This is best expressed by showing a real concern for subordinate interests and needs.

Finally, whenever the opportunity presents itself, managers should identify individuals who would be most desirable to have in their unit and then actively recruit them (Yukl, 1981).

Utilizing Expert Power

Managers should make every effort to become knowledgeable in special areas. When they develop special skills needed by others within the organization, then they have an expert power base.

Managers should work diligently at maintaining a specialized skill once it has been attained because it adds to credibility. At the same time, managers should readily admit any lack of knowledge and never try to bluff their way through—in almost every instance it will catch up with them and jeopardize their reputation. The best position to take is, "I will find the answer to that question."

Expert power can be reinforced by presenting an image of being an expert. When making presentations or discussing issues related to your expertise, it is essential to be direct, decisive, and above all, believable. When explaining things to those less knowledgeable in a specific area, do not use jargon or attempt to impress them with your expertise. Present material at the lowest possible level and make sure everyone understands it. If there is any doubt, go over the material again and make a point of singling out those who look puzzled and provide them with the help they need to understand the topic or issue under discussion. Above all, never do anything that would threaten a subordinate's self-esteem (Yukl, 1981).

Subordinate Power

Managerial power is never absolute but always seems to be modified. This is also true of subordinate power. In law enforcement, officers in line units have a great deal of power because they are the collectors of a lot of information needed by managers so they can perform effectively. This is especially true in officer-initiated actions, seldom monitored by supervisors. If such activities are reported, it adds to the department's information base. Information can be withheld or incorrect information is put into the system—all of which alters the power relationship between managers and subordinates (Staw, 1984). If the information is unreported, it adds to the power base of the officer, for example, field interrogations and informants.

Subordinates can also exert a definite influence on police managers when they have a skill not possessed by the manager. Police departments, as they grow in size, are becoming increasingly dependent on specialists, so it is necessary for managers to delegate authority and responsibility.

When officers join unions or associations, they develop a unique power base to which police managers must respond if the unit is to exercise a united

CASE STUDY

Captain Stewart Parsons

Capt. Stewart Parsons supervises the mounted patrol unit in a large city. The city has a population of 900,000 and is a tourist mecca. Numerous conventions are held throughout the year. Parades, rallies, and demonstrations are commonplace and the mounted horse detail serves at all functions. The police department has 2,232 sworn officers of which 27 are assigned to the mounted detail.

During the last calendar year the unit was very active—not only in terms of arrests made but also in the number of traffic citations issued. There were arrests for 129 felonies and 2,657 misdemeanors. The unit also confiscated 102 weapons including rifles, shotguns, pistols, and knives. Mounted patrol officers issued tickets for 18,921 parking violations and citations for 194 moving violations.

Fines from the traffic violations brought in $354,233 to the city's coffers. The mounted unit logged 12,395 hours of patrol. When not working special events, they patrolled the city parks. Currently the unit has 38 horses and horse carts for transporting the animals.

The city is faced with a large budget deficit and the mayor's office is recommending that the mounted patrol unit budget allocation be eliminated. Capt. Parsons has always been involved in community activities and holds membership in two civic organizations. He decided to circulate a petition throughout the community asking the city to restore the unit's budget. He obtained the support of both civic groups to which he belonged. Seven police officers assigned to the mounted patrol unit assisted in the circulation of the petition during their off-duty hours.

The petition drive proved to be highly successful and approximately 21,000 signatures were obtained. Capt. Parsons and the presidents of the two civic organizations presented the petition to the City Council.

The mayor is really upset about the whole matter—especially because it became apparent Capt. Parsons had initiated the process and a number of officers had assisted in the gathering of signatures. The mayor called in the chief of police and told him the officers were trying to erode his power base and had no business becoming involved in the political process.

The chief pointed out that in this instance neither Capt. Parsons nor the officers had violated any city or departmental policy. He stated the signatures were obtained by the officers when they were off duty. This is the first time this activity has ever occurred. The mayor is convinced these departmental employees have exceeded their authority and officers should not attempt to influence budgetary decisions. He asked the chief to develop a departmental policy prohibiting such activity.

Should police officers be prohibited from circulating petitions designed to alter budgetary support for the police department? Develop a position paper that prohibits officers from circulating such petitions. Write a policy limiting the way officers can influence budget allocations.

voice. For many years, police associations served a social role which (for the most part) has changed so that currently these units function as full-fledged unions. More than three-fourths of all the police departments in the United States are unionized. They are exercising real power in their relationships with police, city managers, and city councils.

In the states allowing collective bargaining, a formal written agreement can be negotiated concerning wages, hours to be worked, and conditions of employment (More, 1985). In one large department, the memorandum of understanding named two specific elements in the contract, altering the relationship between management and the police association (City of San Jose, 1983):

> 1. Labor/Management Committee. This committee is established to maximize communications between the Police Administration and the Peace Officer's Association. Representatives of either side shall be entitled to bring to any meeting, subject matter or experts as deemed appropriate.
> 2. Sergeants Transfer Policy. A committee will be established having the following representatives: the Police Administration; the Peace Officer's Association; and the Assistant Personnel Director.

These two sections of the memorandum were only part of a collective bargaining agreement containing 41 separate items.

In this same police department the memorandum of understanding provided for time off for nine employees elected directors of the Police Protective League, so they could perform employee organizational activities. The same section required the league to reimburse the city for all the release time (City of Los Angeles, 1982).

It can readily be seen that police associations have definitely altered the management-employee relationship. Fortunately managerial power is decreasing while employee power has increased. This is entirely different (and certainly an improvement) from the days when management possessed all the power.

Summary

Power is the ability, the vigor, and the strength to influence others and to control one's own destiny. When a manager is using power correctly, it generally involves bringing together resources to accomplish something. Effective managers are those who understand the uses, limitations, sources, and the characteristics of power.

Power has meaning not only to the individual, but to groups and organizations. When considering power and its implications, we can identify five types of power: reward, coercive, legitimate, referent, and expert. Within police departments, managers will have greater control over reward power in direct proportion to their higher position in the organization. Some common reward powers are praise, commendations, special assignments, additional responsibility, and two-way communication.

Coercive power is based on fear of punishment and the sanctions a police manager can utilize to control the behavior of subordinates. Punishment may take many forms including suspension, demotion, official reprimand, or more subtle sanctions such as giving an officer an undesirable assignment.

Legitimate power is associated with one's position, role, and status within the organization. In law enforcement, rank is closely associated with legitimate power, and power generally increases along with rank. Everyone in a police organization is aware of their relative position in the organization, who they are immediately responsible for, and to whom they are accountable.

Managers are said to have referent power when their employees can easily identify with them. A key element of this type of power is trust. When an officer trusts a manager it enhances the working relationship.

The last power base is expertise. It involves the skill a manager possesses because of knowledge, experience, or judgment. Information relevant to the organization, gained by an employee, increases the power base used to deal with an increasingly complex society and its accompanying social problems.

An effective manager is one who influences the behavior of others in the work environment by using either personal or positional sources of power. Positional power is the power gained from the actual formal position a manager holds in the organization. Personal power is something entirely different. It is the personal characteristics and traits a manager possesses.

How police managers use power sources and bases is important if they are to be truly effective. There are times when one technique can be used effectively to influence subordinate or peer behavior while at other times the choice of a different tactic will be needed.

Key Concepts

The bureaucrat
The controller
The competitor
The incompetent
The realist
Power base
Reward power
Coercive power
Legitimate power
Referent power
Expert power
Charisma
Power sources
Position power
Personal power

Discussion Topics and Questions

1. What distinguishes a bureaucratic managerial style from the realist type?
2. What are the specific rewards police managers can use?
3. As a police manager using coercive power, what specifically can be done when strictly supervising an officer?
4. Compare and contrast personal and positional power.
5. What techniques can a manager use to influence others?
6. What can a police manager do to expand expert power?
7. Differentiate between legitimate and reward power.
8. How can a manager utilize referent power?
9. How does a manager deal with subordinate power?
10. What are the limitations of personal power?

References

Chapman, Elwood N. 1981. *Scrambling*. Los Angeles: J. P. Trachner.

City of Los Angeles. 1982. *Memorandum of Understanding 1982–1984*. Los Angeles, CA.

City of San Jose. 1983. *Memorandum of Understanding 1983–1985*. San Jose, CA.

Cohen, Allan R., Stephen L. Fink, Herman Gadon, and Robin D. Willits. 1980. *Effective Behavior in Organizations*. Homewood, IL: Richard D. Irwin.

Cohen, Herb. 1980. *You Can Negotiate Anything*. Secaucus, NJ: Citadel Press.

Dressler, Gary. 1983. *Applied Human Relations*. Reston, VA: Reston.

Duncan, W. Jack. 1981. *Organizational Behavior* (2nd ed.). Boston: Houghton Mifflin.

Epstein, Earl B. 1979. *No More Mr. Nice Guy*. New York: Farnsworth.

French, John R. P., and Bertram Raven. 1959. "The Bases of Social Power." In Darwin Cartright (Ed.), *Studies in Social Power.* Ann Arbor: University of Michigan Press.

Gordon, Maynard M. 1985. *The Iacocca Management Technique*. New York: Dodd, Mead.

Griffin, Ricky W., and Gregory Moorhead. 1986. *Organizational Behavior.* Boston: Houghton Mifflin.

Grothe, Mardy, and Peter Wylie. 1987. *Problem Bosses: Who They Are and How to Deal with Them*. New York: Facts on File.

Hawkins, Brian L. 1981. *Managerial Communication*. Santa Monica, CA: Goodyear.

Hellriegel, Don, John W. Slocum, Jr., and Richard W. Woodman. 1983. *Organizational Behavior* (3rd ed.). St. Paul, MN: West.

Jenks, James M., and John M. Kelly. 1985. *Don't Do. Delegate*. New York: Ballantine Books.

Kanter, R. M. 1979. "Power Failures in Business Circuits," *Harvard Business Review*, 34(2).

Kipnis, D., S. M. Schmidt, C. Swaffin-Smith, andI. Wilkinson. 1984. "Patterns of Managerial Influence: Shotgun Managers, Tacticians, and Bystanders," *Organizational Dynamics*, Winter, 4.

Korda, Michael. 1977. *The Power Broker.* New York: Random House.

Kotter, John, P. 1985. *Power and Influence*. New York: Free Press.

Lee, James A. 1980. "Leader Power:" In Paul Hersey and John Stinson (Eds.), *Perspectives in Leader Effectiveness*. Athens, OH: Center for Leadership Studies.

More, Harry W. (Ed.). 1985. *Critical Issues in Law Enforcement* (4th ed.). Cincinnati: Anderson.

More, Harry W., and O. R. Shipley. 1987. *Police Policy Manual—Personnel*. Springfield, IL: Charles C Thomas.

Reece, Barry L., and Rhonda Brandt. 1987. *Effective Human Relations in Organizations* (3rd ed.). Boston: Houghton Mifflin.

Ringer, Robert J. 1974. *Power: How to Get It and How to Use It*. New York: Fawcett.

Ringer, Robert J. 1983. *Looking Out for Number One*. New York: Fawcett.

Robbins, Stephen P. 1986. *Organizational Behavior—Concepts, Controversies, and Application*. Englewood Cliffs, NJ: Prentice-Hall.

Rue, Leslie, and Lloyd L. Byars. 1986. *Management Theory and Practice* (4th ed.). Homewood, IL: Richard D. Irwin.

Salancik, Gerald, and Jeffery Pfeffer. 1983. "A Social Information Processing Approach to Job Attitudes and Task Design," *Administrative Science Quarterly*, 23(2).

San Jose Mercury News. 1988. "Outspoken, Provocative Police Chief Will Be Missed," August 14, pp. 1A and 19A.

Schermerhorn, John R., James G. Hunt, and Richard N. Osborn. 1988. *Managing Organizational Behavior* (3rd ed.). New York: Wiley.

Staw, Barry M. 1984. "Organizational Behavior: A Review and Reformulation of the Field's Outcome Variables." In Mark R. Rosenzweig and Lyman W. Porter (Eds.), *Annual Review of Psychology*. Palo Alto, CA: Annual Reviews.

Swingle, Paul G. 1976. *The Management of Power.* New York: Erlbaum.

UNSINGER, PETER C., and HARRY MORE. 1989. *Police Management-Labor Relations*. Springfield, IL: Charles C Thomas.

WAITLEY, DENIS, and RENI L. WITT. 1985. *The Joy of Working*. New York: Dodd, Mead.

WILSON, MARLENE. 1981. *Survival Skills for Managers*. Boulder, CO: Johnson.

WOFFORD, JERRY C. 1982. *Organizational Behavior*. Boston: Kent.

YUKL, GARY A. 1981. *Leadership in Organizations*. Englewood Cliffs, NJ: Prentice-Hall.

For Further Reading

FUNKHOWSER, G. RAY. 1986. *The Power of Persuasion*. New York: Time Books.

A definitive work stating there is only one process of power that operates in four ways: performance power, structure power, agreement power, and persuasive power. The author also describes the ten basic persuasion tactics of special interest to police managers.

KORDA, MICHAEL. 1975. *The Power Broker*. New York: Random House.

Discusses the means used in developing a style of power based on one's character and desires. Presents five rules to be used to obtain and keep power. The author's position is that power can be used to obtain whatever one wants.

KOTTER, JOHN P. 1985. *Power and Influence*. New York: Free Press.

Presents some of the central problems and issues created by modern organizations. Of special interest is the discussion of the life cycle of leadership including a consideration of how to develop an adequate power base and how to use power without abusing it.

MOBERG, DENNIS, and DAVID CALDWELL. 1988. *Interactive Cases in Organizational Behavior*. Glenview, IL: Scott, Foresman.

This book has an excellent discussion of personal power. Tactics that a manager should use include persuasion, pressure, coalitions, and alternative relationships. There is also an excellent discussion of organizational politics.

CHAPTER 9

Decision-Making: The Essential Element in Applied Management

LEARNING OBJECTIVES

1. Identify key elements in the definition of a managerial decision.
2. Describe the dynamics involved in the decision-making process.
3. Show the relationship between problem-solving and decision-making.
4. Make a distinction between personal and organizational decisions.
5. Discuss what are viewed as the cardinal sins in decision-making.
6. Show correlation in rank to scope of decision-making authority.
7. Identify internal, external, and personal constraints on decision-making.
8. Differentiate between the various types of managerial decisions.
9. Demonstrate steps involved in the rational decision-making process.
10. Describe the mechanics and utility of comparative analysis.
11. Define the terms *bounded rationality* and *satisficing*.
12. List and explain guidelines to improve individual decision-making.
13. Discuss group decision-making in light of a humanistic philosophy.
14. Consider the advantages and disadvantages often associated with group decision-making.
15. Compare and contrast a variety of techniques designed to improve the group decision-making processes.
16. Consider the impact that group decision-making is going to have on the role of tomorrow's police administrator.

*I*n the most general sense, to decide is to make up one's mind (Kast and Rosenzweig, 1985). A decision is a choice from among a set of available alternatives (Albanese, 1981). Managerial decisions are choices between alternative courses of action translated into administrative behavior designed to achieve an organization's mission through the accomplishment of specifically targeted goals and objectives. The key elements in this definition of a managerial decision are (1) choices, (2) alternatives, (3) targets, and (4) purposeful behavior.

INTRODUCTORY CASE

Chief Gary Pirsig

Lyndora is a small, relatively affluent community adjacent to a major industrial city in the Midwest. It appeared, until quite recently, that Lyndora would escape the drug epidemic. The crack cocaine death of a very popular local high school basketball player shattered this illusion, however. The coroner's inquiry into the young man's death concluded that teenage drug abuse was common and represented a serious health problem. Based on the coroner's report, the news media demanded more drug enforcement activity by the police.

Gary Pirsig, the new chief of police who came from outside of the department and serves at the pleasure of city council, was reluctant to act. The chief was, by his own admission, uncomfortable making unanticipated decisions in unsettled circumstances. He was sensitive to the political liabilities inherent in making the "wrong decision" and wanted to avoid criticism at all costs. After a particularly nasty editorial in the local newspaper, Pirsig's anxiety level skyrocketed to the point where he became physically ill and had to take three days off from work.

The chief—in order to let things cool down—refused all requests for interviews and issued a news release indicating his department's drug enforcement policy was under review. He admitted to a close friend that he was using this in-process gimmick in order to avoid making hasty decisions.

The ploy did not work. The media continued to press its demands for action. In an effort to get the media off of his back, the chief prepared and circulated the rough draft of a new drug enforcement policy emphasizing full enforcement and user accountability. Police officers were—in addition to arresting all pushers—instructed to apprehend and prosecute everyone who possessed illegal drugs or drug paraphernalia regardless of their age. The new get tough policy was scheduled to go into effect in ten days.

After receiving some negative feedback on the policy from school administrators, elected officials, and concerned parents, the chief had second thoughts and put the drug enforcement policy on hold for further study. Chief Gary Pirsig's indecisiveness has caused a morale problem in the police department and has strained his relations with members of city council. There have, in fact, been some calls for his resignation.

Chief Pirsig has a big problem. He violated some very basic principles and committed the two cardinal sins associated with decision-making. How should this situation have been handled? Based on the information contained in this chapter, what process would you have used to decide how to deal with this particular problem? Be specific.

1. *Choices.* If a police administrator does not have the opportunity or the ability to make a choice, there is no real decision. Following rules, obeying orders, or being coerced to act in certain ways cannot—without a great deal of distortion—be construed as making decisions.

2. *Alternatives.* There must be more than one possible course of action available in order for the police administrator to have a choice.

Effective managers look for and/or try to create realistic options for resolving problems.

3. *Targets.* Goals and objectives come together to perform a vital function. They activate and give direction to the decision-making process (Tansik, Chase, and Aquilano, 1980).

4. *Behavior.* Making decisions is irrelevant unless they are translated into action. To paraphrase a quote from one top-level executive:

> To look is one thing. To see what you are looking at is another. To really understand what you see is a third. To learn from what you understand is something else again. *But to act on what you have learned is all that truly matters* [italics added]. (LeBoeuf, 1985)

Decision-making is the complex process of generating and evaluating alternatives and making choices based on relevant knowledge, beliefs, and judgments. Decision-making also involves the application of our own experience and moral orientation in determining what should be done to resolve a particular problem. Logic is used to test our conclusions, and ethics serve to test our judgment (Swanson, Territo, and Taylor, 1988).

Decision-making is a natural and ubiquitous human activity. It is, in terms of modern organization and management, one of the most important, if not the most important, of all managerial activities (Baron, 1983). Virtually every management action is contingent, to one degree or another, on decision-making. Chester I. Barnard (1976) identified decision-making as one of the "functions of the executive." Two other management theorists, Claude George (1964) and Herbert Simon (1977), go so far as to say that management is, in fact, synonymous with decision-making. While this may be an overstatement, it helps to explain why so much attention is being focused on decision theory and its application in complex criminal justice organizations.

Problem-Solving and Decision-Making

The terms *problem-solving* and *decision-making* are used interchangeably in the context of management because managers spend most of their time making decisions to resolve problems. Managers are paid to identify desirable end states of existence (goals) and select the most appropriate means (methods) formulated to achieve them. The decision-making/problem-solving process consists of three distinct stages: (1) intelligence, (2) design, and (3) choice. These stages have been described as follows:

1. *Intelligence.* Intelligence involves scanning the environment for conditions that require a decision. Some police administrators are much more perceptive than others. They relish the opportunity to process data and make decisions. They are the movers and the shakers.

2. *Design.* Design entails creating, developing, and analyzing possible courses of action. Some police administrators are much more imaginative than others. They live on the margin and are not afraid to try something new. Creative problem-solving is viewed as challenging, not threatening.

3. *Choice.* Choice refers to the actual selection of a particular course of action from among available alternatives. Some managers are much more

decisive than others. They are proactive and thrive on converting decisions into action. It is choice that gives meaning to their existence. (Rue and Byars, 1980).

Based on these concepts, decision-making can be described as a multistep process through which problems are recognized, diagnosed, and defined. Alternative solutions are generated, selected, and implemented. This process helps produce personal commitment to a given course of action and is manifest in one's willingness to invest energy, effort, expertise, and other resources in order to achieve a desired end state of existence.

All managers are obligated to make decisions designed to resolve problems that fall within the scope of their authority. These decisions can be broken down into two categories: (1) personal decisions and (2) organizational decisions. Personal decisions are those which, due to their nature and complexity, cannot ordinarily be delegated to others. Making a major decision (e.g., to terminate the employment of a high-ranking exempt manager) may require several subsidiary judgment-based decisions that can only be made by the chief executive. In other situations, a major decision (like where to build a new jail) may be announced by the chief of police even though many subsidiary decisions were made by different people acting in their organizational capacity. Graham T. Allison (1971) calls this the organizational process model. While chief executives do not make all decisions personally, they are ultimately responsible for all of the decisions made by their subordinates (Holden, 1986).

Some General Principles

There is a growing tendency to evaluate managers primarily on the results of their decisions (Mondy et al., 1986). Three general principles can be applied to the philosophy of decision-making:

Rule 1. Make a decision. Effective managers are graded on their ability to make decisions rather than on the absolute number of correct decisions they make. The two cardinal sins in decision-making are procrastination and vacillation (Steinmetz and Todd, 1986). Even if they occasionally make the wrong decision, the fact that managers take action when action is needed is usually better than if they take no action at all. Decisiveness has a stabilizing influence on subordinates. Indecisiveness is easily perceived and generates disrespect, destroys confidence, lowers morale, and adversely affects performance (Iannone, 1987).

Rule 2. Don't worry. Since decision-making goes with the territory, effective police administrators learn not to waste time or energy worrying about decisions that have already been made. They avoid anxiety by living in "day-tight compartments" and trying not to second-guess themselves (Carnegie, 1948). The only time a manager should reconsider a decision is if it is wrong or if there is a genuine need to consider alternative courses of action. Vacillation has often been the kiss of death for managers.

Rule 3. Expect criticism. Criticism is inevitable in complex organizations. In a positive sense, it means the manager is doing something that is worthy of attention. Competent police administrators know it is impossible to meet the needs and/ or expectations of everyone who is affiliated with the department. As part of a management team, they are required to satisfy the expectations of their superiors while trying to earn the respect of their subordinates. Good managers do what they can under the circumstances and put up an umbrella to keep the rain of criticism from running down the back of their neck (Carnegie, 1948).

While these principles cannot guarantee successful decision-making on the part of each and every police administrator, they provide guidelines for activating and managing the decision-making process (Lynch, 1975).

The ability to make reasonable, correct, and timely decisions is an important skill that is normally found in the repertoire of effective managers (Steinmetz and Todd, 1986). Police administrators who know what is happening and what is to be accomplished garner respect from their peers as well as their subordinates. On the other side of the coin, police executives lose confidence in and respect for those lower level managers who are plagued by indecision or who are unable to forge a link between decisions and actions.

Organizational Decision-Making

While all of us make a wide variety of personal decisions, only about 10 percent of the members of any organized work group have the ability and the desire to exercise formal decision-making authority (Graham, 1984). Even when people have the ability and desire to make decisions, they are not, under normal circumstances, empowered to make them unless they have been granted specific authority to do so. There must be some type of rationale to stipulate who within a particular organization has the responsibility for which decisions. The lack of specificity in this area produces ambiguity, anxiety, and a sense of anomie.

One generally accepted rationale is based on two factors: (1) the scope of the decision and (2) the designated level of management. The scope of the decision is the proportion of the total organization the decision is likely to affect. The greater the proportion, the broader the scope of the decision. The levels of management are arranged in a hierarchical order indicative of formal authority and/ or position power.

1. *Upper-level managers* are the appointed or elected top executives who serve as agency administrators, department heads, and program directors. Executive work is not that of the organization per se, but the specialized work of maintaining the organization in operation (Barnard, 1976). These top executives are expected to establish a sense of purpose, formulate overall policy, and make those decisions that affect the organization as a whole.

2. *Middle-level managers* are located between the top and lower levels of the organization. They are the bureau chiefs and division heads who act on behalf of their superiors to interpret department policies, coordinate the activities of work units, motivate employees, and maintain discipline. Middle-level managers make decisions designed to achieve results. Their decision-making authority is limited and always constrained by preexisting policy.

3. *Lower-level (supervisory) managers* are responsible for the job-related activities of others. They are the work-group leaders charged with getting their subordinates to carry out specific tasks as set down by middle managers. Lower level managers are expected to motivate workers to perform these tasks within a framework of established policies, procedures, rules, and regulations. Consequently, decision-making is highly structured and related almost exclusively to operational considerations (McKinney and Howard, 1979). The rationale is fairly simple: The broader the scope of a particular decision, the higher the level of the manager who is likely to make it (Certo, 1989). Figure 9.1 is designed to illustrate this point.

Nothing just stated precludes any manager who has the primary responsibility for making a decision from seeking the advice of other management personnel or subordinates. Only fools try to make decisions in a vacuum. Top-notch police managers tap every available resource. They also know that it might be desirable to allow members of the work group to make certain decisions (Certo, 1989). We discuss group decision-making later in this chapter.

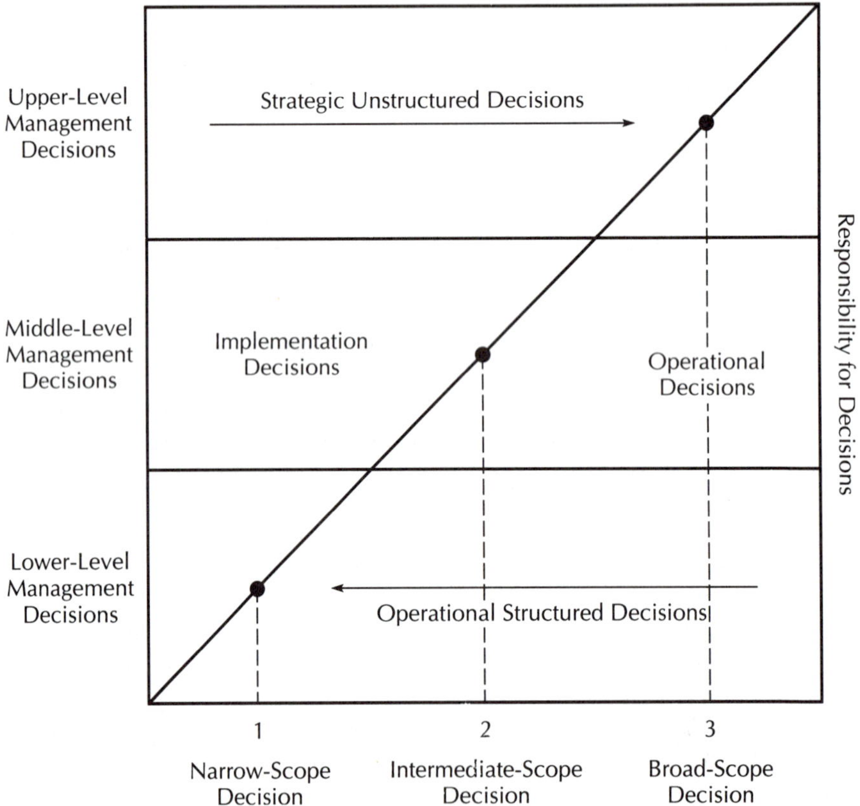

FIGURE 9.1 Levels of Management and Scope of Decisions.
Source Adapted from Samuel C. Certo, *Principles of Modern Management: Functions and Systems* (Boston: Allyn & Bacon, 1989).

Influences on Decision-Making

As we noted, no decision is made in a vacuum. Decisions are made by people at different levels in the organization, and every decision is influenced to one degree or another by the environment, the dynamics of the decision situation, and the personal characteristics of the decision maker. These factors should not be viewed as independent variables. As a matter of fact, they work in conjunction with one another to produce idiosyncratic decisions. We discuss each of the factors to help you gain more insight into the decision-making process.

Decision theorists frequently discuss what is called the state of nature. *State of nature* refers to those aspects of a decision maker's environment that affect choice. Environmental factors can be grouped into two basic categories: (1) the internal environment and (2) the external environment. Some of the internal factors that affect choice are as follows:

1. The specificity of the organization's mission, goals, and objectives.
2. The delegation of sufficient authority to enable managers to carry out their assigned duties.
3. The degree of autonomy given to management personnel at different levels in the organization.
4. The leeway granted to managers by departmental policies, procedures, rules, and regulations.
5. The availability of valid, reliable, and objective information on which to base decisions.
6. The time and energy used to select, train, and retain well-qualified managers.
7. The nature, extent, and effect of intraorganizational conflict.
8. The restrictions imposed on management via the collective bargaining process.
9. The adequacy of the reward system in promoting timely and effective decision-making.

The external factors that affect choice include, but are not limited to, the following:

1. Social instability
2. Rising expectations
3. Professional ethics
4. Legal constraints
5. Dwindling resources
6. Political conflict
7. Technological change

Internal and external environmental factors are never under the direct control of the decision maker. Effective decision makers learn to accept and cope with this uncertainty, complexity, volatility, and risk. Good managers are willing to take a calculated risk. Since they see decision-making as a challenge, they are seldom immobilized by fear of the unknown (Albanese, 1981).

Situational Variables

No two decision situations are exactly the same. There are simply too many variables. Every problem that elicits a decision is unique in terms of its

1. Nature
2. Extent
3. Difficulty
4. Urgency
5. Seriousness
6. Complexity
7. Solution

Each decision is a unique product of the dynamic interaction between the decision maker, environmental factors, and situational variables. No one makes correct decisions all of the time. Good managers are usually decisive and process information in such a way that they make right decisions more often than wrong decisions. Effective decision makers dare to be different. They unshackle themselves from the past and use creative problem-solving as a ticket to success.

Personal Variables

There is a personal dimension to managerial decision-making in all complex criminal justice organizations. Even in the most favorable environment and in relatively stable situations, the personal characteristics of managers have a great influence on the quality of their decisions. Two police administrators evaluating identical data related to the same problem based on identical criteria may reach a different conclusion. Decision theorists account for this disparity in terms of unique personal factors (Sisk and Williams, 1981) such as the following:

1. *Mental health.* While they do not always make the right choice, emotionally healthy managers tend to be adequate decision makers. Managers with strong self-concepts know themselves and are inner directed. Those who see themselves as problem solvers are unlikely to avoid or to postpone decisions. They do not fear that decisions will lead to failure or personal loss. Emotionally unhealthy managers, on the other hand, usually have difficulty in processing information and making decisions. Psychotics are out of touch with reality and neurotics distort it. Impulsive managers become anxious and irritable over delays. They take action without adequate fact-finding or analysis. Compulsive managers are just the opposite. They are detail-minded, overly cautious people who seek refuge in procrastination. Compulsive managers are very insecure. They allow decision situations to deteriorate due to their emotional need to minimize risks. Understanding the role of the personality in making decisions is important. It has practical value in improving the overall quality of managerial decision-making.

2. *Intellectual capacity.* Because of the formal education usually required of personnel who enter management in the private sector, people with average or below-average intelligence seldom get the chance to test their abilities.

Most of the middle- and top-level managers in the private sector are in the upper 10 percent of the general population in terms of intelligence. There is little doubt that this intelligence contributes to their ability to make decisions. Due to the nature of the promotion process in most police departments, police administrators exhibit a much wider range of intelligence. Within this range, the qualitative aspects of a police administrator's intelligence may exert more influence on decisions than the IQ itself. A division chief with an IQ of 120 and a great deal of common sense is in a better position to make good decisions than another upper level manager with an IQ of 130 and little or no common sense. It is likely that the division chief will make even better decisions if he or she is knowledgeable, competent, mature, and emotionally healthy. While intelligence is positively correlated with managerial performance, the relationship is extremely complex.

3. *Education and experience.* The more complex, technical, or global a decision, the more important it is for the decision maker to have access to a broad reservoir of related information. Consequently, education and experience can make a significant contribution to the overall quality of managerial decisions. Decision theorists are quick to point out that the level of relevant knowledge is not necessarily correlated with the years of education or experience, however. It is dependent on the strength of the individual's motivation as well as the nature, extent, and quality of the learning experience. In some cases, too much experience can have a negative influence on decision-making. Some managers become experience bound and make major decisions based on past successes when the current situation calls for creative problem-solving and a break with tradition. The effect is also negative when a police administrator's education and experience has led to the development of undesirable managerial practices.

4. *Values, attitudes, and perception.* As discussed in Chapter 4, managers bring their beliefs, values, attitudes, and perceptions with them to the workplace (Hodgetts, 1979). Values are expressions of what a person considers to have worth and potential for need satisfaction. Attitudes are predispositions to evaluate and act in some favorable or unfavorable way. Values and attitudes are factored into and help to shape our perception. Perception is our view of the world. Colored by our values and attitudes, perception can short-circuit rational decision-making (Hitt, Middlemist, and Mathis, 1979). Under these circumstances, a manager's values and attitudes have a direct influence on the identification of problems, alternatives, and choice criteria in decision-making. Good police administrators strive diligently to overcome the negative aspects of selective perception. While there is no such thing as objective reality, history is replete with examples of value systems getting in the way of sound decision-making.

5. *Motivation to act.* Managers are unique individuals who are different from one another in terms of their motivation to act. Identifying problems, evaluating data, and searching for solutions requires analytical ability as well as creativity. It does not require courage. Making a decision to act based on these processes is another matter altogether. Taking action, which is the essence of decision-making (Allison, 1971), requires managers to risk their reputation, position, and, at times, even their career. Good managers have confidence in themselves and are motivated to take risks. Police managers

who have a healthy need to acquire power usually feel comfortable making tough decisions. They find decision-making pleasurable and self-affirming. Making decisions is an expression of power and a symbol of their value to the organization. Managers with a strong need for affiliation often have a very hard time making organizational decisions. An unhealthy dependence on others detracts from the decision task, distorts perception, and lowers their resolve to take unpopular actions. The excessive need for safety and security almost always has the same effect because decision-making involves risk taking. Managers who are offended by constructive criticism, who feel threatened when their subordinates make suggestions, and who fear change frequently make decisions that meet their emotional needs but fail to solve organizational problems (Sisk and Williams, 1981). It is essential for police departments to recruit, screen, select, and train managers who have the ability to make correct decisions and to link those decisions with action.

Types of Organizational Decisions

Management personnel at all levels make many kinds of decisions. Some are fairly simple. Others are very complex. Top executives make strategic decisions that affect and guide the total organization. Lower level managers spend most of their time making operational decisions involving limited actions designed to achieve a work unit's goals and objectives. Middle-level managers play a dual role: They (1) help executives develop long-range strategies and (2) see to it that line managers convert available resources into valuable goods or services. As Focus 9.1 indicates, a corporate model of decision making is evolving in public-sector police administration. Refer to Figure 9.1.

Another way to categorize organizational decisions is in terms of how routine or well structured they are as opposed to how novel or unstructured they happen to be. Routine decisions include those that recur frequently, involve standardized decision-making procedures, and entail a minimum of uncertainty. Decision makers rely on policies, procedures, and past precedents. Probably 90 percent of all management decisions are routine. Nonroutine decisions, on the other hand, are those which prove to be difficult because of their novel, nonrecurring, and unstructured nature. Their complexity is compounded by incomplete data and the absence of proven methods of resolution. Much more intuition and subjective judgment is involved in nonroutine decision-making (Longenecker, 1977).

Some theorists conceptualize managerial decisions on a continuum ranging from those that are well structured to those that are very poorly structured. Partially structured decisions fall somewhere between the two end points (Radford, 1981). Herbert Simon (1977) referred to these end points as programmed and nonprogrammed. *Programmed decisions* are made repeatedly, on a routine basis, and in concert with preestablished alternatives. *Nonprogrammed decisions,* on the other hand, are elicited by new and unique problems. They are normally made in poorly structured situations where there are no preexisting or ready-made courses of action. Programmed and nonprogrammed decisions can ordinarily be distinguished from one another by

FOCUS 9.1

Corporate Strategies for Policing

MARK H. MOORE/ROBERT C. TROJANOWICZ

Police departments embody a substantial public investment. Each year, the nation spends more than $20 billion to keep police departments on the street and vigilant.[1] More important, each year society puts its freedoms in the hands of the police by empowering them to use force to compel obedience to the nation's laws. That, too, is an investment, for the grant of legitimate authority is a resource granted to police by the citizens. As the Philadelphia Study Task Force explained:

> The police are entrusted with important public resources. The most obvious is money; $230 million a year flows through the police department. Far more important, the public grants the police another resource—the use of force and authority. These are deployed when a citizen is arrested or handcuffed, when an officer fires his weapon at a citizen, or even when an officer claims exclusive use of the street with his siren.[2]

These resources—money and authority—potentially have great value to society. If wisely deployed, they can substantially reduce the level of criminal victimization. They can restore a sense of security to the nation's neighborhoods. They can guarantee civility and tolerance in ordinary social interactions. They can provide a first-line response to various medical and social emergencies such as traffic accidents, drunkenness, domestic disputes, and runaway youth.

Stewardship over these resources is entrusted to the nation's police executives. They largely decide how best to use these assets. They make such decisions every time they beef up a narcotics unit, or establish priorities for the dispatching of calls, or write new policies governing the use of deadly force or the proper use of high-speed auto chases. At such moments, the police executives redeploy the money and authority entrusted to them in hopes that their organizations will produce greater value for society.

Judging how best to use the assets and capabilities of a police department is the principal task of police executives. As Professor Kenneth Andrews of the Harvard Business School says:

> The highest function of the executive is . . . leading the continuous process of determining the nature of the enterprise, and setting, revising, and achieving its goals.[3]

Performing this function well is no trivial task. It requires vision, judgment, and imagination, as well as disciplined analytical abilities.

In the private sector, executives seek to perform this function through the development of a "corporate strategy." A "corporate strategy" defines the principal

[1] Katherine M. Jamieson and Timothy J. Flanagan, eds., *Sourcebook of Criminal Justice Statistics—1986*, Washington, D.C., Bureau of Justice Statistics, 1987:2.

[2] *Philadelphia and Its Police: Toward a New Partnership*, A Report by the Philadelphia Police Study Task Force, March 1987: 129.

[3] Kenneth R. Andrews, *The Concept of Corporate Strategy*, Homewood, Illinois, Richard D. Irwin, 1980: iii.

financial and social goals the organization will pursue, and the principal products, technologies, and production processes on which it will rely to achieve its goals. It also defines how the organization will relate to its employees and its other constituencies such as shareholders, creditors, suppliers, and customers....

Recently, some police executives have begun considering different corporate strategies of policing. While these executives see enormous value in the knowledge and skill that have accumulated within police departments over the last 50 years, they are increasingly aware of the limitations of the past conceptions. They are reaching out for new ideas about how police departments should define their basic goals, deploy their assets, and garner support and legitimacy in the communities they now police....

SOURCE. Mark H. Moore and Robert C. Trojanowicz, *Corporate Strategies for Policing* (Washington, DC: National Institute of Justice, U.S. Department of Justice, November 1988).

(1) the uniqueness of the problem, (2) the degree to which one solution is specified, (3) who is responsible for making the decision, and (4) the organizational setting in which a decision is made (Baron, 1983). It is clear that deciding how to schedule police personnel is much easier than deciding what to do in a union-initiated work stoppage. Figure 9.2 illustrates graphically the difference between programmed and nonprogrammed organizational decisions.

Heuristic versus Objective Decisions

Managerial decisions can also be classified in terms of the processes used to make them. *Heuristic decisions* are gut-level choices based on intuition and personal judgment. The most common heuristic approaches to problem-solving are rules of thumb and trial and error (Hodgetts, 1979). Decisions are made on the basis of similar past experiences or the advice of significant others. The essence of the heuristic model is that the criteria used to validate a decision are internal to the personality of the decision maker, not external to it (Gore, 1964). Consequently, heuristic decisions—while they may be perfectly rational—are subjective and uniquely personal. Sam Souryal (1977), speaking on behalf of the police management theorists who stress the need for objective or fact-based decision-making, contends that reliance on hunches, rules of thumb, and gut feelings is an indication of organizational underdevelopment, personal immaturity, and the lack of training. *Objective decisions* are logical, fact-based choices that are expected (in terms of probability) to solve problems (Janis and Mann, 1977). Reaching objective decisions is much more difficult than using one's sixth sense. Objective decision-making involves the following:

1. Scanning for problems
2. Identifying problems
3. Listing probable causes
4. Designing solutions
5. Evaluating solutions
6. Choosing an alternative
7. Implementing a decision
8. Analyzing feedback
9. Making adjustments

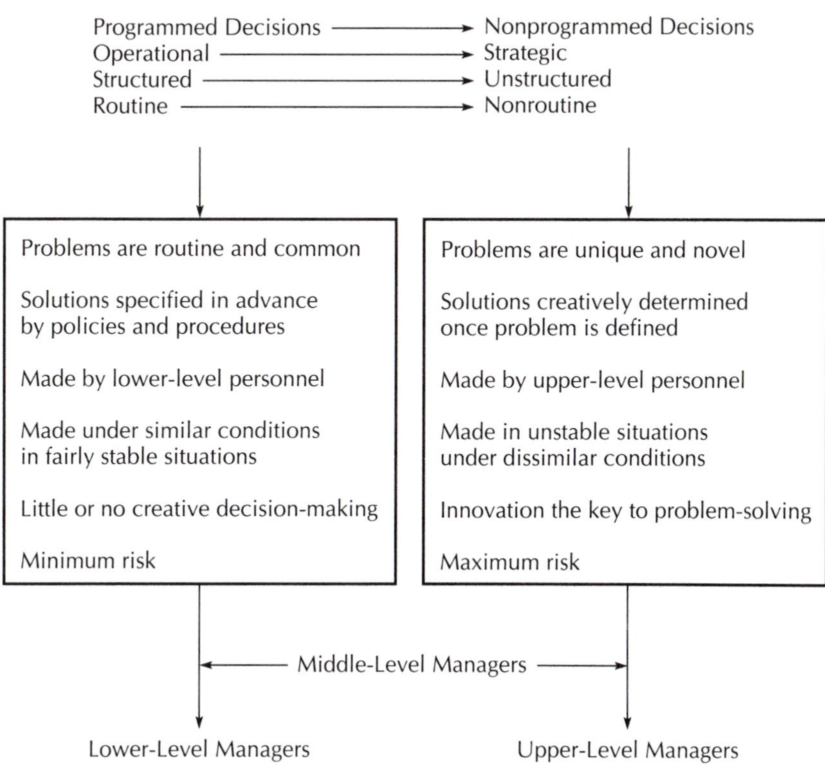
Programmed Decisions → Nonprogrammed Decisions
Operational → Strategic
Structured → Unstructured
Routine → Nonroutine
Problems are routine and common
Solutions specified in advance by policies and procedures
Made by lower-level personnel
Made under similar conditions in fairly stable situations
Little or no creative decision-making
Minimum risk
Problems are unique and novel
Solutions creatively determined once problem is defined
Made by upper-level personnel
Made in unstable situations under dissimilar conditions
Innovation the key to problem-solving
Maximum risk
Middle-Level Managers
Lower-Level Managers
Upper-Level Managers

FIGURE 9.2 Programmed and Nonprogrammed Management Decisions.

Here again, organizational decisions are on a continuum ranging from heuristic to objective. Most decisions fall somewhere in between the two end points. Good police administrators are multidimensional in that they base decisions on affective as well as cognitive input (Whisenand and Ferguson, 1978). This is why effective decision-making will continue to be as much of an art as it is a science.

Reactive versus Proactive Decisions

Organizational decisions may also be grouped into categories based on one's motivation to act. *Reactive decisions* are a response to a perceived problem the decision maker has a need to resolve. The nature of the stimulus and strength of the drive to resolve the problem helps establish the urgency of the response. Crisis decisions at either the strategic or operational level are always made under pressure. Crisis situations are characterized by surprise, urgency, stress, anxiety, and threat to high-priority goals (Smart and Vertinsky, 1977). Crisis decisions are often made heuristically based on intuition, past experience, instantaneous analysis, and emotional considerations rather than objective rationality. Even though these crisis decisions may lack scientific objectivity and can be very difficult to justify on a logical basis, they may actually solve the problem. *Proactive decisions,* on the other hand, are geared toward the future. They are a by-product of the planning process and prepare police managers to deal with the problems they could face down the road. Proactive decision-making involves predetermining future courses of action by deciding what, when, where, how, and by whom a task or set of tasks will be accomplished. Proactive decisions are preparatory in nature and normally made in an orderly manner, under calm conditions, without the pressure generated by time constraints. Contingency plans (products of proactive decision-making) are designed to counteract the chaos generated by fear of the unknown. While a good tactical plan for dealing with hostage situations cannot guarantee successful negotiations, it sets the stage for a coordinated response during a crisis.

The authority to make organizational decisions is distributed according to institutional norms. Managers in bureaucratic organizations normally exercise what Max Weber called rational-legal authority (Wren, 1987). While they may seek advice, bureaucratic managers view themselves as single rational actors when it comes to making decisions that fall within the scope of their authority (Allison, 1971). Consequently, individual decisions are the rule rather than the exception. Bureaucratic managers equate decision-making with power and resist any encroachment on that power. Under these circumstances, they control the speed of the decision-making process and the content of the decisions. As the humanistic philosophy of management (see Chapter 11) has displaced traditional bureaucratic thinking, emphasis has shifted away from exercising power over to sharing power with subordinates. As a result, group decisions are much more common. Teams, committees, task forces, and review panels have become well-established aspects of organizational life. Group decision-making helps satisfy workers' need to participate in making those decisions that affect them. While there are a number of disadvantages, there is evidence that in complex situations—where there is one clear-cut solution—groups using a consensus agreement approach tend to be more effective than individuals. Where problems are less complex and special skill is required, individual managers with proper education and training tend to excel (Tansik, Chase, and Aquilano, 1980). Group decision-making is explored in more detail later in this chapter.

Problem-Solving Through Rational Decision-Making

Given the complexity of modern police work and the crucial need for effective decision-making in the administration of justice, decisions can no longer be relegated to seat-of-the-pants best guessing. David Holt (1987) argues that rational decision-making must replace impromptu thinking. In this context, rational decision-making refers to a sensible, logical, and objective approach based on investigation rather than heuristic intuition. Rational decision-making is a process involving several very distinct steps designed to help managers discover optimal solutions. It is a structured approach that allows them to identify opportunities and zero in on the real problem to be solved. The problem-solving process we describe here is illustrated in Figure 9.3.

The best organizational decisions are made via a series of steps that lead to a particular conclusion. The steps in the decision-making process are as follows:

Step 1. Awareness of the need to make a decision. Decision-making is activated by opportunities and problems. A prerequisite for effective decision-making

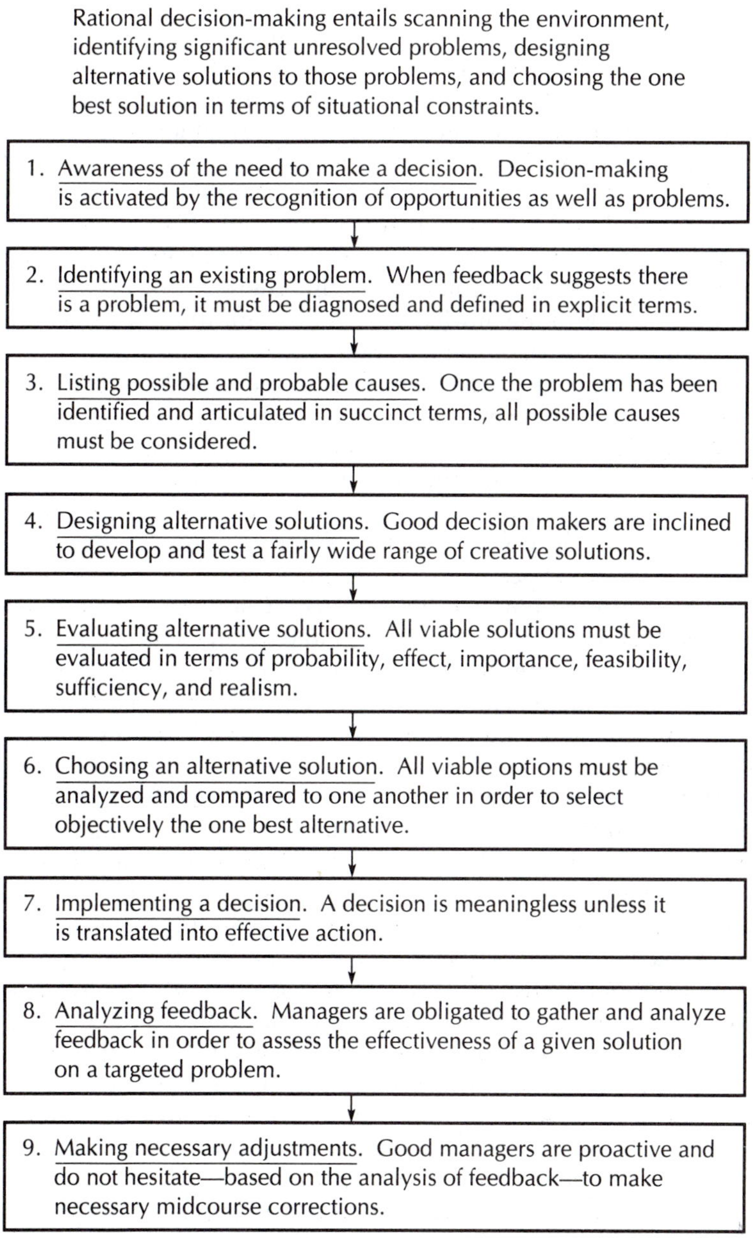

Rational decision-making entails scanning the environment, identifying significant unresolved problems, designing alternative solutions to those problems, and choosing the one best solution in terms of situational constraints.

1. Awareness of the need to make a decision. Decision-making is activated by the recognition of opportunities as well as problems.

2. Identifying an existing problem. When feedback suggests there is a problem, it must be diagnosed and defined in explicit terms.

3. Listing possible and probable causes. Once the problem has been identified and articulated in succinct terms, all possible causes must be considered.

4. Designing alternative solutions. Good decision makers are inclined to develop and test a fairly wide range of creative solutions.

5. Evaluating alternative solutions. All viable solutions must be evaluated in terms of probability, effect, importance, feasibility, sufficiency, and realism.

6. Choosing an alternative solution. All viable options must be analyzed and compared to one another in order to select objectively the one best alternative.

7. Implementing a decision. A decision is meaningless unless it is translated into effective action.

8. Analyzing feedback. Managers are obligated to gather and analyze feedback in order to assess the effectiveness of a given solution on a targeted problem.

9. Making necessary adjustments. Good managers are proactive and do not hesitate—based on the analysis of feedback—to make necessary midcourse corrections.

FIGURE 9.3 Nine Steps in Rational Decision-Making.

is being aware that a decision is required. The most serious situation exists when dire consequences are possible and the decision maker is unaware that a problem even exists. When police managers are blindsided by an unanticipated problem, it is often very difficult for them to regain their equilibrium. According to an old adage, "forewarned is forearmed." In the final analysis, problem awareness is a function of the manager's knowledge, perception, and motivation to know what is going on. Good police administrators have very sensitive antennae and relish the thought of resolving organizational problems through proactive decision-making (Thibault, Lynch, and McBride, 1985).

Step 2. Identifying an existing problem. When feedback suggests there might be a problem, it is the manager's job to recognize it, examine it, and determine what caused it. A common mistake in organizational decision-making is concentrating on finding the right answer rather than identifying the right problem. Finding the real problem can be difficult. Good managers focus their attention on what is and compare it to what should be (Plunkett, 1983). Focusing on the real problem saves time, energy, and effort. It gives managers the opportunity to mobilize the resources needed to correct the problem. Managers often confuse symptoms (indicating there is a problem) with cause and spin their wheels tilting at windmills. As organizations become more complex and the decision environment becomes more complicated, police administrators are required to gather and analyze more and more information in a concerted effort to ensure an accurate diagnosis. Because of errors in conceptualization, managers more frequently fail to identify the right problem than fail to solve the problem they eventually take up.

Step 3. Listing possible and probable causes. Once managers have identified and articulated the problem in very succinct terms, they are ready to look for the cause or causes of the problem. A cause may be a person, fact, or condition that is responsible for an effect. Good police administrators try to think of all possible reasons that help to explain the existing state of affairs. They may, depending on the importance of the decision, even consider a few that seem impossible (Fulmer and Franklin, 1982). Good managers are creative, imaginative, and resourceful. They have an innate or acquired ability to recognize cause and effect no matter how oblique the relationship might be. This ability is critical because it sets the stage for the development of alternative solutions. Causes are arranged along a continuum from possible to probable. Those at the probable end of the continuum become the focus of further inquiry and the catalyst for decision-making.

Step 4. Designing alternative solutions. If there is only one solution to a particular problem, managers—no matter how competent they happen to be—are not in a position to devise alternatives and no decision is required. In most situations, however, police administrators are called on to develop viable options. Formulating alternatives is more of an art than a science. The artistry comes from considering an appropriate range of solutions while reaching out for creative ideas not made obvious by scientific investigation (Holt, 1987). Poor decision makers settle for the easiest and most available solutions. They have little or no desire to find the best possible solution. Poor decision makers rely very heavily on intuition and similar past experiences to fashion alternative solutions to new problems. They lack both the imagination and the motivation to attempt creative problem-solving. Poor decision makers are victimized by perceptual predispositions (or mind sets) that interfere with the free association of ideas. This prevents new and useful solutions from emerging. Breaking the mind sets produced by experience, education, prejudice, and emotional conflict is the primary task of those who aspire to think creatively (Sisk and Williams, 1981). Effective police administrators are aware of and learn to work creatively within the authoritative, biological, physical, technological, and economic constraints that limit their discretion in making decisions (Tannenbaum, Weschler, and Massarik, 1961).

Step 5. Evaluating alternative solutions. The way that alternative solutions are designed and expressed almost always depends on the manager's problem-solving skills, his or her perception of the problem to be solved, and the nature of the problem itself. It is at this stage that decision makers attempt to assess the advantages (benefits) and disadvantages (costs) of each alternative. All solutions are evaluated in terms of their probability, possible effects, and importance (Tansik, Chase, and Aquilano, 1980). Solutions are also evaluated in relation to sufficiency, feasibility, realism, and rationality. According to Simon (1976), the psychological act of evaluating alternatives consists of measuring them vis-à-vis certain value indices that are associated with the realization of our values. The correctness of a particular decision is a relative matter. It is correct if it selects appropriate means to achieve desired ends. Rational decision-making is concerned with the selection of preferred alternatives in terms of some system of values whereby the consequences of the police administrator's behavior can be evaluated. There are several types of rationality. A decision is *objectively rational* if it is the correct behavior for achieving maximum results. It is *subjectively rational* if it achieves maximum results in relation to real knowledge of the subject. It is *consciously rational* to the degree that the adjustment of means to ends is an intellectual process. It is *deliberately rational* when the adjustment of means to ends is intentional (Holden, 1986). A decision is *ethically rational* when it conforms to the moral standards of the individual and is considered proper by those in the appropriate reference group. Decisions that appear to be irrational may be very rational in light of the dynamics of the situation or based on the decision maker's goals.

Step 6. Choosing an alternative solution. It is a grievous error to make decisions based on inadequate data. Information is the raw material out of which effective decisions are made. Once the real problem is identified and realistic solutions have been designed, managers seek to find the alternative that will maximize results in terms of specific objectives. Good police administrators weigh the truly viable alternatives in terms of effort, cost, risk, or other criteria. These criteria are used to measure or judge the various alternatives in order to discriminate among them and rank them in relation to the probability that they will resolve the problem. Comparative analysis is the data-based comparison of viable alternatives, in light of explicit criteria, to select the optimum line of action. This type of comparative analysis is not a substitute for managerial intuition or a denial of its worth. It is a technique to make decisions more effective by reducing imprecision and error. One of the most useful analytical techniques is known as the *decision matrix.* The matrix approach utilizes data, criteria, alternatives, and judgment

Comparative analysis is the data-based comparison of viable alternatives, in light of explicit criteria, to choose an optimum line of action designed to solve a given organizational problem.

The problem: To determine which semiautomatic pistol will be purchased to replace department-issued service revolvers.

Criteria		Alternatives			
		Pistol A	Pistol B	Pistol C	Pistol D
1. Operation	(05)	5 [25]	4 [20]	4 [20]	4 [25]
2. Power	(08)	4 [36]	4 [36]	5 [40]	5 [40]
3. Capacity	(07)	4 [28]	4 [28]	5 [35]	5 [35]
4. Cost	(03)	3 [09]	3 [09]	3 [09]	2 [06]
5. Maintenance	(06)	4 [24]	3 [18]	5 [30]	2 [12]
6. Reliability	(10)	3 [30]	4 [40]	5 [50]	4 [40]
7. Safety	(09)	4 [36]	3 [27]	4 [36]	4 [36]
	Total	188	178	<u>220</u>	194

Legend: The numbers in parentheses are weights indicating the importance of a criterion. Those in brackets are scores that reflect how well an alternative satisfies a criterion. Totals show how the alternatives compare to one another in terms of all the criteria. All other things being equal, the alternative with the highest total represents the best solution to a particular problem.

FIGURE 9.4 Decision Matrix.

as the basis for choosing a particular course of action. As illustrated in Figure 9.4, viable alternatives (solutions) are listed horizontally. The criteria used to judge alternatives are listed vertically. Managers assign a numerical weight to each criterion (from most important to least important) expressing its relative importance. Each alternative is scored numerically (from excellent to poor) in relation to how well it satisfies the criterion. The score is then multiplied by the weight to produce the numerical value of each alternative/criterion relationship. The optimal solution is determined by the total value for each alternative. If—after very careful analysis—there is no significant difference between the alternatives, personal preference becomes the most important factor in the decision ("The Analytical Process," 1979).

Step 7. Implementing a decision. While the analysis of data and decision-making based on the outcome of that analysis is inherent in the manager's role, deciding what to do is only part of the process. The next step is to translate the most beneficial alternative into action. Unless organizational decisions are supported by appropriate managerial action, there is little or no chance that they will be successful (Certo, 1989). Once the solution has been chosen, it is the police administrator's job to plan its implementation. The decision maker must determine who will do what, where, when, and how to carry out the decision. In terms of percentage of time, decision-making takes up a relatively small portion of each manager's workday. Much of managers' time is spent organizing the environment, mobilizing resources, and motivating others to implement the decision. Emphasizing the decision-making activities of police administrators may produce a distorted view of their function (Longenecker, 1977). It can be argued that for every decision, there must be an implementation strategy. The best decision, left unimplemented, will have no more effect than if the problem was never recognized and a decision never made (Tansik, Chase, and Aquilano, 1980). This is what some managers mean when they say, "The way to hell is paved with good intentions and no action."

Step 8. Analyzing feedback. After a decision has been made and implemented, managers are obligated to do a follow-up evaluation. It is their job to keep track of who is doing what and to gather feedback in a conscientious effort to assess the effect of that particular solution on the targeted problem (Plunkett, 1983). Managers need to know whether an action is accomplishing the intended results. While doing something separates dreamers from achievers, action is only part of the equation. It is learning from experience that is important. This requires evaluation of one's action related to a given decision. Good police administrators keep their eyes and ears open. By understanding the dynamics that produce correct decisions, they can better assess environmental factors, problems, solutions, implementation strategies, and so on, as they prepare themselves to handle subsequent decision situations. Only the naive believe in final solutions. Like the rings created when a rock is thrown into still water, decisions invariably lead to the need for more decision-making somewhere within the organization. Without adequate feedback, decision makers are doomed to repeat the mistakes of the past (Hitt, Middlemist, and Mathis, 1979).

Step 9. Making necessary adjustments. The quality of a decision is determined by factors such as the (1) sufficiency of data, (2) accuracy of the database, (3) perceptual ability of the decision maker, (4) problem-solving skill of the manager, (5) adequacy of the implementation strategy, and (6) nature of the follow-up. Proactive police administrators take decision-making in stride. They are not afraid to admit they have made a mistake or that a solution they have chosen is inadequate to resolve a particular problem under a given set of circumstances. Good managers are eager to take action and do not hesitate—based on feedback discussed in step 8—to make rational midcourse corrections as environmental conditions change or as the unknowable future becomes the experience of the present (Sisk and Williams, 1981). Effective decision makers tend to be intelligent, perceptive, creative, and proactive. Getting the job done right is almost always more important to them than the

CASE STUDY

Captain Jayson Moore and Lieutenant Royce Strauss

Capt. Jayson Moore, a 17-year veteran of the police department, is a colorful character who learned his trade in the school of hard knocks. While he has had little or no formal training as a manager, he is acknowledged to be a good decision maker. He uses his past experiences as a prologue to the future and chooses between alternatives based on hunches, gut-level feelings, and rules of thumb. He is right most of the time. Capt. Moore and the heuristic tradition he represents are an anathema to the cadre of college-educated managers who control the department.

In an effort to become more systematic and objective in his decision-making, Capt. Moore enrolled in a senior-level management course offered through the police academy. According to the syllabus, the course was to emphasize managerial problem-solving based on rational decision-making and comparative analysis.

Concerned that his lack of formal education might put him at a disadvantage for mastering the material, Capt. Moore set up an appointment with the instructor (Lt. Royce Strauss). He asked the lieutenant to explain the rational decision-making process and to illustrate it through the use of comparative analysis. Capt. Moore also wanted to know at what point decision-making becomes a science rather than an art.

If you were the lieutenant, how would you explain the mechanics involved in the rational decision-making process to Capt. Moore? What steps are required to identify, compare, and choose from among viable alternatives? Define comparative analysis and give an example of how it might be used in police work. Would you argue that it is always the police administrator's duty to select the best alternative in each and every decision situation? If not, why not? Is there any need for judgment in objective decision-making?

ego trip associated with being right all of the time. Only fools make decisions and then dismiss them. Good managers track decisions and are prepared to make those adjustments that become necessary to ensure the efficiency, effectiveness, and productivity of the organization.

There is nothing magical about the nine-step decision-making process just discussed. There is no intrinsic value to such a list. Its value lies in describing problem-solving behavior (Albanese, 1981). When it comes to routine problems, most managers go through this thought process quickly and without much conscious effort. Unique organizational decisions require more attention. Since relatively few organizational decisions require split-second action, it may be advisable to move in a deliberate step-by-step fashion in order to arrive at the very best decision. Most administrative problems do not require immediate resolution. Consequently, managers have some flexibility in the timing of their decision-making. In most important decisions, this cushion is measured in terms of hours, if not days. While a rush to judgment can have catastrophic effects, procrastination is an unacceptable alternative. Competent police administrators adapt their decision-making to the situation.

Limitations on Rational Decision-Making

Decision-making lies at the center of the administrative process. Under ideal conditions, police managers are expected to make rational data-based decisions utilizing the model just described. Since organizational decisions are usually made in an environment of uncertainty and risk by people who differ greatly in terms of their basic values, acumen, knowledge, and problem-solving skills, complete rationality is an unachievable goal. While it is often assumed that decision makers investigate and decide logically on the basis of their investigation, empirical studies indicate that the decision-making process involves a great deal of competition and even conflict. Some management theorists refer to decision-making as the art of compromise (Souryal, 1977). They reject the so-called economic man assumptions generally associated with rational decision-making.

Herbert Simon, one of the leading opponents of the economic man model, argues that the model simply does not describe actual decision-making behavior in complex organizations. Simon contends that instead of searching for and choosing the best option, many managers settle for decisions that are only good enough to get by. Other decision scientists believe that since people are involved, the best possible decision is seldom made (Hitt, Middlemist, and Mathis, 1979).

Bounded Rationality

Responding to what he considered to be the unrealistic assumptions of the economic model, Simon developed an alternative set of assumptions. According to him, decision makers are not guided by perfect rationality but by *bounded rationality* (Reitz, 1981). He argues that all administrators have limitations on their ability to process information and make rational decisions. Their ability to reason is limited by constraints such as the following:

1. *Organizational anomie:* conflicting and continually changing goals or objectives.
2. *Lack of relevant data:* insufficient and often less than objective information.
3. *Physiological factors:* energy levels, reflexes, habits, and physical skills.
4. *Psychological factors:* beliefs, values, motives, experiences, and perceptions.
5. *Knowledge of the job:* the actual job-related knowledge of the decision maker.

All organizational decisions are made within these boundaries (Holden, 1986). Consequently, it is not unusual for police administrators to misread a decision situation, fail to see a problem, recognize only a limited number of alternatives, or miscalculate the consequences associated with a particular solution. When this happens, they are not being irrational. They are simply making the most rational decision possible within a bounded information set (Tansik, Chase, and Aquilano, 1980). The goal of any organizational decision maker is to expand these boundaries just as far as they can.

While it is clear that there is a natural desire to make the best decision possible, possible and best are not always compatible concepts. In addition to the constraints just discussed, the capacity of the human mind to formulate and solve complex problems is very small when compared to the size of those problems. As a result, managers are inclined to settle for adequate solutions to organizational problems. They take the path of least resistance. Instead of searching for and choosing the best possible option, they accept decisions that are good enough in a given situation. This phenomenon is known as satisficing (Janis and Mann, 1977).

Satisficing

Satisficing is best described as decision-making behavior through which police administrators choose a satisfactory alternative, one that is considered adequate but not necessarily the best (Holt, 1987). In satisficing, managers ask themselves whether the decision is good enough to produce an adequate solution to a particular problem. This pragmatic approach to decision-making, which Charles E. Lindblom calls "the science of muddling through" (1959), adapts to each situation in a fragmented way and provides flexibility for those managers who want to avoid failure or mistakes that could jeopardize future promotions, pay raises, continued employment, and so on. Satisficing is a strategy designed to lessen the danger associated with uncertainty and risk.

Many management theorists believe that satisficing is necessary, if not desirable in some situations because of the following constraints:

1. Managers have a limited amount of time they can devote to organizational decision-making.
2. Managers deal with many complex and competing problems on a simultaneous basis.
3. Managers access only a relatively small amount of the data concerning a given problem.
4. The cost of procuring and utilizing information to make a better decision may be prohibitive.
5. Some data may not be available to the decision maker regardless of the cost.
6. Bureaucratic managers are not necessarily well trained in using research, logic, or advanced reasoning.
7. Public problems are value laden, and there is no real consensus about how to approach them.
8. Managers do not always have the independence necessary to make totally objective or impartial decisions.
9. Major decisions often require public funds controlled by independent legislative bodies (Souryal, 1977).

Satisficing occurs in all aspects of decision-making. During the problem identification stage of the process, for example, police managers ordinarily gather just enough data to give them an adequate picture of what is causing the increase in a particular type of crime. Then, based on their knowledge and problem-solving skills, they develop a short list of viable options that appear to be adequate to solve the problem. If the feasible alternatives all have unacceptable negative consequences, administrators will usually not pick the best of the negatives but will continue to search for another alternative with positive aspects (March and Simon, 1958). It is better to compromise and make a less than optimal decision than to make no decision at all. Satisficing decisions buy time. While they are not perfect solutions, they do provide an incremental approach to problem-solving. At least some progress can be made while managers continue their search for a better decision (Hitt, Middlemist, and Mathis, 1979). Over time, we may be better off moving toward perceived and bounded alternatives via incremental steps of reasonable size rather than taking great strides based on the rational pursuit of perfect, yet virtually unattainable, solutions (Miller and Starr, 1967).

Learning by Doing

Henry Sisk and J. Clifton Williams (1981) argue that there is no way for a manager to become a superior decision maker except through the sometimes painful experience of deciding and then living with the consequences of those decisions. Police administrators can improve the quality of their decisions and help to ensure their acceptance by following some of the guidelines formulated by decision theorists. Good decision makers do the following:

1. Collect available, relevant, factual, and sufficient data on which to base a logical decision.
2. Evaluate alternatives based on knowledge, experience, and inner feelings about what is or is not appropriate.
3. Time all important decisions to coincide with positive as opposed to negative attitudes.
4. Avoid making assumptions and being unduly influenced by gut-level intuition.
5. Communicate decisions clearly to everyone who will be affected by them in any way.
6. Design flexible alternatives that allow adjustments based on unforeseen occurrences or new information.
7. Implement major decisions expeditiously rather than wasting time perfecting never-used plans.
8. Exhibit courage in designing, evaluating, selecting, and implementing viable solutions to unresolved problems.
9. Assume full responsibility for those decisions that fall within the scope of their authority (Fulmer and Franklin, 1982).

While it is impossible to give advice for improving decisions that is applicable to every decision situation, the following recommendations are important because they deal with some of the common faults exhibited by managerial decision makers:

1. Learn to distinguish between personal and organizational decisions.
2. Minimize the number of decisions to be made under crisis conditions.
3. Expect subordinates to make decisions they are capable of making.
4. Seek out problems and opportunities that elicit proactive decisions.
5. Anticipate the potential political fallout generated by major decisions.
6. Involve subordinates and staff specialists in all aspects of decision-making.
7. Recognize the values, biases, and perceptual sets that influence decisions.
8. Approach rational decision-making from a problem-solving perspective.
9. Assess problems in terms of their importance and priority status.
10. Formulate viable and creative solutions designed to solve major problems.
11. Evaluate and select the most appropriate solution under the circumstances.
12. Implement the chosen option as quickly and completely as possible.
13. Assume that all major decisions will require follow-up and adaptation (Williams, DuBrin, and Sisk, 1985).

Effective Decision-Making

Good managers follow a few fairly simple rules to enhance the quality of their decisions. According to Lawrence Steinmetz and H. Ralph Todd (1986), these managers are able to make "ulcerless decisions" because they have learned the importance of the following guidelines:

1. *Differentiate between really big decisions and little problems.* Big problems require attention and should be considered in detail. They merit the time, energy, effort, and expertise necessary to construct a decision matrix that analyzes viable alternatives in terms of cost, contribution to objectives, feasibility, side effects, and so on. Little problems, on the other hand, do not warrant this type of time-consuming consideration. Prioritization is a key to effective decision-making.

2. *Rely on existing policies, procedures, rules, and regulations whenever possible.* There is no need to reinvent the wheel when it comes to routine decisions. Good police administrators do not hesitate to use the problem-solving mechanisms that are known to work in routine situations. It saves time and gives them an opportunity to delegate duties to their subordinates. Specific policies, procedures, rules, and regulations also help ensure consistency in the decision-making process.

3. *Consult and check with significant others before making major organizational decisions.* Good police administrators avoid making decisions based on insufficient data. While other people may not be authorized to make a particular decision, they can provide valuable insight and advice to the decision maker. Successful managers never hesitate to seek guidance from significant others who have expertise in the problem area. They know there is a commonality in decision-making experiences that can be shared by those who have held a similar position.

4. *Avoid making crisis decisions.* Making major decisions under stressful conditions is not an ideal situation and should be avoided whenever possible.

While this is sound advice, it is very difficult to translate into practice. Successful police administrators learn to cope with pressure and to develop various stress-reduction techniques. When confronted with a crisis, they (1) relax and think, (2) go through the decision-making process as outlined in Figure 9.3, and (3) make the best decision possible under the circumstances. Thinking logically helps them maintain a rational presence of mind and avoid making emotional decisions in pressure-packed situations.

5. *Do not attempt to anticipate all eventualities associated with resolution of the problem.* While it is impossible to anticipate all eventualities, many police administrators become inept decision makers and end up worrying needlessly because they try to think of everything that can possibly happen. They overload themselves. Even though Murphy's law declares, "Whatever can go wrong will go wrong," the odds are that most of the things that could go wrong will never go wrong. As a result, managers are ill-advised to consider everything that might happen. Good managers concentrate on the probable as opposed to the possible.

6. *Do not expect to make the right decision all of the time.* Some managers with ego problems insist on always being right. It becomes a fetish that must be satisfied irrespective of the consequences. While it is usually nice to be right, even the best managers make incorrect decisions. Due to various institutional constraints, few major organizational decisions are totally right or totally wrong. More often than not, police administrators satisfice by choosing the middle ground between the best possible solution and the worst solution. Pragmatic managers recognize that rightness is almost always a question of degree rather than absolute perfection. This helps them avoid paralysis by analysis.

7. *Cultivate decisiveness.* Good managers are aware that indecision creates tension in people. They also know that too much tension is a psychological stressor that produces even more reluctance to make tough decisions. Indecision becomes a self-perpetuating and destructive phenomenon. Poor decision makers procrastinate and vacillate. Procrastination is the failure or inability to make a decision when all of the necessary data is there and a decision should be made. When no decision is made, time is wasted. Work goes unfinished or is done improperly. Vacillation refers to a switch in alternatives once a viable course of action has already been selected. Vacillation leads to the misallocation of resources and a waste of time. Good police administrators do not change their major decisions unless they are proven to be wrong or ineffective.

8. *Implement major decisions once they have been made.* Most good decision makers contend that once a major decision has been made, prompt implementation becomes a critical factor in its success or failure. A firm commitment to execution is crucial. Implementation of a decision is far more important than the correctness of that decision. It gives police administrators an opportunity to assess their own judgment, capitalize on unanticipated circumstances, and make those changes that are necessary to correct wrong or defective decisions. Unless they are implemented competently and in a timely manner, major decisions are of no real value when it comes to resolving problems in complex criminal justice organizations.

9. *Accept decision-making as a challenge rather than an unwanted chore.* Good managers are turned on by the unknown and relish the opportunity to

demonstrate personal competence by making substantive organizational decisions. Poor decision makers fear the unknown. They avoid decision situations like the plague. Many are hedonists who rely on benign incrementalism in order to get by. They are content to engage in the ritualism of going through the motions. Poor decision makers are often inept human beings who lack the basic problem-solving skills needed to create and choose between viable alternatives. Others are afraid to rock the boat or jeopardize their career by making tough decisions.

The best managerial decision makers tend to be intelligent, knowledgeable, competent, collegial, decisive, and action-oriented. They respect their subordinates and incorporate them into the organizational decision-making process.

Group Decision-Making

For all practical purposes, the unilateral decision-making associated with autocratic management in complex organizations is heading down the path toward extinction. As police departments move away from the quasi-military model to a more humanistic configuration, much more emphasis is placed on delegating authority and nurturing participative decision-making. Many organization/management theorists contend that operational decisions should be made collectively at the "lowest level possible" by those people who are directly affected by the decisions (Halloran, 1981). Modern organizations have become so complex that the single rational actor (one-person) model of decision-making is gradually being replaced by group approaches to problem-solving and decision-making (Kast and Rosenzweig, 1985).

Group decisions are collective decisions produced by specifically designated groups such as committees, study teams, task forces, and review panels. Group decision-making occurs when members of the group provide input and actively participate in the problem-solving process. Group decision-making is particularly appropriate for making important nonprogrammed decisions (like how to deal with a unique hostage situation or what to do about police corruption). Since these decisions are likely to be complex, few managers have all of the intelligence, acumen, knowledge, skills, and temperament necessary to make the best decision possible (Hitt, Middlemist, and Mathis, 1979). Good managers know their own limitations. They are not afraid to share the power to make certain types of decisions with other people in the organization if it will help to produce better decisions.

Many organization/management theorists argue that groups are in a position to make better decisions than individuals. There are three assumptions inherent in this argument:

1. Groups tend to be more vigilant than individuals because more people are involved in scanning the environment for problem-solving and decision-making opportunities.

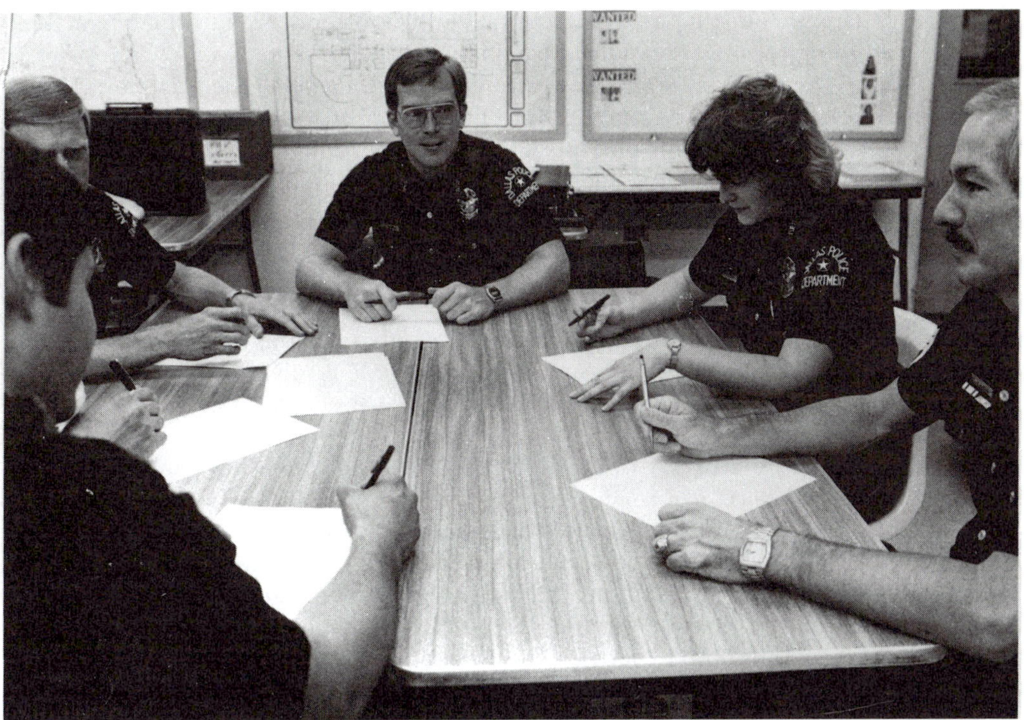

Valued Input Members of the Dallas Police Department share in the decision-making process at a Quality Circle meeting *(Courtesy of Dallas Police Department).*

2. Groups, based on the synergistic effect of social interaction, tend to generate more and more creative solutions than individuals acting alone.
3. Groups tend to evaluate alternatives more thoroughly than individual decision makers (Johns, 1988).

Whether group decisions are, in fact, better than those made by a single rational actor depends on personal as well as situational factors. Good managers are flexible. They use the decision-making model that is most likely to produce the best result under the circumstances.

Research on group decision-making reveals that it has both advantages and disadvantages over idiosyncratic decision-making. If its potential can be harnessed and its deficiencies can be avoided, group decision-making can attain a level of proficiency that is ordinarily not achieved. The key to achieving a high level of performance in any group decision-making hinges on the availability of people-oriented managers who have the ability to maximize the group's assets and to minimize its liabilities. With the proper training, police administrators can learn to perform this function. Under these circumstances, they serve as the group's central nervous system (Swanson, Territo, and Taylor, 1988). It is their job to activate and give direction to the collective decision-making process.

Individual and group decisions each have their own strengths and weaknesses. As we indicated, neither one is suitable for making decisions in all situations. The major advantages that groups offer over individuals in making nonprogrammed decisions are as follows:

1. *The greater sum total of knowledge and information.* There is more knowledge and information in a group than in any of its members. Consequently, decisions that require the utilization of knowledge—internal and external to the police department—generally give groups an advantage over individual decision makers. By pooling the resources of several people, there is much more data on which to base a sound decision.

2. *A greater number of approaches to resolving the problem.* In addition to more input, groups tend to bring more heterogeneity into the organizational decision-making process. Since members of the group have different perceptions and unique approaches to problem-solving, they contribute to the decision-making process by knocking each other out of old ruts in their thinking. Diversity in thinking gives police administrators the opportunity to choose from an array of creative approaches and innovative solutions.

3. *Involvement in decision-making increases acceptance.* Many decisions fail after the final choice is made simply because people do not accept the solution. As noted earlier in the discussion of participative management, employees want to be involved in making organizational decisions that affect them. They become more committed to a decision in which they have invested their time, energy, effort, and expertise. This translates into support for the decision and satisfaction among those required to implement it. When groups solve problems, more people accept and feel responsible for making the solution work.

4. *Better communication of the decision.* Decisions made by an individual must be communicated to those who are expected to carry them out. Failures in the communication process detract from the merit of the decision. Chances of communication failures are greatly reduced when those who must work together in implementing decisions have participated in making them. Members of a decision-making group understand the solution. They are aware of the alternatives and know why they were rejected. Communication is maximized when significant others are incorporated into the organizational decision-making process.

5. *Increased legitimacy.* American society values democratic methods. The group decision-making process is consistent with democratic ideals. As a result, collective decisions are often perceived as being more legitimate than those made by a single rational actor. When police administrators, as principal decision makers, fail to consult with significant others before making important organizational decisions, the exercise of complete power may create the perception that decisions are made arbitrarily as well as autocratically (Robbins, 1989). This perception can lead to intraorganizational conflict and poor morale.

Drawbacks

There are drawbacks to group decision-making. The negative or downside of group decision-making in complex organizations includes these five factors:

1. *Social pressure.* The desire to be a good group member and to be accepted by one's peers tends to squelch disagreement and promote consensus (Dessler, 1979). Psychosocial factors may become more important than ob-

jective decision-making. Reaching agreement in the group is often confused with finding the right solution and making the correct decision (see Chapter 7 for a more detailed discussion of group dynamics).

2. *Valence of solutions.* Possible solutions (alternatives or options) elicit critical and supportive comments from members of the group. When one proposed solution receives considerably more positive than negative reaction, it may—based on its relative strength, or valence—be acted on regardless of its actual capacity to solve the problem. This is the transition point where idea-getting is turned into decision-making via intuition rather than through objective analysis.

3. *Domination by a few.* In most groups, a few dominant individuals emerge and capture more than their fair share of influence on outcomes. They achieve this power through a greater degree of participation, persuasive ability, and/ or stubborn tenacity. This has been called the iron law of oligarchy. If the dominant coalition is composed of those members with low-to-medium ability, the group's overall effectiveness tends to suffer. The quality of every group decision is influenced—to one degree or another—by the knowledge, abilities, and human skills of its (formal and informal) leaders.

4. *Conflicting secondary goal: Winning the argument.* When a decision-making group is confronted with a problem, the initial goal is to resolve it. The formulation of several competing alternatives or options causes another problem. Members have a natural inclination to adopt and support a particular position. They take it upon themselves to sell the favored solution. Converting those with neutral viewpoints and refuting those with opposing views becomes part of the decision-making process. The goal shifts to having one's own solution chosen rather than finding the best solution possible under the circumstances. This new goal is totally unrelated to objective analysis or the quality of the decision. Ego-centered decisions of this kind can result in lowering the overall quality of managerial decisions in complex criminal justice organizations.

5. *Consumption of time.* It takes time to assemble and lead a productive decision-making group. The dynamic interaction that occurs once the group has been formed is often inefficient. As a result, groups almost always take more time to reach a decision than would be the case if a single rational actor were making the final choice. Unskilled managers may be so concerned with finding a solution they terminate the discussion before consensus is achieved or tend to be so interested in getting input that the discussion becomes redundant and boring. Both of these conditions limit management's ability to act quickly and decisively when the need arises (Maier, 1969).

Group decision-making—with its assets and liabilities—has become a permanent fixture in the landscape of contemporary organization and management. In a Delphi study concerning the future of American law enforcement, 20 management experts expressed the belief that police personnel will continue their demand for more meaningful participation in the organizational decision-making process. The experts concluded that real on-the-job satisfaction will be associated with shared decision-making (More, 1984). Group consensus will become the dominant characteristic of police administration. As the shared decision model evolves, the distinction between supervisors and subordinates will become much less significant (More and Wegener, 1990).

Police managers will serve as group facilitators who share decision-making power with others.

Humanistic Approach

Interest in group decision-making can be traced back to the human relations school of management and theorists like Mary Parker Follett, Elton Mayo, Abraham Maslow, Keith Davis, Douglas McGregor, and Warren Bennis. Humanism stresses the importance of group dynamics and participative management in achieving an organization's mission, goals, and objectives. They see participation in decision-making as democracy in action, opening communications, diffusing authority, and motivating people to make a much greater commitment to the organization (Wren, 1987). Humanistic managers, like their Japanese counterparts, believe that people—not capital spending or automation—are the primary source of productive gain. They see workers as their most important asset and treat them with dignity and respect. Good managers treat co-workers as partners (Peters and Waterman, 1982). They strive to achieve genuine consensus, collaboration, and collegiality. Humanists believe that group decisions are far superior to those made by single rational actors as they exercise formal authority.

Current research tends to support the humanistic approach when it comes to nonprogrammed organizational decisions. Researchers have found that decision-making groups make more and better decisions than individuals working alone (Shaw, 1981). Some management theorists argue that controlled conflict between group members helps to improve the quality of its decisions. Skillful police administrators try to create a climate of disagreement (without causing hard feelings) because they know that properly managed disagreement can be a source of creativity and innovation. They adopt a Hegelian perspective and view disagreement as producing ideas rather than as the source of difficulty or trouble. Managers who perceive those who disagree with them as being troublemakers obtain fewer innovative solutions and achieve far less acceptance of group decisions than managers who see them as people with valuable ideas (Swanson, Territo, and Taylor, 1988). Good managers have the ability to differentiate between the decisions they must make and those that should be made by the group.

In comparing group decisions with the individual decisions of members within the group, evidence suggests there are some important differences. What appears to happen in groups is that discussion leads to a shift in the positions of members toward a more extreme position in the direction they were leaning before the discussion took place. In some cases, group decisions are more conservative than individual decisions. More often than not, however, the shift is toward greater risk taking when it comes to nonprogrammed decisions (Robbins, 1989). This can be explained, in part, by the concept of "spreading the risk" and "defusing responsibility." If a risky nonprogrammed decision turns out poorly, all members of the group share the negative consequences and no individual is likely to be singled out for punishment (Johns, 1988). Laboratory experiments show that unanimous group decisions are consistently more risky than the average of the individual decisions (Rue and Byars, 1980). The positive aspects of group decision-making are summarized in Table 9.1.

TABLE 9.1 Benefits of Group Decision-Making

1. Broad knowledge base
2. Access to more information
3. Accuracy in diagnosis
4. Multidimensional analysis
5. Multiple alternatives
6. Collaborative problem-solving
7. Ease of acceptance
8. Accuracy in communication
9. Inherent legitimacy
10. Synergistic disagreement
11. Generally better decisions
12. More comprehensive decisions
13. Inclination to take risks
14. Greater creativity
15. Increased job satisfaction
16. Sense of self-fulfillment
17. Greater unity of purpose

Improving Group Decision-Making

The most common form of collective decision-making takes place in goal-oriented groups where members interact with each other on a face-to-face basis. But as our prior discussion of group decision-making's liabilities demonstrated (see Table 9.2), interacting groups often censor themselves and pressure individual members to discard their own thoughts and to adopt the group's perspective. This phenomenon is known as groupthink and becomes pathological if it is taken to an extreme. *Groupthink,* in this context, is the natural tendency for members of a cohesive decision-

TABLE 9.2 Negative Aspects of Group Decision-Making

1. More time consuming
2. Less consistent
3. Pressure to conform
4. Domination by a few
5. Interpersonal games
6. Emphasis on winning
7. Illusion of valence
8. Groupthink
9. Escalation of risk*

*While risk taking can be a very positive attribute, extreme group-generated and reinforced risk is antithetical to rational decision-making. A lynch mob is a group in which the risk shift takes the concept of law and order to an illogical extreme.

making group to become emotionally bound to suboptimal conclusions without making an individual or a critical analysis of those decisions (Holt, 1987). Leader training, brainstorming, nominal group, and Delphi techniques have been developed in order to deal with the problems caused by traditional group dynamics. Each of these techniques is outlined here.

Leader Training

Group decision-making is bound to increase over the next decade and may become the dominant approach to solving organizational problems. As a result, police administrators must now be trained as work-group facilitators as well as rational decision makers. When group decision-making is used, they will be expected to convene the group and guide the discussion. Since this is a new role for most police administrators, they must be trained to manage group dynamics without trying to manipulate them. As group leaders, they can make or break the decision. If managers act like autocrats and try to sell preconceived decisions, the advantages of participative management will be lost and acceptance of these decisions will almost certainly be reduced. If, on the other hand, managers abdicate their duty to provide adequate guidance for the group, the group may produce low-quality decisions that are not effective in meeting the needs of the organization. Managers should be trained so they acquire the following skills:

- Initiate group decision-making by identifying and defining those problems to be resolved.
- Review the standards that have been set for the group in order to avoid decisions in conflict with those standards.
- State the problem in a nondefensive and objective manner that does not suggest solutions or preferences.
- Supply essential information and specify the nature and extent of any constraints that are to be imposed on solutions.
- Make it possible for all members to contribute by managing group dynamics to prevent domination by one person and protect group members from being attacked or severely criticized.
- Wait out pauses and avoid filling in gaps with suggestions or leading questions.
- Ask provocative questions designed to elicit input and move the discussion forward.
- Focus group attention by elaborating on issues, alternatives, implementation strategies, and the effect they are likely to have on the organization as a whole.
- Summarize and clarify related ideas at several points during the decision-making process in an effort to mark progress.
- Determine (by asking cogent questions) whether members of the group are nearing consensus on a decision or if they are still far apart.
- Be prepared to go along with and implement any reasonable solution that is proposed by an authorized decision-making group (Lynch, 1986; Maier, 1973).

These skills are not abstract concepts, but specific behaviors. They can be learned through training and tested in practical situations. There is good evidence to indicate that this training can best be accomplished through the use of simulation and role playing (Holt, 1987). Leader training improves the overall quality of group decisions and helps to ensure their acceptance by others in the organization (Maier, 1970).

Brainstorming

Brainstorming is a special type of group decision-making process that was initially developed in the advertising industry to help trigger creativity and promote innovation. It is an idea-generation technique that encourages consideration of any and all ideas while prohibiting criticism of those ideas. Managers who use brainstorming in problem-solving have identified several factors that tend to improve the overall effectiveness of brainstorming sessions:

- The length of the sessions should be regulated and last from 40 minutes to an hour.
- The session should be held in reasonably comfortable surroundings.
- The participants should be shielded from outside distractions.
- A small conference table that facilitates face-to-face communication should be used.
- The topic of discussion should not ordinarily be revealed before the session.
- The problem should be stated in a clear, concise, and uncomplicated manner (Whiting, 1955).

Brainstorming sessions are always structured in such a way as to maximize the group's creativity. The following rules are common and have been designed to generate an array of solutions:

- Absolutely no criticism of proposed solutions is permitted.
- Freewheeling thinking is invited, rewarded, and reinforced.
- Quantity is desired and seen as a critical factor in creative problem-solving.
- Piggybacking on the ideas of others is always encouraged.
- Leaders serve as gatekeepers, facilitators, and coordinators (Baron, 1983).

In the typical brainstorming session, 6 to 12 individuals sit around a table designed to promote interaction and communication. The manager or designated group leader states the problem in clear and concise terms so that all participants understand it. Members of the group are allowed to freewheel just as many solutions as they can within the allotted time. All of the proposed alternatives are recorded for subsequent discussion and analysis. Once the analysis has been completed and the options have been narrowed down to a reasonable number, the group or an authorized decision maker selects the option that appears most appropriate given the circumstances. This approach—while it is not always effective—can be useful in dealing with public policy and administrative problems. It is particularly valuable when the problem necessitates trying to find new ways of dealing with a situation (Swanson, Territo, and Taylor, 1988).

Nominal Group Technique (NGT)

The nominal group technique for decision-making represents a refinement in the brainstorming approach. It follows many of the guidelines used in brainstorming but members of the group function independently. Unlike traditional brainstorming, NGT is concerned with the generation of ideas and the continuous evaluation of those ideas throughout the entire decision-making process. Ideas are generated nominally (i.e., without group interaction) in order to prevent inhibition and conformity. Interaction and discussion take place during the evaluation phase. It is structured in such a way as to make sure that each and every idea gets adequate attention. True collaboration occurs when group members consider the merit of each fully articulated alternative collectively. NGT attempts to minimize the biases inherent in and reinforced through group dynamics. Once the problem has been presented to the decision-making group for resolution, the following steps take place:

- Members meet as a group but work independently to develop and list their own ideas on resolving the problem. These ideas are conceived and recorded without interaction or discussion between participants.
- After the silent period during which individual participants design possible solutions to the problem, members present their ideas to the group. They take turns going around the table presenting one idea at a time until all of the alternatives have been recorded on a flip chart or chalkboard. No discussion is allowed until after all of the alternatives have been listed.
- Once all of the alternatives are on the table, members of the decision-making group discuss, clarify, elaborate, and evaluate them in terms of their advantages and disadvantages. At this stage in the process, members are expected—based on group dynamics—to exert an influence on one another.
- At the conclusion of this synergistic group session, individual members silently and independently vote on various alternatives by assigning a rank order or using predetermined rating scales. The results are collected and tallied next to each of the alternatives. The final decision is determined by the highest aggregate rating (Delbecg and Van de Ven, 1971).

An effective variation in the NGT process is to go back and repeat the first three steps. This gives the group an opportunity to flesh out new ideas or amplify recommendations prior to taking the final vote (Holt, 1987). If there is no clear consensus, the entire process can be repeated until the members reach a mutually acceptable compromise. One variation of the NGT process is shown in Figure 9.5.

Delphi Technique

The Delphi technique used in group decision-making was originally developed by the prestigious Rand Corporation (a think tank) to predict changes in technology. This process is similar to the nominal group technique just

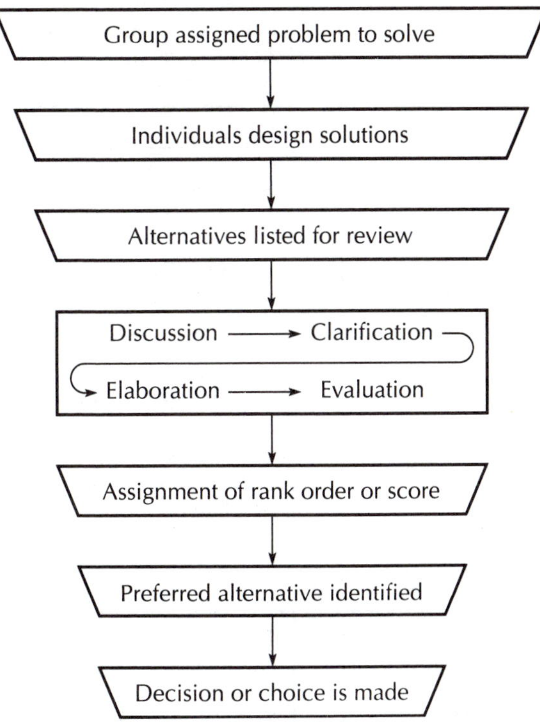

FIGURE 9.5 The Nominal Group Technique.

discussed except that it does not require the physical presence of the participants. There is, in fact, no face-to-face interaction. Consequently, it is possible to poll a group of experts without bringing them together in the same place at the same time. The people who are selected to serve as members of the group do not actually make final decisions. Their job is to generate information (in the form of conceptually sound alternatives) for consideration by organizational decision makers. The heart of the Delphi approach is to determine expert opinion through a series of questionnaires. According to Stephen Robbins (1989), the process consists of the following six sequential steps:

1. A specific problem is identified and the members of the Delphi group are asked to provide potential solutions via a series of carefully designed questionnaires. These questionnaires are usually general in nature and elicit uninhibited responses to the problem.
2. Members of the Delphi group independently and anonymously complete the survey instrument. Creative thinking is encouraged and absolute candor is required.
3. Ideas (i.e., "solutions," "alternatives," or "options") gathered from the initial questionnaire are compiled by a Delphi group facilitator, transcribed, and reproduced. No attempt is made to interpret the data.
4. Members of the Delphi group are given a copy of the results derived from the first questionnaire.

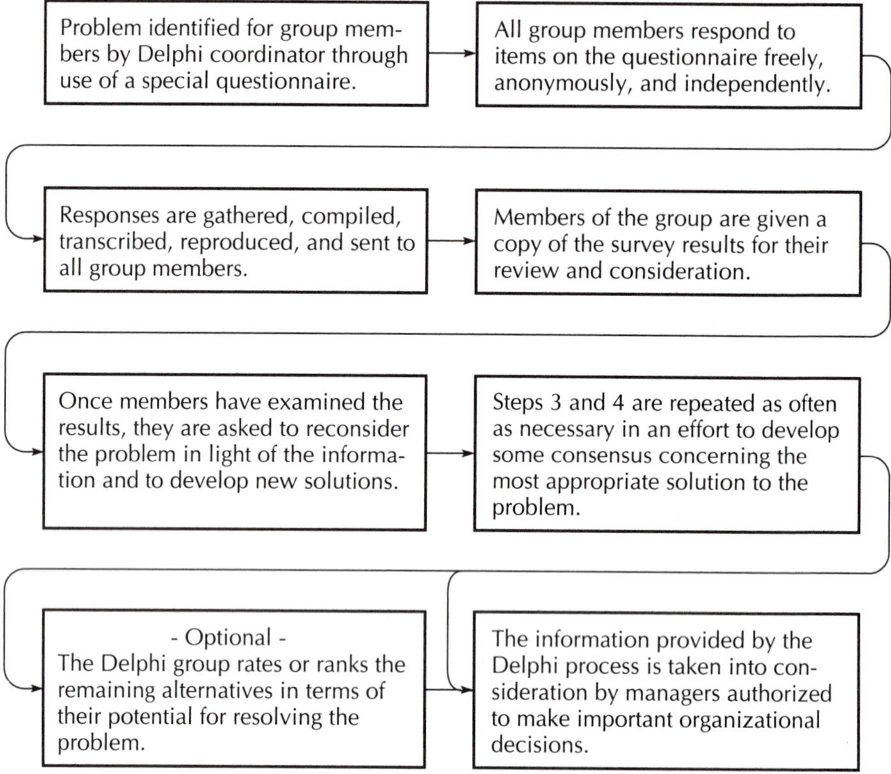

FIGURE 9.6 The Delphi Approach to Decision-Making.

5. After examining the results, the Delphi group members are once again asked for their own ideas on how to solve the problem. Some sort of synergistic piggybacking usually leads to new solutions or substantive shifts in the original position.
6. Steps 4 and 5 are repeated just as often as necessary to achieve consensus. A final questionnaire may be sent asking the group to rate or rank the remaining solutions in terms of their viability. Under these circumstances, the Delphi coordinator would be responsible for merging the ratings or rankings mathematically and presenting them to the authorized decision maker for action.

The Delphi technique is illustrated in Figure 9.6. Like the nominal group technique (NGT), the Delphi approach insulates group members from the undue influence of others (Robbins, 1989). It gives police administrators the opportunity to explore complex issues without unwieldy analysis. Experts are kept on tap and valued for sharing their personal beliefs and values as well as accumulated knowledge. One drawback to the Delphi method is the fairly lengthy time frame involved in the questionnaire phases. Quick decisions are the exception rather than the rule. Another problem is that consensus can

CASE STUDY

Lieutenant Coleman J. Karras

Lt. Karras earned a BA in sociology before he joined the police department in 1969. He continued his education and was awarded an MBA several years later. Lt. Karras is an intelligent, caring, and committed person who puts the welfare of the organization ahead of his own interests. During his 20 years with the Metropolitan P.D. he has served in various capacities. The lieutenant is viewed by his superiors and subordinates as a hard-working and self-disciplined professional.

The lieutenant, who until recently was commander of an intensive patrol unit assigned to an inner-city precinct, was reassigned and designated as director of the department's graphic arts bureau. This is a staff position and considered a stop on the fast track to higher rank.

The previous director, an alcoholic, had given bureau personnel little or no direction. Due to the lack of management, the unit was in chaos. It had become the laughingstock of the police department. Lt. Karras's job was to clean up the mess. Since he was not familiar with the work of the bureau and had never been in a staff position before, he realized that he was not, by himself, prepared to manage the unit in an efficient, effective, and productive manner.

After seeking advice from other administrators and doing a great deal of introspection, Lt. Karras came to the conclusion that in order to succeed in the new assignment he needed to share some decision-making authority with his subordinates. He was absolutely convinced that, except in a limited number of situations, the single rational actor model would not work. He viewed participative management and group decision-making as the most realistic approach. Based on his education and training, he was willing to share power with subordinates rather than exercise power over them. Lt. Karras was glad to play the role of group coordinator and facilitator.

If you were Lt. Karras's adviser, which of the three group decision-making techniques would you recommend he use in order to identify problems and generate creative solutions to those problems? Explain to the lieutenant how the process works and the results that you would expect him to achieve.

be achieved through compromise. The best solution may be ignored if group opinion shifts toward a compromise decision. Despite these disadvantages, the Delphi technique is an efficient method of pooling and drawing on expert judgment while avoiding the problems of conformity and domination that often occur in interacting groups (Johns, 1988).

Much more emphasis is now placed on participative management and formal group decision-making in complex criminal justice organizations. Many police organization/ management theorists believe that collective decision-making may become the dominant form of organizational problem-solving during the next decade. They support this trend and argue that meaningful employee involvement in the decision-making process will increase job satisfaction as well as produce better decisions. Research indicates that due to the synergistic effect of social dynamics, groups tend to be more vigilant than individual decision makers. They generate more and more creative solutions to organizational problems. Employees who share power with management and who are allowed to make meaningful decisions do a more thorough job of evaluating alternatives than individuals acting alone.

On the downside, these are some negatives associated with the group decision-making process. Group decision-making is complex, time consuming, and slow. The quality of group decisions can be adversely affected by (1) inherent pressure to conform, (2) undue influence on the part of a few dominant individuals, (3) conflicting personal goals, or (4) an unintended escalation in risk taking. These negative aspects of group decision-making can be offset, however. More and more emphasis is being placed on the manager's role as a group facilitator. Managers are being trained as group leaders who share power with rather than merely exercise power over their subordinates. They are learning how to enhance the effectiveness of group decision-making through brainstorming, nominal group techniques, and the Delphi method.

There is absolutely no doubt that group decision-making will play an increasingly important role in police administration. Harry More's Delphi group hit the nail on the head. Collective decision-making is here to stay.

Summary

A decision is a choice from among a set of alternatives and is intended to accomplish a goal or resolve a problem. The key elements in decision-making are targets, alternatives, choices, and behaviors. Managers continuously scan the environment for conditions that require a decision, design appropriate courses of action, and select the solution (option or alternative) they believe—based on their own knowledge, expertise, and experience—will work in a given situation.

Good managers avoid procrastination and vacillation. They are decisive decision makers who expect criticism and refuse to worry about it. They know that external constraints and personal limitations have an influence on the quality of their decisions.

The most challenging part of any police administrator's job is to make proactive nonprogrammed decisions. For all practical purposes, modern management has abandoned the heuristic model and embraced the scientific approach emphasizing fact-based, objective, and rational decision-making that involves the following:

- Perceiving the need to make a decision.
- Identifying the specific problem.
- Listing all possible and probable causes.

- Designing viable options or alternatives.
- Evaluating alternatives in light of specific and detailed criteria.
- Choosing the most appropriate alternative.
- Implementing the decision in a timely way.
- Analyzing feedback to assess effectiveness.
- Making necessary midcourse corrections.

Since external and personal constraints make absolute rationality impossible, good managers learn how to compromise and are often willing to settle for less than optimal decisions that are good enough to get by. Satisficing decisions are considered to be adequate, not the best.

Some organizational decisions are made by single rational actors in a position of authority. In order to do a good job, they need to know what institutional constraints have been imposed on their decision-making power. They must also

- Distinguish between personal and organizational decisions.
- Minimize the number of decisions made in crisis situations.
- Let subordinates make decisions they are capable of making.
- Anticipate the political fallout that might be generated.
- Realize that beliefs and values influence decision-making.
- Approach decision-making from a problem-solving perspective.
- Assess problems in terms of importance, priority, and status.
- Formulate viable and creative solutions for major problems.
- Select the most appropriate alternative given the situation.
- Monitor their decisions and make all necessary corrections.

Good managers see decision-making as a challenge rather than a chore. They rely on existing policies, procedures, rules, and regulations to solve problems whenever possible. In addition, they make it a policy to consult with significant others prior to making major nonprogrammed decisions. The best decision makers do not attempt to anticipate every eventuality that might be associated with the choice of a particular alternative nor do they expect to make the right decision all of the time.

Key Concepts

Decision
Scanning for problems
Decision-making
Managerial decisions
Levels of decisions
Decision environment
Personal constraints
Programmed decisions
Nonprogrammed decisions
Heuristic decision-making
Rational decision-making
Comparative analysis
Bounded rationality
Satisficing decisions
Individual decisions
Group decision-making
Participative management

Discussion Topics and Questions

1. What are the four elements in the operational definition of a managerial decision?
2. Why are the terms *problem-solving* and *decision-making* used as synonyms in management? Identify the three stages in this process.
3. Discuss the cardinal sins in decision-making. Give an example of how one of these sins has affected you personally.
4. How does one's level in the managerial hierarchy affect the scope of the police administrator's decision-making authority?
5. Discuss the influence of internal, external, and personal constraints on managerial decision-making. Which do you feel are the most important? Justify your answer.
6. What is the difference between a programmed and nonprogrammed organizational decision? Give at least three examples to illustrate the point.
7. Why are objective decisions perceived as better than heuristic decisions even when heuristic problem-solving techniques work?
8. What series of steps should a single rational actor follow while making important nonprogrammed decisions? Discuss each of these steps in light of a problem with which you are familiar.
9. Define *comparative analysis*. Explain how it can be used by police administrators.
10. What did Herbert Simon mean by the term *bounded rationality?* How is this term related to the concept of *satisficing?*
11. How can individual decision makers improve on the quality of their decisions? What are the do's and don't's of ulcerless decision-making?
12. Discuss the advantages and disadvantages of group decision-making. How does it fit into the humanistic philosophy of management? What role does the manager play in the group decision-making process?
13. Discuss four ways to improve group decision-making. Which one do you think is best? Why? Give an example of how it might be used in a police department.

References

ALBANESE, ROBERT. 1981. *Managing Toward Accountability for Performance*. Homewood, IL: Richard D. Irwin.

ALLISON, GRAHAM T. 1971. *Essence of Decision: Explaining the Cuban Missile Crisis*. Boston: Little, Brown.

BARNARD, CHESTER I. 1976. *The Functions of the Executive*. Cambridge: Harvard University Press.

BARON, ROBERT A. 1983. *Behavior in Organizations: Understanding and Managing the Human Side of Work*. Boston: Allyn & Bacon.

CARNEGIE, DALE. 1948. *How to Stop Worrying and Start Living*. New York: Pocket Books.

CERTO, SAMUEL C. 1989. *Principles of Modern Management: Functions and Systems*. Boston: Allyn & Bacon.

DELBECQ, ANDRE L., and ANDREW H. VAN DE VEN. 1971. "A Group Model for Problem Identification and Program Planning," *Journal of Applied Behavioral Science*, No. 7.

DESSLER, GARY. 1979. *Management Fundamentals: A Framework* (2nd ed.). Reston, VA: Reston.

FULMER, ROBERT M., and STEPHEN G. FRANKLIN. 1982. *Supervision: Principles of Professional Management* (2nd ed.). New York: Macmillan.

GEORGE, CLAUDE. 1964. *Management in Industry* (2nd ed.). Englewood Cliffs, NJ: Prentice-Hall.

GORE, WILLIAM. 1964. *Administrative Decision Making: A Heuristic Model.* New York: Wiley.

GRAHAM, GERALD. 1984. "Strong Managers Are Decisive: The Weak Are Not," *The Kansas City Star,* August 5.

HALLORAN, JACK. 1981. *Supervision, The Art of Management.* Englewood Cliffs, NJ: Prentice-Hall.

HITT, MICHAEL A., R. DENNIS MIDDLEMIST, and ROBERT L. MATHIS. 1979. *Effective Management.* New York: West.

HODGETTS, RICHARD M. 1979. *Management: Theory, Process and Practice.* Philadelphia: Saunders.

HOLDEN, RICHARD N. 1986. *Modern Police Management.* Englewood Cliffs, NJ: Prentice-Hall.

HOLT, DAVID H. 1987. *Management, Principles and Practices.* Englewood Cliffs, NJ: Prentice-Hall.

IANNONE, NATHAN F. 1987. *Supervision of Police Personnel.* Englewood Cliffs, NJ: Prentice-Hall.

JANIS, IRVING L., and LEON MANN. 1977. *Decision Making: A Psychological Analysis of Conflict, Choice and Commitment.* New York: Free Press.

JOHNS, GARY. 1988. *Organizational Behavior: Understanding Life at Work* (2nd ed.). Boston: Scott, Foresman.

KAST, FREMONT E., and JAMES ROSENZWEIG. 1985. *Organization and Management: A System and Contingency.* New York: McGraw-Hill.

LEBOEUF, MICHAEL. 1985. *GMP: The Greatest Management Principle in the World.* New York: Barkley Books.

LINDBLOM, CHARLES E. 1959. "The Science of Muddling Through," *Public Administration Review,* March/April.

LONGENECKER, JUSTIN G. 1977. *Principles of Management and Organizational Behavior* (4th ed.). Columbus, OH: Charles E. Merrill.

LYNCH, RONALD G. 1975. *The Police Manager.* Boston: Holbrook Press.

LYNCH, RONALD G. 1986. *The Police Manager* (3rd ed.). New York: Random House.

MAIER, NORMAN. 1969. "Assets and Liabilities in Group Decision-Making: The Need for an Integrative Function," *Psychological Bulletin,* 74 (4).

MAIER, NORMAN. 1970. *Problem Solving and Creativity in Individuals and Groups.* Belmont, CA: Brooks/Cole.

MAIER, NORMAN. 1973. *Psychology in Industrial Organizations* (4th ed.). Boston: Houghton Mifflin.

MARCH, JOHN C., and HERBERT A. SIMON. 1958. *Organizations.* New York: Wiley.

MCKINNEY, JEROME B., and LAWRENCE C. HOWARD. 1979. *Public Administration: Balancing Power and Accountability.* Oak Park, IL: Moore.

MILLER, D. W., and M. K. STARR. 1967. *The Structure of Human Decisions.* Englewood Cliffs, NJ: Prentice-Hall.

MONDY, R. WAYNE, ARTHUR SHARPLIN, ROBERT E. HOLMS, and EDWIN B. FLIPPO. 1986. *Management: Concepts and Practices.* Boston: Allyn & Bacon.

MOORE, MARK H., and ROBERT C. TROJANOWICZ. 1988. "Corporate Strategies for Policing," *Perspectives in Policing,* National Institute of Justice. Washington, DC: U.S. Government Printing Office.

MORE, HARRY W. 1984. "Delphi Analysis on the Quality of Working Life in the Police Field." Unpublished paper.

MORE, HARRY W., and W. FRED WEGENER. 1990. *Effective Police Supervision.* Cincinnati: Anderson.

PETERS, THOMAS J., and ROBERT H. WATERMAN, JR. 1982. *In Search of Excellence: Lessons from America's Best-Run Companies.* New York: Warner Books.

PLUNKETT, W. RICHARD. 1983. *Supervision: The Direction of People at Work.* Dubuque, IA: Wm. C. Brown.

RADFORD, K. J. 1981. *Modern Managerial Decision Making.* Reston, VA: Reston.

REITZ, H. JOSEPH. 1981. *Behavior in Organizations.* Homewood, IL: Richard D. Irwin.

ROBBINS, STEPHEN P. 1989. *Organizational Behavior: Concepts, Controversies and Applications* (4th ed.). Englewood Cliffs, NJ: Prentice-Hall.

RUE, LESLIE W., and LLOYD L. BYARS. 1980. *Management: Theory and Application.* Homewood, IL: Richard D. Irwin.

SHAW, M. E. 1981. *Group Dynamics* (3rd ed.). New York: McGraw-Hill.

SIMON, HERBERT. 1976. *Administrative Behavior: A Study of Decision-Making Processes in Administrative Organization* (3rd ed.). New York: Free Press.

SIMON, HERBERT. 1977. *The New Science of Management Decisions* (2nd ed.). Englewood Cliffs, NJ: Prentice-Hall.

SISK, HENRY L., and J. CLIFTON WILLIAMS. 1981. *Management and Organization* (4th ed.). Cincinnati: South-Western.

SMART, CAROLYN, and IIAN VERTINSKY. 1977. "Designs for Crisis Decision Units," *Administrative Science Quarterly,* December.

SOURYAL, SAM S. 1977. *Police Administration and Management.* St. Paul, MN: West.

STEINMETZ, LAWRENCE L., and H. RALPH TODD, JR. 1986. *First-Line Management: Approaching Supervision Effectively.* Plano, TX: Business Publications.

SWANSON, CHARLES R., LEONARD TERRITO, and ROBERT W. TAYLOR. 1988. *Police Administration: Structures, Processes and Behavior.* New York: Macmillan.

TANNENBAUM, ROBERT, IRVING R. WESCHLER, and FRED MASSARIK. 1961. *Leadership and Organization: A Behavioral Science Approach.* New York: McGraw-Hill.

TANSIK, DAVID A., RICHARD B. CHASE, and NICHOLAS J. AQUILANO. 1980. *Management: A Life Cycle Approach.* Homewood, IL: Richard D. Irwin.

"THE ANALYTICAL PROCESS: INSTRUCTIONS FOR PARTICIPANTS." 1979. Fort Lauderdale, FL: Nova University.

THIBAULT, EDWARD A., LAWRENCE M. LYNCH, and R. BRUCE MCBRIDE. 1985. *Proactive Police Management.* Englewood Cliffs, NJ: Prentice-Hall.

WHISENAND, PAUL M., and R. FRED FERGUSON. 1978. *The Managing of Police Organizations.* Englewood Cliffs, NJ: Prentice-Hall.

WHITING, CHARLES S. 1955. "Operational Techniques of Creative Thinking," *Advanced Management Journal,* 20 (28).

WILLIAMS, J. CLIFTON, ANDREW J. DUBRIN, and HENRY L. SISK. 1985. *Management and Organization* (5th ed.). Cincinnati: South-Western.

WREN, DANIEL. 1987. *The Evolution of Management Thought* (3rd ed.). New York: Wiley.

For Further Reading

DUBRIN, ANDREW J. 1985. *Contemporary Applied Management: Behavioral Science Techniques for Managers and Professionals* (2nd ed.). Plano, TX: Business Publications.

An excellent text for humanistic managers who want to upgrade the performance of their organization's human resources. Emphasis is placed on group leader training, team building, quality circles, and Japanese management techniques. The text contains a great deal of information on how to increase productivity through improved human relations. DuBrin promotes participative decision-making (PDM). He views it as a very good strategy to combat employee burnout and alienation.

KELLY, JOE. 1980. *How Managers Manage.* Englewood Cliffs, NJ: Prentice-Hall.

The book deals with applied management. In addition to the usual information on rational decision-making, it discusses how to stimulate creative thinking. The text also presents some general information on decision-making through operations research. The author explores quantitative techniques, modeling, queuing, networking, cost-benefit analysis, and the use of simulation.

ROBERG, ROY R., and JACK KUYKENDALL. 1990. *Police Organization and Management: Behavior, Theory and Process.* Pacific Grove, CA: Brooks/Cole.

This publication deals with traditional police administration in behavioral terms. The authors see employees as a valuable resource. They argue that a set of cooperative goals would help police managers improve the quality of work life (QWL) in their organizations. These goals include (1) sharing initial expectations, (2) development of humane relationships, (3) open communication, (4) participative decision-making, and (5) the capacity for revitalization. One way to achieve these goals is through quality circles like those used in the Dallas Police Department. Researchers have concluded that the participative management approach enhances morale and improves the quality of work life.

WHISENAND, PAUL. *The Effective Police Manager.* 1981. Englewood Cliffs, NJ: Prentice-Hall.

Whisenand, taking cues from other human relations-oriented authors, stresses the importance of human resources. It is the manager's job to help personnel become more efficient, effective, and productive. One way to accomplish this goal is to let people participate in making those decisions that directly affect them. Another way is to seek expert opinion via the Delphi technique. The Delphi technique is explained in some detail and sample questionnaires are provided.

WHISENAND, PAUL M., and R. FRED FERGUSON. 1978. *The Managing of Police Organizations* (2nd ed.). Englewood Cliffs, NJ: Prentice-Hall.

This is a well-written text that covers the traditional material and also adds a human dimension. The chapter on decision-making is very good. Even though the authors emphasize the importance of delegating decision-making authority, they recognize that participative management is not a panacea. They argue that too much autonomy in decision-making could be detrimental to the organization. The success or failure of participative decision-making depends on the skill of those involved and on interactions that increase feelings of trust, caring, and empathy.

CHAPTER 10

Managerial Communications: The Vital Process

LEARNING OBJECTIVES

1. Describe why it is important for a manager to become a skillful communicator.
2. Define *communications.*
3. Describe and diagram the elements of a communications system.
4. Identify how the chain of command supports communications.
5. Identify the nature and extent of informal communications.
6. Write a short essay on inhibitors to communication.
7. Describe the critical features of the grapevine.
8. Describe the importance of body language.
9. Identify the key elements of a suggestion system.
10. Compare and contrast survey and feedback techniques used to improve communication.

Effective communication is vital. When communication is faulty, many officers feel they have been left out, rules and regulations can be misinterpreted, rumors overwhelm the communications process, and the transmission of information is inhibited (Gray, 1984).

Communications is the process whereby the organization and its managers translate policy and procedures into agreeable day-to-day decisions and acceptable operational activities. A manager uses communications as a vehicle for motivating, disciplining, and training officers in an effort to achieve organizational goals. In addition, a police manager plans and organizes work, issues directives, gives orders, and evaluates employees' unit and departmental performance—all in an effort to attain objectives and create a safe community (Boyd, 1984).

INTRODUCTORY CASE

Lieutenant Donald Bear

Donald Bear has just been promoted to lieutenant and assigned to field operations. In this position he reports directly to the assistant chief of the department and serves as the watch commander on the swing shift.

Lt. Bear has been a member of the department for nine years and prior to his promotion served as a first-line supervisor for three years. His appearance fits the stereotype of a manager. He is 6 feet 4 inches tall, weighs 210 pounds, and keeps himself in top physical shape. He has taken numerous courses at the local university and is currently working on an MBA.

All Bear's time as a first-line supervisor was spent in records and planning. He gained a world of experience in preparing operational plans and the annual departmental budget. In this capacity he functioned primarily as a numbers cruncher, so his relationship to line personnel was limited.

Immediately upon promotion he was fortunate enough to attend an 80-hour management course offered at a local university and funded by the State Police Training Commission. Armed with theory, it is now time for its application. After a honeymoon of five and a half months, the first major issue needing his administrative expertise involves communications.

Lt. Bear has verbally disciplined Officer George Mandering for engaging in horseplay on two separate occasions over a three-week period. In both instances Officer Mandering left typewritten notes (in mailboxes of other officers) allegedly signed by the assistant chief, stating the officer is scheduled for transfer to the midnight shift. In both instances the officers who received the notes became very upset because the change conflicted with prescheduled vacations.

The lieutenant was caught in the middle in both instances because he was totally unaware of the incidents until the officers came to him and complained. Lt. Bear identified the perpetrator and feels an oral reprimand is sufficient discipline under the circumstances. But when the assistant chief heard about the incidents, he became very upset and expressed the opinion that Officer Mandering should receive formal punishment for unduly harassing other employees.

This is clearly a problem of communications that can be listed under the heading *Why didn't he/she tell me?* It is a question often asked in organizations. Lt. Bear thought he was doing what was right, but his superior disagreed.

In your judgment, what action should Lt. Bear have taken? Or do you agree the oral reprimand was enough? How much and what things should he communicate to the assistant chief? Should all instances of discipline be communicated to one's superior?

Defining Managerial Communications

It is difficult to establish a definition of managerial communications acceptable to everyone. The problem is the extensive number of definitions of just the word *communications,* let alone the term *managerial communications.* In fact, one research project found there were 95 definitions of communication. The dictionary defines communications as a process by which information is exchanged between individuals through a common system of symbols, signs, or behavior. On the other hand, the definition of managerial communication is the process through which modification of interpersonal and organizational outcomes occur as a result of message exchange (Hawkins and Preston, 1981).

Thus managerial communications involves two entirely different and distinct functions (see Figure 10.1). The first aspect is *organizational communications* and includes standard operating procedures, rules, regulations, memoranda, and policy statements. The other element is *interpersonal communications,* in which a great deal more is communicated than specific messages. It includes emotions, needs, and feelings modifying and conditioning verbal messages (Williams, DuBrin, and Sisk, 1985).

There is a critical need for managers to understand the complexity of the communications process and strive for enhancement and improvement until it is open, continuous, and related positively to goal attainment (Boyd, 1984). Communications among members of an organization is extremely important. When communication is faulty, problems abound and resolving them consumes a major portion of managerial time.

Effective communications between individuals is problematic when one party assumes everyone concerned is aware of all aspects of the issue, whereas, in fact, many are still uninformed. If the basic assumption is faulty, then (in all likelihood) the results will be defective. Interpersonal communications involves the exchange of information. Not only must information be transmitted—it must be understood.

This may sound simple, but it is not. When communication is poor it can be exceedingly costly and in some cases harmful (Rue and Byars, 1986). If there is a vital force of an organization, it is communication. It is the binding ingredient of an organization. When a message is not understood, the immediate reaction is to find fault. Generally, blame is placed on a *communications gap,* or *barrier* (Hawkins and Preston, 1981).

Organizational Communications

Managerial Communications

Interpersonal Communications

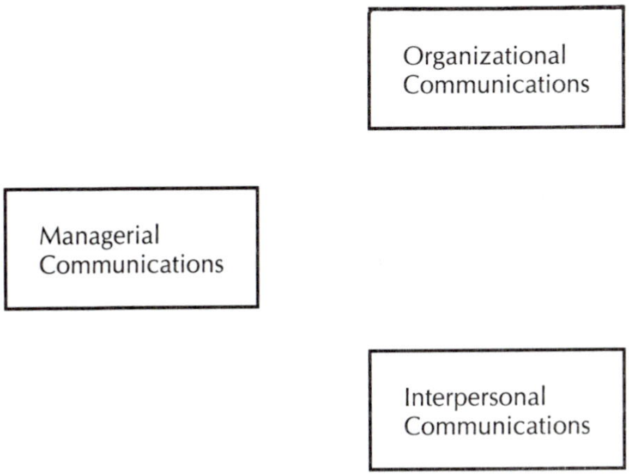

FIGURE 10.1 Components of Communications.

In many instances a great deal of effort is expended to find a scapegoat to blame for inadequate communication. This proves to be a lot easier than dealing with the problem directly. While a common source of organizational problems is faulty communications, just the act of improving communications will not make up for poor leadership or an inadequately structured organization. Good communications supports and reinforces the managerial processes of planning, organizing, directing, and controlling a law enforcement agency.

Managerial Functions

The role of communications is distinctly different for each of the major managerial functions. Effective management calls for a different application of communications skills, which vary from level to level within the organization. If communication is to be effective it must be nurtured by all levels of management from the top down. It is also essential for managers to recognize the human processes involved in communicating and utilize a variety of techniques when dealing with different managerial functions (Leonard and More, 1987).

Communications and Planning

Planning serves as the integrating function for a manager. It ties together separate entities as goals evolve and objectives of each function are identified. Plans must be developed in a positive and outgoing manner. A useful plan must be based on current information, and in many instances officers at varying levels throughout the organization will have important information to contribute.

One of the problems in some agencies is that plan(s) are developed in isolation and those responsible for plan implementation are never consulted. It seems logical to involve people in the preparation of plans especially when the plans affect the way something is done.

A police department should continually gather pertinent information, convert it to a usable format, and distribute it to all personnel. The success of a plan depends on how successfully it is implemented—one of the keys to success is communications. Planning is affected by the degree to which managers can depend on information provided by employees or organizations (Hawkins and Preston, 1981).

Good planning requires a manager to communicate with all information sources continually (many of which involve personnel in other organizations). All information received should be evaluated even if it is not received through the normal chain of command. To reject vital information could lead to an unsuccessful plan when implemented.

An effective police manager should view planning as fulfilling the following communications criteria (More and O'Neill, 1984):

1. Openness within the organization to an extent that communications are encouraged.
2. Organizational climate fostering communications.

3. Suggestion system allowing for continuous input.
4. Access outside the chain of command so input can be received from all personnel.
5. Continuous and responsive feedback.

When a police manager is firmly committed to an interactive type of planning involving (as frequently as possible) agency personnel at all levels, then that manager will be assured the agency will operate with a greater degree of effectiveness as it deals with a dynamic and constantly changing society (Leonard and More, 1987).

Communications and Organizing

The organizing function of police managers brings together various activities and groups, placing them within a structure of authority so agreed-upon objectives and goals can be attained. Organizational structure provides the framework for transmitting formal communications. The advantage is, formal communications are predictable—they follow the chain of command serving as a filtering system as messages are sent and modified at each level of the organization. In some instances the filtering process can dilute a message to such a point that the original meaning is distorted. Usually, however, formal messages are given serious consideration because they come from known and reliable sources.

SPAN OF MANAGEMENT. In structuring an organization, several factors must be taken into consideration. One of these is the span of management, sometimes referred to as span of control. The term *span of management* implies not only control, but planning, organizing, and directing (Williams, DuBrin, and Sisk, 1985). Span of control was first introduced into the literature by the writers of traditional management theory.

V. A. Graicunas and Lyndall Urwick in the 1930s stated, "No executive should attempt to directly supervise the work of more than five, or at most six, immediate subordinates whose work interlocks" (Urwick, 1974). Others recommended different numbers. Ralph Davis suggested that the span should be limited to 3 to 9 when supervising subordinate managers and the work is difficult. When supervising operative employees, an acceptable span can range from 10 to 30 (Davis, 1951). Another expert has suggested that when limited supervision is needed the span can range from 6 to 15 (Davis, 1962).

Graicunas quantified the relationships between superiors and subordinates. It is interesting to note how rapid the potential relationships increase each time an additional subordinate is added to the group (see Table 10.1). When there are only 2 subordinates, the number of relationships is only 6, but when there are 3, the relationships increase to 18. Note that when there are 8 subordinates, the number of relationships increases to 1,080 (Graicunas, 1937).

It is generally accepted that as one moves up through organizational levels to the top of the agency, the number of subordinates should be reduced. First-line supervisors can interact with a larger number of subordinates. From the behavioral viewpoint of management and the implementation of problem-

TABLE 10.1 Potential Number of Interactions Between Superiors and Subordinates

Number of Subordinates	Number of Relationships*
2	6
3	18
4	44
8	1,080

SOURCE: V. A. Graicunas, "Relationship in Organizations," in Luther H. Gulick and Lyndall F. Urwick (Eds.), *Papers on the Science of Administration* (New York: Columbia University, 1937).

*The number of relationships can be determined by utilizing the following formula: $r = n(2^{n-1} + n - 1)$.

solving, there is a definite need to be flexible when determining the number to be supervised (Urwick, 1938).

This leads then to the obvious question: How many subordinates should report to a police manager? The answer is short and to the point: It depends. Table 10.2 lists factors to be considered when attempting to determine an operational span of management. Each of these factors interact to either reduce or expand the span of management.

For example, managers must assess their own ability. Individuals who delegate authority and practice a style of leadership emphasizing trust are capable of supervising more subordinates. When the manager is adept at communicating effectively, the span can be expanded because less time is spent on discussing trivia and clarifying distorted messages (Leonard and More, 1987).

It is also true that when subordinates are well trained and self-motivated a manager can easily supervise a larger number of employees. Overall, a police manager functioning within the concept of community problem-solving will find a greater number of subordinates can be supervised when the system is fully operational. If the span is too broad, the following symptoms may occur: communications between managers is poor, feedback fails to provide

TABLE 10.2 Factors Influencing the Span of Management

1. Complexity of the work to be performed by the subordinate.
2. Competence of the superior and the subordinates.
3. Value system of the manager and the subordinates.
4. Stability of the organization.
5. Extent of standardization.
6. Nature and number of interactions between the manager and others.

SOURCE: J. Clifton Williams, Andrew J. DuBrin, and Henry L. Sisk, *Management and Organization* (5th ed.) (Cincinnati; South-Western, 1985), and Robert J. Thierauf, Robert C. Klekamp, and Daniel W. Geeding, *Management Principles and Practices* (New York; Wiley, 1977).

viable information needed to control operations, and performance standards prove to be unrealistic (Gray, 1984; Leonard and More, 1987).

LINE AND STAFF. Another organizational problem arises when a law enforcement agency becomes large enough for a distinction to be made between line and staff. Recognition of the concept of line and staff is the first step toward arranging related functions into specific units. The value of this distinction is that it provides for the proper location of the two major functions of police organization—preparation for the delivery of police services and their actual delivery (Leonard and More, 1987).

The key to determining what is line and what is staff is not the function they perform, but the extent to which they make a direct contribution to the attainment of departmental goals. In this context the staff services the line, supplying it with records, data, transportation, and material so the line can discharge its functions.

In smaller organizations, staff units do not exist, but as a department grows in size, specialization is necessary to provide support services. Initially, functions such as communications, records, and evidence control evolve. As the agency continues to grow, such units as psychological service, crime analysis, and research and development are added.

The concept of line and staff acknowledges there are two types of managerial authority. When this distinction is blurred, it can result in confusion and impede effective communications. One of the problems is that specialized staff functions become somewhat vague. In most law enforcement agencies, we find three types of staff authority (Williams, DuBrin, and Sisk, 1985):

1. *Service authority*. Some staff personnel have authority to provide a specific service to the total organization.
2. *Advisory authority*. Staff in these positions limit their activities to providing advice and normally function in a very narrow area of expertise.
3. *Functional authority*. Staff members in this area have authority to perform specific activities and generally function with a great deal of independence.

Considering these three types of staff authority, you can readily see that they overlap operationally. In some instances a single staff unit can exercise all three types of authority. Problems between the line and staff occur in many agencies, generally when staff members exceed their authority by ignoring their advisory position. Thus, rather than recommending, they give orders. What starts out as an advisory function or a service function by a staff member suddenly blossoms into a threat to unity of command when authority is exceeded and there are conflicting orders.

Effective communications can be thwarted when line personnel perceive that line and staff conflicts are ignored and poor conditions are allowed to continue. For example, in one department when the research and development unit recommended the implementation of a Field Training Officer (FTO) program, the head of the unit became operationally involved. Line personnel felt the staff member clearly exceeded proper authority and responsibility. The conflict was ignored by the chief, so the effectiveness of the program was sabotaged by both line commanders and line officers. Detailed plans were ignored as well as staff orders. Over a period of time, the evaluation of the FTO program showed it was not working and the program was abandoned.

There was never a question of the viability of an FTO program because it had proven successful in other departments. Thus the FTO program was never given an opportunity to succeed. Line managers resented the intrusion of authority. They perceived they were losing control of the situation so they stifled communication, ignored written guidelines, and did not provide adequate feedback (Thierauf, Klekamp, and Geeding, 1977).

When the chief supervises an excessive number of immediate subordinates, the office tends to become a bottleneck where effective communication decreases and work is impeded. When a communications network functions at maximum effectiveness, it serves to unify the organization, reduce confusion, and improve efficiency.

DUAL REPORTING. Some police agencies have organized under a matrix system. This type of structure alters the traditional concept of unity of command and allows for multiple supervision. Under such circumstances it is essential for police managers to learn how to function under a dual reporting system (see Figure 10.2). It calls for the strengthening and formalization of secondary reporting systems.

The problem-solving police department must learn to overcome the barriers to communications occurring under dual reporting. It is a question of

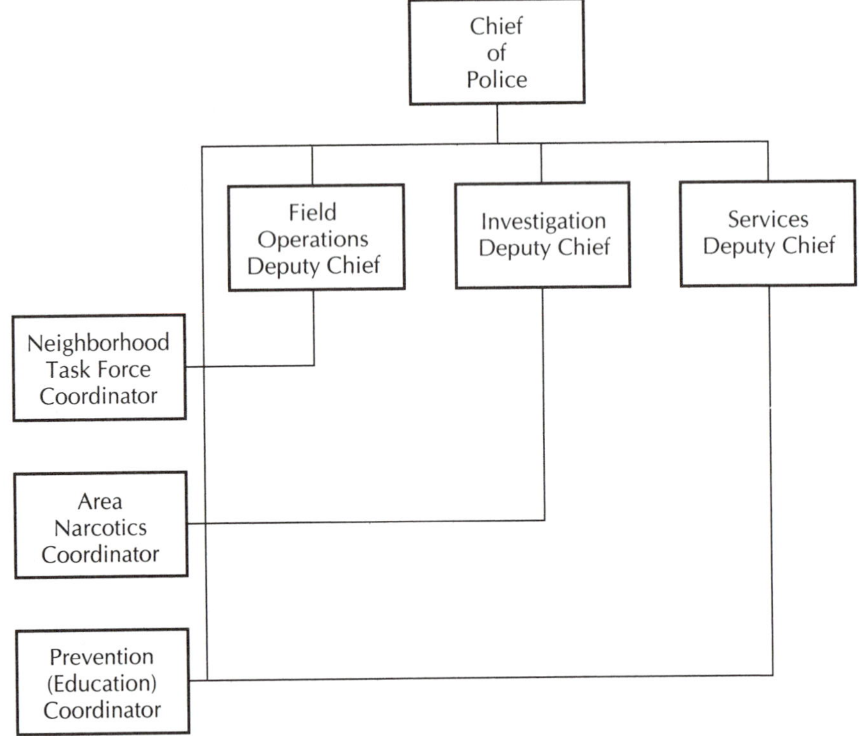

FIGURE 10.2 Dual Reporting System in a Matrix Organization.

shared power and decision-making, best handled by formalizing frequent interaction between managers. In other words, *talk,* but above all, *listen.*

Lastly, communication becomes increasingly complex when a new unit is created. Both formal and informal lines of communication are changed. It will usually take a considerable period of time before units adapt to each other and communication becomes effective (Hawkins and Preston, 1981).

Communications and Directing

A large part of a police manager's time is spent communicating. A manager's effectiveness is influenced by the capacity to send appropriate messages. Accurate organizational communications will be more effective and without distortion when properly filtered and routed within the organization. While this is not always possible, the police manager should work diligently to maximize this ideal within the organization (Wofford, 1982).

Positive leadership can be attained by establishing and utilizing communications networks in the organization. When communications networks are managed effectively, information is moved from one point to another within the organization for the greatest benefit of every member.

Communications networks fostering effective attainment of departmental goals take into account the following four considerations (Sigband, 1982):

1. The *regulatory* network serves as a vehicle for transmitting messages dealing with directing and providing guidance to the department. Typical examples include policy statements, standard operating procedures, and rules and regulations. It is not uncommon for one department to need six separate binders to hold all the detailed procedures.

2. The *innovative* network provides the police manager with a way of adapting to change and meeting the needs of the community. Typical examples of tapping the resources within the organization include either a suggestion system, quality circles, or task forces. The changing composition of the typical law enforcement agency places a premium on utilizing the expertise of every employee within the department.

3. The *integrative* network focuses on employee morale and places a strong emphasis on motivating every officer. Examples of communications in this area include praising an individual who does a good job, awarding citations for exceptional accomplishments, and promotion.

4. The *informative* network is comprised of all types of communications not included under the other networks. Examples are newsletters, training bulletins, annual reports, and bulletin board notices (see Table 10.3).

A positive leadership style can contribute directly to organizational effectiveness by creating an organizational climate fostering *real* communications. A manager should view every employee as someone who has the capacity

TABLE 10.3 Communications Network

Regulatory
Innovative
Integrative
Informative

to make a positive contribution to the department. A working relationship should be established allowing for continuous employee input. Officers should be viewed as genuine assets and communications as the primary process to ensure that everyone's skills are utilized.

If communication is to be effective, it must be nurtured at every level of management from the chief to the first-line supervisor. A police manager should work diligently at improving communication by utilizing each of the networks just described.

Communications and Control

Control is utilized extensively in law enforcement agencies to measure the performance of other managerial functions. Feedback provides a means of assessing the planning process, and (as just indicated) directing emphasizes the control of officer behavior. Finally, the organization is usually structured so as to place responsibility and authority in specific subunits of the department. Control, then, can certainly be viewed as an important ingredient and an integral part of the other managerial functions (Gray, 1984).

Control involves comparing the actual outcomes with planned outcomes, which can only be accomplished when communication is adequate and reliable. Controlling is after the fact; planning is before the fact (Rue and Byars, 1986). Controls are designed to provide a police manager with information regarding progress. *Good* information allows the manager to do the following:

1. *Prevent or ameliorate crises.* A manager must know what is going on in his or her unit—otherwise something that could be solved at an early stage can mushroom into a major problem. An example is an operating procedure becoming obsolete because it has not kept pace with changing conditions. This occurred in one agency allowing officers to fire a warning shot when pursuing a fleeing felon. In one instance an innocent bystander was killed. The community responded so strongly that the policy was reviewed. The outcome was that warning shots are now prohibited.

2. *Appraise performance.* In the instance of employee performance, a standard is established against which activities are evaluated. When appropriate, corrective action is taken. In some instances the standard reflects a combination of quality and quantity. The time an officer takes to complete a report when responding to a call differs greatly from appraising the quality of the report to determine whether the problem was handled appropriately (Williams, DuBrin, and Sisk, 1985).

3. *Update plans, procedures, and policies.* Change and unintended consequences are inevitable—therefore it is necessary to institute controls that provide the information needed to update or alter the database. Without corrective information, it is nearly impossible to judge the effectiveness of the organization (Gray, 1984). Police managers should review standards constantly to ensure their contribution to goal achievement.

Deciding what information is needed in order to have a positive control process requires a manager to review the control system constantly and evaluate it in terms of its impact on employees. It has been found that compliance with standards is higher when employees find them to be realistic.

Managerial Communications

The importance of communications cannot be disputed, but it still serves to confuse and confound some managers. Every manager strives to communicate successfully. Communications must be carefully studied and continuously readjusted for proper clarity in order to avoid confusion. Unfortunately, a poorly written document or a misinterpreted verbal message can create serious problems. Frequently managers believe they are communicating when exactly the opposite is true.

Police officers constantly make decisions (as they enforce the law) that deny citizens their freedom. Likewise, law enforcement managers make innumerable daily decisions having either a positive or negative impact on officers as well as citizens. Police managers cannot perform any of the elements of the managerial process of planning, organizing, directing, or controlling without communicating either formally or informally.

Communicating with any degree of effectiveness is demanding and time consuming. It is not easy, nor does it just happen. The process of communicating requires the attention of everyone in the organization. It cannot be turned off and on based on the whim of a manager. It must be constantly refined and adjusted to the current situation.

The exchange of information is vital to the success of any law enforcement agency, and police managers spend a large part of their working day communicating either orally or in writing. When the work week of police executives was studied, it was found they spend approximately 70 percent of their time communicating in one form or another: telephone, 7.47 percent; scheduled meetings, 39.80 percent; and unscheduled meetings, 23.07 percent (Mayo, 1983).

Another way to analyze the communications process of executives is to see who they contact. The largest amount of time (45 percent) is spent with subordinates, followed by contacts with citizens (27 percent), both individuals and groups. The third highest amount of time is spent with superiors (17 percent) and involves consulting with the city manager, members of the city council, or (in some instances) supervisors. Lastly, slightly over 10 percent of the time is spent communicating with other law enforcement officials such as another chief, the city attorney, or the prosecuting attorney. Also note that police executive managers interact with other law enforcement officials by attending local or regional meetings and conferences (see Table 10.4).

TABLE 10.4 Managerial Communications by Level and Type of Contact

	Percentage		
	Executive Manager	*Middle Manager*	*Supervisory Manager*
Subordinates	45	50	55
Superiors	17	21	26
Citizens	27	12	15
Other law enforcement personnel	11	17	4
	100	100	100

CASE STUDY

J. Fred Sullivan

The chief executive officer of a county law enforcement agency recently was the subject of controversy when a full page ad intending to publicize a shopping center appeared in a local newspaper. The heading for the ad read, "Crimes of Fashion" and featured a young handcuffed model attired in a tight-fitting black evening gown, leaning forward, with her eyes closed and lips pouting. Off to one side of the ad was a shadowy male figure wearing dark glasses. In the background, a police vehicle was clearly identifiable.

The male figure in the ad was the sheriff, J. Fred Sullivan, who was running for election. Two other candidates for the position lost little time in criticizing the sheriff. The ad was viewed by the opposing candidates as antifeminist and a vivid expression of sexual bondage.

The sheriff posed for the ad at the request of the shopping center, which contacted him through his campaign manager, Virginia Marsh. Sheriff Sullivan was not compensated for appearing in the ad, but $200 was donated to two different charitable organizations.

Women's organizations are expressing shock over the incident, claiming that the ad is negative toward women and condones violence. Their concern is that the ad damages their years of effort to change the attitudes of the public and law enforcement toward women.

Both the sheriff and his campaign manager say that the ad was done for charity without intent to insult or demean anyone.

The women's groups find the ad to be so offensive they are considering picketing the sheriff's home and office, as well as the shopping center. The sheriff and his campaign manager have apologized. The shopping center claims the ad will not be used again and an apology appeared in the following issue of the newspaper. In addition, the shopping center donated money to a women's organization.

In this instance the message the sheriff and the shopping center wanted to convey was interpreted by the women's group as supporting violence against women. Why was the message viewed negatively by the women's groups? Would the ad have had the same negative response if the young model had not been handcuffed? Could the ad have been designed in a way that would have been less controversial? Should a public figure appear in an ad to promote specific business interests?

Middle managers are also highly involved in communicating. In fact, they spend more than twice as much time communicating with subordinates (50 percent) as they do with superiors (21 percent). Citizen contact (12 percent) is the lowest amount of time devoted to any category; 17 percent of their time involves interacting with peers, other agency personnel, and external law enforcement representatives.

At the supervisory level of management, only 4 percent of the time is spent dealing with internal and external law enforcement personnel; 15 percent is spent communicating with citizens. Approximately one-fourth of the time involves interacting with superiors; the vast majority of the time (55 percent) is spent communicating with subordinates.

Generally speaking, the police chief executive officer serves as the spokesperson for the agency as well as the leader and figurehead (see Chapter 2). The other two managerial levels focus on internal communications and subordinate interaction. Interestingly enough, all the managerial levels have a reasonable amount of contact with members or groups of citizens, but liaison contact is the least for the supervisory manager.

It can readily be seen that communication defines the nature of a law enforcement agency and is a time-consuming process (Johns, 1983). Communicating is exceedingly complex and managerial effectiveness depends on identifying and overcoming communications barriers.

Realistic Communications Process

One expert points out that effective communications is built on a free and open exchange between all levels of management. Typical of the communications dilemma is the observation that no matter what level is occupied in the organization, it always seems to the supervisor that everything subordinates need to know is given to them, but administration could do a much better job of passing information down to the supervisory level (Lundy, 1986).

Communications in organizations involves three major communicators: individuals, groups, and the organization itself (Higgins, 1982). Communicating is a mental maze to be mastered. If it is to be improved, we must become aware of what constitutes effective communications and what should be avoided. Poor communications is a waste of time and energy—so the goal is to avoid inadequate communications at all costs. The sender of a message is responsible for transmitting with clarity and ensuring the message is not only received but understood (Department of the Navy, 1982). Focus 10.1 discusses further the need for effective communication.

An individual sending a message must do everything possible to affect the behavior of the recipient. Communications can only be effective when one person is communicating with another if (1) the message is encoded, (2) transmission is effectuated, (3) the message is decoded, and (4) the receiver of the message interprets it correctly and the message is understood (Keys and Miller, 1984).

The communications process provides a means of viewing the complexity of making oneself understood in an organizational context. There are six stages of a communications model and two modifiers of the process (see Figure 10.3).

Sender

The source of a message can be anyone in or outside the organization. It is important to note when someone is trying to function as a message sender and communicating either formally or informally. If the sender has a great deal of expertise and is viewed as knowledgeable, added attention is paid to the communication. This is also true if the sender holds a position of rank. Certainly when the sender is the chief, the message receives immediate attention. The same is usually true when the sender is the city manager or a member of the city council (Williams, DuBrin, and Sisk, 1985).

FOCUS 10.1

Who Needs Effective Communications?

Who needs effective communications? Quite simply... all of us. We all need to communicate... ideas, concepts, fish stories, golf scores... all incidental repetitive information is necessary. How effective that communication is, depends largely on you... the sender. Don't assume everything you say is clearly and immediately understood. Hearing is not synonymous with understanding—without understanding, there is no effective communication.

If you are the sender in the communication process, it's up to you to be sure your message is not only transmitted, but also received and understood. And that's one of the first barricades you'll encounter along the road.

There has to be a receiver for your message, and that receiver must be sensitive to your message. No matter how much sending you do, without a sensitized receiver, you are not communicating. And if you don't believe it, think back to the last time you were talking to someone who wasn't really interested in what you were saying ...you get the feeling you're a television, blasting away in an empty room. Performing in an empty hall can be pretty frustrating.

SOURCE. Director, Navy Publications and Printing Service, *Don't Talk... Communicate* (Washington, DC: U.S. Government Printing Office, 1980).

The sender of a message is the one who determines the relevance of each and every message. This is known as *gatekeeping* because the sender determines not only the importance of the message but the relevancy. The sender also exercises control over the flow of the information. When a police manager is the sender, the chain of command serves as a vehicle of transmission, and decisions are constantly made about what messages should be sent.

Encoding

When the message is converted into a readily understandable form, it is said to be *encoded*. A message can either be verbal or nonverbal. It is desirable to

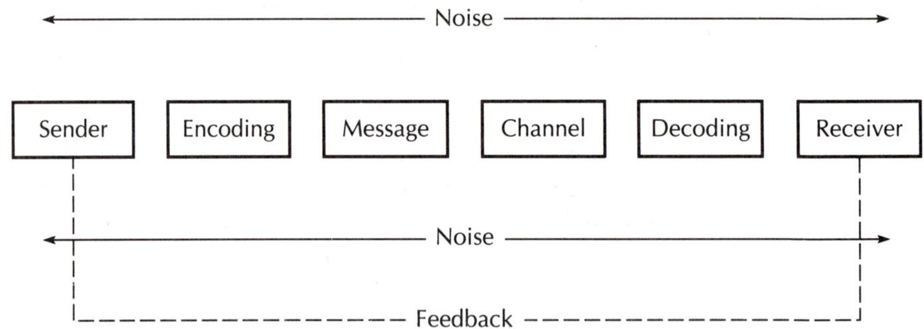

FIGURE 10.3 Realistic Communication Process.

make a choice of symbols (e.g., read the Miranda warning) that everyone can understand. Many things influence the encoding process. One of the major variables is the personality of the sender (or organizational members) who actually encodes the message. Every member of an organization has his or her own perception of what a message should accomplish and how it should be encoded (Higgins, 1982).

Vocabulary and expertise can play major roles in the sender's ability to encode data, ideas, or the interpretation of information (Hellriegel, Slocum, and Woodman, 1983). Encoding is not easy. It requires a manager to select some type of symbol representing exactly what is to be communicated (Higgins, 1982).

Message

The specific information transmitted constitutes the message—it might be some type of symbol creating an awareness of need, pointing out a problem, or expressing an opinion about a matter of concern to the department. Whatever the intent of the message, it is to the sender's best interest to be sure it gets through loud and clear. Neither officers nor managers can react to a message when it cannot be understood (Department of the Navy, 1982).

One of the most difficult tasks for police managers is to write standard operating procedures, rules, regulations or departmental policies. It seems such documents have to be written and rewritten several times before every level in the organization places a stamp of approval on them (Higgins, 1982).

Semantics (the study of the meaning of words) is one of the problems. A single word may have a very different meaning to someone else. Therefore it is essential that words be carefully chosen and clearly defined for effective communication (Rue and Byars, 1986).

Each police manager who prepares a message should seek answers for the following questions:

1. What is the real message I want to send?
2. Is there sufficient information to support the message?
3. Does any word or phrase imply something not intended?
4. Is there any possibility the message can be misinterpreted?
5. What will be the reaction to the message?
6. Will the message produce the intended results?

Good communications means clearly expressing one's intentions in a message. More importantly, when a police manager prepares a message, keep in mind it must be worded in plain English. The ability to express one's thoughts is one of the most important distinctions separating successful managers from those who prove to be ineffective (Waitley and Witt, 1985).

Channel

In law enforcement agencies, a number of communications channels are available for transmitting messages, including radio, teletype, computer,

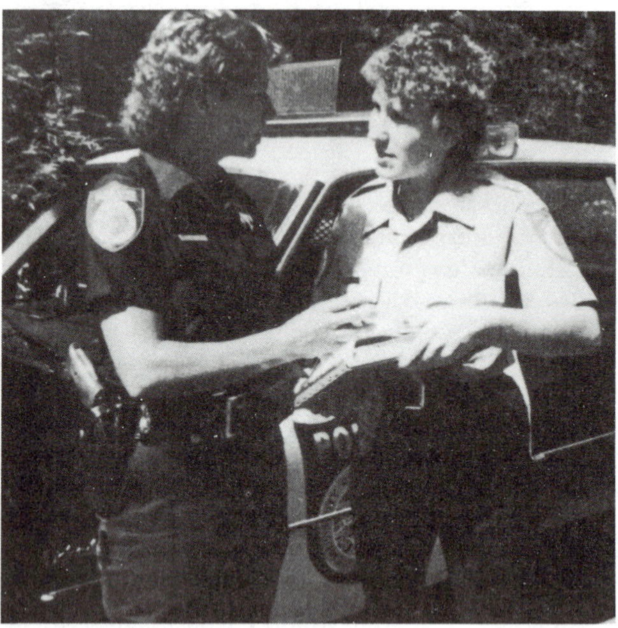

Communicating It is the manager's responsibility to insure that the message is understood and interpreted correctly. *(Courtesy of the Sacramento, California, Police Department)*

teleconferencing devices, telephone, electronic mail, and voice mail (Williams, DuBrin, and Sisk, 1985). Other potential channels include bulletin boards, departmental newsletters, or when appropriate, verbal and/or nonverbal communications. In general the supervisory police manager spends more time communicating verbally than managers at higher levels in the chain of command.

As police departments grow in size and become more decentralized, there is a tendency for communications to become depersonalized. The terminal on the desk or in the police vehicle becomes the major channel for the transmission of a message. The screen and the keyboard increasingly dominate the communications process—the in basket and the mailbox are slowly being replaced. Messages can be sent and received, police records checked, license numbers processed, case files reviewed, and bookings checked without ever leaving one's vehicle or desk.

Decoding

When a message is received it undergoes decoding. Thus it is interpreted and meaning is given to the message and the receiver. If the message is decoded improperly it will not be understood (Gray, 1984).

A message becomes significant when meaning is given to symbols (e.g., book the suspect). When decoding, a receiver should ascertain the following (Naval Education and Training Program, 1984):

1. What did the sender *intend* to say.
2. What was *actually* said.
3. What the receiver *heard.*
4. What the receiver *thinks* was heard.
5. What the receiver *said.*
6. What the sender *thinks* the receiver said.

Each of these factors serves to modify the decoding process, and the accuracy of the interpretation will depend on the ability of the receiver to respond adequately to each factor.

Receiver

The receiver is the individual(s) to whom the message is sent, and (similar to the sender) many things occur that potentially distort the message or allow for its misinterpretation (Williams, DuBrin, and Sisk, 1985). Motives, emotions, and how one perceives a message all have a tendency to impair effective communications. Selective perception in many instances will cause the receiver to distort a message. This is actually a filtering system preventing messages from being completely understood. Meaning has to be subscribed to a message before it can be followed by a reaction.

Selective perception is more apt to occur when a message is transmitted orally and less apt to occur when the message is written. Perception of the received information is modified by personality, previous experience, and some type of stimulus. This actually means different people will react to messages differently (Rue and Byars, 1986).

Miscommunications can also occur because some words allow for different interpretations, some receivers are poor listeners, feedback is inadequate, and nonverbal communications can be interpreted differently.

Feedback

Until feedback occurs, communication cannot be described as being a viable two-way process. It only occurs when a receiver responds to the sender. Feedback can be something as simple as a nod of the head or it may require the preparation of a detailed report (Hellriegel, Slocum, and Woodman, 1983).

If it were not for feedback, the sender would never know if a message had been received. If feedback is to be effective it should have the following characteristics (Wofford, 1982):

1. *Descriptive and not evaluative.* The receiver can describe his or her reaction to the message, but should not evaluate the message or the sender. In other words, the message should not be responded to emotionally or become a source of argument.

2. *Specific rather than general.* Important points in the message should be selected for a response. An example would be the difference in meanings

between "That was a good arrest" as compared to saying, "Successful prosecution is inevitable because of your interrogation of the suspect and the evidence obtained with a search warrant." The latter leaves no doubt about what the sender meant.

Feedback is most effective when accomplished face to face; thus managers are encouraged to hold meetings with subordinates as often as possible. The sender will receive more feedback verbally than when undue emphasis is placed on written memos (Gray, 1984).

If communication is to be improved, it is essential for police managers to provide four different kinds of feedback (Karlins, 1981; Philip, 1983).

1. *Immediate feedback.* Part of the message being transmitted, whether oral or written, should indicate a specific time limit during which a reply is required or a conference or meeting time is established. Ask for input. Do not leave it up to a person's imagination to determine what something means. If appropriate, have the message receiver explain the message to ensure there are no discrepancies between what was meant and how it is interpreted.

2. *Informational feedback.* This type of feedback should provide someone with information unfamiliar or unavailable to them. It should be used to clarify issues and provide for better decision-making. It should also be specific enough to tell someone how well he or she is communicating. Above all, this type of feedback should be made as often as possible and not limited to periodic evaluations.

3. *Corrective feedback.* A manager should provide corrective feedback when appropriate. Managers (since they might have information more pertinent to the issue) have a responsibility to correct message errors as a means of improving the accuracy of all types of messages. This should be done in such a way that it informs someone and does not punish or criticize.

4. *Reinforcing feedback.* When a manager receives an excellent report, whether written or oral, praise should be forthcoming. If the situation warrants, write the acclaim. It is amazing how fast this recognition will be noticed within the unit or organization. In other words, reward good communicators with whatever means are at your disposal—from just telling someone about an outstanding report to awarding the person with a special assignment. Tailor the reward to the needes of the individual (Peters, 1987).

Feedback, when used properly, will not only improve the communications process, it will provide a foundation for better departmental morale and heighten the potential for attaining objectives and goals (see Table 10.5).

Noise

The last feature of the communications process is *noise*—defined as anything disrupting communications. It includes not only physical noise, but attitudes

TABLE 10.5 Kinds of Feedback

Kinds of Feedback
Immediate
Informational
Corrective
Reinforcing

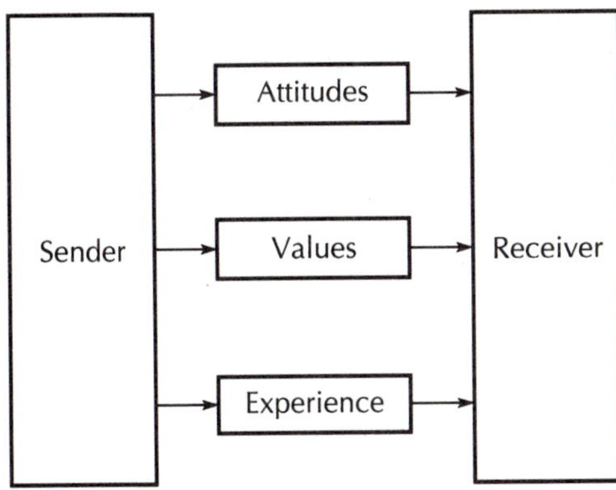

FIGURE 10.4 Emotional Bias and Communication Noise. Source Adapted from Jerry L. Gray, *Supervision* (Boston: Kent, 1984).

and emotions interfering with either interpreting the message or providing adequate feedback. In recent years, substantial job stress has been identified as a type of noise that makes it difficult for some individuals to concentrate on a message (Williams, DuBrin, and Sisk, 1985).

At the beginning of the communications process, noise can interfere with the conceptualization of the message, making it unclear. When a message is encoded, the wrong symbol may be selected. This can happen when slang, jargon, or unknown technical terms are used. When the message is transmitted, it can be garbled—especially when it is oral rather than written. Decoding can be the next stage at which noise appears when perceptions are different. Finally, the receiver's attitude or values can cause a message to be misunderstood (Higgins, 1982).

Finally, emotional bias plays a very important part in communications noise. The receiver's attitudes, values, and experience all serve as a filter within the communications process and can cause a message to be altered or misinterpreted (see Figure 10.4). Filtering can be either intentional or unintentional, but in either instance, it can result in only part of the message being transmitted or interpreted. An awareness of emotional bias is the first step in working to reduce noise in the communications process.

Formal Organizational Communications

Effective communications within a police organization becomes increasingly difficult as the agency becomes larger and decentralized. Based on the military model, many police organizations have formalized communications channels—as we have noted, a strict chain of command best describes the typical police organization.

The communications networks reflect the hierarchical nature and the differentiation of functions within the department. Consequently communications flow horizontally as well as vertically. The functions performed by police departments call for an extensive amount of communication. Decisions made by managers are generally dependent on information received from operational personnel who are assigned to various departmental units.

Police bureaucracies are unique in this respect—line personnel are usually the ones at the focal point of activities generating an organizational response to an incident. Consequently the information an officer feeds into the communication network is crucial to the department's operations (Hochstedler and Dunning, 1983).

Downward Communications

Police managers devote a great deal of their time to downward communications, whereas many business managers rely on a constant flow of information from the bottom of the organization. With the information received, managers usually respond by controlling the discretion of the line officer. This is done by issuing orders and developing standard operating procedures.

The chain of command determines the usual flow of messages as priority is given to the information that starts at the top and filters down throughout the organization (see Table 10.6). Except for critical situations, managers will give priority to a memo from the chief before responding to memos from subordinates or other managers (Wofford, 1982).

Generally, downward communications concerns itself with the following types of messages:

1. Policies
2. Procedures
3. Rules and regulations
4. Performance feedback
5. Schedules
6. Operational plans
7. Training bulletins
8. Informational memorandum
9. Legal decisions

Even though downward communications has the cloak of power and is backed by organizational authority, a police executive manager should create an environment that allows for two-way communications. If communication is limited to one way, then those at lower levels in the organization will resort to modifying or filtering the messages as they come down the chain of command.

Managers should not be overly optimistic about their skills as communicators. It is something that must be questioned continuously, especially as they achieve higher rank. Managers often have problems with downward communications because of one of the following problems (Frank, 1982):

1. *Overcommunicating.* In a sincere effort to communicate with employees, a manager can send so much information to subordinates that just taking time to read it all detracts from work. The manager's excessive duplicating costs is a major problem. A greater concern, however, is that recipients might miss something important if they get into the habit of putting most of the com-

TABLE 10.6 Sample Departmental Policy

Rewards, Gifts, or Gratuities

Background

Rewards, gifts, and gratuities can compromise the integrity of a police department.

1.0 *Policy*

1.1 The personnel rules and regulations manual states:

Officers and employees shall not. either in the course of regular duty or when off duty, through the representation of any position or connection held with the department, solicit, directly or indirectly, any person, firm, or organization for any reward, gratuity, contribution, or gift.

Officers shall not accept any gratuity, fee, loan, reward, or gift whatsoever, directly or indirectly, from any person liable to arrest or to complaint, or in custody, or after discharge or from any friend or friends, or person acting on behalf of any such person. They shall not conduct business with or engage in any business transaction with any person while he/she is confined in the city or county jail.

2.0 *Gifts and Gratuities*

2.1 In order that all employees may be aware of the gift policy, this statement is to be promulgated by delivery to each employee. While the Christmas season is the problem time, this policy shall prevail all year long.

2.2 In our city, employees have made many friends and may even have relatives doing business with the city. This policy is not intended to interfere with the exchange of gifts in those situations. It does affect, however, the acceptance of gifts given solely because of employment by the city. . . .

2.3 This policy is not intended to eliminate the box of candy type of gift sent to be enjoyed by a whole office or division of employees, and which can be consumed on the working line within a day or two. It is also not intended to stop the small reasonable donations to groups of employees associated with each other for a benevolent purpose. It is intended to stop the receiving of individual gifts from people or firms with which a certain small number of employees work as a part of doing their jobs.

2.4 No employee shall accept a gift from any person or firm, which gift is offered because of the employee-donor relationship. Every effort will be made to avoid an embarrassing situation by notifying those who offer such gifts, of this policy. They will be relieved to be free of this unnecessary, expensive tradition and they will think all the more of the city exmployees for the extra effort to be completely fair and honest in applying the services police render. If a gift is left or forced upon an employee, that person should notify the donor the gift cannot be accepted. This must be done tactfully, for there is no ill-will intended, and the donor should be given a sincere expression of gratitude.

2.5 This policy is an administrative directive affecting all employees. Its violation will be considered grounds for disciplinary action.

SOURCE: Harry W. More and O. R. Shipley, *Police Policy Manual—Personnel* (Springfield, IL: Charles C Thomas, 1987). Reprinted with permission.

munications they receive from an overzealous manager in the wastebasket. Employees simply are supersaturated with trivial information.

2. *Undercommunicating.* Controlling information is a source of power for managers, so if they share information, they lose a degree of control. This is a barrier that managers must overcome if they are to follow the dictate that work is accomplished through the efforts of others. Information must be given freely, especially what is needed to attain objectives or goals. When

a new procedure is instituted, a manager should provide a rationale for the decision as a means of keeping officers informed of why this new course of action is being instituted.

3. *Evaluation of the communication process.* A police manager should evaluate the communications process periodically to see if it is effective. Discuss important departmental memos with employees in order to reduce defensiveness. These meetings should be open, frank, and all officers should be given an opportunity to participate in the discussion. Communications channels must be kept open between superiors and subordinates if the department is to operate effectively.

Upward Communications

Upward communications starts with each line officer. As each message goes up through each level of the organization, it is filtered and distorted more than it is in downward communications. Upward communications is vital because it provides managers with a means of evaluating their messages that have been sent down the chain of command. It is a way of identifying problems, and in many instances, it is the quickest way of really finding out what is going on in the organization.

Many things should be communicated upward, but at least information about the following should be included (Rue and Byars, 1986):

1. What tasks have been completed, progress achieved, and what has to be done to complete a task or an assignment.
2. Unforeseen problems that arise requiring management input or clarification.
3. Suggestions that will improve working conditions or recommendations to make the department more efficient and effective.
4. Feelings of officers about their immediate working environment and other related work issues.

As a manager, it is very important to determine whether the information received from subordinates is accurate. When there is mutual respect for each other in the working relationship, accurate information will be available. Subordinates must trust a boss and be willing to forward negative information when necessary. Upward communications of a negative type should not place someone at risk—it should be accepted as a challenge to change or alter something that has gone wrong.

Managers will also be denied information when it becomes known that forwarded information is either rejected without comment or just ignored. An environment of give and take must be established if communications are to flow freely from the bottom of the organization to the top (Sigband, 1982). An example of how one can be placed at risk occurred to a deputy chief of police for a medium-sized city when he openly criticized the way the department handled a situation involving a barricaded police officer who finally was talked out of a motel room without anyone being injured. After the departmental investigation, the officer was allowed to resign from the department. The deputy chief publicly voiced his displeasure with the handling of the case and soon found himself on administrative leave and then retired in short order.

Horizontal Communications

Horizontal communications is part of the normal working conditions within a department. For example, two officers talk with each other about a common problem, or an officer discusses a case with a detective or a criminalist, or a records supervisor is consulted about information on a suspect or a defendant.

Most of the messages transmitted horizontally provide for the following (Moberg and Caldwell, 1988):

1. Interdepartmental and intradepartmental coordination of activities.
2. Emotional and social support among peers.
3. Problem-solving of mutual interest.
4. Rapid exchange of information.
5. Information about work attitudes.
6. Influencing the distribution of resources.
7. Mutual decision-making.

Communicating across horizontal lines is fraught with difficulty. First, it is outside the chain of command and unless encouraged, it will not occur to the extent it should. Second, it threatens the traditional authority relationship of individuals of different ranks. If it is to occur, it must be based on persuasion and not authority. Finally, a real value is that it tends to reduce the amount of communications through official channels and it reduces the errors by placing employees in direct contact with each other (Stoner, 1982).

Horizontal communications was formalized by several law enforcement agencies when they structured their organization along the lines of a matrix. When executive management accepts horizontal communications as inevitable it can be made an integral part of the communications process by creating task forces, special teams, committees, or any other type of temporary organization facilitating problem-solving (Frank, 1982).

As horizontal communications assumes an increasingly important place in the overall communications process, it will bring greater balance to organizations and serve as a major vehicle in improving the delivery of police services.

Communicating in the Informal Organization

As we have observed, a vast majority of the problems occurring in organizations is the result of faulty communication. Effective police managers become adept at solving such problems by becoming sensitive to one additional communications system—the informal system (Moberg and Caldwell, 1988).

The bureaucratic organization sets forth the communications relationship between members of an organization in explicit detail while the informal organization identifies, in most instances, the individuals with whom organizational members prefer to communicate. When left to personal choice, a great deal of communications occurs between individuals who feel comfortable working together (Frank, 1982).

For the most part, the informal organization is composed of small groups because of the overriding need to have constant interaction. Emphasis here is placed on the term *groups* because there are usually a number of informal groups in a typical police organization (Frank, 1982):

1. *Task groups.* These are usually a number of organizational members who are brought together by the formal organization to accomplish a specific task(s). As a consequence, the personal relationships facilitate the exchange of information and channel it to where it is needed.

2. *Friendship groups.* The largest number of friendship groups in law enforcement agencies are those composed of peers. It can be officers who are on the same shift and socialize together after work, or it may be graduates of the same academy class maintaining contact throughout their careers.

3. *Ethnic minority or special groups.* In recent years a number of ethnic groups such as blacks and Hispanics have been organized within law enforcement agencies in order to promote their own interests. As other minorities enter law enforcement, it is anticipated they will follow the same trend. In addition, women have organized in order to express their views and to exchange information. Historically other groups (Catholics, Masons, Jews, and Irish) have exerted a great deal of influence within organizations. Currently, in one large department, the born-again Christians dominate.

A word of caution is necessary when considering the informal aspects of organizations because one individual can belong to more than one group and the membership within any single group is constantly changing. Nonetheless, the informal organization is a vital part of the communications process.

The Grapevine

A unique form of informal communications within an organization is the grapevine. In fact, it is an inevitable part of human behavior and a vitally important element of a communications system. It cannot be eliminated, even though it can be harmful as well as helpful (Gray, 1984). The grapevine never appears on the department's organizational chart, but it carries a large number of messages.

For the most part, the messages are verbal—although in some instances, written messages are sent through this informal communications system. Examples include the selective circulation of a report to reorganize the department or an internal affairs investigative report. The grapevine in an organization has no respect for rank or authority and can link members in any combination of directions (Stoner, 1982).

The grapevine functions constantly. Sometimes it is transmitting a great deal of information; in other instances, the messages (of any reasonable importance) are few, and the grapevine then performs a more social function. One unique characteristic of the grapevine is that it usually operates at a faster rate of speed than the formal communications system. Another feature of the grapevine is distortion. Messages can easily become garbled as they move through the grapevine at a rapid pace.

Grapevines are usually activated when the following conditions exist (Frank, 1982):

1. Information is new.
2. Significant changes are anticipated such as promotions, pay raises, unusual punishment of an officer, reduction in force, or unusual occurrences.
3. Organizational members are given a greater opportunity to interact. Examples are the creation of a task force or when a number of officers are sent to the same training program.

Rumors are definitely identified with the grapevine. A rumor is an unverified belief flowing freely through the grapevine. A rumor is seldom factual but cannot be refuted easily. As a message moves through the grapevine the gaps are filled in and embellishment can become significant. If the message is exceedingly complex, the rumor mill will simplify it (Johns, 1983).

The grapevine cannot be managed, but when it is understood, its negative effects can be minimized or eliminated. When a rumor arises, it is best for a manager to deal with it immediately by taking these actions (Wofford, 1982):

1. Providing accurate and detailed information especially when the rumor involves any emotional issue.
2. Correcting information as errors are detected.
3. Openly discussing rumors at roll call, during staff meetings, or whenever the opportunity presents itself.

A police manager should tap into the grapevine by making a sincere effort to know what messages are being carried. The best plan of action is to make relevant inquiries of those who are part of the informal communications network. It is always amazing what different people in an organization know. Ask the secretaries, clerks, janitors, or active members of employee groups. Any or all of them can help identify current areas of concern.

The grapevine can be an important addition to the formal communications process. It can give a manager insight into employee emotions, attitudes, and concerns. It can also be used to monitor the overall morale of organizational personnel.

Improving Communication

Several techniques are helpful in improving communication. Each of the techniques we describe has advantages as well as disadvantages so a manager should select the technique(s) appropriate to measuring communications within the organization.

Survey Feedback

Surveys can be useful to managers because they provide information about employee perceptions. Surveys may be conducted by personally interviewing officers and other employees or by using the telephone. Face-to-face interviewing is time consuming, but it allows the interviewer to ask a large number of probing questions (Duncan, 1981). A telephone survey allows the interviewer an opportunity to talk with a larger number of agency personnel.

It is not necessary to contact every member of the department when conducting a survey. That is why the sampling technique is recommended. A survey can be conducted dividing the sample by rank, gender, age, ethnic origin, or any other compelling critical element. A random sample results when the manager or a researcher selects each participant in such a way that everyone has an equal chance of being selected.

An employee survey can provide management with information about the communications process, as well as serving as an excellent vehicle for improving and increasing the flow of information upward.

One survey (to determine the attitudes of police middle managers toward departmental communications) ranked the following statements as being most descriptive of police department communications (More, 1986):

1. Channels of communications are well defined.
2. Written communication is preferred over verbal communication.
3. The chain of command provides the employees with sufficient information.
4. Official channels of communication emphasize upward communications.
5. There is a limited open-door policy.
6. Bulletin boards are an important source of communication.
7. The administration ignores the informal communications system.

At the same time, another survey was conducted measuring line officer perceptions of communications and ranked the following statements as being most descriptive of the departmental communications system (More, 1986):

1. Communications violating the chain of command are discouraged.
2. Upward communication channels are poorly defined.
3. The grapevine is discouraged.
4. The department has an ineffective open-door policy.
5. Meetings to solicit line officer input are nonexistent.
6. Officers do not receive all the information necessary in order to perform effectively.

Thus the middle managers of the police department describe the communications system quite differently than line officers. This information (obtained by questionnaire) served as the basis for a follow-up study and the eventual institution of a number of changes in the communications system. It illustrates how a survey-feedback instrument can be used to change and improve the department's communications process.

To be most effective, a survey-feedback approach should follow a continuous cycle (Wofford, 1982):

CASE STUDY

Jerry Olsen

Jerry Olsen has been with the Seaville Police Department for the last nine years. He is currently assigned to the patrol division and is on the swing shift. He is regarded as a excellent officer and during his service with the department has received 12 commendations for outstanding performance.

Officer Olsen is extremely well liked by his peers and is respected as a real street cop. He attended college for two years and made the decision not to pursue any additional formal education. He really enjoys his job and has no desire to achieve higher rank. In fact, he has been eligible to take the sergeant's examination twice but refused both times.

Recently the department adopted the rewards, gifts, and gratuities policy (see Table 10.6), which (in part) states, *Officers shall not solicit, directly or indirectly, any person, firm, or organization for any reward, gratuity, contribution, or gift.* This new policy was discussed at length at roll call, and its intent and implications seemed to be understood by everyone.

The officers on Officer Olsen's team always have a coffee break at Lillie's Grill and they do not pay for their coffee. The manager of the café strongly supports the practice, and it is clear to the staff that the presence of the officers provides added security. The café is located in a high crime area and is unquestionably an oasis in the desert. Even the patrons like to see the officers come into the café because their presence is calming.

Lt. Eric Ammerman, watch commander, advised the officers that free coffee is in violation of the new departmental policy. The officers feel very strongly that a couple of cups of coffee cannot be considered a gratuity or gift. Officer Olsen, serving as the spokesperson for the team, points out that although the officers do not pay for the coffee, they actually leave tips exceeding its price.

Lt. Ammerman is adamant. He claims that the free coffee is a violation of policy. On the other hand, the officers feel strongly that the policy is not intended to cover such a minor thing as a cup of coffee. All parties involved attended roll call when the policy was discussed, but there is obviously a misunderstanding about the actual intent of the policy.

How might communications be improved at the roll call meeting other than reading the policy and limiting the discussion to answering questions? The question of a cup of coffee never came up during the original discussion. How can the roll call session be conducted? How should the policy be rewritten to cover Lt. Ammerman's concern (which actually is interpreted as prohibiting such things as free coffee)?

1. Survey personnel periodically.
2. Make data obtained from the survey available to all personnel.
3. Hold meetings with agency personnel to discuss the data and to identify what action should be taken.
4. Follow up to see that plans developed from the survey are implemented.

When survey results are transmitted back to officers and civilian employees it has proven to be an effective means of improving communications in all directions (Johns, 1983).

Exit Interview

Whenever employees are dismissed, resign, or are retired, they should be interviewed to obtain information useful for improving the department's communications process. The interview should be conducted by a manager or someone from the personnel unit, and every effort should be made to obtain accurate information. During the interview, emphasis should be placed on the process and not the personalities involved. It is also useful to conduct a second interview (after a waiting period) to verify the accuracy of the information obtained the first time.

Summary

Communications is the vehicle that police managers use to translate policy and procedures into conforming day-to-day decisions and acceptable operational activities. Managers utilize communications to motivate, discipline, and train officers and civilian employees in order to achieve organizational goals.

Managerial communications involves two entirely different and distinct types of communications—organizational and interpersonal. The former concerns itself with standard operating procedures; the latter deals with emotions and feelings modifying and conditioning messages.

The role that communications plays is distinct for each of the major managerial functions: planning, structuring, directing, and controlling. The manager must nurture communications at all levels of the organization and learn to recognize the human processes involved in communicating as well as utilize a variety of techniques for each of the managerial functions.

A study of police executives showed that 70 percent of their time was spent communicating; 45 percent of this was consumed dealing with immediate subordinates. The remainder of the time was spent communicating with citizens, superiors, and personnel from other law enforcement agencies.

Communications in organizations involve three major communicators: individuals, groups, and the organization itself. There are six stages of a communications model: sender, encoding, message, channel, decoding, and the receiver, and two modifiers—feedback and noise.

Characteristics of the formal organizational communications system are dominated by three types: downward, horizontal, and upward communications. Each influences the agency differently and places unique demands on police managers at different levels in the organization.

The informal organization identifies the individuals and groups with which members actually communicate. The informal groups include task groups, friendship groups, and other special interest groups. The formal system of communications is further modified by the grapevine, making the communications process even more complex.

Finally, a police manager can use several different techniques in an effort to improve organizational communication. Two of these are survey feedback and the exit interview. They can be used to determine employee perception. Once data is obtained after utilizing one of the techniques, police managers should develop a plan to improve the communications process.

Key Concepts

Organizational communications
Interpersonal communications
Regulation network
Innovative network
Integrative network
Informative network
Span of management
Dual reporting
Grapevine
Survey feedback
Decoding
Receiver
Feedback
Noise
Downward communications
Upward communications
Horizontal communications
Informal communications
Sender
Encoding
Message
Channel
Exit interview

Discussion Topics and Questions

1. Compare and contrast organizational communications and interpersonal communications.
2. When a police department operates with a dual reporting type structure, what are the communications problems?
3. What can a manager do to create an organizational climate fostering *real* communications?
4. Do supervisory managers and middle managers have the same type of communications problems? Discuss.
5. Differentiate between noise and feedback as part of the communications process.
6. Is undercommunicating more serious than overcommunicating?
7. Describe how a manager can deal with a rumor.
8. What is the difference between service and functional authority?
9. Discuss the relationship between superiors and subordinates as conceptualized by V. A. Graicunas.
10. Discuss the importance of semantics when a manager is communicating.

References

Boyd, Bradford. 1984. *Management-Minded Supervision* (3rd ed.). New York: McGraw-Hill.

Davis, Keith. 1962. *Human Relations at Work* (2nd ed.). New York: McGraw-Hill.

Davis, Ralph C. 1951. *The Fundamentals of Top Management.* New York: Harper and Brothers.

Department of the Navy. 1982. *Don't Talk—Communicate.* Washington, DC: Navy Publications and Printing Service.

Duncan, W. Jack. 1981. *Organizational Behavior* (2nd ed.). Boston: Houghton Mifflin.

Frank, Allen D. 1982. *Communicating on the Job.* Glenview, IL: Scott, Foresman.

Graicunas, V. A. 1937. "Relationship in Organizations." In Luther H. Gulick and Lyndall F. Urwick (Eds.), *Papers on the Science of Administration.* New York: Columbia University.

Gray, Jerry L. 1984. *Supervision.* Belmont, CA: Kent.

Hawkins, Brian L., and Paul Preston. 1981. *Managerial Communications.* Santa Monica, CA: Goodyear.

Hellriegel, Don, John W. Slocum, Jr., and Richard W. Woodman. 1983. *Organizational Behavior* (3rd ed.). St. Paul, MN: West.

Higgins, James D. 1982. *Human Relations.* New York: Random House.

Hochstedler, Ellen, and Christine M. Dunning. 1983. "Communication and Motivation in a Police Department," *Criminal Justice and Behavior,* Vol. 10, No. 1.

Johns, Gary. 1983. *Organizational Behavior—Understanding Life at Work.* Glenview, IL: Scott, Foresman.

Karlins, Marvin. 1981. *The Human Use of Human Resources.* New York: McGraw-Hill.

Keys, J. Bernard, and Thomas R. Miller. 1984. "The Japanese Management Theory Jungle," *Academy of Management Review,* Vol. 9.

Leonard, V. A., and Harry W. More. 1987. *Police Organization and Management* (7th ed.). Mineola, NY: Foundation Press.

Lundy, James L. 1986. *Lead, Follow or Get Out of the Way.* San Diego, CA: Avant Books.

Mayo, Louis A. 1983. *Analysis of the Role of the Police Chief Executive.* Ann Arbor: University Microfilms International.

Moberg, Dennis J., and David F. Caldwell. 1988. *Interactive Cases in Organizational Behavior.* Glenview, IL: Scott, Foresman.

More, Harry W. 1986. *Communications in Law Enforcement.* Unpublished research paper.

More, Harry W., and Michael O'Neill. 1984. *Contemporary Criminal Justice Planning.* Springfield, IL: Charles C Thomas.

More, Harry W., and O. R. Shipley. 1987. *Police Policy Manual—Personnel.* Springfield, IL: Charles C Thomas.

Naval Education and Training Program. 1984. *Human Behavior.* Washington DC: U.S. Government Printing Office.

Peters, Thomas J. 1987. *Thriving on Chaos, Handbook for a Management Revolution.* New York: Knopf.

Philip, Harris. 1983. *New Worlds, New Ways, New Management.* New York: AMACOM.

Rue, Leslie, and Lloyd L. Byars. 1986. *Management—Theory and Application* (4th ed.). Homewood, IL: Richard D. Irwin.

Sigband, Norman B. 1982. *Communications for Management and Business.* Glenview, IL: Scott, Foresman.

Stoner, James A. F. 1982. *Management* (2nd ed.). Englewood Cliffs, NJ: Prentice-Hall.

Thierauf, Robert J., Robert C. Klekamp, and Daniel W. Geeding. 1977. *Management Principles and Practices.* New York: Wiley.

Urwick, Lyndall F. 1938. *Scientific Principles and Organization.* New York: American Management Association.

Urwick, Lyndall F. 1974. "V. A. Graicunas and the Span of Control," *Academy of Management Journal,* June.

Waitley, Denis, and Reni L. Witt. 1985. *The Joy of Working.* New York: Dodd, Mead.

Williams, J. Clifton, Andrew J. DuBrin, and Henry L. Sisk. 1985. *Management and Organization* (5th ed.). Cincinnati: South-Western.

Wofford, Jerry C. 1982. *Organizational Behavior—Foundations for Organizational Effectiveness.* Boston: Kent.

For Further Reading

FRANK, ALLAN D. 1982. *Communicating on the Job*. Glenview, IL: Scott, Foresman.

This book was designed to help employees improve their understanding of the forms of communications most crucial to their growth and success on the job. It is written from the employee's rather than the supervisor's point of view.

GOLDHABER, GERALD M. 1983. *Organizational Communications* (3rd ed.). Dubuque, IA: William C. Brown.

This text was written by one of the leading experts in the field. It provides a comprehensive analysis of all the traditional areas of organizational communications.

HOCHSTEDLER, ELLEN, and CHRISTINE M. DUNNING. 1983. "Communication and Motivation in Police Departments," *Criminal Justice and Behavior,* Vol. 10, No. 1.

This study reports the results of a survey completed by 1,000 police officers in a large southwestern police department. The satisfaction indicators used in the study showed that the most important kind of communications was vertical.

LEWIS, P. V. 1980. *Organizational Communications: The Essence of Effective Management.* Columbus, OH: Grid.

The author uses communications as the central issue in a detailed analysis of such organizational elements as control, leadership, motivation, and structuring.

CHAPTER 11

Leadership: The Integrative Variable

LEARNING OBJECTIVES

1. Identify essential managerial tasks.
2. Define *leadership*.
3. Describe management leadership.
4. Distinguish between task and people orientations.
5. Contrast knowledge areas with leadership skills.
6. Compare and contrast select theories of leadership.
7. Describe organizational humanism.
8. Define participatory management.
9. Assess adaptive management as an alternative to "the one best way."

*H*elp Wanted ads, like the one displayed in Figure 11.1, emphasize three distinct yet interrelated aspects of police administration. Top executives are expected to motivate, manage, and lead employees as they strive to accomplish the organization's mission, goals, and objectives. Like the proverbial horse and carriage, motivation, management, and leadership form a natural unit, or *gestalt*. Under ideal circumstances, "you can't have one without the other."

The term *motivation* is derived from a Latin word meaning to move. It involves the use of incentives to encourage or reinforce member behavior that is consistent with and contributes to the organization's purpose. It is incumbent on management to create a hospitable milieu within which police officers are able to satisfy personal as well as organizational needs. Motivation is the key to personal productivity. According to Michael LeBoeuf (1985), good managers have the ability to turn on subordinates and convert collective efforts into productive work. *Things that get rewarded get done!* There is a very direct and inextricable link between motivation and productivity in all complex criminal justice organizations.

INTRODUCTORY CASE

Captain Karl Hammiker

Karl Hammiker, former officer in charge of the police department's planning and research unit, was recently promoted to captain. Based on departmental policy, he was transferred and placed in charge of a medium-sized precinct on the lower east side of the city. While the captain gets along with most of his subordinates, they see him as a desk jockey and have the uneasy feeling he lacks the leadership skills needed to do the job. A hostage situation occurred late last week that fueled the fire and reinforced these negative perceptions. Capt. Hammiker appeared to be indecisive in dealing with the crisis. Most police personnel—based on the nature of their work—regard decisiveness as an absolutely essential leader trait.

Two young males, members of a notoriously violent street gang, had been selling crack to students at a local high school. As an undercover officer from the city's drug task force tried to apprehend them, he was knocked to the ground and stomped. His backup was unable to act without endangering several uninvolved students. The men fled from the scene and took the undercover officer as hostage. Police officers from Capt. Hammiker's precinct cornered the actors in an abandoned house a block away from the school. The men threatened to kill their hostage. All escape routes were sealed off and the captain was notified of the situation.

The captain responded to the scene and quickly established a command post. His objective was to obtain the release of the police officer without violating the department's policy against making concessions in order to free the hostage.

Capt. Hammiker was committed to and had successfully used a system 4 approach to management when he was in charge of planning and research. In what could be considered a textbook example of participatory leadership, he sought input from his immediate subordinates before trying to deal with the hostage situation. He and his close advisers worked very diligently to identify the exact problem, to explore alternatives, and to select the best alternative. After what amounted to a two-and-one-half-hour planning session, the captain was ready to take action. The SWAT team was ordered to storm the building, neutralize the offenders, and rescue the hostage. Using a precision timing protocol, the SWAT team entered the building successfully and captured the unarmed gang members without incident. The hostage was in a coma induced by the injuries inflicted during the beating. The officer died three days later.

The police union has called for the captain's immediate suspension and asked for an independent investigation of the incident. The union has alleged that Capt. Hammiker is incompetent.

If you were the chief of police what would you do? Based on the information you have, what do you think happened in this situation? What can be done to help ensure that it does not happen again?

Police Commissioner

SUFFOLK COUNTY
NEW YORK

We are located on Long Island, a location renowned for its natural beauty and high quality of life, approximately 2 hours from New York City. Our county covers an area of approximately 1,000 square miles with a population of 1.3 million.

The successful candidate will direct a 3,200 employee department with a current budget of $186 million. The Commissioner is appointed by the County Executive subject to the approval of the County Legislature. Our compensation package includes a salary in the $80,000 range and a diversified, all inclusive benefit plan.

We require an individual with a progressive record of success who has proven adept at solving major problems in prior positions. As a minimum, the individual should have a bachelor's degree, 8 years of administrative/management experience in a large major law enforcement agency (minimum of 500 employees) and an unblemished record of integrity. We are seeking a candidate with excellent communications skills, an ability to organize, manage and implement programs and systems, and who has substantial knowledge of the principles and practices of modern police administration. The ideal candidate will also have the initiative, flexibility and dedication to lead a department which is operating under a consent decree resulting from a Justice Department lawsuit. A sensitivity to the problems of minorities is essential.

Successful candidate will be subject to a thorough background investigation and physical examination.

Please send resume and cover letter, both of which will be maintained in confidence, detailing your qualifications before August 15, 1987 to:

Suffolk County Search Committee
P.O. Box 352
Hauppauge, NY 11788

Dr. David G. Salten, Chair
Provost, New York Institute of Technology

The Honorable Leon D. Lazer
Justice of the Appellate Division, Ret.

Michael J. Murphy, Police Commissioner
City of New York, Ret.

Laure C. Nolan, Deputy Suffolk County Executive

Alan Schneider, Suffolk County Personnel Director

FIGURE 11.1 Multidimensional Leadership.

Management is the art of getting things done in conjunction with and through others in formally organized, task-oriented groups. Truly effective managers use legitimate authority and real power to create a work environment in which police personnel perform as individuals yet cooperate with one another to achieve a common purpose. They devise strategies and use various techniques designed to remove roadblocks to productivity. Experienced managers rely on their knowledge of the behavioral sciences to motivate employees and to enhance the efficiency, effectiveness, and productivity of the organization.

Managers plan, direct, and control police operations. An organization is inert until it is fused with leadership to become a dynamic force with a compelling thrust toward the achievement of its overall mission (Leonard and More, 1987). Proactive leadership is a behavioral transaction that involves the art of influencing, guiding, instructing, directing, and controlling human beings in an effort to gain their willing obedience, cooperation, confidence, support, and respect (Iannone, 1987). Effective management is built on a foundation of trust. Managerial leaders have the ability to elicit productive work that is well above and beyond the minimum required of employees in a particular job (Albanese, 1981). Police managers are expected to generate a sense of purpose, motivate and direct the work force, and lead subordinates so that individual police officers voluntarily make meaningful contributions to the department.

Perspectives on Leadership

Empirical evidence and common sense suggest that an organization's performance is closely related to the quality of its leadership. While leadership may not be the only important variable in the success or failure of a collective effort, it is an essential one. There is absolutely no doubt that inept leaders lower employee morale and hamper police operations. A strong and resourceful leader, on the other hand, can—in the right environment and with proper resources—transform a disparate group of individuals into a cohesive, aggressive, and very successful organization (Longenecker, 1977). The leader is the person who energizes the group, knows how to elicit initiative, and has the ability to draw from employees what they have to give (Follette, 1977). V. A. Leonard and Harry W. More (1987) contend that leadership could well be the most important single factor in successful police work. They note that the fundamental basis for success in any police enterprise is found in the energy, effort, and expertise of the chief executive officer.

Leadership Defined

Leadership is a very difficult term to define. While most people are able to recognize leaders, few can explain satisfactorily exactly what makes a leader different from a nonleader. Defining leadership is even harder since there is no direct relationship between the ability to lead and those who are chosen to provide leadership in any given situation. Scholars have expended considerable time and effort trying to explain the phenomenon of leadership and yet—after more than 50 years of theory construction and research—there are still no provable generalizations (Bennis, 1976). H. Joseph Reitz (1981) feels that the years of research have not been very fruitful. Genuine leadership appears to be something internal to a given individual and is nurtured by the situation. Real leadership (as opposed to formal authority) is not a commodity to be dispensed by those in positions of power.

The word *leadership* is a fairly recent addition to the English language. It has been in use for a little over 200 years, and describes the traits, behavior, and/or style of those persons who—either formally or informally—assume responsibility for the activities of a goal-oriented group. In simple terms, leadership is the knack of getting others to follow and to do willingly those things the leader wants them to do (Bittel, 1980). Leadership is a group phenomenon involving interaction between two or more persons. It also involves an influence process whereby intentional influence is exerted by the leader over followers. The concept of leadership implies that there is an observable difference between those who lead and those who are content to follow (Yukl, 1981).

Related Concepts

There is a symbiotic relationship between leadership and followership. They are best viewed as two different sides of the same coin. Leaders—based on their position or power—exert influence on and motivate followers to act in certain ways. Followers, on the other hand, have a self-imposed *zone of acceptance* within which they willingly allow themselves to be activated, directed, and controlled by a leader. They establish psychological parameters and permit leaders to influence personal choices within those limits (Simon, 1976). Once a leader/follower relationship develops, leaders are thrust into a group maintenance role. Effective leaders focus the group's energy and help members function in such a way that the police department is able to accomplish its mission, goals, and objectives.

The term *leadership* means different things to different people. Our definition evolved from a chain or series of related definitions:

1. *Influence:* To cause some behavior in another human being without the use of authority or physical force. Influence is manifest in one's ability to affect the character and actions of others. Influence is the major process, function, or activity involved in the leadership role (Lynch, 1986). The behavior of the leader is also influenced by its consequences. A major consequence of leader behavior is predictable follower behavior. Follower behavior tends to reinforce, diminish, or extinguish leadership.

2. *Power:* The ability of a leader to influence other human beings in such a way as to produce a particular behavior. Whether it is formal (authority) or informal (influence), power carries with it the means necessary to ensure that subordinates respond positively to suggestions, instructions, and orders. According to Richard Plunkett (1983), power is the capacity to command, to get others to do what the leader wants when the leader wants it and in the manner prescribed. Leader power comes from different sources (e.g., reward power, coercive power, legitimate power, referent power, and expert power). Real power may or may not coincide with the theoretical distribution of formal authority depicted on an organizational chart. See Chapter 8 for a

thorough discussion of power and its relationship to police organization and management.

3. *Authority:* Legitimate power vested in some person for a specific purpose. This is institutionalized power that is inherent in the position rather than the individual. Authority is the right to act or cause others to act in an effort to accomplish the organization's mission. Ultimate authority rests with the police chief executive. Appropriate authority is delegated down through the formal chain of command to all personnel within the department. The delegation of authority is controlled by law, policies, procedures, rules, and regulations. Management personnel and supervisors are granted formal authority to determine, direct, control, and regulate the behavior of subordinates. While they are often treated as synonyms, authority and power should be viewed as fairly distinct yet related concepts. There are those police administrators who occupy positions with a great deal of formal authority but no real power to influence the behavior of the men and women who work for them. Others have no formal authority per se yet exercise a great deal of influence over the people they work with. Effective leaders have the authority and power to fulfill their role in management of complex criminal justice organizations (Schermerhorn, Hunt, and Osborn, 1982).

4. *Reciprocal response:* Mutual influence between parties to a behavioral transaction. Leadership simply cannot exist in a social vacuum. There is a functional relationship between leaders and followers. Mary Parker Follette (1977), a well-known management theorist, noted that a stimulus is always influenced to some degree by the resulting response. Each party to the transaction reacts not just to the other person but to the total situation he or she helped to create. The result is a situation that neither person could have produced alone. Leadership—much like life in general—is reflected in a series of social situations orchestrated by synergistic relationships. Each and every situation is dynamic. They are, according to Alvin Toffler (1972), in process and subject to kaleidoscopic change.

5. *Zone of acceptance:* The parameters within which followers are inclined to do willingly what is asked of them by their leaders. This zone, or area reflects the exercise of power and formal authority that subordinates voluntarily accept as legitimate (Figure 11.2). The zone of acceptance, which Chester Barnard calls the zone of indifference, lies in the mind and is manifest in the behavior of the follower, not in a position or a leader. It represents follower-imposed limitations on the power and authority of superiors (Holden, 1986). The zone of acceptance is getting smaller. People do not blindly follow orders today even if they are in religious or military organizations (Tansik, Chase, and Aquilano, 1980). This makes the job of the police manager much more complex and difficult. Leadership is slowly but surely displacing autocratic control in police departments throughout the nation.

Functional Leadership

Emphasis has shifted away from charismatic and autocratic leadership models to a new form of leadership based on function. The evidence is clear. A subordinate's zone of acceptance is flexible. It expands and contracts based on the police administrator's formal authority, real power, managerial know-how, competence, credibility, leadership style, and interpersonal skills.

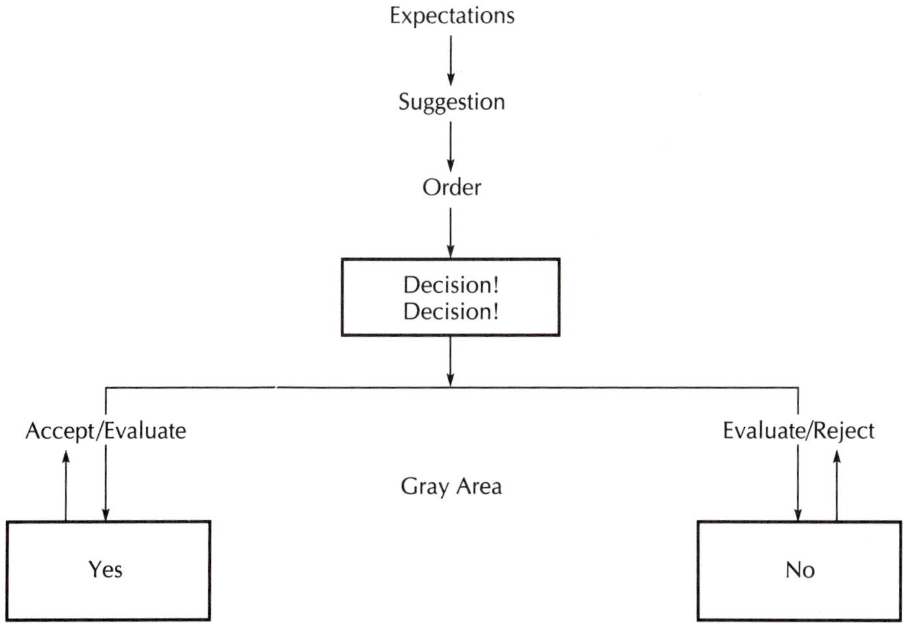
Expectations
Suggestion
Order
Decision!
Decision!
Accept/Evaluate
Evaluate/Reject
Gray Area
Yes
No
Expectations, suggestions, and orders that fall within the zone of acceptance are adopted with a minimum of analysis. Those that fall outside of the zone of acceptance are not easily converted into voluntary or willing behavior; they may become insurmountable obstacles to human productivity.

FIGURE 11.2 Zone of Acceptance.

The origin of the word *leadership* can be traced to early Greek and Latin. It is derived from an archaic term meaning "to act" and/or "to carry out" (Arendt, 1958). Every act of leadership consists of two elements: (1) initiation by a leader and (2) execution by followers. Based on this concept, leadership theorists have developed an almost endless array of definitions. Since leadership is a very complex, multifaceted phenomenon, there is no real agreement on what the term means. For our purpose, *leadership* can be defined as follows:

> An interactive goal-oriented process through which individual human beings are (for a variety of reasons) induced to follow someone and in so doing receive psychosocial satisfaction for willingly doing what the leader wants them to do.

Leader effectiveness is measured by diverse criteria ranging from the group's performance to the leader's tenure (see Figure 11.3). Two commonly used measures of leader effectiveness in law enforcement are the degree to which police officers work and how well they accomplish the department's mission, goals, and objectives.

Police Administrators as Leaders

Police administrators are responsible for and expected to provide competent managerial leadership. In fulfilling this role expectation, they initiate goal-

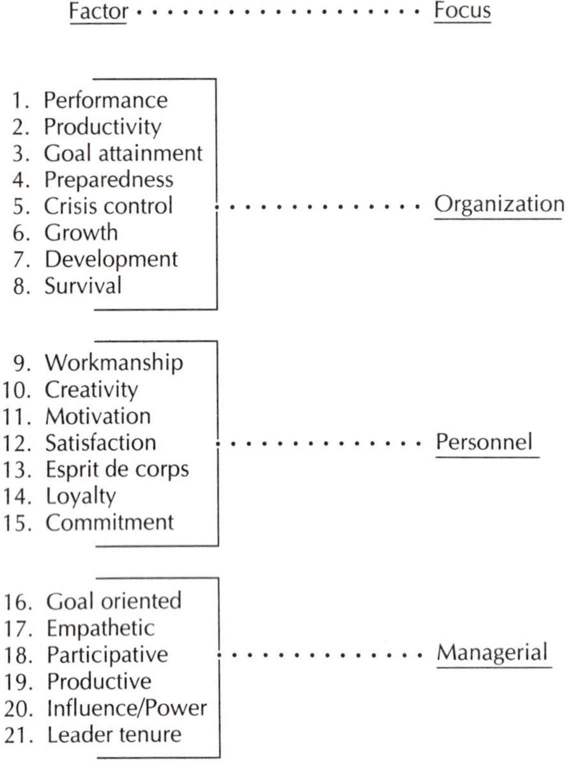

FIGURE 11.3 Criteria for Determining Leadership Effectiveness.

oriented action by others and manage those assigned to do the work. Executives and other upper-level managers perform the specialized task of maintaining the organization in operation (Barnard, 1968). As managerial leaders, police administrators

1. Formulate and refine the organization's mission, goals, and objectives in terms of perceived needs.
2. Fulfill the department's mission through the goal-oriented and proactive management of available resources as illustrated in Focus 11.1.
3. Motivate police personnel to invest time, energy, effort, and expertise in job-related activities.
4. Make police work an intrinsically more rewarding and productive occupation.
5. Set a moral and professional tone to guide the behavior of others within the organization.
6. Use power and formal authority in an effort to help their employees become more efficient, effective, and productive.
7. Create a milieu in which police officers do willingly what the manager wants them to do.

According to Sam Souryal (1977), the essence of management leadership is in the administrator's ability to identify the needs of people in work groups and to meet work-related needs in ways designed to produce optimal productivity.

FOCUS 11.1

Accrediting Law Enforcement Agencies

As early as 1967, the President's Commission on Law Enforcement and Administration of Justice recognized the need for standards for law enforcement agencies as one strategy for improving the overall provision of police services in America. As a result, in 1979, the International Association of Chiefs of Police, the National Organization of Black Law Enforcement Executives, the National Sheriffs' Association, and the Police Executive Research Forum joined forces to establish the Commission on Accreditation for Law Enforcement Agencies (CALEA). CALEA was charged with developing a body of standards that would enhance the quality and efficiency of law enforcement services and with establishing a voluntary program through which interested agencies could become accredited.

Standards

CALEA has promulgated more than 940 standards for agencies to use in assessing their capabilities. Major categories of standards include law enforcement roles; responsibilities and relationships; organization and administration; personnel practices; traffic and other law enforcement operations; court-related activities; and auxiliary/technical services. The standards generally indicate what an agency should do rather than how it should go about doing it. The sheriff or police executive is responsible for transforming the standards into specific policies and procedures that are appropriate for that agency given its size, structure, and mandate. In order to become accredited, an agency must comply with all of the mandatory and at least 80 percent of the nonmandatory standards that apply to departments of its size. CALEA has established six size groups ranging from one to nine to 1,000 and above. CALEA does charge a fee for conducting the assessment phase of the accreditation process that is based on agency size, and recent figures from CALEA indicate that these fees range from $5,000 to $20,000.

Commonwealth Participation

Currently, there are approximately 120 law enforcement agencies that have been accredited. Police agencies within the Commonwealth [of Pennsylvania] have recently begun to recognize the potential for participating in the accreditation process. In July 1989, the Mount Lebanon Police Department in Allegheny County and the Harrisburg City Police Department in Dauphin County joined the Tredyffrin Township Police Department in Chester County as the state's only accredited agencies. In becoming accredited, these agencies cited a number of benefits, including enhanced administrative and operational effectiveness, greater public confidence in the agency, state and local recognition of professional competence, diminished vulnerability to civil law suits and a reduction in liability insurance costs, and stronger relationships with neighboring agencies and other components of the justice system.

As the future of accreditation evolves in Pennsylvania, there is the potential for this type of program among departments with 25 or more full-time sworn law enforcement personnel. Recognizing that accreditation can serve as a useful tool in enhancing police services in the Commonwealth, PCCD is currently exploring strategies for facilitating the program on a statewide basis. . . .

SOURCE. Pennsylvania Commission on Crime and Delinquency, *PCCD Quarterly,* "Accrediting Law Enforcement Agencies," Winter 1989–90.

Managerial Leadership

Managerial leaders make an effort to identify and understand the needs of subordinates and to mesh them with those of the organization. While these needs vary from person to person, one organization to the next, and over time, they are normally separated into two distinct categories:

1. *Task-oriented needs* are work-centered and directly related to defining goals, making policy, building programs, establishing process, and creating organization based on the efficient division of labor. Management organizes the elements of productive enterprise (money, material, equipment, and human resources) to accomplish its stated goals and objectives.

2. *People-oriented needs* are employee-centered and related to improving interpersonal relations, facilitating communications, motivating personnel, providing support, generating morale through meaningful participation, and resolving destructive conflict. The task of management is to create conditions that allow people to achieve their own goals by directing their productive effort toward organizational objectives (McGregor, 1960).

The task and people dimensions of management leadership are not, and never have been, mutually exclusive. They are interdependent. Effective managers exhibit both orientations simultaneously. They seek to create work environments that are productive as well as satisfying for human beings. People-oriented leadership—interactive behavior based on mutual trust, friendship, support, and respect—is directly related to on-the-job performance and employee satisfaction in a wide range of organizations. Those leaders who are more considerate of others usually have the most satisfied subordinates (Dessler, 1979).

Modern police work is labor intensive. Somewhere between 70 and 85 percent of the budget is earmarked for recruiting, screening, training, nurturing, and retaining personnel. Under these conditions, managerial leaders must possess the knowledge and skills required to maximize the efficiency, effectiveness, and productivity of the organization's human resources. Researchers have identified the major knowledge areas and leadership skills associated with good management:

KNOWLEDGE AREAS	*LEADERSHIP SKILLS*
1. Organization theory (work flow)	1. Conceptual skills
2. Industrial engineering (job)	2. Human skills
3. Behavioral science (attitudes)	3. Technical skills

We now explore these knowledge areas and leadership skills to provide you with a foundation for a more detailed discussion of managerial leadership in law enforcement.

Frederick Herzberg (1968) refers to organization theory, industrial engineering, and behavioral science as the eternal triangle. Contemporary managerial leaders utilize organizational theory to structure work in a logical and sequential manner and ensure coordinated efforts by all personnel in order to achieve a work unit's goals and objectives. They function as industrial engineers in the sense that it is their task to create and/or modify individual jobs so that the employee is productive and makes a substantive contribution to the organization. As applied social scientists, managerial leaders use their knowledge of human behavior to motivate employees, nurture positive attitudes toward work, and cultivate appropriate norms, values, and ethical orientations (see Figure 11.4). Good police managers bring the disparate elements of the eternal triangle into dynamic equilibrium to preserve and strengthen the organization as a consciously coordinated and goal-oriented system of human interaction (Barnard, 1968).

Managerial leaders understand human nature. They know that subordinates learn, participate, and produce best when they are allowed to set some of their own goals, choose activities related to achievement of those goals, and exercise freedom of choice in other important areas of life within the organization. An effective leader acts as a catalyst, a consultant, and a resource person for the work group. The leader's job is to help the group emerge as a collective entity, grow in terms of solidarity, and become less dependent on external direction or outside control.

Managers serve the interests of the group best when, as leaders, they are spontaneous, empathetic, direct, open, and honest in dealing with their subordinates (Gibb, 1976). They have a unique ability to apply knowledge readily and effectively in any given situation. In addition to knowledge, police managers draw on and exhibit a dynamic mix of leader skills. In this particular context, management leadership requires *conceptual skills, human skills, and technical skills* (Katz, 1974).

Conceptual skills are used to organize and integrate experience. They involve the ability to comprehend and ascribe meaning to bits and pieces of information as data is converted into comprehensive thought. This is not merely an intellectual exercise. It is a part of a process that allows the manager

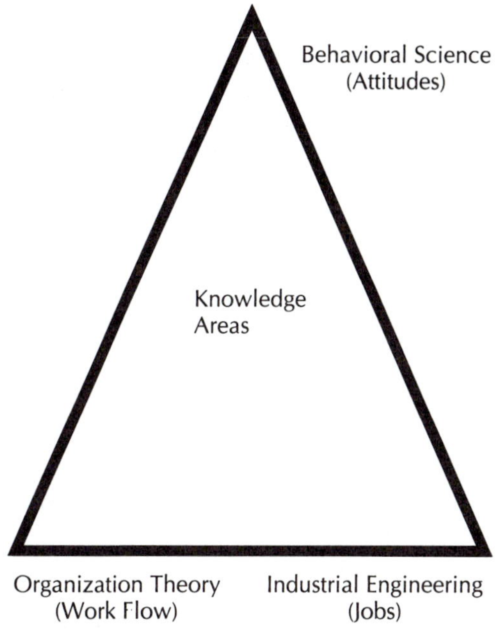

FIGURE 11.4 Herzberg's "Eternal Triangle."

to translate knowledge into action. Police administrators with well-developed conceptual skills are able to perceive of themselves in relation to the department and learn to really appreciate how their behavior affects interpersonal transactions and functional relationships within the organization. Effective managers evaluate their own personal worth in terms of their leadership role in the police department, the criminal justice system, and the government itself. While conceptual skills are required at every level in police work, the standards for handling different kinds of information become less clear and the level of abstraction increases dramatically as one moves up in the hierarchy of authority (Thibault, Lynch, and McBride, 1985).

Human skills involve those aspects of behavior and/or personality that influence the individual's ability to interact in a positive way with other persons in the organization. They include, but are certainly not limited to, tolerance for ambiguity, empathetic understanding, and interpersonal communication skills. Tolerance for ambiguity refers to the managerial leader's capacity to deal effectively with problems even though the lack of information might preclude making a totally informed choice from among the available alternatives. Empathy is the ability to position oneself to see a situation or series of situations from the perspective of others. Empathy is a prerequisite for understanding human behavior. Communication represents an idea transplant from the mind of one person to the mind of another (Fulmer, 1983). Effective communication is a critical variable in the success or failure of any cooperative effort. Tolerance for ambiguity, empathetic understanding, and goal-oriented communication help translate idiosyncratic behavior into coordinated human effort designed to accomplish the police department's mission, goals, and objectives. Managerial leaders have a unique ability to function as members of an organization while fostering a cooperative spirit and guiding its activities.

The technical skills utilized by police personnel vary depending on the level they have attained within the organization. According to Robert Katz (1974), technical skill represents specialized knowledge, analytical ability related to the speciality, and competence in the use of those tools and techniques associated with police work. The technical skills needed in law enforcement are diverse and normally acquired through on-the-job experience or job-related training programs. These skills are much more operational than managerial. The techniques and mechanics of arrest, for example, have little or nothing to do with the use of preventative detention to protect the community from potentially dangerous criminals. The ability to shoot a revolver accurately is unrelated to the manager's decision to control the use of deadly force through the imposition of policies, procedures, rules, and regulations.

As police officers attain rank and move up the chain of command, the leadership mix needed to function properly changes to reflect the task-oriented and people-oriented demands placed on managerial leaders at that level in the hierarchy. Without attempting to split hairs about what constitutes a conceptual, human, or technical skill, Figure 11.5 demonstrates the relative mix of leadership skills needed by line supervisors (corporals/sergeants), middle-level managers (lieutenants/captains), and top managers (division chief/deputy chief/chief executive officer). Only those officers with leadership skills or the ability to acquire them through education, training, and supervised practical experience should be promoted to higher rank in the police department (National Advisory Commission on Criminal Justice Standards

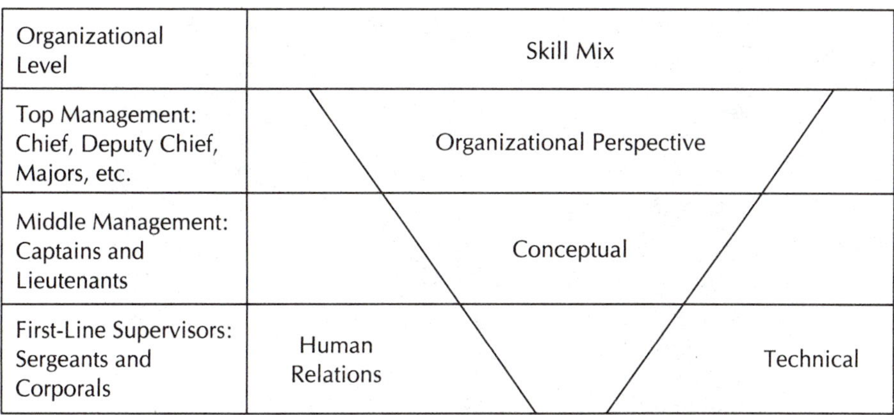

Organizational Level
Skill Mix
Top Management: Chief, Deputy Chief, Majors, etc.
Organizational Perspective
Middle Management: Captains and Lieutenants
Conceptual
First-Line Supervisors: Sergeants and Corporals
Human Relations
Technical

FIGURE 11.5 Rank-Specific Leadership Skill Mix. Source Adapted from Charles Swanson et al., *Police Administration* (New York: Macmillan, 1988).

and Goals, 1973). Once promoted, they should be judged on their performance as managerial leaders. Accountability based on performance appraisal is a critical variable in the success or failure of an ongoing enterprise.

Theories of Leadership

Many theories have been developed to explain those factors thought to produce leaders and sustain leadership in complex organizations. The conceptual approaches used to study leadership are ordinarily grouped into two basic categories: (1) universal theories and (2) situational theories. Universal theories search for an explanation of leadership unrelated to follower behavior or the social environment within which it develops. To the extent that these theories are truly universal in nature, they fail to shed much light on managerial leadership in very specific situations (Albanese, 1981). Situational theories, on the other hand, tend to place undue emphasis on contingency variables in an effort to explain the emergence of leaders (and leadership) in a particular set of circumstances. While neither approach has proven to be satisfactory per se, both of them provide us with a starting point for further discussion.

Venerable names like August Vollmer, William Parker, O. W. Wilson, and J. Edgar Hoover almost always surface when there is a serious discussion about leadership in law enforcement. Someone will point out that their personal traits, their leadership style, and the overall situation came together in such a way to guarantee them a place in history. Experts in management leadership agree. Gary Dessler (1979) contends that there are at least four components in effective management leadership:

1. Positive personal traits
2. Congruent leader style
3. People-oriented approach
4. Meaningful participation

Successful Leadership As the Commissioner of the New York City Police Department and President of the International Association of Chiefs of Police, Lee P. Brown has emerged as one of the most influential law-enforcement leaders in the world. *(©John Sotomayor: NYT Pictures)*

We discuss these factors here in order to describe the ideal-type police administrator.

Trait Theory

Trait theory, one of the earliest approaches used to study leadership, was very popular until the mid-1950s and is still viable in one form or another. Trait theories were formulated by luminaries like Thomas Carlyle, Georg Friedrich Hegel, and Francis Galton and are based on the assumption that some people are born leaders. Carlyle saw leaders as unusually endowed and talented people who made history. Hegel took a different approach. He argued that events brought out the latent leadership potential in great men and women. Francis Galton believed that leadership skills were simply inherited biologically (Swanson, Territo, and Taylor, 1988).

Trait theory is based on the concept that good leaders always have certain physical, mental, and character traits that poor leaders do not possess. There is an implicit assumption that one's ability to lead develops concurrently with the personality during the formative years of childhood (Holden, 1986). According to trait theory (Baron, 1983), leaders differ from followers with respect to several specific key traits that do not change much over time. Persons with these special traits are virtually predestined to exercise informal as well as formal leadership in a variety of situations. Those who worked to refine trait theory and apply it to police administration were confident that adequate leadership could be obtained through a fairly simple two-step process. First of all, good leaders would be studied and compared to nonleaders in order to determine special traits that only the leaders possess. Secondly, police officers with these special leadership traits would be identified and promoted to managerial positions within the department.

Researchers have been trying to identify those special traits that set effective managerial leaders apart from poor managers for over 50 years. Different researchers—depending on their philosophy and/or academic training—have reached radically different conclusions concerning exactly what constitutes an absolutely essential leadership trait. A review of selected research data helps to illustrate this problem.

Based on extensive survey data regarding the qualifications of an executive, Ralph C. Davis (1940) found 56 different characteristics or traits that he considered important. While admitting it was unlikely that any manager would exhibit all 56, he claimed that the following 10 were required for executive success:

1. Intelligence
2. Experience
3. Originality
4. Receptiveness
5. Teaching ability
6. Personality
7. Knowledge of human behavior
8. Courage
9. Tenacity
10. Sense of justice and fair play

Davis made no attempt to rate these factors in terms of their relative importance in determining effective management leadership.

Cecil Goode's research (1951) determined that the following traits were essential for successful leadership in complex organizations:

1. Leaders are more intelligent than the average of their followers. They are not, however, so superior that they cannot be easily understood by those who work for them.
2. Leaders are well-rounded persons from the standpoint of knowledge, interests, and aptitudes.
3. Leaders have an unusual facility with language. They speak and write intelligently, persuasively, understandably, and simply.
4. Leaders are physically as well as mentally and emotionally mature.
5. Leaders have a powerful inner drive or motivation which compels them to strive for accomplishment.
6. Leaders are fully aware of the need for cooperative effort in getting things done. They understand the need for and practice effective human skills.
7. Leaders rely on their administrative (or conceptual) skills to a far greater extent than the technical skills associated with their work.

Goode's list of traits tends to emphasize the people-oriented aspect of managerial leadership.

Typical of the later studies is one using 306 managers employed by 90 different companies carried out by Edwin Ghiselli (1971) at the University of California. Several characteristics were found to have a significant relationship to managerial performance: supervisory ability, achievement orientation, intelligence, self-assurance, decisiveness, and the need for self-actualization.

In a comprehensive analysis of more than 280 trait studies conducted from 1904 to 1970, Ralph M. Stogdill (1948, 1974) described a managerial leader as someone who acquires status through purposeful social interaction and a demonstrated ability to facilitate efforts of the work group in achieving its goals and objectives. The traits most often associated with the assumption and performance of this role were intelligence, sensitivity to the needs of others, understanding of the task, initiative and persistence in handling problems, and a desire to accept responsibility and occupy a position of dominance and control. Based on this research, Stogdill developed a trait profile designed to describe successful managerial leaders. According to the profile, effective leaders exhibit

1. Strong needs for responsibility and task completion.
2. Vigor and persistence in pursuit of their goals.
3. Adventuresomeness and originality in problem-solving.
4. Drive to exercise initiative in social situations.
5. Self-confidence and a sense of personal identity.
6. Willingness to accept consequences for their actions.
7. Skills in coping with interpersonal stress.
8. Patience when dealing with ambiguity and frustration.
9. Power as they influence the behavior of other people.
10. Talent in organizing the group into a cohesive whole.

The leader traits (and corresponding leadership skills) emphasized by Stogdill are summarized in Table 11.1.

TABLE 11.1 Traits and Skills of Successful Leaders

Leader Traits	Leadership Skills
Adaptable in various situations	Resourceful
Aware of social environment	Ability to conceptualize
Ambitious/achievement oriented	Creative
Assertive	Diplomatic and tactful
Collaborative	Facile with language
Decisive	Understands the task
Desires to influence others	Organizational ability
Energetic and proactive	Persuasive
Self-confident	Socially interactive
Tolerant of ambiquity/stress	Empathetic understanding
Needs to assume responsibility	Ability to motivate others
Positive "*can do*" attitude	Collegiality
Respects co-workers	Teaching/coaching ability

SOURCE: Adapted from Gary A. Yukl, *Leadership in Organization* (Englewood Cliffs, NJ: Prentice-Hall, 1981).

In a thorough review of the literature on trait theory, Joe Kelly (1974) produced what he considered to be a definitive list of those traits most often identified in research as having a positive correlation with managerial leadership. This list of leader traits included intelligence, initiative, extroversion, a sense of humor, enthusiasm, fairness, sympathy, and self-confidence. While these traits seem to be important, there is simply no way to prove whether they are or are not essential elements in effective managerial leadership.

There has been and will continue to be an avid interest in those physical, social, and psychological traits that separate leaders from nonleaders and good managers from poor managers. There is, however, no quick and easy test to assess leadership potential. In fact, most management theorists now agree that there are no universal leader traits (Albanese, 1981). Applied research has failed to discover a definite, consistent correlation between genetically determined traits and truly effective leadership (Reitz, 1981).

There are inherent methodological problems involved in defining, identifying, and measuring leader traits. Consequently, no particular set of traits has emerged to differentiate effective leaders from nonleaders in any theoretically meaningful sense (Schermerhorn, Hunt, and Osborn, 1982). Based on the analysis of available data, the opposite is true. It is clear that situational factors and pressures are critical variables in determining who becomes an effective police manager. Robert Baron (1983) argues that different situations require managers with different personal characteristics, leader styles, and leadership skills. In some situations, direct and forceful action by the leader is necessary. It enhances productivity and morale. In others, this type of behavior creates resentment and becomes counterproductive. A flexible, unstructured approach works best. In some circumstances, an autocratic style of decision-making—in which the designated leader gathers information and then acts unilaterally—may be effective. In other circumstances a participative approach involving consultation and collaboration with one's subordinates might be necessary to ensure that important decisions are acceptable to various members of the work group. In short, there is no evidence to support the contention that one particular set of traits produces effective leadership in all situations.

The age-old assumption that leaders are born and develop their conceptual, technical, and human skills independent of situational variables has been completely discredited. The notion that effective managers possess specific leader traits and leadership skills has not been confirmed by research. Consequently, we have been developing a more reasonable and balanced paradigm concerning the importance of traits. It is now believed that certain traits and functional skills increase the likelihood that a given person will be an effective manager. There are no guarantees, however. According to Gary Yukl (1981), the relative importance of the police administrator's personal traits and skills will be determined by the leadership situation.

Leader Behavior Approach

Behavioral scientists abandoned trait theory because it provided few clues as to exactly what caused effective leadership. Researchers wanted to identify those proactive leadership strategies that elicited superior performance by human resources and were consistently effective. As a result, they shifted their attention to the study of actual leader behavior. There were important implications involved in this shift in paradigms. First, by focusing on what leaders do and how they do it (as opposed to who they are), there is a tacit assumption that there is some best way to lead. Secondly, since personal traits remain fairly stable over time, leader behavior can be learned (Tansik, Chase, and Aquilano, 1980). Most management theorists reject the notion that leaders are born and accept the idea that they are created in an interactive social milieu.

Researchers began to study how leader behavior affected follower performance and job-related satisfaction. As a result, leadership was viewed as a process of maintaining supportive social relationships in an organized work unit while getting members of that unit to perform assigned tasks at some acceptable level. Although this inquiry did not uncover a list of behaviors that always distinguish leaders from nonleaders, it served to identify major patterns or styles of leader behavior. It also demonstrated that management style has a significant influence on the productivity and morale of personnel within any type of complex criminal justice organization.

Leadership Styles

Early studies, using the methodological approach pioneered by Kurt Lewin, Ronald Lippit, and Ralph White (1939), viewed leadership style as an interaction continuum ranging from people-centered to task-centered managerial behavior. The focus of style theory is to determine which leadership style produces the greatest increase in productivity. Three basic styles have been identified and described as autocratic, democratic, and laissez-faire (Lewis, 1983):

1. *Autocratic leaders* are power oriented. They prefer to make decisions and give orders rather than to invite group participation. Loyalty and obedience are rewarded. This style is useful when there is a genuine need for strict control and quick decision-making. While the autocratic approach might be effective in the short run, the organization simply may be unable to function properly when the leader is absent. This type of police management stifles the development of leadership ability in subordinates because they are rarely allowed to make meaningful, independent decisions.

2. *Democratic leadership* is people oriented. There is an emphasis on participation and collaboration. Leaders work with subordinates to help them achieve the organization's goals and objectives. These managers strive to establish positive relationships based on mutual respect and trust. Democratic leaders create administrative environments in which they consult with and draw ideas from their personnel. They delegate sufficient authority to accomplish the task. In crisis situations requiring a highly structured response, a democratic leadership style might prove to be far too time consuming or awkward to be effective. While participative management has merit in police work, it also has its downside.

3. *Laissez-faire leadership* represents a hands-off approach to management in complex organizations. In this style, the leader is actually a nonleader who acts as an information center and exercises almost no control. The organization runs itself with little or no input from management. This places the entire organization in jeopardy. Many theorists no longer consider this to be

a true style. The laissez-faire approach is now viewed as a form of administrative abdication (Holden, 1986).

In a somewhat more sophisticated approach, Robert Tannenbaum and Warren Schmidt (1973) identified four basic leadership styles they described as tell, sell, consult, and join (see Figure 11.6). Phillip Applewhite (1965), on the other hand, divided managerial leadership into four very distinct categories including authoritarian, democratic laissez-faire, bureaucratic, and charismatic. While bureaucratic management is based on the process model of leadership, charismatic management is completely idiosyncratic and fueled by personal magnetism.

One of the problems associated with the leadership style approach is that it does not permit management personnel to rate high at both ends of the continuum. It implies that managers are one-dimensional players who are unable to exhibit people-oriented and task-oriented behavior at the same time. Most leadership theorists now feel that the people and task dimensions of leader behavior are not mutually exclusive. They are, in fact, independent variables that can be exhibited simultaneously (Dessler, 1979). A large body of applied research data suggests that the either/or view of leadership is out of sync with reality.

Much of our knowledge about leadership in complex criminal justice organizations is rooted in studies conducted by Ohio State University and the University of Michigan in the late 1940s. While the researchers used different methodologies and focused their attention on different aspects of

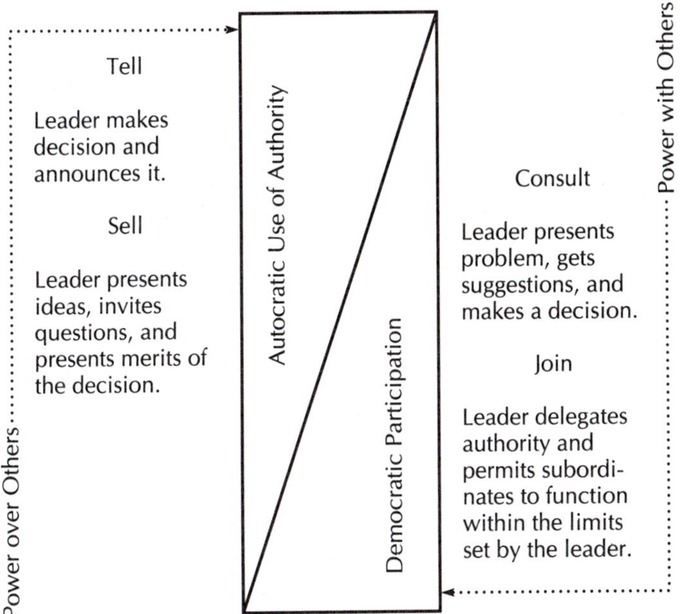

FIGURE 11.6 The Leadership Continuum. Source Adapted from Paul Hersey and Kenneth H. Blanchard, *Management of Organizational Behavior* (Englewood Cliffs, NJ: Prentice-Hall, 1972).

leadership, they reached very similar conclusions. They cast doubt on the validity of viewing leader behavior as a single continuum and developed a two-dimensional independent factor approach to management. The factors identified in the Ohio State University studies were consideration and initiating structure. The University of Michigan researchers defined them as people-oriented and production-oriented aspects of leadership. These factors are, regardless of the terminology used, now considered to be the two most important dimensions of managerial leadership (Leonard and More, 1987).

Leadership Quadrants

Based on an analysis of extensive survey data, E. A. Fleishman and his colleagues at Ohio State University (Fulmer, 1983) discovered that subordinates tend to think of leadership in terms of the consideration and initiating structure provided for them by those in positions of authority. Consideration was measured by behavior items such as openness, communication, consultation, friendship, supportiveness, appreciation, respect, and empathetic understanding. These human relations-oriented behaviors help leaders to establish and maintain positive relationships with their subordinates. Initiating structure was measured by behavior items such as planning, coordinating, monitoring, evaluating, directing, and problem-solving. These task-related behaviors promote the efficient utilization of personnel and resources in achieving the organization's mission, goals, and objectives. Effective police administrators are not one dimensional. They have learned to emphasize both consideration and initiating structure in a concerted effort to influence, motivate, coordinate, and control their subordinates (Yukl, 1981).

The patterns of management leadership described in the Ohio State studies form a composite model with four quadrants plotted along two separate axes. Each axis represents a leader style vis-á-vis initiating structure and consideration for employees (see Figure 11.7). It is clear, based on an analysis of the research data, that police managers can and often do exhibit concern for their subordinates as well as the task. The underlying assumption is that truly effective managers rank high in both areas (Albanese, 1981). Since leader behavior and leadership skills are learned, police managers might benefit from exposure to leader-effectiveness training. Altering one aspect of their style could lead to an appreciable increase in work-group productivity.

Numerous research projects have been conducted to determine the effects of consideration and initiating structure on the performance, productivity, and morale of subordinates. The assumption that managers who adopt leadership styles which are high in both consideration and initiating structure will be effective in all situations has simply not been proven. Many studies have, in fact, concluded that *no single leadership style is best in all situations*! In a review of 24 studies related to leadership behavior, 13 found a significant (or positive) relationship between showing consideration and initiating structure for subordinates, 9 studies found no relationship between the two, and 2 studies found a negative correlation (Reitz, 1981). Researchers began to realize that what sounds good in theory may not prove out in practice. There is no consistent pattern of research results to demonstrate that one leader style is superior to another (Longenecker, 1977). Even Ralph Stogdill (1974),

− Consideration +	− Structure +	
+	High Consideration and Low Structure (Unproductive)	High Structure and High Consideration (Democratic)
−	Low Structure and Low Consideration (Laissez-Faire)	High Structure and Low Consideration (Authoritarian)

FIGURE 11.7 The Ohio State Leadership Quadrants. Source Adapted from Robert M. Fulmer, *The New Management* (New York: Macmillan, 1983).

one of the originators of the Ohio State leadership studies, believes it may be overly simplistic to claim that an effective manager merely needs to behave in a considerate and structuring manner. As stated earlier, an adequate analysis of leadership must take into consideration the leader, the followers, and the situation.

While they do not provide the aspiring police administrator with a comprehensive "how to do it" explanation of proactive leadership in complex criminal justice organizations, the importance of the Ohio State leadership studies should not be underestimated. The Ohio State research stimulated interest in a systematic study of leaders, leader behavior, and leadership. The Ohio State studies set the stage for further inquiry and provided a conceptual framework for the well-known managerial grid and the situational leadership theories proposed by Paul Hersey and Kenneth Blanchard.

The University of Michigan launched its own program of research on leadership behavior at about the same time as Ohio State. The focus of the research was to identify relationships between leadership behavior, group processes, and group performance. A major objective of the project was to determine what pattern or style of leadership behavior most often leads to efficient, effective, and productive work by subordinates.

Researchers used field studies and survey data in an effort to discover how effective managers differed from ineffective managers. They came up with a two-dimensional leadership profile. *Employee-oriented* behavior included taking an interest in individual employees and their needs, encouraging two-way communications, developing supportive interpersonal relations, and dealing with conflict. *Production-oriented* behavior, on the other hand, dealt with planning, establishing goals, giving instructions, monitoring performance, stress-

CASE STUDY

Lieutenant Kevin Stern

Lt. Stern is a shift commander in a relatively large municipal police department. He is a pragmatic, no-nonsense type of person who sets high performance standards for himself as well as his subordinates. While he does not have an abrasive personality, the lieutenant is aloof and somewhat insensitive to the needs of his personnel. Lt. Stern's management style is definitely located at the task-oriented end of the leadership continuum. He respects competence and rewards achievement.

A probationary patrol officer assigned to Lt. Stern's unit has been lagging behind other members of the work group in the number of traffic tickets issued and is well below the departmental average. In an effort to correct the problem, the lieutenant has placed this person in the marginal performer category and ordered the officer's sergeant to intensify supervision. The sergeant is to monitor the officer's performance and overall productivity on a regular basis. He was advised to create a paper trail for use when and if the termination of employment becomes necessary. Since the traditional Theory X approach worked for the lieutenant in the past, he is convinced that it will work again. He subscribes to the authoritarian philosophy summed up in the phrase, "Do it my way or you're fired."

Capt. Harrison Blyler, chief of the patrol division and Lt. Stern's immediate superior, was briefed on the problem and the proposed solution. The captain, who is more personable and people-oriented than his lieutenant, agreed with the diagnosis but disagreed with the remedy. He argued that traditional authoritarianism is passé and counterproductive in most leadership situations. He urged the lieutenant to become more open, honest, empathetic, and trusting in his relations with subordinates. Capt. Blyler discussed the value of collaboration, mutual goal setting, and joint decision-making. He stressed the manager's role as a motivator, teacher, and team builder.

Capt. Blyler also encouraged the lieutenant to become familiar with various leadership theories and to begin to assess his own strengths and weaknesses in terms of those theories. He placed a great deal of emphasis on the importance of developing supportive relationships throughout the entire organization. What started out as a mere exchange of information quickly became a seminar in the human relations approach to management in complex criminal justice organizations.

Immediately following his meeting with the captain, Lt. Stern removed the probationary patrol officer from the marginal performer program and ordered the sergeant to reduce the level of supervision. The officer's performance continued to deteriorate and he was terminated prior to the completion of his probationary period. Lt. Stern believes that Capt. Blyler's human relations approach made the problem worse and led to the dismissal.

Which of the two approaches just discussed—authoritarian or human relations—do you feel would work with you if you were the probationary officer? Why? What would you have done differently if you were in the lieutenant's shoes? How did his reaction to the captain's suggestions make the problem worse?

ing productivity, and assigning people to specific tasks (Reitz, 1981). These two aspects of leader behavior were found to be independent, yet complementary to one another.

The University of Michigan researchers also found that effective managerial leaders do not spend most of their time and effort doing the same kind of work as their subordinates. Effective leaders concentrate on supervisory functions like planning, scheduling work, coordinating worker activities, and distributing resources (supplies, equipment, and technical assistance). This production-oriented behavior did not detract from their concern for human relations. Effective managers were more considerate, supportive, and helpful with their subordinates. They were likely to use general supervision rather than close supervision. After establishing goals and general guidelines, effective leaders allowed their subordinates some freedom in deciding how to do the work and how to pace themselves while doing the work (Yukl, 1981).

While the University of Michigan studies unearthed a great deal of information about leadership, they tell only part of the story. These studies are susceptible to the same criticisms as were leveled at the Ohio State leadership studies. Leaders are but one element in the mosaic of human interaction.

The Managerial Grid®

Robert Blake and Jane Srygley Mouton have also dealt with the task and people dimensions of managerial leadership. They proposed a framework whereby leader style is plotted on a two-dimensional grid. The *Managerial Grid*—a charting technique developed independently of the Ohio State studies—identifies five normative leadership styles based on the relationship between concern for production and concern for people. Leadership style is determined according to how a particular manager ranks in both of these areas. The Managerial Grid is used as a diagnostic tool to help individual managers assess their own leadership style (Brittel, 1980).

The Managerial Grid is a 9 by 9 matrix. As illustrated in Figure 11.8, the horizontal axis indicates gradated concern for production. A rating of 9 reflects maximum concern for production. The vertical axis, on the other hand, shows regard for subordinates as human beings. The higher the rating, the greater the concern. A 9 on this axis is indicative of maximum concern for people (Blake and Mouton, 1985). Since the grid is a 9 by 9 matrix, there are 81 possible combinations, or styles of managerial leadership. Only the five basic styles are represented in Figure 11.8. This is sufficient to understand the concepts behind grid theory, however.

The five basic managerial leadership styles identified by Blake and Mouton are (1) impoverished management, (2) task-oriented management, (3) country club management, (4) middle-of-the-road management, and (5) team management.

1,1 *Impoverished management.* People are hired, placed in a job, and left alone. Managers exert minimum effort. They sense little or no conflict between production goals and needs of subordinates. Very little is expected from these managers. They are out of it and seem to be lost among rather than actively managing people. A 1,1 style is sometimes referred to as laissez-faire management and represents an abdication of professional responsibility.

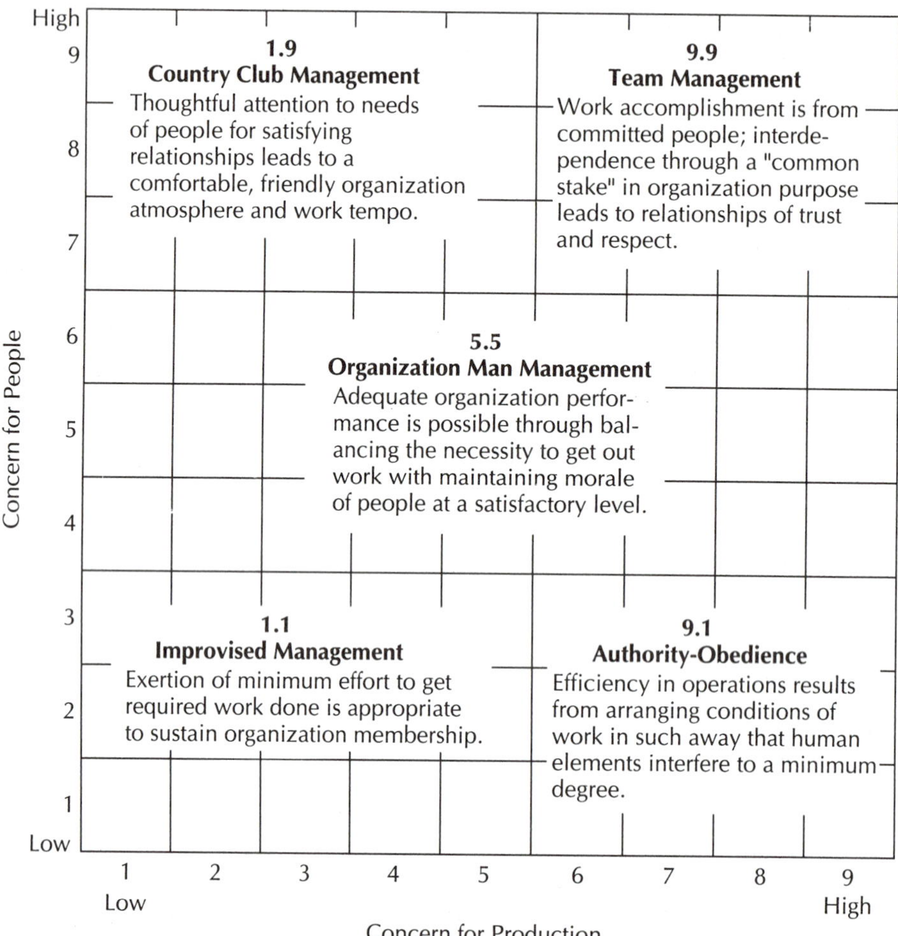

FIGURE 11.8 The Managerial Grid®. Source Adapted from *The Managerial Grid III: The Key to Leadership Excellence,* by Robert R. Blake and Jane Srygley Mouton (Houston: Gulf, Copyright©1985, page 12). Reproduced by permission.

9,1 *Task-oriented management.* The leader exhibits a very strong interest in productivity and almost no concern for employee needs or morale. The manager is a proverbial taskmaster. Human considerations are not allowed to interfere with productivity and/or efficiency. 9,1 represents an autocratic management style in which the end justifies the means and the exploitation of personnel becomes the rule rather than the exception.

1,9 *Country club management.* Leaders are overly concerned with creating and maintaining a friendly atmosphere. They spend much of their time placating employees in an effort to meet human needs. The attitudes and feelings of subordinates are their only real concern. People always come first. 1,9 managers exhibit a low functional concern for productivity. Work becomes a ritualistic exercise designed to sustain the employee's personal lifestyle.

5,5 *Middle-of-the-road management.* Leaders exhibit basic concern for production and people. Their managerial behavior reflects an intermediate level of interest in productivity and a modest concern for subordinates. While they assume that there will be a conflict between organizational goals and personal needs, they seek to strike a balance between the two. The manager's survival often depends on creating and maintaining a state of equilibrium. The 5,5 manager believes most people are practical and will normally put forth some effort based on self-interest. The middle-of-the-road approach to managerial leadership is very common in modern police work.

9,9 *Team management.* 9,9 managers rate high in terms of their concern for productivity and personnel. They assume there is no conflict between the goals of the organization and the needs of their subordinates. There is an emphasis on meaningful participation. Integration of organizational goals and employee needs is achieved by involving all personnel in determining the goals, methods, and conditions of work (Leonard and More, 1987).

Blake and Mouton argue that 9,9 on the grid represents an ideal-type leadership style that all managers should try to adopt (Tansik, Chase, and Aquilano, 1980). They contend that the 9,9 leadership style is the one most positively associated with efficiency, effectiveness, productivity, and employee satisfaction (Blake and Mouton, 1985). According to W. Richard Plunkett (1983), 9,9 managers succeed because they motivate others to join with them in accomplishing the work of the organization. They cultivate a sense of commitment and interdependence by providing their employees with a common stake in the organization. Effective managerial leaders develop goal-oriented relationships with subordinates based on influence, trust, and mutual respect.

Managers ordinarily adopt and retain a dominant mode or style of management. Their actions are normally consistent with this grid style unless it fails to work. Under these circumstances, they may shift into a backup style keyed to the situation. Consequently, where individual managers fit on the grid at any given point in time is not entirely up to them. A variety of factors must be taken into consideration. The demands of the situation as well as the manager's personality, managerial philosophy, administrative acumen, and interaction patterns influence the placement. While police administrators should strive to achieve the 9,9 position on the grid, they must be flexible enough to adapt to changing situations and changes in their personnel when necessary. Truly effective leaders know and have an appreciation for those forces that affect their managerial behavior. They understand themselves, the interpersonal dynamics of the work group, and the situational context within which they function (Plunkett, 1983).

Due to the paramilitary structure of most police departments, there has not been much of an emphasis on team management in law enforcement. As a result, the grid approach has been used infrequently. In a recent study of 76 police administrators, however, nearly 70 percent of the respondents reported that the team management approach was their dominant leadership style. They identified middle-of-the-road management as their primary backup style (Leonard and More, 1987). In a study of 25 managers from a large police department, Jack Kuykendall (1977) discovered that 45 percent of them had 9,9 leadership styles. While these studies are certainly encouraging, they should not be used to make far-reaching generalizations.

In related research, Jack Kuykendall and Peter Unsinger (1982) found that police managers tended to have either no dominant leadership style or used the sell approach to accomplish the organization's goals and objectives. They were most effective when using leader styles placing an emphasis on the task and least effective in styles requiring delegation of authority and/or work-group participation. According to Roy Roberg and Jack Kuykendall (1990) there is simply no proof to support the assertion by some management theorists that the team management style of leadership is superior to other styles in all situations. While concern for both production and people is important, concern alone cannot ensure effective managerial leadership in complex police organizations.

All behavioral approaches to leadership are based on similar concepts even though they may be couched in different terms and generate a different set of labels. The notion that effective managerial leaders seek to influence both work output and social factors is a fundamental assumption inherent in all behavior theories. Even though their basic approach was different, Blake and Mouton came to the same conclusions as the OSU researchers. Ohio State used a behavioral model to examine leader actions as perceived by subordinates in the work force. The managerial grid, on the other hand, is an attitudinal model that has been designed to measure the predispositions of effective managers. Both discovered a positive relationship between the production-oriented and people-oriented dimensions of proactive managerial leadership. The work of these leader behavior theorists provided the foundation for further study of managerial leadership because it strongly suggested that the most effective way to lead is a dynamic and versatile process that adapts itself—in terms of dominant and backup styles—to unique situations (Whisenand and Rush, 1988).

Supporters of the managerial grid concept believe the 9,9 leadership style is the one best way to lead and to manage. They view leadership as the interaction between two interdependent variables (i.e., concern for production and concern for people). Emphasis is placed on using all available resources to determine the optimum course of action. The 9,9 police leader seeks to achieve coordinated direction through multiloop, open communication designed to find the best alternative or course of action congruent with the logic inherent in a given situation. Even in crisis situations, 9,9 managers continue—to the extent possible—to rely on superordinate goals and the processes of participation, conflict resolution, and group problem-solving. Their behavior remains consistent with humanistic principles of openness, involvement, and participatory management. The 9,9 leader seeks input, contributions, recommendations, reservations, and doubts from those involved and acts quickly to define problems and devise solutions. According to Blake and Mouton (1985), 9,9 participation is an interaction process predicated on the following:

1. Openness
2. Candor
3. Strong initiative
4. Thorough inquiry
5. Effective advocacy
6. Conflict resolution
7. Delegation
8. Teamwork
9. Two-way critique

If the 9,9 approach fails, police managers may be compelled to shift into a backup style keyed to the needs of the situation. Once the crisis is over, the 9,9 orientation tends to reemerge as the dominant style of management. This is known as 9,9 versatility (see Blake and Mouton, 1985, for a more detailed discussion of this particular concept).

Some situation theorists discount the importance of philosophical and behavioral continuity in the managerial process. They regard effective leadership as a very complex multidimensional social phenomenon which can only be understood from an interactionist perspective that emphasizes contingency factors. Managerial leadership is thought to be the product of an interaction/influence system in which leaders exert influence on and are influenced by other people in a concrete situation (Luthans, 1977). The key variables in the situational approach to leadership are the leaders themselves, the followers, and unique situational factors (see Figure 11.9).

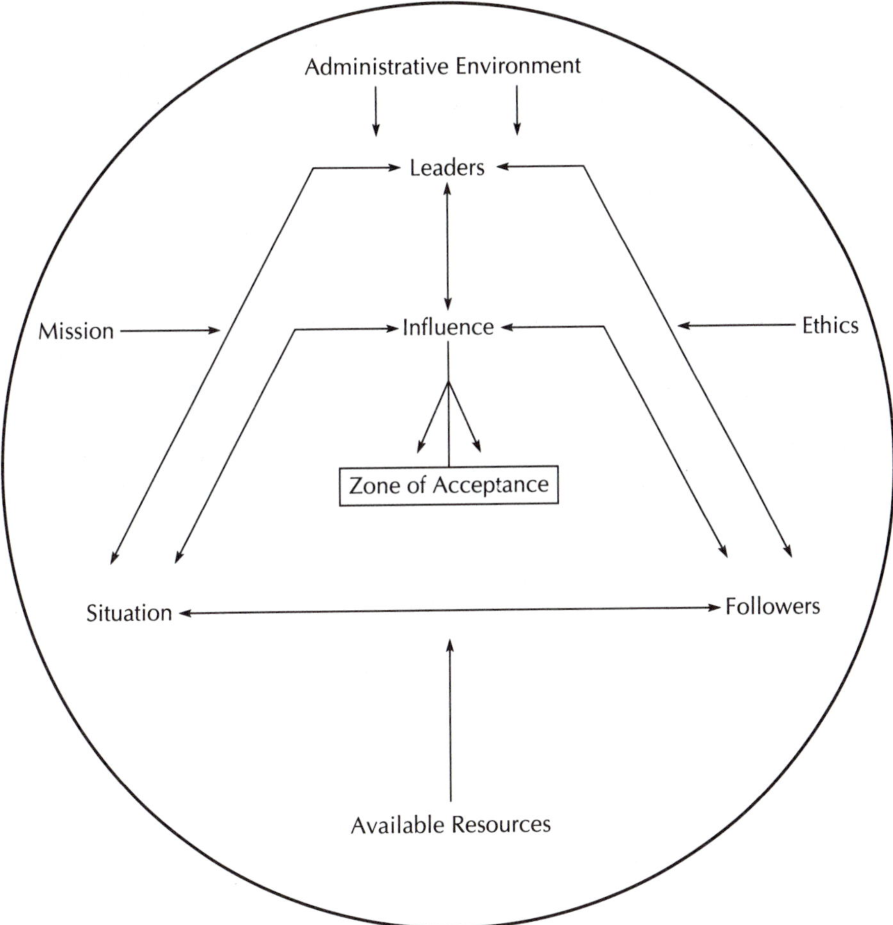

FIGURE 11.9 Leadership Influence Interaction System. Source Adapted from Fred Luthans, *Organizational Behavior* (2nd ed.) (New York: McGraw-Hill, 1977).

Situational Leadership Approach

Situational leadership theories attempt to explain effective managerial leadership in terms of the interaction/influence system just discussed. The situational approach is based on the implicit assumption that leadership is always exercised in specific situations that involve real people in a given physical environment (Longenecker, 1977). It utilizes contingency variables to explain leader behavior. *Contingency variables* are those factors within situations or followers that determine the style of management leadership most likely to be effective in a given set of circumstances (Albanese, 1981). In other words, different situations call forth and reinforce different kinds of leadership.

While situational theories cannot explain exactly what causes a human being to become an effective leader, they do provide an analytical frame of reference for thinking about it. Situational theory says, in effect, that managerial leadership is linked to adaptability. Success is contingent on the individual manager's ability to sense, interpret, and deal with various issues shaped by situational forces and unfolding events. According to Robert Fulmer (1983), the situational approach to leadership is expressed symbolically as L = f (LP, GP, S): Leadership equals the function of the leader's personality, the work-group's personality, and the dynamic situation.

Situational approaches are conceptual tools that leaders use to assess circumstances in which their leadership may become an important factor. A careful analysis of each potential leadership situation is of critical importance and is part of the process used by effective managers as they contemplate the most appropriate leadership style. Effective management is dependent on the degree to which the leader's style fits a given situation.

One of the most important aspects of the managerial role is to diagnose and evaluate the disparate factors that could have either a positive or negative effect on leadership. An accurate assessment of the situation involves identifying and understanding the influence of factors such as individual differences, group dynamics, and organizational policies, procedures, rules, and regulations. As Paul Whisenand (1981) pointed out, an accurate diagnosis in a given situation requires police administrators to examine four extremely important areas: (1) managerial characteristics, (2) subordinate characteristics, (3) work-group structure and the nature of the task, and (4) organizational factors.

1. *Managerial characteristics.* Leader behavior in a given situation depends on the forces or personal characteristics of the individual manager. The most important factors seem to be maturity, personality, needs, motives, past experience, and reinforcement.

2. *Subordinate characteristics.* Before managers adopt a particular leadership style, they assess intuitively the personal characteristics and behavioral patterns of others within the work group. Police officers, like their managers, have many internal forces that affect them and shape their behavior in a given set of circumstances. These factors include maturity, personality, needs, motives, past experience, and reinforcement.

3. *Work-group structure.* Groups are an omnipresent feature in modern society and represent a keystone in the structure of all complex criminal justice organizations. The characteristics of the work group usually have a direct im-

pact on a manager's ability to exercise effective leadership. The significance of the group's influence depends on factors such as its proficiency, cohesiveness, structure, maturity, and work ethic. Work groups that are engaged in ambiguous activities, for example, are much more likely to require a totally different kind of leadership than those performing routine tasks. As a rule, the truly effective managerial leader is flexible when it comes to dealing with the collective needs of the group.

4. *Organizational factors.* One of the most crucial yet least understood aspects of a leadership situation is the organization itself. Some of the more important considerations relate to its assigned mission, the influence base (power and legitimate authority) utilized by leaders, department policies, procedures, rules and regulations, the skill and professional competence needed to do the job, and the time allotted to make decisions and/or to achieve the goals and objectives of the work group. The complexity of the task, the size of the organization, the work-group's interaction pattern, and the reward system help determine the most appropriate leadership style (see Figure 11.10).

Managerial leadership is an art, not a science. Effective managers have the unique ability to create and maintain an interaction/influence system based on a dynamic equilibrium between themselves, their followers, and the leadership situation. They derive inner satisfaction from achieving the organization's goals and meeting the psychosocial needs of their subordinates.

It has—after decades of theory construction and research—become apparent that there are no universal leadership traits and no one best way to manage complex, goal-oriented organizations. In reality, the effective police

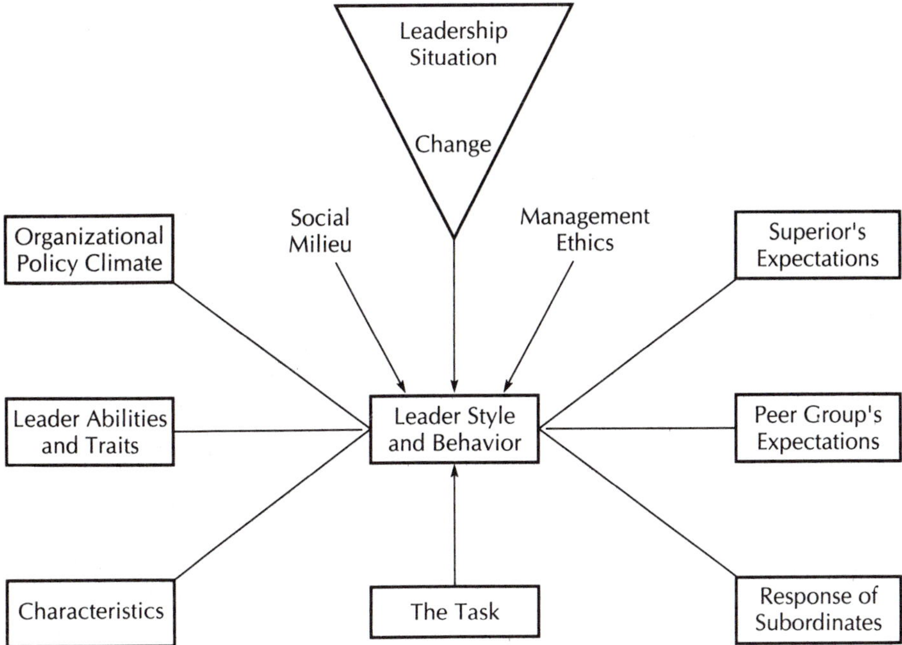

FIGURE 11.10 Sources of Influence on the Choice of Leader Style.
Source Adapted from H. Joseph Reitz, *Behavior in Organizations* (Homewood, IL: Richard D. Irwin, 1981).

manager is one who is able to call on and integrate all of the available leader styles in order to adapt to the demands of a given situation. Good management requires adaptive leadership. In essence, police managers who are able to adjust their style according to the demands of the situation and the needs of their subordinates are those who will be most effective in achieving personal as well as organizational objectives (Lynch, 1986). Paul Whisenand and Fred Furguson (1978) contend that adaptive leaders are much more likely to be successful than those who remain inflexible in the face of change. Being flexible enough to shift into and out of various leadership styles creates a complete manager. Flexibility is the element in dynamic leadership that permits managers to adjust their style to fit the situation.

Contingency Management

The contingency approach to understanding leadership effectiveness attempts to combine elements of both trait theory and situation theory in a single model. It is based on the fundamental assumption that elements in the leadership situation influence the effectiveness of the manager's leadership style. According to the contingency model developed by Fred Fiedler (1964) and his associates, the most important situational factors are (1) leader-member relations, (2) task structure, (3) position power of the leader, and (4) the overall favorableness of the situation. Since their personality is set and not easy to change, an effective manager is one who is able to alter the elements of a leadership situation to effect a proper fit between leader style and the unique demands of a particular situation.

According to contingency theory, group effectiveness in achieving organizational goals and objectives ultimately depends on the leader's personality as manifest in the person's leadership style and the dynamics of the situation in which managerial leaders and their subordinates find themselves. The leader's personality, leadership style, and situational control—based on real power and the legitimate authority to reward or punish subordinates—determine exactly what can be achieved through the efforts of others.

Contingency theorists contend that managerial leaders are primarily motivated either by tasks or interpersonal relationships with their subordinates. Task-oriented managers seek accomplishments in order to reinforce their sense of self-esteem and competence. Relationship-oriented managers, on the other hand, seek admiration and respect from subordinates to fortify social and esteem needs. The orientation of the manager can be identified through Fiedler's Least Preferred Co-worker (LPC) Scale. The LPC classifies leadership orientation by measuring the manager's perceived psychological distance from the least preferred co-worker. The Least Preferred Co-worker Scale—using a set of bipolar adjectives like rejecting/accepting and quarrelsome/harmonious separated on an 8-point scale—assumes that if managers are inclined to describe in positive terms those persons with whom they work least well, they are motivated by interpersonal relationships. If they describe these people in clearly negative terms, they are task motivated (Plunkett, 1983). The LPC measures leader attitudes and values. Low-LPC managers emphasize the task. High-LPC managers are more concerned with establishing and maintaining good relationships in the workplace. They are more cognitively complex than low-LPC leaders and are much more adaptable to changes in the situation (Reitz, 1981).

Whether a task or relationship orientation is most appropriate depends on the nature of the leadership situation. Situational factors determine the power and influence the manager has at any given time. Contingency theory is built on an assumption that all managerial leaders are likely to find themselves in one of three leadership situations:

1. *High-control situations.* Managers are allowed by their subordinates—based on positive relationships, task structure, and position power—to exercise a great deal of influence and control. This creates a predictable organizational environment in which to direct the work of their employees.

2. *Moderate-control situations.* Managers are faced with a number of different problems but tend to deal with them all in the same manner. They either have good relationships with little emphasis on task structure and low position power or poor relationships because of task structure and high position power.

3. *Low-control situations.* Managers are not permitted to exercise much influence or control because members of the work group do not support them. Neither task structure nor position power give managers much influence or control. Low-control situations breed chaos.

V. A. Leonard and Harry More (1987) emphasize that leader-member relationships, task structure, and position power determine whether or not a manager has situational control of the job. These factors are critical and may be described as follows:

1. *Leadership-member relations* measure just how well managers and members of the work group get along. Close leader-follower relationships are normally favorable to the manager. Well-liked and respected leaders can influence a work group far beyond what their legitimate reward and coercive power would suggest.

2. *Task structure* measures how clearly goals, procedures, and performance expectations are defined. Well-defined tasks with minimal ambiguity provide the most favorable situation for the manager. There are four characteristics of structured tasks:

- The goal is clearly understood by members of the group.
- There are relatively few correct solutions to a problem.
- There are only a few ways to accomplish a specific task.
- Decisions about work tasks can be evaluated objectively.

3. *Position power* measures how much authority managers have to hire, reward, discipline, and fire subordinates. Managers who have the real power and formal authority to direct, reward, and punish their employees find themselves in a very favorable leadership situation.

Interaction between these factors determines the favorableness of the situation for the leader.

Contingency theory's criterion for organizational effectiveness is productivity. In very favorable situations, those in which the manager has real power, group support, and a well-structured task to accomplish, members of the work force volunteer to be led and do willingly all that is expected of them.

In relatively unfavorable situations, however, the work group tends to disintegrate unless there is active intervention and control by the leader. Consequently, it appears that a more autocratic and task-oriented leadership style is best when situational factors are very favorable or very unfavorable for the leader (Tansik, Chase, and Aquilano, 1980). A substantial body of research utilizing Fiedler's contingency model has shown a positive correlation between high-LPC (human relations) leadership and productivity in intermediate to moderately difficult situations. Under these conditions, effective leaders seek to create a nonthreatening and much more democratic atmosphere in which subordinates are encouraged to participate in solving the problems faced by the work group. In other words, a high-LPC leadership style seems to work well in average leadership situations but not in very favorable (good) or very unfavorable (bad) situations (Longenecker, 1977).

Contingency theorists argue that it is often necessary for managers to change their normal leadership style in order to meet the challenges presented by a given situation. They contend that both types of leaders should be able to shift gears and play both kinds of roles. Task-oriented leaders may, as the need arises, be required to adopt a human relations approach to motivate their subordinates. On the other hand, a relationship-oriented manager might have to emphasize getting the job done during a crisis or when time constraints demand it, but will revert to the high-LPC approach when the situation returns to normal. According to W. Richard Plunkett (1983) and nearly all situationalists, this flexibility is the hallmark of a true leader. Unfortunately, not everyone has this flexibility.

According to Leonard and More (1987), police managers can modify the situation if they find that their leadership style is out of sync with the demands of the situation in which they are working. Managers can engineer their job by adjusting the three factors involved in situational control (human relations, task structure, and position power). A number of research studies suggest that the contingency approach has practical implications for the training of leaders. Recent research shows that we can improve organizational performance by teaching managers how to diagnose and modify situational control in order to achieve an optimal match between leadership style and the situation as it unfolds in a constantly changing organizational environment (Fiedler, 1978).

While there have been criticisms of the LPC Scale and other aspects of Fred Fiedler's contingency model of leadership, it still represents one of the major thrusts in leadership theory. It is a valuable frame of reference that emphasizes the interaction between the manager (based on a consideration of traits), followers, and the leadership situation. The model is antithetical to the notion that there is one best way to manage complex interaction/influence systems like a police department. Successful police administrators learn to adapt their managerial style to the requirements, constraints, and opportunities presented in the leadership situation (see Figure 11.11).

Path-Goal Leadership Model

The path-goal theory of leadership was formulated by Robert J. House to explain how the behavior of the manager influences the motivation and satis-

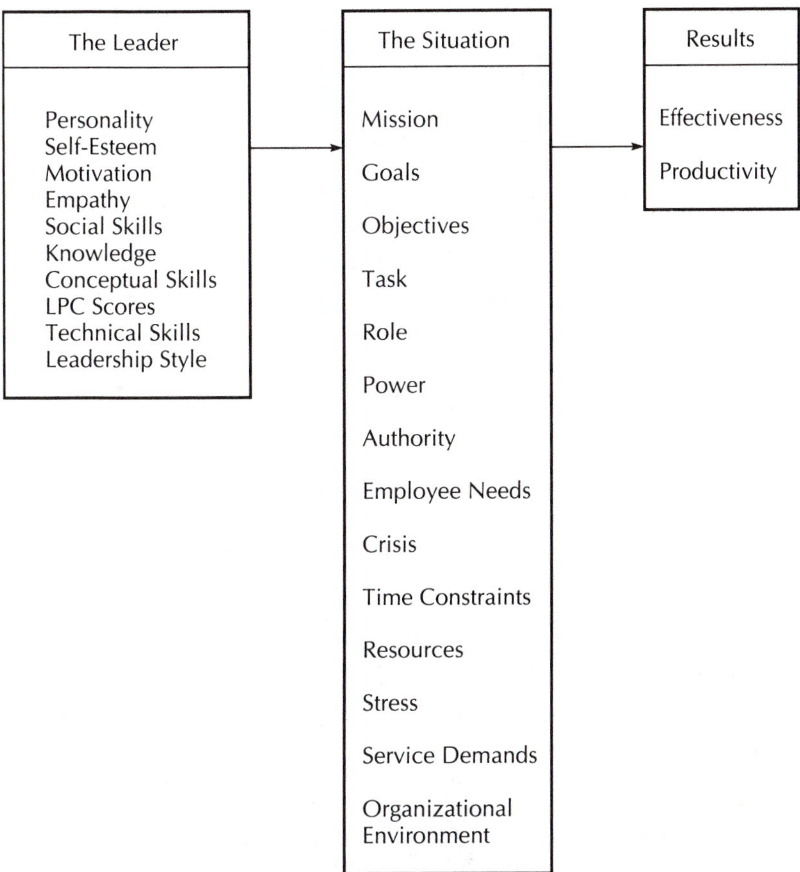

FIGURE 11.11 Contingency Leadership Model.

faction of subordinates. According to House (1971), the managerial leader's motivational function consists of increasing the personal payoffs associated with work goal attainment and making the path to these payoffs easier to follow by clarifying it, removing roadblocks, and increasing the opportunities for personal satisfaction while en route. In other words, leaders set goals for their subordinates and clear the path to accomplish them. The basic assumption underlying path-goal theory is that certain leadership approaches will be much more effective in situations where leader behavior contributes to achievement of the employee's work-related goals. Managers play a supplemental role in the sense that they provide their subordinates with coaching, guidance, and performance incentives that are otherwise not provided by either the organization or the work group.

The path-goal model views leadership as being potentially the most important factor in determining what is to be accomplished (goals) and exactly how it is to be done (job behavior) within the parameters of the situation. Leaders engage in activities designed to identify proper methods (paths) by which their subordinates are allowed to accomplish organizational goals. The key to path-goal leadership is that effective managers create, nurture, and reinforce a meaningful connection between organizational goals and worker goals (Johns, 1983). The manager affects the relationship between legitimate goals and appropriate means by

1. Delegating sufficient authority and assigning proper tasks.
2. Supporting the efforts of subordinates as they strive to accomplish work-related goals.
3. Determining the amount and kinds of extrinsic rewards to be made available.
4. Recognizing, reinforcing, and rewarding goal accomplishment.
5. Enhancing subordinate satisfaction, reducing stress in the workplace, and removing the barriers that frustrate goals (Reitz, 1981).

Path-goal theorists have identified four very basic leader behavior systems, or styles, commonly found in complex organizations: (1) achievement-oriented leadership, (2) instrumental leadership, (3) supportive leadership, and (4) participative leadership.

1. *Achievement-oriented leadership.* Managers set challenging goals, expect subordinates to perform at the highest level, and constantly seek improvements in on-the-job performance. Achievement-oriented managers emphasize excellence and are confident their subordinates will meet these high standards.

2. *Instrumental leadership.* This type of directive leadership is similar to the initiating structure discussed earlier and emphasizes planning, organizing, controlling, and coordinating by the manager. The manager lets subordinates know what they are expected to do and controls their on-the-job behavior through formal policies, procedures, rules, and regulations.

3. *Supportive leadership.* Supportive leadership is similar to consideration as used in the original Ohio State studies. Supportive managers pay attention to the people dimension of leadership. They are concerned with the social needs of subordinates and exhibit a sincere interest in their well-being.

4. *Participative leadership.* Participative managers share information with and seek input from subordinates in order to reach group consensus. They consult with their employees and permit them to have a meaningful role in the decision-making process.

The manager's leadership style is an important factor in determining the kinds of rewards that will be used in a given situation. A relationship-oriented manager uses praise, emotional support, encouragement, and various sociopsychological strokes to supplement standard rewards like pay raises and promotions. They value individual differences and are inclined to tailor reward packages to meet the needs of their employees. Task-oriented managers, on the other hand, use a narrower set of rewards normally unrelated to individual needs. They tend to stress pay and job security. In order to be effective managers, the police administrators' leadership style must coincide with the rewards being sought by their subordinates.

There are two very important situational or contingency variables in the path-goal approach. The first one relates to the personal characteristics of subordinates in terms of their individual needs (need for achievement, affiliation, and autonomy); their ability to perform the task (job skills, knowledge, and experience); and their personality (emotional stability, self-esteem, and self-confidence). The second variable relates to the nature of the task and the environment in which it is performed. Some are certainly much more demanding and stressful than others. According to Robert Albanese (1981), three aspects of the organizational environment have a significant impact on leader behavior: (1) the nature and complexity of the task, (2) the formal authority system, and (3) primary group relations. Both variables influence the manager's leadership style as it relates to motivating subordinates. Motivation, in turn, is presumed to influence employee satisfaction and on-the-job performance. Subordinates perceive leadership behavior to be legitimate and accept it when it is an immediate source of satisfaction or when they anticipate that it will lead to future satisfaction (Yukl, 1981).

Path-goal theory assumes subordinates will respond differently depending on the leadership style. Situational factors help determine their preference for certain types of leader behavior. For example,

1. When subordinates are involved in a task that is stressful, tedious, boring, frustrating, time consuming, dangerous, or otherwise unpleasant, effective managers make the work more tolerable by acting in an empathetic, caring, and supportive manner designed to minimize (moderate) the negative aspects of the job. Supportive relationships tend to increase the intrinsic value (valence) of the task. Increased satisfaction, at least in theory, leads to more effort on the part of most employees.

2. Directive leadership increases subordinate satisfaction and effort where there is role ambiguity. This condition occurs when the task is relatively unstructured, there is little or no formalization, and employees are inexperienced in relation to the task. Role ambiguity causes subordinates to have a low expectation of success when it comes to performing a complex task even if they plan to exert maximum effort. The path-goal model assumes that role ambiguity is dysfunctional, dissatisfying, and counterproductive. Under these circumstances, directive leader behavior will increase employee satisfaction with work and with the leader. There is a possibility that increased satisfaction will lead to an overall increase in productivity.

3. Directive leader behavior is much more likely to motivate subordinates who have a need for autonomy, responsibility, and self-actualization yet find themselves in very complex and ambiguous situations. They want to know what is expected of them. They need to know the parameters within which they are expected to operate (Dessler, 1979).

In those situations where organizational goals and the paths for achieving them are unambiguous, competent workers who have a strong self-image seek autonomy and want to work for a supportive, relationship-oriented manager. Less skilled, more passive employees are much more amenable to task-oriented leaders. The trick, of course, is for police managers to make sure that their leadership style is in sync with the needs of subordinates and the demands of the situation.

The path-goal model (see Figure 11.12) just discussed represents a fairly complex view of leadership. It is designed to deal with the interaction between leader behavior and situational factors. In essence, it views the managers' role as that of motivating employees when subordinates are not motivated sufficiently by intrinsic satisfaction or extrinsic rewards. The goal is to increase productivity. The ability of managers to satisfy employee needs and to generate increased productivity will be contingent on their leadership style, the

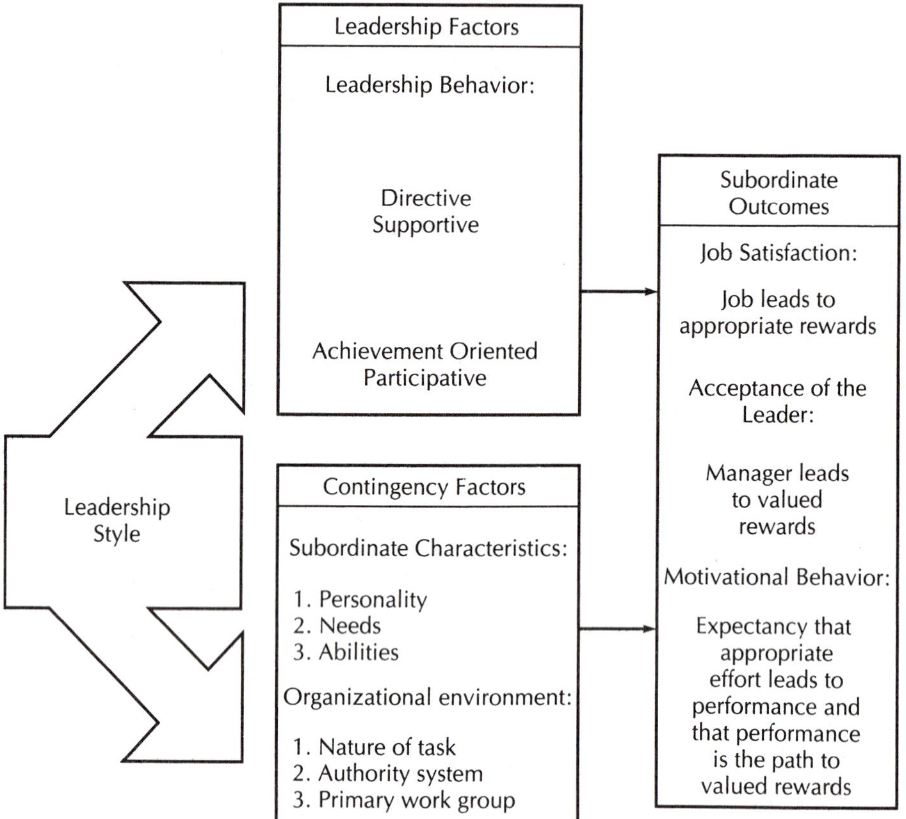

FIGURE 11.12 Path-Goal Approach to Leadership.

moderating effect of subordinate characteristics, and various environmental factors. As principal actors in the motivation process, managerial leaders are expected to establish legitimate and realistic goals, to identify and clear the most direct path to follow in achieving those goals, and to reward appropriate goal-oriented behavior. A leader style (achievement-oriented, instrumental/directive, supportive, or participatory) which corresponds with employee needs and situational variables will, at least in theory, satisfy subordinates and lead to increased productivity on the part of individual employees and the work group as a whole.

Research on path-goal theory has produced mixed results. Some studies support the concept; others do not. Most support is found for the notion that leader behavior has a direct effect on subordinate satisfaction. In one recent study (of 110 bank employees and 205 manufacturing employees), investigators found that task structure moderated the effects of leader behavior on subordinate satisfaction. When tasks were varied, provided little or no feedback, and offered few opportunities for meaningful social interaction, directive leader behavior (initiating structure) increased employee satisfaction. When tasks were routine, provided feedback, and offered opportunities for social interaction, initiating structure became dysfunctional and dissatisfying (Schriesheim and DeNisi, 1979). It has been much more difficult to demonstrate the link between satisfaction and increased productivity (Reitz, 1981).

Participatory Leadership

As noted earlier in this chapter, several leadership studies link managerial style to group performance and have developed classification systems to depict this relationship. These classifications (or ideal types) are usually viewed as elements on a conceptual continuum ranging from completely autocratic to completely democratic leadership. One popular way to illustrate this range of leadership styles is shown in Figure 11.13. The continuum identifies and differentiates between seven styles based on the degree of managerial authority and group involvement. Given the fact that no style is necessarily superior to another, the most appropriate leadership style will depend on the situation and the criteria used to judge what is considered to be appropriate. If productivity is the criterion, any leader style could be effective. If decisive and quick decision-making is the criterion, a leadership style at the leader-centered end of the continuum might be the best one. If, on the other hand, optimizing group participation is the objective, group-centered styles are much more effective than those emphasizing the unilateral exercise of authority by managers in positions of power. According to Robert Albanese (1981), the value of a particular leader's style must be assessed in terms of the desired outcomes.

Group-oriented leadership—known as participatory management—involves the *consults, joins,* and *delegates* styles and is specifically designed to involve employees in the leadership process. Participatory leaders make a sincere effort to get their subordinates involved in the task of creating and maintaining pro-

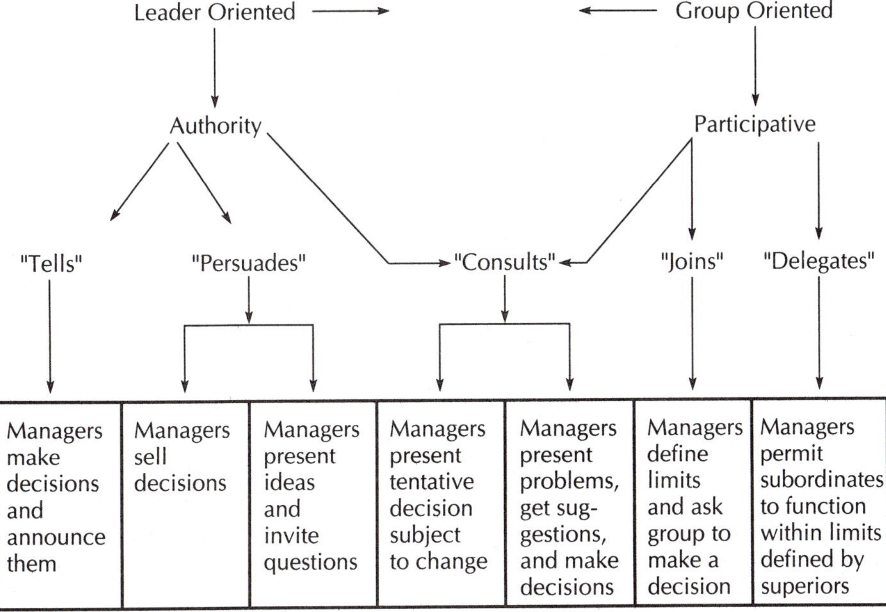

FIGURE 11.13 Seven Leadership Styles. Source Adapted from R. Tannenbaum and W. H. Schmidt, "How to Choose a Leadership Pattern," *Harvard Business Review*, No. 36 (March–April 1958).

ductive work environments. The participatory management model assumes that employees prefer some form of self-governance to autocratic control and that, as achievement-oriented human beings, they have an absolute need to be included in the group decision-making process (Peters and Waterman, 1982).

Management by participation is an essential part of the credo of the organizational humanists (Leonard and More, 1987) and an extension of the human relations school of thought. The implicit assumption is that meaningful participation in the management process meets employee needs, enhances the satisfaction derived from work, and increases organizational as well as individual productivity. (see Focus 11.2, on Effective Followership.) According to the late Douglas M. McGregor (1960), decentralization and delegation are ways of freeing people from the close control of traditional bureaucratic organizations. They give subordinates a degree of freedom to direct their own activities, to assume responsibility, and to satisfy their egoistic needs, which include the following:

1. The needs that relate to the employee's self-esteem, for example, needs for knowledge, for achievement, for self-confidence, for competence, and for independence.
2. The needs that relate to the employee's reputation, for example, needs for recognition, for appreciation, for status, and for the respect by one's peers.

In the right circumstances, participatory management provides employees with sufficient encouragement to direct their creative energies toward organizational goals, gives them a voice in decisions that affect them, and produces significant opportunities for satisfaction of both social and egoistic needs.

The concept of participatory managerial leadership is rooted in the humanistic theories developed by people like Mary Parker Follett ("power with vs. power over" in industrial democracy), Elton Mayo (the Hawthorne effect), Abraham Maslow (the hierarchy of needs), Frederick Herzberg (motivation-hygiene theory), and Douglas McGregor (Theory X and Theory Y). These theories are built on the assumption that an increase in follower participation will usually have a favorable effect on subordinates who have relatively high needs for independence, a readiness to assume responsibility, the necessary knowledge and expertise to deal with problems, and identification with the mission, goals, and objectives of the organization (Eddy et al., 1976).

Participatory management is often touted as the one best way to develop organizational conditions and operational procedures that will motivate individual employees to attain their (social and psychological) goals as they direct their efforts toward achievement of organizational goals and objectives. In fact, some humanist ideologues argue that participatory leadership is the only way to enhance employee satisfaction, performance, and morale in complex organizations. They contend that most people will voluntarily commit to and accept those decisions they helped to make.

The human relations approach to managerial leadership is consistent with American ideals as they relate to equity, democracy, and individual dignity. In a fairly recent study, J. M. Rosow (1979) found that 54 percent of all

FOCUS 11.2

Effective Followership

Transformational leadership is dynamic in that leaders enter into a purposeful and mutually supportive relationship with followers who are activated, motivated, and sustained by it. The challenge for the police chief executive is to help police officers redefine their role and accept responsibility for following in a constantly changing, transformational environment. The key ingredients in developing an effective leadership/followership strategy are

1. Genuine participation
2. Communication
3. Shared decision-making
4. Equity
5. Self-control
6. Interdependence

The transformational approach emphasizes the importance of (1) people, (2) commitment, (3) leadership, (4) fun, and (5) empowerment. Leadership is not the exercise of power, but the empowerment of others to help set and achieve mutually acceptable goals or objectives. Good police administrators cultivate effective followership by creating and nurturing collective ownership of the enterprise based on common culture, shared values, mutual respect, trust, problem-solving, and collaborative risk taking.

SOURCE. Keith M. Rippy, "Effective Followership," *The Police Chief*, September 1990.

Americans feel they have a right to participate in making decisions that affect their job. Sixty-two percent of the younger workers concurred. There is every reason to believe that the demand for worker participation in organizational decision-making will continue to grow. American workers want to be treated as adults and as partners in the search for excellence (Peters and Waterman, 1982).

Organizational humanists have advanced a number of propositions to explain why meaningful participation enhances employee satisfaction and improves performance. Some of those explanations have been synopsized here:

1. Participation leads to a greater understanding and acceptance of managerial decisions by reducing the anxiety and fear normally associated with substantive social change.
2. Participation leads to a greater acceptance of managerial decisions and a personal commitment to implement them efficiently and effectively.
3. Participation leads to a greater understanding of the objectives of a particular managerial decision and the plan designed to achieve those objectives.
4. Participation provides subordinates with a more accurate perception concerning the intrinsic and extrinsic rewards available within the organization.

5. Participation is consistent with the (social and psychological) needs of mature adult subordinates in terms of autonomy, achievement, self-identity, personal growth, and self-actualization.
6. When a work-group decision is made through a collegial process perceived as legitimate, the group itself will pressure individual members to accept the decision and comply with it on a voluntary basis.
7. Group decision-making gives its members an opportunity to engage in collaborative problem-solving that tends to increase teamwork and facilitate continued cooperation.
8. Some participative procedures create an informal bargaining relationship between managers and subordinates in which differences are resolved by mutual concessions.
9. Participation results in better decisions when members of the work group have relevant information and analytical skills not possessed by the leader and are willing to cooperate in making sound decisions (Yukl, 1981).

Humanist police managers attempt to deal with the people-oriented problems of bureaucracy by emphasizing management by participation or team management. They try to create an organizational environment in which subordinates are kept fully informed and given a meaningful role in the decision-making process. These administrators spend much of their time counseling, training, and developing personnel. Humanists embrace change and stress the human relations approach in which their subordinates are treated in an empathetic and supportive manner to enhance morale. Morale is seen as a pathway to efficiency, effectiveness, and productivity.

Once again, the results of the research on participatory management have been mixed. While participation is important, Roy Kaplan and Curt Tausky (1977) believe that the ideological air of organizational humanism has distorted the true relationship between participation and motivation. Some research indicates that participatory leader behavior is most effective when the tasks being performed are ego-involving, ambiguous, and nonroutine (House and Baetz, 1979). Other studies have concluded that participatory management is most effective when subordinates have enough knowledge and competence to make a meaningful contribution to the organization's decision-making process. According to Robert Albanese (1981), the effects of participation on employee satisfaction and performance will depend on the characteristics of the actors, task variables, and situational factors. Consequently, participation should not be considered as a panacea for creating congruence between employee needs and organizational needs. In some situations and for certain types of personnel, participatory leadership techniques might be very effective. In other situations, however, they are definitely inappropriate (Leonard and More, 1987).

Management Systems Model

Participative leadership, as espoused by the human relationists and organizational humanists, is predicated on the fundamental assumption that there is a genuine need for power equalization in the management of complex organizations. They argue that it is absolutely essential to reduce the power and status differential between superiors and subordinates in order to facilitate meaningful participation. The goal is to deemphasize hierarchial authority, to give workers a collective voice in the decision-making process, to encourage a creative response to change, and to overcome apathy by a morale-building approach in which employees become involved with and committed to achieving the organization's mission, goals, and objectives (Wren, 1987).

The late Rinsis Likert was a leading advocate of participatory management. Likert's management systems model represents a continuum of styles ranging from autocratic to participatory. The model contrasts traditional management (Theory X) with democratic managerial leadership (Theory Y). Using the well-known Likert scale to measure attitudes and values, he identified four basic management styles, or climates:

1. Exploitive authoritative	System 1
2. Benevolent authoritative	System 2
3. Consultive	System 3
4. Participative group	System 4

Each of these management systems reflects a different approach to handling major organizational processes like motivation, communication, decision-making, goal setting, coordination, and control (Tansik, Chase, and Aquilano, 1980).

Ronald Lynch explored Likert's climate concept in his book *The Police Manager* (1986). A synopsis of his findings is presented here:

System 1. Management is seen as having no confidence or trust in its personnel and seldom involves them in any aspect of organizational decision-making. Top management makes virtually all decisions, sets goals, and issues policies, procedures, rules, and regulations through the chain of command. Employees are kept in line through the use of intimidation, fear, and manipulation of the reward system. The emphasis is on meeting (what Maslow called) basic and security needs. Managerial contacts with subordinates are often initiated through the disciplinary process in an effort to correct mistakes or misconduct on the part of police personnel. While there are pockets of resistance, the trend in police work is to move away from system 1 and toward the other end of the continuum.

System 2. Management places some degree of confidence and trust in lower level police personnel, but the organization still retains its rigid paramilitary structure. Most decision-making and goal setting takes place at the top and is filtered down through the chain of command. System 2 managers accept some input from lower levels and permit personnel in lower level positions to make some of the less important decisions. Rewards, punishments, and the threat of punishment are used to motivate employees. Managers still inject fear and caution in their employees. While there is some delegation and decentralization, rank-and-file police officers continue to be distrustful of their superiors.

System 3. Police departments utilizing system 3 management exhibit substantial but not total trust between leaders and subordinates. Under this arrangement most decisions are made at lower levels. Effective leaders tend to manage by exception. Policy-making and high-level decisions remain in the hands of top administrators. Communication flows upward and downward. Rewards and occasional punishments are used to motivate personnel. Since there is more and more interaction between leaders and followers, mutual trust and confidence replace fear and suspicion. Both the higher and lower levels feel a responsibility for increasing productivity and maintaining quality. A system 3 managerial style places emphasis on (what Maslow called) the belongingness and self-esteem needs of working police officers.

System 4. The leader behavior and managerial practices associated with system 4 are indicative of the total trust and confidence that middle- and executive-level managers have in their subordinates. Decision-making is widely dispersed and promoted throughout the organization. Communication flows not only up and down within the organization but horizontally among peers as well. Lower level employees get involved in (1) establishing organizational goals, (2) improving on techniques, procedures, and operations, and (3) evaluating the overall success of the organization in accomplishing its mission, goals, and objectives. System 4 managers create a warm and friendly atmosphere in which all levels are fully involved in decision-making and the control process flows from lower units to the top. System 4 leadership is based on empathetic understanding, mutual trust, meaningful participation, and teamwork in very complex influence/interaction structures.

According to Daniel Wren (1987), Rensis Likert's system 4 management style is built on three basic concepts:

1. Supportive relationships
2. Group decision-making and supervision
3. High-performance goals

The principle of supportive relationships means leaders must ensure that each member of the work group views the experience as supportive in that it creates and maintains a sense of personal worth and self-esteem. The second concept (group decision-making and supervision) involves a collective decision-making process in an overlapping group structure by which individual work groups are linked to the rest of the organization through persons who are members of more than one group (these people are known as linking pins). In order to be efficient, effective, and productive, members of the organization must be encouraged to set high-performance goals for themselves. These high-performance goals should be keyed to the employee's personal needs as well as to the needs of others within the work group. System 4 management allows personnel at all levels of the organization to move toward what Abraham Maslow described as self-actualization.

Organizational humanists contend that a system 4 management style improves employee morale and that good morale is the harbinger of increased productivity. They are convinced that leadership styles at the system 1 end of the continuum lead to frustration, dissatisfaction, apathy, and decreased productivity (Albanese, 1981). Likert believed that system 2 management styles are the most common and that the conceptual tools available to many of

CASE STUDY

Chief Martin "Buddy" Strock

Buddy Strock is the chief of police in a small municipal police department in the midwestern United States. He was hired to be a change agent and given a mandate for reform. As the first outside chief in the department's history, he inherited a legacy of suspicion, distrust, and outright hostility. Morale was nonexistent and the local community had lost faith in its nine-person police department.

The chief, a competent, emotionally secure, goal-oriented, and very decisive manager, took immediate action to deal with the chaotic situation. Using emergency powers given to him by the city council and the mayor, Chief Strock fired three veteran officers, suspended a civilian clerk, and put the rest of the employees on notice that they had to pull their load or get out. It was obvious to everyone that the chief was a man with a mission and that he planned to upgrade his department by whatever means necessary. After the smoke cleared, it was obvious that the chief was in charge, and he would determine the rules by which the game would be played.

After the initial flurry of autocratic activity, the chief convened a series of meetings designed to incorporate all of the remaining personnel into the decision-making process. The meetings were held on a regular basis and were designed to reestablish trust through open and honest dialogue. The chief encouraged participation and acted more as a teacher and group facilitator than a dictator. The officers were given an opportunity to help formulate short-term goals and devise strategies for achieving them. Chief Strock made every attempt to strike an appropriate balance between the needs of the department (for efficiency, effectiveness, and productivity) and the physical, psychological, and social needs of his subordinates. He was convinced that his brand of organizational humanism would lead to more efficiency, effectiveness, and productivity.

Things began to fall apart. The officers rejected Chief Strock's efforts to draw them into the decision-making process. They were content to sit back and complain about things as they waited for the chief to fail. They were used to being spectators, not participants in the management process. The officers were paranoid and saw participative management as a setup. They did not want to become scapegoats for the administration.

The mayor and city council also expressed concerns about the social experimentation going on in the police department. They wanted their man to be in charge and viewed participative management as a wishy-washy abdication of authority. The mayor asked Chief Strock to explain what was going on, and the city council demanded a thorough investigation of the police department.

Chief Strock was unable to understand why mature adults acted like a bunch of children. He refused to subject himself to further criticism and resigned. In his letter of resignation, the chief blamed everyone but himself for his failure. He complained that he had not been given a chance to succeed.

Several factors led to Chief Strock's resignation. He made a number of mistakes. What was his most serious miscalculation? What would you—as an aspiring police administrator—have done differently in this particular situation?

today's managers do not fit into the system 4 approach, which most employees now prefer.

Assuming there is a demonstrable link between theory and practice, we would expect to find that most employees find themselves in a system 2 climate. In one recent study of 18 local police departments of various sizes in 15 different states, Charles R. Swanson and Susette Talarico asked 629 uniformed police officers assigned to field duties to describe their department's management climate. The results were interesting and tended to confirm Likert's management systems model. Some 16.6 percent of the officers reported a system 1; 42.9 percent claimed a system 2; 35.9 percent identified their situation as a system 3; and a mere 4.6 percent thought their department used the system 4 approach to management (Swanson, Territo, and Taylor, 1988).

Research on the participation factor has—much like the other theories discussed in this chapter—produced mixed results. There is no reason to believe that participatory leadership is the one best way to manage complex criminal justice organizations. Finding the promised land has been an elusive task. The etiology of effective leadership continues to be a mystery.

Summary

There is absolutely no doubt that leadership plays a pivotal role in organizational dynamics. Police administrators are expected to be leaders as well as managers. Management leadership, as we have called it, is a behavioral transaction that involves influencing, motivating, guiding, and controlling human resources in a cooperative effort to accomplish the organization's mission, goals, and objectives. It is an interactive—achievement-oriented—process through which individual members of the work group are induced to follow a leader and, in so doing, receive psychosocial satisfaction from willingly behaving the way the leader wants them to behave. Part of the task of the leader is to get subordinates to participate in the leadership process.

Many types of people make good leaders. No one leadership style has proven to be effective in all situations. Consequently, management theorists tend to define leadership in terms of their own perspective and/or those aspects of the phenomenon that interest them the most. As we have seen, the concept of leadership has been explored in terms of traits, behavior, style, influence, role, interaction, and situational variables. Five major explanatory paradigms have emerged and dominated the study of leadership, in general, and managerial leadership, in particular. They are the (1) trait approach, (2) leader behavior approach, (3) situational approach, (4) interaction/influence approach, and (5) human relations approach. After more than 50 years of contemplation and applied research, theoretical pragmatists have come to the conclusion that there is no one best way to manage complex organizations.

While participatory leadership is often touted as the ultimate form of management, the situational approach is much closer to reality. When the chips are down, the most appropriate leadership style will depend on the synergistic interaction between the actors, the task, and the environmental factors that coalesced to create the particular leadership situation.

Many management theorists now believe that adaptive leaders—those who are able to change their style of leadership based on the situation and the needs of their subordinates—will be the most effective when it comes to achieving both personal and organizational objectives. They see adaptive management as a pathway to effective police administration in the 21st century.

Key Concepts

Management
Leadership
Managerial Leadership
Task-oriented management
People-oriented management
Knowledge areas
Leadership skills
Eternal triangle
Leadership skill mix
Trait theory
Leader behavior approach
Leadership styles
Leadership quadrants
Managerial grid
Situational leadership
Influence/Interaction system
Contingency management model
Least-preferred co-worker
Path-goal leadership model
Organizational humanism
Participatory management
Management systems model
Adaptive management

Discussion Topics and Questions

1. Define *leadership* and explain its relationship to effective management in complex law enforcement organizations.
2. Why has it been so difficult to identify and describe those leader traits common to effective police managers?
3. What two dimensions of leader behavior were identified in both the Ohio State and University of Michigan leadership studies? What specific terms did they use to describe these particular concepts?
4. Based on the managerial grid, what is 9,9 management and how does it relate to Rensis Likert's system 2 approach?
5. What is the LPC Scale and what does it tell the contingency theorist about the manager who fills it out?
6. Define *interactionist perspective* and explain how it relates to L = f (LP, GP, S).
7. Participatory management and organizational humanism are rooted in human relations theory. Name some theorists who are closely identified with this paradigm.
8. Why do most police officers find themselves working in a system 2 climate?
9. What is adaptive police management and why is it likely to become the dominant approach in the 21st century?

References

ALBANESE, ROBERT. 1981. *Managing: Toward Accountability for Performance*. Homewood, IL: Richard D. Irwin.

Applewhite, Phillip B. 1965. *Organizational Behavior.* Englewood Cliffs, NJ: Prentice-Hall.

Arendt, Hannah. 1958. *The Human Condition.* Chicago: University of Chicago Press.

Barnard, Chester I. 1968. *The Functions of the Executive.* Cambridge: Harvard University Press.

Baron, Robert A. 1983. *Behavior in Organizations: Understanding and Managing the Human Side of Work.* Boston: Allyn & Bacon.

Bennis, Warren G. 1976. *The Unconscious Conspiracy.* New York: AMACOM.

Bittel, Lester R. 1980. *What Every Supervisor Should Know: The Basics of Supervisory Management.* New York: McGraw-Hill.

Blake, Robert R., and Jane Srygley Mouton. 1985. *The Managerial Grid III: The Key to Leadership Excellence.* Houston: Gulf.

Davis, Ralph C. 1940. *Industrial Organization and Management.* New York: Harper and Brothers.

Dessler, Gary. 1979. *Management Fundamentals: A Framework.* Reston, VA: Reston.

Eddy, William B., Warner Burke, Vladimir Dupre, and Oron South. 1976. *Behavioral Science and the Manager's Role.* LaJolla, CA: University Associates.

Fiedler, Fred E. 1964. "A Contingency Model of Leadership Effectiveness." In L. Berkowitz (Ed.), *Advances in Experimental Social Psychology.* New York: Academic Press.

Fiedler, Fred E. 1978. "Situational Control and a Dynamic Theory of Leadership." In B. King, S. Streufert, and F. E. Fiedler (Eds.), *Managerial Control and Organizational Democracy.* Washington, DC: V. H. Winston.

Follett, Mary Parker. 1977. "Leader and Expert," In E. M. Fox and L. Urwick (Eds.), *Dynamic Administration.* New York: Hippocrene Books.

Fulmer, Robert M. 1983. *The New Management.* New York: Macmillan.

Ghiselli, E. E. 1971. *Explorations in Management Talent.* Pacific Palisades, CA: Goodyear.

Gibb, Jack R. 1976. "Dynamics of Leadership." In W. B. Eddy et al. (Eds.), *Behavioral Science and the Manager's Role.* LaJolla, CA: University Associates.

Goode, Cecil E. 1951. "Significant Research on Leadership," *Personnel,* March.

Hersey, Paul, and Kenneth H. Blanchard. 1972. *Management of Organizational Behavior.* Englewood Cliffs, NJ: Prentice-Hall.

Herzberg, Frederick. 1968. "One More Time: How Do You Motivate Employees?" *Harvard Business Review,* January–February.

Holden, Richard N. 1986. *Modern Police Management.* Englewood Cliffs, NJ: Prentice-Hall.

House, Robert J. 1971. "A Path-Goal Theory of Leader Effectiveness," *Administrative Science Quarterly,* 16(5).

House, Robert J., and M. L. Baetz. 1979. "Leadership: Some Empirical Generalizations and New Research Directions." In B. M. Staw (Ed.), *Research in Organizational Behavior* (Vol. 1). Greenwich, CT: JAI Press.

Iannone, Nathan F. 1987. *Supervision of Police Personnel.* Englewood Cliffs, NJ: Prentice-Hall.

Johns, Gary. 1983. *Organizational Behavior.* Dallas: Scott, Foresman.

Kaplan, H. Ray, and Curt Tausky. 1977. "Humanism in Organizations," *Public Administration Review,* 37(2).

Katz, Robert L. 1974. "Skills of an Effective Administrator," *Harvard Business Review,* 52(5).

Kelly, Joe. 1974. *Organizational Behavior: An Existential Systems Approach.* Homewood, IL: Richard D. Irwin.

Kuykendall, Jack L. 1977. "Police Leadership: An Analysis of Executive Style," *Criminal Justice Review,* 2(1).

Kuykendall, Jack L., and Peter Unsinger. 1982. "The Leadership Styles of Police Managers," *Journal of Criminal Justice,* 9.

LeBoeuf, Michael. 1985. *The Greatest Management Principle in the World*. New York: Berkley Books.

Leonard, V. A., and Harry W. More. 1987. *Police Organization and Management*. Mineola, NY: Foundation Press.

Lewin, Kurt, Ronald Lippit, and Ralph K. White. 1939. "Patterns of Aggressive Behavior in Experimentally Created 'Social Climates,' " *Journal of Social Psychology*, 10.

Lewis, Phillip V. 1983. *Managing Human Relations*. Boston: Kent.

Longenecker, Justin G. 1977. *Principles of Management and Organizational Behavior*. Columbus, OH: Charles E. Merrill.

Luthans, Fred. 1977. *Organizational Behavior*. New York: McGraw-Hill.

Lynch, Ronald G. 1986. *The Police Manager: Professional Leadership Skills*. New York: Random House.

McGregor, Douglas, M. 1960. *The Human Side of Enterprise*. New York: McGraw-Hill.

National Advisory Commission on Criminal Justice Standards and Goals. 1973. *Police*. Washington, DC: U.S. Government Printing Office.

Pennsylvania Commission on Crime and Delinquency. *PCCD Quarterly*, Winter 1989–1990.

Peters, Thomas J., and Robert H. Waterman, Jr. 1982. *In Search of Excellence*. New York: Warner Books.

Plunkett, W. Richard. 1983. *Supervision: The Direction of People at Work*. Dubuque, IA: Wm. C. Brown.

Reitz, H. Joseph. 1981. *Behavior in Organizations*. Homewood, IL: Richard D. Irwin.

Rippy, Keith M. 1990. "Effective Followership," *The Police Chief*, September.

Roberg, Roy, R., and Jack Kuykendall. 1990. *Police Organization and Management: Behavior, Theory, and Process*, Pacific Grove, CA: Brooks/Cole.

Rosow, J. M. 1979. "Quality-of-Work-Life Issues for the 1980s." In C. Kerr and J. M. Rosow (Eds.), *Work in America: The Decade Ahead*. New York: D. Van Nostrand.

Schermerhorn, John R., James G. Hunt, and Richard N. Osborn. 1982. *Managing Organizational Behavior*. New York: Wiley.

Schriesheim, Chester A., and Angelo S. DeNisi. 1979. "Task Dimensions as Moderations of Effects of Instrumental Leader Behavior: A Path-Goal Approach." Academy of Management *Proceedings*.

Simon, Herbert A. 1976. *Administrative Behavior*. New York: Free Press.

Souryal, Sam S. 1977. *Police Administration and Management*. St. Paul, MN: West.

Stogdill, R. M. 1948. "Personal Factors Associated with Leadership: A Survey of the Literature," *Journal of Psychology*. Vol. 25, No. 1.

Stogdill, R. M. 1974. *Handbook of Leadership*. New York: Free Press.

Swanson, Charles R., Leonard Territo, and Robert W. Taylor. 1988. *Police Administration*. New York: Macmillan.

Tannenbaum, Robert, and Warren H. Schmidt. 1973. "How to Choose a Leadership Pattern," *Harvard Business Review*, 51(3).

Tansik, David A., Richard B. Chase, and Nicholas J. Aquilano. 1980. *Management: A Life Cycle Approach*. Homewood, IL: Richard D. Irwin.

Thibault, Edward A., Lawrence M. Lynch, and R. Bruce Mcbride. 1985. *Proactive Police Management*. Englewood Cliffs, NJ: Prentice-Hall.

Toffler, Alvin. 1972. *Future Shock*. New York: Bantam Books.

Whisenand, P aul. M. 1981. *The Effective Police Manager*. Englewood Cliffs, NJ: Prentice-Hall.

Whisenand, Paul M., and R. Fred Ferguson. 1978. *The Managing of Police Organizations*. Englewood Cliffs, NJ: Prentice-Hall.

Whisenand, Paul. M., and George E. Rush. 1988. *Supervising Police Personnel: Back to Basics*. Englewood Cliffs, NJ: Prentice-Hall.

Wren, Daniel. 1987. *The Evolution of Management Thought*. New York: Wiley.

Yukl, Gary A. 1981. *Leadership in Organizations*. Englewood Cliffs, NJ: Prentice-Hall.

For Further Reading

ARCHAMBEAULT, WILLIAM G., and BETTY J. ARCHAMBEAULT. 1982. *Correctional Supervisory Management.* Englewood Cliffs, NJ: Prentice-Hall.

A well written text that emphasizes the relationship between motivation and leadership. The authors believe that flexibility is the key to good management. Managers should develop a repertoire of styles and skills and adapt them to the leadership situation.

HOLT, DAVID H. 1987. *Management: Principles and Practices.* Englewood Cliffs, NJ: Prentice-Hall.

Defines leadership as the management function of influencing others to strive toward performance that achieves organizational objectives. A state-of-the-art textbook with comprehensive coverage of the topic.

STEINMETZ, LAWRENCE L., and H. RALPH TODD, JR. 1986. *First-Line Management.* Plano, TX: Business Publications.

A good basic textbook. Discusses the multicratic approach to leader style. The author compares "hard-nosed" management to "no-nosed" management, in which the leader abdicates responsibility and defers to the work group.

CHAPTER 12

Change: Coping with Organizational Life

LEARNING OBJECTIVES

1. Define and explore change as a natural phenomenon in complex criminal justice organizations.
2. Differentiate between planned and unplanned change.
3. Compare and contrast proactive police administrators with reactive police administrators.
4. Describe internal and external forces or pressures that precipitate substantive organizational change.
5. Identify and explain common indicators or symptoms of malfunctioning organizations.
6. Discuss management's role in creating and maintaining a positive climate for planned change.
7. List and discuss the most frequent targets of planned change efforts in complex organizations.
8. Distinguish between the three basic power approaches to planned organizational change.
9. Assess the importance of proactive and participative management in achieving an organization's mission, goals, and objectives.
10. Discuss the three-stage process that leads to permanent personal and/or organizational change.
11. Explain the dynamics involved in almost all successful organizational change efforts.
12. Identify and explore issues related to diagnosis, resistance, implementation, evaluation, institutionalization, and diffusion.
13. Evaluate the need for creating and maintaining a healthy, dynamic equilibrium between stability and change in complex organizations.

We live in a world of kaleidoscopic change. As it is used here, the term *change* refers to any alteration that occurs in the organization of the total

INTRODUCTORY CASE

Mayor Clifford Yarnell

Bill Orion is a traditional Theory X manager who has ruled the Smithton Police Department with an iron fist for the last two decades. The department has an authorized strength of 17 sworn personnel and 3 civilians. A very weak and easily manipulated civil service system has produced a staffing pattern based on political patronage and nepotism rather than merit. Under the existing circumstances, loyalty to the chief is considered more important than developing professional competence in police work. As a result, routine departmental decision-making has been centralized to the point where virtually all decisions are made by the police chief executive. Subordinates are rewarded for subservience not creative problem-solving.

Several incidents have served to focus media attention on problems within the police department. The most recent incident, involving the suicide of a prisoner, has become something of a cause célèbre.

The prisoner—a young man who had been arrested for a relatively minor crime—was placed in a holding cell pending completion of the booking process. The arresting officer observed the prisoner trying to hang himself with a noose made from his own shirt. The officer intervened, took the shirt away, and reported the incident to his immediate supervisor. Sgt. John Caperton talked with the prisoner and concluded that he was emotionally disturbed. Since he did not want to make a decision on how to handle the situation, Sgt. Caperton spent ten minutes on the phone discussing the matter with Chief Orion. When he returned to the holding cell, he found the young man's body. He had hanged himself using a tube stocking attached to a bar in a window opening. It was the second suicide in the holding cell in three months.

According to one political insider, "all hell broke loose!" The dead man's family excoriated the police for failing to provide proper supervision or care for mentally ill offenders, the media clamored for an objective investigation by a neutral third party, and the Smithton city council called on Mayor Yarnell to fire Chief Orion.

If you were the mayor, what would you do in this situation? Why does it often take an incident of this magnitude to precipitate substantive change in complex bureaucratic organizations? What are the most common indicators of the need for planned organizational change? Why is it better to be proactive rather than reactive in circumstances like these?

environment (Fulmer, 1983). According to Alvin Toffler (1972), change is the process by which the future invades our lives and shapes our behaviors. He argues that change is not merely a necessary aspect of life. It is life.

Change is a natural and inevitable manifestation of organizational life. Police departments change on a continuous basis because they are organic and relatively open social systems. They exchange information, energy, and material with various environments (Kast and Rosenzweig, 1985). Police departments are not static structures. They consist of dynamic interrelationships between people performing those functions necessary to achieve the mission, goals, and objectives of the organization. As goals, relationships, and people change, the need for a modification in organizational structure and function increases (Sisk and Williams, 1981). One of the most important measures of an organization's strength is its ability to adapt to and incorporate change.

John R. Schermerhorn and his colleagues (1982) divide organizational change into two basic categories: (1) unplanned change and (2) planned change.

Unplanned change: Change that occurs at random and spontaneously, without the direct intervention of a change agent acting as a catalyst or assuming responsibility for managing the change process.

Planned change: Change that is produced as the result of the intervention of a change agent trying to make things different.

Change agents are individuals and/or groups who act as catalysts and assume responsibility for managing the change process. A change intervention is an intentional action on the part of someone to make things different. Most planned changes are problem-solving efforts initiated by managers acting in their capacity as change agents (see Chapter 9). For all practical purposes, initiating and coping with change is the essence of the modern police administrator's job (Reitz, 1981).

Unfortunately, most substantive organizational change occurs only when managers find themselves under intense pressure to act (Holt, 1987). The hard fact is that most individuals and organizations resist change. *Reactive* police administrators try to keep the department on a fairly steady course. They are wedded to the past and glorify the status quo. They rely on cosmetic changes as they attempt to adjust to new conditions. The problem is that change is synergistic and cumulative. A series of small incremental changes can accumulate to cause a significant alteration in the operation of the organization (Tansik, Chase, and Aquilano, 1980).

Proactive managers, in contrast to their reactive counterparts, are future oriented and much more inclined to embark on a program of planned change. They believe in the systematic approach to initiating and managing organizational change. Planned change involves deliberate actions to alter the status quo. Proactive police administrators set out to change things, to chart a new course rather than maintain the current one. They want to anticipate changes in the environment and to develop ways of dealing with predicted conditions (Tansik, Chase, and Aquilano, 1980).

There is absolutely no doubt that due to the rapidity, intensity, and complexity of change facing law enforcement in contemporary American society, police administrators must learn to utilize as well as understand planned change strategies. Robert Albanese (1981) states flatly that a proactive response to change is a *sine qua non* when it comes to organizational survival, growth, and development (in terms of efficiency, effectiveness, and productivity). Learning how to initiate and manage planned change is one of the most important functions of a manager. Managers in complex criminal justice organizations are no exception. They do not, as a rule, have the option of not initiating and managing substantive change because those organizations that fail to adapt to the changes in their environment almost always fail to accomplish their mission, goals, and objectives (Tansik and Elliott, 1981). While they may not actually disappear, these organizations tend to wither away and die on the vine.

Police administrators face a somewhat paradoxical situation. They must respond to the need for both organizational stability and change. Good managers create and maintain environments that balance the demand for stability and change. They are responsible for maintaining a dynamic equilibrium by diagnosing situations and designing adjustments appropriate for altered or anticipated conditions. Dynamic equilibrium in a healthy police organization consists of the following four dimensions:

1. Enough stability to facilitate the achievement of current goals and objectives.
2. Enough continuity to ensure an orderly change in either goals (ends) or methods (means).
3. Enough adaptability to react appropriately to external opportunities and demands as well as changing internal conditions.
4. Enough innovativeness to allow the organization to be proactive in initiating change when conditions warrant it (Kast and Rosenzweig, 1985).

Whether change is good or bad depends on how it affects the organization. The pace and scope of change is important. There can be too much as well as too little change. From an organizational perspective, change for the sake of change is not a good thing. A police department that is in a constant state of flux will ordinarily be unable to establish and maintain the regularized patterns of collaborative behavior needed to ensure effectiveness.

Forces Influencing Organizational Change

Police administrators face a variety of factors that dictate the necessity for changes in structural relationships and/or organizational behavior. The most important dimension of each factor is the degree to which it can be influenced by the intervention of management. Some problems are easily resolved because the solution is apparent. Others are much more complicated and may well be beyond the control of a particular manager. Good managers concentrate their effort on making needed changes in areas where they have responsibility and in which there is a reasonable expectation of success. Rationality and judgment are critical components in creative problem-solving. Creative problem-solving is a key to the successful implementation of a planned change (Bobbitt et al., 1978).

All organizations are confronted with two basic sources of pressure to change. These sources are usually classified as being either external or internal to the organization. While this distinction is somewhat arbitrary, it provides a fairly convenient basis for discussing forces for change.

External forces. Modern police departments are open systems that take inputs from the environment, transform some of the inputs into public safety services, and send them back into the environment as outputs (Katz and

Kahn, 1978). Like other organisms, police departments consume external resources in order to survive. This means that they must be able to attract resources—such as capital, personnel, equipment, and knowledge—and must be able to market what they produce in the way of services. External sources of change are those factors outside of an organization that modify the organization's ability to attract resources or market its services. These factors include competition and changes in economic conditions, the labor force, public expectations, the physical environment, social norms and values, and legal constraints. Cognizant of these external factors, Shirley Terreberry (1968) argues that an organization's adaptability and survival depends increasingly on its ability to learn and perform according to environmental changes.

Internal forces. The internal sources of pressure to change come from within complex organizations and include conflict, administrative changes, technical changes, and people changes (Leavitt, 1964). A certain amount of intraorganizational conflict is normal and healthy. Under the right conditions, it leads to creative problem-solving and produces adaptive change. Administrative changes involve restructuring the organization or revising policies, procedures, rules, and regulations. Technological changes include new paradigms, methods, tools, equipment, and so forth. People changes are concerned primarily with changes in values, attitudes, motivation, skills, and on-the-job behavior. Since change is both synergistic and cumulative, a change in one area leads to changes in the others. Problems occur in police organizations because many administrators do not recognize the interdependencies of these internal change areas (Tansik and Elliott, 1981).

Technological, Sociocultural, and Organizational Factors

A few of these factors warrant special consideration because they have had a major impact on police organization and management. They are as follows: (1) technological, (2) sociocultural, and (3) organizational.

Technological change has made an enormous impact on American law enforcement (Leonard and More, 1987). The ongoing knowledge explosion has revolutionized modern police work and created a legion of specialists to deal with crime in an enormously complex society. The development and deployment of technology in the guise of hand-held radios, computers, computer-assisted fingerprint identification, offender profiling, infrared surveillance, field drug testing, electronic eavesdropping, voice print analysis, thermo tracking, genetic fingerprinting (see Focus 12.1), forensic odontology, operations research, mechanical speed detection, and so on, has changed policing forever. If the recent past is indicative of the future, today's mind-boggling technology will become obsolete tomorrow. With police work poised to plunge headlong into the 21st century, new police administrators must acquire the skills required to keep up with and manage rapidly escalating technological change (Toffler, 1972).

Profound social and cultural changes are taking place in American society as it moves toward a rendezvous with its future. These changes are reflected in our changing values concerning life, human existence, social equity, productive work, and the government's role in dealing with the revolution in rising expectations. As the population has expanded, it has become increasingly more diverse. It is aging, becoming more ethnically diverse, and much

FOCUS 12.1

State Police Plan DNA Unit

BY CHRISTINE S. TOMSEY

Forensic laboratories continuously search for new technology to help individualize evidence linking victim to perpetrator. Since the advent of fingerprinting, none of the currently used scientific techniques has made a greater impact on supplying this direct link than DNA. What is this powerful tool that one cannot see with the naked eye? Quite simply, DNA (deoxyribonucleic acid) is a molecule that carries with it a "blueprint" of our bodies. It is the genetically controlling material found in the chromosomes of each of our nucleated cells that makes us separate and distinct.

Under a microscope, DNA appears as a tangled mass of string. Distinct areas of that string govern such factors as hair color, eye color, disease factors, or some genetic characteristic. There are also areas of this "thread-like mass" that show marked variations from individual to individual that do not code for a particular function. Research has revealed that the likelihood of any two individuals, except identical twins, having exactly the same variations is extremely remote. Consequently, a technique was developed to identify these variations and serve as a genetic identification. The technique involves extracting the DNA from a blood or semen stain, cutting the DNA into fragments, arranging the fragments according to size, applying a radioactive probe specific to those areas of variability, and ultimately obtaining a banding pattern. These patterns are compared and a statistic assigned to each variant within each probe. These patterns can be computerized and placed into a database for detection of repeat offenders.

This technology far exceeds the current capabilities of serology testing. It is stable much longer than traditional blood grouping systems; has a much greater discrimination; and is detectable in mixtures of fluids. DNA results can indicate the probability of a stain coming from an individual in the one-in-a-million range. It has an even greater impact in rape and rape-homicide cases where the only evidence is a semen sample mixed with vaginal fluid. Traditional serology testing cannot separate these fluids and routinely gives only a one in ten probability.

Court Acceptance

Forensic DNA technology is continuously earning a more secure place in the judicial system. The technology itself has not been successfully challenged and Pennsylvania has had several successful FRYE hearings, which are hearings to determine the acceptability of new scientific technology. In addition, nine state governments (Arizona, California, Colorado, Florida, Iowa, Minnesota, Nevada, Virginia, and Washington) have enacted legislation authorizing data banking of DNA results of convicted sex offenders, and, in varying degrees, of those convicted of other serious felonies. Maryland, Minnesota, Nevada, and Louisiana legislatures have declared it admissible in the courtroom.

The Pennsylvania Commission on Crime and Delinquency has recognized the value of this tool and has provided a grant of Federal Drug Control and Systems Improvement funds to the Pennsylvania State Police to develop a DNA capability. The State Police Laboratory System is establishing a DNA unit in its Greensburg Regional Laboratory. . . .

Upon completion of certification, the DNA unit will open for casework in early 1991. It is the objective of the unit to provide DNA analysis to all local, county and state law enforcement agencies at no cost. ... If demand increases, additional laboratories may become DNA complete.

SOURCE. Christine S. Tomsey, "State Police Plan DNA Unit," Pennsylvania Commission on Crime and Delinquency, *PCCD Quarterly,* Summer 1990.

more litigious in pursuit of social justice. Police departments are beginning to mirror the society at large. Based on changing demographics and Equal Employment Opportunity/Affirmative Action programs, more women and minorities have joined the police service. In some cases, homosexuals are being recruited by urban police departments. More and more of these non-traditional employees are moving into supervisory positions. More women have been elevated to executive positions. All organizations are vulnerable

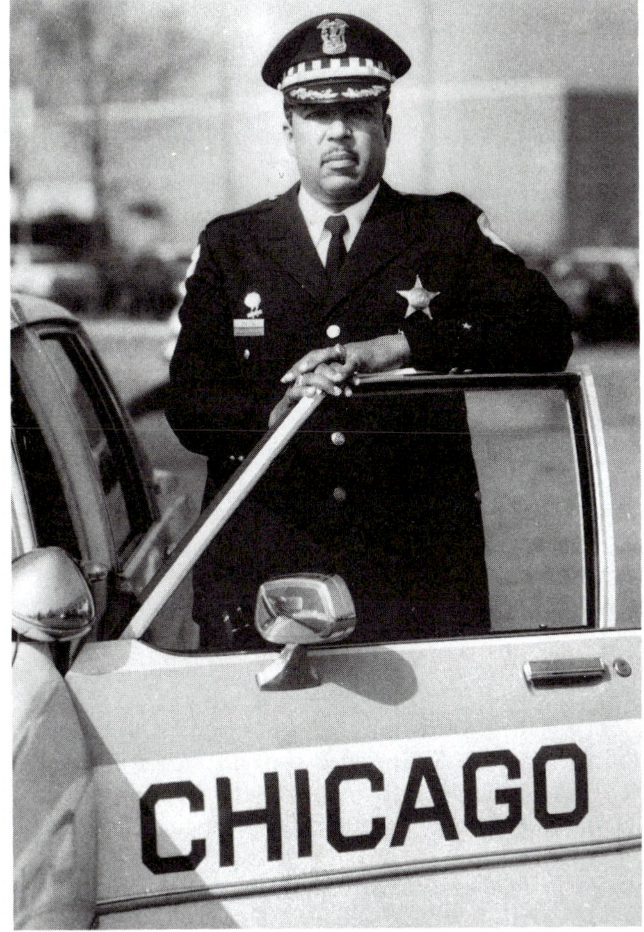

Altering the Status Quo A mind-boggling rate of social change has buffeted American society and altered the composition of many police departments. (©*Steve Kagan: NYT Pictures*)

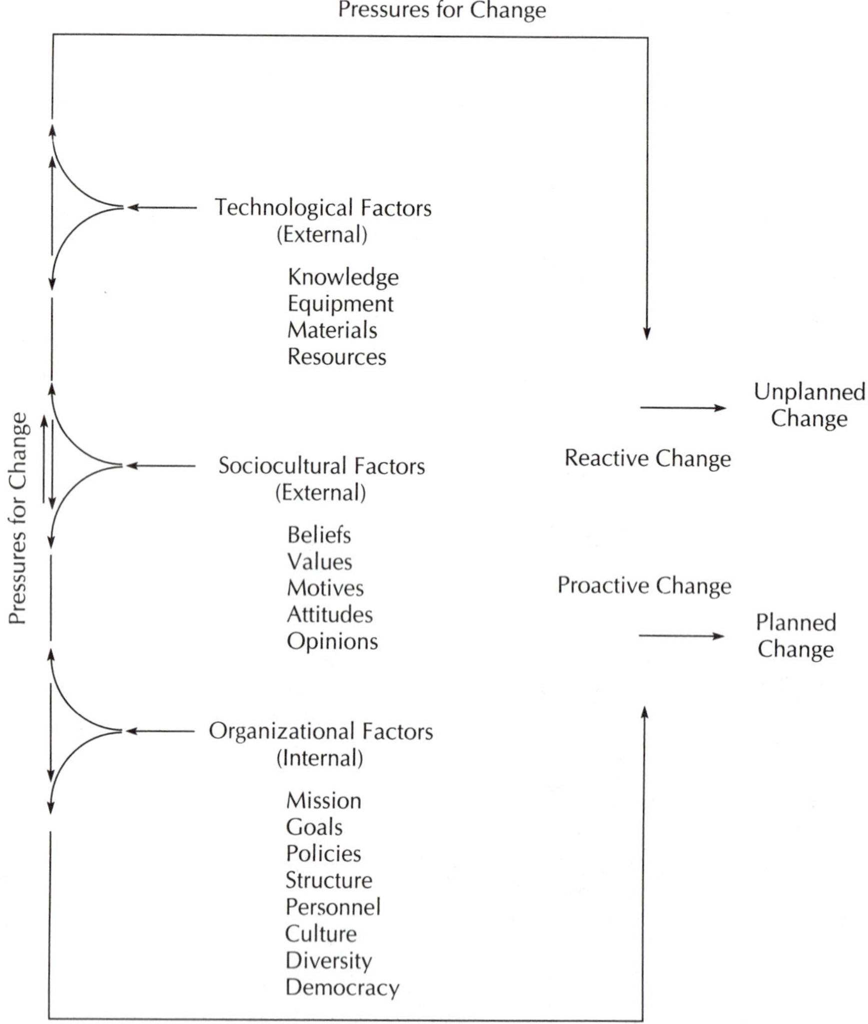

FIGURE 12.1 Forces Affecting the Need for Organizational Change.

to social influence (Hitt, Middlemist, and Mathis, 1979). According to Dan Costley and Ralph Todd (1978), the success of managers in dealing with social change will depend on their sensitivity to rapidly changing values, awareness of the forces that cause change, and their flexibility in adjusting policy and/or organizational style.

The impetus or pressure for organizational change may come from inside as well as outside of the organization (see Figure 12.1). Internal change is often precipitated by administrative changes and/or changes in people.

Administrative pressures come from intentional, managerially induced changes in goals, practices, procedures, policies, deadlines, and reward systems. Newly appointed police chief executives are likely to be enthusiastic, energetic, and proactive in changing things they perceive as creating problems within the organization. They see themselves as managers as well as initiators of change.

Intrapersonal pressures are generated by changes in values, interests, attitudes, skills, motivation, and on-the-job performance. Some of these changes are elicited and reinforced by managers. They are achieved and nurtured through a strong personnel selection procedure, specialized training, and continuous review in the form of performance appraisals. Others occur due to changes in the overall composition of the work force. New and nontraditional employees bring new values, aspirations, and goals with them into the workplace. While hierarchical bureaucracies require individual employees to accept subordinate status within the organization, people today are less willing to be subordinates (Hampton, 1977). Whether managers are ready for it or not, the ethic of participation has spread bottom up across America and is having a radical impact on the way employees expect to be treated by their employers. People whose lives are affected by managerial decisions are demanding a meaningful role in making those decisions. Participatory democracy has seeped into the core of our value system (Naisbitt, 1984). Police officers are the avant-garde of this movement in that they have more education, place far greater emphasis on achieving self-fulfillment, and exhibit an instinctive need to redesign the job or reconfigure organizational relationships in terms of their own values, interests, motives, and abilities (Reitz, 1981).

Internal factors are a powerful force for change in complex criminal justice organizations. The importance of these factors cannot be overestimated.

Most organizational/management theorists subscribe to a synergistic point of view. They contend that a change in any one of the areas just discussed leads to changes in the others. Based on this particular concept, the dynamics that produce change are the same as those in the fabled perpetual motion machine. Consequently, the absence of change is viewed as abnormal under any and all circumstances. The realization that change is a natural and inevitable aspect of organizational life has led to a resurgence of interest in initiating and managing planned change.

Recognizing the Need for Planned Change

Good police administrators are good because they are multidimensional human beings. They have the ability to process large amounts of abstract information and to learn from their own personal experiences. Competent managers possess better than average problem-solving skills. They also exhibit a great deal of flexibility in adjusting their own managerial style vis-à-vis changing conditions. Proactive managers continuously scan the internal as well as the external environment for symptoms calling for some type of organizational change. The remainder of this chapter is designed to create a paradigm that will help police administrators do the following:

1. Recognize the internal indicators that signal the need for some type of planned change.

2. Implement the required change via a planned intervention strategy.
3. Regulate change by monitoring, evaluating, and managing the process.

As stated in Chapter 9, decision-making is a form of problem-solving and is, in fact, the essence of management. Police organizations are not static structures. They are organic in the sense that they are an entity composed of dynamic interrelationships between people performing those functions necessary to achieve the organization's mission, goals, and objectives. As people or goals change, the need for some modification in the organization's structure or function arises. In order for police managers to function effectively in their role as problem solvers, decision makers, and organization change agents, they must perceive problems that exist and have the ability to create solutions to resolve them. Henry Sisk and J. Clifton Williams (1981) have identified four symptoms that are indicative of a malfunctioning organization in need of change through a planned intervention. They are (1) faulty decision-making, (2) failure in functional areas, (3) poor communications, and (4) the lack of real innovation (see Table 12.1).

Faulty decision-making. Decision-making can become too fragmented or slow to take full advantage of situational factors. Erroneous decisions may also create problems. In either case, the difficulty can often be traced back to placement of decision-making authority in the hands of those who, for whatever reason, lack the inclination, information, or expertise needed to make sound decisions. Faulty decision-making is also produced by bureaupathic behavior that insists on a very rigid hierarchical review of all decisions; exaggerated aloofness on the part of those responsible for making major decisions; excessive control in terms of policies, procedures, rules, and regulations; and institutionalized resistance to substantive change (Munro, 1977). Excessive bureaucratization saps police departments of their vitality and leads to inflexibility, indecision, and poor performance.

Failure in functional areas. Inefficiency or failure in any of the major functional areas (like patrol, traffic, criminal investigation, staff services, etc.) should alert perceptive police administrators to organizational problems that require attention in the form of a planned intervention. Poor performance, a reduction in service, and citizen dissatisfaction are symptomatic of organizational malfunction and must be addressed in order to restore functional equilibrium. Functional failure is often rooted in poor personnel selection, inadequate training, ineffective supervision, debilitating internal conflict, or the misallocation of rewards. Without appropriate corrective action, problems like these fester and continue to undermine the organizational health and well-being of the entire police department (Holden, 1986; LeBoeuf, 1985).

Poor communications. It is quite possible that a failure in one functional area may be the result of poor communications between organizational subunits

TABLE 12.1 Indicators of Malfunctioning Organizations

1. Faulty decision-making
2. Failure in functional areas
3. Poor communications
4. Lack of real innovation

as opposed to any deficiency in the functional area itself. Unit alignment and functional interdependence are critical variables in determining the success or failure of any complex criminal justice organization. Good managers strive to prevent articulation problems and try to correct them when, and if, they occur. Their job is to structure, direct, and coordinate the activities of the enterprise as it seeks to accomplish its authorized mission, goals, and objectives (McKinney and Howard, 1979). This would be impossible without effective communication. According to the late Chester I. Barnard (1976), the primary function of management is to establish and maintain a system of internal communication. It holds the organization together and helps keep everyone flying in proper formation.

Lack of real innovation. Bureaucratic organizations tend to become less organic (open and adaptive) and more mechanistic (closed and mechanical) as they mature and begin to age. Ritualistic behavior often displaces innovation (Smith and Preston, 1982). There may be a dearth of ideas concerning new services or new and better ways of performing present functions. Those who venerate the status quo are the most tenacious when it comes to resisting change. When innovation ceases, organizational growth and development cease as well. The lack of innovation is symptomatic of an unhealthy organization (see Table 12.2) and should precipitate a planned intervention designed to remedy the situation.

The presence of any of the symptoms just discussed is cause for alarm and indicates the need for a planned change. Sometimes, as the result of a crisis, routine organizational analysis, or negative feedback about an organization's effectiveness, immediate intervention is required. Emphasis is placed on structural change that can be implemented within a relatively short period. At other times, change is the result of a long-range plan of organizational development designed to strengthen the organization by altering certain aspects of its internal environment. The organizational development (OD) approach is discussed in Chapter 14.

TABLE 12.2 Unwritten Rules That Stifle Innovation in Unhealthy Bureaucratic Organizations

1. *Bureaucrats* must keep their jobs at all costs. You keep the lid on things and create the illusion of productive work by filling days with an assortment of relatively meaningless activities. *Impression management* is the real name of the game.
2. *Bureaucrats* must shield superiors from both criticism and embarrassment. Regardless of your assigned duties, your task is to protect the boss from unpleasant information and demands by outsiders.
3. *Bureaucrats* should spend all allocated funds by the end of the fiscal year (regardless of need). A budget surplus causes problems and makes it difficult to justify an even larger budget for the next year.
4. *Bureaucrats* should keep all existing programs alive regardless of their usefulness. As long as your programs survive, you survive. The organization's formal goals are secondary to those of the bureaucracy.
5. *Bureaucrats* should cultivate friendships with influential people and interest groups outside of government as support for themselves and the organization. Connections are a hedge against unanticipated change.

SOURCE: Matthew Dumont, "Down the Bureaucracy," *Transaction,* No. 7 (1970).

Climate for Change

A climate for planned change is created when recognition of the need for change is coupled with a heightened sense of dissatisfaction and a genuine desire to alter the status quo. Since even the slightest change can be frightening, painful, or disruptive to the employees involved, it must be initiated very carefully and managed with sensitivity. Many well-meaning and necessary organizational changes fail to get off of the ground or achieve what they are expected to achieve simply because police administrators are unable to create a win-win atmosphere that is conducive to substantive change in complex criminal justice organizations.

To become successful change agents, managers must learn to work with people in such a way that their subordinates are psychologically willing to make an effort to change. This is not nearly as easy as it might appear. Good police administrators operate on the following set of assumptions:

1. Change is not something to be feared; planned change is a normal aspect of life in all healthy, goal-oriented organizations.
2. Any change process involves not only learning something new, but unlearning what has already been integrated into one's personality and social relationships.
3. No substantive change is likely to occur unless there is motivation to change and, when motivation is lacking, instilling that motivation is usually the most difficult part of the process.
4. Substantive changes in power, authority, structures, processes, and systems occur only as the result of individual change in key members of the organization.
5. Substantive change requires the alteration of values, motives, and attitudes as well as behavior.
6. Lasting change is the product of a multistage process or cycle of behavior modification.
7. Managers activate the planned change process and are responsible for coordinating, directing, and regulating the pace of the process (Schein, 1980).

It is the police administrator's job to create a positive atmosphere for change by demonstrating that the rational planning of change is superior to and far less risky than seat of the pants decision-making (More, 1977). Police officers will be more inclined to take the ambiguity, confusion, and fear associated with change in stride if they are allowed to participate in the process and learn to perceive change as an opportunity as opposed to a threat (Whisenand and Rush, 1988).

After reviewing a number of research studies, Ronald Corwin (1972) identified several factors that portend success in planned change efforts. He contends that an organization can be changed more easily if the following conditions are present:

1. If the organization attracts many liberal, creative, and unconventional outsiders with fresh perspectives.

2. If these outsiders are exposed to creative, competent, and flexible socialization agents.
3. If managers are young, proactive, supportive, and generally competent.
4. If the organization's structure is decentralized as well as complex.
5. If the organization has sufficient revenue to create a financial cushion to lessen the cost of innovation.
6. If members of the organization are sufficiently secure and protected against the status risks associated with change.
7. If the organization is located in a modern, dynamic, and urban setting in close proximity to other progressive organizations that can supplement its skills and resources.

Police departments differ in terms of the degree to which these conditions are met. They run the gamut from tenaciously resisting change to openly embracing it.

The success or failure of a planned change effort can usually be traced back to the attitudes of those to be affected by the change. In any proposed change, police officers must be convinced they will benefit from the change or at least not be adversely affected by it. A history of fair, honest, and competent management lays a foundation for trust and the acceptance of change (Chruden and Sherman, 1976).

Targeting Change

Managers can, at least in theory, change just about any aspect of the organization they wish. Since change is such a broad concept, however, it is useful to identify those areas in which planned change has been most common.

Goals and strategies. Organizations are often compelled to change their goals and the strategies used to reach them in an effort to adapt to major changes in the external environment. Many police departments, for example, are moving away from the law enforcement model and are placing more emphasis on crime prevention through community-oriented policing.

Technology. Technological change, depending on the applicability of the innovation, can vary from minor to major. DNA fingerprinting has the potential to revolutionize modern law enforcement when it comes to identifying, apprehending, and successfully prosecuting criminals.

Job Design. Jobs can be redesigned and enriched in order to offer more variety, autonomy, identity, significance, feedback, and self-fulfillment. The police agent concept focuses on the development and deployment of generalists instead of specialists.

Structure. Structure may be modified in an effort to enhance efficiency, effectiveness, and productivity. Many police departments are revising their policies, procedures, rules, and regulations to broaden the span of control and decentralize decision-making.

People. The membership of an organization can be changed in terms of its (1) composition (through hiring and firing) and (2) skills and attitudes (via

CASE STUDY

Captain John C. Holleran

"J.C." Holleran is an administrative captain in a large municipal police department. The department is heading into a budget deficit and must reduce costs or cut services. Capt. Holleran has been ordered by the deputy chief of police to find ways to reduce the amount currently being spent on personnel. They have tentatively agreed to seek a 10 to 15 percent across-the-board reduction in personnel costs.

Adopting the shared power perspective inherent in participatory management, Capt. Holleran formed a deficit reduction task force to analyze the available data, determine the cause or causes of the problem, and recommend appropriate solutions. The task force consisted of managers and rank-and-file police officers appointed by the collective bargaining agent (union). The task force was authorized to access all of the department's financial data. After extensive deliberations, the task force formulated a cost-containment plan in lieu of recommending cuts in service.

The task force's cost-containment plan called for a temporary freeze on all hiring, restrictions on overtime, a minimal reduction in court-time reimbursement, and expansion of the telephonic complaint reception/screening program. Once the specifics of the plan were reduced to writing, Capt. Holleran and Deputy Chief Ray Runion met with union leaders as well as the chief in order to elicit support for the proposal.

During the briefing, Chief Bear asked a series of questions. He wanted to know the following:

1. Who was most likely to be affected by the proposed changes.
2. How employees, the department, and the public would be affected by the proposed changes.
3. What kind of resistance could be expected if the proposed changes were put into effect.
4. What strategies could be used to minimize resistance to the proposed changes.
5. What the odds are of achieving the projected savings in personnel costs.

He asked Capt. Holleran to prepare a position paper outlining answers to these questions.

Assume that you are Capt. Holleran. Prepare a position paper for submission to Chief Bear. Address each of his concerns to the best of your ability. Use the information presented in this chapter as the basis for your narrative.

training). Professional police departments, like almost all other successful organizations, have developed sophisticated personnel systems and emphasize the importance of training (Johns, 1988). Nearly every state has enacted comprehensive legislation establishing minimum qualifications for police personnel and mandating extensive job-related training.

The choice of what to change and how to change it is up to management and depends, in large measure, on the analysis of the internal as well as the external factors that signal there is a need for some kind of change.

Three Basic Approaches to Planned Organizational Change

The power to effect change in complex goal-oriented organizations has been analyzed by Larry E. Greiner (1967). He found that managers ordinarily use one of three basic power alternatives, or approaches, when it comes to initiating substantive organizational change. He arranged them on a continuum ranging from unilateral through shared to delegated. The continuum and its relation to subordinate participation is illustrated in Figure 12.2. Professor Greiner described his three approaches to organizational change in the following way:

1. *Unilateral Power*
   A. *The decree approach.* A one-way policy announcement originating with a person in a position of authority and passed on to those at lower levels.
   B. *The replacement approach.* People occupying one or more key positions are replaced with other individuals on the assumption that substantive organizational changes are a function of the new manager's ability.
   C. *The structural approach.* Instead of issuing a decree or injecting new blood into work relationships, upper-level managers reorganize in or-

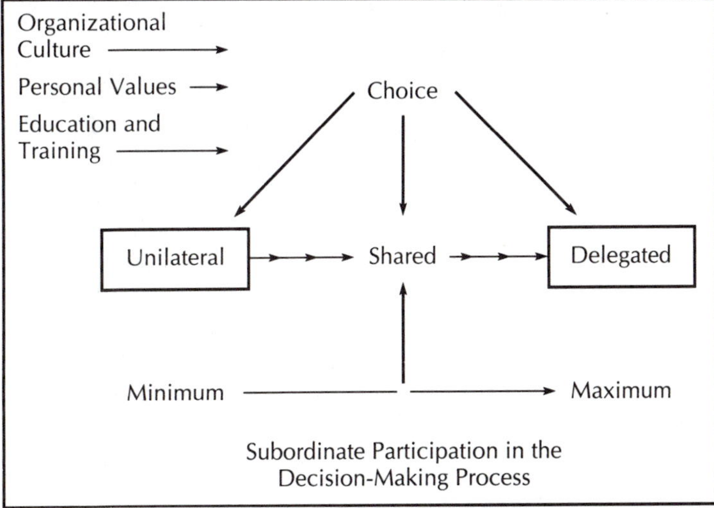

FIGURE 12.2 Greiner's Power Approaches to Change. Source Adapted from David A. Tansik, Richard B. Chase, and Nicholas J. Aquilano, *Management: A Life Cycle Approach* (Homewood, IL; Richard D. Irwin, 1980).

der to initiate changes in required relationships and elicit new behavior from existing personnel.

2. *Shared Power (Participation)*
   A. *The group decision approach.* Participation by members of the work force is limited to selecting a preferred alternative from an array of alternatives determined in advance by management.
   B. *The group problem-solving approach.* Work groups within the organization are encouraged to help identify real problems and construct viable solutions to them through the dynamics of the group problem-solving process. This is the essence of participatory management.
3. *Delegated Power*
   A. *The data discussion approach.* Once a problem has been identified, the work group is permitted to develop its own analysis of data (from survey findings, consultant reports, etc.), to construct an array of alternatives, to choose the best solution, and to implement that solution (or change) in an attempt to solve the problem.
   B. *The sensitivity training approach.* Sensitivity training places emphasis on achieving organizational change through improvements in employee self-awareness. It is based on the assumption that changes in work patterns and/or work-based relationships follow changes in each employee's interpersonal relationships.

There is no one best approach to introducing planned change in complex organizations. From a contingency perspective, any one of the three might be appropriate depending on the circumstances. A unilateral approach may be appropriate in chaotic situations or when timing is a critical factor. Delegation may be appropriate for dealing with other problems. More often than not, it is the middle-of-the-road shared power approach that civilian managers are finding most useful (Dessler, 1979).

The Winds of Change

Due to the paramilitary nature of policing, there has been (and in all probability will continue to be) heavy reliance on the use of unilaterally imposed change. Top police administrators, by virtue of their accountability for the efficient and effective operation of the department, still insist on playing a key role in defining, determining the need for, and directing planned change. Even so, it is now clear that more and more police administrators are beginning to recognize the value and appropriateness of the shared power approach (Albanese, 1981). Police officers are certainly adaptable to change and accept it readily when they become actively involved in the decision-making process (More and Wegener, 1990).

The Process of Planned Change

Change involves a sequence of psychological adjustments, behavioral adaptations, or organizational transformations that occur over time. Most modern views concerning planned change involving individuals in organizations can be traced back to the work of Kurt Lewin (1951) and Edgar H. Schein (1961). They both argue that all planned change is produced as the result of a very basic three-stage process. The three stages involve (1) unfreezing the status quo, (2) moving to a new state, and (3) refreezing the new state in order to make it permanent (see Figure 12.3).

Unfreezing. Unfreezing occurs when there is dissatisfaction with the status quo and a felt need to alter the current state of affairs. Unfreezing generally involves the realization that the existing technology, job design, or structure is ineffective or that the attitudes or skills of employees are no longer appropriate. Support for current values and behavior is withdrawn. The old way is no longer desirable or acceptable given the circumstances. Unfreezing is often precipitated by a crisis of some kind. It may, on the other hand, be produced as the result of a routine organizational analysis. Good managers utilize organizational analysis to scan the internal and external environments for potential problems and initiate planned change before a crisis occurs (Robbins, 1989).

Moving. Moving (change) occurs when driving forces overcome restraining forces and a program or plan is initiated by the change agent to introduce different attitudes and behaviors into the vacuum created during the unfreezing of the status quo. These change efforts range from minor to major. Significant change takes place only when members of the work force identify with and accept new ideas, approaches, and relationships (Fulmer, 1983). The mere introduction of change does not ensure the elimination of the prechange condition or the permanence of that change.

Refreezing. Change must be internalized. Internalization is the social/psychological process of trying, adopting, and becoming committed to new attitudes or behaviors. Without some type of positive reinforcement, newly acquired attitudes and behaviors cannot become a permanent part of the individual's normal repertoire. According to Stephen Robbins (1989), refreezing involves stabilizing the change by balancing both driving and restraining forces.

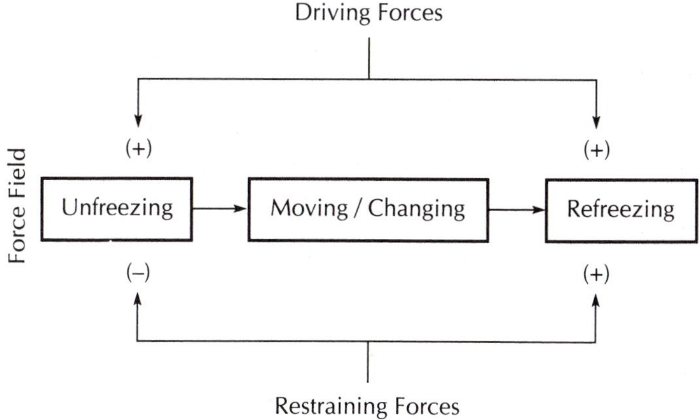

FIGURE 12.3 Planned Change Process.

The mechanics of planned change are the same for organizations as they are for people because changing people is the critical variable in changing the structure and/or function of any complex criminal justice organization.

Police management training is a very good example of the planned change process. Trainers (on behalf of the police chief executive) facilitate the unfreezing process by inducing a certain amount of stress in trainees to create a felt need for change. Trainees are then exposed to new ideas, values, and skills. Moving begins when these newly introduced ideas, values, and skills are given credence by the trainees and get translated into new forms of behavior. Once new ideas, values, skills, and behaviors elicit appropriate reinforcements in terms of internal or external rewards/punishments, the refreezing process takes over. Trainees accept, identify with, and internalize the change. As a result, it is incorporated into their personality structure. It also becomes a recurrent, predictable, and intrinsically rewarding aspect of their on-the-job behavior.

While there is great value in being aware of and understanding the dynamics involved in unfreezing-moving-refreezing theory, good police administrators know that using this knowledge effectively requires a tremendous amount of skill. As Robert Fulmer (1983) has pointed out, planned change happens easier and faster in a textbook than it does in the mind of the person or organization being changed. As illustrated in Focus 12.2, the manager/change-agent concept is applicable to small and mid-sized departments as well as large urban law enforcement agencies.

Dynamics of Planned Organizational Change

Based on a study of successful planned change in a number of complex organizations, Larry E. Greiner (1967) developed a comprehensive model to explain the dynamics involved in the process. Greiner's model consists of six steps or phases:

Phase 1. Pressure on and arousal of upper-level management to take some action. Top management perceives the need, or pressure to change something. This pressure is ordinarily caused by a significant problem or problems like a sharp decline in performance, labor unrest, deteriorating community relations, corruption, and so on.

Phase 2. Intervention by a respected person (acting in the capacity of a change agent) and reorientation to the internal problem. Outside consultants are often brought in to define the problem and to help members of the organization focus on it. In other situations, internal staff members who are trusted and considered to be experts may be assigned responsibility for attacking a particular problem.

Phase 3. Diagnosing the data and identification of the problem. Information is gathered from a variety of sources. The information is analyzed by the change agent and others with responsibility for initiating and managing planned change in the organization. The real problem is defined in concrete terms.

FOCUS 12.2

Current Theory on Police Management—A Book Review

CIZANCKAS, V. I., AND D. G. HANNA. 1977. *MODERN POLICE MANAGEMENT AND ORGANIZATION.* ENGLEWOOD CLIFFS, NJ; PRENTICE-HALL.

Written by two working police chiefs, this text provides a critical examination of the American police, police organizational change, and effective management of police services. Offered as an alternative to traditional police management practices, it focuses on aspects of organization that have received relatively little attention in small- and medium-sized police agencies in America. In the first section, the authors address the process of change. They criticize traditional police management, offer alternatives, and provide a precise analysis of the problems that the American police face and the possible solutions for these problems. The second section presents several case studies of police organizational development. Studies are drawn from Menlo Park (CA), Ohio State University, Charlotte (NC), and St. Petersburg (FL). In the final section, the authors deal with controversial police problems—citizens' complaints, police secrecy, police cynicism, police corruption, police brutality, public relations, role of women officers, police discretion, and others. Some of the police management subjects in the book are basic change strategies, managing police resources, organizational change considerations, team concept, effective police organization, and the police manager as a change agent.

SOURCE. National Institute of Law Enforcement and Criminal Justice, *Police Management* (Washington, DC: U.S. Department of Justice, 1978).

Phase 4. Development of a number of creative alternatives as well as an organizational commitment to action. Successful change agents stimulate thought and avoid using the same old methods. Participatory problem-solving is encouraged. Subordinates who are allowed to participate in making decisions that affect them will, in all probability, be much more committed to the course of action that is finally selected.

Phase 5. Experimentation with various alternatives and the analysis of results. The creative solutions developed during the previous phase are pilot tested on a limited scale and evaluated in terms of their effectiveness prior to implementation on an organization-wide basis. The structure of large police departments lends itself to this type of exploration.

Phase 6. Reinforcement from results and acceptance of the planned change. If the course of action has been tested and found to be valid, it is likely to be more willingly accepted by those to be affected. As an organization improves, the improvement—in and of itself—functions as a reinforcer and fosters a continuing commitment to planned change. This process is outlined in Figure 12.4.

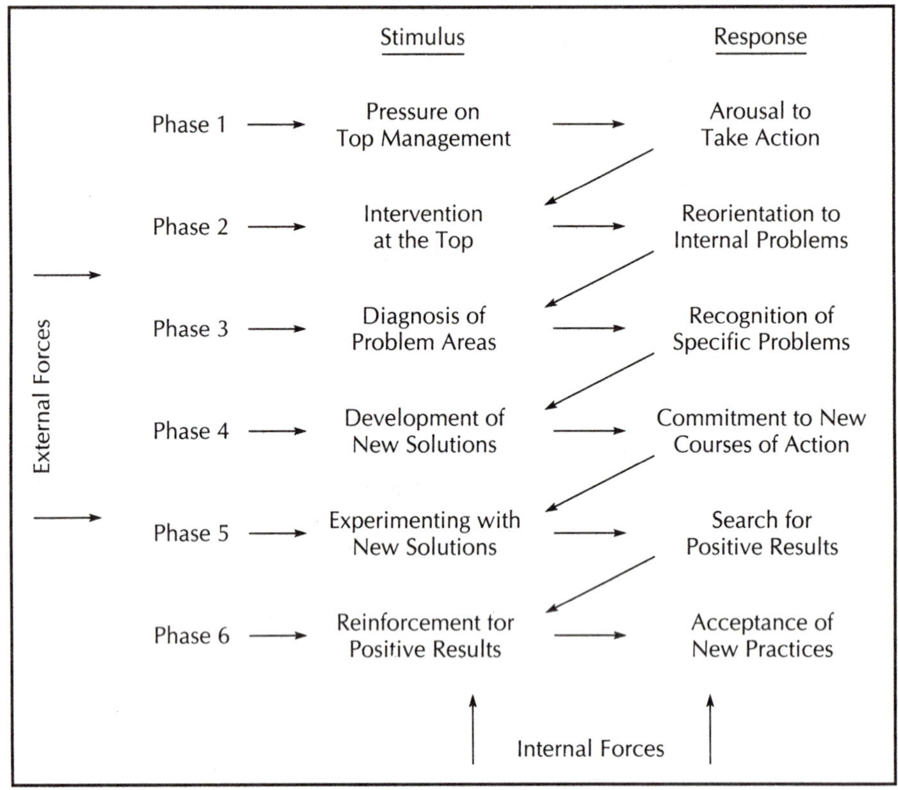

FIGURE 12.4 Dynamics of Planned Change. Source Adapted from Larry E. Greiner, "Patterns of Organization Change," *Harvard Business Review*, No. 5 (1967).

Greiner's model provides police administrators with a convenient checklist approach to planned change. It is complete and presented in a logical, sequential order that reflects reality (Tansik, Chase, and Aquilano, 1980).

Too many managers are inept when it comes to dealing with planned change. They venerate the status quo and actively resist change. Due to their personal biases and lack of managerial skill, they fall back on comfortable courses of action fitted to the past. Preexisting solutions seek problems irrespective of the real problem. This type of tunnel vision creates and exacerbates organizational problems. Poor police administrators are part of the problem instead of being part of the solution.

Issues in the Planned Change Process

According to Gary Johns (1988), several very important issues must be confronted during the change process. They represent problems that must be overcome if the process is going to become more effective. The issues relate to (1) diagnosis, (2) resistance, (3) implementation, (4) evaluation, (5) institutionalization, and (6) diffusion. We discuss each of these issues in turn.

Diagnosis

The very first step in any planned change effort is to diagnose the real problem, and this step is often missed (Dessler, 1979). The accurate diagnosis of organizational problems serves two crucial functions. First of all, diagnosis provides information that contributes to unfreezing by showing all of those concerned that the problem does, in fact, exist. Secondly, once the unfreezing takes place, further diagnosis helps clarify the problem and suggests the type of change that is required. It is one thing to feel that police officer morale has fallen dramatically but quite another to be sure that it is true and to develop an effective intervention strategy designed to resolve the problem. Accurate diagnosis ensures that managers have the opportunity to deal with root causes rather than mere symptoms.

Diagnosis takes various forms and can be performed by a variety of individuals. Routine problems (requiring change) are best handled by those in the existing chain of command. In the event that the problem is nonroutine and/or complex, police administrators may be ahead to seek specialized diagnostic help from a change agent. Change agents, whether they are on staff or come from outside of the agency, bring an independent, objective perspective to the diagnosis while working with those who are to undergo change. Diagnosis involves analyzing the organization, recognizing performance deficits, and identifying problems. Diagnosticians acquire their information from a variety of sources: (1) observations, (2) interviews, (3) questionnaires, and (4) record review. Careful diagnosis is a critically important factor in the success or failure of any planned change effort. If the diagnosis is done properly, it clarifies the problem, indicates what needs to be changed (in terms of technology, structure, or people), and suggests the appropriate strategy for implementing the change with a minimum of resistance.

Resistance

People are hedonistic creatures of habit. As a result, they tend to resist both unfreezing and change. At the unfreezing stage of the process, defense mechanisms may be used to deny or rationalize away the signals that substantive change is needed. Even when there is some agreement that change is necessary, any particular plan or program may be rejected. It takes a great deal of hard work and skill to achieve consensus when change is involved.

Police officers resist change when they fear the costs associated with the change outweigh its benefits to them. This resistance takes many forms and ranges from simply ignoring something to open rebellion. Resistance can be rational or emotional. Robert Albanese (1981) believes there are four basic reasons why people openly resist change:

1. *Parochial self-interests.* Individuals see themselves as being in a position to lose something of value as the result of the proposed change.
2. *Misunderstanding/lack of trust.* People who do not fully understand the implications of the change or have a lack of trust in management tend to perceive change as being more costly than beneficial to them.

3. *Different assessments.* Employees affected by the proposed change may have a totally different perspective than managers who plan to implement a change and feel that management is making a mistake.
4. *Low tolerance for change.* Some people are obsessed with maintaining the status quo and are unable to cope with the ambiguity generated by change.

Resistance to change is not necessarily bad. It gives managers the opportunity to reevaluate the situation. Resistance is often a red flag signaling that something is going wrong. It may indicate there is a need for better communication or better strategy for initiating and managing organizational change.

It appears that the best way to minimize resistance to change is to create an environment in which those to be affected by the change are permitted to participate in the decision-making process. According to Kenneth Benne and Max Birnbaum (1969), the effectiveness of any particular planned change is directly related to the degree that members at all levels of the organizational hierarchy take part in fact-finding and diagnosing needed changes. This strategy should also help increase commitment to the change by giving those involved in the decision-making the ownership of the change process. Good police administrators have learned to share power with employees in order to effect substantive organizational change.

Implementation

In American society, decisions have traditionally been made at the higher levels and articulated downward through the bureaucratic chain of command. Change strategies have ordinarily followed a similar pattern. This approach assumes that a few top executives make unilateral decisions without involving lower level managers or nonmanagement employees. While this Theory X approach to management is onerous to all organizational humanists, it may be absolutely necessary in emergency situations, in unusually complex organizations, or in those cases where employees are either incapable of or refuse to play any major role in the organizational decision-making process.

Comprehensive change normally requires a top-down initiative. The two main advantages of this approach are speed and breadth of change. Since relatively few people are involved in the decision-making, decisions can be made in a timely manner and communicated quickly to the lower levels of the organization. This process sets in motion a change strategy that carries great weight and is capable of reaching deeply into all aspects of the organization (Holt, 1987). There are drawbacks to the top-down approach, however. Unilateral decision-making by top managers may alienate employees, lower morale, reduce productivity, and increase the risk of disruption if members in the lower ranks question the need for or reject the planned change. Unilateral decision-making tends to create a one-dimensional work force and sets the stage for an increase in intraorganizational conflict. The absence of participation (based on management's compulsive need to control) is symptomatic of an unhealthy organization.

A new management paradigm has been developing in this country. As a result, more emphasis is being placed on bottom-up problem solving, decision-making, and initiation of change. The philosophy of organizational humanism, along with its commitment to shared governance and participatory management, is beginning to find its way into complex criminal justice organizations. Progressive police departments are moving toward classic Theory Y management styles. Everything indicates that Mary Parker Follett (1973) was right when she predicted there would be movement toward democratization in the workplace. This trend was confirmed by Thomas Peters and Robert Waterman (1982) in research for their widely acclaimed bestseller, *In Search of Excellence*.

In the bottom-up approach, top management makes organization-wide policy and encourages people to make those operational decisions that directly affect their own work. Well-managed organizations that encourage bottom-up changes are human relations oriented and emphasize the importance of creativity within the work group. Managers strive to reduce anxiety and eliminate fear for employees who make suggestions, change their approach to work, or seek to alter the way things are done (Holt, 1987). There are drawbacks as well as advantages. The process is time consuming and slow. In addition, lower level employees may be unwilling to expend the time, effort, or energy necessary to make this approach work.

Managing change through shared responsibilities is a comprehensive approach in that it consolidates the best aspects of both top-down and bottom-up processes. Top management provides leadership, support, and coordination; lower level managers and nonmanagement personnel—working in diagnostic problem-solving groups—make and implement operational change decisions. Team and community policing are both steps in this direction.

Evaluation

For all practical purposes, evaluation has been the weak link in most planned change efforts. This is particularly true when it comes to plans or programs that are designed to change attitudes or improve interpersonal skills through human relations training programs. Under ideal circumstances, plans for evaluation of the change effort should be built into the process during the diagnostic phase. Effective evaluation protocols are almost always designed to assess the following factors as they relate to the planned change:

1. *Reactions.* Do the participants like or dislike the basic change? To a degree, reactions measure resistance to and provide managers with feedback concerning change.
2. *Learning.* What knowledge or skill was acquired as a result of the planned change effort? Newly acquired data help activate unfreezing and may precipitate substantive interpersonal or organizational change.
3. *Behavior.* What changes in job-related behavior have occurred as a result of the planned intervention? Behavior reflects movement and refreezing.
4. *Outcomes.* What changes in performance and productivity have occurred? Outcomes clearly indicate whether or not the change (in structure, technology, or people) is useful to the organization (Catalanello and Kirkpatrick, 1968).

Unfortunately, many evaluations of planned change efforts never go beyond the measurement of reactions. Sometimes the change effort is only ritualistic, and there is simply no motivation to measure its impact on the organization or the people in the organization. Some managers are afraid of evaluation. They fear reprisals if the change effort fails.

Institutionalization

As we indicated, organizational change is manifested in new behavior and outcomes. If the outcome of a planned change effort proves favorable to a police department, the administration may wish to institutionalize that particular change. This means that members of the organization are socialized to accept, identify with, and internalize the change. As a result, the change becomes a permanent part of the department's culture. It is translated into a sociocultural fact that persists over time despite inevitable turnover by those who originally conceived, initiated, implemented, or experienced that change. The psychosocial dynamics of institutionalization are exactly the same as those involved in other forms of learning. Whether or not a planned change is accepted and passed on from one generation to the next is a function of intrinsic rewards and strategic reinforcement.

The degree of effort required to institutionalize a given change will depend on the nature, scope, and complexity of the change involved (Shanahan and Whisenand, 1980). Some changes are relatively innocuous and fall within just about everyone's zone of acceptance. They are implemented and become permanent fixtures of the organizational landscape with little or no real scrutiny. Making and institutionalizing substantive change is an altogether different matter. The status quo always has a constituency. Broad-based organizational change calls for commitment and may require great sacrifices by those concerned. Unless it is nurtured and carefully managed, the change may be cosmetic and life will go on as usual.

Studies of complex change efforts reveal that a number of different factors can inhibit the institutionalization of a planned change. According to Gary Johns (1988), the institutionalization process may fail to work if the following conditions exist:

1. Promised extrinsic rewards (such as pay increases, promotions, etc.) are not developed to accompany the change.
2. The initial change provides intrinsic rewards that create higher expectations which cannot be fulfilled.
3. Newly hired personnel are not carefully socialized to understand the unique environment of the changed organization.
4. Key management supporters of the change effort retire, resign, or are transferred to new assignments.
5. External pressures cause managers to back off, revert to familiar behavior, and abandon the change effort.

It is management's responsibility to remove the roadblocks to planned change. Good police administrators learn to anticipate the threats to institutionaliza-

CASE STUDY

Chief Charles S. Ahern

Charles Ahern, a veteran law enforcement officer, has been chief of the Johnson County Police Department for a little over three years. This county is in a border state and part of a major metropolitan area. With an authorized strength of 272 sworn officers and 37 civilians, it is one of the largest law enforcement agencies in a six-county megalopolis.

The Johnson County Police Department has long been considered to be one of the most professional police organizations in the state. It has an excellent pay scale and attracts top-notch personnel. As a result, the department has been able to avoid most of the problems and almost all of the criticism leveled at other large police departments in the area. In fact, Chief Ahern was recently elected to serve as the third vice president of the nation's most prestigious professional law enforcement association.

Since personnel complaints were few and far between and the JCPD had never experienced a bona fide case of corruption, management adopted a fairly casual attitude concerning internal discipline. Although it violated generally accepted standards, supervisors in the normal chain of command were assigned to investigate personnel complaints lodged against their own subordinates.

When a high-ranking police official was indicted on a RICO (or racketeer-influenced corrupt organization) charge related to drug trafficking, it became obvious that there was a glitch in the system. It was clear there was no objective mechanism to investigate and resolve allegations of corruption. Due to the magnitude of the case and the heat it generated, Chief Ahern realized that corrective action (in the form of a planned change) was required.

Chief Ahern contacted the executive director of the International Association of Chiefs of Police (IACP) and arranged for its consultants to come in. Their job was to define the problem and help members of the department focus their attention on it. After reviewing the available data, analyzing the organization, and comparing the JCPD with departments of similar size, the consultants recommended creation of an internal affairs unit.

A representative task force was formed and assigned to work with the IACP consultants in an effort to develop structural models congruent with the department's culture. After exploring several different configurations, the task force constructed a model similar in both its structure and function to the one recommended by the National Advisory Commission on Criminal Justice Standards and Goals. The commander of the internal affairs unit was to report directly to the chief, and unit personnel would remain outside of the normal chain of command. According to the model, the internal affairs unit would investigate all personnel complaints (including corruption) and make recommendations concerning disciplinary action to the chief police executive.

The Internal Affairs Unit became an operational component of the JCPD per Executive Order 6734. It was later upgraded to division status.

Identify the six phases in the dynamics of a successful organizational change. Are they all accounted for in the case study? If not, which are missing?

tion and plan programs or strategies to overcome them. Being forewarned is forearmed!

Diffusion

Many planned change efforts begin as limited experiments or pilot projects in one unit, section, or division of an organization. This is a cautious and reasonable way for management to ascertain what will or will not work given situational constraints. If the change effort produces a desirable outcome, it might be appropriate to diffuse it by institutionalizing the same change in other parts of the organization. Diffusion is based on the assumption that it makes little or no sense to keep reinventing the wheel.

Diffusion is not quite as simple as it might appear. In a pioneering study of the diffusion process associated with major change efforts in eight large corporations, Richard Walton (1975) found that while all of the pilot projects were considered to be successful, diffusion occurred in only one case. He identified several factors that may account for this poor track record:

1. Lack of commitment and support by top-level management.
2. The setting or technology of the pilot project differs significantly from other elements of the organization.
3. Attempts to diffuse specific techniques rather than goals that can be tailored to other situations.
4. Management reward systems that place emphasis on traditional performance measures while ignoring successes at initiating, implementing, and managing planned change.
5. Union resistance to expanding negotiated exceptions designed to accommodate the original pilot project.
6. Fears that pilot projects begun in nonunionized areas might be implemented in unionized portions of the organization.
7. Conflict between the pilot project and the bureaucratic structures in the rest of the organization.

Without diffusion, many change-oriented innovations are bound to fail.

Summary

Change is a natural and inevitable aspect of organizational life. Police administrators are expected to cope with spontaneous change as well as to initiate, implement, manage, and evaluate planned change in their departments. Proactive managers are future oriented. They are inclined to change things and chart new courses of action. In order to be effective, proactive managers anticipate change and are prepared to adapt to it. In order to be successful as change agents, managers must understand the internal (organizational) as well as external (environmental) factors pushing for change. Good administrators pay special attention to technological, sociocultural, and organizational factors.

Managers must know how to recognize the need for change. Faulty decision-making, functional failure, poor communications, and the lack of innovation should be considered red flags. It is up to management to determine who or what to target for change. They also choose how to effect the change. The shared power approach to organizational problem-solving is gaining in popularity.

No matter which approach is used, the basic change process is the same. Successful change requires unfreezing, movement to a new state, and refreezing the change to make it permanent. The dynamics of planned change involve pressure on and arousal of top management to take action; intervention by a respected person; diagnosing the data and identifying the real problem; developing creative alternatives; experimenting with the alternatives; and reinforcing the results.

In order to be effective change agents, police administrators must work on their diagnostic skills. Identifying the right problem is half the battle. Good managers reduce resistance to change by incorporating subordinates into the problem-solving process whenever it is feasible. The unilateral imposition of planned change is being abandoned in favor of a combined top-down/bottom-up approach. Participatory management has become one of the most influential concepts in contemporary management theory.

Police administrators have a responsibility to assess the impact of a planned change in terms of member behavior and organizational outcomes. If changes in behavior or outcomes are beneficial, they should be institutionalized through positive reinforcement techniques. Once refreezing has taken place, all changes must be passed on to others through the organization's socialization process. Modern police managers need to acquire an understanding of and appreciation for their role in the change process. One thing is certain: Police administrators will be spending more of their time initiating, implementing, and managing planned change during the next decade.

Key Concepts

Change
Planned change
Change agent
Reactive management
Proactive management
Internal forces
External forces
Driving forces
Restraining forces
Interpersonal factors
Administrative factors
Dynamic equilibrium
Resistance to change
Climate for change
Scanning
Symptoms/Indicators
Diagnosis
Targeting change
Creating alternatives
Group problem-solving
Approaches to change
Change process
Dynamics of change
Participatory management
Institutionalization

Discussion Topics and Questions

1. Define *change*. Explore the difference between spontaneous change and planned change. Which occurs most often?
2. What is a change agent? Why are proactive managers considered to be change agents? Explain your reasoning.
3. What are the characteristics of a police organization that is in a state of dynamic equilibrium when it comes to change? Be specific.
4. List and discuss the forces or pressures that precipitate the need for planned change in complex criminal justice organizations. Identify those that warrant special consideration.
5. Identify and describe the four basic symptoms of a malfunctioning organization. What role does perception play in this process?
6. When does a positive climate for planned change exist? What does willingness have to do with it? How would you hedge your bet to ensure that the planned change takes root and is institutionalized?
7. Identify the target areas in which planned change has been the most common. Describe each of these areas. Who is ultimately responsible for determining what is to be changed and how it is to be changed?
8. Why is the shared power approach to change ordinarily superior to the other two approaches? What are the mechanics of this process? Give one or two examples.
9. Describe the unfreezing, moving, and refreezing process as it relates to organizational change as well as changes in personal behavior. Illustrate this process through the use of examples.
10. What are the six phases normally associated with any successful organizational change? Elaborate on each one and show their dynamic relationship to one another.
11. What is the first step in any planned change effort? What two functions does it serve?
12. Why do so many people resist substantive change in the workplace? If resistance is not all bad, what function or functions does it serve?
13. Why do good police administrators try to consolidate the very best aspects of top-down management with bottom-up management? What are the practical advantages in terms of efficiency, effectiveness, and productivity?
14. What factors should be used to evaluate the success or failure of a planned change effort? Which two are the most important from a management point of view? Why?
15. Explain why institutionalization is so critical in any planned change effort. What factors tend to inhibit the refreezing process? Why is early recognition of these factors so important? Give an example to illustrate your point.

References

ALBANESE, ROBERT. 1981. *Managing: Toward Accountability for Performance*. Homewood, IL: Richard D. Irwin.

BARNARD, CHESTER I. 1976. *The Functions of the Executive*. Cambridge: Harvard University Press.

BENNE, KENNETH D., and MAX BIRNBAUM. 1969. "Principles of Change." In Warren G. Bennis, Kenneth D. Benne, and Robert Chin (Eds.), *The Planning of Change*. New York: Holt.

BOBBITT, H. RANDOLPH, ROBERT H. BREINHOLT, ROBERT H. DOKTOR, and JAMES P. MCNAUL. 1978. *Organizational Behavior* (2nd ed.). Englewood Cliffs, NJ: Prentice-Hall.

CATALANELLO, R. F., and D. L. KIRKPATRICK. 1968. "Evaluating Training Programs: The State of the Art," *Training and Development Journal,* No. 22.

CHRUDEN, HERBERT J., and ARTHUR W. SHERMAN, JR. 1976. *Personnel Management* (5th ed.). Chicago: South-Western.

CORWIN, RONALD G. 1972. "Strategies for Organizational Intervention: An Empirical Comparison," *American Sociological Review,* No. 8.

COSTLEY, DAN L., and RALPH TODD. 1978. *Human Relations in Organizations*. New York: West.

DESSLER, GARY. 1979. *Management Fundamentals: A Framework* (2nd ed.). Reston, VA: Reston.

DUMONT, MATTHEW. 1970. "Down the Bureaucracy," *Transaction,* No. 7.

FOLLETT, MARY PARKER. 1973. "The Illusion of Final Authority." In Elliot M. Fox and L. Urwick (Eds.), *Dynamic Administration*. New York: Hippocrene Books.

FULMER, ROBERT M. 1983. *The New Management* (3rd ed.). New York: Macmillan.

GREINER, LARRY E. 1967. "Patterns of Organizational Change," *Harvard Business Review,* No. 3.

HAMPTON, DAVID R. 1977. *Contemporary Management*. New York: McGraw-Hill.

HITT, MICHAEL A., R. DENNIS MIDDLEMIST, and ROBERT L. MATHIS. 1979. *Effective Management*. New York: West.

HOLDEN, RICHARD N. 1986. *Modern Police Management*. Englewood Cliffs, NJ: Prentice-Hall.

HOLT, DAVID H. 1987. *Management Principles and Practices*. Englewood Cliffs, NJ: Prentice-Hall.

JOHNS, GARY. 1988. *Organizational Behavior: Understanding Life at Work* (2nd ed.). Boston; Scott, Foresman.

KAST, FREMONT E., and JAMES E. ROSENZWEIG. 1985. *Organization and Management: A Systems and Contingency Approach* (4th ed.). New York: McGraw-Hill.

KATZ, DANIEL, and ROBERT L. KAHN. 1978. *The Social Psychology of Organizations* (2nd ed.). New York: Wiley.

LEAVITT, HAROLD J. 1964. "Applied Organizational Change in Industry: Structural, Technical and Human Approaches." In W. W. Cooper, H. J. Leavitt, and M. W. Shelly (Eds.), *New Perspectives in Organization Research*. New York: Wiley.

LEBOEUF, MICHAEL. 1985. *GMP: The Greatest Management Principle in the World*. New York: Berkley Books.

LEONARD, V. A., and HARRY W. MORE. 1987. *Police Organization and Management* (7th ed.). Mineola, NY: Foundation Press.

LEWIN, KURT. 1951. *Field Theory in Social Science*. New York: Harper & Row.

MCKINNEY, JEROME B., and LAWRENCE C. HOWARD. 1979. *Public Administration: Balancing Power and Accountability*. Oak Park, IL: Moore.

MORE, HARRY W. 1977. *Criminal Justice Management*. St. Paul, MN: West.

MORE, HARRY W., and W. FRED WEGENER. 1990. *Effective Police Supervision*. Cincinnati: Anderson.

MUNRO, JIM L. 1977. *Administrative Behavior and Police Organization*. Cincinnati: Anderson.

NAISBITT, JOHN. 1984. *Megatrends: Ten New Directions Transforming Our Lives*. New York: Warner Books.

NATIONAL INSTITUTE OF LAW ENFORCEMENT AND CRIMINAL JUSTICE. 1978. *Police Management* (Bibliography). Washington, DC: U.S. Department of Justice.

Peters, Thomas J., and Robert H. Waterman, Jr. 1982. *In Search of Excellence: Lessons from America's Best-Run Companies.* New York: Warner Books.

Reitz, H. Joseph. 1981. *Behavior in Organizations.* Homewood, IL: Richard D. Irwin.

Robbins, Stephen P. 1989. *Organizational Behavior: Concepts, Controversies and Applications* (4th ed.). Englewood Cliffs, NJ: Prentice-Hall.

Schein, Edgar H. 1961. "Management Development as a Process of Influence," *Industrial Management Review,* No. 5.

Schein, Edgar H. 1980. *Organizational Psychology* (3rd ed.). Englewood Cliffs, NJ: Prentice-Hall.

Schermerhorn, John R., James G. Hunt, and Richard N. Osborn. 1982. *Managing Organizational Behavior.* New York: Wiley.

Shanahan, Donald T., and Paul Whisenand. 1980. *The Dimensions of Criminal Justice Planning.* Boston: Allyn & Bacon.

Sisk, Henry L., and J. Clifton Williams. 1981. *Management and Organization* (4th ed.). Cincinnati: South-Western.

Smith, Ronald W., and Frederick W. Preston. 1982. *Sociology: An Introduction* (2nd ed.). New York: St. Martin's Press.

Tansik, David A., Richard B. Chase, and Nicholas J. Aquilano. 1980. *Management: A Life Cycle Approach.* Homewood, IL: Richard D. Irwin.

Tansik, David A., and James F. Elliott. 1981. *Managing Police Organizations.* Monterey, CA: Duxbury Press.

Terreberry, Shirley. 1968. "The Evolution of Organizational Environments," *Administrative Science Quarterly,* No. 4.

Toffler, Alvin. 1972. *Future Shock.* New York: Bantam Books.

Tomsey, Christine S. 1990. "State Police Plan DNA Unit," *PCCD Quarterly,* Summer.

Walton, Richard E. 1975. The Diffusion of New Work Structures: Explaining Why Success Didn't Take," *Organizational Dynamics,* No. 3.

Whisenand, Paul M., and George E. Rush. 1988. *Supervising Police Personnel: Back to the Basics.* Englewood Cliffs, NJ: Prentice-Hall.

For Further Reading

Broderick, John J. 1987. *Police in a Time of Change* (2nd ed.). Prospect Heights, IL: Waveland Press.

> Good analysis of change at the personal and organizational level. The author applies basic concepts to changes in law enforcement. He maintains that the pressure to change is not pressure to change from one static organizational form to another, but the pressure to change and to keep changing as the situation warrants.

Certo, Samuel C. 1986. *Principles of Modern Management: Functions and Systems* (4th ed.). Boston: Allyn & Bacon.

> Explores change from a practical perspective. The author offers specific guidelines for reducing resistance to change. He discusses what can be changed in relation to structural factors, technological factors, and people. The thesis is that managers who can make changes successfully are highly valued in organizations of all types. The evaluation of change may increase the organizational benefit derived from that change.

Mondy, R. Wayne, Arthur Sharplin, Robert E. Holms, and Edwin B. Flippo. 1986. *Management: Concepts and Practices* (3rd ed.). Boston: Allyn & Bacon.

Well-written chapter on organizational culture, change, and development. Authors outline the change sequence and discuss the value of participatory management in facilitating change efforts. Identifies specific sources of resistance to change and approaches to reducing that resistance. Moves on to a good discussion of organizational development (OD).

CHAPTER **13**

Conflict: Nature, Causes, and Management

LEARNING OBJECTIVES

1. Define and discuss the nature of human conflict in complex criminal justice organizations.
2. Describe the dynamics of the collaboration–aggression continuum.
3. Contrast intergroup conflict with interpersonal conflict in organizational settings.
4. List and discuss the recognizable steps involved in the conflict development cycle.
5. Distinguish the historical phases of management thinking as it relates to organizational conflict.
6. Identify and discuss the most common causes of conflict in complex organizations.
7. Differentiate between functional conflict and dysfunctional conflict.
8. Describe the conflict management strategies and techniques that are applicable to police work.
9. Describe the management styles that evolved in response to the need for conflict resolution.
10. Define *contingency management* and *economic humanism* as they relate to conflict management.
11. Describe the structure and function of employee assistance programs (EAPs).

Human behavior is diverse and varies tremendously in terms of its interpersonal dimensions. Viewed on a continuum, it ranges from collaboration at the positive end to overt aggression on the negative side (see Figure 13.1). Collaboration exists when mutual assistance is emphasized and personal antagonisms are kept to a minimum in an effort to help members of a group accomplish their collective goals. *Cooperation* is a basic form of interaction in

INTRODUCTORY CASE

Chief Anson Weller

Anson Weller is 54 years old. He is a high school graduate who worked his way up through the ranks at the Harmerville Police Department. Weller has been the chief of police since 1975.

Harmerville is a relatively small, economically depressed town in what is known as the rust bucket area of the northeastern United States. The department's authorized strength is 15 (FTE, or full-time equivalent) police officers. Most of the officers are part time. Chief Weller is the only command officer. The department's only sergeant, Nick Pason, is in charge of the night shift.

Chief Weller is, and always has been, an autocratic Theory X manager. He runs an incredibly tight ship and has been dubbed "Captain Hook" because of his propensity to fire people. The city council has always acquiesced and rubber-stamped these personnel actions even though some of them were of questionable legality.

While there has always been an undercurrent of discontent within the department, most officers kept their complaints to themselves for fear of being fired. Some officers have become much more vocal over the last couple of years.

Some newly hired part-time officers openly criticized the chief's methods and—as a group—urged their colleagues to unionize under the State Labor Relations Act. They also discussed the situation with the executive director of the Fraternal Order of Police. The FOP expressed an interest in organizing the work force in the department. In order to focus public attention on the issue, the FOP leaked the story to a friendly reporter. The banner headline said it all:

POLICE MORALE PLUMMETS, OFFICERS WANT UNION PROTECTION.

The chief was livid. He denounced the unionists as radicals who were trying to destroy the police department. After an internal investigation, Chief Weller fired two of the part-time officers for conduct unbecoming an officer and actions detrimental to the welfare of the department. After a rancorous public hearing in which both sides impugned the motives of the other, the city council upheld the dismissals. Conflict between the chief and his subordinates continued unabated and got progressively worse.

The FOP filed an unfair labor practice charge with the State Labor Relations Board (SLRB). The SLRB ruled that Chief Weller had, in fact, interfered with the lawful activities of his employees. It ordered its staff to determine if there was sufficient interest to hold an election to select a collective bargaining agent. An election was held and the employees voted unanimously to affiliate with the FOP. The city and the FOP are now in the process of negotiating the first collective bargaining agreement (CBA). Chief Weller is not actively involved in the negotiating process.

Chief Weller and his employees are still at odds with each other. There is no end in sight as far as personal animosity goes. The chief has vowed, on a number of occasions, to "bust the union." Union members continue to attack the chief as a petty dictator who should be forced out of office. While much of this vitriolic rhetoric is designed to influence the ongoing negotiations, it is clear that the conflict is far from over.

What kind of social dynamics were involved in this conflict situation? How would you classify the chief's basic philosophy vis-à-vis his reaction to the conflict? Identify the different stages in the development of this conflict episode. What do you feel could have been done by the chief to deal with this conflict before it got out of hand?

which two or more individuals coordinate their behavior in order to achieve a particular objective. *Competition* emerges when individuals attempt to maximize their own advantage while disadvantaging others. Mutual assistance and personal antagonism are both low in healthy competitive situations. *Conflict* arises in those situations where someone or something has thwarted or is about to thwart someone else's goals. *Aggression,* on the other hand, is produced as the result of conflict. It is intentional or unintentional behavior that is designed to injure the people or things perceived to be the source of the conflict (Baron, 1983). This chapter examines the nature, causes, and management of conflict in complex criminal justice organizations.

Interpersonal Conflict

Conflict within an organization can be described as the breakdown or disruption of normal activities to a point where individuals and/or groups experience real difficulty in working with one another (Reitz, 1981). In a general sense, interpersonal conflict is a condition in which two or more people have a mutual difference of opinion involving scarce resources, perceptions, values, and goals, where there is behavior or threat of behavior through the exercise of power to control the situation or gain something of value at the expense of the other participants (Roark and Wilkinson, 1979). Conflict is a

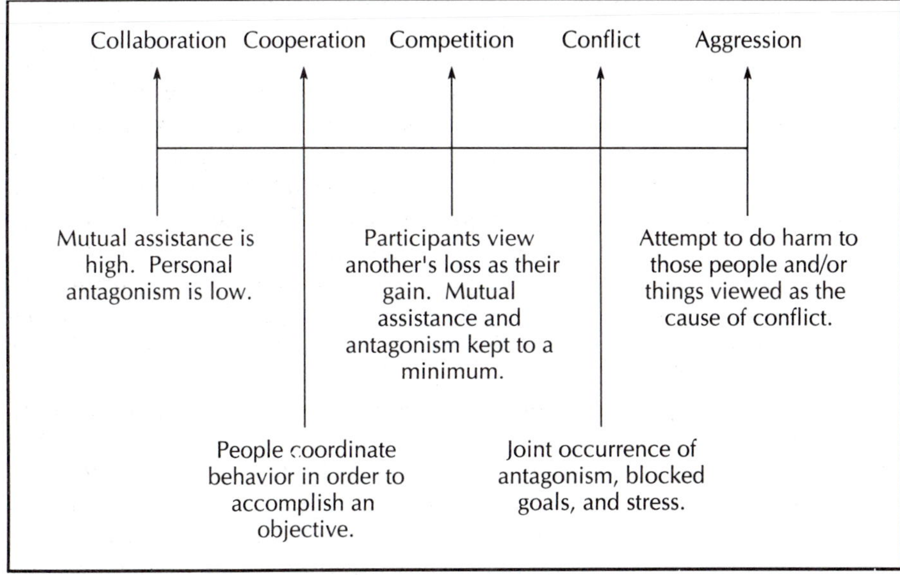

FIGURE 13.1 Collaboration–Aggression Continuum.

process in which an effort is purposely made by one person or a group of people to offset the efforts of others through some sort of blocking action designed to frustrate them in achieving goals or furthering their interests (Robbins, 1989). Conflict begins once one party perceives another person or group has frustrated or is about to frustrate them in an area they consider to be important (Thomas, 1976).

Conflict is built into human nature and exacerbated by intergroup dynamics. It is a pervasive and perhaps inevitable part of our human existence (Swanson, Territo, and Taylor, 1988). In order to be successful managers, police administrators must learn to understand conflict and develop the skills needed to manage it. This is not an easy task. In fact, learning how to deal effectively with conflict is one of the most challenging aspects of any manager's job.

Types of Interpersonal Conflict

Behavioral scientists who specialize in the study of social interaction have identified the following three distinct types of interpersonal conflict:

1. *Conflict between individuals.* Probably the most common type of conflict is conflict between individuals. Some people simply dislike one another. There is, in fact, a personality conflict. Some of these so-called personality clashes are rooted in and nurtured by various role conflicts, however. The two people in conflict tend to disagree with each other concerning role expectations and/or appropriate performance. The intensity of the conflict will depend on the issues, the personality of people involved (in terms of intellect, problem-solving skills, mental health, etc.), internal inhibitions, external constraints, and situational variables.

2. *Conflict between individuals and groups.* Conflicts can also occur between individuals and the groups they interact with. These clashes are normally precipitated by differences in opinion concerning appropriate norms, values, ethical orientations, and behaviors. Individuals who violate group-shared expectations are usually isolated, punished, and labeled as deviant. Conflict over work norms creates special problems. Most work groups establish informal yet binding norms that prescribe certain behaviors and prohibit others. When a person falls short of or exceeds the norms established by the group, social distance is increased. Offenders may be excluded from group-related social activities or cut off from the informal communication process (known as the grapevine). This eliminates a very important source of job satisfaction. If there is a serious conflict between individual behavior and group norms, the group will do everything within its power to change the individual's "deviant" behavior. Here again, the intensity of the conflict will depend on a wide variety of different factors.

3. *Conflict between groups.* American society represents a collage of multiform informal as well as formal social groups interacting with each other as they pursue their own goals and objectives. Each social group develops an identity in terms of its specialized task, function, structural configuration, location, size, and degree of cohesion. As indicated in Chapter 7, all social groups develop a unique personality based on racial, ethnic, and cultural considerations. Task-oriented work groups generate their own distinct culture built on a foundation of shared beliefs, values, attitudes, interests,

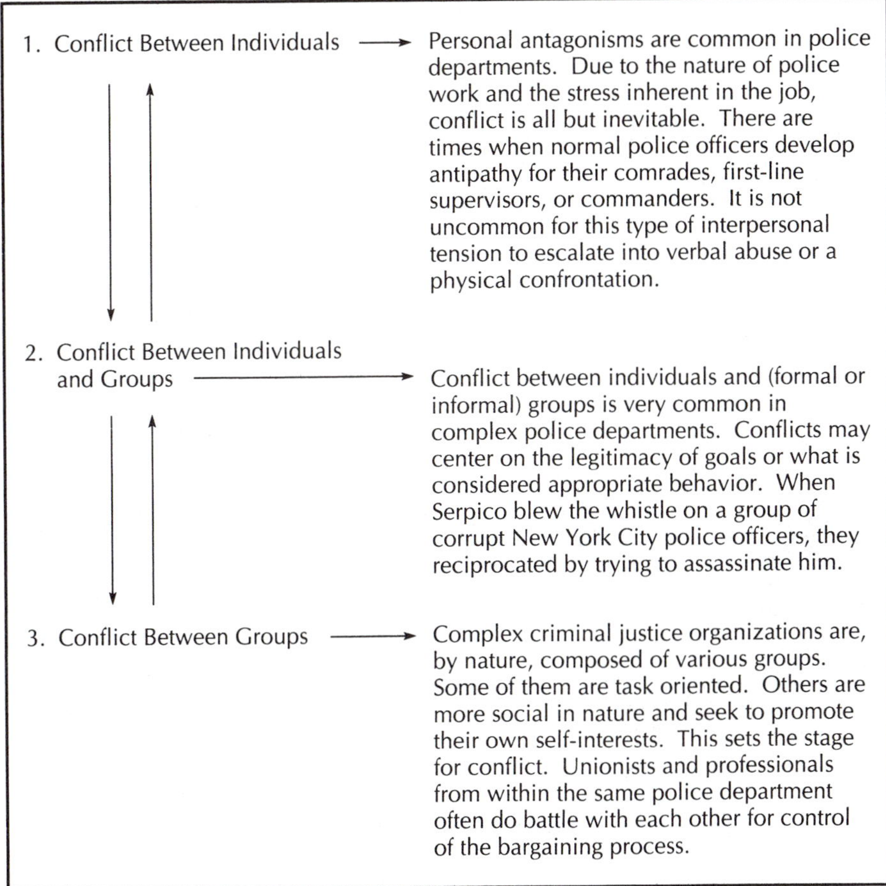

1. Conflict Between Individuals
Personal antagonisms are common in police departments. Due to the nature of police work and the stress inherent in the job, conflict is all but inevitable. There are times when normal police officers develop antipathy for their comrades, first-line supervisors, or commanders. It is not uncommon for this type of interpersonal tension to escalate into verbal abuse or a physical confrontation.
2. Conflict Between Individuals and Groups
Conflict between individuals and (formal or informal) groups is very common in complex police departments. Conflicts may center on the legitimacy of goals or what is considered appropriate behavior. When Serpico blew the whistle on a group of corrupt New York City police officers, they reciprocated by trying to assassinate him.
3. Conflict Between Groups
Complex criminal justice organizations are, by nature, composed of various groups. Some of them are task oriented. Others are more social in nature and seek to promote their own self-interests. This sets the stage for conflict. Unionists and professionals from within the same police department often do battle with each other for control of the bargaining process.

FIGURE 13.2 Types of Interpersonal/Intergroup Conflict.

and behavioral norms. As a particular group becomes more cohesive, the differences between it and other social groups tend to be accentuated. This often leads to polarization between competing groups. The polarization of competing groups in the same sociocultural milieu (a society, a nation, or an organization) almost always sets the stage for destructive intergroup conflict. As indicated in Focus 13.1, the nature, extent, and intensity of the conflict will depend on the specific issue in dispute, relative group strength, collective rationality, internal control mechanisms, leadership, external constraints, and situational variables (Holt, 1987).

Police work is an extraordinarily complex goal-oriented human activity and, as such, provides a natural habitat for all three types of interpersonal/intergroup conflict (see Figure 13.2).

As we noted, conflict is a disruptive situation between two or more individuals (or groups of people) stemming from substantive disagreements over scarce resources, beliefs, values, attitudes, goals, or normative behavioral expectations. Conflict is ubiquitous. It is also endemic to human nature. From an organizational point of view, conflict is antithetical to development of the collaboration that is needed to achieve collective goals and objectives. The

FOCUS 13.1

FOP Chief Disputes City Police Complaint Data

BY CLARK HALLAS

The president of the Fraternal Order of Police has accused the Department of Public Safety of issuing misleading statistics on complaints against police officers and the number of current police who have poor disciplinary histories.

Lt. Patrick McNamara, head of the FOP's Fort Pitt Lodge, said Friday that Public Safety Director Glenn Cannon has refused to release to him the names of police officers whose disciplinary histories were cited in a Pittsburgh Press article July 22. The officers were not identified.

The article cited complaint figures provided by the department's Office of Professional Responsibility which indicated that several officers still in uniform have had a pattern of drawing complaints, either from citizens or superiors, throughout their careers.

The OPR figures showed the 26 officers have been the subject of five or more complaints during their careers and that one of them had 25 complaints, only one of which was upheld after an internal investigation.

In the story, Cannon said the statistics reinforced the need for a revised trial board procedure, which is the subject of current negotiations between the department and FOP.

"I don't know where they're coming up with these figures," McNamara said. "My records don't show anywhere near the number of complaints or disciplinary actions." The union maintains its own records on disciplinary actions sought against officers.

He said the union is considering filing a lawsuit to force Cannon to release the names of officers on whose disciplinary histories the statistics were based.

"The OPR is a tool to further Glenn Cannon's own political aims," McNamara said, adding that his membership has lost confidence in the partly civilian office that replaced the old police internal affairs unit.

Cannon's office last week provided the FOP with the same information it gave The Pittsburgh Press, but those figures did not identify officers by name.

Cannon said Friday that the total yearly complaint figures included complaints against some firefighters and paramedics. But he said the information about individual officers' disciplinary histories was correct and still supported his stance about the need for departmental reform.

Cannon said the identities of the officers are confidential and not a matter of public record and therefore McNamara was not entitled to the information.

McNamara said that unless the officers' names are revealed, he cannot verify the accuracy of the OPR figures.

McNamara also challenged yearly complaint figures against police that were mentioned in the story, accusing the department of deliberately inflating police totals by adding in those of firefighters and paramedics.

Carla Gedman, acting assistant chief of OPR, said the inclusion of nonpolice complaints was unintentional.

The original figures included 906 complaints between 1987 and 1989 lodged against police officers, firefighters, paramedics, and other Public Safety employees. The OPR figures did not break down the totals complaint by job description.

A second chart provided to the newspaper gave complaint figures broken down by jobs for only the first six months of 1989.

"There was no intent to mislead anyone," Gedman said. "The whole thing was a breakdown in communication."

Actually, there were 684 complaints, or an average of 228 per year, against police between 1987 and 1989, Gedman said.

That is about one complaint per every five officers a year, not one per four officers as originally reported. The remaining 222 complaints over the three-year period, or about 74 a year, were against firemen, paramedics, and other DPS personnel.

The breakdown of figures by bureau also shows that 655 investigations of complaints against police officers, instead of 845 as originally reported, were completed between 1987 and 1989. In that instance, other bureau figures also were included with police statistics.

The results of completed investigations involving only police, according to OPR:

- 40.4 percent, or 265, were not sustained because there was insufficient evidence to establish guilt or innocence.
- 20.7 percent, or 136, were sustained because the allegations were proved by available evidence.
- 13.2 percent, or 87, were unfounded, meaning the charges were proved to be inaccurate. Beginning this year, noncriminal complaints brought against officers more than 90 days after the incident also are classified as "unfounded" as part of the new police labor agreement.
- 14.4 percent, or 92, were "closed by memo" for various reasons including lack of cooperation from a complainant.
- 8.2 percent, or 54, were exonerated – not only cleared of all charges but found to have followed all proper police procedures.

With the other bureaus eliminated from the total figure for completed investigations, the 40.4 percent of unsustained complaints against police actually was higher than the 34.4 percent, or 291, originally reported.

For the other categories, the earlier figures reported were: "unfounded," 135 or 15.9 percent; closed by memo, 130 or 15.4 percent; and exonerated, 57 or 6.7 percent.

The six-month report of OPR complaint figures for 1989 showed that 126 of 150 complaints had been lodged against police. Eleven complaints involved fire personnel, 10 were against Administration Bureau employees, and three were for Emergency Medical Services employees.

About 46 percent, or 69 of those complaints, involved allegations of verbal abuse or use of excessive force.

The department's release of statistics describing individual officers' disciplinary histories was in response to a request by The Pittsburgh Press to review disciplinary case files. The newspaper submitted a list of 88 names, most of whom had been identified in court records and news accounts as having allegedly used excessive force against citizens or having allegedly committed other civil rights violations.

McNamara said that his own review of the list of names submitted to the department by The Pittsburgh Press found six were not Pittsburgh police officers, 12 were retired officers, and 47 were police who have never been the subject of a disciplinary action report.

"That's why if he (Cannon) commingled these with other names and misled everybody, I want to know how many," McNamara said.

Gedman said OPR eliminated from the newspaper's list the names of officers who had retired or were found not be members of the department and "added 20 names of our own—people whose disciplinary histories we were already familiar with."

The statistics for this group released to the newspaper showed that the department had called for discipline against them 137 times. Such a recommendation is called a Disciplinary Action Report.

The OPR report showed that two current officers have been cited 10 times, 11 have drawn five or more recommendations for punishment, 28 have been cited at least twice, and 46 received at least one DAR.

McNamara disputed the figures, saying that the number of DAR's contained in his files do not match the number cited by OPR.

He said the complaint and DAR figures are misleading since complaints do not always result in a recommendation for discipline, nor are all of OPR's recommended DAR's sustained by supervisors.

Gedman said that McNamara would not have a record of all complaints since the OPR is required to notify the FOP only when a disciplinary case is completed and a finding issued. Officers can review their own disciplinary files, she said.

"He (McNamara) is not entitled to know about every complaint filed against an officer. That is part of the officer's private file."

SOURCE. *The Pittsburgh Press,* August 26, 1990. Reprinted with permission.

---

average police administrator spends anywhere from 20 (Albanese, 1981) to 45 percent of his or her time dealing with interpersonal/intergroup conflicts (Graham, 1984).

Conflict Development Cycle

It is important that police administrators learn to understand the dynamics of conflict. Under normal circumstances, conflict does not appear suddenly out of the blue. In fact, it passes through a cycle of progressive stages as tension builds. The steps or stages in the conflict development cycle are as follows:

1. *Latent conflict.* At the latent stage, all of the basic conditions for future conflict exist but have not been recognized as a problem by potential adversaries. The most likely sources of substantive disagreement in an organizational setting are competition for scarce resources, role conflicts, and incompatible expectations.

2. *Perceived conflict.* The cause(s) of the conflict are recognized by one or both of the parties. Some latent conflicts are never perceived as conflicts per se and do not cross the threshold of awareness.

3. *Felt conflict.* At this point, tension starts to build between the participants. Felt conflict differs from perceived conflict in that at least one of the parties begins to experience discomfort, stress, or anxiety.

4. *Manifest conflict.* The struggle begins in earnest and the behavior of the participants makes the existence of the conflict obvious to others who are not directly involved in the dispute. Manifest conflict takes the form of overt behavior such as apathy, withdrawal, minimum job performance, sabotage, and open aggression.

5. *Conflict resolution.* Attempts to resolve the conflict can range from approaches that simply ignore the conflict to strategies designed to confront the conflict head on and resolve it in such a way that all parties can achieve their goals (Fox and Urwick, 1973).

6. *Conflict aftermath.* The conflict is ended by resolution or suppression. This establishes new conditions that may lead to more effective cooperation or a new conflict, which could be much worse than before (Pondy, 1967).

Based on this perspective, conflict is viewed as an unfolding process rather than a discrete event that occurs at one moment in time. The process consists of a series of conflict episodes. Each episode involves an escalation in tension via stages in the conflict development cycle. The resolution of conflict sets the stage—in a dialectical sense—for new life experiences. While this process is fairly simple to understand, it is much more complicated than it might appear, since not all conflict passes through every stage in the cycle. In addition, the participants in the conflict may not be at exactly the same stage. One party might be at the manifest stage (ready to launch attack) while the other person is at the latent stage and totally unaware that a confrontation is brewing (Rue and Byars, 1980).

Conflict theorists also use the cyclical approach to illustrate the processing of events in the conflict development cycle. In destructive conflict situations, for example, winning becomes the object and is considered far more important than coming up with mutually acceptable solutions to substantive disagreements. The antagonists begin to conceal relevant information or pass on distorted information in an effort to mislead their opponents. Based on psychosocial dynamics, individuals become more committed—at an emotional level—to their original position. Groups, on the other hand, become more cohesive and substitute groupthink for rational analysis. Any deviation from the party line results in the imposition of immediate and severe sanctions. Contact with adversaries is discouraged except under controlled circumstances. Contrast conceptions are formed and projected on opponents through the use of negative stereotypes. These stereotypes fuel the fire of discontent and are used to justify escalation in the level of conflict. Inherently aggressive people, who have the ability to turn others on and the tactical skill needed to exploit conflict, tend to emerge as strategists and/or group leaders. This usually intensifies hostility and perpetuates the struggle until someone wins (Johns, 1988). Destructive conflict is almost always a zero-sum equation. "To the victor go the spoils."

Conflict in Formal Organizations

Management theorists often disagree with one another when it comes to defining conflict and assessing its role in organizations. The literature suggests that there have been three relatively distinct phases in the development of thinking concerning conflict in organizational settings. They are usually referred to as (1) the traditional phase, (2) the human relations phase, and (3) the interactionist phase. Traditionalists viewed conflict as pathological and something to avoid at all costs. Behavioralists perceived conflict as a natural yet resolvable disturbance in the balance or equilibrium of an organization. Modern interactionists contend that a certain amount of conflict is necessary if goal-oriented groups are to perform effectively.

1. *The traditionalists.* This early approach to conflict assumed that all interpersonal/intergroup conflict was bad. Traditional theorists believed that

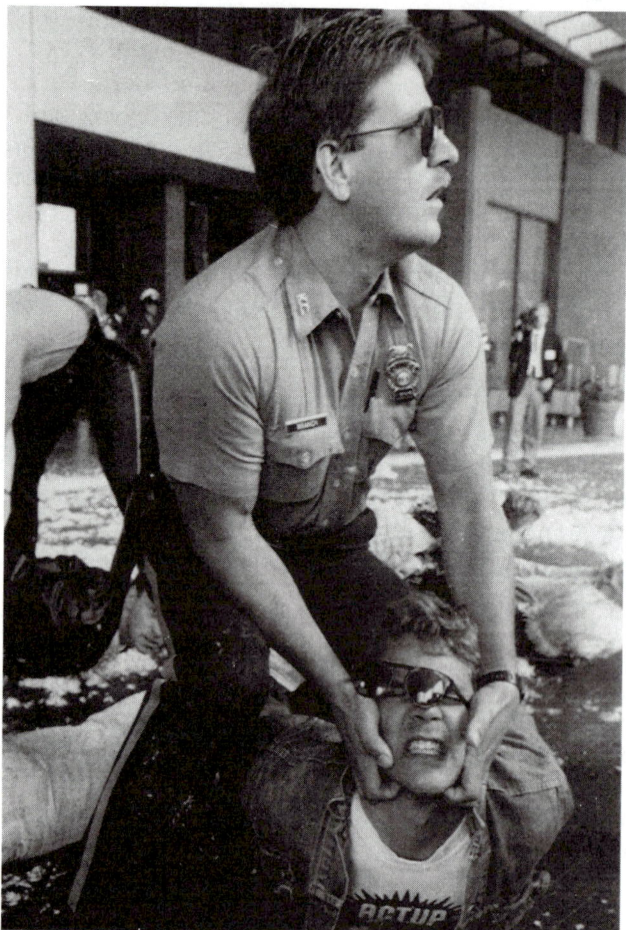

Multifaceted Conflict While officers face physical conflict on the street, police managers wrestle with other forms of conflict within the organization. *(AP/Wide World Photos.)*

there would always be positive cooperation between labor and management in well-managed organizations. Conflict was viewed as a dysfunctional outcome caused by factors like poor communication, the lack of openness and trust between people, and the failure of management personnel to respond to the needs or aspirations of their subordinates. If conflict reared its ugly head, it was management's job—through the use of logic and rational analysis—to determine the cause of the malfunction and correct it on management's terms. The traditionalists subscribed to a Theory X perspective. Anyone who created conflict within the organization was considered to be persona non grata. In the past, disruptive police officers were often fired for the good of the service.

2. *The behavioralists.* During the late 1940s, the human relations approach displaced traditionalism as the dominant view of conflict in formal organizations. Behavioralists accepted conflict as an inevitable fact of life whenever

people were required to work together. Conflict was seen as a natural yet resolvable disturbance in the balance or equilibrium of an organization. The root causes of conflict were seen as idiosyncracies in people themselves. Human relations theorists focused their attention on the use of group dynamics (encounter groups, T-groups, guided group interaction, OD, etc.) to resolve disruptive interpersonal and intergroup conflict. A modified behavioral approach emerged during the late 1960s. Its proponents maintained that conflict created a paradox in complex organizations. While it often led to serious problems and dysfunctional behavior, it could also be beneficial if it evoked enough anxiety to motivate the parties to resolve their substantive differences through cooperative problem-solving and participative management. Emphasis began to shift to the positive aspects of conflict management.

3. *The interactionists.* A refinement of the human relations approach is to assimilate conflict when it is beneficial and discourage it only when it becomes harmful. Interactionists actually encourage some forms of conflict on the grounds that harmonious, peaceful, tranquil, cooperative, and collaborative work groups tend to become static, apathetic, and openly resistant to innovation or change. They believe in introducing and maintaining a minimum level of conflict in order to keep the group viable, self-critical, and creative. Functional conflict is considered to be constructive in the sense that it heightens anxiety to the point where the organization is forced to take proactive steps designed to find a realistic solution to the problem. Dysfunctional conflict, on the other hand, always has a negative influence on group performance and is detrimental to the welfare of all group members. The actual demarcation between functional and dysfunctional conflict is neither clear nor precise. It all depends on the situation, the players involved, and the dynamics between the two. There is a paradox, however. While some conflict is, in fact, healthy and contributes to overall group performance, most groups and formal organizations try to eliminate it whenever possible (Robbins, 1989).

The American preoccupation with modern Japanese management techniques has led to a substantive reevaluation of the role of conflict in complex task-oriented organizations. Even though Japanese managers subscribe to the concept that conflict is inevitable, they also feel that it is inexcusable to allow uncontrolled conflict to have an adverse effect on the efficiency, effectiveness, and productivity of the organization. Based on their Buddhist culture, with its emphasis on the goodness of harmony and tranquility, Japanese managers always see persistent conflict as a reflection of personal imperfection as well as professional incompetence (Maruta, 1983). The emerging view of conflict—based on this Japanese model—assumes that a relatively high degree of interpersonal/intergroup harmony is required if complex organizations are to survive and thrive. It is the manager's job to elicit cooperation, reinforce collaborative relationships, and maintain the organization in operation through effective team building and participatory management. The anxiety necessary to motivate people and to produce organizational change need not come from distress or conflict but can occur as the result of healthy competition or a debate that is designed to avoid conflict (Holt, 1987).

A police department is not one of Max Weber's ideal types. It is a microcosm of the society at large. Consequently, conflict is the rule rather than the exception. As public officials who are responsible for getting things done through others and managing conflict, police administrators have an affirmative duty to study the causes of conflict and develop strategies designed to control them.

Causes of Organizational Conflict

Although it is possible to identify a great number of factors that can lead to conflict, much of the conflict in organizations appears to come from one of six sources:

1. Interdependence
2. Differences in power, status, and culture
3. Organizational ambiguity
4. Competition for scarce resources
5. Drive for autonomy
6. Bifurcation of subunit interests

1. *Interdependence.* Conflict always occurs within a context of mutual interdependence. There is a potential for conflict whenever people or organizational subunits are dependent on each other to achieve their own particular goals. Three common types of interdependence are pooled, sequential, and reciprocal. Pooled interaction is where the output of two relatively independent groups is combined to help the organization achieve its goals. In the case of sequential interdependence, one group depends on the other for input (data, raw materials, clientele, etc.), but the dependency is only one way. Reciprocal interdependence exists when groups exchange inputs as well as outputs. Interdependence sets the stage for conflict in that the participants are required to interact with one another and exercise some power over each other. Large police departments are composed of many specialized work groups that interact to varying degrees in a coordinated effort to accomplish specific goals and objectives.

2. *Differences in power, status, and culture.* Intergroup conflict is very likely to erupt when there are significant disparities in power, status, and culture in a particular organization. Because of the complexity of police work, the following factors are important:

- The real power to influence individuals, groups, and organization outcomes is seldom, if ever, distributed in the manner depicted by the chain of command on the organization chart. There is a very natural tendency for people and/or groups to acquire a disproportionate amount of power and use that power to their advantage. Conflict is inevitable whenever there is a struggle for power.
- As is the case with power, not every person or group within a complex organization shares the same status. In fact, differential status is the rule rather than the exception. Status (or the value conferred on someone by significant others) is often related to education, training, assignment, rank, and political influence. Status differences normally do not create interper-

sonal/intergroup conflict when those with lower status are dependent on those of higher status. This is the way most formal organizations are supposed to work. Group members are socialized to expect and accept this kind of order in work-oriented relationships. Due to the inordinate complexity of modern police work, there are times when individuals or groups with technically lower status find themselves in a position to control the action and give orders to persons with higher status. There is, for example, a great potential for status-based conflict in situations where detectives—the so-called prima donnas of the police profession—find themselves under the functional supervision of uniformed patrol personnel. In addition, unbridled competition for status can, in and of itself, degenerate into debilitating conflict in complex criminal justice organizations.

- An organization's culture, or way of life (see Chapter 7) consists of shared beliefs, values, motives, norms, and behaviors exhibited by members of a group as they pursue their collective interests, goals, and objectives. Since complex organizations are composed of many work groups, some cultural diversity is normal. When two or more distinct cultures develop within the same organization, the clash in beliefs, values, motives, and behavioral expectations almost always leads to some type of overt conflict. The nature and extent of this conflict will depend on the issue, the emotional response it generates, the resources available, the tactical skills of the combatants, the subcultural orientation to winning or losing, and the overall level of reinforcement derived from mindless groupthink. John Broderick, in his insightful book *Police in a Time of Change* (1987), argues that there is and will continue to be a great deal of conflict between those police officers who subscribe to the due process model of American law enforcement (the idealists) and those for whom crime control is the sole objective of police work (the realists). One group places an emphasis on functioning within constitutional constraints. The other group is utilitarian and operates on the implicit assumption that the end justifies the means.

It is the police administrator's responsibility to manage—not eliminate—the conflict caused by differences in power, status, and culture within complex criminal justice organizations. Trying to eliminate all conflict would, in the words of the famous man from La Mancha, be "to dream the impossible dream."

3. *Organizational ambiguity*. Task uncertainty in nonroutine situations coupled with organizational ambiguity tends to create a sense of anomie (or normlessness) that exacerbates the potential for serious interpersonal/intergroup conflict. The lack of clarity and specificity in terms of jurisdictions, goals, behavioral expectations, and performance criteria becomes a precursor for truly spontaneous conflict. Under these circumstances, the formal as well as informal rules that govern task-oriented interaction break down. The lack of purposeful interaction makes organizations less efficient, effective, and productive. It also leads to the formation of factions. Once factions (cohesive subgroups) form and develop a distinct cultural orientation, they begin to pursue their own interests as opposed to those outlined in the organization's mission statement. Organizational ambiguity of one kind or another is the most frequent cause of substantive conflict between man-

agers and their subordinates. The emphasis on collective bargaining in law enforcement can be traced to the human need to minimize conflict-causing ambiguity in the workplace. Nearly three-fourths of all American police officers are members of labor unions (Cole, 1986). Collective bargaining is based on the assumption that a certain amount of controlled conflict (via negotiation) is healthy and represents an appropriate alternative to the spontaneous, often destructive, conflict that is generated by organizational ambiguity (More and Wegener, 1990).

4. *Competition for scarce resources.* Every organization operates with a finite amount of resources in terms of its budget, personnel, and equipment. What one component (or subunit) gets in terms of budget, personnel, or equipment, other subunits do not get. As dependence on the same resource increases, so does the likelihood that competition will degenerate into open conflict (Reitz, 1981). The chances that conflict will occur are increased in direct proportion to the degree of scarcity. As illustrated in Focus 13.2, battle lines are drawn as people or groups jockey for the power to capture the resources needed to achieve their own goals. Scarcity has a way of converting dormant or latent hostility into overt conflict (Johns, 1988). Overt conflict manifests itself in disputes between individuals, between individuals and groups, or between groups. It can range all the way from an episodic show of disrespect to intentional sabotage. It is not uncommon for specialized units to siphon resources off of the patrol division. This reduces the patrol division's ability to protect life and property, preserve the peace, prevent crime, and apprehend criminals (Leonard and More, 1987). Patrol officers feel exploited and become very cynical because they have been denied the resources required to do their job. Cynicism creates and then perpetuates conflict in complex criminal justice organizations (Baker, 1985).

5. *Drive for autonomy.* Complex organizations are created, structured, and maintained in an effort to coordinate the activities of people in the work force as they pursue mutually acceptable goals and objectives. As a rule, most newly hired employees enter the organization with a fairly broad zone of indifference. In other words, they are willing to voluntarily accept direction from significant others in the organization who have either the power or legitimate authority to issue orders and expect compliance (Barnard, 1976). This helps to stabilize interaction patterns within the group. Superior-subordinate conflict often occurs when the participants do not agree with each other on the bounds of the zone. Conflict erupts when subordinates resist direction and assert their autonomy. Most managers do not fully appreciate the fact that human beings perceive themselves as having certain freedoms (a "set of free behaviors") and that they are—over time—motivated to resist threats to, or abridgment of, those freedoms (Brehm, 1966). If a freedom is eliminated, they are very likely to try to reestablish it. The most direct way of reestablishing a freedom is to challenge the authority of the manager as a representative of the status quo. Under these conditions, those managers who feel threatened frequently respond by invoking policies, procedures, rules, and regulations in an effort to regain control of the recalcitrant employee's on-the-job behavior. While this strategy may ensure minimum conformity, it can have dysfunctional consequences. It allows the problem to fester as a continuous

FOCUS 13.2

Fourth Reverse-Bias Suit for Dallas PD Promotion Policy

Dallas Police Chief Mack Vines, former chief Billy Prince, Mayor Annette Strauss, City Manager Richard Knight, and the Dallas City Council are among the defendants named by 24 white police lieutenants in a reverse-discrimination suit that claims the lieutenants were passed over for promotion to captain in favor of the highest ranking black and Hispanic candidates.

The suit, filed in U.S. District Court on March 16, is the fourth filed since 1988 by Dallas police officers alleging reverse discrimination in the promotional practices of the Dallas Police Department. One of the suits, filed by three police officers who say they were passed over for promotion to the rank of sergeant, will go to trial in September [1990], and the rest are in the pretrial discovery phase, said Joseph E. Scuro, Jr., the lawyer representing the plaintiffs in all four cases.

At issue in the latest suit is a change in promotional policies ordered this year by city officials, which set up promotional goals for minorities in city agencies, including supervisory positions in the 2,600-officer Police Department. Previously, promotions were based on candidates' placements on a list that ranked candidates according to their scores on a written promotional exam and an oral assessment. Vines ordered the change in the Police Department's promotional policy to make it conform to that of the city government. The revised policy says that 25 percent of all promotions are to go to black candidates, while Hispanics are allocated 10 percent.

"The city said [the change] was implemented to achieve goals; the officers contend that goals are a pretext for quotas," said Scuro.

Scuro said the promotional list drawn up in January 1989 comprised 35 candidates eligible for the rank of captain. During a Civil Service hearing in February 1989, the top-ranking officer, who was white, was promoted, but officials then dropped down to the number-seven position to promote a Hispanic, and to number 33 to promote the highest scoring black candidate. As a result, Scuro said, one of the minority candidates promoted to captain in 1989 ranked lower on the promotional list than 19 of the 24 officers who joined in the suit, and two other minority candidates ranked lower than five of the 24 officers.

The officers are seeking $38 million in damages, along with promotions to the rank of captian with back pay and benefits. Scuro said the suit also seeks to have the plan declared unlawful.

Police spokesman Ed Spencer said the department could not comment on the suit since it is pending, but noted that the agency has met goals for minority promotions that it had set for 1989. Spencer said 26 percent of the promotions to sergeant, lieutenant, and captain went to blacks last year, 12 percent to Hispanics, and 16 percent to females.

Assistant City Attorney Sam Lindsay said the affirmative action measures taken by the city are "defensible and we intend to show that in court" because the Supreme Court has ruled that promotions can be made on the basis of race or sex if there is a "manifest imbalance."

Lindsay said that all of the minority candidates were qualified for promotion, and added that no existing local, state, or Federal rule compels officials to make promotions based on the order of rank on a promotional list.

SOURCE. Reprinted with permission from the March 31, 1990 issue of *Law Enforcement News,* John Jay College of Criminal Justice, New York City.

---

source of conflict and perpetuates minimally acceptable performance on the part of the employee (Bobbitt et al., 1978). The rigid paramilitary structure in most police departments tends to exacerbate the psychological reactance syndrome that we just outlined.

6. *Bifurcation of subunit interests.* The bifurcation of subunit interests is a natural source of conflict in complex organizations. Conflict is created by the delegation of tasks that, while they are subgoals of the organization as a whole, become major—if not the exclusive—goals for various subunits within the organization. These subgoals become desired ends in and of themselves. In the worst case scenario, there is head-to-head competition between subunit goals and the goals of the organization itself. The potential for conflict increases dramatically when two or more specialized work groups whose goals differ are functionally dependent on one another. This is a particularly important consideration when one group's success at reaching its goals or accomplishing its task depends not only on what it does but on the behavior of other people or groups as well (Bobbitt et al., 1978). The desire of a special investigative team to "apprehend dopers and put them behind bars" can become so intense it may cloud their judgment to the point where they make a deal to help spring a potentially violent burglar (who terrorized a particular neighborhood) in exchange for information. The detectives in a situation like this have allowed their own goals to supersede those of the police department, the legislature, and the community at large.

Dysfunctional Conflict

Interpersonal-intergroup conflict is clearly dysfunctional when it creates intolerable anxiety, disrupts healthy relationships, wastes an excessive amount of time and energy, keeps an organization from accomplishing its lawfully prescribed mission (goals and objectives), and/or leads to destructive behavior. It is the manager's job to neutralize debilitating conflict and reward those who make positive contributions to the work group. Police administrators must do everything in their power to foster loyalty, cooperation, and a sense of teamwork. They have an affirmative duty to deal with the troublemakers who thrive on creating unnecessary conflict. If wholesale adversity continues to exist, the reward system probably encourages confrontation and conflict instead of teamwork (LeBoeuf, 1985).

Functional Conflict

While the destructive effects of dysfunctional conflict are obvious and fairly easy to articulate, the positive effects of functional conflict are far more subtle. Good managers have learned to recognize the dual nature of conflict and evaluate it in terms of a cost/benefit analysis (Rue and Byars, 1980). Some of the useful aspects of conflict are as follows:

CASE STUDY

Lieutenant Michael Parks

Lt. Michael "Mickey" Parks is a 19-year veteran of the Sparta Police Department. He is a fatherly, college-educated man with the demeanor of an empathetic elementary school teacher. The lieutenant has an easy-going personality and the unique ability to establish almost instantaneous rapport with other police officers. Under normal circumstances, he is an ideal mentor and coach.

Raymond Perkoski, a newly promoted sergeant, was initially assigned to the patrol division. He reported directly to Lt. Parks. They bonded spontaneously and became very good friends. Lt. Parks was the teacher and Sgt. Perkowski was an eager student. He was a protégé who enjoyed picking the brain of his mentor. Perkowski didn't object to the fact that the lieutenant called most of the shots and made nearly all of the important decisions. After all, it eased his (Perkowski's) anxiety and made him look good to the brass.

As the sergeant became more comfortable with his role as a supervisor and started to believe in himself as a professional, he began to question his relationship with Lt. Parks. He felt a need to distance himself from the lieutenant.

Since Sgt. Perkowski liked Parks as a person, he did not want to hurt the man's feelings. He sent subtle messages designed to tell the lieutenant to back off. When the subtle approach failed and the lieutenant kept interfering in his professional life, Perkowski got angry. Since he was unable to vent his frustration, the anger turned to resentment.

Sgt. Perkowski began to avoid the lieutenant whenever possible. He cooled their relationship as much as he could.

One night, Lt. Parks—without Perkowski's knowledge—took disciplinary action against one of Sgt. Perkowski's patrol officers. When Perkowski heard about the incident, he got so angry that he initiated a confrontation with the lieutenant. He burst into the lieutenant's office and challenged his authority. After a heated exchange, Perkowski told Lt. Parks that he was "sick and tired of being mothered" and that he wanted to be left alone to do his job. He told the lieutenant to "butt out" of his life.

Lieutenant Parks was mystified by Perkowski's bizarre behavior and vowed never to talk to the "ungrateful S.O.B." again.

What would you, as a conflict management theorist, tell the lieutenant about the cause or causes of this conflict episode? What can he do to ensure that it does not happen again? Be very specific.

1. Conflict wakes people up, turns them on, and energizes them.
2. Strategic conflict usually involves the search for a resolution to an underlying issue or problem.
3. Conflict often provides a forum for better communication.
4. Conflict may serve as an outlet for pent-up frustrations resulting in a psychosocial catharsis.
5. Conflict can be an educational experience in which the parties become much more aware and understanding of each other (Templeton, 1969).

TABLE 13.1 Functional and Dysfunctional Conflict

Conflict is functional when	Conflict is dysfunctional when
1. It turns on and energizes people.	1. It creates unhealthy and debilitating anxiety.
2. It leads to goal-oriented interaction.	2. It siphons off energies that could otherwise be spent on productve activities.
3. It helps people sharpen their goals, methods, and procedures.	3. It disrupts/destroys normal interpersonal or intergroup relationships.
4. It moves individuals or groups to higher levels of achievement.	4. It creates a situation in which "might" is used to conquer what is "right".
5. It opens up channels for more communication.	5. It keeps the organization from accomplishing its assigned mission, goals, and objectives.
6. It helps to release pent-up frustration and acts as a healthy catharsis.	6. It focuses on personalities rather than issues.
7. It leads to more awareness and greater understanding.	7. It leads to abnormal frustration, unhealthy anxiety, withdrawal, obstructionism, aggression, and other forms of destructive group behavior like slowdowns, strikes, and "jungle warfare."

The positive value of any conflict episode will depend, to a great degree, on the problem-solving skills of the manager who is responsible for resolving it. Effective police administrators are utilitarian in that they are willing to use any conflict management strategy which they feel is appropriate given the circumstances inherent in the conflict situation. Table 13.1 contrasts functional with dysfunctional conflict.

Reacting to and Managing Conflict

Conflict, as with all other elements in the administrative process, must be managed so that it is not allowed to run amok. It is the managers' job to keep conflict functional and within the parameters of organizational necessity (Holden, 1986). They know that in order to motivate their personnel and to increase the overall productivity of the work force, they must try to stimulate healthy competition while minimizing the negative influence of dysfunctional conflict in the organization. Police administrators react to conflict issues, episodes, and situations in a variety of ways and, depending on the circumstances or their own managerial skills, either resolve the conflict or make it worse (Albanese, 1981). Conflict resolution techniques run the gamut from cosmetic to functional.

Based on a review of the literature, it is clear that there are many strategies for dealing with conflict in complex organizations. While each may be effective under certain circumstances or in certain situations, some are of limited value because they fail to get at the sources of the conflict. Others have the potential to be effective but may be very difficult to implement. It is the manager's job to sort through the alternatives and choose the conflict resolution strategy or technique most likely to succeed given existing constraints (Holt, 1987).

Techniques

Management theorists have identified, described, and analyzed the conflict management techniques most often used by practitioners. The most common ones are as follows:

1. Avoidance
2. Dominance
3. Soothing
4. Compromise
5. Resource acquisition
6. Superordinate goals
7. Structural change
8. Behavioral change
9. Conflict stimulation
10. Problem-solving
11. Integration

Avoidance. Rather than dealing with conflict, many managers choose to close their eyes and pretend that it does not exist. Avoidance may be the most common method of addressing conflict, although it is, in reality, a strategy that is designed to ignore it. Stalling while a problem is being studied is the administrative equivalent to turning a blind eye on the conflict situation in hopes that things will sort themselves out and the problem will resolve itself. While this does not happen often, it does happen. Avoidance may be reasonable if the consequences of the conflict are perceived as being inconsequential, there is little chance of winning, or the costs far outweigh the benefits. Avoidance creates a problem, however. A pattern of avoidance can lead to crisis management (Holden, 1986). Crisis management occurs when important conflict issues, episodes, or situations are ignored to the point where they become so big they must be resolved immediately and without regard to the cost. The most effective managers are inclined to confront conflict head on and least likely to ignore it (Burk, 1970).

Dominance. The autocratic response to conflict is to rely on one's formal authority (i.e., position power) to force others to cease and desist. The hierarchical structure of complex organizations consists of superior-subordinate relationships. Managers occupy strategic positions and are responsible for resolving dysfunctional conflicts (Tansik, Chase, and Aquilano, 1980). Due to the paramilitary nature of police work, many police administrators have learned to rely almost exclusively on their formal authority to force decisions on their subordinates. They wield this authority by virtue of their position in the chain of command. This type of autocratic command can be useful in making quick decisions designed to achieve short-term results. It seems to be a misguided response in most situations, however. The coerced cessation of conflict treats only the symptoms, not the cause or causes of the problem. As a result, the unresolved conflict is almost certain to erupt again. It may be even more destructive the second time around.

Soothing. Soothing, or smoothing things over is really not much more than a diplomatic plea for more sensitivity or understanding. It is designed to defuse dysfunctional conflict by calming things down and straightening out ruffled feathers. If there are no substantive conflict issues involved, soothing may, in fact, be the appropriate managerial response. By applying salve to the egos of those who are in conflict with one another, the manager helps eliminate much of the friction. Both sides can focus on points of agreement and downplay differences. The risk in this strategy is that real conflict may go unresolved. It may be pushed under the rug and allowed to fester. Under these circumstances, the conflict may become much worse (Holt, 1987).

Compromise. Compromise is a practical and popular approach to conflict management because it fits in with the realities of life in complex organizations. It consists of the mutual trading of offers, counteroffers, and concessions between those involved or their representatives (Baron, 1983). The distinguishing feature of compromise is that each party is required to give something up in order to come to a mutually acceptable middle ground. There are no clear winners or losers. Everybody gets a little piece of the action. Compromise is one of the principal techniques used to resolve conflict in police departments throughout the United States (Whisenand and Rush, 1988). In some ways, it is the worst. Compromise puts expedience ahead of principle. As a result, the root cause or causes are ignored. They also continue to fester. In addition, compromise decreases accountability and ensures that mediocrity prevails. Two good ideas are often merged into one mediocre, or bad, idea. Under these circumstances, everybody loses. Richard Holden (1986) argues that organizations are better off if compromise is avoided. He believes that everyone should be allowed to win, as well as lose, on occasion. This will bolster morale and generate better ideas designed to resolve interpersonal or intergroup conflict.

Resource acquisition. A very important source of conflict in complex task-oriented organizations is unhealthy competition for scarce resources. The best way for managers to defuse this conflict is to acquire additional resources and to distribute those resources in an equitable manner. While this sounds fairly simple, it is often difficult to achieve (Hitt, Middlemist, and Mathis, 1979). Police departments are funded by legislative bodies from a finite and exhaustible tax base. Consequently, additional resources may simply not be available. More and more police departments are being confronted by this reality every day. Retrenchment and cutback management are here to stay. The rank structure in police departments may turn healthy competition into a form of dysfunctional conflict. When the chances for promotion are valued and scarce, there is certain to be intense conflict between those competing for that particular resource. One conflict management strategy is to diversify the rank structure and increase the total number of administrative positions. While the addition of managerial positions may increase morale, job satisfaction is usually temporary because the level of expectation also increases. Top-heavy organizations are seldom, if ever, efficient, effective, or productive.

Superordinate goals. A superordinate goal is a highly valued end state of affairs that two or more parties desire but which cannot be achieved without the mutual cooperation of those who are otherwise involved in conflict. Conditions are arranged in such a way that people and groups must work together to overcome a common threat or achieve shared goals. The creation of superordinate goals is a functional strategy designed to transform "them" (out-group members) into "us" (in-group members). If this strategy works as anticipated, the overall level of destructive conflict will almost always be reduced (Baron, 1983). Labor and management may put aside their deep-seated differences and work together if they are convinced that survival of the organization is contingent on collaboration. Concession and take back contracts are very common in the hostile world of shrinking resources. The use of superordinate goals should not be viewed as a panacea, however. Since they do not really deal with the cause or causes of the conflict, superordinate goals may only delay the conflict. Current research suggests that substantive conflict often remains unresolved even after a superordinate goal is achieved (Hunger and Stern, 1976). In addition, most police administrators find that there are real limitations on their ability to generate tailor-made superordinate goals.

Structural Change. Reorganization is a common conflict management strategy. Conflict can be reduced through transfers, developing new organizational relationships (setting up new departments, creating new coordinator positions, or uncoupling conflicting units), enlarging administrative areas to accomodate different units, and realigning managerial responsibilities within the organization. Transfer is one of the most popular methods used to manage dysfunctional conflict in complex organizations. Difficult employees are frequently reassigned to positions in which the potential for destructive behavior is quite limited. Police administrators often find that it is much easier to isolate recalcitrant personnel in relatively innocuous positions than it is to terminate their employment. Every police department has some very low-status positions where troublemakers are placed in order to minimize their negative influence on work-group dynamics. There are two basic problems with this strategy, however. Even these low-status positions require personnel who are interested in and competent enough to do the job. Once a position has been identified as an undesirable disciplinary assignment, good people will—no matter how important the job is—avoid it like the plague for fear that it will destroy their career. This tends to debilitate the whole organization. Television's "F Troop" is a classic example of this phenomenon. It should also be noted that transfers do not necessarily resolve conflicts. They may just move them from one location to another within the police department (Holden, 1986).

Behavioral change. Inducing specific changes in behavior is one of the most difficult conflict management techniques. One approach involves the use of planned interventions designed to change the beliefs, values, attitudes, and motives of one or more of the antagonists. Managers often try to help those in conflict understand and empathize with one another as they come to grips with personal emotions, values, and behaviors in conflict situations. The social learning approach is quite different, however. The concept of psychosocial motivation is discarded in an attempt to understand and change the behavior that produces conflict. Managers identify the kind, category, or class of behavior (verbal, nonverbal, emotional response, etc.) that must be changed. They try to determine the "stuff" that the person has learned and which now controls his or her behavior. Once these bits and pieces of information have been factored into a comprehensive diagnosis of the conflict situation, techniques (like modeling, direct reinforcement, persuasive communication, etc.) which are likely to produce a desired change in behavior can then be applied. In other words, by changing the expected consequences associated with a given behavior, managers can alter and direct the behavior of their subordinates (Zimbardo and Ebbesen, 1969). Changing behavior is not nearly as simple as it might appear. Resocialization and behavior modification techniques may produce harmful results in the hands of amateurs. They are also costly and time-consuming. Consequently, resocialization and behavior modification have not been used extensively in law enforcement.

Conflict stimulation. As indicated earlier in this chapter, some purposefully initiated (or strategic) conflict may be required to produce needed changes within the organization. There are times when managers feel the need to stimulate conflict rather than reduce it. Under these circumstances it is assumed that a conflict stimulation strategy will result in a beneficial change. Police administrators may choose to induce a modicum of conflict when everyone has settled into a relatively nonproductive, yet friendly, rut. Stimulation may also be needed in situations where those who should be interacting closely have chosen to withdraw from one another in an effort to avoid overt conflict. A third signal manifests itself when any conflict is downplayed by denying differences, ignoring controversy, and exaggerating points of agreement (Johns, 1988.) According to Paul Whisenand and George Rush (1988), properly harnessed and channeled conflict can produce the following positive results:

1. Stimulates productive change
2. Fosters creativity and innovation
3. Helps to clarify issues and goals
4. Encourages individuality
5. Enhances communication
6. Piques professional interests
7. Increases energy within the unit
8. Promotes in-group solidarity
9. Nurtures psychological health

While a certain amount of conflict is healthy in any complex organization, there is always a danger that strategic conflict will generate unanticipated negative consequences. The strategic use of conflict must be handled carefully and should be part of an overall management strategy. Like a forest fire started by a tiny spark, even well-meaning conflict can spread to the point where it threatens the entire organization. Discretion is always the better part of valor when it comes to dealing with conflict.

Problem-solving. One way to prevent dysfunctional conflict is to encapsulate it (Etzioni, 1964). This is usually done through the formulation of reasonable policies, procedures, rules, and regulations. They specify how group members are to interact with each other. When dysfunctional conflict does arise, problem-solving techniques similar to those discussed in Chapter 9 are normally used to deal with it. Problem-solving confronts issues directly. It focuses on identifying and clarifying the cause or causes of the conflict and moving systematically toward its resolution. Emphasis is placed on issues rather than personalities. The objective is to identify mutually acceptable ways of dealing with problems (Tansik, Chase, and Aquilano, 1980). Managers are not really expected to resolve conflicts by themselves. They normally act as referees and counselors who help antagonists reach an acceptable solution. It is their job to help those who are in conflict by

1. Determining why the conflict exists.
2. Specifying the issue to be resolved.
3. Providing the information needed to reach an acceptable solution.
4. Regulating the frequency of contact between the parties.
5. Establishing a climate for problem-solving.
6. Keeping the parties moving toward a true resolution of the conflict.
7. Intervening and imposing a solution when the participants have failed and it is in the best interest of the organization to do so (Rue and Byars, 1980).

Problem-solving is the best approach to conflict management when participants share a common perspective and/or the conflict was caused by a misunderstanding. If the antagonists have different value systems, problem-solving may be nothing more than an exercise in futility and can, in fact, make the conflict much worse.

Integration. According to Mary Parker Follett (Fox and Urwick, 1973), integration is the best way to manage conflict in complex organizations. Managers seek solutions by which the parties achieve their desires (or goals) while neither side is forced to sacrifice anything. This is known as "a moment of interacting desires." True collaboration requires creativity and the ability to think outside of the boundaries of two alternatives that are mutually exclusive. Integration is an ideal state in which all parties transcend the conflict mode and move into genuine collaborative problem-solving. The philosophy is win-win (DuBrin, 1985). The bases of integration are to

1. Bring basic differences out into the open by laying all the cards on the table.
2. Encourage the simultaneous reevaluation of interests on both sides.
3. Find the substantive rather than the dramatic features of the conflict.
4. Break whole problems up into constituent elements in order to examine them.
5. Anticipate conflicts and formulate appropriate responses to them ahead of time.
6. Respond as dictated by circumstances inherent in the situation.
7. Prepare for a circular as well as a linear response from other people because our behavior always triggers behavior in others.
8. Avoid the innate propensity to dominate and/or compromise in conflict situations.
9. Seek collaboration in an effort to achieve the mutually acceptable desires of all parties in the conflict (Fox and Urwick, 1973).

While there is no doubt that integration is a superior method for resolving conflict in many situations, it may not be very practical. The biggest problem is that it is alien to the bureaucratic thinking that is so pervasive in modern-day law enforcement. As a result, very few police administrators possess the skills or have the training required to make the integration approach to conflict management a really viable alternative to the status quo.

Managerial Styles and Conflict Management

Police administrators, like all other managers, eventually settle into a pattern, method of operation (MO), or style of conflict management that reflects their personalities and meets their own unique needs. Researchers have identified five basic types of managers and usually describe them in terms of their approach to conflict resolution. Theses five typologies are outlined here:

1. *Competitors ("Sharks")*. Competitive managers are self-confident, assertive, and aggressive. They use power, intimidation, and domination to achieve their own goals in a win-lose environment. They are driven to win in a zero-sum game.
2. *Avoiders ("Turtles")*. Avoiders are lose-lose managers who choose to remain neutral and duck dysfunctional conflict at all costs. They fear the potential damage of confrontation and are willing to limp along within the constraints imposed by the status quo.
3. *Accommodators ("Teddy bears")*. These managers formulate and live by a utilitarian lose-win philosophy designed to ensure their survival. Accommodators are not assertive or aggressive and usually give way to conflict by folding under pressure. They go along to get along.
4. *Compromisers ("Foxes")*. Compromise-oriented managers put expedience before principle as they seek short-term solutions to long-term problems. Compromise is a lose-lose strategy that tends to deify the middle ground. Compromisers are always willing to make concessions in order to achieve consensus.
5. *Collaborators ("Owls")*. These are the win-win managers who accept the premise that conflict is inevitable and—depending on its nature and extent—a potentially positive aspect of life. They look for creative solutions to problems through the purposeful integration of divergent perspectives (Graham, 1984; Thomas, 1976).

Each style has both positive and negative features. As a result, good managers tend to favor a contingency approach. The contingency view of conflict resolution is based on the fundamental assumption that an effective managerial response is dependent on the synergistic interaction between the manager, the antagonists, and the totality of circumstances inherent in the situation (Albanese, 1981). In other words, they pick and choose the style they feel is most likely to produce a desired result.

The Problem Employee as a Source of Conflict

Most police officers are intelligent, hardworking, and helpful human beings. They usually exhibit a positive mental attitude and work in concert with their colleagues and managers to accomplish the police department's mission, goals, and objectives. Unfortunately, most work groups have at least one or two members who are a continuous source of dysfunctional conflict. It is the manager's job to transform these recalcitrant troublemakers into productive human resources or to purge them from the organization. Under these circumstances, termination of employment is generally the court of last resort.

Problem employees are usually honest people who—for one reason or another—simply do not fit into the organization and, as a result, engage in disruptive behaviors. They may be suffering from health problems, stress-induced burnout, mental illness, or social malfunctions related to unhealthy relationships, marital discord, drug abuse, alcoholism, and so on. These personal problems can lead to apathy, absenteeism, interpersonal conflict, intergroup antagonisms, overt aggression, and other destructive forms of dysfunctional human behavior (Wambaugh, 1973).

There is absolutely no doubt that an employee's personal, medical, and emotional problems may seriously affect on-the-job performance and can generate a considerable amount of internal organizational conflict. In a police department with 100 employees or less, one single employee can create significant problems for the entire organization. A few unhappy, dissatisfied, and conflict-oriented workers can and do consume more of a police administrator's time and energy than do hardworking, productive employees (Williams and Bratton, 1990).

In the past, troublesome employees were considered to be throwaways. People who were perceived as the cause of organizational conflict got warned, disciplined, or transferred depending on their willingness to conform to the expectations of management. Those who could not or would not change their behavior were terminated for the good of the service (Leonard and More, 1987). Things have changed rather dramatically, however. The human, financial, and organizational costs associated with firing experienced personnel have become prohibitive. Police administrators are now expected, where possible and when it is in the best interest of the department, to salvage rather than to fire people (Robinette, 1985). Managers coach and counsel problem employees in an effort to contain dysfunctional conflict and improve performance. This kind of *economic humanism* is on its way to becoming the norm in police administration.

Employee Assistance Programs

Most managers do not have the clinical training or expertise needed to deal with all of the personal, physical, and emotional problems of their subordinates. Consequently, more and more police departments are establishing employee assistance programs (EAPs). These EAPs are designed to improve personal and/or organization performance by making prevention, diagnostic, and treatment services available to ill or troubled personnel (Thibault, Lynch, and McBride, 1990).

There are more than 3,000 EAPs operating in all kinds of organizational settings throughout the United States. They vary tremendously in terms of their size, scope, and overall level of sophistication. Comprehensive EAPs usually provide prevention, intervention, and treatment services to those who are at risk or in need:

1. *Prevention.* Prevention (intended to educate employees) is designed to keep potential problems from becoming real problems.
2. *Intervention.* Intervention (stepping into a situation) is a proactive attempt on the part of management to influence the course of events.
3. *Treatment.* Treatment (the application of remedies) represents a concerted effort by a professional staff to cure problems.

EAPs may be organized in various ways. They can be operated by (1) in-house specialists, (2) outside agencies, or (3) some combination of the two. The larger the organization, the more likely it will be to have its own EAP (DuBrin, 1985).

Police administrators play a dual role in an EAP. First of all, they monitor on-the-job behavior and evaluate actual job performance. If an employee's behavior becomes unacceptable or job performance is below par, it is the manager's job to determine whether the problem is being caused by organizational or personal factors. Secondly, if unacceptable behavior or poor performance is caused by personal factors, it is the administrator's job to confront the employee in a constructive manner. As part of this confrontation process, the problem employee should be encouraged to seek help through the EAP. According to Andrew J. DuBrin (1985), managers are responsible for tracking the progress of those subordinates who choose to deal with their own personal problems through an EAP.

EAPs establish a clear division of labor. Managers detect problems, confront employees, make necessary referrals, and perform a follow-up function. Prevention, intervention, and treatment services are provided by a professional staff with the training as well as the expertise needed to help troubled employees cope with personal problems that cause disruptive behavior or performance deficits. If problem employees elect not to participate in an EAP or fail to benefit from participation in a program, they must—under normal circumstances—be dealt with through the formal disciplinary process. Figure 13.3 illustrates these options.

The direct costs (hospitalization, sick leave, severance pay, etc.) and indirect costs (in terms of lost productivity and managerial time spent disciplining personnel) generated by troubled employees are phenomenal. It is estimated that problem employees cost employers approximately 25 percent of their annual budgets in lost time, accidents, and higher insurance premiums (Pati and Adkins, 1983). These costs may run into billions of dollars.

While EAPs may not be the panacea some claim, they are tools that police administrators can use to help troubled employees overcome personal, physical, emotional, and social problems that have a negative impact on job performance. Alcoholism has, for any number of reasons, been a relatively persistent problem in American law enforcement. The direct and indirect costs associated with alcohol abuse are incalculable. In the past, alcohol-impaired officers were hidden away in "rubber gun squad" jobs or separated from the service. Things are very different today. Economic humanists try to modulate conflict and salvage alcoholic employees. The New York City Police Department has been in the avant-garde. It is estimated that 75 percent of the alcohol-impaired officers who are referred to and participate in the EAP recover and begin making a more positive contribution to the organization. Treatment programs in the private sector report similar results (DuBrin, 1985).

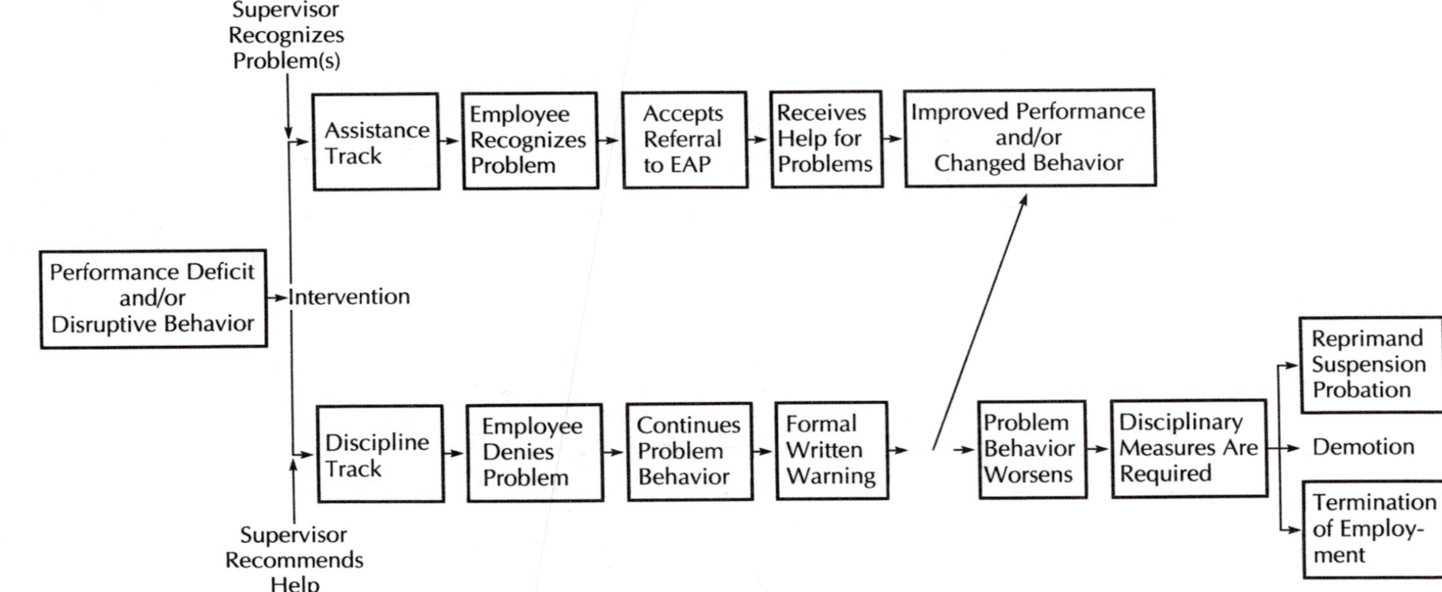

FIGURE 13.3 Dealing with Performance Deficits and Disruptive Job-Related Behavior.

CASE STUDY

Lieutenant Barry Simpson

Barry Simpson is a bright, street-wise police officer with a degree in human resources management. He was just promoted and has been assigned to the research and planning unit of a fairly large municipal police department. The department has been plagued by personnel problems and has lost a great deal of its credibility. Lt. Simpson's job, as a human resources development specialist, is to pinpoint the cause or causes of the problem and recommend managerial strategies designed to remedy the situation.

Based on an in-depth analysis of over 90 cases that resulted in severe disciplinary action, Lt. Simpson concluded the interpersonal conflict between police officers or between police officers and civilians was a significant precipitating factor. He also found the much of this dysfunctional conflict was rooted in the physical, emotional, and social problems of troubled employees. It became obvious to him that these personal problems were exacerbated by the stress inherent in law enforcement and the inhospitable psychosocial environment within which police officers ply their trade.

Lt. Simpson's research helped him to understand that interpersonal conflict (induced by unresolved personal problems) exacts an incalculable toll on any complex organization in terms of poor performance, lost productivity, absenteeism, disciplinary action, and turnover. He came to the conclusion that the traditional response—to terminate problem employees—may be "penny wise and pound foolish" in that it is a short-run solution to a long-range problem. The cost of replacing otherwise competent alcohol or drug dependent employees is often much more costly than salvaging them. The same is true when it comes to dealing with those in physical discomfort or emotional distress.

In a preliminary report to the deputy chief in charge of research and planning, Lt. Simpson called for an emphasis on economic humanism in the police department. The deputy chief signed off and forwarded Lt. Simpson's report to the chief of police.

What is economic humanism? Why is it such an important concept? If you were Lt. Simpson, what specific recommendations would you give to your superiors? How should they go about minimizing dysfunctional interpersonal conflict and salvaging troubled employees?

Every police department should establish or have access to an independent EAP that works with management and for employees. The program must be designed to protect each employee's rights (including the right to privacy), yet provide managers with the information necessary to protect the health and welfare of the citizens served and the employees seeking help. Once the EAP is up and running, self-referral should be encouraged. In addition, management should adopt a strong disciplinary policy that incorporates mandatory participation is the EAP as an alternative to appropriate punitive action in conflict situations (Williams and Bratton, 1990).

Summary

Interpersonal and intergroup conflict is a ubiquitous and normal fact of life in complex criminal justice organizations. Conflict arises in situations where someone or something thwarts or is about to thwart someone else's goals. It is an unfolding process rather than a discrete event.

Many police administrators harbor traditionalist views about conflict. They view all conflict as dysfunctional and bad. Their goal is to eliminate it regardless of the cost. Modern-thinking police administrators, on the other hand, view conflict somewhat differently. They accept beneficial conflict and try to neutralize destructive conflict. The interactionists believe conflict is beneficial when it forces the parties to reevaluate the situation and take proactive steps designed to find realistic solutions to divisive problems.

The common sources of conflict in complex criminal justice organizations are (1) interdependence, (2) differences in power, status, and culture, (3) organizational ambiguity, (4) unbridled competition for scarce resources, (5) drive for autonomy, and (6) the bifurcation of subunit interests. Conflict is dysfunctional when it creates too much anxiety, disrupts healthy relationships, consumes an excessive amount of time and energy, keeps the organization from accomplishing its mission, or leads to destructive behavior. Functional conflict, on the other hand, energizes people, enhances communication, provides an outlet for pent-up frustration, and becomes an educational experience.

While there are a number of potentially effective conflict management strategies that can be used in police work, the most promising techniques are problem-solving and integration. Problem-solving is designed to confront conflict issues in a direct manner. It focuses on identifying the problem, diagnosing the cause (causes) of the problem, constructing viable solutions to the problem, and moving systematically toward resolution of the conflict. Integration, on the other hand, is an approach to problem-solving in which police managers seek solutions so that both parties to the conflict can achieve their own desires (or goals) without sacrificing anything of value. Integration is an ideal state in which all parties transcend the conflict mode and move on to genuine collaboration.

Problem employees are often a source of dysfunctional conflict in complex criminal justice organizations. Under these conditions, it is management's responsibility to neutralize the conflict or reduce it to an acceptable level. Based on the emerging philosophy of economic humanism, many police departments have established employee assistance programs. EAPs are designed to improve organizational as well as personal performance by making prevention, intervention, and treatment services available to ill, troubled, or disruptive personnel. Competent police administrators learn how to develop and manage all kinds of human resources rather than to waste them.

Key Concepts

Collaboration
Cooperation
Competition
Aggression
Interpersonal conflict
Intergroup conflict

Conflict cycle
Traditionalists
Behavioralists
Interactionists
Organizational conflict
Causes of conflict
Functional conflict
Dysfunctional conflict
Conflict management
Management strategies
Management techniques
Strategic conflict
Problem-solving
Integration
Managerial styles
Problem employees
Employee assistance
EAP

Discussion Topics and Questions

1. What are the basic components in the collaboration/aggression continuum? Describe them and give an example of each one.
2. Define *interpersonal conflict*. How does it differ from intergroup conflict in an organizational context?
3. List the steps or stages in the conflict development cycle. Explain how they fit together as part of a dynamic, unfolding process.
4. Identify the three distinct phases in management thinking as it relates to organizational conflict. How do the modern-day interactionists differ from traditionalists? Explain the Japanese view of organizational conflict.
5. What are the six primary causes of conflict in complex criminal justice organizations? Give examples.
6. Contrast and compare functional with dysfunctional conflict. Discuss the most useful aspects of organizational conflict.
7. Identify the most common conflict management techniques used by police administrators. Why have problem-solving and integration become so important in police work?
8. What are the basic managerial typologies used to describe police administrators in terms of their approach to resolving interpersonal and/or intergroup conflict? Explain why good managers normally subscribe to a contingency perspective.
9. Define *economic humanism*. How has it been translated into action in the employee assistance movement? What is an EAP? Discuss the role that managers play in the referral process.

References

ALBANESE, ROBERT. 1981. *Managing: Toward Accountability for Performance*. Homewood, IL: Richard D. Irwin.

BAKER, MARK. 1985. *COPS*. New York: Pocket Books.

BARNARD, CHESTER I. 1976. *The Functions of the Executive*. Cambridge: Harvard University Press.

BARON, ROBERT A. 1983. *Behavior in Organizations: Understanding and Managing the Human Side of Work*. Boston: Allyn & Bacon.

BOBBITT, H. RANDOLPH, ROBERT H. BREINHOLT, ROBERT H. DOKTOR, and JAMES P. MCNAUL. 1978. *Organizational Behavior* (2nd ed.). Englewood Cliffs, NJ: Prentice-Hall.

BREHM, JACK W. 1966. *A Theory of Psychological Resistance*. New York: Academic Press.

BRODERICK, JOHN J. 1987. *Police in a Time of Change*. Prospect Heights, IL: Waveland Press.

BURK, RONALD J. 1970. "Methods of Resolving Superior-Subordinate Conflict: The Constructive Use of Subordinate Differences and Disagreements," *Organizational Behavior and Human Performance*, No. 5.

COLE, GEORGE F. 1986. *The American System of Criminal Justice*. Monterey, CA: Brooks/Cole.

DUBRIN, ANDREW J. 1985. *Contemporary Applied Management* (2nd ed.). Plano, TX: Business Publications.

ETZIONI, AMITAI. 1964. "On Self-Encapsulating Conflicts," *Journal of Conflict Resolution*, No. 4.

FOX, ELLIOT M., and L. URWICK. 1973. *Dynamic Administration: The Collected Papers of Mary Parker Follett*. New York: Hippocrene Books.

GRAHAM, GERALD. 1984. "Strong Managers Are Decisive: The Weak Are Not,"*The Kansas City Star*, August 5.

HALLAS, CLARK. 1990. "FOP Chief Disputes City Police Complaint Data,"*The Pittsburgh Press*, August 26.

HITT, MICHAEL A., R. DENNIS MIDDLEMIST, and ROBERT L. MATHIS. 1979. *Effective Management*. New York: West.

HOLDEN, RICHARD N. 1986. *Modern Police Management*. Englewood Cliffs, NJ: Prentice-Hall.

HOLT, DAVID H. 1987. *Management: Principles and Practices*. Englewood Cliffs, NJ: Prentice-Hall.

HUNGER, J. D., and L. W. STERN. 1976. "An Assessment of the Functionality of the Superordinate Goal in Reducing Conflict," *Academy of Management Journal*, No. 19.

JOHNS, GARY. 1988. *Organizational Behavior: Understanding Life at Work* (2nd ed.), Boston: Scott, Foresman.

Law Enforcement News. 1990. "4th Reverse-Bias Suit for Dallas PD Promotion Policy," March 31.

LEBOEUF, MICHAEL. 1985. GMP: *The Greatest Management Principle in the World*. New York: Barkley Books.

LEONARD, V. A., and HARRY W. MORE. 1987. *Police Organization and Management*. Mineola, NY: Foundation Press.

MARUTA, YOSHIO. 1983. "Tetsuri: Guidelines for Management, Research and Development." Unpublished paper presented at the 2nd Annual Japan-U.S. Business Conference.

MORE, HARRY W., and W. FRED WEGENER. 1990. *Effective Police Supervision*. Cincinnati: Anderson.

PATI, GOPAL C., and JOHN L. ADKINS. 1983. "The Employer's Role in Alcoholism Assistance," *Personnel Journal*, No. 7.

PONDY, LOUIS. 1967. "Organizational Conflict: Concepts and Models," *Administrative Science Quarterly*, No. 9.

REITZ, H. JOSEPH. 1981. *Behavior in Organizations*. Homewood, IL: Richard D. Irwin.

ROARK, ALBERT E., and LINDA WILKINSON. 1979. "Approaches to Conflict Management," *Group and Organizational Studies*, No. 4.

ROBBINS, STEPHEN P. 1989. *Organizational Behavior: Concepts, Controversies and Applications* (4th ed.). Englewood Cliffs, NJ: Prentice-Hall.

ROBINETTE, HILLARY M. 1985. "The Police Problem Employee." In James J. Fyfe (Ed.), *Police Management Today*. Washington, DC: International City Management Association.

RUE, LESLIE W., and LLOYD L. BYARS. 1980. *Management: Theory and Application*. Homewood, IL: Richard D. Irwin.

SWANSON, CHARLES R., LEONARD TERRITO, and ROBERT W. TAYLOR. 1988. *Police Administration: Structures, Processes and Behavior* (2nd ed.). New York: Macmillan.

TANSIK, DAVID A., RICHARD B. CHASE, and NICHOLAS J. AQUILANO. 1980. *Management: A Life Cycle Approach*. Homewood, IL: Richard D. Irwin.

TEMPLETON, JANE. 1969. "For Corporate Vigor, Plan a Fight Today," *Sales Management*, No. 13.

THIBAULT, EDWARD A., LAWRENCE M. LYNCH, and R. BRUCE MCBRIDE. 1990. *Proactive Police Management* (2nd ed.). Englewood Cliffs, NJ: Prentice-Hall.

THOMAS, KENNETH. 1976. "Conflict and Conflict Management." In Marvin D. Dunnette (Ed.), *Handbook of Industrial and Organizational Psychology*. Chicago: Rand-McNally.

WAMBAUGH, JOSEPH. 1973. *The Choirboys*. New York: Delacorte Press.

WHISENAND, PAUL M., and GEORGE E. RUSH. 1988. *Supervising Police Personnel: Back to the Basics*. Englewood Cliffs, NJ: Prentice-Hall.

WILLIAMS, FRANK E., and JOAN E. BRATTON. 1990. "A Step-By-Step Guide to Developing Employee Assistance Programs in Small Police Agencies," *The Police Chief*, No. 2.

ZIMBARDO, PHILIP, and EBBE B. EBBESEN. 1969. *Influencing Attitudes and Changing Behavior*. Menlo Park, CA: Addison-Wesley.

For Further Reading

EWING, DAVID W. 1983. *Do It My Way or You're Fired: Employee Rights and the Changing Role of Management Prerogatives*. New York: Wiley.

An informative text that explores the changing role of management in a humanistic environment emphasizing participative management and self-discipline. The author suggests that by encouraging industrial democracy and reducing dysfunctional conflict between labor and management, public agencies will make fewer mistakes in accomplishing their mission, goals, and objectives. He also believes society will benefit from esprit de corps and élan vital in the work force. The author concludes that voluntary collaboration will become the norm and pave the way for the creation of more efficient, effective, and productive organizations.

LYNCH, RONALD G. 1986. *The Police Manager* (3rd ed.). New York: Random House.

A durable police management text containing a good discussion of the five styles of conflict management available to modern police administrators: (1) win/lose, (2) yield/lose, (3) lose/leave, (4) lose/lose (compromise), and (5) win/win (synergism). The author argues that while the synergistic style may be the best, the style that is eventually chosen will depend on the situation, the people involved, the time available, and the manager's philosophical orientation.

SCHERMERHORN, JOHN R., JAMES G. HUNT, and RICHARD N. OSBORN. 1982. *Managing Organizational Behavior*. New York: Wiley.

This text contains an excellent discussion of interpersonal conflict in complex work-oriented organizations. The authors differentiate between constructive and destructive conflict. They explore the conflict development cycle and discuss various conflict resolution strategies. Blake and Mouton's conflict grid is utilized to illustrate the five basic conflict management styles of avoidance, authoritative command, soothing, compromise, and problem-solving. Some additional conflict management techniques are discussed.

WHISENAND, PAUL M., and FRED FERGUSON. 1989. *The Managing of Police Organizations* (3rd ed.). Englewood Cliffs, NJ: Prentice-Hall.

The authors discuss conflict and its consequences in complex law enforcement organizations. They also examine the concept of principled negotiation and offer it as an all-purpose strategy for conflict resolution. If managers really want to be effective in dealing with conflict, they must learn to be problem solvers. Being nice is not the answer. They must be objective, analytical, creative, and tough. Good managers do not bargain over position. They know how to separate the people from the conflict. Creative managers generate a number of options and adopt objective criteria. They are always willing to take calculated risks in order to resolve dysfunctional conflicts.

CHAPTER 14

Developing the Organization: Techniques for Improving Performance

LEARNING OBJECTIVES

1. Define *organizational development* (OD).
2. Describe the functions performed by a change agent.
3. List the values that are inherently a part of OD.
4. Describe team building as a technique of planned change.
5. Identify the characteristics of a healthy police organization.
6. Describe the 14-point QWL program.
7. List the key characteristics of survey feedback.

Today, as never before, change is occurring at such a rapid pace that ambiguity is becoming an everyday part of the managerial process. Thus police managers have to seek out new tactics or strategies by thinking about problems differently. Managers must learn to contribute to the development of subordinates, which in turn will lead to the formation of a creative and highly responsive organization.

Ambiguity is not new—it is something all police officers and managers deal with daily. It would be ideal to have everything fall into place, but such is seldom the case (McCaskey, 1982). In reality, managing ambiguity is what police managers are paid for, and they must accept the challenge of each contradiction. In ambiguous situations (where programs, procedures, or rules and regulations just do not work) a police manager should turn to the human resources within the department, preferably by utilizing one or more of the organizational development techniques.

INTRODUCTORY CASE

Chief Robert Miller

Chief Robert Miller assumed command of the Quail Valley Police Department after being selected via an assessment center. He was previously a captain in another department where he had served for 14 years. It is well known his predecessor had a drinking problem and retired early on disability. During the last three years of the chief's tenure, the morale of the officers in the department had gone down considerably, and the officers performed their duties with a minimum of managerial guidance from the chief's office.

The department has 42 sworn officers and 9 civilians. The city has a population of 37,000 and is governed by a city manager and a weak mayor. The city is located at the edge of a metropolitan area and still has vestiges of open land and some truck farming. In recent years the city has grown because a number of people have opted to live in the community and commute to other cities to work.

It is anticipated that within 20 years the population of the city will double and the tax base will be improved considerably. The racial mix of the city is currently 12 percent black, 26 percent Latino, and the remainder Caucasian. Projections are that the racial mix will remain the same. The city has a moderate crime rate and the greatest problem is residential burglary.

Mark Rogers, the city manager, has given the chief a mandate to professionalize the department. In the current table of organization there are three divisions: services, investigation, and uniform—each headed by a lieutenant. In addition, there are 6 sergeants, 5 detectives, and the remainder are patrol officers. One-half of the patrol officers have less than 3 years service and the remainder have an average of 12 years service. There are 2 black officers, 5 Latinos, and the remainder are Caucasian. The department does not have any policewomen. One was hired 3 years ago and did not complete the probationary period.

The chief has decided to call a meeting of the lieutenants and sergeants to discuss the reorganization of the department and determine what can be done to improve the organization.

Prepare an agenda for the initial meeting. Justify the inclusion of each item. How would you involve the lieutenants and sergeants in the meeting? What would be the next thing you would do after the initial meeting? How would you go about involving the other employees? What would be the first organizational development (OD) technique you would use? How would you handle individuals who feel OD is a waste of time?

Definition

Organizational development (OD) is the process of planned change and the improvement of organizations through the application of the behavioral sciences (Griffin and Moorhead, 1986). OD has varying definitions. In its most extended sense, W. Warren Burke has suggested it actually means organizational change (Burke, 1982). Implicit in the definition is that if OD is to succeed, it has to have the support of top management. It is a long-range process, so those expecting immediate results are probably going to be disappointed. Some have even suggested that when organizational renewal takes place, it might be seven years before significant changes can be observed.

An OD intervention is essentially solving an organizational problem through the application of knowledge of the behavioral sciences, including psychology, sociology, and cultural anthropology. The focus of an OD intervention is to change the culture of the organization whether it involves individuals, groups, or the total structure.

Organizational development is goal oriented, with its ultimate purpose to improve organizational effectiveness. It is not surprising that organizational development is complex, includes a variety of approaches for introducing change, makes assumptions about human behavior, and is a process emphasizing the evaluation and implementation of organizational choices (Williams, DuBrin, and Sisk, 1985).

Organizational Development Objectives

A police manager can make better use of OD by being fully aware of its potential for solving current problems and creating an organizational climate maximizing the effective use of resources. Objectives of OD include the following (Lorsch, 1987):

1. Creation of an open departmental culture focusing on problem-solving.
2. The building of trust between individuals and groups.
3. Moving decision-making responsibilities to the lowest possible location in the organization.
4. Maximizing individual self-control and self-direction.
5. Helping managers achieve organizational objectives.
6. Fostering an organizational climate stressing a commitment to organizational objectives.
7. Maximizing collaborative efforts.

Attainment of these objectives creates a working environment allowing for individual and group initiative, building mutual support, and acquiring individual and departmental goals.

Basic Values of Organizational Development (OD)

A manager's ability to contribute significantly to the development of human resources depends not only on having a humanistic view of people, but going one step further and employing a managerial style in support of such

Mutual Benefit Management-sponsored continuing education programs can fulfill an officer's need for growth and development while benefiting the organization as a whole. *(Courtesy of* Police Chief *Magazine)*

a belief system. There are many police managers who have received excellent management training and know all the latest buzz words, but still operate in the same manner they always have—which in many instances is authoritarian.

OD assumptions about people in organizations are genuinely optimistic and require a manager to function humanistically and in a participative manner (Pascarella, 1984). The following are underlying values of OD (French and Bell, 1984; Robbins, 1986; Schermerhorn, Hunt and Osborn, 1988):

1. Most individuals enjoy working in a challenging environment.
2. Officers, for the most part, have a need for growth and development.
3. When problems occur they should be confronted immediately—not ignored.
4. An atmosphere of trust and cooperation enhances both individuals and the organization.
5. Participation in decision-making will make the participants more committed to the changes caused by the decision.
6. Individuals must be treated with respect and viewed as capable of assuming responsibilities for their own actions.
7. Participation in groups will help satisfy organization members' needs.
8. Groups can work either for or against an organization.

9. Collaboration can benefit both the organization and individuals.
10. An organization can be structured to meet the needs of the department as well as groups and individuals.

The basic values of OD present a clear-cut challenge to police managers of the future. The values just expressed call for the redefinition of work and working relationships. They are not a threat to the vast majority of managers, but are definitely a menace to autocratic managers (Pascarella, 1984).

One of the primary objectives of an OD effort is to develop the organization to the point where the culture is based on *openness and trust* (see Table 14.1). Its achievement might even be said to be a significant breakthrough in the relationship between employees and management. It is most difficult to have real communications in a police department when one constantly hears such comments as, "I don't trust that guy" or, "She is a manipulator and will do anything to get ahead" or, "If anything goes wrong he will always find someone to blame."

When a manager does not trust officers, it creates resentment and eventually a negative working environment. In a trusting atmosphere subordinates are allowed to make independent decisions. Trust does not just happen—it has to be cultivated and it must become the foundation of any OD effort (Leonard and More, 1987). Trust means allowing subordinates to function with a sense of confidence that they are supported by superiors (Dyer, 1983). Trust is based on managers believing that officers have the capacity to contribute to the organization.

Feedback is an essential aspect of communicating (see Chapter 10) and helps a manager create a climate where employees feel safe when they share information. It is difficult to underestimate the importance of feedback. Without it, communication does not exist. Effective feedback is not easily achieved (Reece and Brandt, 1987). It requires a manager to be especially sensitive to employees because many people find they are uncomfortable when speaking to someone about their performance. A manager should keep in mind that some employees will remain silent rather than share information with someone in a position of power (Dyer, 1983).

To determine what impact they have on others when soliciting feedback, managers should use a variety of techniques including personal discussion with peers or subordinates, written communication, group meetings, or questionnaires to obtain anonymous feedback (Dyer, 1983). Whatever technique is used, employees must feel free to express their impressions about work issues. Focus 14.1 discusses managing change.

TABLE 14.1 Foundations of a Successful OD Effort

Trust and openness
Feedback
Confronting conflict
Risk taking

FOCUS 14.1

Future-Shock Absorbers

PROFIT IN A CHANGING WORLD BY INVESTING IN OTHER PEOPLE

After you have set your goals, external events may alter circumstances in ways requiring you to adjust your approach, or even your mission itself. The most important factor in managing the changes will be the cooperation you get from others—both those who work for you and the outsiders who want to help you because the things you are doing helps them as well. If you can form an alliance of minds and make them cooperators with you, they will keep you in touch with what's happening out there; they'll happily help you figure out what to do about it.

But how do you make them want to help you? My late friend and colleague Napolean Hill said, in the 1920s, it was simply a matter of "learning to live harmoniously with others." His language may sound simplistic, but his method is as effective as ever.

1. First, learn to like people, whether or not they think and act as you do.
2. Second, make it a practice to let people know you like them, through words and deeds.
3. Third, and most important, go the extra mile, by rendering favors or some form of service to them that you are not required to provide.

SOURCE. W. Clement Stone, "Future-Shock Absorbers: Profit in a Changing World by Investing in Other People," *Success*, October 1987, p. 80. Reprinted with permission from *Success* magazine, Copyright ©1987 by HAL Holding Corporation.

Another value of importance to organizational development is the desire and ability to *confront conflict*. Whenever individuals interact, the potential for conflict is inevitable. Conflict can be positive if it is directed constructively. In police departments, discord occurs not only between individuals and groups, but between units and divisions. For instance, in some agencies, traffic units dominate the department; in others, the detective bureau holds the commanding position. In either instance it can lead to operational discrepancies when one unit always seems to receive greater support than the other.

In patrol-dominated police departments, real police work is viewed as working the street, and all other specialties are perceived as second-class efforts. In these situations, conflict is inevitable as these priorities surface. All this calls for some type of adjustment by police managers. In this instance, an OD effort can prove to be an effective means of dealing with the conflict, especially when the organization is open and there is a definite feeling of trust between managers and employees.

The last value of importance to organizational development is *risk taking*. Ambiguity occurs when a police manager engages in risk-taking activities. When responsibilities are delegated, pressure is placed on everyone involved. Mistakes will be made but they must be turned into learning situations (not scapegoating, or finding someone to blame). People must be allowed to grow, not vegetate. Risk taking calls for the sharing of power and a deep understanding of the needs of employees (Pascarella, 1984).

When a police organization acknowledges the existence of and need to control conflict, creates a working environment emphasizing openness and trust, provides for feedback, and allows managers to assume risk-taking postures, then the organization is reaching a point where it can maximize organizational productivity (Randall, 1979).

The Healthy Organization

When organizational development is successful, the organization becomes healthier and more responsive to the community it serves. The real purpose of OD is to improve organizations as much as possible. A totally healthy organization might be idealistic, but striving for it is certainly worthwhile. The healthier the organization, the more it represents the values of OD we have discussed (see Table 14.2).

In the healthy police organization many goals are established by statute or ordinance, but some goals and most objectives are arrived at jointly. Everyone is truly supportive of departmental objectives, and personal objectives are integrated into the organization whenever possible. Departmental objectives are carefully spelled out and everyone is aware of the relationship between goals and objectives. Managers define a goal as a statement of broad direction, general purpose, or intent; in contrast, the definition of an objective, which is a desired accomplishment that can be measured within a given timeframe and under specific conditions. For example:

Goal: to reduce the opportunities for the commission of some crimes through preventive patrol and other measures.

Objective: to reduce residential burglaries by 33 percent during the next fiscal year as compared to previous fiscal years.

The healthy organization has problems but they are handled effectively—not conveniently ignored. Officers talk about problems when they occur and then work with managers to resolve them. Constructive feedback is a continuing process and two-way communication is stressed.

TABLE 14.2 Characteristics of a Healthy Police Organization

1. Objectives are jointly developed by managers.
2. Problems and issues are confronted.
3. Informality in relationships is acceptable conduct.
4. Decision-making is delegated to the lowest possible problem-solving location.
5. Responsibility is shared.
6. Personal needs are considered important.
7. Collaboration between management and employees is considered essential.
8. Conflict is encountered and managed.
9. Feedback is two-way and continuous.
10. Managerial styles vary according to the situation.
11. Within the organization there is an atmoshpere of trust between managers and employees.
12. Risk is accepted when making decisions and conducting operations.
13. Poor performance is confronted and dealt with objectively.
14. Policy, procedures, and the organizational structure are utilized to support goal attainment.
15. Employees are treated as responsible individuals capable of performing at a high level.

SOURCE: Thomas H. Patten, Jr., *Organizational Development Through Teambuilding* (New York: Wiley, 1981).

Task accomplishment is seen as paramount—thus a reasonable degree of informality in personal relationships is encouraged. Emphasis is placed on problem-solving instead of the organizational structure. The chain of command is utilized (only as a frame of reference for facilitating communication) but is never allowed to disrupt goal attainment. What really counts is achievement rather than a concern with rank, status, or position power.

Employees who have problems are referred to those who have the expertise to help resolve them and can render the most appropriate decision. This process maximizes the participation of those who are both knowledgeable and also more apt to be motivated to solve the problem(s).

In a healthy organization, the managerial approach emphasizes sharing responsibility. It is definitely the opposite of the *we/they* style of management, which takes the position that it is top management's job to tell everyone what to do and how to do it. Shared responsibility improves communications, reduces ambiguity, and creates a support base to facilitate implementation. In addition, sharing responsibility demonstrates the willingness of top management to accept the judgment of lower-level managers and employees.

Personal needs in the healthy organization are given serious consideration. There is a commitment to the integration of personal needs with organizational needs. Job satisfaction is emphasized with a focus on satisfying subordinates' needs for self-actualization in their work. Motivators such as recognition, achievement, and responsibility are stressed (Leonard and More, 1987).

In a healthy police department, managers and employees work together to achieve objectives. This type of collaboration rejects the competition and petty jealousy quite common in unhealthy police organizations. Information is shared, and the knowledge one possesses (not rank) is what counts. Collaboration is encouraged (regardless of one's position in the organization) and training programs promote the development of expertise.

Conflict is viewed as inevitable because of differing attitudes of individuals and groups. It must be managed instead of ignored or rejected. Conflict is accepted as a challenge and dealt with openly and candidly. The goal is to manage conflict with all the resources at the command of the organization (see Chapter 13).

Feedback in the healthy organization is viewed as an integral component of the managerial process. Feedback never concerns itself with personality, but views performance as essential. It is two-way and is actively sought by employees at all levels and in every rank. Feedback is used in order to grow and meet the challenges of a constantly changing work environment.

Leadership style is flexible. When tasks are varied and complex, the manager utilizes a directive leadership style. When tasks are routine, the manager limits control and utilizes an employee-centered supportive managerial style. During unusual occurrences or emergencies, the leadership style is shifted to authoritarian.

Members of the organization work in an atmosphere of trust. Involvement is emphasized and employees have the freedom to work for departmental goals and determine work strategies. Control is minimal and records are limited to those needed for achieving objectives.

In the healthy organization, risk is accepted as a necessary part of the managerial process and essential to growth and development. When the outcome cannot be controlled, developments are monitored carefully so as to minimize negative consequences. Risk taking is perceived as a managerial challenge rather than a negative inhibitor.

When poor performance occurs in the healthy organization it is dealt with quickly, and the process treats those involved with care and understanding. Standards are clear-cut and known to all. Discipline is used as a last resort and a strong effort is made to administer it judiciously. Training, coaching, and supervision are used to resolve problems. Expectations are high and mediocrity is not acceptable employee conduct (Patten, 1981).

As change occurs, the healthy organization responds by altering the structure to meet the new situation. Policies and procedures are viewed as flexible guidelines and not absolute dogma. When policies and procedures become dysfunctional, they are reviewed and changed and thus are never allowed to become a refuge for incompetent employees.

The healthy organization encourages every employee to develop to the maximum. A job description is never allowed to limit the achievement of objectives. Employees are given wide latitude in their performance and the necessary authority to carry out their work. They are encouraged to support each other in order to achieve teamwork (Patten, 1981).

Goal attainment by the most effective means possible is what counts. The goal of the contemporary police manager is the creation of a healthy working environment. As change occurs, it is accepted as an inevitable consequence of striving to be more effective. The healthy organization is based on trust and a culture promoting job satisfaction.

Intervention Techniques

Organizational development uses a number of techniques to change an organization and influence either individuals or groups. It implies a great deal more than making people happy or teaching them how to get along with fellow employees. OD concentrates on changing conditions so officers can work more effectively and achieve their goals (Quick, 1980).

Intervention techniques utilized in organizational development have the following common characteristics (Beer, 1980):

1. They are applied to the total organization.
2. Members of the organization identify the issues and the problems to be solved.
3. Organizational members are taught how to solve both immediate and future problems.
4. Emphasis is placed on the joint collection of data, its analysis, and the developing of a planned intervention followed by an evaluation.
5. An effort is made to create an environment that is committed to change.

Focusing human energy toward specific organizational goals can be accomplished by utilizing OD intervention techniques that deal with the environmental conditions of an organization. Specific intervention techniques can be applied to either individuals, groups, or the total organization. Values, attitudes, relationships, and the organizational environment are all issues of great concern to consultants and agency personnel (Leonard and More, 1987).

Once the decision is made to alter the organizational environment, an OD effort usually consists of the following elements (Rue and Byars, 1986): (1) diagnosis, (2) planning, (3) training, and (4) evaluation.

The diagnosis phase of an OD effort can be quite simple or exceedingly complex. It involves the gathering and analysis of data in order to determine what areas need to be improved. Information can be obtained by utilizing questionnaires, conducting interviews, holding meetings, observation, or examining rules, regulations, and procedures (French and Bell, 1984). The information sought may include superior/subordinate relationships, how conflict is resolved, techniques of goal setting, or how problems are solved. For example, when determining communications patterns, the following questions can be addressed: Is communication two-way? Who talks to whom, for how long, about what? Are communications filtered? Who initiates communications? (French and Bell, 1984).

After the diagnosis phase, it is necessary to develop plans for dealing with the identifiable problems and issues. This can include how to develop organizational flexibility, providing a frame of reference for decision-making, how to maximize employee involvement, or the development of indicators for measuring individual and unit performance (More and O'Neill, 1984).

Training is the next phase in altering the organizational environment. It consists of sharing information on a one-on-one basis or by more traditional methods such as group discussion or lecture. The key is to involve everyone who will be affected by the planned change. The training can be done by in-house personnel or by consultants, depending on which method will bring the best results.

The final phase is evaluation and involves the gathering of data in order to determine the effects of the OD effort on the organization. The evaluation includes identifying the need for additional training, determining the need for obtaining additional information (in order to refine the initial plan), or fact-finding leading to the creation of change-oriented program(s) (Rue and Byars, 1986). (See Focus 14.2 for a discussion of one OD effort.)

Sensitivity Training

Sensitivity training, also known as laboratory training or T-group, is one of the earlier OD techniques. It is an intensive process designed to foster interpersonal awareness and personal growth. Participants share their feelings and receive feedback on their own behavior from group members. In recent years it has been partially supplanted by other intervention techniques such as process consultation (French and Bell, 1984; Robbins, 1986).

Sensitivity training is conducted with a group of 8 to 15 members. Meetings are held without an agenda and are leaderless. Normally the group meets

FOCUS 14.2

The Use of Quality Circles by Police Departments

Quality circles are currently being used by many public and private sector organizations in the United States. Of the 300 police departments responding, 48 (16 percent) reported having used quality circles sometime during the previous three years.

A quality circle is typically composed of nonsupervisory employees and a circle leader, who is usually the first-line supervisor for the work unit (for instance, a patrol sergeant or communications supervisor). However, some other person, such as another member of the work unit, can be the leader. Circle members receive considerable training, particularly in techniques for group interaction and problem-solving. A quality circle facilitator, chosen by the department from outside the work unit, provides the training, helps the circle get under way, and provides continuing help and guidance to the circle on any problems it may encounter.

The facilitator helps the group remain focused on the problem at hand and develop feasible solutions. The facilitator also acts as liaison between the circle and other units when the circle needs information, assistance, or cooperation from organizational units external to its own area. The circle is allowed to select its own problems for study.

Although there is no consensus on the purpose of quality circles, objectives usually include the improvement of services provided by the members of the unit, working conditions, worker morale and/or communication within the organization, and the personal development of circle members.

SOURCE. Harry P. Hatry and John M. Greiner, *Improving the Use of Quality Circles in Police Departments*, National Institute of Justice (Washington, DC: U. S. Department of Justice, 1986).

away from work and the time devoted to the effort generally ranges from a weekend up to two weeks. In some instances the group is composed of employees who work together; in others the group consists of employees who work for the same organization but not with each other, or the group includes individuals from different organizations (Johns, 1983).

When a T-group meets, there is a change agent who serves as a catalyst and facilitator for the group. Generally the first session starts with a brief introduction, which specifies that the primary objective for the group is to learn more about itself. As the program moves along, the change agent will take a very passive role, but if needed can present conceptual material on such topics as interpersonal relations and group dynamics (French and Bell, 1984).

The group is process oriented; consequently, the participants learn through observation and participation rather than being lectured by the change agent.

If frustration or even hostility occurs, it can be directed against the change agent who in many instances will appear to be inept and ineffective because of his or her passive position. This allows the change agent to focus on the specific event, such as hostility, and encourage participants to express their ideas, beliefs, and attitudes (Johns, 1983).

Every effort is made to assure feedback is nonevaluative; however, the process can still be quite stressful for some participants. It is felt, however, that a certain degree of anxiety helps the participants learn from the process. Generally, the expected outcomes of sensitivity training include the following (Campbell and Dunnette, 1978):

1. A greater awareness and sensitivity to the behavior of others.
2. A better understanding of group dynamics.
3. The ability to analyze one's own behavior.
4. The capacity to act based on what has been learned.
5. Improved diagnostic skills.
6. An ability to improve interpersonal relations.

Sensitivity training has strong supporters as well as a certain number of detractors. It has been difficult to predict how the training will affect an employee. In fact, sensitivity training with its accompanying frustration and anxiety caused by the feedback process has caused psychological problems for some participants. Another problem, many former T-group participants have found, is the difficulty of transferring the newly acquired knowledge back to the working environment (Johns, 1983). An effort has been made to solve the first problem by a more careful selection and screening of applicants for T-groups. The second problem has been addressed by making the training more job-oriented or by utilizing real organizational problems to work on (Johns, 1983).

Currently sensitivity training is used by some organizations to increase interpersonal awareness as a means of integrating the individual into the organization. It is the view of many change agents that sensitivity training has its place, but it is only one of a number of intervention techniques used as part of an overall OD effort.

Team Building

During the last decade, team building has become increasingly popular and is now one of the most widely used intervention techniques to improve the health and effectiveness of police departments. Team building is a training technique involving both managers and employees. It might involve a team of offices on the same shift, a special unit such as a SWAT team, or a task force created to address a specific problem (for a detailed discussion of groups, see Chapter 7). Team-building efforts by change agents can involve the more traditional emphasis on interpersonal relations, but one major difference is the special weight placed on tasks to be performed (Johns, 1983).

CASE STUDY

Chief Wally Partin

Chief Wally Partin has been the chief of police for three years in the city of Popular, which has a population of 113,321. The community has an excellent tax base because of a large number of light industrial plants and two major shopping centers. It is fortunate to have a below-average crime rate (in terms of felonies) with the exception of residential burglaries.

The department has 132 sworn police officers and 42 civilians. There are three major divisions: investigations, field services, and administration. Specialized units include a SWAT team, a traffic unit, a youth bureau, and a crime prevention unit. In addition, officers are detailed to a metropolitan narcotics unit.

During the last two years the community has been up in arms over the large number of residential burglaries. The situation is to the point that a number of influential community organizations are pressuring the city administration and the police department. The mayor has told the chief she wants something done about the problem. The research assistant who works in the chief's office has compiled a report on residential burglaries showing the incidents occur throughout the city and the vast majority of the burglaries are committed by youths between the ages of 15 and 20 followed by young persons ages 21 to 25. During the preceding calendar year, 16 percent of the reported residential burglaries were solved.

During the weekly staff meeting, attended by the heads of the three major divisions and all special units, the problem is discussed extensively and two recommendations are presented to the chief. The first recommendation is to expand the youth services bureau and use the added personnel to target the burglary problem. The second recommendation is to adopt team policing and restructure the department accordingly.

The chief, with the approval of the mayor and city council, has decided to adopt the concept of team policing and the department will be allocated 12 new positions. The chief realizes such a major change in the way the department operates may be resisted by many of the line officers as well as some of the managers. Of special concern to the chief is the resistance he anticipates from middle managers.

In the past, the lieutenants in the department have resisted all efforts they perceived as diluting their authority. As a group, they were most comfortable in a leadership style relying on the power of their position and they tolerated little deviation from departmental procedures. The one word best describing their relationship with subordinates can only be *control*.

The other group that the chief anticipates will resist team policing consists of 12 senior patrol officers, all of whom work the swing shift. These officers have been in the department for 18 years or more, and for the most part are just putting in enough time to retire. As a group, they do not want to do anything that rocks the boat.

The chief has consulted several organizational behavior experts at the local university and has made the decision to institute an OD effort.

If you were the chief, what type of OD effort do you believe could reduce the anticipated resistance from the two groups? Would you hire an outside consultant or use departmental personnel? How would you present the team policing concept to the public?

Team-building efforts are usually conducted to achieve one or more of the following goals (Patten, 1981):

1. Creation of a working environment where there is mutual trust between all the components of the organization.
2. Development of managerial skills in the following areas:
   a. Resolving conflict with individuals and groups
   b. Interpersonal relations with superiors, peers, and subordinates
   c. Confronting issues
   d. Open and honest communications
3. Understanding motivation techniques and how to alter work through job enrichment.
4. Reviewing and examining the basic managerial skills such as work planning, setting objectives, controlling activities, controlling time, solving problems, and soliciting employees' participation.
5. Learning how to use nonfinancial rewards.

Before a team-building effort can be effective, it is necessary to follow an OD process including the following: problem identification, gathering of data, diagnosis, planning, implementation, and evaluation (Dyer, 1977). Table 14.3 identifies the sequence and also shows the interrelationship of each phase.

The team-building process is unique because it involves participation throughout the process. Generally a change agent is used during the initial steps of the process, but such involvement can be lessened as the team becomes more cohesive and a trusting relationship is established (Kellogg, 1984). Key factors in a successful team-building endeavor are the changing composition of teams and the need for the continuing integration of personnel into the team. In some departments the turnover of personnel exceeds 10 percent annually from transfers, retirements, or resignations, so a change agent may be needed over an extended period of time in order to work with continually evolving teams (Griffin and Moorhead, 1986).

TABLE 14.3 The Team-Building Process

Identification of the problem by all members of the team.

Gathering of data by all available means and methods including survey-feedback instruments.

Diagnosis of the problem by analyzing the data and determining problem areas, establishing priorities, and developing some preliminary recommendations.

Development of an action plan based on the data gathered. Such a plan should include the identification of what should be changed, who is responsible, and a timetable for completion of the effort.

Evaluation of the developmental effort by all of the participants.

SOURCE: Ricky W. Griffin and Gregory Moorhead, *Organizational Behavior* (Boston: Houghton Mifflin, 1986), and Jerry C. Wofford, *Organizational Behavior* (Boston: Kent, 1982).

During initial sessions of the team-building process it is usually beneficial for members of the team to clarify member roles and responsibilities. The change agent should serve as a catalyst and a resource person as goals are established and the team process is analyzed (Robbins, 1986).

Team strengths and weaknesses should be identified and a list of changes compiled. Differing perceptions should be resolved and priorities established. As the diagnosis phase progresses, the training sessions should become increasingly task oriented with special techniques taught to those who need them in order to deal with the problems identified. Once the skills training is completed, the way the team is performing can be analyzed in an effort to improve the process with the goal of maximizing effectiveness (Johns, 1983).

Team-building should emphasize teaching individuals how to take their share of team responsibilities so they can participate in consensual decision-making. In addition, members should be brought up to a point where they have a minimal level of relationship skills that accompanies the requisite technical knowledge (Bradford, 1984).

When members learn on the job, they become a viable part of the team because they usually find the newly acquired technical, managerial, and interpersonal knowledge not only builds up their personal competency but increases the probability of successful task accomplishment.

Team-building is most successful when it is an ongoing process. It should never be used as a one-shot operation. Regular training sessions can serve to energize and motivate team members. As new problems are identified it gives team members the opportunity to grow and respond to the challenge presented by each new situation (Griffin and Moorhead, 1986).

Survey Feedback

An intervention technique being given increased attention is survey feedback. It involves collecting data from the department and feeding it back to organizational members and groups during a series of meetings, with the intent of identifying corrective action to be taken to improve the department.

Survey feedback can be used as part of a team-building effort, but when used independently it focuses on the collection of valid data rather than interpersonal processes (Johns, 1983). Early in the development of survey-feedback techniques, the Institute for Social Research at the University of Michigan specified five steps to make a survey effective (Mann, 1961):

1. Top management supports and is involved in the preliminary planning.
2. All departmental members complete the survey instrument.
3. Top management is provided with the results of the survey, followed by its being revealed to all other participants.
4. A manager presides at a meeting in which everyone interprets the data; then plans are made for constructive change and introduction of the data throughout the department.

5. At each meeting a change agent is present to assist the manager and serve as a resource.

Survey feedback has proven to be most useful when it is periodically administered and results are compared from one year to the next. Generally, cost considerations require the change agent to utilize questionnaires rather than conducting structured interviews with each member of the organization. Most questionnaires ask members for their perceptions and attitudes on a wide range of topics such as communications and decision-making (Robbins, 1986).

Some consultants use prepacked survey instruments; others design a special instrument for each agency. One standardized survey instrument that can be utilized to determine the current management style of a police department concerns itself with the following variables:

1. Leadership
2. Motivation
3. Communications
4. Decisions
5. Goals
6. Interaction
7. Control

Most people expect police departments to be rigid bureaucracies run by managers who have no confidence in subordinates. Compliance is expected, and if necessary it will be accomplished by creating an atmosphere of fear with a liberal use of punishment. We can describe this management style as *exploitative authoritative* (system 1). Figure 14.1 is an abridged version of Rensis Likert's survey-feedback instrument.

One study of police organizations utilized the instrument by surveying 171 officers who were students attending the National Academy of the Federal Bureau of Investigation. Of that number, 83 percent had a college degree or were currently enrolled in a college program. The same officers were surveyed two years later. When comparing the responses, it was found that the agencies represented had moved from the upper part of system 2 (*benevolent authoritative*) to close to the midpoint of system 3 (*consultative*). Of the eight dimensions measured, three of the categories changed the most—communications, training, and decision-making. This suggests that over the two-year period the departments surveyed had become more open (Shanahan, Hunger, and Wheelen, 1979).

Feedback is an essential ingredient of the survey process. It is most effective when done face to face. When the data is simply summarized and distributed to each participant it defeats the whole process. Positive participation, done in small groups such as a team of officers or a special unit, is the key. It is also best to have the immediate supervisor of the team or unit conduct the meeting to demonstrate interest and commitment to the data being discussed (Johns, 1983).

		SYSTEM 1 Exploitive authoritative	SYSTEM 2 Benevolent authoritative	SYSTEM 3 Consultative	SYSTEM 4 Participative group
Leadership	How much confidence is shown in subordinates?	None	Condescending	Substantial	Complete
	How free do they feel to talk to superiors about job?	Not at all	Not very	Rather free	Fully free
	Are subordinates' ideas sought and used, if worthy?	Seldom	Sometimes	Usually	Always
Motivation	Is predominant use made of 1 fear, 2 threats, 3 punishment, 4 rewards, 5 involvement?	1, 2, 3, occasionally 4	4, some 3	4, some 3 and 5	5, 4, based on group-set goals
	Where is responsibility felt for achieving organization's goals?	Mostly at top	Top and middle	Fairly general	At all levels
Communication	How much communication is aimed at achieving organization's objectives?	Very little	Little	Quite a bit	A great deal
	What is the direction of information flow?	Downward	Mostly downward	Down and up	Down, up, and sideways
	How is downward communication accepted?	With suspicion	Possibly with suspicion	With caution	With an open mind
	How accurate is upward communication?	Often wrong	Censored for the boss	Limited accuracy	Accurate
	How well do superiors know problems faced by subordinates?	Know little	Some knowledge	Quite well	Very well
Decisions	At what level are decisions formally made?	Mostly at top	Policy at top, some delegation	Broad policy at top, more delegation	Throughout but well integrated
	What is the origin of technical and professional knowledge used in decision-making?	Top management	Upper and middle	To a certain extent, throughout	To a great extent, throughout
	Are subordinates involved in decisions related to their work?	Not at all	Occasionally consulted	Generally consulted	Fully involved
	What does decision-making process contribute to motivation?	Nothing, often weakens it	Relatively little	Some contribution	Substantial contribution
Goals	How are organizational goals established?	Orders issued	Orders, some comment invited	After discussion, by orders	By group action (except in crisis)
	How much covert resistance to goals is present?	Strong resistance	Moderate resistance	Some resistance at times	Little or none
	How concentrated are review and control functions?	Highly at top	Relatively highly at top	Moderate delegation to lower levels	Quite widely shared
	Is there an informal organization resisting the formal one?	Yes	Usually	Sometimes	No—same goals as formal
	What are cost, productivity, and other control data used for?	Policing, punishment	Reward and punishment	Reward, some self-guidance	Self-guidance problem-solving

FIGURE 14.1 Diagnose Your Management. Source Rensis Likert, *The Human Organization: Its Management and Values* (New York: McGraw-Hill, 1967). Reprinted with permission of McGraw-Hill, Inc.

The change agent should help the manager prepare for the feedback meeting by reviewing the data and suggesting techniques to be used to stimulate discussion, pointing out how problems can be identified and solved (Griffin and Moorhead, 1986). The change agent can attend meetings and serve as a resource for the manager as well as other participants.

The meetings should result in moving from analysis to action. Managers should be especially careful not to get bogged down in minutiae. After a thorough discussion of the issues and identification of problems, action plans should be developed. Such plans should include a follow-up procedure to see if the desired results are actually attained. One way of doing this is to administer an additional questionnaire, possibly one year later, in order to measure the change (Smithers, 1988).

Confrontation Meeting

One means of determining the health of an organization is through a confrontation meeting, which involves the total management group of a police organization. The key for effectiveness in law enforcement is the chief executive's identification of those individuals who are considered managers. It is strongly recommended to include first-line supervisors. A confrontation meeting needs commitment on the part of the chief executive law enforcement officer to solve a problem. It can take place in a relatively short period of time—the initial meeting usually takes only one day. Because time is of the essence, the confrontation meeting is a widely accepted tool (Beckhard, 1967).

In one large department, the confrontation meeting was especially useful because it served to clarify the problems associated with decentralizing the department. During the meeting, the chief was made aware of the problems of coordination and communication and plans were made to direct and resolve them.

In another department, conflict between the patrol unit and youth service bureau had created so much difficulty that the chief, with the assistance of a consultant, set up a confrontation meeting to analyze the underlying causes of the problem between the two units. It was determined the key issue was one of departmental policy on how juveniles would be handled. A plan was developed and a task force set up to correct the problem. Within three months the task force had drafted a new policy acceptable to everyone concerned. Its work resulted in a memorandum of understanding setting forth specific departmental procedures for handling juveniles.

A confrontation meeting has six specific steps (see Table 14.4). At the beginning of the meeting the chief sets the tone by inviting everyone to express an opinion about the issues under consideration. This is a key feature, and the chief should reinforce it as needed throughout the meeting, continually emphasizing the need to deal with issues, not personalities. If a consultant is used, that individual can address ground rules for problem analysis and resolution. This initial step is critical and can really make or break the confrontation effort (French and Bell, 1984).

TABLE 14.4 Steps in a Confrontation Meeting

1. Tone setting
2. Information gathering
3. Sharing of information
4. Development of a plan
5. Follow-up by police executive managers
6. Evaluation

SOURCE: Richard Beckhard, "The Confrontation Meeting," *Harvard Business Review,* 45,(2) (1967).

The second step in the one-day meeting is to divide the group into smaller teams of no more than ten members. Managers for each team should represent different units within the department; the top executives in the organization should meet separately (Beckhard, 1967). The overall health of the organization should be the major topic of discussion and can include such subjects as morale, job satisfaction, departmental policies, goal achievement, organizational structure, communications, and job enrichment or job enlargement.

After the information is collected by the smaller team, the entire group reconvenes and recorders from each team present the results of their meetings. Normally the chief will combine the items presented by recorders into groups such as leadership, motivation, communications, decision-making, goal attainment, or policy.

The next step is most critical—setting priorities and establishing an action plan. The list of items developed in step 3 are distributed to all involved, and the members of the group are divided into normal work groups such as patrol, investigations, traffic, juvenile, and administration. Each group discusses the problem areas and identifies potential situations with which top management will have to deal. Solutions can then be addressed (by individual units) (Beckhard, 1967).

Then the top managers in the department meet to discuss what they have learned and determine what follow-up activities should be taken. The final step occurs sometime later (one to six months) and is a progress report (Wofford, 1982).

The confrontation meeting is most useful in law enforcement. It is inexpensive, practical, responsive, and results oriented. It is an excellent method for determining organizational health and dealing with organizational problems. It opens channels of communication, involves key personnel, and generates a commitment to getting something done (French and Bell, 1984).

Grid Organizational Development

One of the best known and widely used organization techniques is *grid organizational development,* which was developed by Robert R. Blake and Jane

S. Mouton. An integral aspect of this type of development is the managerial grid, discussed in Chapter 11. It is a two-dimensional depiction of leadership styles based on a concern for production and a concern for people. Grid OD utilizes a number of specially designed questionnaires allowing managers to identify their existing style of management and then develop an improved managerial style.

The introduction of this system into a department is based on a desire to move an organization to a point of true excellence. The program extends over a period of time (two to five years) and is conducted by agency personnel who have been trained in grid organizational development (French and Bell, 1984). Typically, the grid OD program has six phases. Central to the program is a concern to improve both communications and planning. The initial phases of the program concentrate on communications (see Table 14.5); the last three parts are concerned with planning and goal setting (Blake and Mouton, 1969):

1. Laboratory-seminar training is designed to encourage managers to analyze their own managerial style and work on improving skills such as group problem-solving, communications, and team development. During this phase, numerous managers can be trained including top managers and those who will train the other managers in the organization.

2. The second phase is team development. During this time, consideration is given to analyzing the traditions and culture of the organization. This is followed by training sessions in superior/subordinate relationships, planning, problem-solving, and other key functions performed by managers. Additional emphasis is placed on feedback to each individual as a means of improving team effectiveness.

3. The third phase of the program focuses on intergroup development. Groups or teams are selected because there is a need to improve coordination and cooperation with the goal of changing the focus from win/lose to a relationship concerned with problem-solving and joint resolution of problems.

4. Next, the grid OD effort encourages the development of an ideal organizational model by top management. Emphasis is placed on evaluating the status of the current organization and how it can reach a position of excellence. The process involves the review of policy, procedures, rules and regulations, structure, and other significant organizational factors. The end result is development of an ideal model and a plan for changing the organization.

TABLE 14.5 Phases of Grid OD

1. Laboratory training
2. Team development
3. Intergroup development
4. Creation of a model organization
5. Implementation
6. Evaluation

5. Implementation is the next phase. This is accomplished by teams in each major unit of the organization. It is a matter of reorganization by utilizing the expertise of team members in an effort to create the ideal organization. If team members need assistance, consultants are brought in to advise and help with the implementation of corrective action.

6. The last phase is the measurement and evaluation of the changes made. The evaluation can be made by departmental personnel or by outside experts. Efforts are made to stabilize positive changes implemented and identify areas still needing to be improved. It can be a matter of determining to continue reorganization, or possibly additional OD efforts will be needed.

A grid OD effort is time consuming, and as we noted, it is implemented over a relatively long period of time. Its real value is its systematic effort to change a total organization rather than dealing with subunits or a few individuals. Striving to create the ideal organization is not only a challenge but a most rewarding experience for police managers.

Quality of Work Life (QWL)

The quality of work-life programs is quite comprehensive and points out the need for improving employee productivity and job satisfaction. Quality of work life is defined as "a process by which all members of an organization, through appropriate channels of communications set up for this purpose, have some say about the design of their jobs in particular, and the work environment in general" (Glaser, 1980).

Quality of work-life (QWL) programs have the following characteristics (Berstein, 1980):

1. Reasonable compensation and fringe benefits.
2. Job security.
3. A safe and healthful work environment.
4. Recognition for achievement through promotion, pay, or other rewards.
5. Due process in the settlement of grievances, separation, or other work-related problems.
6. Participation in decision-making.
7. Some responsibility for and autonomy over the immediate work process.
8. Flexible time arrangements such as flextime or the compressed work week.
9. Emphasis on education, training, and career development.
10. Use of nonbureaucratic forms of work organization.
11. Consideration of social aspects of life on the job.
12. Open communication and adequate feedback.
13. Recognition of the competing demands of work, family, community, and leisure.
14. Redesign of work.

A review of the points just listed clearly establishes the breadth and depth of a QWL program. Similar to other OD efforts the QWL program should be tailored to the specific needs of the police department. This can only be done after a careful diagnosis of the problems unique to the agency (Williams, DuBrin, and Sisk, 1985).

Where QWL programs have been implemented, the benefits have varied, but generally have resulted in employees having a more positive attitude toward work and the department, which results in greater job satisfaction. In addition, productivity has increased, although it is always difficult to determine whether the increase has been as a result of the QWL effort or some other factor. Finally, the organizations have proven to be more effective in attaining departmental goals (Griffin and Moorhead, 1986).

If there is a police union or association, it should be involved in the design and implementation of the program. Otherwise there is always a possibility of barriers developing to impede the successful implementation of a program. It is also essential when developing a plan to follow through to completion. In some instances the pressure generated by day-to-day operations has allowed even the best plans to become dormant (Suttle, 1977).

Numerous steps can be taken by managers to create a working environment allowing employees to increase their job knowledge and assume the responsibilities generated by the position they occupy. These are set forth in Table 14.6 and have proven to be effective techniques when implementing a QWL program.

The humanistic focus of QWL programs is clearly evident, and it has been found that the interests of the individual are definitely compatible with organizational interests. It is a matter of a joint effort between management and employees handling conflicting issues, enabling them to work toward their resolution (Nadler and Lawler, 1983). When a QWL program is tailored to the organization, it has proven to be an effective means of improving the overall efficiency of an organization.

TABLE 14.6 Steps for Improving QWL Programs

1. Hold meetings with each officer in order to discuss individual skills and goals.
2. Develop a specific plan for each employee that will result in acquiring new skills.
3. Be sure a manager is readily available to meet with employees.
4. Create problem-solving teams that have the responsibility to develop a solution to pressing problems.
5. Review proposals made by problem-solving teams.
6. Reward proven effective performers.
7. When a job is well done, place a notation in the officer's personnel file.
8. Reward outstanding performance by giving officers special assignments that require the application of special skills.
9. Let people know when they are doing a good job.

SOURCE: Martha G. Cox and Jane C. Brown, "Quality of Work Life: Another Fad or Real Benefit?" *Personnel Administrator* 27 (5) (1982).

Successful Implementation of OD Programs

Some OD efforts have been highly successful, but others have failed. The reason for failure varies, so it is definitely more fruitful to review the essential factors for success. First, management must accept the fact that the organization has real problems which must be solved satisfactorily instead of carelessly or deliberately overlooked. An OD effort is both time consuming and usually expensive. Consequently these efforts should only be considered when an organization has a problem for which OD is specifically designed. The idea of engaging in an OD effort because other departments have tried it must be rejected. When there is a sense that the organization is not as effective as it could be, then top management should give serious consideration to using OD (French and Bell, 1984).

Another important characteristic of a successful OD effort is the use of an external change agent, since the internal change agent seldom has the equivalent skills and knowledge. Many times, internal personnel have axes to grind or they are not capable of looking at the big picture. Generally someone outside the organization is in an exceptional position to gain the support of top management. This is especially true if the external change agent has an excellent track record and his or her credentials are impeccable. Experience supports the view that external experts are more apt to be accepted by agency personnel (Grossman, 1974).

An OD effort has a greater potential for success when top management clearly is committed to the program. When top management gives only lip service to an OD program it is, without a doubt, scheduled for failure. Managers must not only support, but become involved in the OD effort (Griffin and Moorhead, 1986).

When top managers are involved in the OD effort it sends a direct signal to lower level managers that the program is important and should be supported by everyone. Managers at all levels must engage in activities designed to improve the effectiveness of the organization. Management must encourage those who are participants in the change process (as a means of reducing resistance to the change effort), and reward those who make a significant contribution to the OD effort.

Managers should also take a holistic view of the organization and the OD effort. Barriers between subunits should be overcome and the traditional competition between organizational units should be replaced with a working environment that stresses cooperation (Griffin and Moorhead, 1986).

An OD effort will have an excellent chance of attaining its goal if there is some success during the early stages. This demonstrates to those involved that positive change can occur and also serves to motivate employees. When early success is missing, it has a tendency to impede the program. The change agent should deliberately design the OD effort in such a way that early success is inevitable (French and Bell, 1984).

Another characteristic of a successful OD effort is open and continuous communications. As uncertainties and ambiguities arise, they must be re-

CASE STUDY

Robert Proctor

Robert Proctor became the chief of police after serving 12 years in the department. He replaced a chief who ran the department in a highly autocratic manner, causing departmental morale to reach an all-time low. Proctor assumed his position with widespread organizational support. It is well known he was just as frustrated as the other officers with the authoritarian style of his predecessor.

Within two years, Chief Proctor reorganized the department and added three new positions with the rank of captain to the department. Each of the captains are assigned as commanders of major units.

Altogether there have been 14 promotions because of personnel changes. During the following three-and-one-half years (commensurate with population growth within the city) the department added 27 new positions to bring the sworn strength up to 92 positions.

The rapid growth of the department is not without difficulties. The large number of personnel changes and bringing so many new officers on board caused a schism between the older patrol officers and those recently hired. The older officers have an average length of service of 11 years and have been passed over for promotion to sergeant. The frustration this caused was compounded because all six sergeants in the patrol division have assumed their positions within the last few years and are still feeling their way as supervisors.

The newly hired officers are well educated, goal oriented, and believe all the new changes are exciting. They appreciate the opportunity to be really involved. The younger officers, as a group, resent the inability of the sergeants to perform effectively and feel they are not being given the necessary guidance for doing their job.

The older officers resent the enthusiasm of the newer officers and feel threatened. There is clearly a we/they relationship beginning to hamper the performance of the unit. Capt. Robert Quick (commander of the patrol division) consulted with Chief Proctor and it was agreed it is necessary for the first-line supervisors to improve their managerial skills. There is also a need for improving interdepartmental harmony. After hearing the situation described in detail, the chief pointed out both problems had to be addressed.

It is apparent to all that something should be done as soon as possible to resolve the two problems. Funding has been approved, and a behavioral scientist has been brought in to assist in the resolution of the problems.

The consultant recommends that everyone in the organization complete a questionnaire to be used for determining the exact nature of the problem. An OD effort can then be designed. As the chief, would you suggest using the instrument entitled Diagnose Your Management? How would you want to use it? Do you think a confrontation meeting would be helpful? Why or why not?

sponded to with facts backed by readily available information for everyone. Rumors should be responded to immediately, and a premium should be placed on the accuracy of the information disseminated. During a period of rapid change, every manager should be especially sensitive to the problems created by uncertainty and the guideline should be communicate, always communicate (Griffin and Moorhead, 1986).

Summary

Organizational development (OD) is a widely accepted method of solving organizational problems through the application of the behavioral sciences. It is normative in nature, goal oriented, and a managerial process.

OD assumptions about people in organizations are genuinely optimistic, and require a humanistic and participative manager. One of the primary objectives of an OD effort is to develop the organization to the point where the culture is based on openness and trust.

Another important value of OD is the desire and ability to deal with conflict constructively and turn it into something positive rather than avoiding it at all costs.

Another characteristic of organizational development is feedback. Police managers can use a variety of techniques to improve communications, including personal discussion with subordinates, written communications, group meetings, or questionnaires.

The last value of importance to OD is risk taking. When mistakes are made by subordinates they must be turned into learning situations. Officers must be allowed to grow as they accept increasing amounts of responsibility, and they should not be punished for exercising the power needed to accomplish a task.

When OD is successful, the organization becomes healthier and more responsive to the community it serves. The healthy police department encourages every employee to develop to the maximum, so goals can be attained by the most effective means. The change occurring from an OD effort is viewed with optimism and accepted as an inevitable consequence of striving to become more effective.

There are a variety of intervention techniques to change organizations and influence the behavior of individuals and groups. No matter which technique is selected, it will follow a set pattern when efforts are being made to alter the working environment. These steps include diagnosis, planning, training, and evaluation.

One of the intervention techniques used extensively is sensitivity training. It is used to increase interpersonal awareness as a means of integrating the individual into the organization. Sensitivity training has both its supporters and its detractors, but it has proven effective when introduced into an organization by a competent change agent.

Team building is another intervention technique involving both managers and employees. Emphasis is placed on interpersonal relations (similar to other techniques), but special attention is given to the tasks to be performed. Team building is most successful when it is an ongoing process. It should never be a one-shot procedure.

Survey feedback is being used extensively. It involves collecting data from the department and feeding this data back to organizational members and groups during a series of meetings, with the intent of identifying corrective action.

Another means of determining the health of an organization is through the confrontation meeting. It is most useful in law enforcement. It is inexpensive, practical, responsive, and results oriented. It opens channels of communication, involves key personnel, and generates a commitment to getting something done.

One of the best and most widely used intervention techniques is grid OD, which was developed by Robert R. Blake and Jane S. Mouton. Change agents utilizing the technique administer a variety of instruments to personnel in an organization in order to identify their existing style of management and then develop an improved managerial style.

Quality of working-life (QWL) programs are comprehensive and emphasize the need for improving employee productivity and job satisfaction. QWL programs have a humanistic focus and are based on the premise that the interest of each employee is definitely compatible with organizational interests.

Some OD programs have proven to be highly successful, but others have failed. Success seems to be predicated on top management support, the use of external change agents, and the managers having a holistic view of the organization and the OD effort.

Key Concepts

Organizational development (OD)
Openness and trust
Feedback
Confronting conflict
Risk taking
The healthy organization
Diagnosis
Planning
Training
Evaluation
Sensitivity training
Team building
Survey feedback
Confrontation meeting
Grid OD
Quality of work life (QWL)

Discussion Topics and Questions

1. What are the objectives of a major OD effort?
2. Discuss the importance of the OD assumption that people in an organization want to participate in the decision-making process.
3. How and when should managers take risks when involved in an OD effort?
4. Compare and contrast sensitivity training and the confrontation meeting.
5. What would limit the effective use of team building as a training technique?

6. How should a police manager use survey feedback?
7. What part should the police association (union) play in an evolving quality of work-life program?
8. Differentiate between a QWL program and a quality circle.
9. Discuss the relationship between managers and line officers when developing a QWL program.
10. Discuss the inherent values of OD.

References

Beckhard, Richard. 1967. "The Confrontation Meeting," *Harvard Business Review*, 45(2).

Beer, M. 1980. *Organization Change and Development: A Systems View*. Santa Monica, CA: Goodyear.

Berstein, Paul. 1980. *Career Education and the Quality of Working Life*. Washington, DC: U.S. Department of Health, Education, and Welfare.

Blake, R. R., and J. S. Mouton. 1969. *Building a Dynamic Corporation Through Grid Organization Development*. Reading, MA: Addison-Wesley.

Bradford, David L. 1984. *Managing for Excellence*. New York: Wiley.

Burke, W. Warner. 1982. *Organization Development: Principles and Practices*. Boston: Little, Brown.

Campbell, J., and M. Dunnette. 1978. "Effectiveness of T-Group Experiences in Management Training and Development," *Psychological Bulletin*, 70.

Cox, Martha G., and Jane C. Brown. 1982. "Quality of Working Life: Another Fad or Real Benefit," *Personnel Administrator*, 27(5).

Dyer, William G. 1977. "Basic Problems and Plans." In William G. Dyer (Ed.), *Team Building: Issues and Alternatives*. Reading, MA: Addison-Wesley.

Dyer, William G. 1983. *Contemporary Issues in Management and Organizational Development*. Reading, MA: Addison-Wesley.

French, Wendell L., and Cecil H. Bell, Jr. 1984. *Organization Development: Behavioral Science Interventions for Organization Improvement* (3rd ed.). Englewood Cliffs, NJ: Prentice-Hall.

Glaser, Edward M. 1980. "Productivity Gains Through Work-Life Improvement," *Personnel*, 57(1).

Griffin, Ricky W., and Gregory Moorhead. 1986. *Organizational Behavior*. Boston: Houghton Mifflin.

Grossman, Lee. 1974. *The Change Agent*. New York: AMACOM.

Hatry, Harry P., and John M. Greiner. 1986. *Improving the Use of Quality Circles in Police Departments*, National Institute of Justice. Washington, DC: U.S. Department of Justice.

Johns, Gary. 1983. *Organizational Behavior*. Glenview, IL: Scott, Foresman.

Kellogg, Dianne M. 1984. "Contrasting Successful and Unsuccessful O.D. Consulting Relationships," *Group and Organization Studies*, 12(2).

Leonard, V. A., and Harry W. More. 1987. *Police Organization and Management* (7th ed.). Mineola, NY: Foundation Press.

Likert, Rensis. 1967. *The Human Organization: Its Management and Values*. New York: McGraw-Hill.

Lorsch, Jay W. (Ed.). 1987. *Handbook of Organizational Behavior*. Englewood Cliffs, NJ: Prentice-Hall.

Mann, Floyd C. 1961. "Studying and Creating Change." In W. G. Bennis, K. D. Benne, and R. Chin (Eds.), *The Planning of Change*. New York: Holt.

McCaskey, Michael B. 1982. *The Executive Challenge*. Marshfield, MA: Pitman.

More, Harry W., and Michael O'Neill. 1984. *Contemporary Criminal Justice Planning*. Springfield, IL: Charles C Thomas.

Nadler, David A., and Edward E. Lawler, III. 1983. "Quality of Work Life: Perspective and Directions," *Organizational Dynamics*, 23(4).

Pascarella, Perry. 1984. *The New Achievers: Creating a Modern Work Ethic*. New York: Free Press.

Patten, Thomas H., Jr. 1981. *Organizational Development Through Teambuilding*. New York: Wiley.

Quick, Thomas L. 1980. *Understanding People at Work*. New York: Executive Enterprises.

Randall, Lyman, K. 1979. "Common Questions and Tentative Answers Regarding Organization Development," *California Management Review*, 13(3).

Reece, Barry L., and Rhonda Brandt. 1987. *Effective Human Relations in Organizations* (3rd ed.). Boston: Houghton Mifflin.

Robbins, Stephen P. 1986. *Organizational Behavior—Concepts, Controversies, and Application*. Englewood Cliffs, NJ: Prentice-Hall.

Rue, Leslie, and Lloyd L. Byars. 1986. *Management Theory and Practice* (4th ed.). Homewood, IL: Richard D. Irwin.

Schermerhorn, John R., James G. Hunt, and Richard N. Osborn. 1988. *Managing Organizational Behavior* (3rd ed.). New York: Wiley.

Shanahan, Gerald W., J. David Hunger, and Thomas L. Wheelen. 1979. "Organizational Profile of Police Agencies in the United States," *Journal of Police Science and Administration*, 7(3).

Smithers, Robert D. 1988. *The Psychology of Work and Human Performance*. New York: Harper & Row.

Stone, W. Clement. 1987. "Future-Shock Absorbers, Profit in a Changing World by Investing in Other People," *Success*, October.

Suttle, J. Lloyd. 1977. "Improving Life at Work—Problems and Prospects." In J. Richard Hackman and J. Lloyd Suttle (Eds.), *Improving Life at Work: Behavioral Science Approaches to Organizational Change*. Santa Monica, CA: Goodyear.

Williams, J. Clifton, Andrew J. DuBrin, and Henry L. Sisk. 1985. *Management and Organization* (5th ed.). Cincinnati: South-Western.

Wofford, Jerry C. 1982. *Organizational Behavior—Foundations for Organizational Effectiveness*. Boston: Kent.

For Further Reading

French, Wendell L., and Cecil H. Bell, Jr. 1984. *Organization Development: Behavioral Science Interventions for Organization Improvement* (3rd ed.). Englewood Cliffs, NJ: Prentice-Hall.

> An excellent publication describing the methods and techniques used in the practice of OD. Of special interest is the discussion of OD intervention techniques of team building, survey feedback, and grid organizational development. There is also a very good discussion of the history of OD.

Patten, Thomas H., Jr. 1981. *Organizational Development Through Teambuilding*. New York: Wiley.

> This book is concerned with OD through team building. It suggests ways that managers can function as a team. The book is written for practitioners who seek improvement of management in work organizations.

SMITHERS, ROBERT D. 1988. *The Psychology of Work and Human Performance*. New York: Harper & Row.

The text reviews OD techniques as a means of introducing change into an organization. It reviews possible services to be provided by a change agent in overcoming resistance to change. Of special interest is the discussion of the problems evaluating OD efforts.

WILLIAMS, J. CLIFTON, ANDREW J. DUBRIN, and HENRY L. SISK. 1985. *Management and Organization* (5th ed.). Cincinnati: South-Western.

The book has an excellent discussion of OD as a human process approach. There is a discussion of quality of work-life (QWL) programs describing how productivity and job satisfaction can be expanded by giving workers greater opportunity and power.

CHAPTER **15**

Managerial Issues

LEARNING OBJECTIVES

1. Describe the current state of police unions.
2. List the types of police unions prevailing in many police departments.
3. Identify the key elements of collective bargaining.
4. Describe the two most common types of police brutality.
5. Identify the types of brutality committed against civilians by the police.
6. List the problems that women police officers face in their employment.
7. Describe a typical minority recruiting program based on quota.

It is widely recognized by contemporary police managers that the scope and complexity of police administration is increasing rapidly. Urbanization, emigration, technological advancement, a large youth population, a changing morality, a more educated populace, greater use of drugs, and an increase in violence are all factors conditioning and reconditioning the way police managers function.

Police department managers are currently facing challenges requiring increased sensitivity, flexibility, and responsiveness to a rapidly changing organization. Successful managers must accept change within the organization as inevitable. In fact, change must be viewed as a challenge, not as a problem.

Other important challenges today for police managers include

1. Labor and management
2. Use of force
3. Women officers
4. Minority officers

The nature and extent of the challenge will vary from organization to organization. In the decade ahead, these challenges potentially could transform

INTRODUCTORY CASE

Sergeant Bud Fredrickson

Bud Fredrickson is a newly appointed sergeant in the patrol division of Mountain Township Police Department. The city covers an area of 18 square miles and may be described as a bedroom suburb located 20 miles from a major metropolitan area. Mountain Township has three major shopping areas and the population is 47,523. The police department has 54 sworn officers. There are 33 officers in the patrol division and Sgt. Fredrickson supervises a team of seven of these officers.

Bud graduated from a local community college with a degree in criminal justice and is enrolled in a four-year college he has attended part time for the last three years. He is married and has two children. He joined the department at the age of 21 and received a promotion to sergeant after just three years. He is the youngest supervisor in the department and has held his current position for nine months. He completed the police supervisory course of 80 hours, graduating first in his class.

All the supervisory officers in the department belong to the police union. The current negotiation between Mountain Township and the police union has broken down and officers are working without a contract. The union has been discussing what should be done to break the impasse and considered such activities as the "blue flu," a work slowdown, or actually striking.

The state in which Mountain Township is located does not provide for collective bargaining, and strikes are prohibited. So the relationship between the city and the union is limited to negotiation in an attempt to reach a mutual agreement. Officers, independent of the union, have almost reached the point where they intend to walk off the job.

Sgt. Fredrickson has very strong personal ties with many of the line officers, but he considers himself a part of management. The city's administration has made a serious effort to separate supervisory positions from the union. A number of officers have been talking with sergeants in the department in an effort to get them to walk out also. Fredrickson feels the officers are being treated unfairly; for years, Mountain Township's administration has ignored the needs of police officers.

Officers have scheduled the strike and intend to leave town and stay in a motel located in an adjacent state. This action will make it difficult for the local court to serve a restraining order. Officers in Mountain Township Police Department are poorly paid—the base salary is 22 percent under the amount paid to officers who work for the nearby metropolitan police department. The department loses eight officers each year primarily because of the low pay.

If you were Sgt. Fredrickson, would you go on strike? Explain your position. Should any officer be allowed to go on strike? Why? Would a state law providing for collective bargaining alleviate such problems?

law enforcement agencies. Many of these issues are not new, and they have been handled with varying degrees of success.

Labor and Management

It was about 25 years ago that labor relations became a concern to law enforcement administrators. Today such terms as *collective bargaining, bargaining unit, grievance procedures, negotiation tactics,* and *memorandum of understanding* have become an integral part of the working environment in which administrators find themselves.

Police managers have an increasingly important part to play in critical aspects of labor relations. In agencies where police managers have demonstrated a continuing interest in the welfare of employees, unions have found limited support. On the other hand, many law enforcement administrators have almost forced officers to join police unions because of poor management practices (Sirene, 1981).

In every agency, the reason for organizing a police union varies, but in most instances it can be attributed to one or more of the following reasons (Crane, 1979; Sirene, 1981):

1. Unsatisfactory working conditions
2. Opportunity for advancement
3. Lack of a grievance procedure
4. Low salary
5. Opportunity to be heard
6. Need to be recognized
7. Poor communications

Once a union becomes an integral part of a police organization, the issues it deals with vary extensively, depending on the needs and desires of its membership. For example, in 1988 New York City announced that officers seeking promotion would be required to have two to four years of college. This policy had a potential effect on more than 18,000 officers planning to take the sergeant's promotional examination.

The Patrolmen's Benevolent Association obtained a court order directing the city to show cause why the new policy should be implemented. The union argued that a college requirement was improper and should have been negotiated with the police union. It also claimed there is no rational relationship between a college education and the ability to be an effective supervisor (*Law Enforcement News,* March 29, 1988).

In another instance, the Police Patrolmen's Association of Boston indicated it planned to file a constitutional challenge against the Commonwealth of Massachusetts's ban on smoking by police officers and fire fighters. An attorney for the association viewed the matter as an unlawful intrusion into the private lives of police officers (*Law Enforcement News,* October 15, 1988).

In recent years, increasing numbers of benevolent associations have become affiliated with more traditional private sector unions such as the AFL-CIO and the Teamsters. For example, the AFL-CIO has chartered its first police union affiliate, the International Union of Police Associations (IUPA). Although the exact membership is not known, it is believed to exceed 40,000 police officers. The best estimates affirm there are more than 10,000 police officers affiliated with the Teamsters (Sirene, 1981).

The largest police labor organization in the United States is the Fraternal Order of Police (FOP), which has a membership of 198,000 (see Table 15.1). It functions as a fraternal organization for the most part, but in some instances a local unit serves as a bargaining unit. In addition the FOP continually updates its membership on the Fair Labor Standards Act and conducts labor and grievance seminars from its national office. It also sponsors a legal and an insurance program for its members (*Law Enforcement News,* December 1988).

With the growth of police unions and benevolent associations, it became increasingly common for municipalities to recognize the right of employees to join unions. In one city, an agreement stated the following (City of Milpitas, California, January 1984):

> Any employee in the City's competitive service may join, organize or maintain membership in a labor organization if he/she so desires. The City neither encourages nor discourages these activities, nor does membership or nonmembership in any labor organization affect the employment standing or right as a City employee.

In recent years there has been a significant growth in the number of rules governing the workplace. As police unions have evolved into meaningful units with considerable power and influence, conflict has increasingly been resolved through negotiation and some type of mediation process.

Management/labor relations govern almost every personnel action taking place in today's police organization. When a manager or an employee decides on an action, it often takes into account some aspect of a labor/management consideration based on a prior agreement between the two parties.

TABLE 15.1 Police Labor Organizations

Unit	Number of Members
Fraternal Order of Police (FOP)	198,000
International Union of Police Associations (IUPA)	20,000
Teamsters	10,000
National Troopers Coalition	17,000
International Brotherhood of Police Officers (IBPO)	38,000
Peace Officers Research Association (PORAC)	18,000
American Federation of State, County, and Municipal Employees (AFSCME)	14,000
Independent Organizations	110,000 (est.)

SOURCE: Correspondence with major organizations.

Memoranda of Agreement/Understanding

In a number of agencies, settlements between labor and management are spelled out in documents called memoranda of agreement/understanding (see Table 15.2). Such agreements have replaced what in the past was viewed by some police officers as arbitrary and capricious management. On the other hand, many police chiefs view such agreements as reducing their managerial prerogatives.

An appreciation of what constitutes a memorandum of understanding will allow both managers and union representatives to perform their roles more effectively. A memorandum of understanding is defined as follows:

> A written agreement prepared by management and an employee organization reached through meet and confer procedures that concerns wages, hours, or working conditions. The agreement may be submitted to the appropriate determining body or a government official for ratification and implementation.

When new situations arise that are not included in an agreement, elaborate mechanisms are implemented to deal with the item(s) (Unsinger and More, 1989).

The typical memorandum of agreement/understanding is a written agreement and generally has a term of from one to three years. In some states a statute requires the negotiators to prepare a written memorandum (California Government Code, 1985):

> If agreement is reached by the representatives of the public agency and a recognized employee organization or recognized employee organizations, they shall jointly prepare a written memorandum of such understanding.

Preparation for the creation of an agreement requires those involved not only to consider the past, but to take into consideration new laws or ordinances and certainly new programs instituted since the last agreement (Coble, 1989). For example, in one community the city manager and department

TABLE 15.2 Typical Categories Included in a Memorandum of Agreement/Understanding

Employee rights	Medical leave of absence
City rights	Court cancellation
Advance notice	Training
Grievances	Attendance
Equal employment opportunity grievance procedure	Safety equipment
Annual vacation leave	Uniform allowance
Sick leave	Retirement plan
Family leave	Pay plan
Military leave	Benefits
Leave of absence	Educational incentive pay

heads developed a classification for training based on the degree of value to the city (City of Milpitas, 1984):

1. *Assigned training.* Training of an immediate, direct, and tangible benefit to the performance of specific city responsibilities.
2. *Recommended training.* Training offered by the city or other agencies or institutions enabling an employee to improve his or her performance.
3. *Mutual benefit training.* Training deemed to be of more benefit to the employee than the city such as general course work toward a degree in a field other than the employee's current career assignment.

The negotiators were required to incorporate the new training classifications into the agreement and to identify types of training specifically for each classification.

Managerial Rights

When unions negotiate with management they are usually concerned with such issues as compensation, job security, time off, payment for court time, personal safety, and general fair treatment (McAndrew, 1989). At other times, a specific union might be concerned with acquiring protection for its shop stewards and officials.

Negotiable items become of special concern to police managers when it appears the union is intruding into what is termed *managerial prerogatives,* or *managerial rights* (Leonard, 1980). Police unions are not interested in running departments, but like all organizations, there is always a push and pull when dealing with other administrative entities. Mangers sit on one side of the table and union representatives on the other. Inasmuch as they are advocates for their respective positions, there is a constant interplay between them. In some instances unions will deliberately present a proposal that is obviously an intrusion into managerial prerogatives and use it as a trade-off for something really wanted as part of a compromise settlement (McAndrew, 1989).

Management rights vary from agency to agency, but generally include the following (City of Milpitas, 1984):

1. Exclusive right to determine the mission.
2. Establishment of standards of service.
3. Determining the procedures and standards for employee selection.
4. Taking disciplinary action.
5. Directing employees.
6. Relieving employees from duty because of lack of work or other legitimate reasons.
7. Maintaining the efficiency of governmental operations.
8. Determining the content of job classification.
9. Determining when an emergency exists and providing a mandate to take all necessary action to carry out the mission in emergencies.

If these and other managerial prerogatives are guarded jealously, police managers will find they have retained the rights needed to function more effectively. In some instances, police labor unions have made inroads by successfully negotiating such things as assignment to specific beats based on seniority, shift assignments, and staffing levels (Favreau and Gillespie, 1978). In addition, some cities protect their rights by always including a statement that stipulates all conditions and terms not specifically covered in the agreement are the exclusive province of management (Hale, 1977).

Collective Bargaining

The Commission on Accreditation for Law Enforcement Agencies has established a number of standards addressing collective bargaining. Their concern is for the disparity found among agencies engaging in collective bargaining. The specific standards include the following (Commission on Accreditation for Law Enforcement Agencies, 1984):

1. Development of a written directive describing the role of the agency in the collective bargaining process.
2. Establishment of a collective bargaining team with one member as the principal negotiator.
3. Specification of the bargaining unit.
4. Development of impasse-resolving procedures.
5. Creation of ground rules prior to negotiation.
6. Adoption of the principle of good faith bargaining based on the Taft-Hartley Act.
7. A written record in the form of a contract or an agreement signed by both parties.
8. Distribution of the agreement to all supervisory and management personnel.

A critique of collective bargaining in the police field strongly suggests it has been beneficial to both management and labor. In states having labor laws that encourage bargaining, the vast majority of communities involved in the process have rated it as a positive influence (More and Wegener, 1989).

Contrary to initial fears, unions are not running police departments, but informal or verbal procedures have become more formal and contractual in nature (More, 1985). In addition, collective bargaining has provided many police officers with a greater opportunity to participate in the decision-making process.

The Negotiations Process

Unquestionably the negotiations process is highly visible and receiving a great deal of attention. In 1982 the U.S. Bureau of the Census estimated that about one-half of the police officers in the United States were engaged in some type of negotiations process (McAndrew, 1989).

The negotiations process replaces the arbitrary rule making of chiefs of police, civil service commissions, and city managers or city officials, and allows for the joint resolution of issues. The initial process generally involves negotiation of a contract or memorandum of understanding to be enforced for one to three years. In many instances it is a matter of revising and updating a previous agreement rather than creating a brand-new one.

Another type of negotiation, known as the *sidebar agreement,* involves issues not included in the original contract or memorandum of understanding. It is often needed because changes in the law or other considerations require more negotiation. Additional negotiation may also be needed to clarify the original memorandum of understanding so that provisions accurately reflect what should have been clear in the beginning. In other words, errors are made, something is left out and needs to be resolved, or a lack of understanding develops as the agreement is interpreted. Successful operation, in many instances, demands resolution because it is impossible to wait until the next time contract negotiation takes place (Coble, 1989).

Possibly there can be day-to-day negotiations between management and labor as the agreement is interpreted and as new problems occur. In addition, grievances have to be resolved and disciplinary cases handled (McAndrew, 1989).

Ordinarily, a law enforcement negotiation unit will consist of all the nonsupervisory sworn personnel of an agency, but this varies considerably. One study found that a major problem is the inability of both management and labor to distinguish clearly what ranks belong to management and who is a member of the employee bargaining unit (N.E.I. Committee on Management's Rights, 1987). One agency typifies this problem—there is one bargaining unit for lieutenants and below and another unit for command officers. At the extreme, there are some bargaining units including everyone in the department from the chief on down.

It seems essential for management to include command personnel and all supervisory personnel as part of the management team. When management personnel belong to bargaining units, there is a tendency for them to look at many contract issues from the viewpoint of line personnel and identify with their needs rather than to take a management perspective. When supervisory personnel are part of management's team, they accept changes more readily and it is more likely they will support management's perspective (N.E.I. Committee on Management's Rights, 1987).

Another dilemma is the part the chief of police plays in the negotiation process. Some chiefs limit their participation to the implementation of the contract after it has been approved by all the interested parties. At the very least, the chief should serve as an adviser to management's negotiators. This expert input will alleviate many problems occurring after an agreement has been approved by both sides (Garmire, 1982).

Grievances

An additional concern for both management and the union is an adequate grievance mechanism. It is a formal process for dealing with disputes arising relevant to the interpretation or application of personnel ordinances, or concerning any rule or regulation governing personnel practices or working conditions (City of Milpitas, 1984).

When an employee has a complaint, it should be brought to the immediate attention of the supervisor and a serious effort should be made to resolve the problem (Lambert, 1989). If the problem is not resolved, the employee has the right to discuss the issue with the supervisor's immediate superior. Again, every effort should be made to work out a mutually acceptable agreement. If this cannot be done and the employee does not agree with the decision, a formal written appeal should be submitted within 15 days after the initial presentation of the informal grievance (City of Milpitas, 1984; More and Shipley, 1987).

Following are the steps to be employed when utilizing formal review:

Step 1. An employee's appeal shall be presented in writing to the employee's immediate supervisor, who shall render a decision in writing within ten days.

Step 2. The division or department head shall review the appeal and complete action within ten days.

Step 3. The personnel committee acts as a grievance board for any employee appealing matters involving working conditions, disciplinary actions, suspension, or reduction.

a. Appeals should be written and filed within 15 days.
b. A hearing date will be set.
c. The appellant, if physically able, will appear before the personnel committee.
d. After conclusion of the hearing, the committee will certify (within ten days) its findings and recommendations to the city manager.

Step 4. The city manager will review the findings and recommendations and may affirm, revoke, or modify the action and shall render a decision within 20 days.

Whenever possible, grievances should be resolved at the lowest possible organizational level. It is essential for police managers to adopt a problem-solving approach (extending beyond the immediate resolution of each grievance) in an effort to identify more broadly based actions management should take. This should involve attempting to find answers to the following questions (Lambert, 1989):

1. Is there a need for changes in policies, procedures, rules, regulations, or contract provisions?
2. Is there a need to provide managers with additional training?
3. Is there a need for providing officers with additional training?
4. Is there either a localized or widespread supervisory problem?
5. Is there a problem attributable to employee misunderstanding of an operational need?

These and similar questions can provide managers with information that, in many instances, can be used to prevent future problems and improve the organization's capacity to respond to emerging problems (Unsinger and More, 1989).

Minorities

A recent study pointed out that by the year 2000, more than 90 percent of the growth in the U.S. labor market will be among minorities and women; only 8 percent will be white males. In other words, minorities and women will be recruited increasingly by police departments because there will be fewer white males in the potential recruitment pool.

An individual is considered a member of a minority group if the group to which he or she belongs is smaller than other dominant groups in a society. An individual, discriminated against, is denied equal treatment or opportunities afforded to members of the dominant group. This selectivity could be evident in recruitment, promotion, job assignments, training, or other work-related privileges. Historically, this has been particularly true in the area of selection and recruitment where law enforcement agencies have had entry requirements not especially related to the actual job to be performed (Reece and Brandt, 1987).

Minority groups are easily identifiable and include blacks, Hispanics, Asians, and Native Americans. Other less obvious minorities, such as homosexuals, may also be discriminated against. The civil rights of everyone must be protected. Title VII of the Civil Rights Act of 1964 prohibits discrimination by employers on the basis of race, color, religion, sex, or national origin. It specifically applies to discrimination in personnel practices including recruitment, hiring, promotion, discharge, classification, training, compensation, and other conditions and privileges of employment (Anderson and Levin-Epstein, 1982).

The Equal Employment Opportunity Commission (EEOC) is the federal agency responsible for administering Title VII. This agency has the authority to investigate all charges of discrimination. In more recent years, it has been given authority to administer the Age Discrimination in Employment Act and the Equal Pay Act (Anderson and Levin-Epstein, 1982). Focus 15.1 describes the mandate of the EEOC.

The EEOC issues standards and guidelines for compliance with antidiscrimination laws. Many of the cases filed with this agency have reached various courts where decisions have been rendered that completely altered many police personnel practices (Swanson, Territo, and Taylor, 1988). For example, in one appeals court decision, a height requirement for police officers was upheld, even though the requirement resulted in the exclusion of a number of female applicants. At the same time, this court struck down a weight requirement (Anderson and Levin-Epstein, 1982). Since that decision, however, some agencies have altered or eliminated height requirements, which has allowed women, Hispanics, and Asians to meet one aspect of police employment prerequisites successfully.

One of the leading cases in this area was *Officers for Justice v. Civil Service Commission,* San Francisco, 395 F. Supp. 378 (Northern District, Calif., 1975) where a federal judge ruled that minimum height requirements for the selection of police officers could not be used because it excluded certain ethnic groups and females (Kenney and More, 1986).

FOCUS 15.1

The Equal Employment Opportunity Commission

The U.S. Equal Employment Opportunity Commission was created by Title VII of the Civil Rights Act of 1964, which prohibits employment discrimination based on race, color, sex, religion, or national origin. Since 1979, the EEOC also has been responsible for enforcing the Age Discrimination in Employment Act of 1967, which protects employees 40 years of age or older; the Equal Pay Act of 1963, which protects men and women who perform substantially equal work in the same establishment from sex-based wage discrimination; and Section 501 of the Rehabilitation Act of 1973, which prohibits federal sector handicap discrimination.

The EEOC staff receives and investigates employment discrimination charges against private employers and state and local governments. If the investigation shows reasonable cause to believe discrimination occurred, the commission will begin conciliation efforts. If the EEOC is unable to conciliate the charge, it will be considered for possible litigation. The commission's policy is to seek full and effective relief for each and every victim of employment discrimination whether it is sought in court or in conciliation. . . .

SOURCE. The U.S. Equal Employment Opportunity Commission, *Commission Enforces EEO Laws,* Office of Communications and Legislative Affairs, November 1988.

This ruling means that applicants can only be held to definitely job-related standards. When standards are arbitrary or are clearly not related to the tasks performed by a police officer, they are discriminatory, and courts have ruled against such standards. Federal law prohibits the use of tests or standards disproportionately disadvantaging minority applicants that are not shown to be job related (U.S. Commission on Civil Rights, 1981).

In recent years, *affirmative action plans* have come into vogue as a means of remedying the effect of past discrimination against ethnic and minority groups. The U.S. Civil Service Commission and various courts reached the conclusion that simply removing inappropriate standards was not eliminating the reality of discrimination or making up for the many past years of discrimination.

For many years the U.S. Commission on Civil Rights has called for law enforcement agencies to work toward developing police departments truly reflective of the racial and ethnic composition of the community they service, including speaking the major language spoken in the community (U.S. Commission on Civil Rights, 1980).

It must be kept in mind that the central issues in EEOC law are concerned with several types of discrimination, including recruiting, hiring, promotion, employment testing, employment conditions, seniority, layoffs, retaliation, and reverse discrimination. The essential components of a nondiscriminatory employment policy include basic procedures for recruiting and selecting new employees that do not intentionally or inadvertently work to screen out minority group members or other protected groups (Anderson and Levin-Epstein, 1982).

If there is any issue immediately arousing the ire of many, it is quota hiring. An explicit ban on quota hiring is contained in Title VII; however, the language of the title has been interpreted to allow quota hiring when it is used to remedy racial imbalance caused by unlawful discriminatory conduct. In other words, a district court *may* impose a hiring quota as a remedy (Anderson and Levin-Epstein, 1982).

In reaction to quotas, white males have filed *reverse discrimination* complaints challenging employers' affirmative action programs. The major case in this area was decided in 1978 by the U.S. Supreme Court in the *Regents of the University of California v. Bakke,* in which the Court found that the university's affirmative action program violated Title VII by providing for a special admissions procedure excluding white applicants from 16 percent of the freshman medical class.

It is important to note that in this case the Court pointed out the university could establish an affirmative action program considering race to be one of the admission factors. When this decision was announced, it was felt by some it would substantially alter affirmative action plans. Note that this decision was made in an educational context and not in employment; hence, the specific meaning and its application to law enforcement agencies is still not clear (Anderson and Levin-Epstein, 1982; More and Wegener, 1989).

The U.S. Commission on Civil Rights has taken the position that the use of racially preferential employment techniques, such as quotas, is not properly viewed as a situation pitting the interests of blacks against the interests of whites. Rather, each specific preferential plan favors members of the preferred group—of whatever race or gender—at the expense of the nonpreferred group, which inevitably includes persons of diverse ethnic, religious, or racial groups (U.S. Commission on Civil Rights, 1984).

The commission also rejects the concept of an operational justification for racial quotas. In one major police department, it was asserted its promotion quota increasing black officers at all ranks was necessary to achieve more effective law enforcement and reduce discriminatory treatment against black citizens. It was the commission's position that this approach amounted to little more than a claim that only black officers can effectively provide law enforcement services to black citizens or supervise lower rank black police officers.

The commission asserted such a claim has no place in a free, pluralist society made up of many diverse ethnic and racial groups striving to achieve the goal of becoming one nation. If accepted, it would justify a claim that members of a racial or ethnic group can be properly served or treated only by fellow members of that group (U.S. Commission on Civil Rights, 1981). Table 15.3 lists selected cities and the number of minority patrol officers serving in those cities in 1981. In another survey in 1983, it was found minorities in police departments averaged 7.6 percent. Minorities were also found to be

TABLE 15.3 Minority Police Officers Working in Selected Cities

City	*Blacks*	*Hispanics*	*Native Americans*	*Other Minorities*
Chicago	1,870	282	5	17
Detroit	801	26	4	4
Miami	103	122	–	–
New York	1,603	977	6	30
Philadelphia	1,075	38	–	14
Seattle	36	15	9	37
St. Louis	260	–	–	–
Washington, D.C.	1,310	26	2	5

SOURCE: Police Foundation, *Survey of Police Operational and Administrative Practices—1981* (Washington, DC: Police Executive Research Forum, 1981).

strongly represented in the larger cities and in the South and the West (Urban Data Services Publications, 1983). Focus 15.2 describes the implementation of the FBI minority hiring plan.

A few court decisions have imposed quotas as a means of achieving greater minority representation in police departments, but this has only been done after a careful investigation showed racial imbalance had been caused by unlawful discrimination. Court decisions vary considerably across the nation. In one community, the court took the position the police department should hire a specific number of employees who were bilingual in Spanish and English. In another department the court issued an order requiring 15 percent of its force to be composed of blacks and Puerto Ricans. Finally, another decision by a district court imposed promotional quotas based on race for the positions of sergeant and lieutenant.

The real goal is to use affirmative action techniques as tools to enhance equal opportunity for *all* citizens rather than as devices to penalize some because they are not receiving the same treatment due to race, gender, or other status. Techniques to be utilized include the following (U.S. Commission on Civil Rights, 1984):

1. Development of recruitment efforts aimed at increasing the number of qualified minority applicants.
2. Training, educational, and counseling programs targeting minority participants and enhancing their opportunities to be hired or promoted on the basis of merit, but open to all applicants and employees.

One way of dealing with its obligations is for an agency to develop a recruitment policy and program having specific measurable goals, evaluated periodically. Law enforcement agencies should have a ratio of minority employees approximately equal to the proportion of such groups within the service area. In the absence of such a ratio, a police department should prepare an affirmative action plan that specifically provides for an equal employment opportunity (Commission for Accreditation for Law Enforcement Agencies, 1984; Hochstedler, 1984).

FOCUS 15.2

FBI Director Unveils Minority Hiring Plan

WASHINGTON (AP)—FBI Director William Sessions, vowing to stamp out any racism or discrimination at the bureau, said Thursday he has approved a new five-year affirmative action program to hire and promote more minority employees.

"From the beginning, I have tried to make the FBI's policy against racism and discrimination crystal clear to every member of the FBI, both by policy statements ...and by personally addressing employees," Sessions said.

The FBI chief outlined steps he has taken to eliminate discrimination over the past 10 months, but he refused to talk about pending legal actions taken by a group of Hispanic agents and by a black agent.

Some 311 Hispanic agents filed a class-action suit in El Paso, Texas, contending that the FBI discriminates in the promotion, discipline, and assignment of Hispanics....

In the other case, Donald Rochon, a black agent in the Philadelphia office, has filed racial harassment charges against the government. The Equal Employment Opportunity Commission has already upheld many of Rochon's complaints stemming from his tenure in the Omaha, Nebraska office....

Out of 9,597 agents, 417 are black and 439 are hispanic. In the U.S. population, blacks account for about 12 percent and Hispanics make up about 8 percent....

SOURCE. San Jose Mercury News, Friday, September 2, 1988. Reprinted with permission of the Associated Press.

Another step can be taken—establish an equal employment opportunity grievance process providing an efficient means for resolving individual or group problems (of a sensitive nature) quickly and with a minimum of formal procedural requirements. This approach should deal with allegations of discrimination regarding application, recruitment, appointment, training, promotion, retention, discipline, or other aspects of employment because of race, religion, color, sex, physical/mental handicap, medical condition, marital status, age, national origin, or ancestry.

Each agency should have an EEO counselor who will respond to a complaint (within 30 calendar days) and do the following (City of Milpitas, 1984):

1. Consult with the aggrieved person.
2. Discuss civil rights laws and EEO guidelines.
3. Make necessary inquiries in an attempt to resolve the complaint.
4. Counsel the aggrieved on issues of the case.
5. Seek informal resolution of the problem(s).

If informal resolution of the aggrieved person's problem(s) is not possible, a formal complaint should be filed with the department's affirmative action officer. An investigation of the complaint should be made and findings and recommendations submitted to the city manager or mayor, who should then provide the complainant with a written decision within a reasonable period of time. An effective affirmative action plan demands a serious and vigorous commitment from top management. A plan must be carried through at every level within the organization because if lower ranks believe the plan is not really supported, it can be sabotaged, ignored, or relegated to a very low priority. Top management should demand periodic reports not only listing the minority members hired or promoted, but also including an in-depth analysis of the positions filled, rate of advancement, and turnover. Management needs quality information indicating how policies are being carried out and the effect they are having on the organization (Reece and Brandt, 1987).

Women

Discrimination based on gender is still a major issue in some police departments, but there has been considerable progress as women have entered what was, for many years, a male-dominated occupation. Title VII of the 1964 Civil Rights Act specifically prohibits discrimination based on gender with respect to compensation, terms, conditions, or privileges of employment. Eight years later, the Equal Opportunity Act coverage was extended to include public employees. In other words, the law requires that women be treated fairly—if they are not, liability will be found (Higginbotham, 1988).

When Title VII was initially passed, the ban on sexual discrimination was inserted into the act, with limited accompanying discussion to clarify the intent of the legislation. Consequently, the EEOC has had considerably more difficulty in interpreting the ban on sexual discrimination than with understanding any other aspect of the act. The EEOC has issued guidelines twice, and many of the issues such as maternity leaves, breast-feeding at work, grooming standards, and stereotyping that women have encountered have been litigated in federal court (Anderson and Levin-Epstein, 1982).

Women have been employed since approximately 1845 in American police departments but through the years their participation has been limited to specific duties and their law enforcement responsibilities have been restricted. Typically, they have served as jail matrons and in a social service role in juvenile units. As time has passed, women have occasionally served as undercover officers in vice and organized crime details. Limited to these types of functions, women have traditionally been relegated to a secondary position in law enforcement, so they have had little opportunity for advancement except for those few women who have risen through the ranks in specialized units (Stone and DeLuca, 1985).

Since 1972 and the passing of the Civil Rights Act, an increasing number of women have entered law enforcement. Generally, these women must

CASE STUDY

Roberta F. Partin

Roberta F. Partin always wanted to be a police officer. She was raised in a family where her father and two uncles were officers. At family gatherings, there was a great deal of discussion of police activities. Roberta joined the Girl Scouts and, as soon as she was eligible, became an Explorer Scout. She was also very active in the town's Police Athletic League.

Upon graduation from high school, she enrolled in the local community college, where she majored in police science and administration. She graduated with honors and continued to pursue her education at the local university. As soon as she was 21, she took the police officer test at Riverwide City and successfully passed the oral examination and the physical agility test. She placed second on the selection list, was subsequently hired, and attended the regional police academy.

She graduated number one from the academy, completed field training easily, and received high marks from all her supervising officers. She was then assigned to patrol and works the midnight shift, where she is the only woman on a team of nine officers. As the first female officer ever hired by the department, she finds herself the object of considerable scorn from the majority of officers on the team. She is the butt of many jokes, and three of the officers on the team refuse to work with her. The team sergeant (Sgt. Rogers) is in a dilemma. Personally, he feels there is no place in law enforcement for women, but the chief of police has taken a very strong position supporting women and has directed Sgt. Rogers to make every effort to assure that Officer Partin be treated fairly.

The only other women in the department are the clerical staff and the dispatchers, so Officer Partin finds she has nobody she can actually turn to other than her father and uncles, who work in another department. The advice she received is just to do her job as best she can and wait for everything to work out. At the end of their shift, the other officers go to a nearby restaurant for coffee, but she has never been included in the group.

Since she is the only woman officer in patrol, everything she does is carefully scrutinized. She feels like she is operating in a fishbowl. Some members of the community responded to her negatively also, but during the last six months, a few of the officers with whom she works find she is very competent and professional in the way she conducts herself.

In several violent confrontations, she remained poised and more than adequately assisted other officers in subduing suspects who appeared to be on drugs. She is 5 feet 4 inches tall and weighs 131 pounds. She has taken extensive self-defense training, at her own expense, and performs effectively and confidently during violent situations. When she responds to family disputes, she has the interpersonal skills to defuse potentially explosive situations.

Partin knows she is doing a good job, and her six-month evaluation confirmed this view. She continues to be unaccepted by the majority of the officers on her shift and is becoming increasingly negative toward the officers who openly oppose her. There is no one she feels she can turn to for help. Her superior notes that whenever *he* is around, she is treated as an equal—but unfortunately he is not around all the time.

If you were Officer Partin, how would you deal with the other officers on the team? Would it be helpful to fight back, either verbally or by filing a grievance? How could Sgt. Rogers help Officer Partin? If you were the chief of police, what would you do?

---

overcome three barriers: the traditional role females are expected to play, the attitudes of males and females within the organization, and the lack of a support system to help the woman stay on the job (Reece and Brandt, 1987). Focus 15.3 makes suggestions to help managers prevent sexual harassment.

It has not been easy for women to enter a male-dominated occupation, especially one like law enforcement, long perpetuating the myth that a good police officer is the combination of John Wayne and Rambo—tall, tough, and unyielding when confronting the criminal. This macho concept has proven to be one of the most difficult for women to deal with, especially for the first women who broke the barriers and entered the male-prevalent world of patrol and traffic regulation (Swanson, Territo, and Taylor, 1988).

Often women go through three stages when they enter the police world. The initial stage is best described as the *honeymoon phase,* as women adjust to the police academy and to the close supervision provided by a field training officer. The newly hired policewoman begins to get positive feedback as she adapts to each new challenge successfully and realizes many of her fears are unwarranted. She begins to believe she can handle a career, a home life, and outside interests.

Next she enters the *ambivalent stage* as she becomes doubtful about her ability to accept the new role. She suffers from internal conflict as the traditional values inculcated through her growing years compete and conflict with the newly defined role she wants to assume in the working environment. Sometimes a woman becomes the victim of the *superwoman syndrome* as she strives to meet the demands placed on her by both her family and employer. With many women, the demands to be all things to all people has led to a variety of pressures, resulting in frustration and exhaustion.

The final stage is called the *transformation time* and begins as internal conflicts are resolved. The working environment begins to provide the working woman with a feeling of status and self-fulfillment. The job becomes meaningful to her and she becomes increasingly motivated and committed. No longer is the home the sole source of role satisfaction (Reece and Brandt, 1987).

These stages are further modified by what might be termed the police personality—characterized as one definitely needing to control the situation (an authoritarian attitude), and needing to be assertive and physically aggressive. Every one of these characteristics reflect our society's traditional male role rather than the female role (Berg and Budnick, 1986).

The situation then becomes a case of a woman adapting to the stereotype of the male police personality. It is an example of true conflict. Women who

FOCUS 15.3

Preventing Sexual Harassment in the Workplace

1. Don't mix business and pleasure. Personal relationships with subordinates expose managers not only to possible complaints from the person with whom the relationship exists, but to complaints from other employees stating favorable treatment is granted only to persons with whom an intimate relationship develops.

2. Avoid the appearance of impropriety as well as any actual impropriety. Think about how a situation will appear to others in the workplace....

One experienced manager always makes sure he's in a group of three, and avoids, if possible, one-on-one after-hours meetings with business associates of the opposite sex.

3. Don't tell off-color jokes with sexual implications in a business situation, even when the day's business is over and it's time to relax....

4. Don't make overly personal comments about an employee's clothing or body....

5. It is impossible to deny that situations occur where men and women become more than business associates. If this happens to you or to people within your sphere of responsibility, a good rule is to separate the individuals into different units. It is important to be equitable to both male and female employees, and not to react by "transferring the woman." To allow a supervisory relationship to be continued between two employees who are involved in a personal relationship exposes your agency to liability that could be translated into... litigation if an equal opportunity complaint were to be brought [against the supervisor].

6. Make sure all managers, supervisors, and employees know what sexual harassment is. Hold a workshop for supervisory staff. Define sexual harassment in plain terms for them. Tell them not to... make inappropriate sexual comments to... coworkers or subordinates....

7. When complaints are made, investigate promptly, confidentially, and follow departmental policy when violations are found....

SOURCE. Reprinted with permission from *Toeing the EEOC Legal Line,* 1989, available from the Alexander Hamilton Institute, 197 W. Spring Valley Ave., Maywood, NJ 07607.

serve as police officers face the difficult choice of retaining their basic femininity or emulating facets of the male police personality. This event is generally termed *defeminization.* Women who adjust in this way to the police occupation believe the male officers will accept them more readily, thus it becomes easier to establish a more trusting relationship (Martin, 1979). In another study, one

Confronting Stereotypes Female police officers are faced with the unique challenge of struggling for acceptance among their co-workers while maintaining their own identity. *(©Rhoda Sidney: Monkmeyer Press)*

researcher pointed out that when women attending a police academy exhibited masculine behavior (rather than feminine) they tended to get along better with their male counterparts (Gross, 1981).

This presents a dilemma to other women officers because if they decide to retain their femininity it will, in all reality, limit their careers. In most instances, assignment to patrol will not occur for these women, which will (in all probability) preclude their consideration for supervisory or managerial positions (Berg and Budnick, 1986).

The woman who wants to become a police officer will, in many instances, encounter discrimination not only from within the department, but by a hostile community still learning to accept women as police officers (Bell, 1982). Obstacles women must overcome are numerous, but one of the most significant is the attitude of male officers of all ranks. Through the years this male-dominated bastion has built numerous barriers into the formal and informal structures of the work organization, prescribing the female role as helping and nurturing. The male attitude can be summed up as "Police work is man's work" (Horne, 1980).

The male view is that women are not physically or psychologically able to handle *real* police work. This view holds that if departments are forced to accept women, they should serve in limited capacities and never be allowed to become a party to the violence and sordidness of daily police work. Not all male officers resist the entry of women into their department, but when it does occur, resistance can range from a rational attitude to an illogical one. Some officers will openly discriminate against a woman officer. For example, when serving as field training officers, they can pressure a woman to such an extent that her judgment finally becomes faulty, and numerous mistakes result in a poor rating. Supervisors have been known to show partiality to men over women when assigning officers to different shifts, when assigning preferred beats, or when selecting an officer for special training. The nature and type of discrimination varies considerably, depending on the male involved. Life can be made most miserable for a policewoman when she becomes the butt of jokes, snide remarks, and sexual innuendoes (Horne, 1980).

A somewhat more rational argument against hiring women police officers, from the male view, has been that women are not physically qualified to serve as police officers. Current data suggest that certain aspects of women's physical capability are limited, such as upper body strength and overall strength, as compared to most males. However, experts feel women can (with careful training) assume a level of fitness well within the demands of police work.

Contrary to popular belief, policing is not a really physically demanding job. There are certainly times when situations become physically demanding. Every officer, male or female, must have a reserve of strength to provide a positive response to a critical incident. Experts state that an officer can stay physically fit through careful and continuous training. This means an officer should exercise two or three times a week, with each session lasting from 30 to 45 minutes, to maintain a good level of fitness (Charles, 1982).

A number of studies have been conducted in recent years refuting the position that women cannot perform effectively when assigned to a police department's patrol division. When an agency has a carefully thought-out recruitment, selection, and training program, women can perform successfully as patrol officers. But there must be adequate supervision, careful planning, proper use of appropriate backup, and clearly spelled out policies and procedures circumscribing patrol operations (Horne, 1980; Lord, 1986).

Success seems to beget success. As more women have entered police departments, the barriers to their employment have eroded and in a few instances been breached. This is not to suggest every policewoman will function effectively any more than it can be said of every male officer (Swanson, Territo, and Taylor, 1988). There are still relatively few women in police departments, especially in supervisory or higher levels. Table 15.4 shows that of 12,149 agencies responding to a survey in 1987, only 7.6 percent of the sworn officers were female.

It is interesting to note that the larger the size of the city, the higher the percentage of female police officers. For example, in 60 cities with a pop-

TABLE 15.4 Law Enforcement Employees by Gender

Population Group	*Total Police Employees*			*Police Officers (sworn)*			*Civilian Employees*		
	Total	*Percentage Male*	*Percentage Female*	*Total*	*Percentage Male*	*Percentage Female*	*Total*	*Percentage Male*	*Percentage Female*
Total agencies: 12,149 agencies; population 226,796,000	641,168	78.2	21.8	480,383	92.4	7.6	160,785	35.9	64.1
Total cities: 9,255 cities; population 153,087,000	404,946	79.9	20.1	320,959	92.9	7.1	83,987	30.2	69.8

SOURCE: Uniform Crime Reports, *Crime in the United States—1987* (Washington, DC: Federal Bureau of Investigation, July 1988, p. 88).

TABLE 15.5 Women in Investigative, Supervisory, and Command Positions in 1981

Cities	*Detective*	*Sergeant*	*Lieutenant*	*Captain*	*Major*	*Above*
123	300	196	25	5	4	5

SOURCE: Police Foundation, *Survey of Police Operational and Administrative Practice*—1981 (Washington, D.C.: Police Executive Research Forum, 1981).

ulation greater than 250,000, the percentage of female police officers was found to be 10.4. There was a lesser representation in cities with populations under 99,999, where the percentage of female officers ranged from 4.1 to 5.3 percent. Fewer female officers were found in rural counties when contrasted with suburban counties. The respective percentages were 6.0 and 10.6 (Uniform Crime Reports, 1988). In another survey of 123 cities, the position that women are latecomers to the field of law enforcement is clearly supported by the fact that only 39 women held positions of lieutenant or higher and there were only 196 sergeants and 300 investigators (see Table 15.5). As the number of women police officers increases, it is anticipated that more females will move into management ranks. At some point in the future, gender will no longer be a factor in promotion decisions.

Use of Force

During the last three decades, no single issue has been of greater concern (not only to police managers but to the community at large) than police shootings and the use of other types of deadly force. For example, police shootings in 1980 and 1989 played significant roles in triggering urban riots in the city of Miami. It has become clear that police shootings can have extreme societal consequences beyond injury or death of a suspect (Geller and Karales, 1981).

The situations vary, as well as the types of deadly force used, but in recent months, a wide range of police confrontations occurred including shooting a prisoner who attempted to escape while being transferred to another jail. In another instance, two detectives fired 12 shots at a prisoner trying to escape. Three of the shots struck and killed the unarmed escapee. In this instance, the prisoner managed to get out of the police vehicle and start running along a driveway. The reason given by the officers for shooting the man was they feared for their lives.

In another community, in 1988, police responded to a report at 3 A.M. On arrival, the police officer approached a man with what looked like a sawed-off shotgun. The officer shot and critically wounded the man, who actually was carrying only a large radio. The officer said darkness and a sudden move by the suspect (when he spun around holding a long black radio at waist level) after he was told to freeze, were contributing factors in the shooting. The officer thought he had been menaced with a weapon. Believing his life and the life of his partner were threatened, he fired one shot, hitting the suspect.

In New York City during 1988, officers responded to a family dispute after receiving a call from the wife stating her husband was distraught at not being able to see his son. The four responding officers were within 5 feet of the subject as they attempted to talk him into surrendering and were being threatened by the subject with a knife. The subject suddenly lunged at an officer and was subsequently shot 11 times. A grand jury found no basis for indicting the two officers who fired the shots killing the subject.

After the shooting, the Police Commissioner of New York City, Benjamin Ward, called for additional training of officers when handling violent people. He pointed out the department has very strict standards on the use of deadly force, but officers need more training in defensive delaying tactics and accepting the idea that officers can retreat from confrontation.

Commissioner Ward announced the department wanted to purchase more protective plastic shields and train officers in their use. Utilizing money confiscated in drug cases, it was hoped each of the department's 1,400 patrol cars would be equipped with a shield. They also planned to put a shepherd's crook in a sergeant's car in each of the 75 precincts. It was explained that while one officer was being protected by a shield, the other office could hook a suspect's leg and pull the person down (*Law Enforcement News,* October 15, 1988).

Other nonlethal weapons used by some departments include a Tasar (electronic stun gun). During 1988, two men died in Los Angeles in separate incidents after being shot by police stun guns. It was later proven by autopsies that they died as a result of drug overdoses, not from the effects of the Tasar that has 50,000 volts. Both subjects violently resisted officers' attempts to subdue them. One subject died from acute phencyclidine (PCP) intoxication and the other from an overdose of cocaine.

The manufacturer of the Tasar points out the stun gun projects two electrically charged barbs at the end of 18-foot wires and there has never been a death attributed to the gun. The U.S. Bureau of Alcohol, Tobacco, and Firearms classifies the gun as nonlethal (*Law Enforcement News,* October 15, 1988).

The situations just described clearly illustrate the complexity of the problems of an officer working the street. There is a big difference between reviewing a case (in the quiet environment of an office where there is plenty of time to consider the alternatives) involving an officer using deadly force as compared to the actual situation in the field when a decision has to be made in a few seconds. This dilemma of using (or not using) deadly force is not new to the police field. As early as 1858, an officer using his personal weapon shot a suspect who was fleeing from the scene of a crime. The grand jury declined to indict the officer. It was not too long afterward that other New York police officers armed themselves. At the turn of the century, police departments started to issue weapons to officers (Matulia, 1982).

Law and the Use of Force

Through the years, the rules governing the use of deadly force have been determined by various states by virtue of statute or court decisions. In most instances, states have followed the English common law rule that was in place when this nation was founded (Hall, 1984). This rule soon became known as the *fleeing felon rule.* Under it, an officer was authorized to use deadly force when it was believed an arrest would be made for a felony. In addition, the officer was required to believe the use of force was necessary for self-protection or to prevent a subject from escaping.

Keep in mind that under English law, during the 18th century, all felonies were considered to be capital crimes punishable by death. It was a logical extension then that killing a fleeing felon was not only justified, but necessary (Hall, 1984).

An alternative to the fleeing felon rule can be found in the Model Penal Code, developed by the American Law Institute in 1962. Under this recommended rule, deadly force could be used against a fleeing felon under the following conditions (Hall, 1984):

1. The crime is a felony.
2. The individual making the arrest is a peace officer or someone who is assisting a peace officer.
3. The officer believes the use of deadly force creates no substantial risk to bystanders.
4. The officer believes the felony committed by a suspect included the actual use or threatened use of deadly force or there is a risk the suspect will cause someone's death or serious bodily harm if the suspect is not harmed.

While many officers can complete a career without ever drawing a weapon, there are enough incidents of police shooting civilians that it is of considerable concern not only to police administrators and the public at large, but also to legislative bodies and the courts. The magnitude of the problem can be illustrated by utilizing statistics from a study of the Chicago Police Department for the period from 1974 to 1978.

During this period of time, 523 civilians were shot by the police and of that number, 85 percent were shot intentionally and 14 percent unintentionally. Table 15.6 shows the majority of the civilians were shot because they threat-

TABLE 15.6 Reasons Given by Police for Shooting Civilians in Chicago

Reason	*Number*	*Percentage*
Gun use/threat	264	51
Other deadly weapon or physical force use/threat	72	14
Flight without resistance	89	17
Accidental	52	10
Stray bullet	17	3
Other deadly weapon possessed without threat	12	2
Other—intentional	7	1
Not ascertained	6	1
Mistaken identification	4	1
	523	100

SOURCE: William A. Geller and Kevin J. Karales, *Split-Second Decisions: Shootings of and by Chicago Police* (Chicago: Chicago Law Enforcement Study Group, 1981).

ened or used a weapon against an officer or a citizen. When suspects were fleeing the scene of the crime, 17 percent of all who had been involved in a forceful felony and were suspected burglars were shot. The category most startling is that 10 percent of the civilians were shot accidentally (Geller and Karales, 1981).

While even the taking of one life is regrettable, it should be placed in perspective. One expert pointed out that even when utilizing the highest estimates of shootings by the police, over a 15-year period fewer than 1 in 60 officers killed anyone. Further data shows the vast majority of shootings occur in metropolitan areas, which would indicate that in smaller jurisdictions, the rate would be much lower (Fyfe, 1982).

The U.S. Commission on Civil Rights in 1980 suggested police officers should receive extensive training in the appropriate use of firearms and other weapons, and such instruction should be sanctioned by a written departmental policy approved by both the executive and legislative bodies of the jurisdiction in question.

The commission has criticized fleeing felon statutes, pointing out that even when it is legally permissible to shoot a person who has just committed a felony (for which the penalty imposed after trial will, in nearly all cases, be much less severe than execution), an officer may have only a few seconds in which to assess the situation and decide whether to fire or not. There is little opportunity to determine the nature of the offense committed, the identity and age of the suspect, the reason for the flight, or whether a weapon is being carried. The commission took the position that the circumstances in which deadly force may be used should be limited to those occasions when it is necessary to protect the officer or another person from death (U.S. Commission on Civil Rights, 1980).

The issue of deadly force was placed in focus when two police officers in Memphis, Tennessee, responded to a night call announcing a residential burglary was in progress. A neighbor reported as she arrived at the scene that she had heard glass breaking from her home next door. One officer radioed in their location while the other officer went to the backyard, heard a door being slammed, and saw someone running. The suspect stopped at a 6-foot chain-link fence and the officer (using a flashlight to see the suspect's face and hands) was reasonably sure the man was not armed.

The officer challenged the suspect—"Police, halt." As the man climbed the fence, the officer fired one shot, killing him. Ten dollars and a purse were found on the body and the man was identified as Eugene Garner, a 15-year-old eighth grader, 5 feet 4 inches tall, and weighing 100 to 110 pounds (Hall, 1988). The use of deadly force to stop the escaping suspect was based on a Tennessee statute permitting the use of "all necessary means" to prevent the escape of a felony suspect if, "after notice of the intention to arrest... he either flees or forcibly resists..." (Hall, 1984).

The father of the suspect filed a suit in federal court seeking damages and eventually the U.S. Supreme Court heard the case. A decision was rendered on March 27, 1985. In a 6–3 opinion, the Court ruled statutory and administrative rules governing shootings of fleeing suspects must restrict officers to firing only when the officers have "probable cause to believe the suspect poses a threat of serious physical harm, either to the officers or to others...."

The Court concluded, "If the suspect threatens the officer with a weapon or there is probable cause to believe he has committed a crime involving the infliction or threatened infliction of serious physical harm, deadly force may be used if necessary to prevent escape and if, where feasible, some warning has been given" (*Tennessee v. Garner*, 1985).

Interestingly enough, the Court based its decision on the fact that the action of the officer violated the Fourth Amendment protections against unreasonable seizures. A seizure was defined as a situation where an officer restrains the freedom of an individual to walk away. It was pointed out there can be no question that apprehension by the use of deadly force is a seizure subject to the reasonableness requirement of the Fourth Amendment (*Tennessee v. Garner*, 1985).

The Court concluded the evidence in the case was such that the mere fact Garner was a suspected burglar could not, without more information, justify the use of deadly force to prevent his escape. The Court stated the officer had no reason to believe Garner was armed or otherwise posed a personal threat, and furthermore, that burglary is commonly characterized by law enforcement agencies as a property crime (Hall, 1984).

One leading expert, William A. Geller, has recommended the easiest way for police departments that do not already comply with or exceed the requirements of the Garner ruling, is to adopt the standards promulgated by the Commission on Accreditation for Law Enforcement Agencies (Geller, 1982). The commission has a number of standards addressing this critical area, which include the following written directives (Commission on Accreditation for Law Enforcement Agencies, 1984):

1. Stating personnel will use only the force necessary to effect lawful objectives.
2. Encompassing the use of all types and kinds of force (whether deadly or nondeadly) and all types of weapons.
3. Stating an officer may use deadly force only when the officer reasonably believes the action is in defense of human life, including the officer's own life, or in defense of any person in immediate danger of serious physical injury.
4. Specifying the use of deadly force against a fleeing felon.
5. Requiring all personnel be issued copies of deadly force policies.
6. Governing the discharge of warning shots.
7. Governing the carrying of sidearms and ammunition while on duty.
8. Governing the use of nonlethal weapons by agency personnel.
9. Establishing criteria for authorizing the carrying of nonissued personal firearms.
10. Requiring officers to be proficient in the use of agency firearms.
11. Requiring each officer to qualify (at least annually) with any firearm the officer is authorized to use.
12. Establishing a procedure to review situations when an officer discharges a firearm, whether on or off duty.

Focus 15.4 illustrates what can occur when deadly force is used inappropriately. The use of deadly force is a complex issue that police managers should

FOCUS 15.4

Ex-Cop Jailed; Acquittal in '80 Sparked Riots

MIAMI, FLA. (AP)—A former police officer whose acquittal in the beating death of a black man led to race riots in 1980 was arrested, along with a federal agent, on drug charges, authorities said yesterday.

The former officer, Alex Marrero, 34, and federal drug agent Jorge Villar, 44, were charged with conspiring to distribute cocaine and conspiring to commit bribery.

Marrero's acquittal in the beating death of businessman Arthur McDuffie sparked a riot that left 18 people dead and caused 80 million dollars in property damage in May 1980. . . .

SOURCE. "Ex-Cop Jailed; Acquittal in '80 Sparked Riots," *Arizona Daily Star*, April 11, 1989. Reprinted with permission of the Associated Press.

review constantly to see that policy is appropriate to a changing society (as can be seen from the 12 standards just listed). It requires a great deal of serious consideration. When drafting a department's deadly force policy, the constitutional boundaries established by *Garner* should be carefully considered. A policy more restrictive than common law may actually permit the use of unconstitutional deadly force, and conversely, an overly restrictive policy can create increased risks to the lives of police officers and others in the community (Hall, 1984).

Summary

The complexity of police administration is such that modern police managers are currently faced with diverse problems requiring not only a sensitive response, but an ability to deal with competing demands. These challenges include the development of police unions and associations, handling the increasing power they have acquired, managing the conflict created by the police's use of deadly force, and hiring women and minority police officers.

Today most police managers are concerned with a wide range of new activities including dealing with bargaining units, implementing collective bargaining, learning how to negotiate with unions effectively, and guiding the development of memoranda of understanding. In recent years, as police unions have grown in size and acquired new power, many police managers have found it necessary to change their management style and learn how to negotiate with unions.

Recently, a growing number of municipalities have recognized the right of employees to organize or maintain membership in a labor organization.

CASE STUDY

Charles A. Sudac

Charles A. Sudac has been a sworn officer for 17 years and although he and others in the department feel he would receive serious consideration for a higher rank (and in all probability be promoted to sergeant or higher), he refuses to take promotional examinations. He is very content to remain a patrol officer, and he prefers to work the graveyard shift in the high crime area of the city.

Over the years he has worked in patrol, vice, narcotics, and traffic investigation. He is currently a member of the department's tactical unit. He is the oldest officer working in the special unit consisting of 18 officers, 2 sergeants, and a lieutenant. The primary function of the unit is to target known multiple offenders, place them under surveillance, and apprehend them in the act of committing a felony.

The methods used by the tactical unit have proven most successful as evidenced by the apprehension of numerous felons and a significant reduction in armed robberies in the city. Assignment to the unit is vigorously pursued, so officers are subject to transfer after three years of service in the unit. This is Officer Sudac's third year in the unit. Because of his long service in the department, he has numerous informants and information sources that are of great value to the unit.

During his service, Officer Sudac has killed three felons as they were leaving the scene of armed robberies. The tactical unit has shot more suspects than any other unit in the police department. In fact, over a period of 22 years, the unit killed 31 suspects and wounded 12. No officer assigned to the unit has ever been wounded or killed. Within the unit, Officer Sudac is considered a model for other officers and is very comfortable in this role. Macho from the ground up, he responds positively to violent confrontations and always gives the appearance of being totally in control of himself.

The use of deadly force is strongly supported by members of the unit. Critics of the operation express grave concern not only for the taking of life, but for allowing the surveillance techniques to reach a stage where the utilization of force becomes all but inevitable. Legal experts point out all the operations are well within legal limits, and in every instance, internal investigations as well as grand jury hearings cleared the officers of any wrongdoing when suspects were killed or wounded.

Officer Sudac is very effective in the tasks he performs and has always received outstanding ratings. He believes (as do other members of the unit) it is best to arrest offenders after they have committed a serious felony as a means of ensuring that the case is prosecutable. In addition, the officers operate under the premise that violence can only be responded to with violence.

The use of deadly force is truly a dilemma facing officers such as Charles A. Sudac as well as police executives. One dimension of the problem is the spirit of the law as well as the letter of the law. Should a suspect under surveillance be allowed to complete the commission of a serious felony before an officer intercedes? Does such an action really reinforce the use of deadly force? Should someone like Officer Sudac be assigned to elite units?

Normally, cities and municipalities take a position of neither encouraging nor discouraging such activities. Membership or nonmembership in a labor organization is viewed as not affecting an employee's standing or rights.

A contract or memorandum of understanding has become increasingly common. It is a written agreement reached through meet and confer procedures, dealing with wages, hours, and other working conditions. The typical agreement runs for one to three years and in most instances contains a section describing how to deal with items not covered in the agreement.

Of concern to most police executives is the issue of what constitutes managerial rights. This generally includes the exclusive right to decide the mission of the department, determining the procedures and standards for employee selection, taking disciplinary action, and relieving employees from duty because of lack of work or other legitimate reasons.

In dealing with police unions, management (in many agencies) has found it necessary to prepare for collective bargaining by (1) establishing a bargaining team and designating one of the members as the principal negotiator, (2) identifying and recognizing the employee bargaining unit, and (3) developing ground rules prior to negotiation.

Ordinarily a police negotiation unit will consist of all the nonsupervisory sworn personnel of an agency (sergeants and all higher ranks are considered part of the management team). Unfortunately this clear-cut distinction has not occurred in every agency. In one instance the bargaining unit even included the chief of police; in another department there were three distinct bargaining units representing different ranks.

Another dilemma in the labor/management arena is the part the chief of police should play in the negotiation process. Some chief executive officers have taken the position they should not be involved but limit their participation to the implementation of approved agreements. Generally, experts in this vital area express the belief the chief should serve as an adviser to management negotiators.

Municipalities should establish a formal grievance mechanism. It is a process for dealing with disputes that arise concerning the interpretation or application of personnel ordinances, or of any rule or regulation governing personnel practices or working conditions.

The number of minorities and women in the police field has increased considerably since the passing of the Civil Rights Act of 1964. Title VII specifically prohibits discrimination by employers on the basis of race, color, religion, sex, or national origin. The Equal Opportunity Act that was passed eight years later extended the Civil Rights Act to public employees. The Equal Employment Opportunity Commission is the federal agency for administering Title VII, and it investigates all charges of discrimination.

The laws enforced by the EEOC are those involving discrimination in recruiting, hiring, promotion, employment testing, employment conditions, seniority, layoffs, retaliation, and reverse discrimination. In recent years, in order to comply with laws and court decisions, numerous police departments have developed affirmative action plans with the intent of recruiting officers from all segments of society so personnel can truly reflect the racial and ethnic composition of the community served, including speaking the major language spoken in the community.

Title VII included a ban on sexual discrimination—thus increasing numbers of women have entered law enforcement. The barriers offering resistance have eroded, and currently 7.6 percent of sworn officers are female. In the next decade, it is anticipated this number will increase rapidly.

During the last 30 years, no single issue has been of greater concern (not only to police managers but to the community at large) than police shootings and the use of other types of deadly force. Through the years the statutes and court decisions have revolutionized the use of deadly force by police officers, and the current trend is to limit the application of force to situations where the officer(s) or members of the community are threatened with death or serious injury.

Key Concepts

Memorandum of understanding
Managerial rights
Collective bargaining
Negotiation
Sidebar agreement
Grievance
Equal opportunity
Affirmative action plans
Discrimination
Honeymoon phase
Transformation time
Deadly force
Fleeing felon rule

Discussion Topics and Questions

1. How does a police manager identify those who are members of the management bargaining unit?
2. What categories of working conditions can be included in a memorandum of understanding?
3. Compare and contrast managerial rights and union rights.
4. What are the steps in a typical grievance procedure?
5. What is the function of the Equal Employment Opportunity Commission?
6. What techniques can be utilized to increase the number of minorities in a police agency?
7. What barriers must women overcome when entering law enforcement?
8. What is the fleeing felon rule?
9. Compare and contrast the fleeing felon rule with the guidelines provided in the *Garner* case.

References

ALEXANDER HAMILTON INSTITUTE. 1989. *Toeing the EEOC Legal Line*. Maywood, NJ.

ANDERSON, HOWARD J., and MICHAEL D. LEVIN-EPSTEIN. 1982. *Primer of Equal Employment Opportunity* (2nd ed.). Washington, DC: Bureau of National Affairs.

ASSOCIATED PRESS. 1989. "Ex-Cop Jailed; Acquittal in '80 Sparked Riots," *Arizona Daily Star*, April 11.

BELL, DANIEL J. 1982. "Policewomen: Myths and Reality," *Journal of Police Science and Administration*, Vol. 10, No. 1.

BERG, BRUCE L. and KIMBERLEY J. BUDNICK. 1986. "Defeminization of Women in Law Enforcement: A New Twist in the Traditional Police Personality," *Journal of Police Science and Administration,* Vol. 14, No. 4.

CALIFORNIA GOVERNMENT CODE. 1985. Section 3505.1.

CHARLES, MICHAEL T. 1982. "Women in Policing." *Journal of Police Science and Administration,* Vol. 10, No. 2.

CITY OF MILPITAS. 1984. *Memorandum of Understanding*. Milpitas, CA: Author.

COBLE, PAUL. 1989. "Memoranda of Agreement/Understanding." In Peter C. Unsinger and Harry W. More (Eds.), *Police Management/Labor Relations*. Springfield, IL: Charles C Thomas.

COMMISSION ON ACCREDITATION FOR LAW ENFORCEMENT AGENCIES. 1984. *Standards for Law Enforcement Agencies*. Fairfax, VA: Author.

CRANE, DONALD P. 1979. *Personnel: The Management of Human Resources* (2nd ed.). Belmont, CA: Wadsworth.

FAVREAU, DONALD, F. and JOSEPH E. GILLESPIE. 1978. *Modern Police Administration*. Englewood Cliffs, NJ: Prentice-Hall.

FYFE, JAMES J. (ED.). 1982. *Readings on Police Use of Deadly Force*. Washington, DC: Police Foundation.

GARMIRE, BERNARD L. (ED.). 1982. *Local Government Police Management*. Washington, DC: International City Management Association.

GELLER, WILLIAM A. 1982. "Deadly Force: What We Know," *Journal of Police Science and Administration,* Vol. 10, No. 2.

GELLER, WILLIAM A. and KERVIN J. KARALES. 1981. *Split-Second Decisions: Shootings of and by the Chicago Police*. Chicago: Chicago Law Enforcement Study Group.

GROSS, S. 1981. *Socialization into Law Enforcement: The Female Police Recruit*. Miami: Southeastern Institute of Criminal Justice.

HALE, CHARLES D. 1977. *Fundamentals of Police Administration*. Boston: Holbrook Press.

HALL, JOHN C. 1984. "Deadly Force: The Common Law and the Constitution," *FBI Law Enforcement Bulletin,* Vol. 53, No. 4.

HALL, JOHN C. 1988. "Police Use of Deadly Force to Arrest," Part 1, *FBI Law Enforcement Bulletin,* Vol. 58, No. 6.

HALL, JOHN C. 1988. "Police Use of Deadly Force," Conclusion, *FBI Law Enforcement Bulletin,* Vol. 58, No. 6.

HIGGINBOTHAM, JEFFREY. 1988. "Sexual Harassment in the Police Station," *FBI Law Enforcement Bulletin,* Vol. 58, No. 9.

HOCHSTEDLER, E. 1984. "Impediments to Hiring Minorities in Public Police Agencies," *Journal of Police Science and Administration,* Vol. 12, No. 2.

HORNE, PETER. 1980. *Women in Law Enforcement* (2nd ed.). Springfield, IL: Charles C Thomas.

KENNEY, JOHN P. and HARRY W. MORE. 1986. *Patrol Field Problems and Solutions*. Springfield, IL: Charles C Thomas.

LAMBERT, JOSEPH. 1989. "Grievance Mechanisms." In Peter C. Unsinger and Harry W. More (Eds.), *Police Management/Labor Relations*. Springfield, IL: Charles C Thomas.

LAW ENFORCEMENT NEWS, March 29, 1988.

LAW ENFORCEMENT NEWS, October 15, 1988.

LAW ENFORCEMENT NEWS, December 15, 1988.

LEONARD, V. A. 1980. *Fundamentals of Law Enforcement*. St. Paul, MN: West.

LORD, LESLI K. 1986. "A Comparison of Male and Female Peace Officers' Stereotypic Perceptions of Women and Women Peace Officers," *Journal of Police Science and Administration,* Vol. 14, No. 2.

MARTIN, S. 1979. "Policewomen and Policewoman: Occupational Role, Dilemmas and Choices of Female Officers," *Journal of Police Science and Administration,* Vol. 7, No. 3.

MATULIA, KENNETH J. 1982. *A Balance of Force*. Gaithersburg, MD: International Association of Chiefs of Police.

MCANDREW, IAN. 1989. "The Negotiations Process." In Peter C. Unsinger and Harry W. More (Eds.), *Police Management/Labor Relations*. Springfield, IL: Charles C Thomas.

MORE, HARRY W. (ED.). 1985. *Critical Issues in Law Enforcement* (4th ed.). Cincinnati, OH: Anderson.

MORE, HARRY W. and O. R. SHIPLEY. 1987. *Police Policy Manual—Personnel*. Springfield, IL: Charles C Thomas.

MORE, HARRY W. and FRED WEGENER. 1989. *Police Supervision*. Cincinnati: Anderson.

N.E.I. COMMITTEE ON MANAGEMENT'S RIGHTS. 1987. *Management Rights*. Washington, DC: National Executive Institute Associates.

POLICE FOUNDATION. 1981. *Survey of Police Operational and Administrative Practices—1981*. Washington, DC: Police Executive Research Forum.

REECE, BARRY L. and RHONDA BRANDT. 1987. *Effective Human Relations in Organizations*. Boston: Houghton Mifflin.

SAN JOSE MERCURY NEWS. 1988. "FBI Director Unveils Minority Hiring Plan," September 2.

SIRENE, WALT H. 1981. "Management: Labor's Effective Organizer," *FBI Law Enforcement Bulletin*, Vol. 52, No. 1.

SWANSON, CHARLES R., LEONARD TERRITO, and R. W. TAYLOR. 1988. *Police Administration* (2nd ed.). New York; Macmillan.

TENNESSEE V. GARNER. 1985. 471, U.S. 1 at 7.

UNIFORM CRIME REPORTS. 1988. "Crime in the United States—1987." Washington, DC: Federal Bureau of Investigation.

U.S. COMMISSION ON CIVIL RIGHTS. 1980. *Police Practices and the Preservation of Civil Rights*. Washington, DC: U.S. Government Printing Office.

U.S. COMMISSION ON CIVIL RIGHTS. 1981. *Who Is Guarding the Guardians?* Washington, DC: U.S. Government Printing Office.

U.S. COMMISSION ON CIVIL RIGHTS. 1984. *Statement on Civil Rights Concerning the Detroit Police Department's Racial Promotion Quota*. Washington, DC: U.S. Government Printing Office.

U.S. EQUAL EMPLOYMENT OPPORTUNITY COMMISSION. 1988. *Commission Enforces EEO Laws*, Office of Communications and Legislative Affairs.

UNSINGER, PETER C. and HARRY W. MORE. 1989. *Police Management/Labor Relations*. Springfield, IL: Charles C Thomas.

URBAN DATA SERVICE PUBLICATION. 1983. *Police Personnel Practices*. Washington, DC: International City Management Association.

For Further Reading

GELLER, WILLIAM A. 1982. "Deadly Force: What We Know," *Journal of Police Science and Administration*, Vol. 10, No. 2.

> This article is an excellent summary of the empirical research representing several dozen studies on the use of deadly force. Discussion includes police-involved shootings—their frequency, their nature, their correlates, and their control. The author recommends research on police-civilian encounters where there was a high potential for the use of deadly force but the situation was resolved without shots being fired.

HOCHSTEDLER, E. 1984. "Impediments to Hiring Minorities in Public Police Agencies," *Journal of Police Science and Administration*, Vol. 12, No. 2.

This study proposes that in order to achieve affirmative action in the hiring of minorities and women, public police agencies must establish and use a hiring quota which has as its goal making the agency work force composition the same as the composition of the general work force.

LEINEN, STEPHEN. 1984. *Black Police, White Society*. New York: New York University Press.

This book, written by a black police officer, describes the working world of the black police officer in New York City. It is based on in-depth interviews with 46 black police officers describing how they are treated by their superiors, how they get along with white officers, and how they view their role in the black community.

TAUBMAN, BRYNA. 1987. *Lady Cop—True Stories of Policewomen in America's Toughest City*. New York: Warner Books.

The book describes in the officer's own words the work and feelings of some of the women police officers on the streets of New York City. The women interviewed represent a broad spectrum of races, ages, and ethnic backgrounds. They hold jobs ranging from detective to patrol duty. The book describes the job of police officer particularly as it affects women who work on patrol.

Index